MONK!

TO SELMA,

TO MOM,
TO MY FAMILY

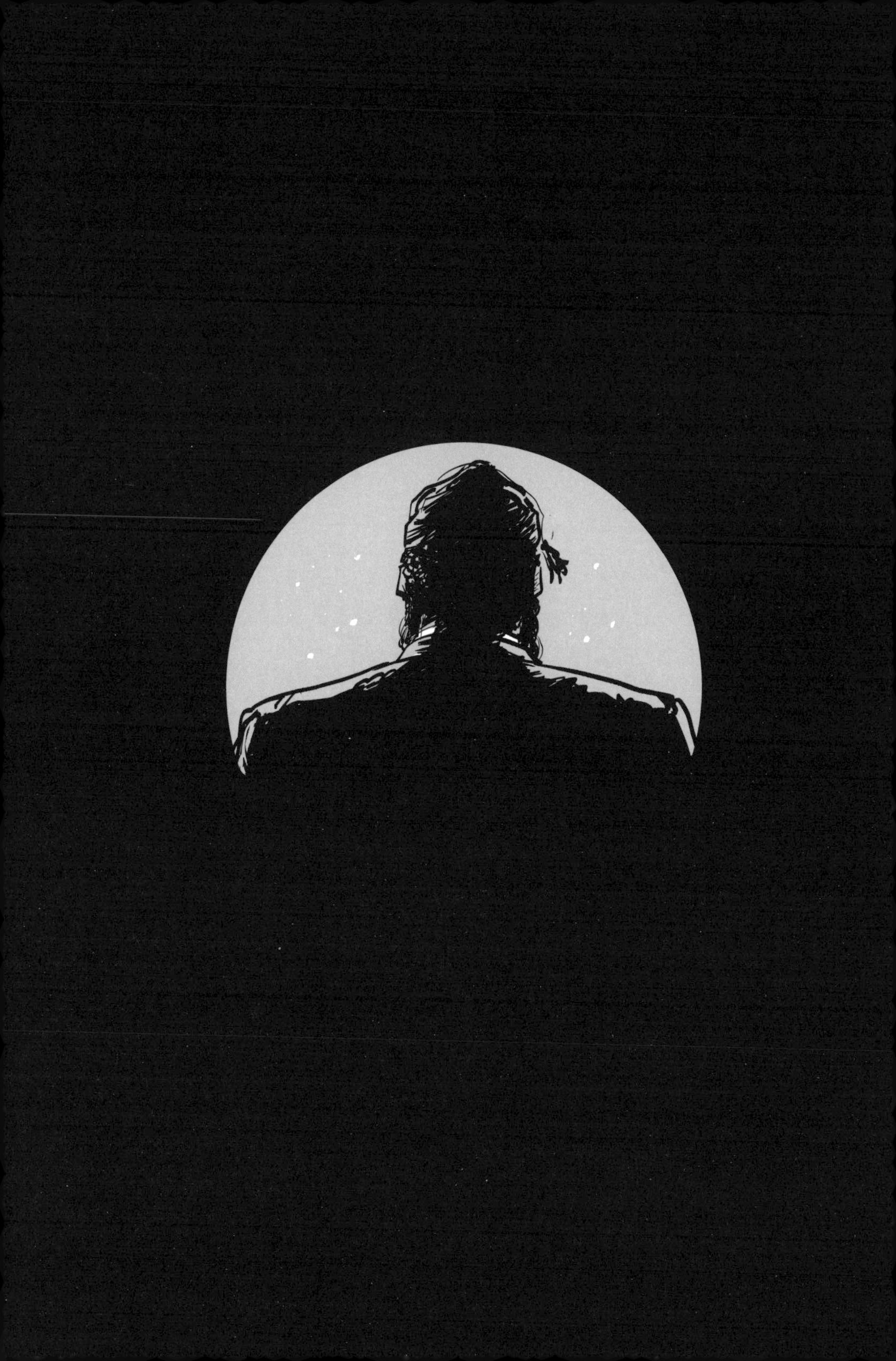

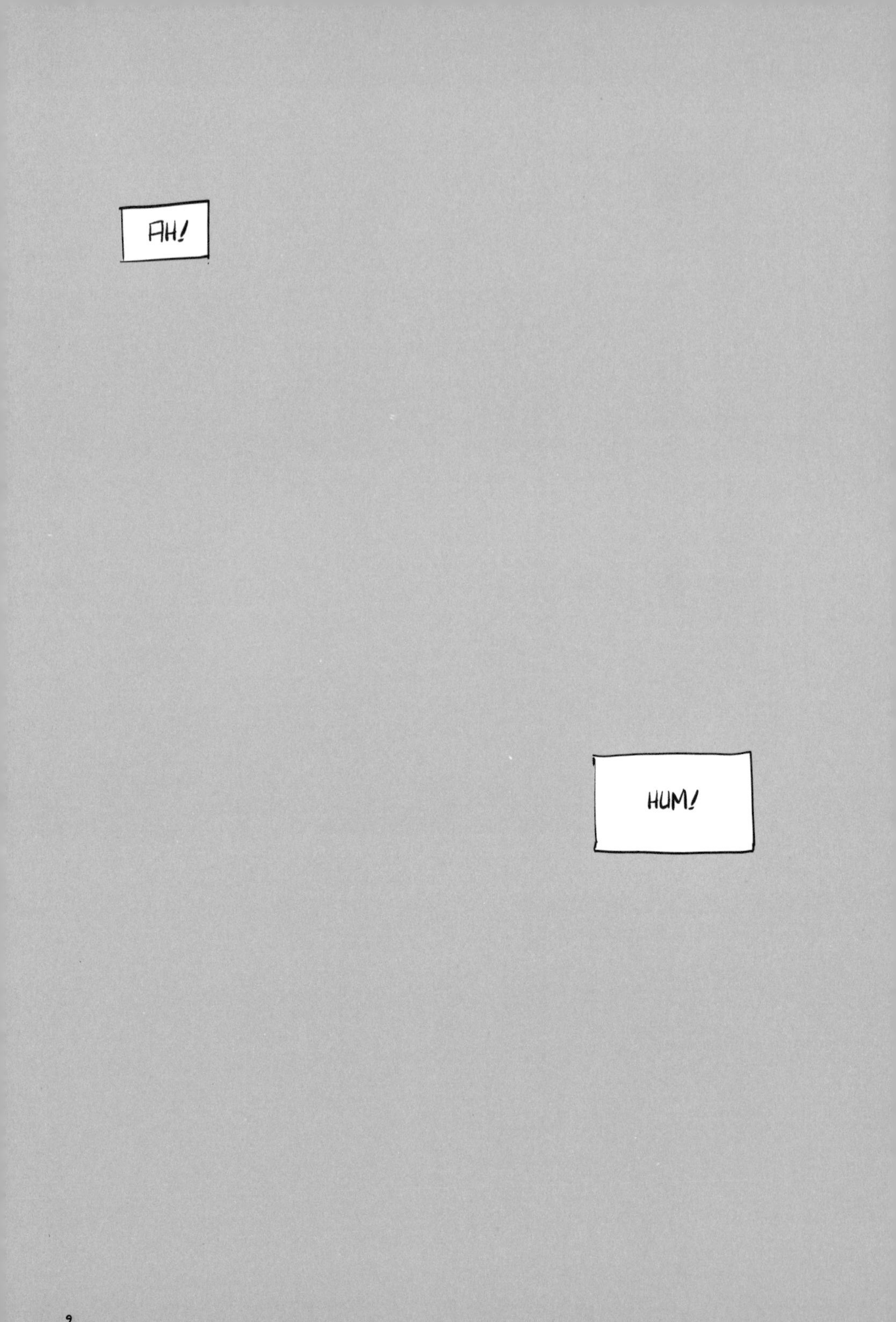
AH!
HUM!

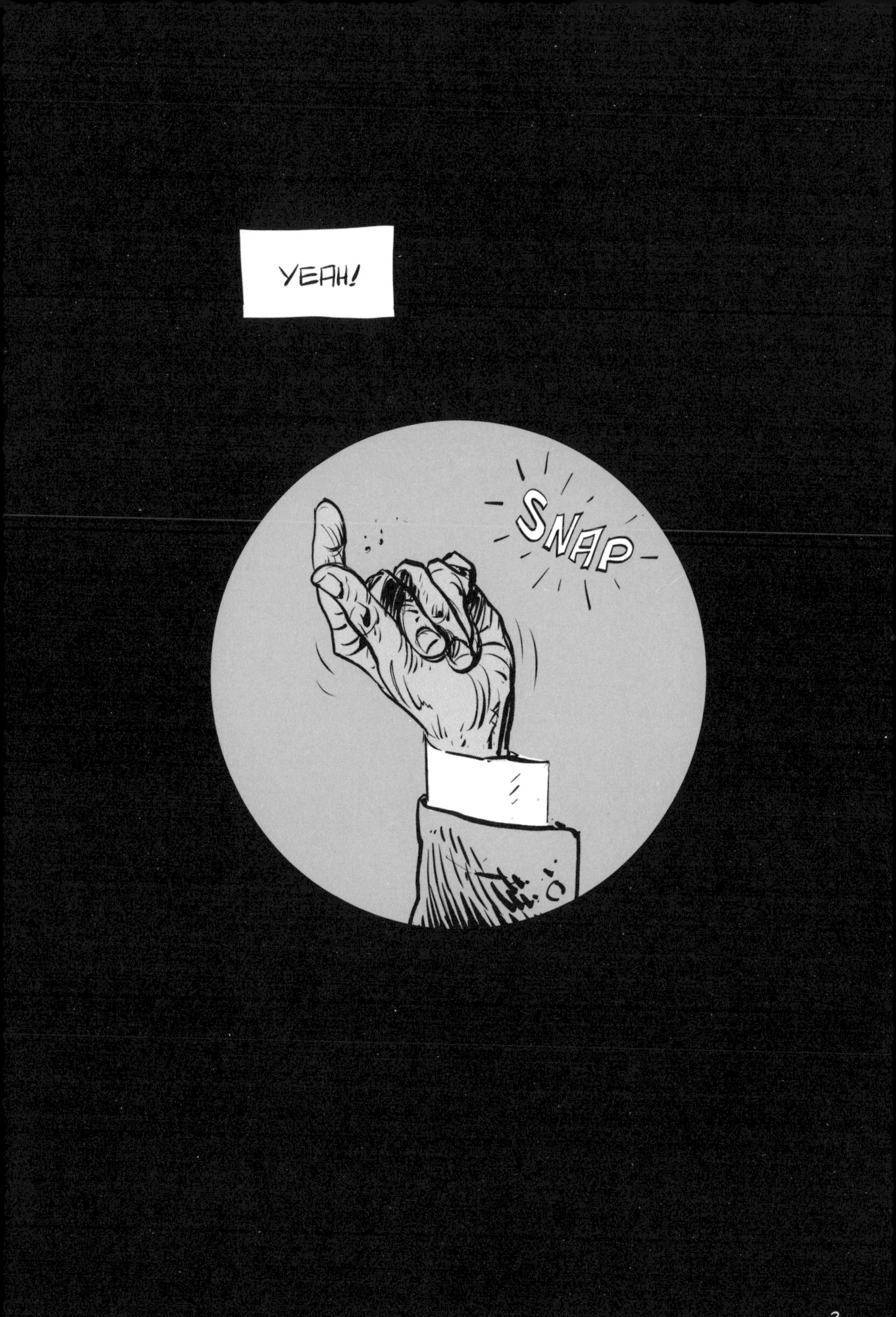
YEAH!
SNAP

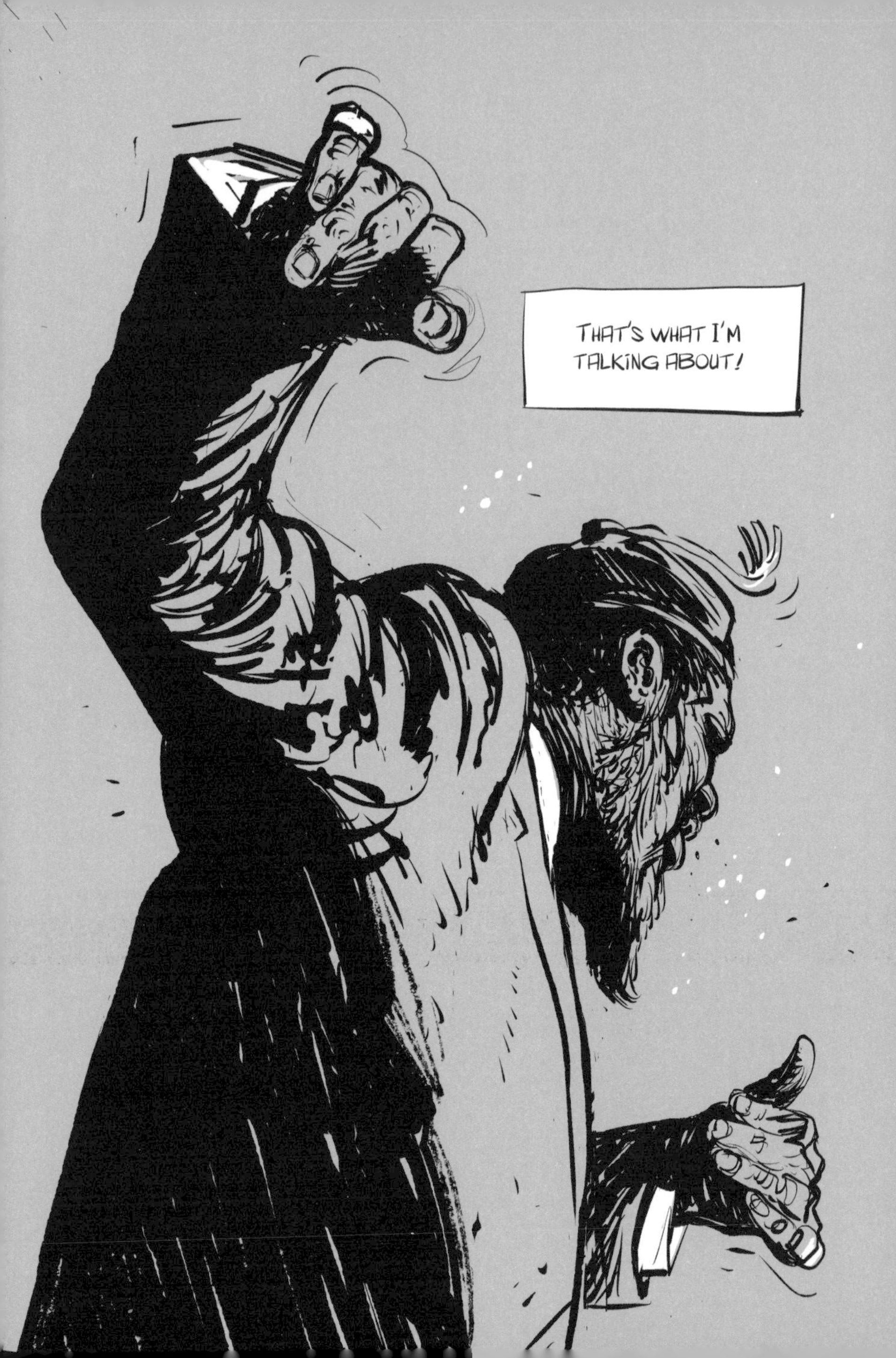
THAT'S WHAT I'M
TALKING ABOUT!

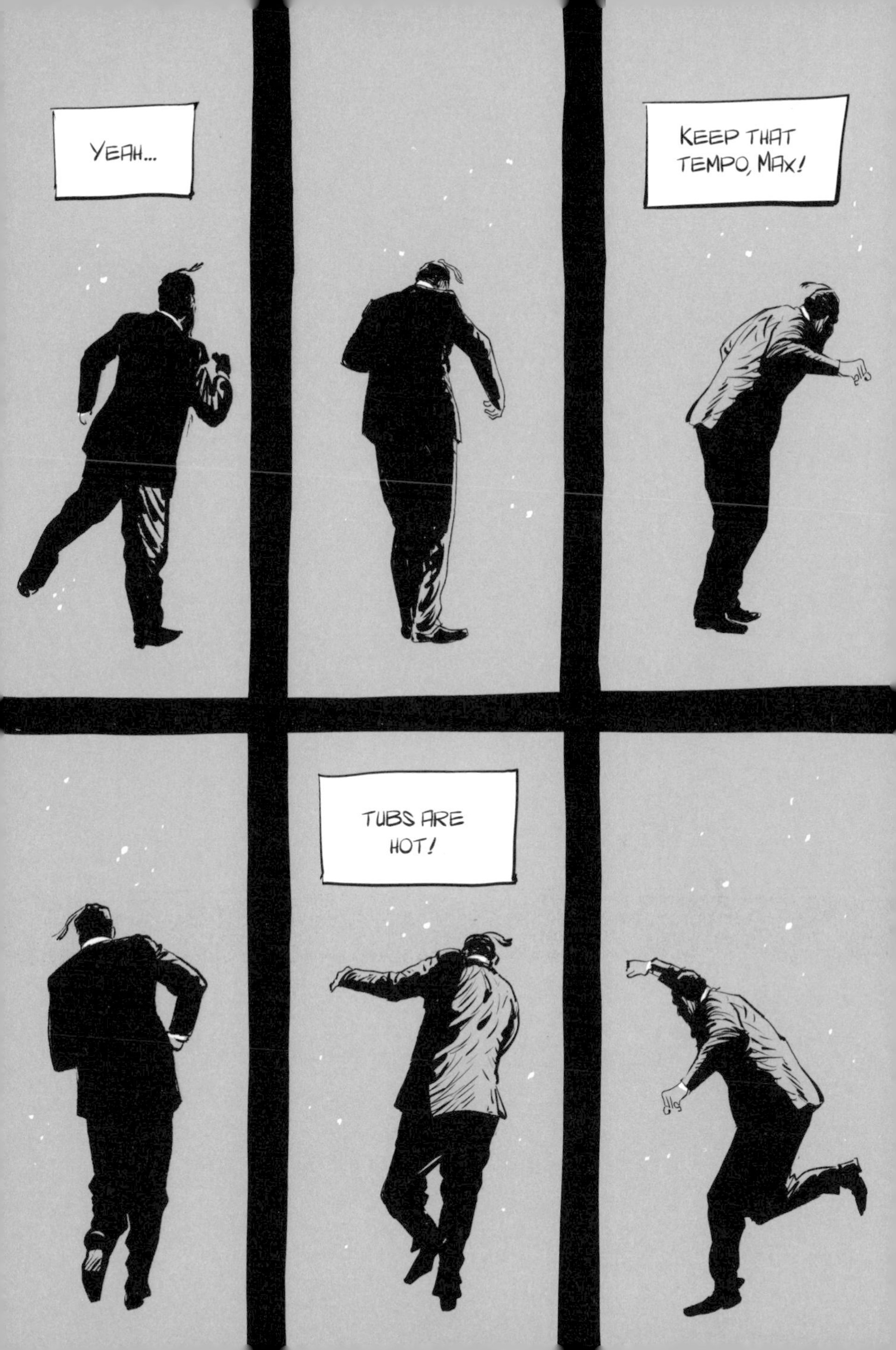
YEAH...
KEEP THAT TEMPO, MAX!
TUBS ARE HOT!

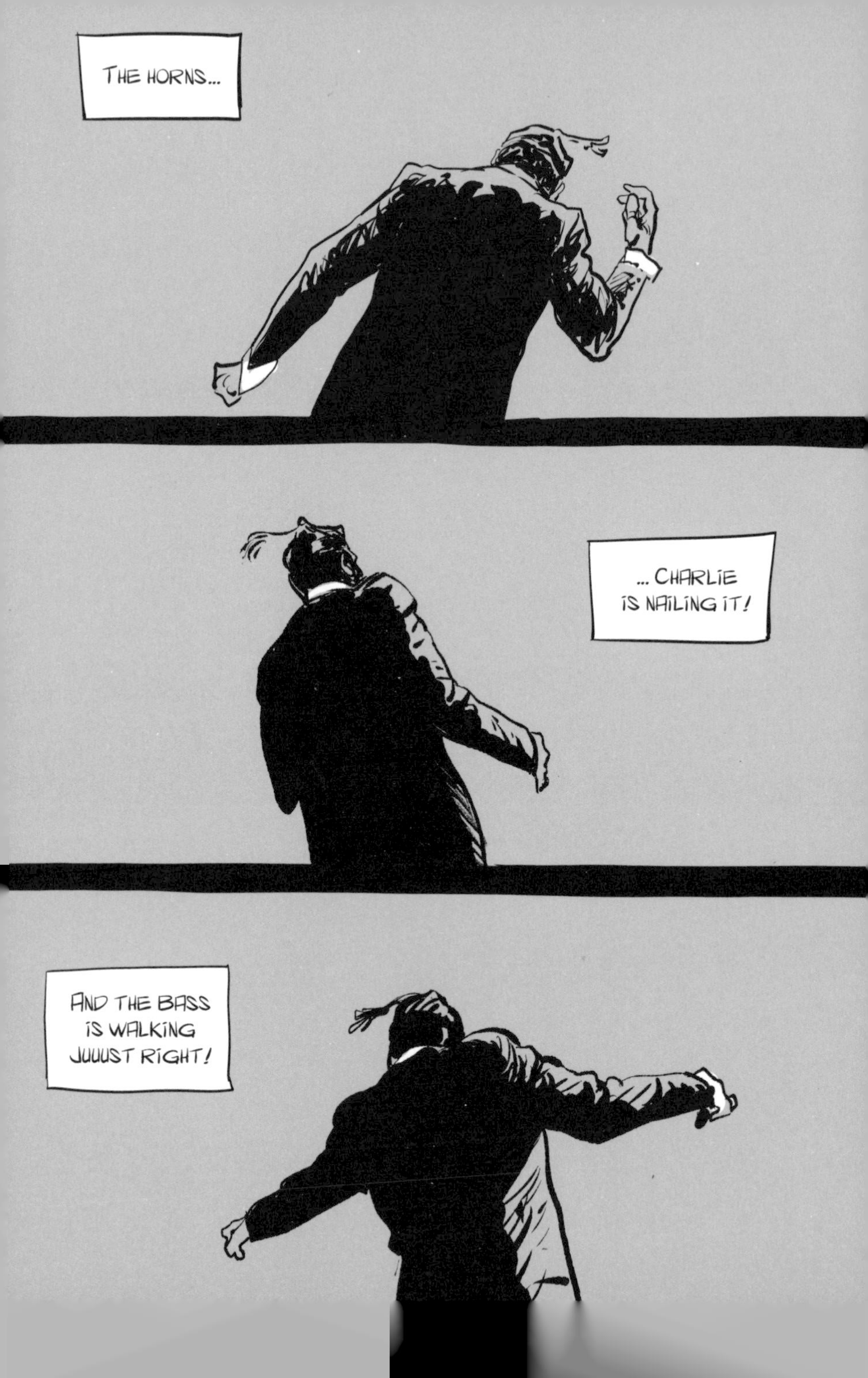
THE HORNS...
... CHARLIE IS NAILING IT!
AND THE BASS IS WALKING JUUUST RIGHT!

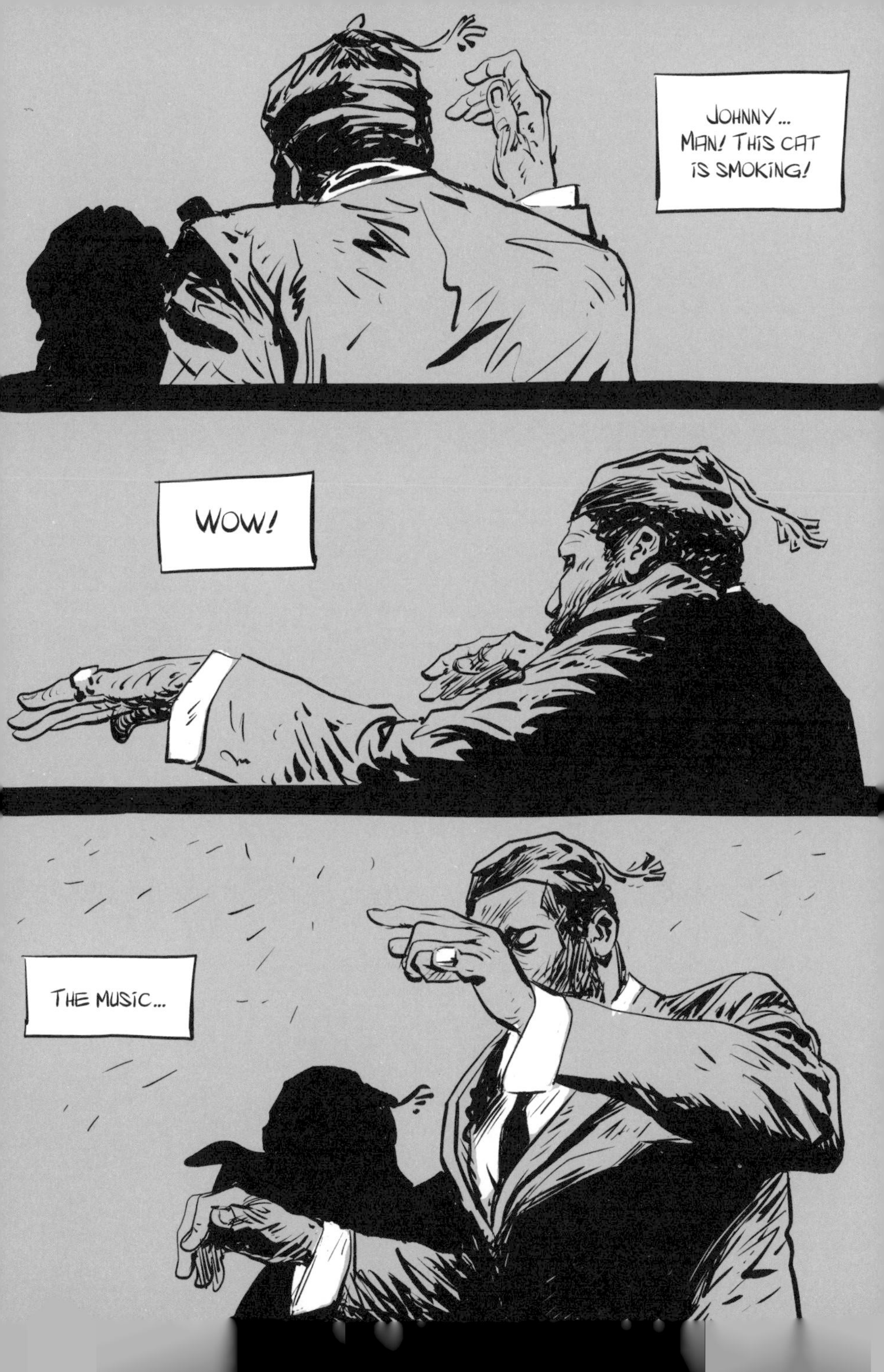
JOHNNY...
MAN! THIS CAT
IS SMOKING!
WOW!
THE MUSIC...

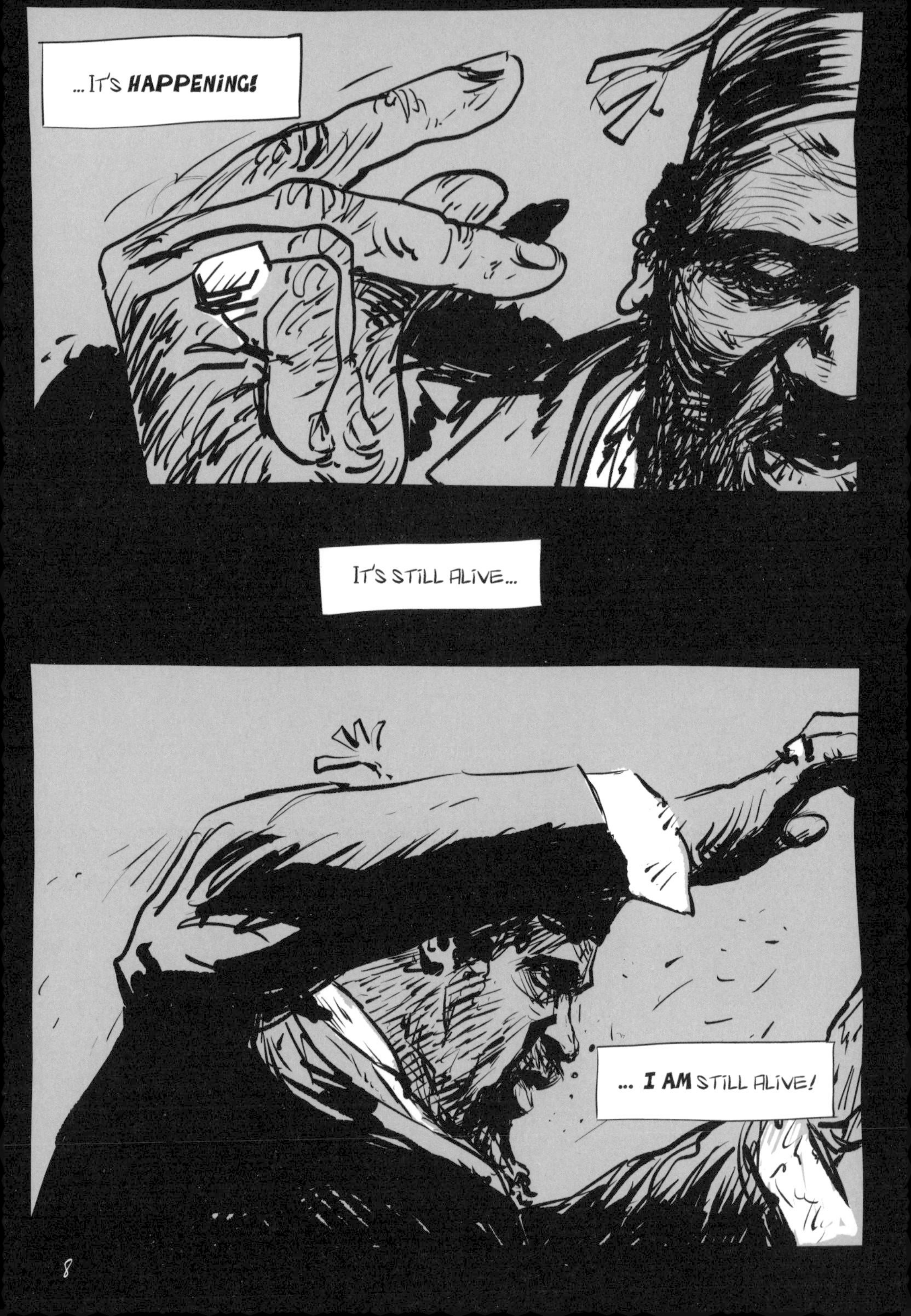
...It's HAPPENING!
It's still alive...
... I AM still alive!

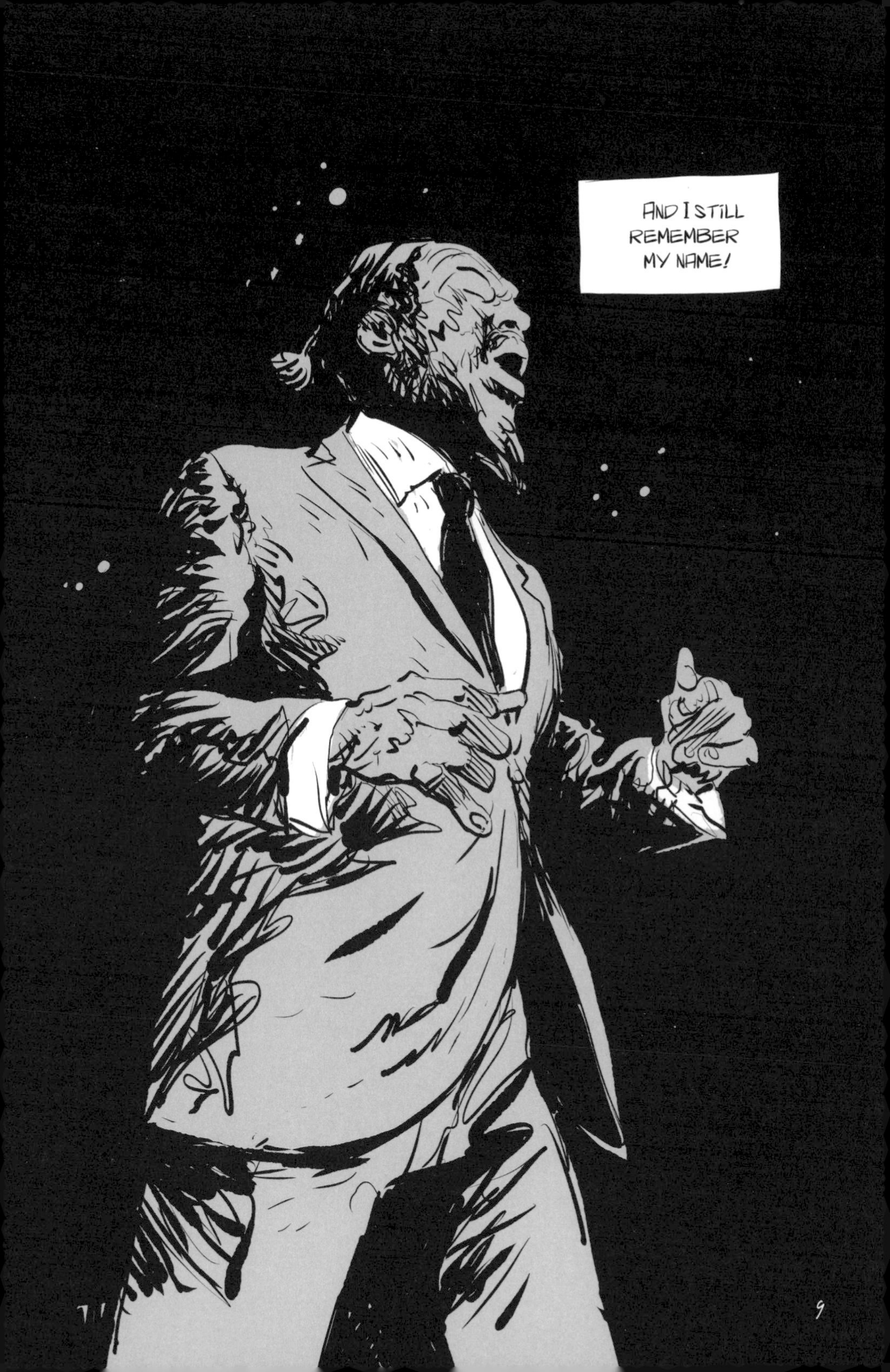
AND I STILL REMEMBER MY NAME!

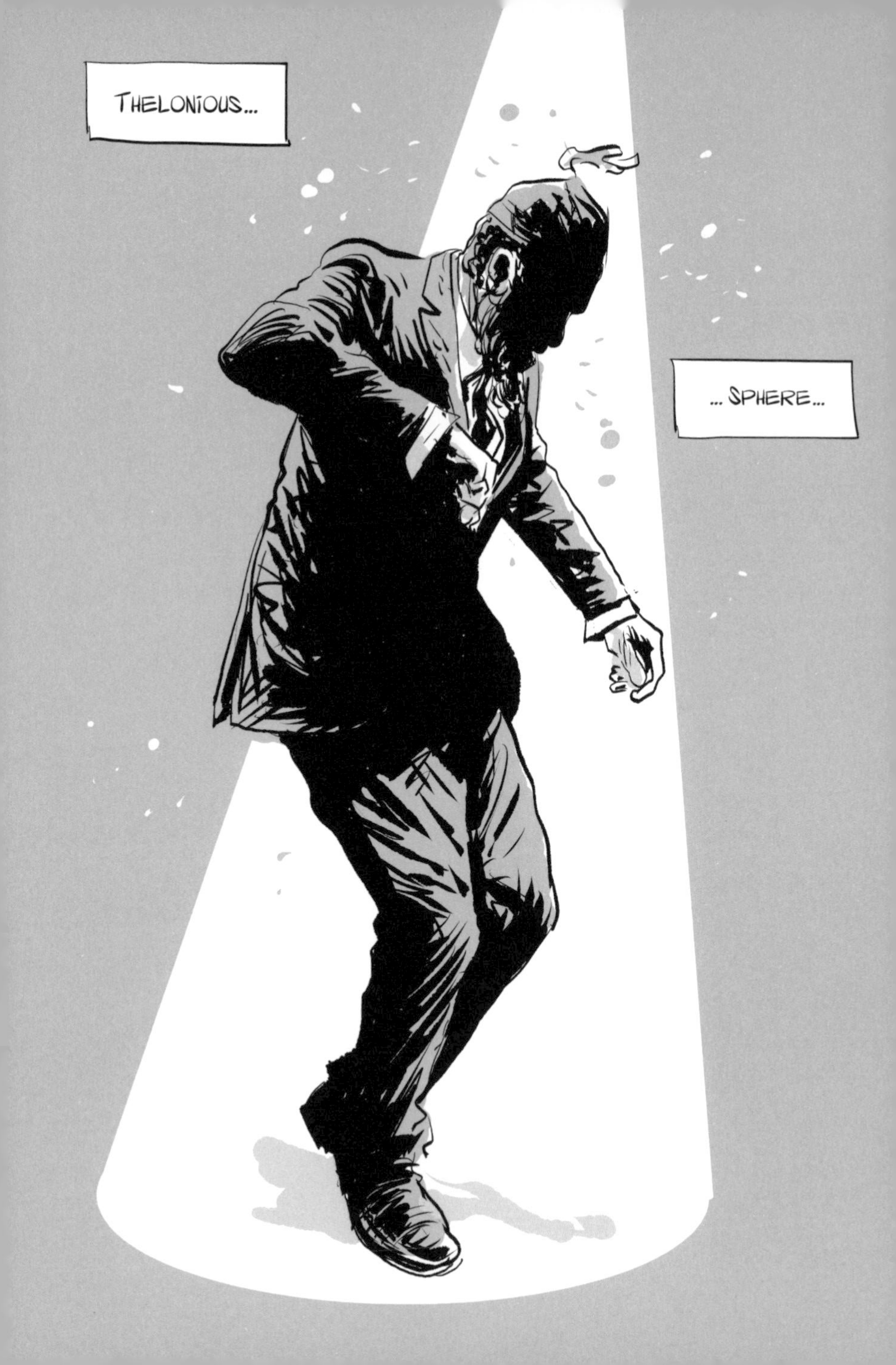
THELONIOUS...
... SPHERE...

MONK!

THELONIOUS, PANNONICA, AND THE FRIENDSHIP BEHIND A MUSICAL REVOLUTION

YOUSSEF DAOUDI

:01

First Second

New York

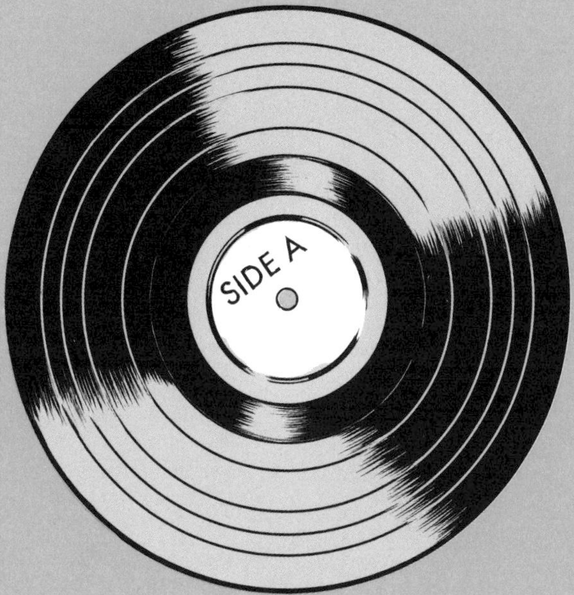
SIDE A

THELONICA

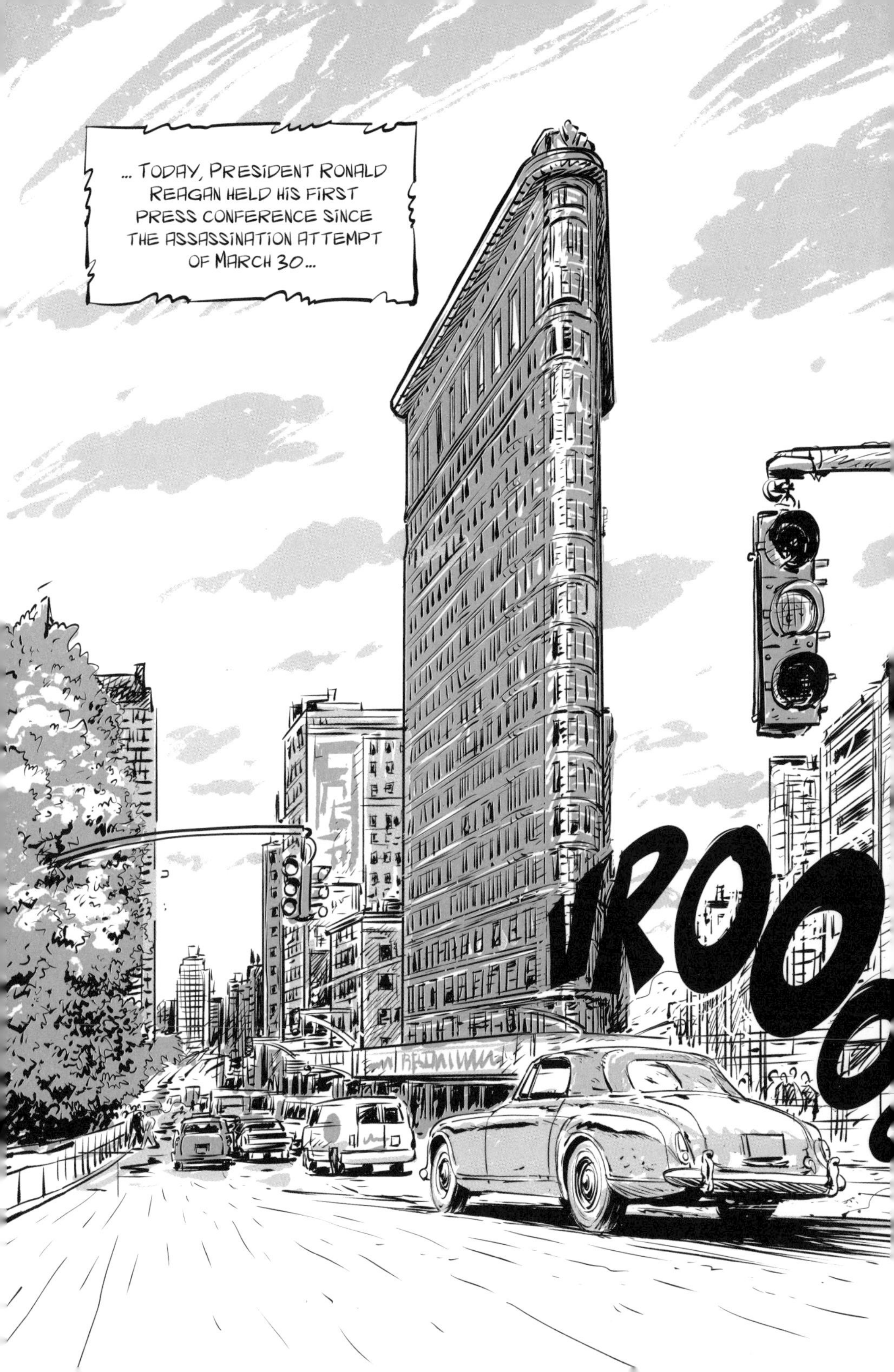
... TODAY, PRESIDENT RONALD REAGAN HELD HIS FIRST PRESS CONFERENCE SINCE THE ASSASSINATION ATTEMPT OF MARCH 30...
VROOO

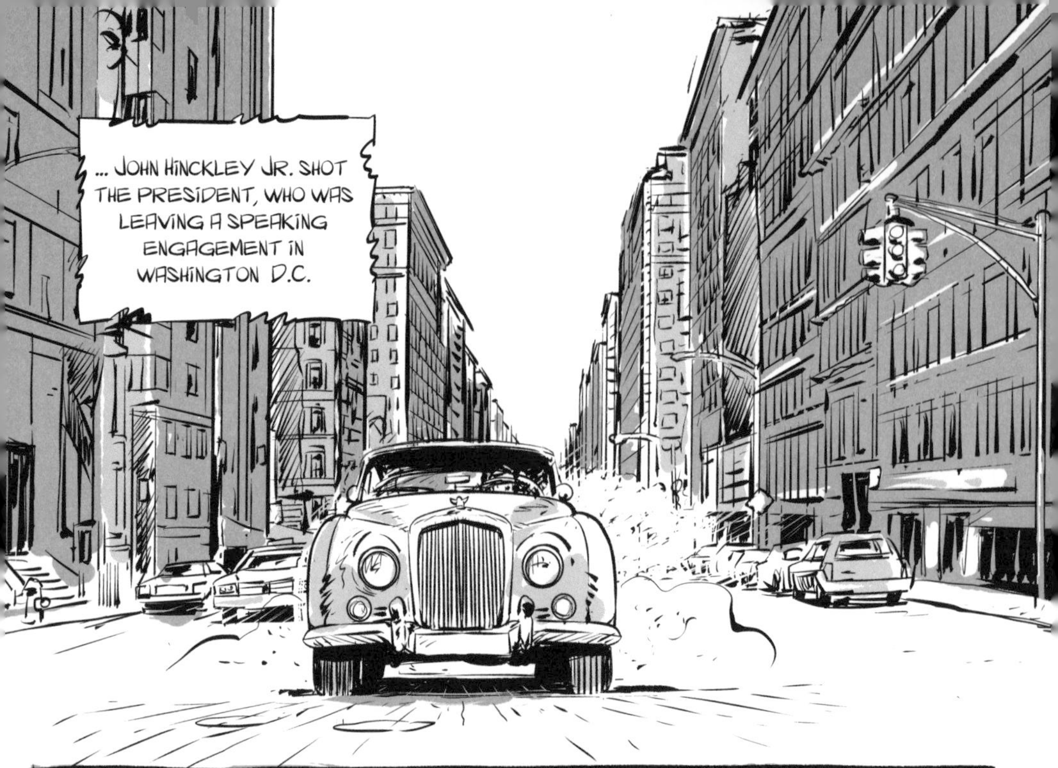
... JOHN HINCKLEY JR. SHOT THE PRESIDENT, WHO WAS LEAVING A SPEAKING ENGAGEMENT IN WASHINGTON D.C.

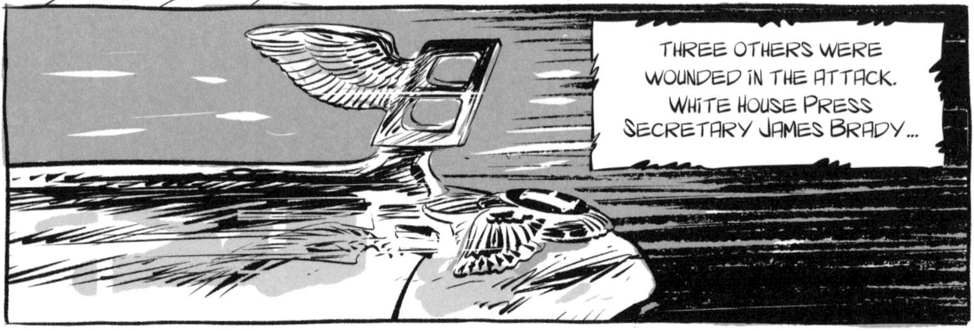
THREE OTHERS WERE WOUNDED IN THE ATTACK. WHITE HOUSE PRESS SECRETARY JAMES BRADY...

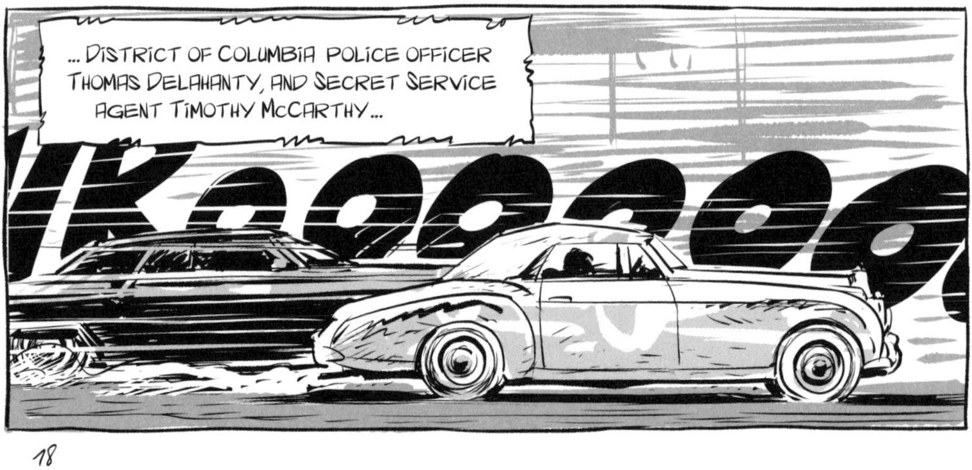
... DISTRICT OF COLUMBIA POLICE OFFICER THOMAS DELAHANTY, AND SECRET SERVICE AGENT TIMOTHY McCARTHY...

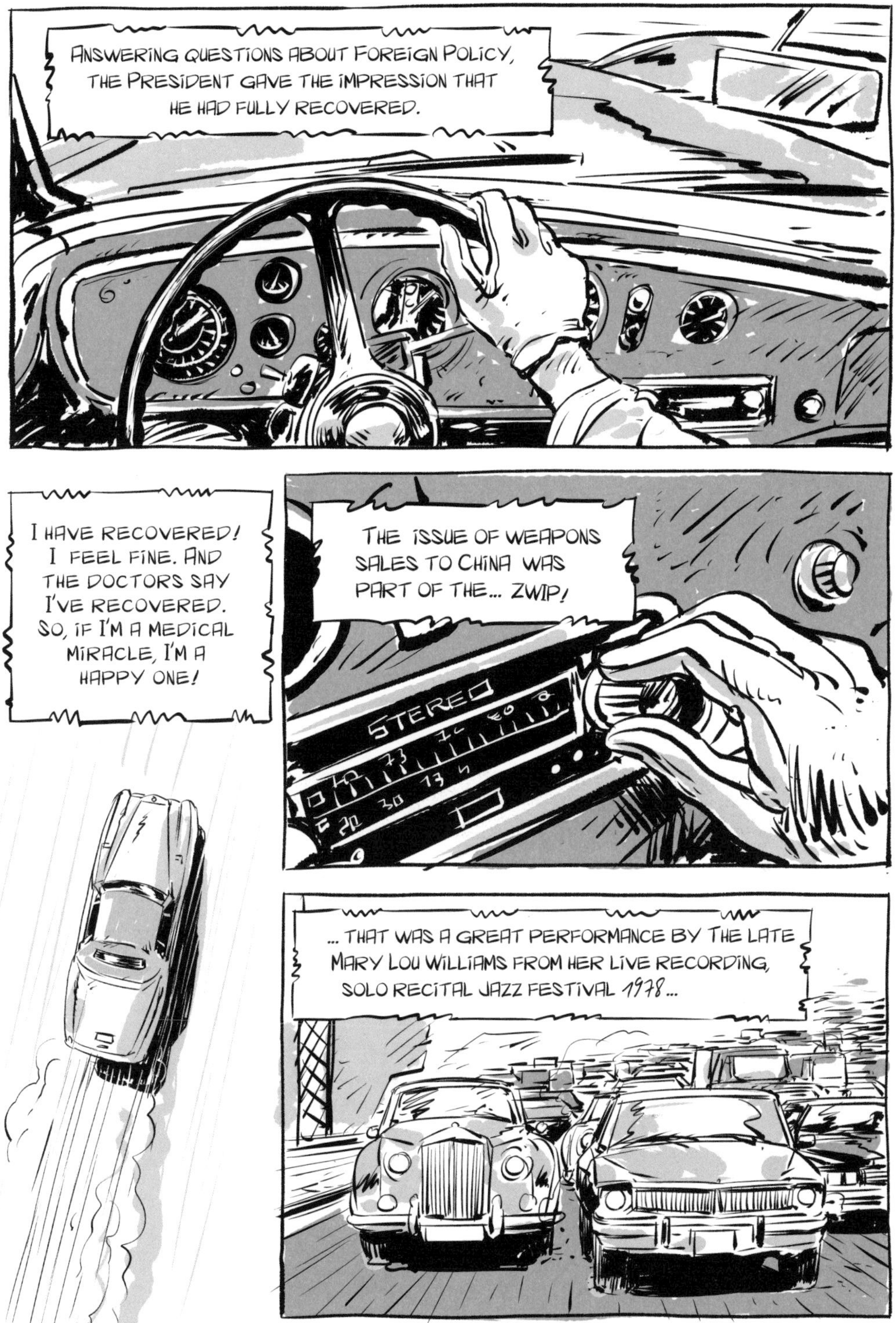
ANSWERING QUESTIONS ABOUT FOREIGN POLICY, THE PRESIDENT GAVE THE IMPRESSION THAT HE HAD FULLY RECOVERED.
I HAVE RECOVERED! I FEEL FINE. AND THE DOCTORS SAY I'VE RECOVERED. SO, IF I'M A MEDICAL MIRACLE, I'M A HAPPY ONE!
THE ISSUE OF WEAPONS SALES TO CHINA WAS PART OF THE... ZWIP!
STEREO
... THAT WAS A GREAT PERFORMANCE BY THE LATE MARY LOU WILLIAMS FROM HER LIVE RECORDING, SOLO RECITAL JAZZ FESTIVAL 1978...

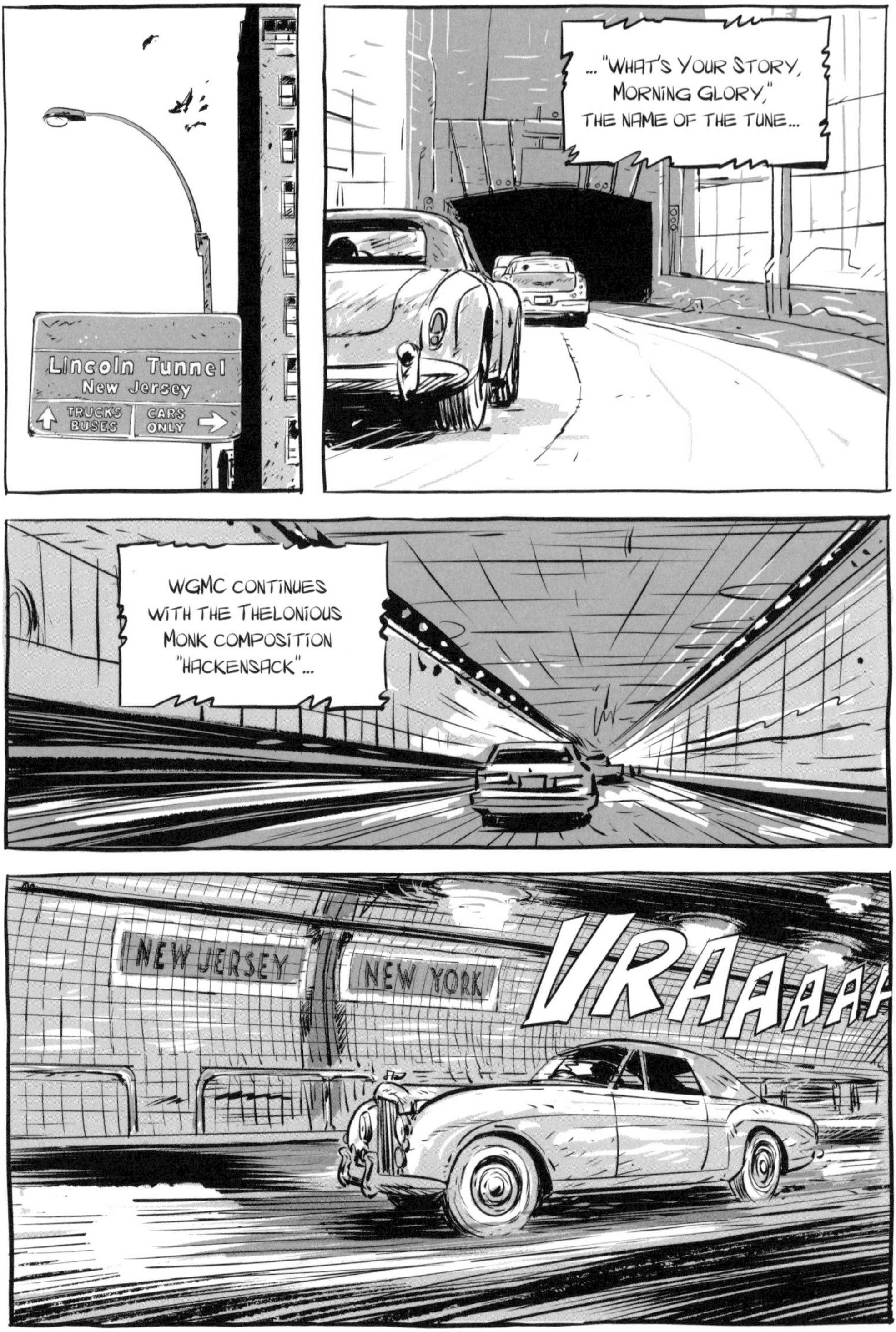
Lincoln Tunnel
New Jersey
TRUCKS BUSES
CARS ONLY
..."WHAT'S YOUR STORY, MORNING GLORY," THE NAME OF THE TUNE...
WGMC CONTINUES WITH THE THELONIOUS MONK COMPOSITION "HACKENSACK"...
NEW JERSEY
NEW YORK
VRAAAAA

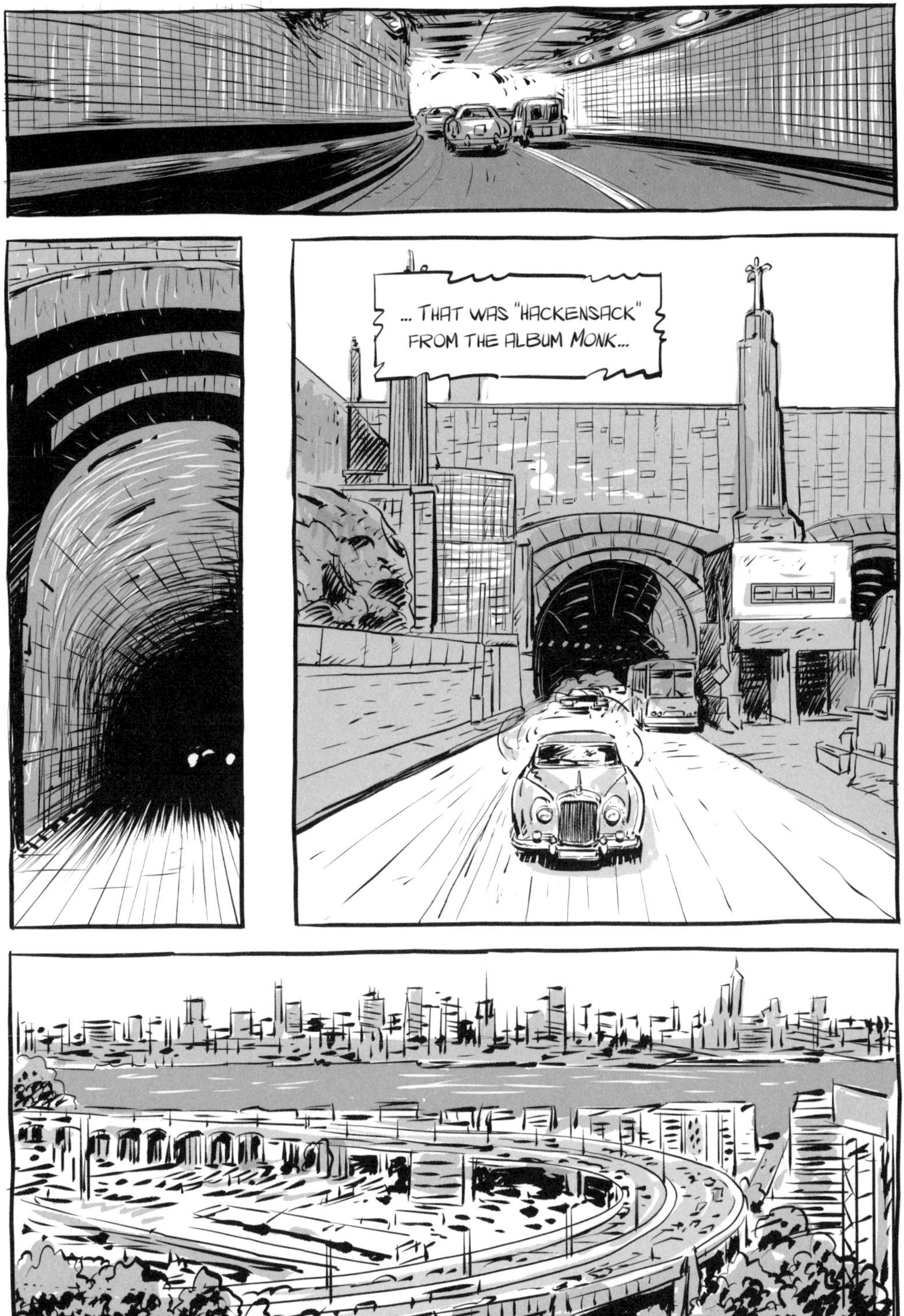
... THAT WAS "HACKENSACK" FROM THE ALBUM MONK...

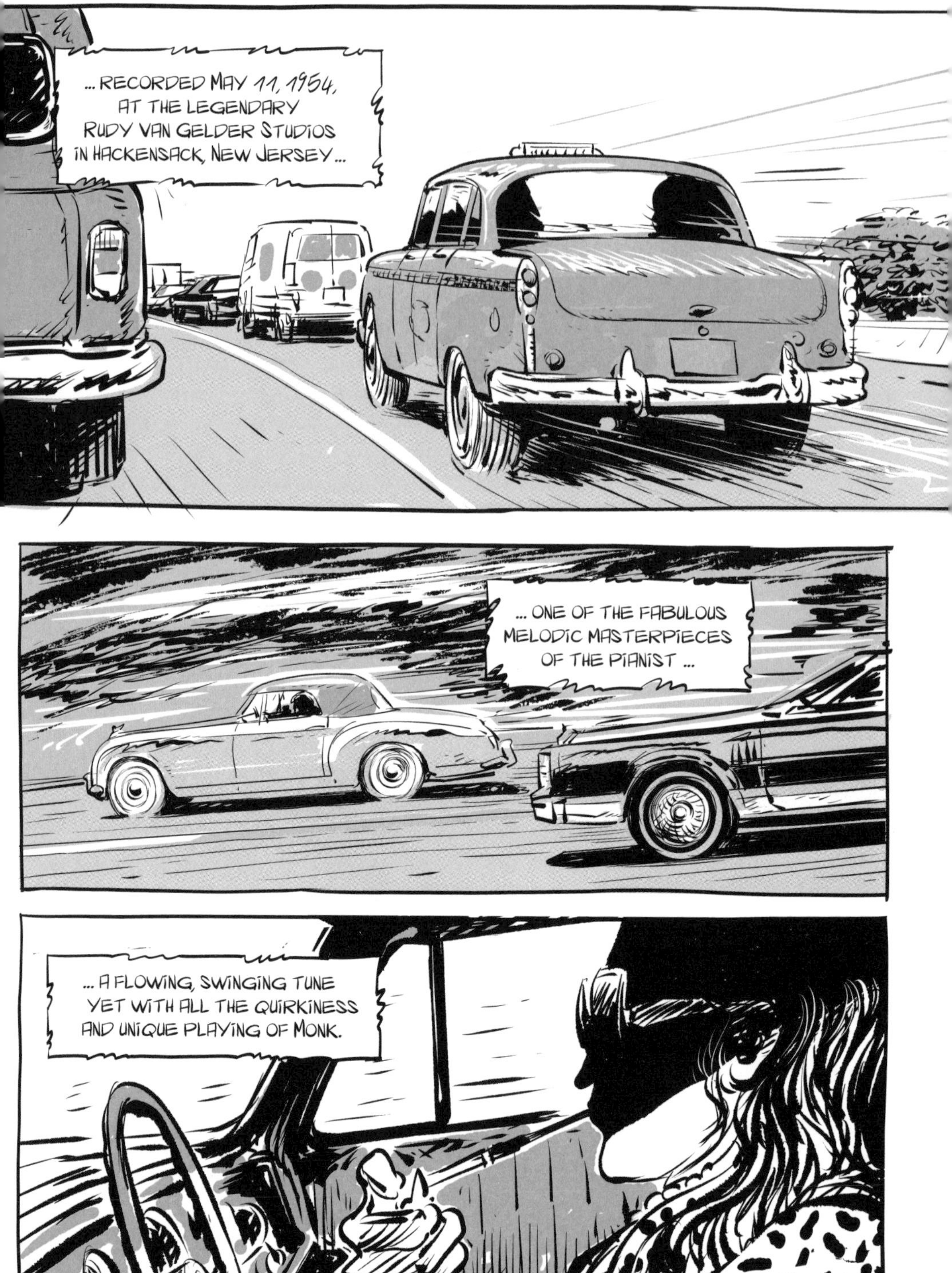
... RECORDED MAY 11, 1954, AT THE LEGENDARY RUDY VAN GELDER STUDIOS IN HACKENSACK, NEW JERSEY...
... ONE OF THE FABULOUS MELODIC MASTERPIECES OF THE PIANIST ...
... A FLOWING, SWINGING TUNE YET WITH ALL THE QUIRKINESS AND UNIQUE PLAYING OF MONK.

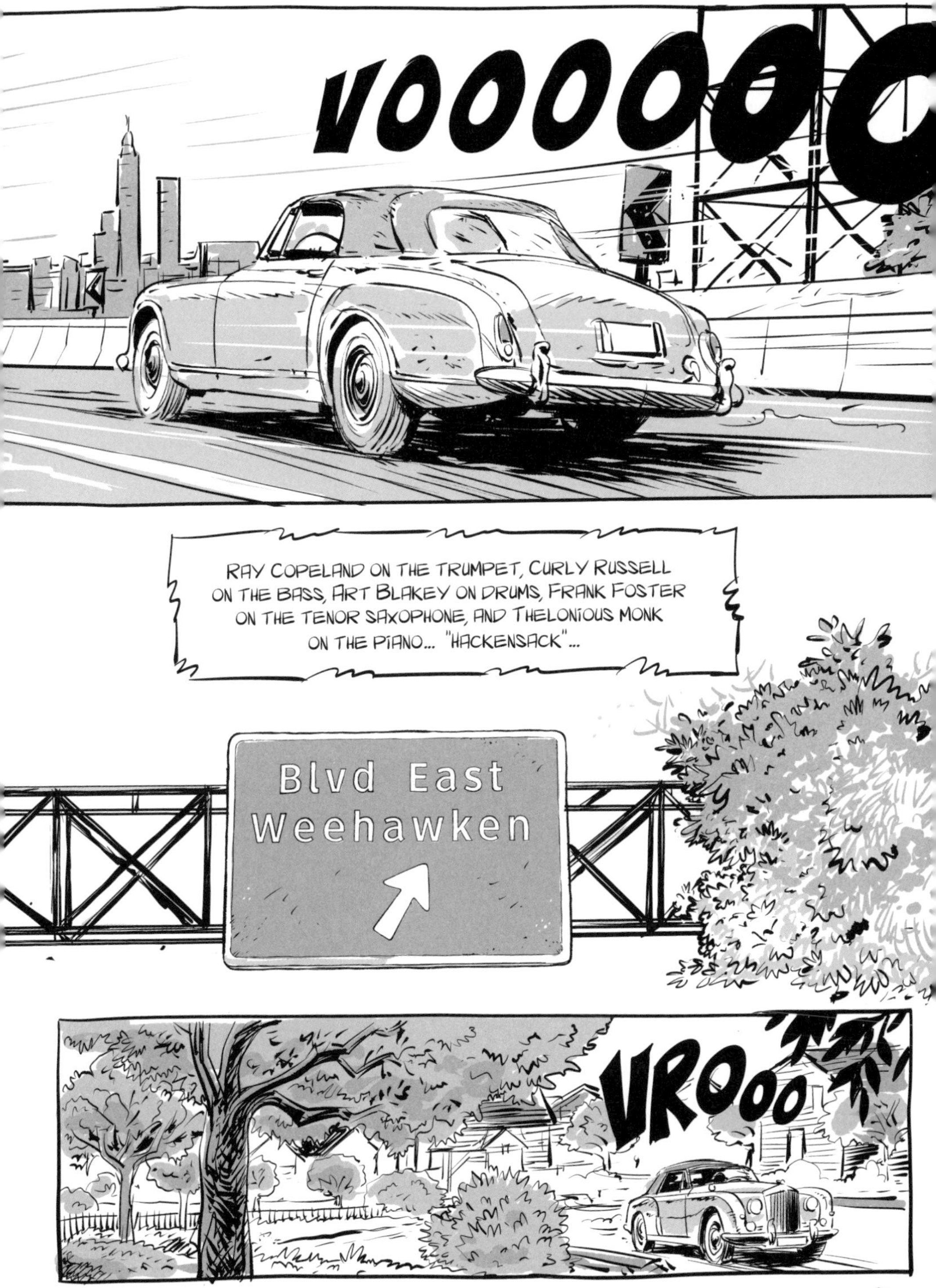
VOOOOOO
RAY COPELAND ON THE TRUMPET, CURLY RUSSELL ON THE BASS, ART BLAKEY ON DRUMS, FRANK FOSTER ON THE TENOR SAXOPHONE, AND THELONIOUS MONK ON THE PIANO... "HACKENSACK"...
Blvd East
Weehawken
VROOO

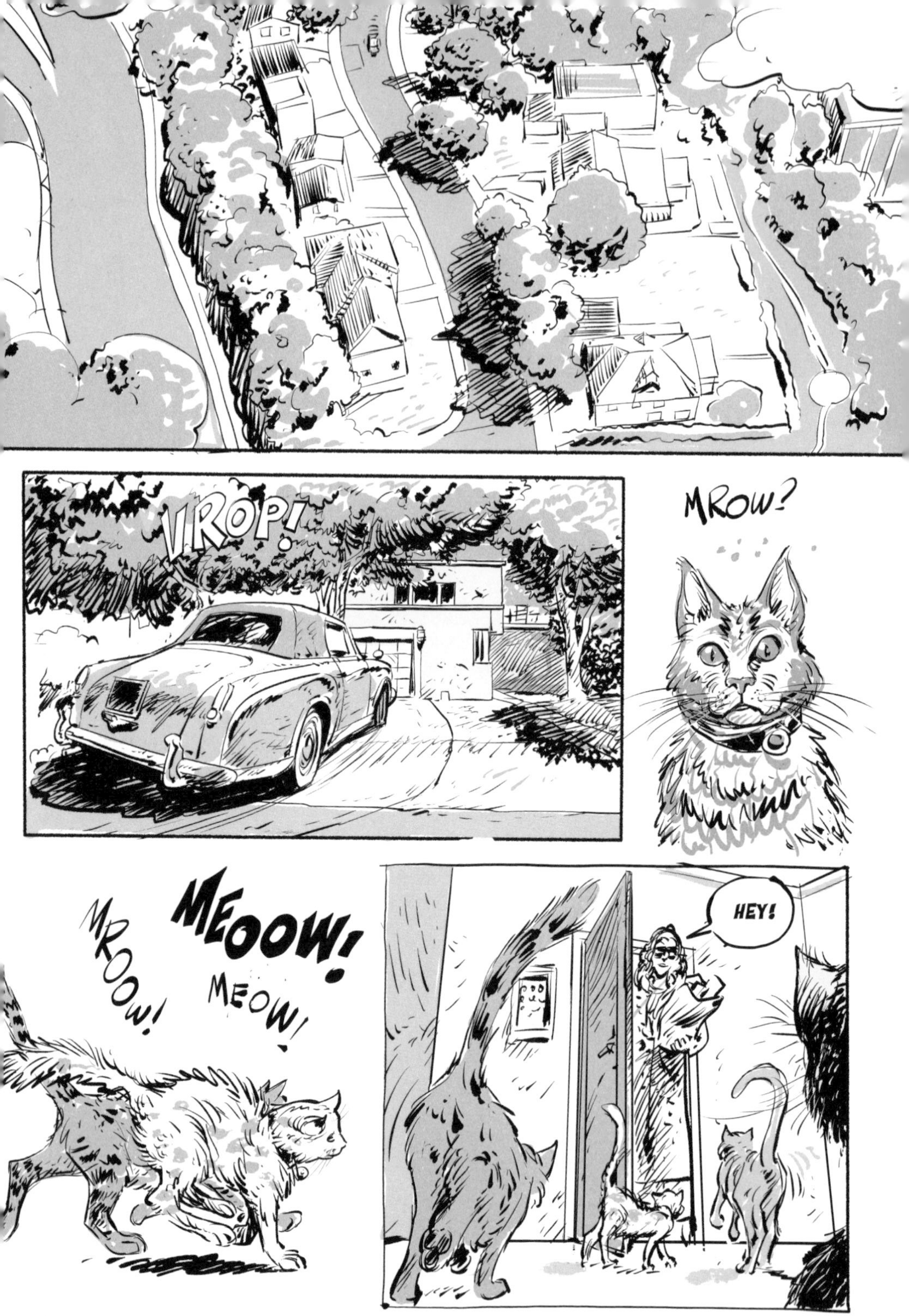
VROP!
MROW?
MROOW!
MEOOW!
MEOW!
HEY!

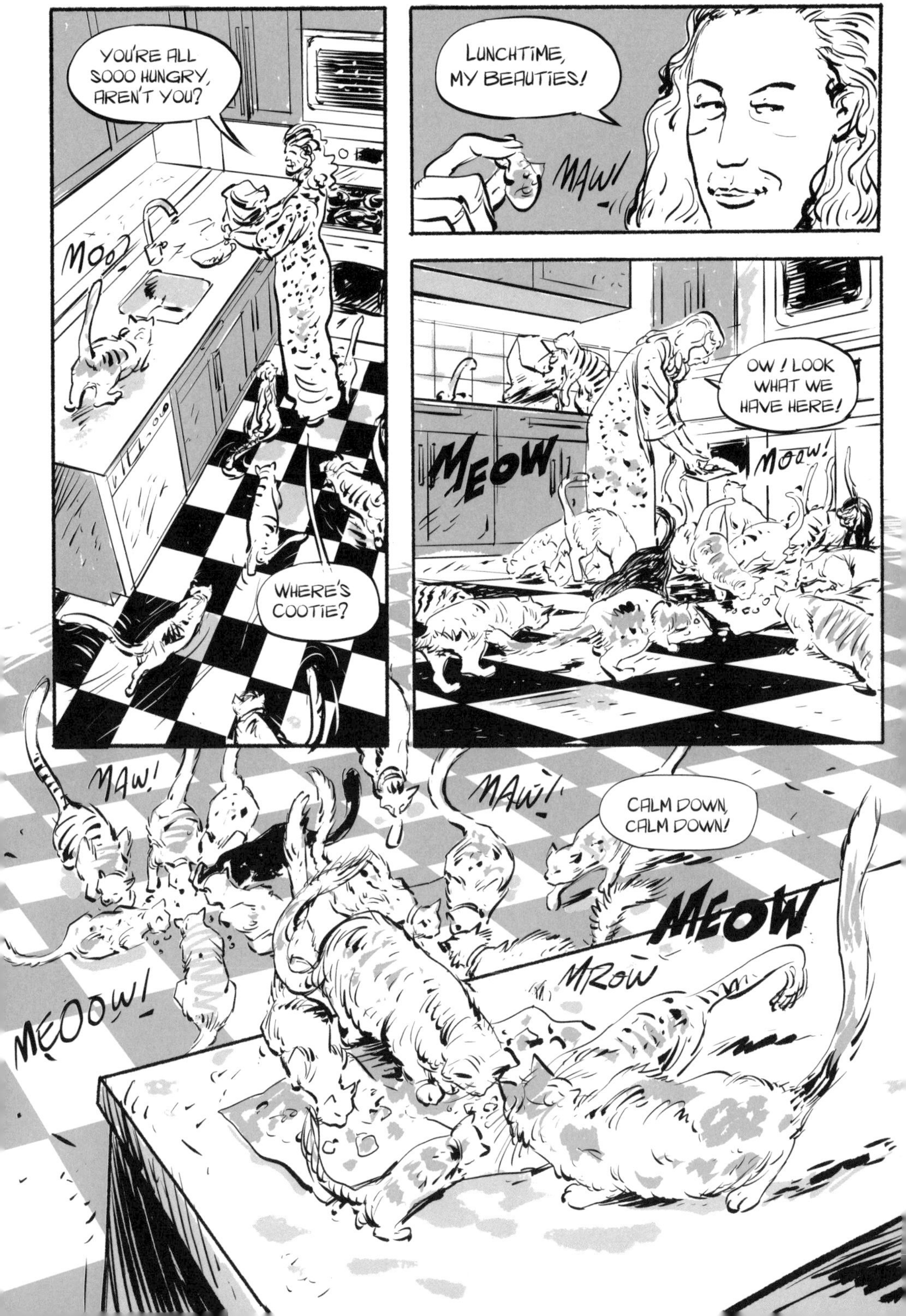
YOU'RE ALL SOOO HUNGRY, AREN'T YOU?
MOO
WHERE'S COOTIE?
LUNCHTIME, MY BEAUTIES!
MAW!
OW! LOOK WHAT WE HAVE HERE!
MEOW
MOOW!
MAW!
MAW!
CALM DOWN, CALM DOWN!
MEOW
MROW
MEOOW!

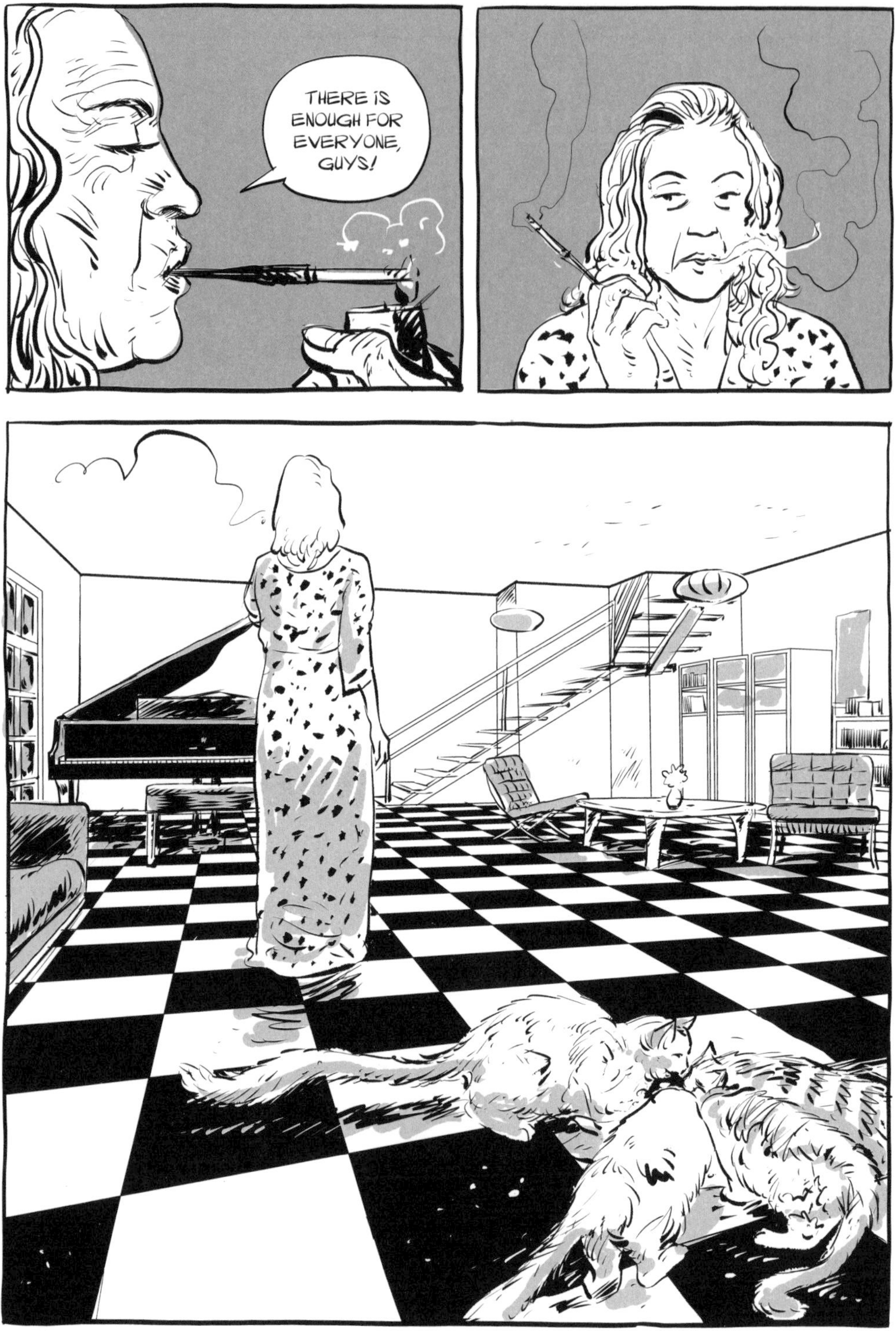
THERE IS ENOUGH FOR EVERYONE, GUYS!

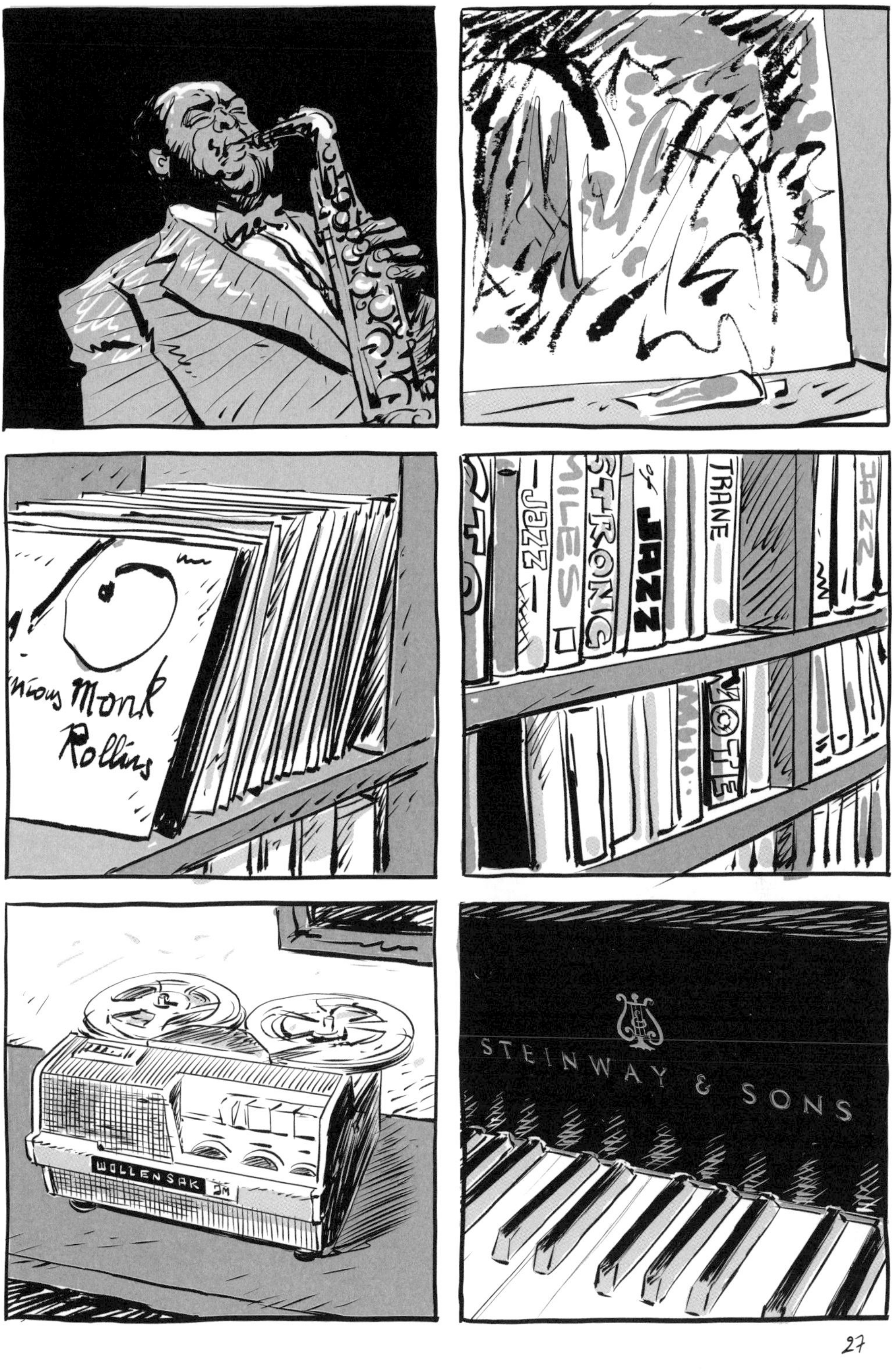
Monk
Rollins
Jazz
STRONG
JAZZ
TRANE
WOLLENSAK
STEINWAY & SONS

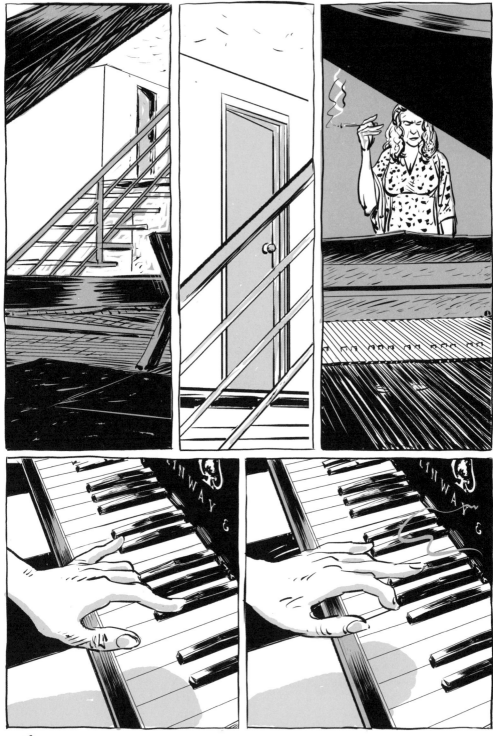

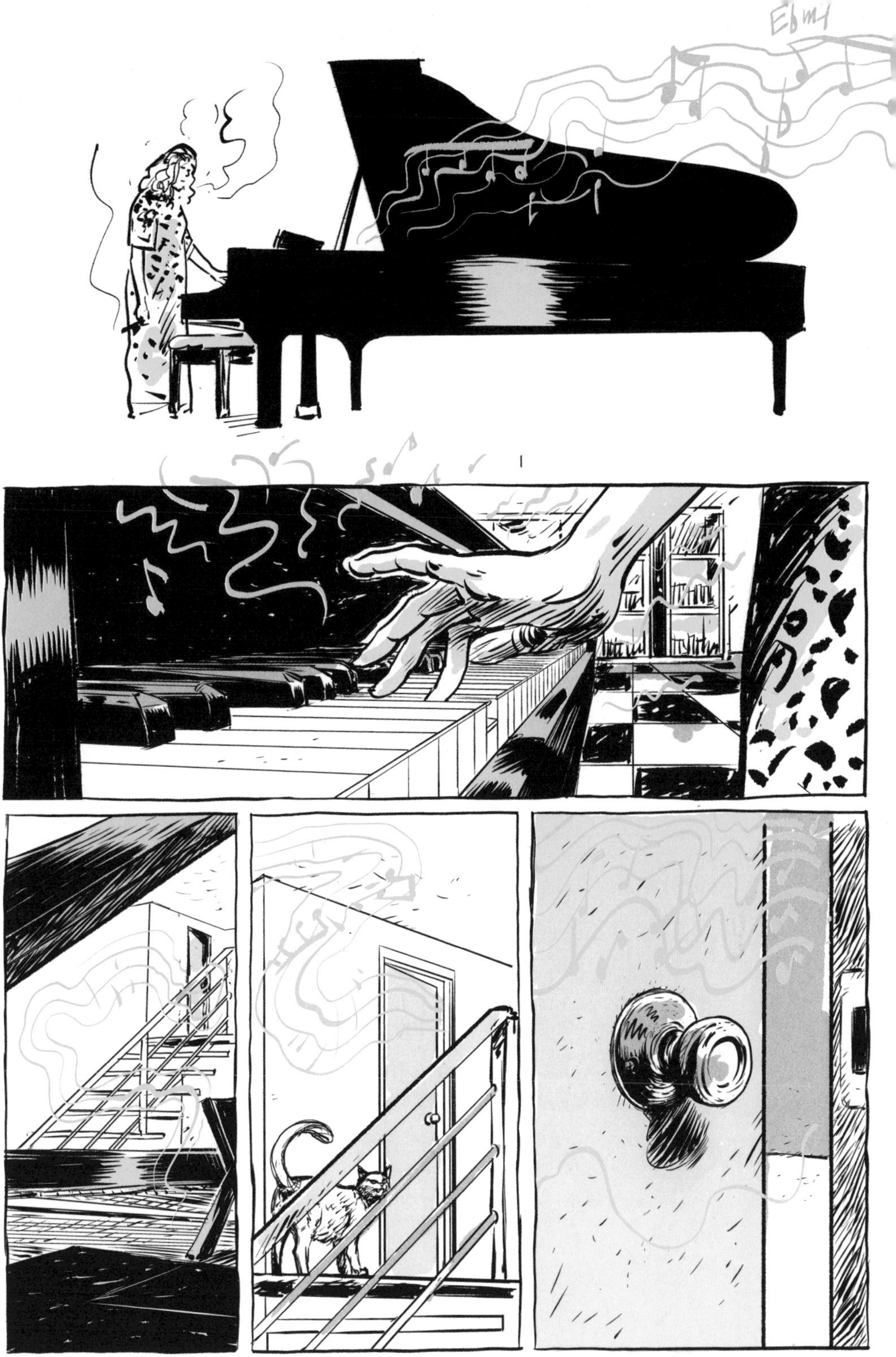

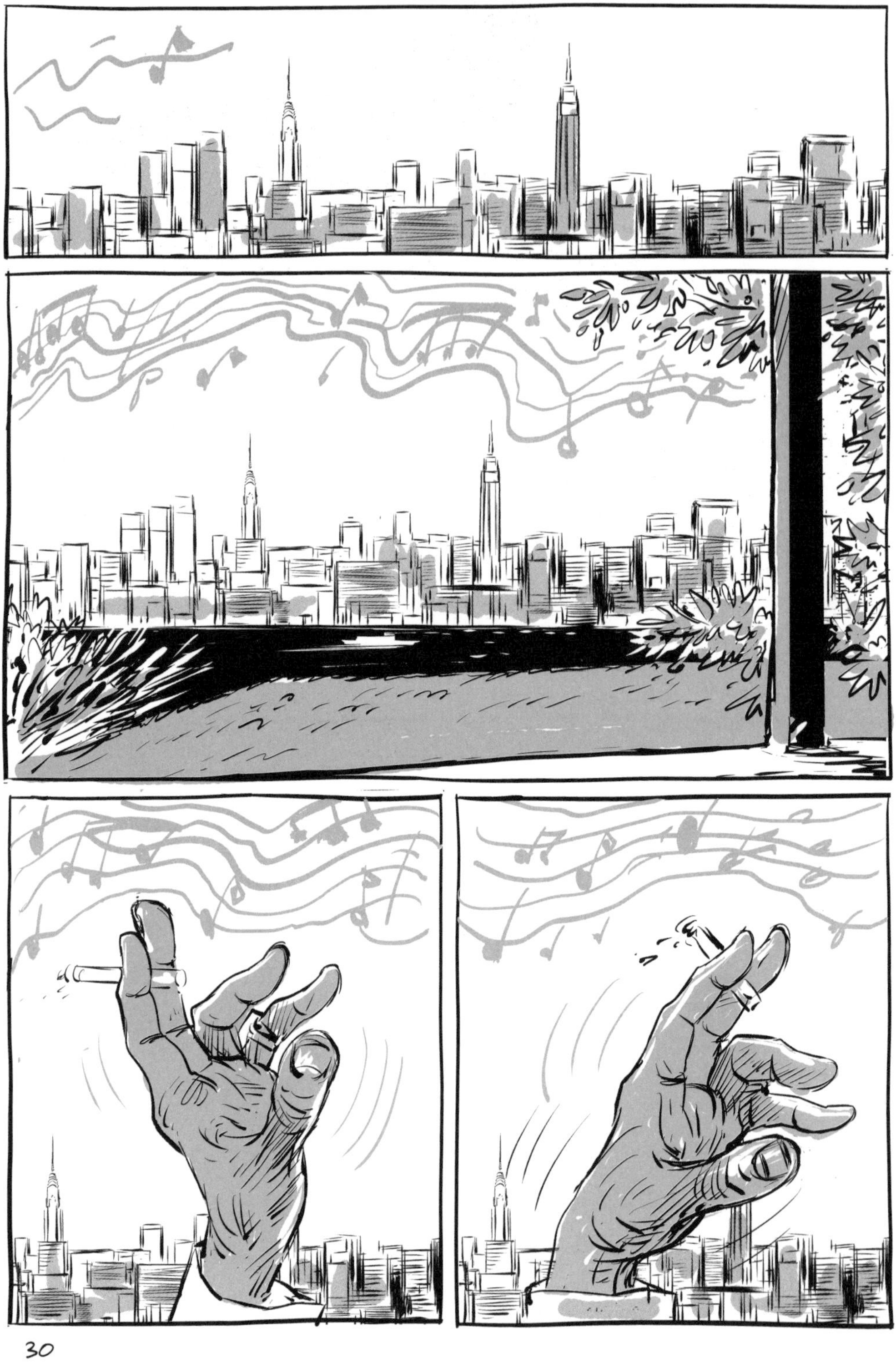

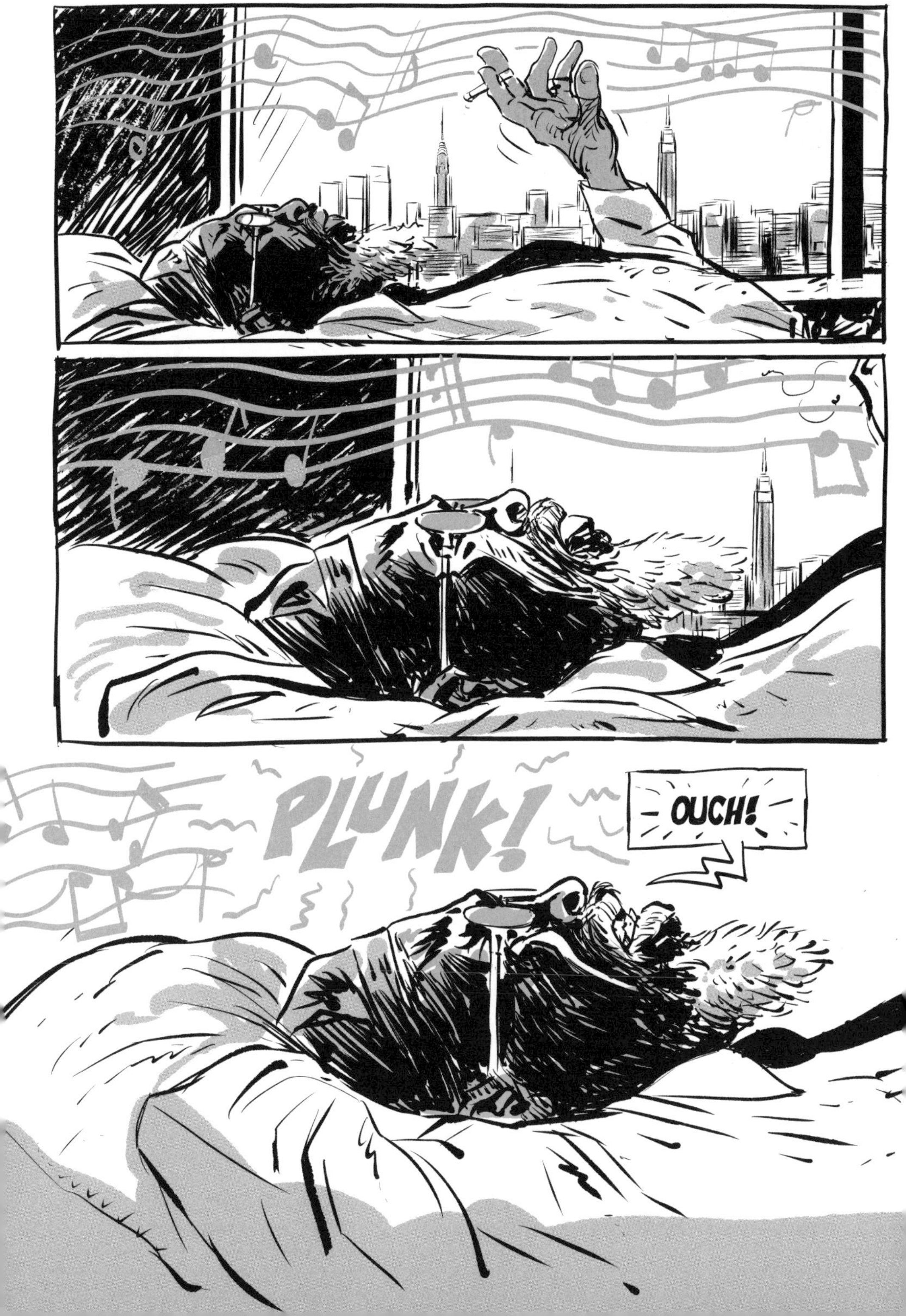
PLUNK!
OUCH!

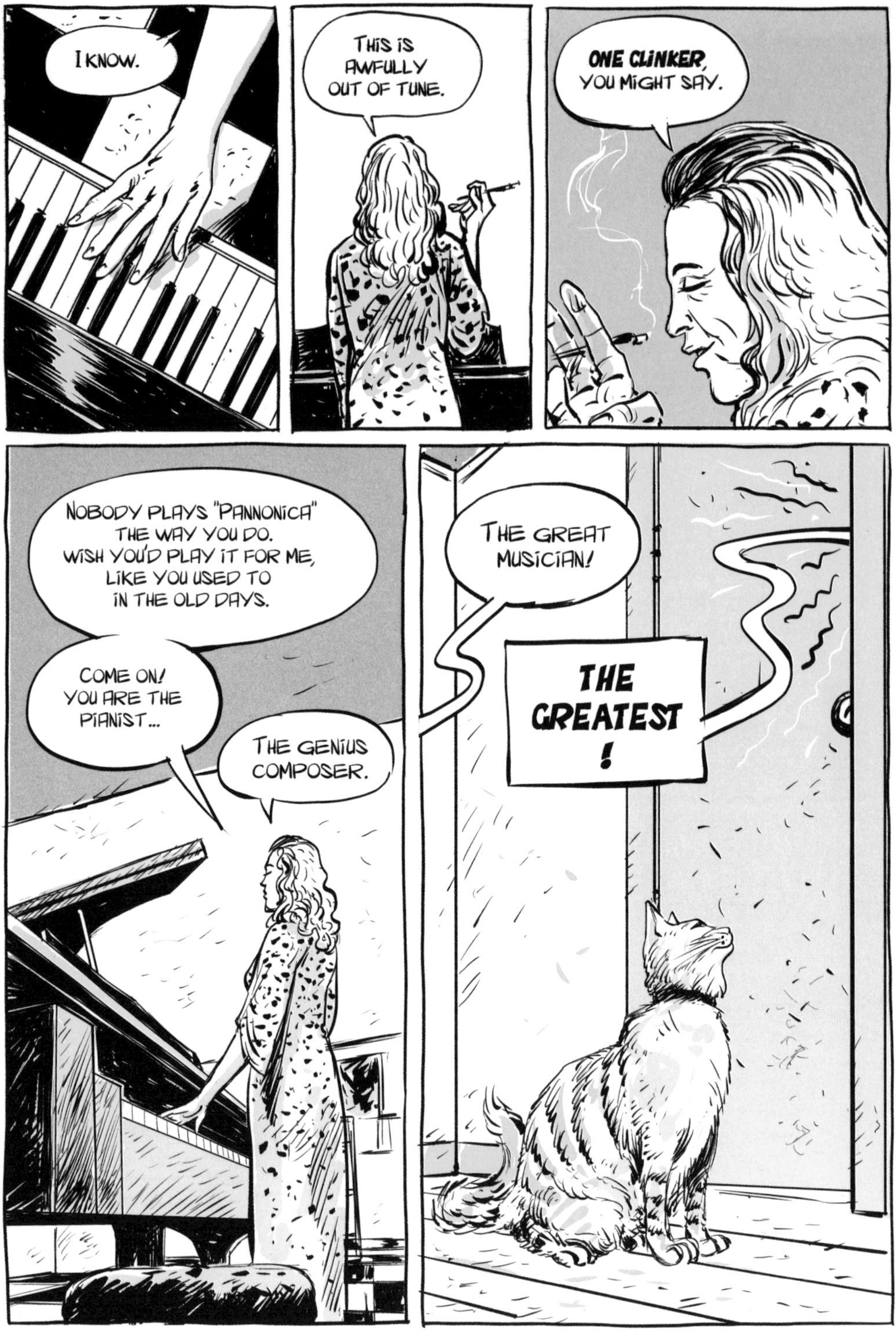
I KNOW.
THIS IS AWFULLY OUT OF TUNE.
ONE CLINKER, YOU MIGHT SAY.
NOBODY PLAYS "PANNONICA" THE WAY YOU DO. WISH YOU'D PLAY IT FOR ME, LIKE YOU USED TO IN THE OLD DAYS.
COME ON! YOU ARE THE PIANIST...
THE GENIUS COMPOSER.
THE GREAT MUSICIAN!
THE GREATEST !

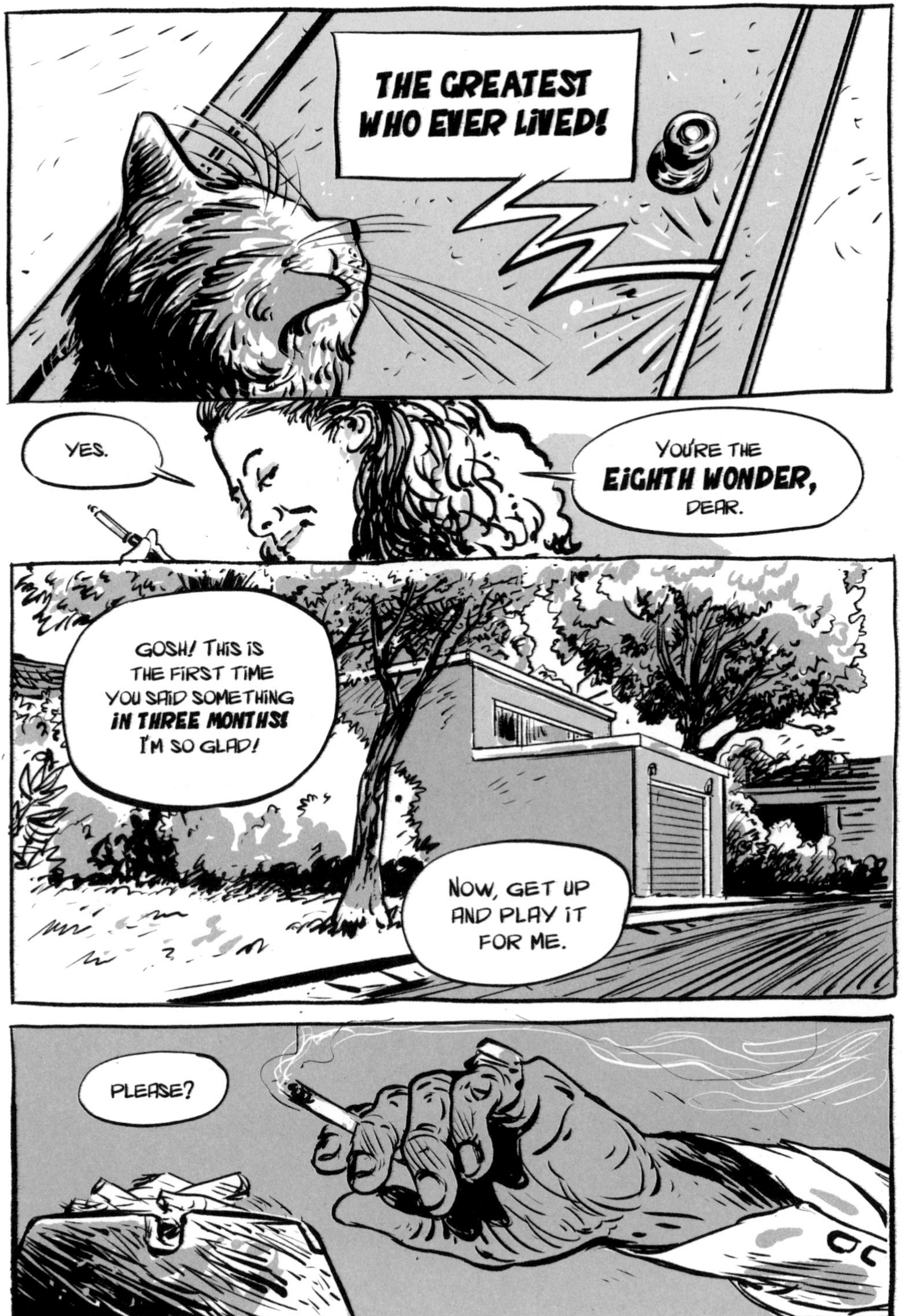
THE GREATEST WHO EVER LIVED!
YES.
YOU'RE THE EIGHTH WONDER, DEAR.
GOSH! THIS IS THE FIRST TIME YOU SAID SOMETHING IN THREE MONTHS! I'M SO GLAD!
NOW, GET UP AND PLAY IT FOR ME.
PLEASE?

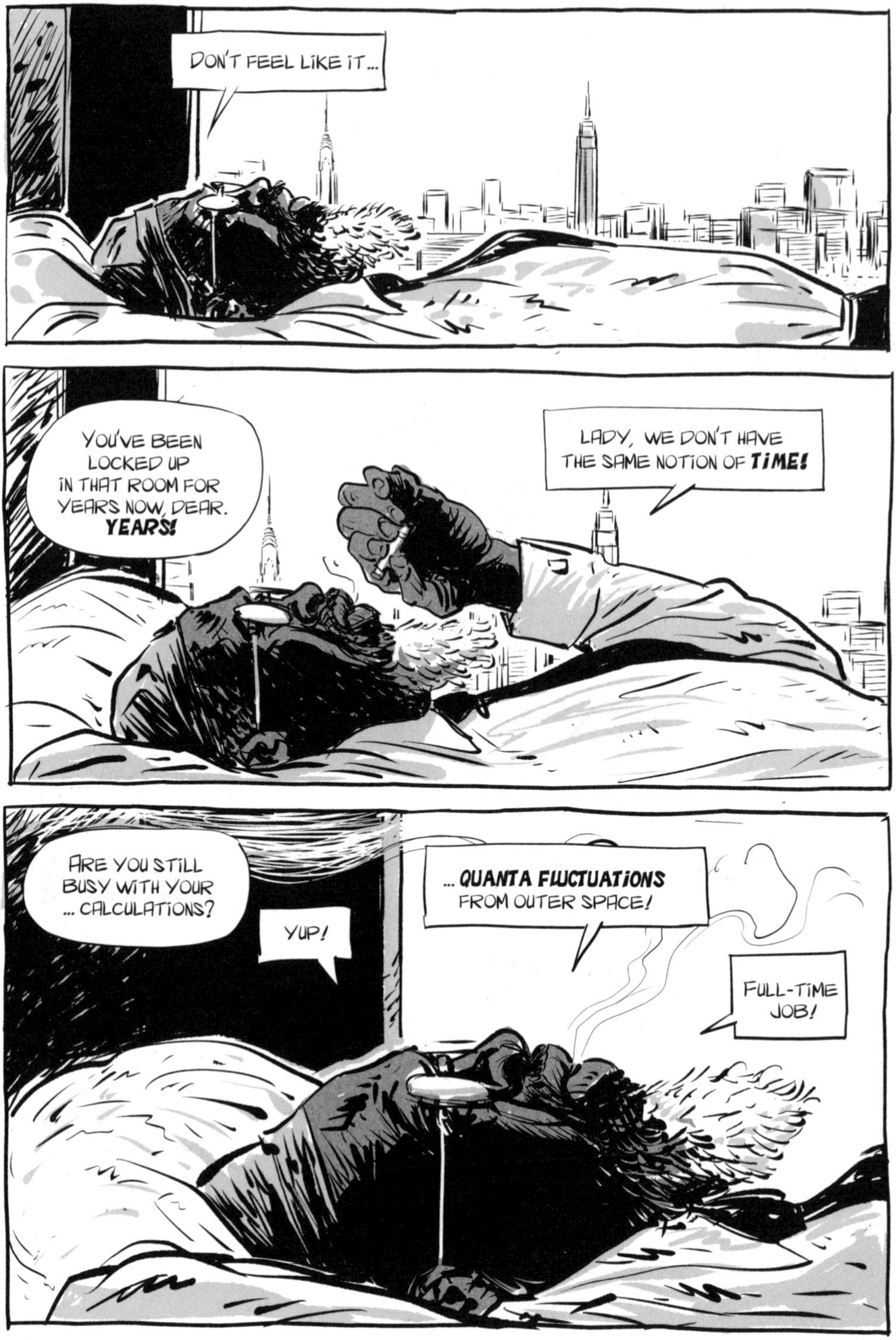
DON'T FEEL LIKE IT...
YOU'VE BEEN LOCKED UP IN THAT ROOM FOR YEARS NOW, DEAR. **YEARS!**
LADY, WE DON'T HAVE THE SAME NOTION OF **TIME!**
ARE YOU STILL BUSY WITH YOUR ... CALCULATIONS?
YUP!
... **QUANTA FLUCTUATIONS** FROM OUTER SPACE!
FULL-TIME JOB!

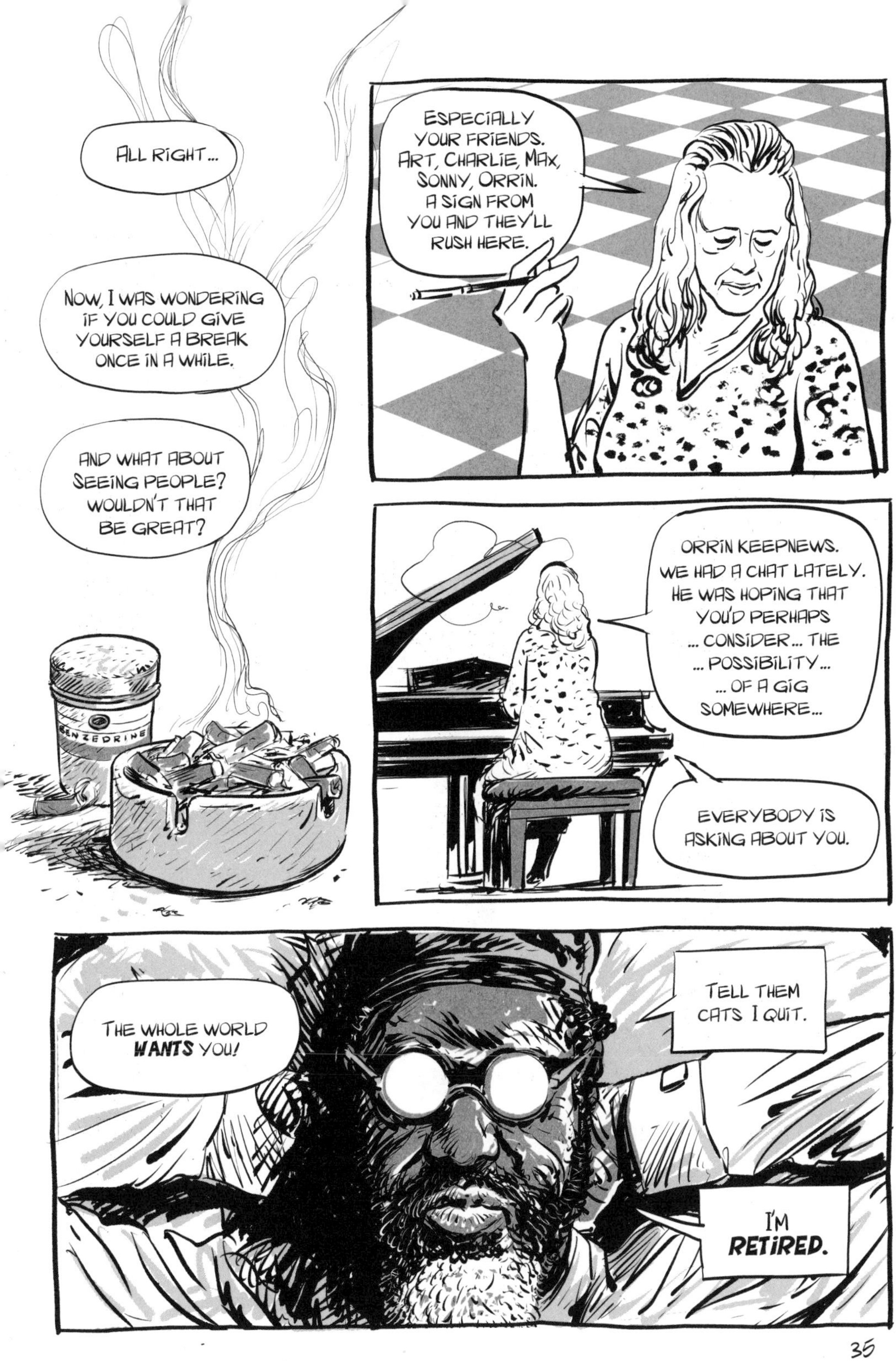
ALL RIGHT...
NOW, I WAS WONDERING IF YOU COULD GIVE YOURSELF A BREAK ONCE IN A WHILE.
AND WHAT ABOUT SEEING PEOPLE? WOULDN'T THAT BE GREAT?
BENZEDRINE
ESPECIALLY YOUR FRIENDS. ART, CHARLIE, MAX, SONNY, ORRIN. A SIGN FROM YOU AND THEY'LL RUSH HERE.
ORRIN KEEPNEWS. WE HAD A CHAT LATELY. HE WAS HOPING THAT YOU'D PERHAPS ... CONSIDER... THE ... POSSIBILITY... ... OF A GIG SOMEWHERE...
EVERYBODY IS ASKING ABOUT YOU.
THE WHOLE WORLD **WANTS** YOU!
TELL THEM CATS I QUIT.
I'M **RETIRED.**

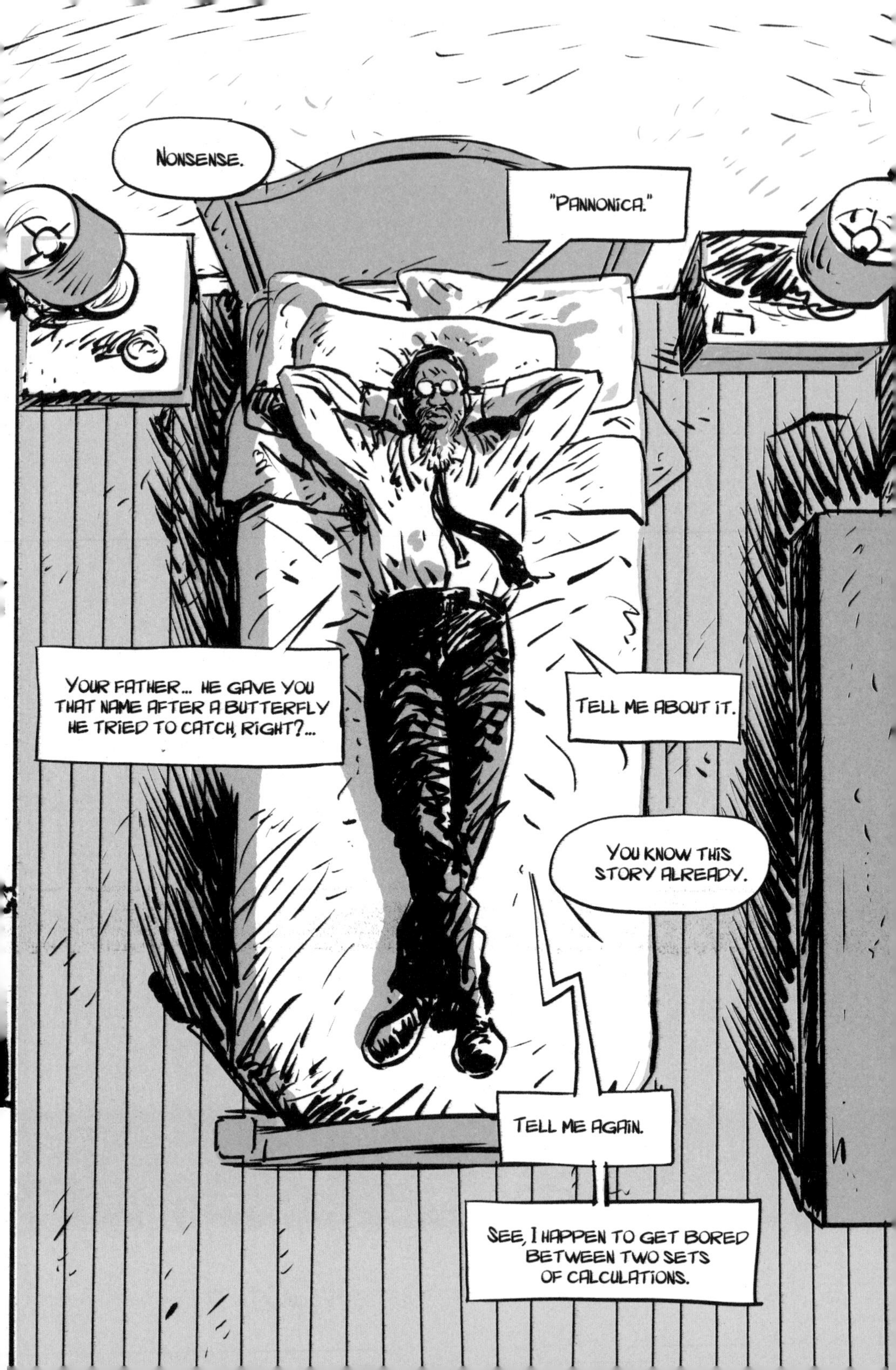
NONSENSE.
"PANNONICA."
YOUR FATHER... HE GAVE YOU THAT NAME AFTER A BUTTERFLY HE TRIED TO CATCH, RIGHT?...
TELL ME ABOUT IT.
YOU KNOW THIS STORY ALREADY.
TELL ME AGAIN.
SEE, I HAPPEN TO GET BORED BETWEEN TWO SETS OF CALCULATIONS.

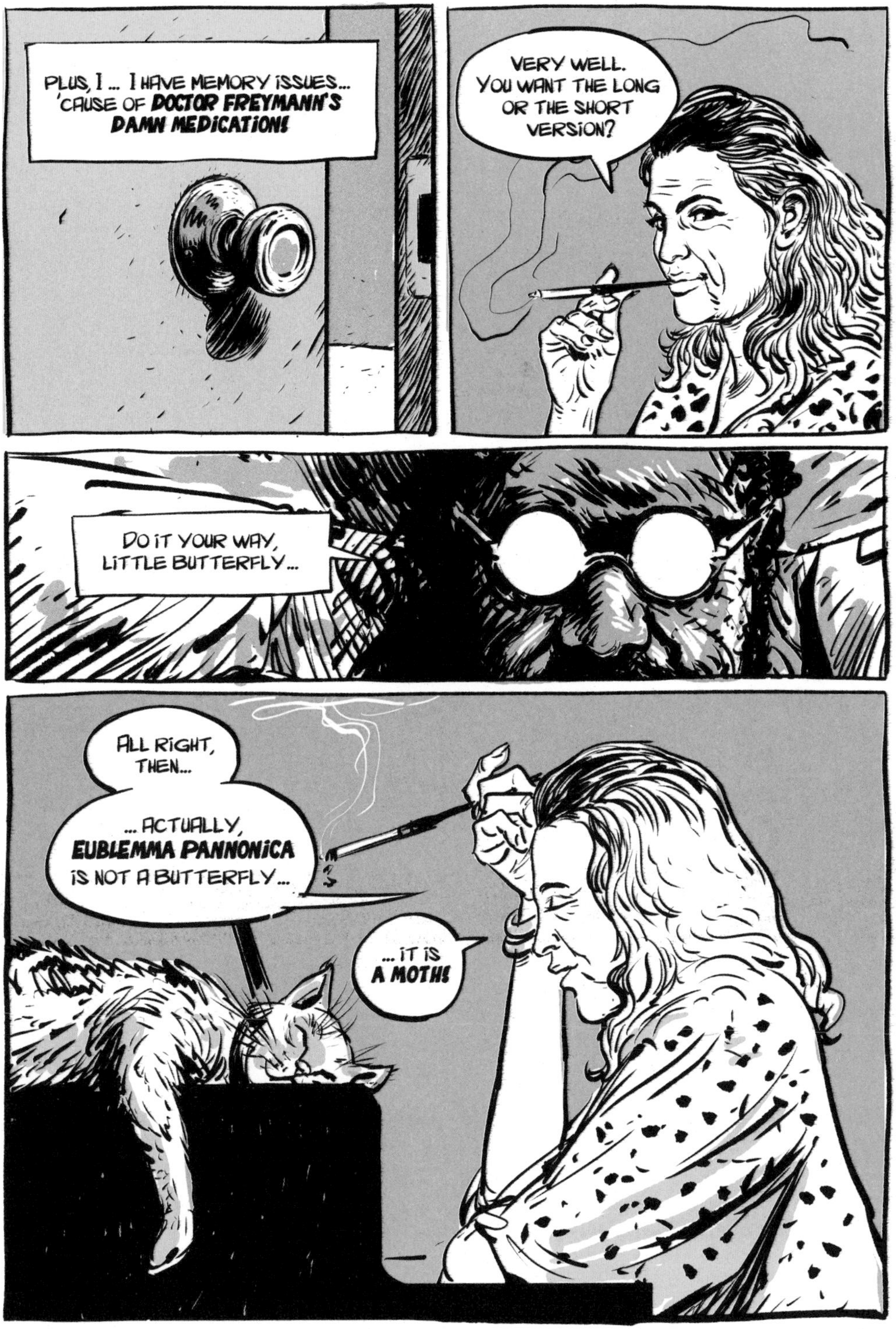
PLUS, I ... I HAVE MEMORY ISSUES... 'CAUSE OF DOCTOR FREYMANN'S DAMN MEDICATION!
VERY WELL. YOU WANT THE LONG OR THE SHORT VERSION?
DO IT YOUR WAY, LITTLE BUTTERFLY...
ALL RIGHT, THEN...
... ACTUALLY, EUBLEMMA PANNONICA IS NOT A BUTTERFLY...
... IT IS A MOTH!

PANNONICA

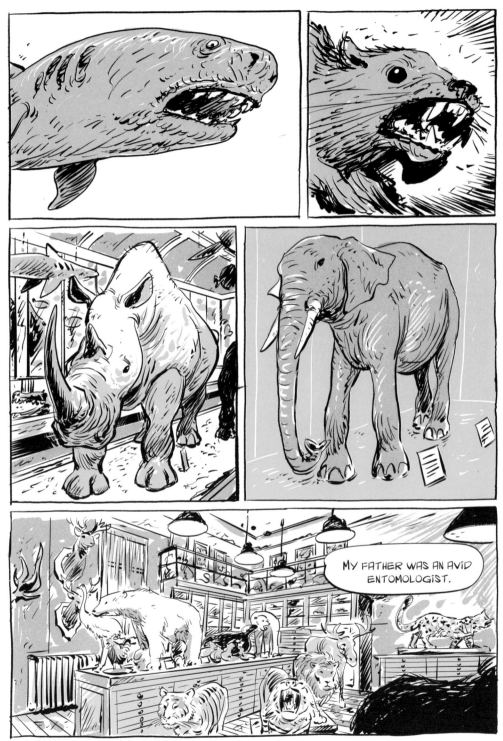

MY FATHER WAS AN AVID ENTOMOLOGIST.

41

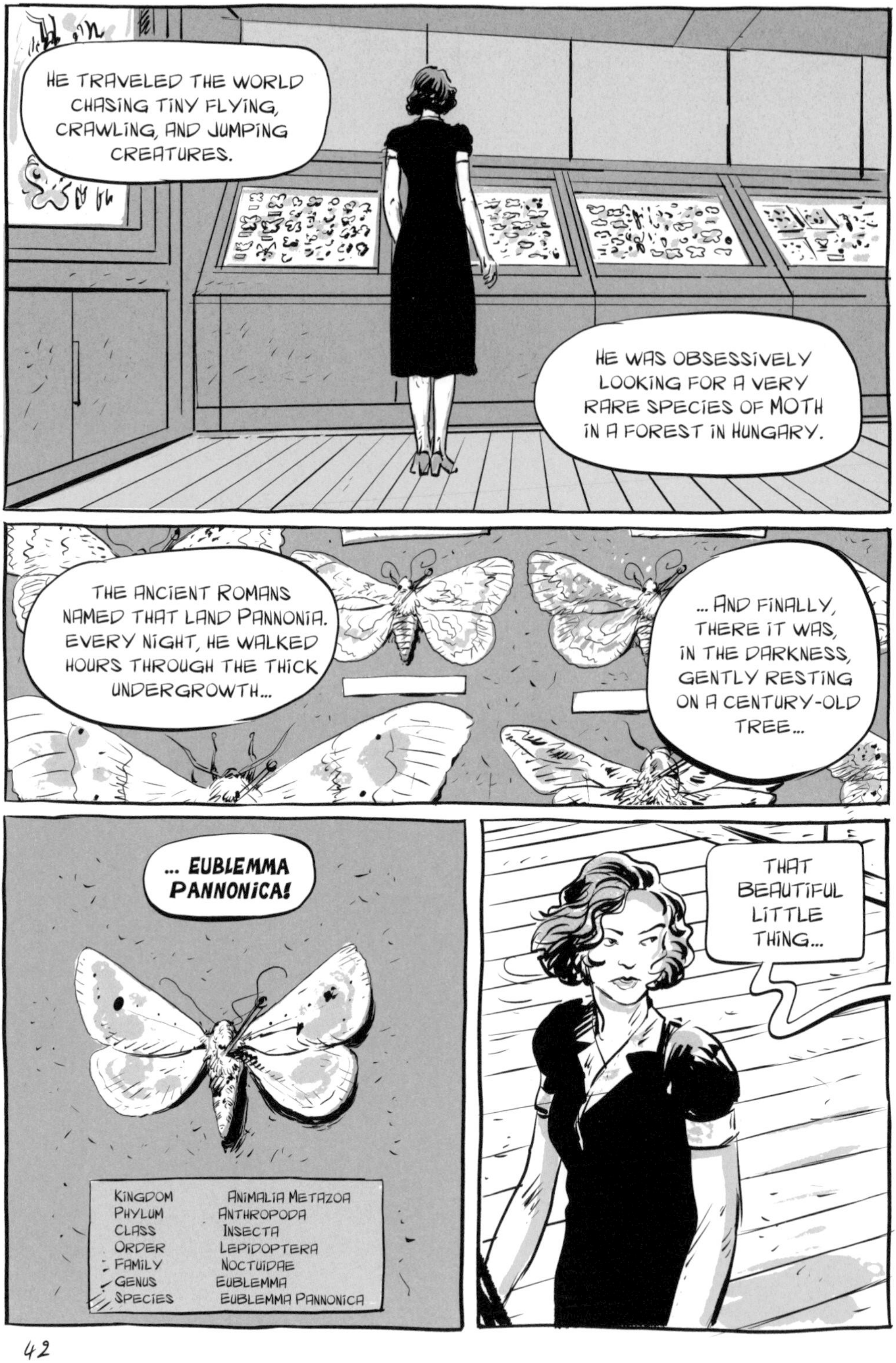
HE TRAVELED THE WORLD CHASING TINY FLYING, CRAWLING, AND JUMPING CREATURES.
HE WAS OBSESSIVELY LOOKING FOR A VERY RARE SPECIES OF MOTH IN A FOREST IN HUNGARY.
THE ANCIENT ROMANS NAMED THAT LAND PANNONIA. EVERY NIGHT, HE WALKED HOURS THROUGH THE THICK UNDERGROWTH...
... AND FINALLY, THERE IT WAS, IN THE DARKNESS, GENTLY RESTING ON A CENTURY-OLD TREE...
... EUBLEMMA PANNONICA!
KINGDOM ANIMALIA METAZOA
PHYLUM ANTHROPODA
CLASS INSECTA
ORDER LEPIDOPTERA
FAMILY NOCTUIDAE
GENUS EUBLEMMA
SPECIES EUBLEMMA PANNONICA
THAT BEAUTIFUL LITTLE THING...

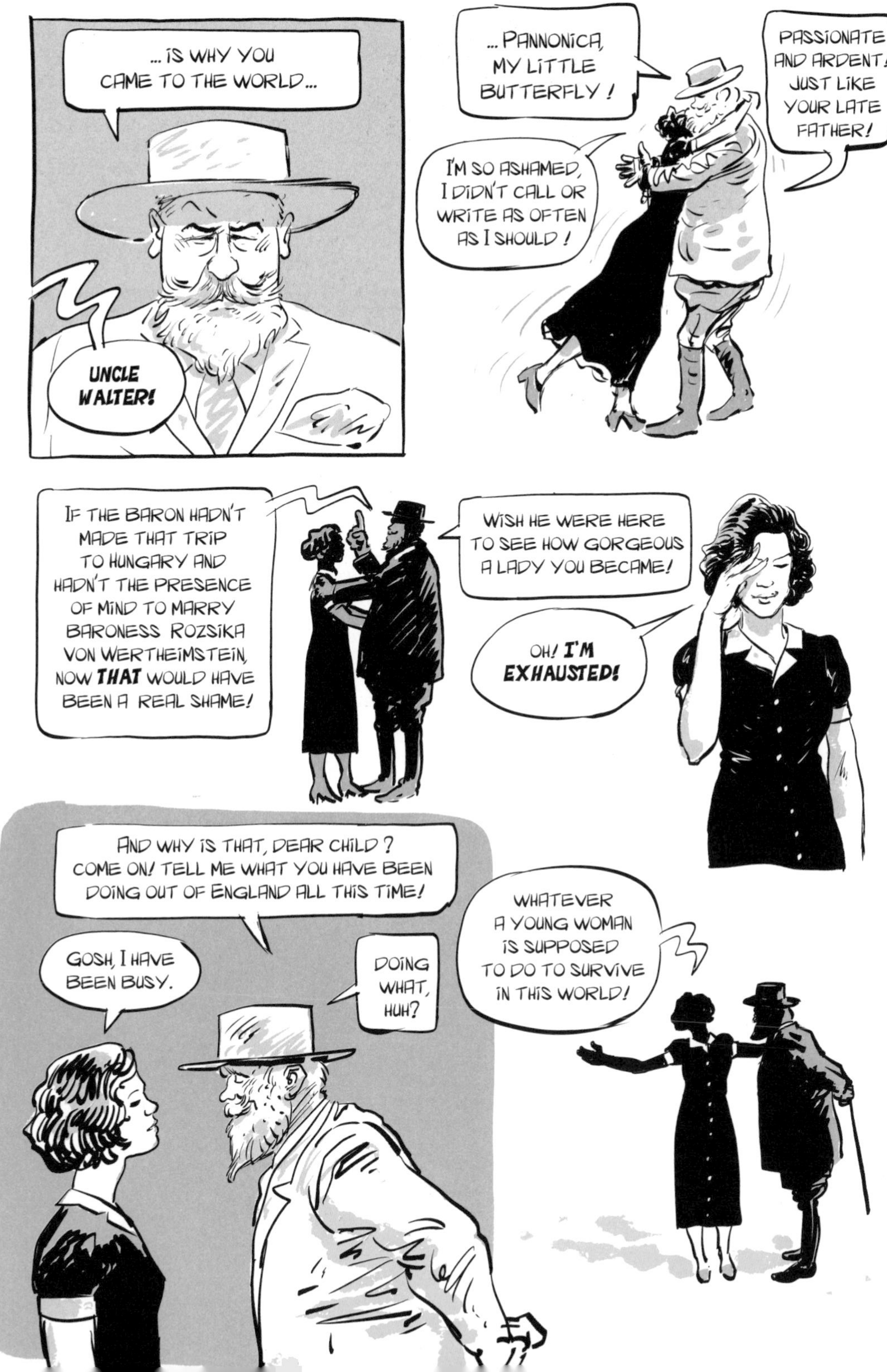
... IS WHY YOU CAME TO THE WORLD...
UNCLE WALTER!
... PANNONICA, MY LITTLE BUTTERFLY!
PASSIONATE AND ARDENT! JUST LIKE YOUR LATE FATHER!
I'M SO ASHAMED, I DIDN'T CALL OR WRITE AS OFTEN AS I SHOULD!
IF THE BARON HADN'T MADE THAT TRIP TO HUNGARY AND HADN'T THE PRESENCE OF MIND TO MARRY BARONESS ROZSIKA VON WERTHEIMSTEIN, NOW THAT WOULD HAVE BEEN A REAL SHAME!
WISH HE WERE HERE TO SEE HOW GORGEOUS A LADY YOU BECAME!
OH! I'M EXHAUSTED!
AND WHY IS THAT, DEAR CHILD? COME ON! TELL ME WHAT YOU HAVE BEEN DOING OUT OF ENGLAND ALL THIS TIME!
GOSH, I HAVE BEEN BUSY.
DOING WHAT, HUH?
WHATEVER A YOUNG WOMAN IS SUPPOSED TO DO TO SURVIVE IN THIS WORLD!

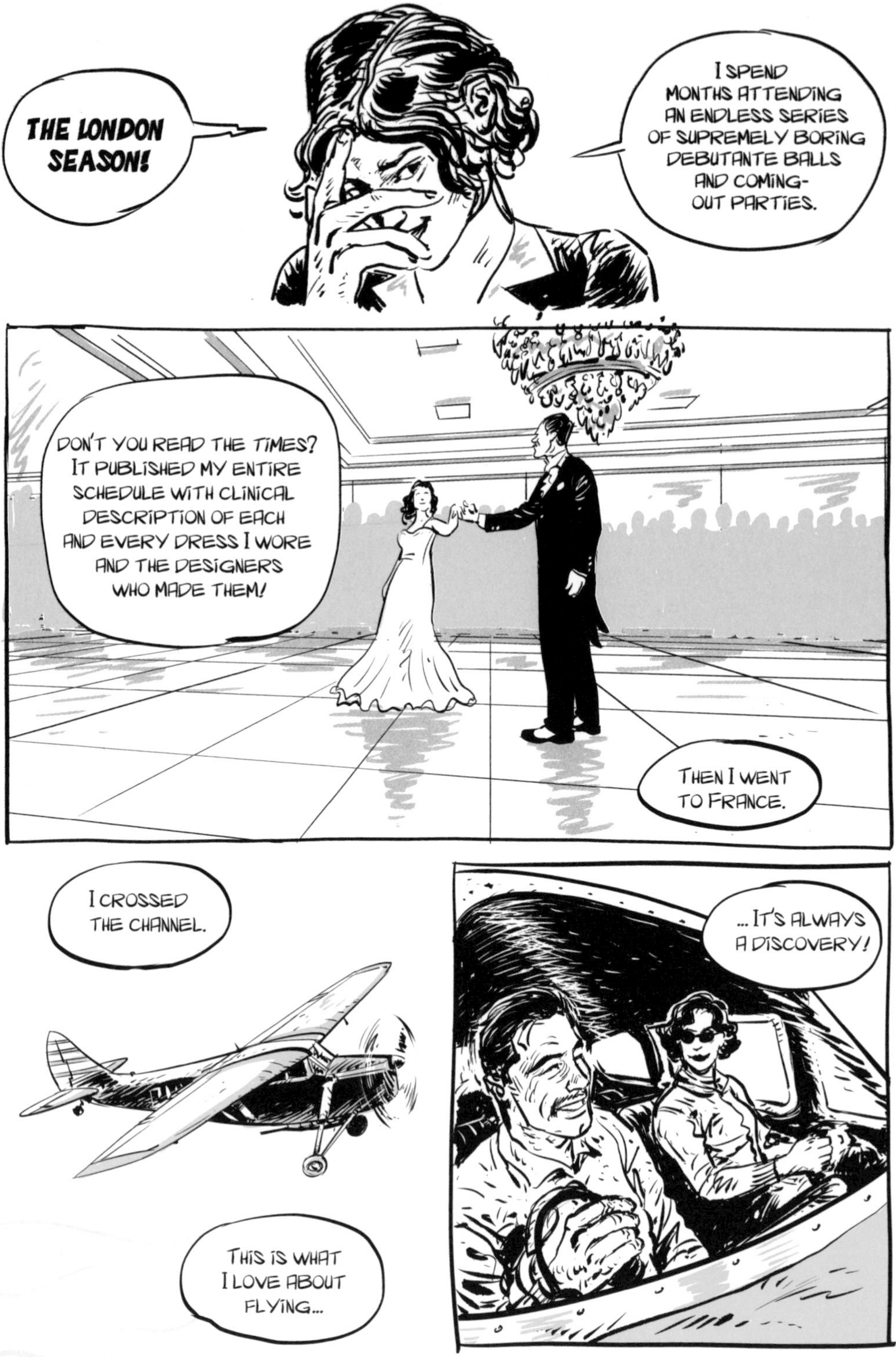
THE LONDON SEASON!
I SPEND MONTHS ATTENDING AN ENDLESS SERIES OF SUPREMELY BORING DEBUTANTE BALLS AND COMING-OUT PARTIES.
DON'T YOU READ THE TIMES? IT PUBLISHED MY ENTIRE SCHEDULE WITH CLINICAL DESCRIPTION OF EACH AND EVERY DRESS I WORE AND THE DESIGNERS WHO MADE THEM!
THEN I WENT TO FRANCE.
I CROSSED THE CHANNEL.
THIS IS WHAT I LOVE ABOUT FLYING...
...IT'S ALWAYS A DISCOVERY!

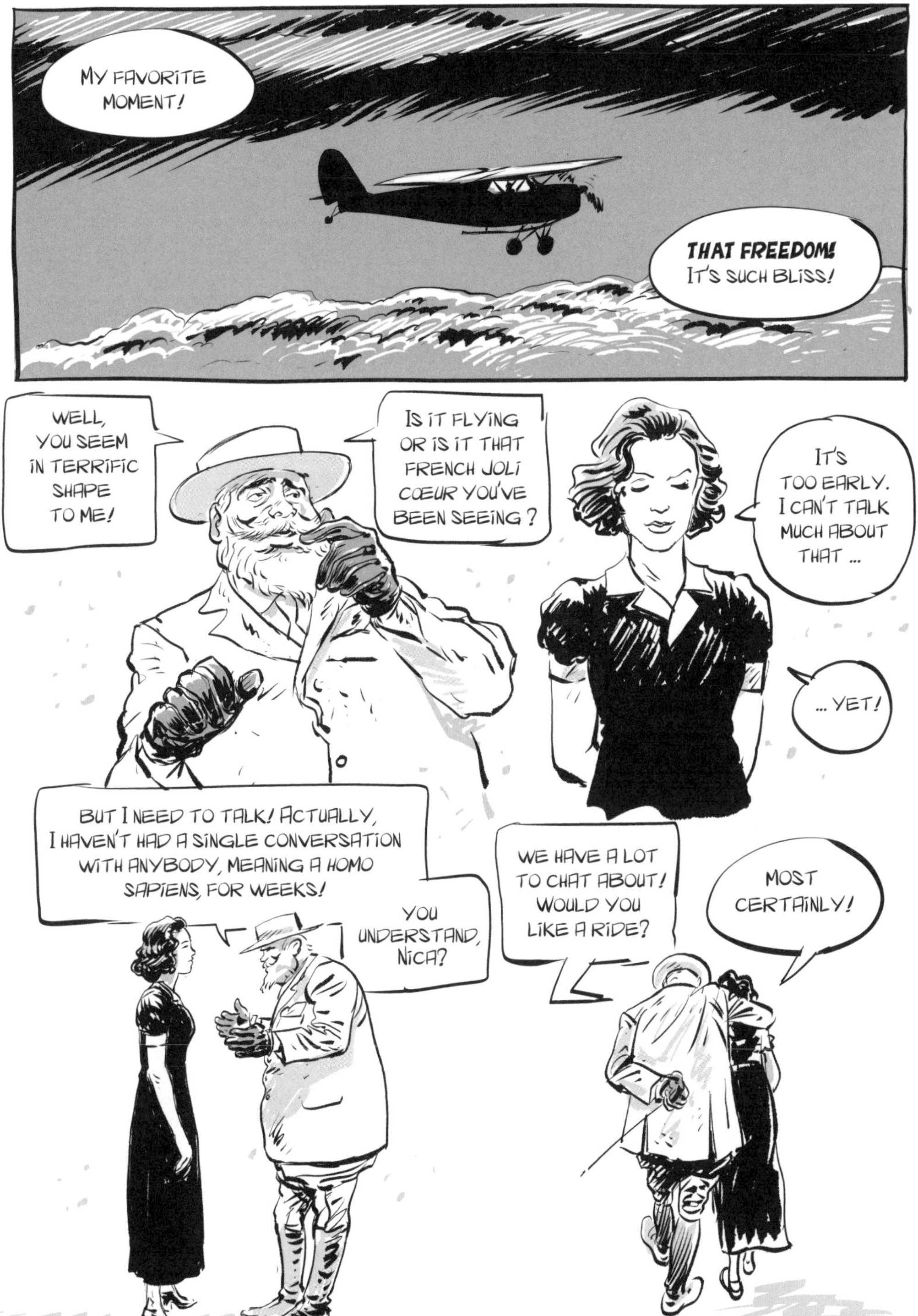
MY FAVORITE MOMENT!
THAT FREEDOM! IT'S SUCH BLISS!
WELL, YOU SEEM IN TERRIFIC SHAPE TO ME!
IS IT FLYING OR IS IT THAT FRENCH JOLI CŒUR YOU'VE BEEN SEEING?
IT'S TOO EARLY. I CAN'T TALK MUCH ABOUT THAT ...
... YET!
BUT I NEED TO TALK! ACTUALLY, I HAVEN'T HAD A SINGLE CONVERSATION WITH ANYBODY, MEANING A HOMO SAPIENS, FOR WEEKS!
YOU UNDERSTAND, NICA?
WE HAVE A LOT TO CHAT ABOUT! WOULD YOU LIKE A RIDE?
MOST CERTAINLY!

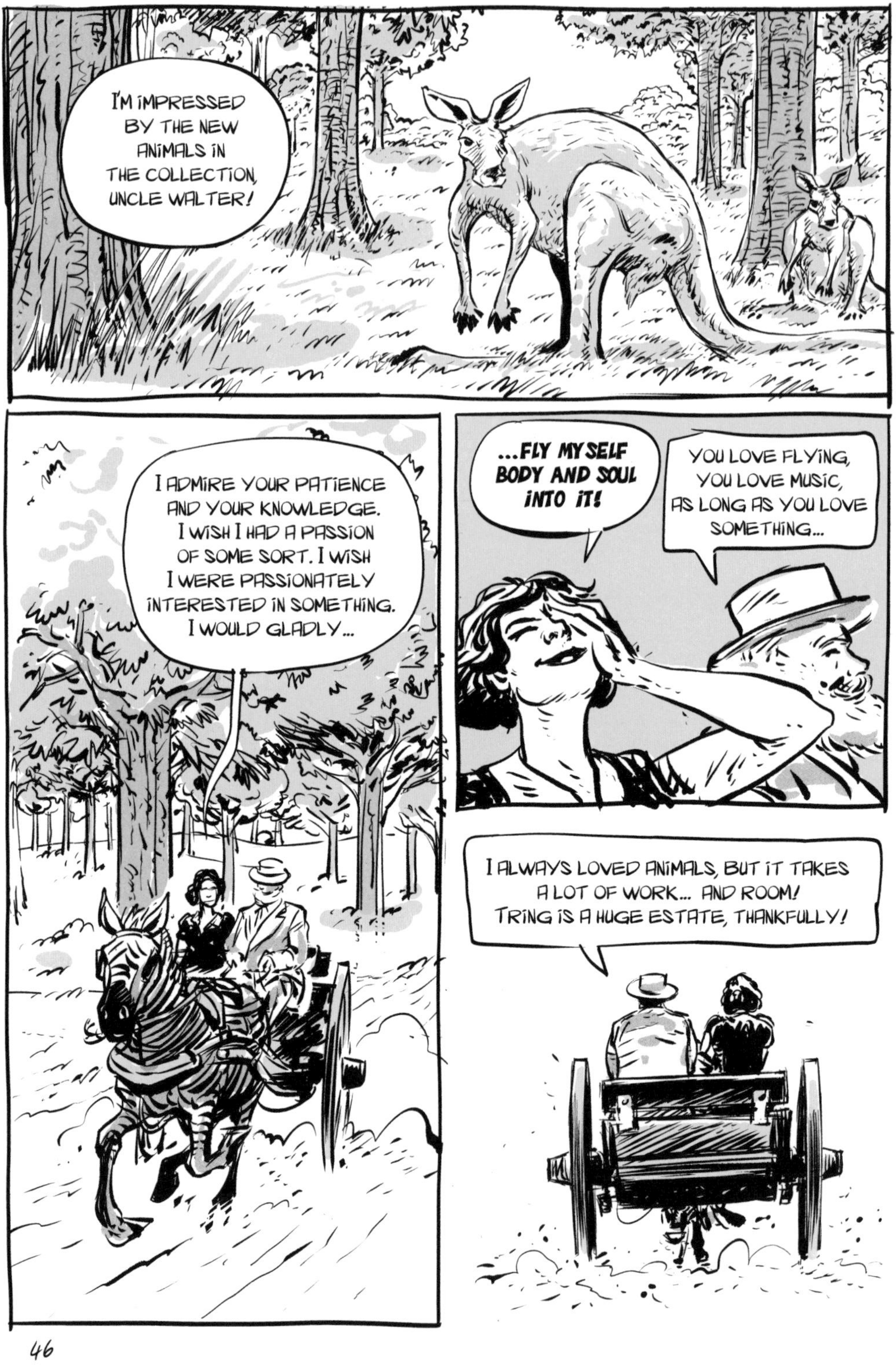
I'M IMPRESSED BY THE NEW ANIMALS IN THE COLLECTION, UNCLE WALTER!
I ADMIRE YOUR PATIENCE AND YOUR KNOWLEDGE. I WISH I HAD A PASSION OF SOME SORT. I WISH I WERE PASSIONATELY INTERESTED IN SOMETHING. I WOULD GLADLY...
...FLY MYSELF BODY AND SOUL INTO IT!
YOU LOVE FLYING, YOU LOVE MUSIC, AS LONG AS YOU LOVE SOMETHING...
I ALWAYS LOVED ANIMALS, BUT IT TAKES A LOT OF WORK... AND ROOM! TRING IS A HUGE ESTATE, THANKFULLY!

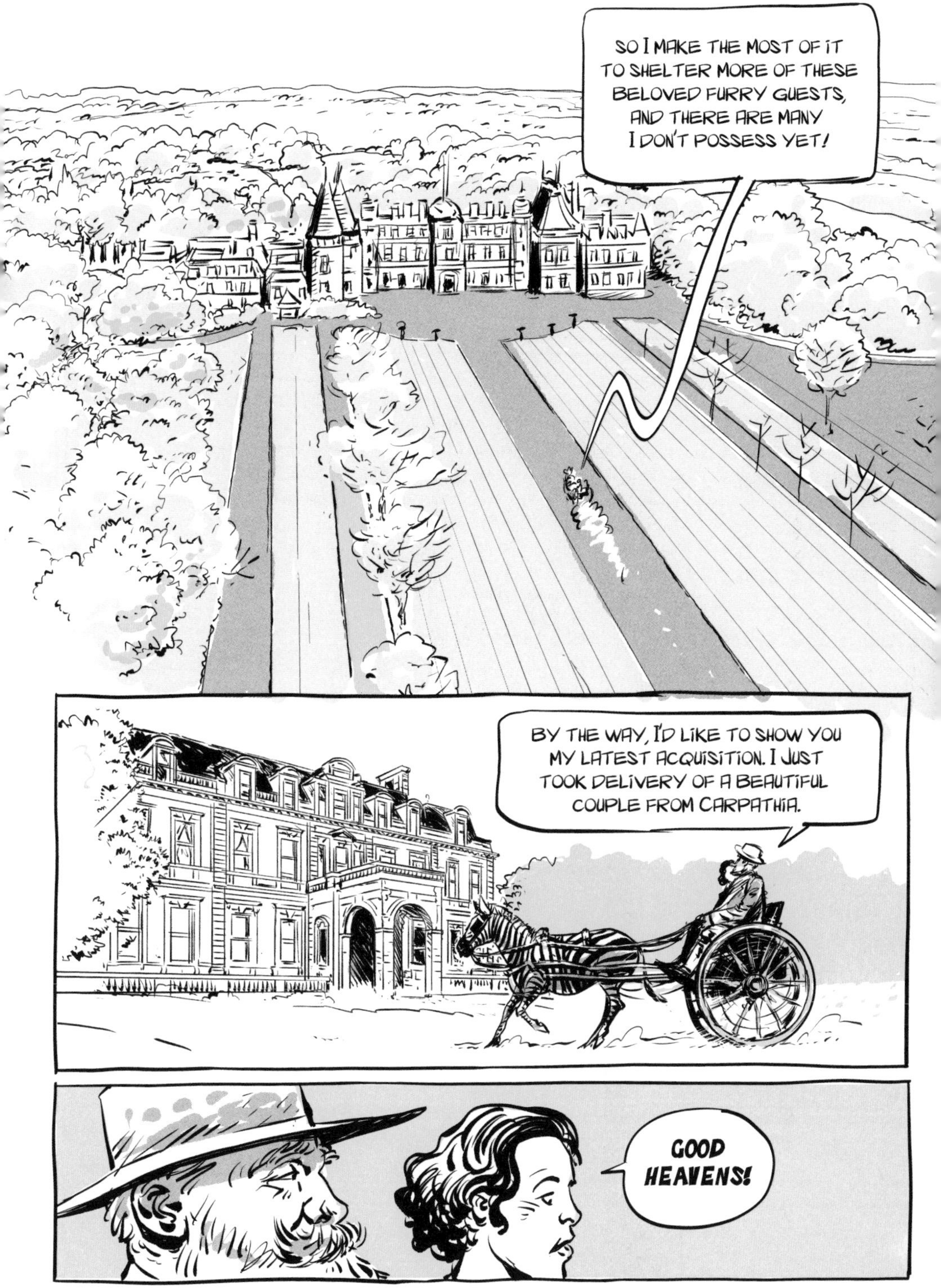
SO I MAKE THE MOST OF IT TO SHELTER MORE OF THESE BELOVED FURRY GUESTS, AND THERE ARE MANY I DON'T POSSESS YET!
BY THE WAY, I'D LIKE TO SHOW YOU MY LATEST ACQUISITION. I JUST TOOK DELIVERY OF A BEAUTIFUL COUPLE FROM CARPATHIA.
GOOD HEAVENS!

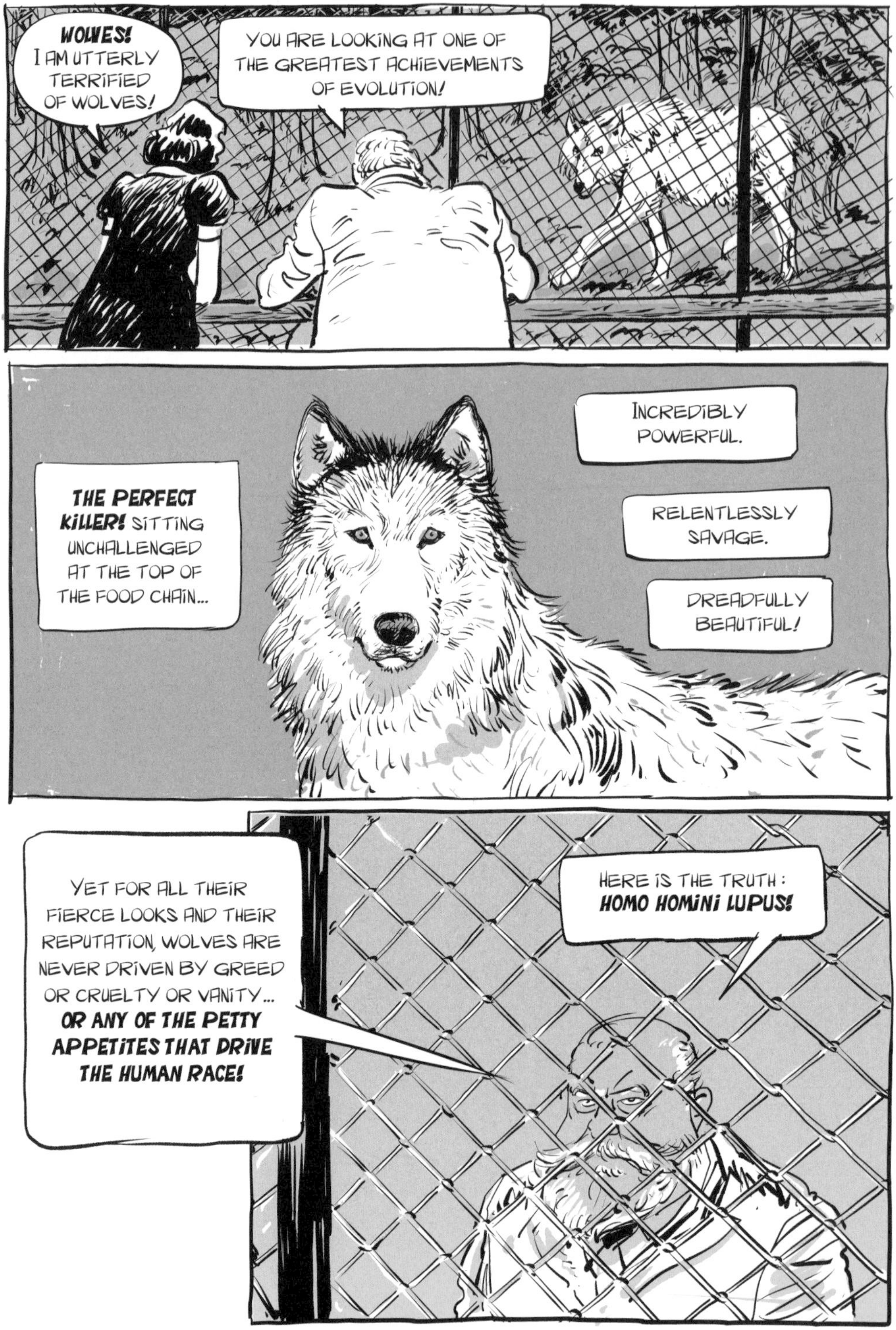

WOLVES! I AM UTTERLY TERRIFIED OF WOLVES!
YOU ARE LOOKING AT ONE OF THE GREATEST ACHIEVEMENTS OF EVOLUTION!
THE PERFECT KILLER! SITTING UNCHALLENGED AT THE TOP OF THE FOOD CHAIN...
INCREDIBLY POWERFUL.
RELENTLESSLY SAVAGE.
DREADFULLY BEAUTIFUL!
YET FOR ALL THEIR FIERCE LOOKS AND THEIR REPUTATION, WOLVES ARE NEVER DRIVEN BY GREED OR CRUELTY OR VANITY... OR ANY OF THE PETTY APPETITES THAT DRIVE THE HUMAN RACE!
HERE IS THE TRUTH: HOMO HOMINI LUPUS!

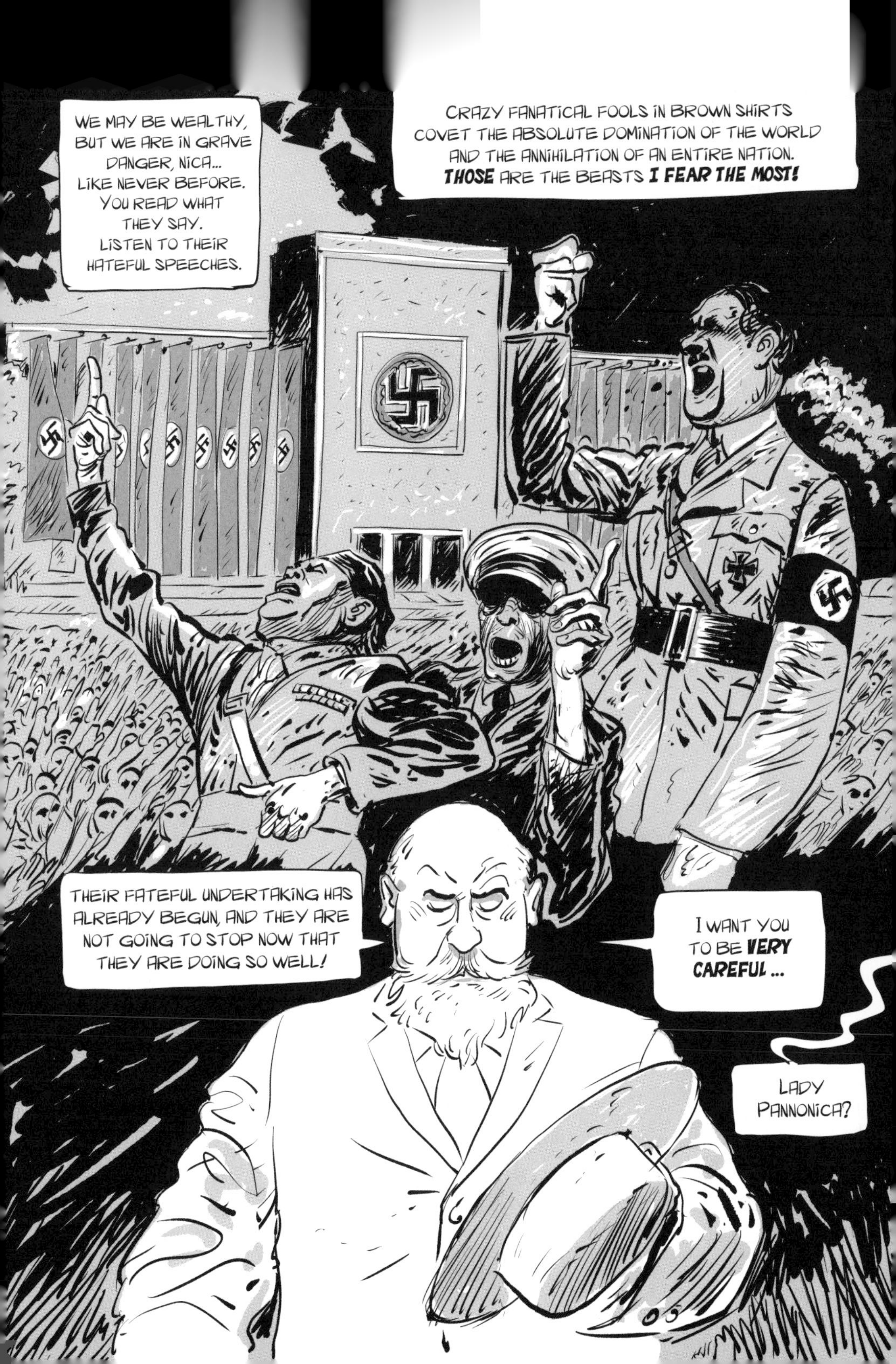
WE MAY BE WEALTHY, BUT WE ARE IN GRAVE DANGER, NICA... LIKE NEVER BEFORE. YOU READ WHAT THEY SAY. LISTEN TO THEIR HATEFUL SPEECHES.
CRAZY FANATICAL FOOLS IN BROWN SHIRTS COVET THE ABSOLUTE DOMINATION OF THE WORLD AND THE ANNIHILATION OF AN ENTIRE NATION. **THOSE** ARE THE BEASTS **I FEAR THE MOST!**
THEIR FATEFUL UNDERTAKING HAS ALREADY BEGUN, AND THEY ARE NOT GOING TO STOP NOW THAT THEY ARE DOING SO WELL!
I WANT YOU TO BE **VERY CAREFUL ...**
LADY PANNONICA?

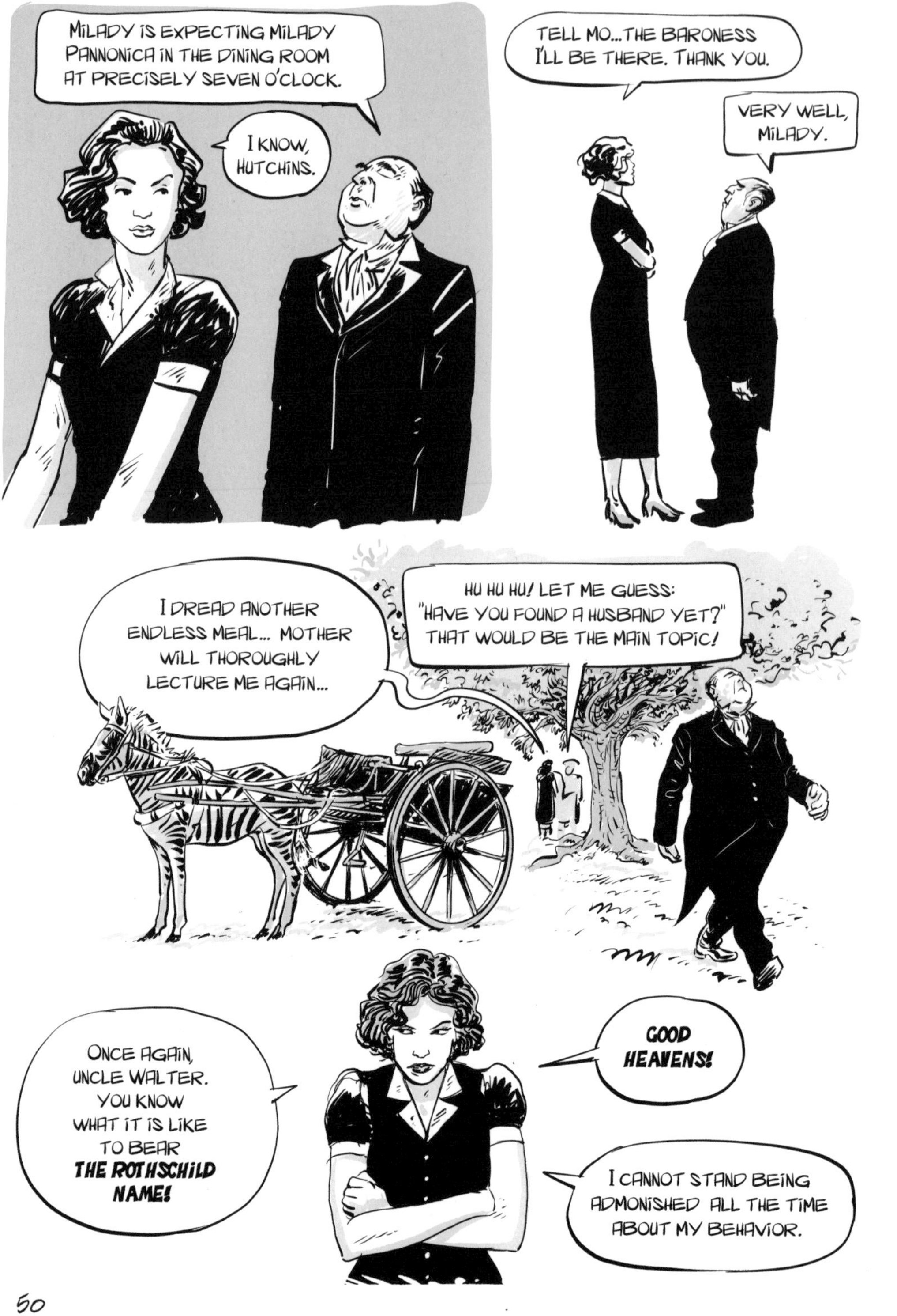
MILADY IS EXPECTING MILADY PANNONICA IN THE DINING ROOM AT PRECISELY SEVEN O'CLOCK.
I KNOW, HUTCHINS.
TELL MO...THE BARONESS I'LL BE THERE. THANK YOU.
VERY WELL, MILADY.
I DREAD ANOTHER ENDLESS MEAL... MOTHER WILL THOROUGHLY LECTURE ME AGAIN...
HU HU HU! LET ME GUESS: "HAVE YOU FOUND A HUSBAND YET?" THAT WOULD BE THE MAIN TOPIC!
ONCE AGAIN, UNCLE WALTER. YOU KNOW WHAT IT IS LIKE TO BEAR **THE ROTHSCHILD NAME!**
GOOD HEAVENS!
I CANNOT STAND BEING ADMONISHED ALL THE TIME ABOUT MY BEHAVIOR.

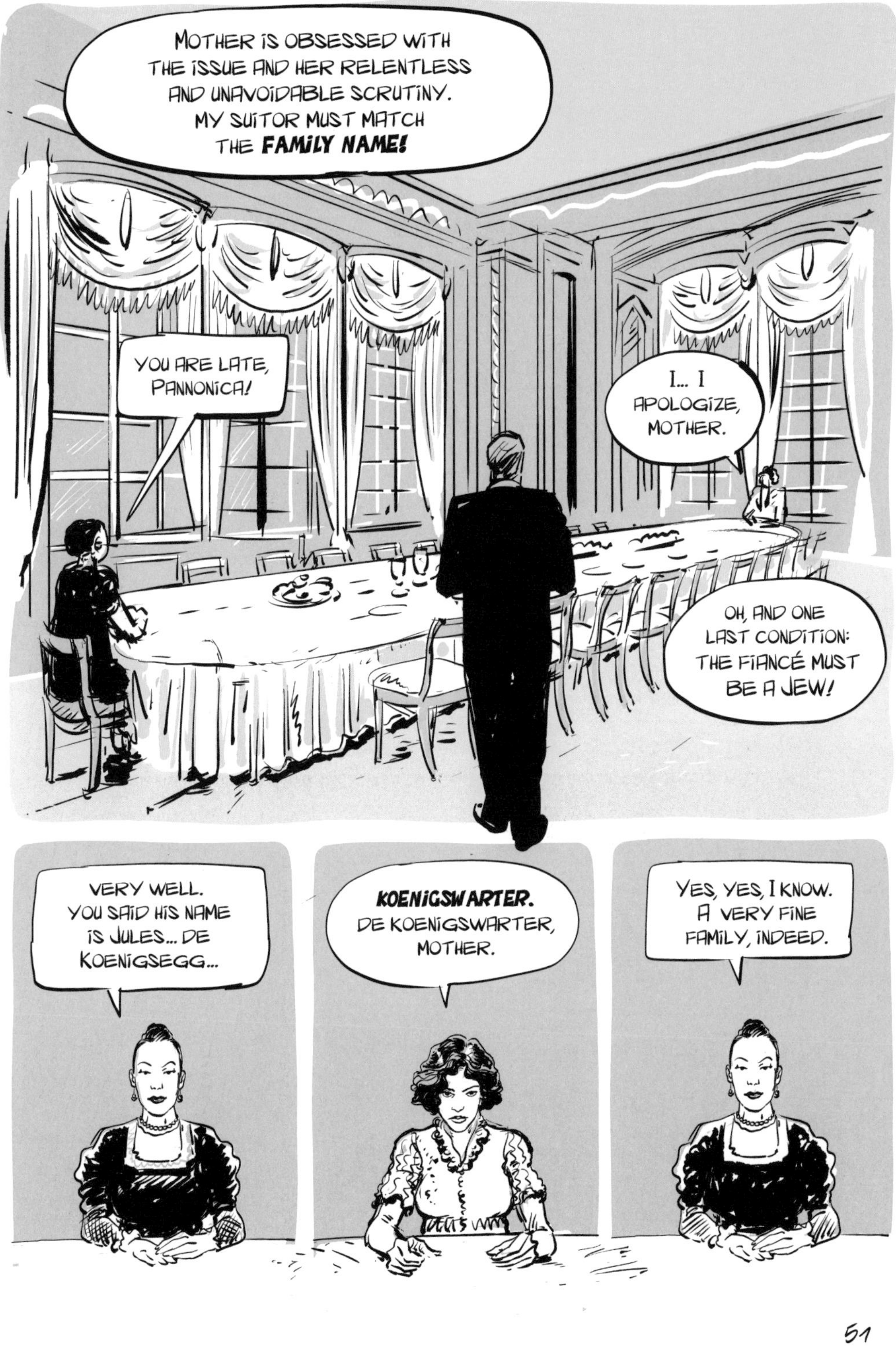
MOTHER IS OBSESSED WITH THE ISSUE AND HER RELENTLESS AND UNAVOIDABLE SCRUTINY. MY SUITOR MUST MATCH THE **FAMILY NAME!**
YOU ARE LATE, PANNONICA!
I... I APOLOGIZE, MOTHER.
OH, AND ONE LAST CONDITION: THE FIANCÉ MUST BE A JEW!
VERY WELL. YOU SAID HIS NAME IS JULES... DE KOENIGSEGG...
KOENIGSWARTER. DE KOENIGSWARTER, MOTHER.
YES, YES, I KNOW. A VERY FINE FAMILY, INDEED.

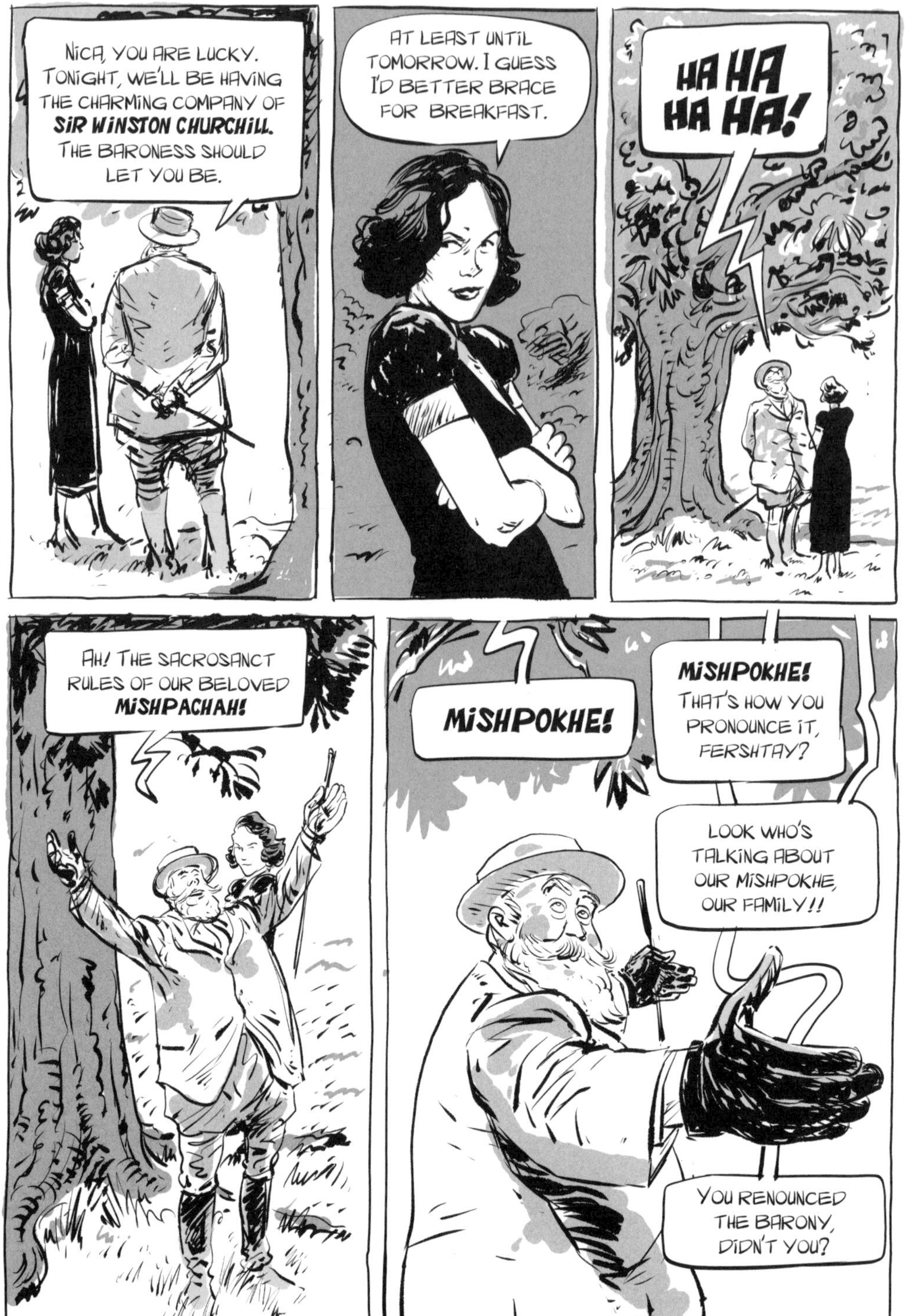
NICA, YOU ARE LUCKY. TONIGHT, WE'LL BE HAVING THE CHARMING COMPANY OF **SIR WINSTON CHURCHILL.** THE BARONESS SHOULD LET YOU BE.
AT LEAST UNTIL TOMORROW. I GUESS I'D BETTER BRACE FOR BREAKFAST.
HA HA HA HA!
AH! THE SACROSANCT RULES OF OUR BELOVED **MISHPACHAH!**
MISHPOKHE!
MISHPOKHE! THAT'S HOW YOU PRONOUNCE IT, FERSHTAY?
LOOK WHO'S TALKING ABOUT OUR MISHPOKHE, OUR FAMILY!!
YOU RENOUNCED THE BARONY, DIDN'T YOU?

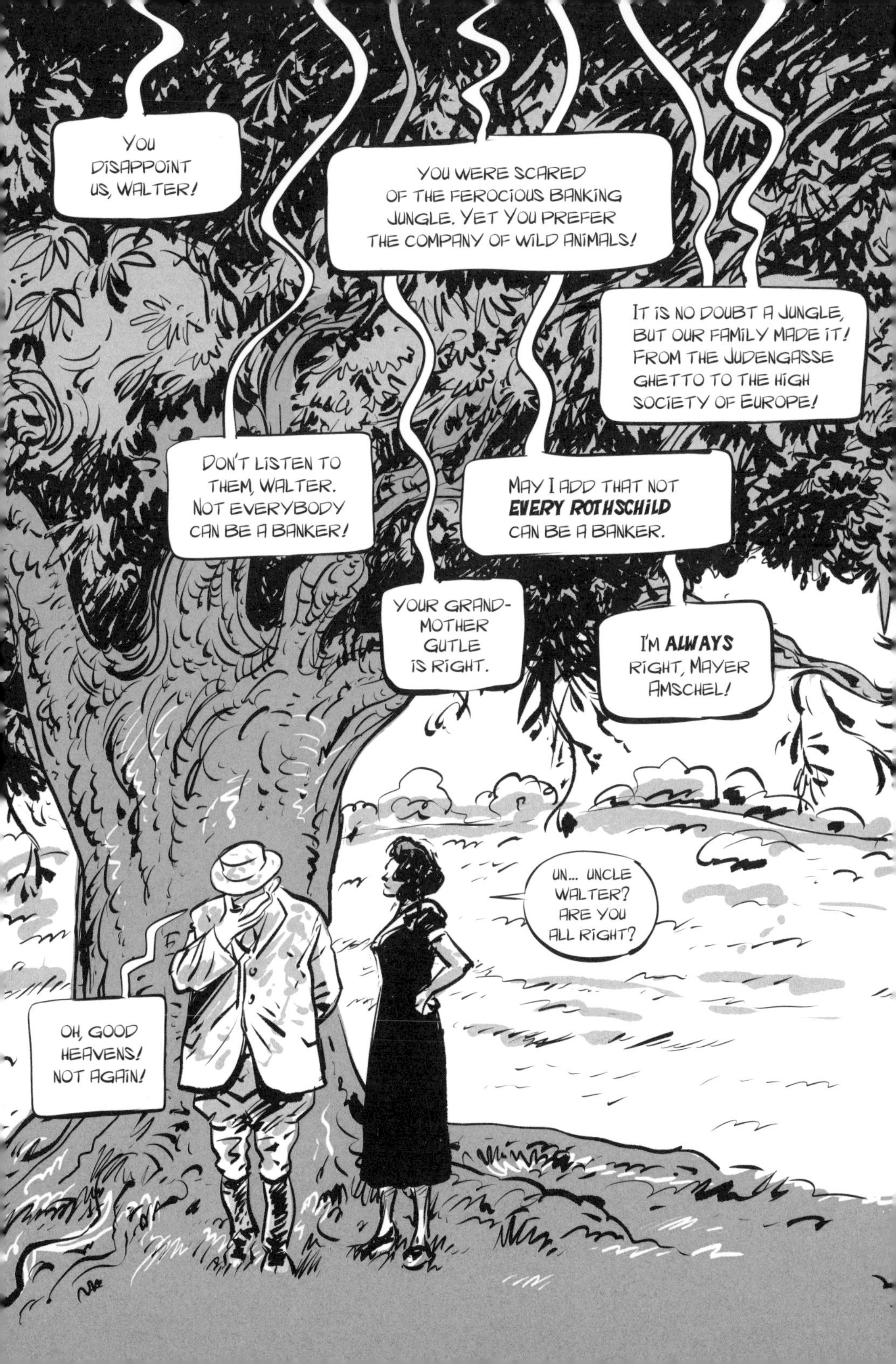

YOU DISAPPOINT US, WALTER!
YOU WERE SCARED OF THE FEROCIOUS BANKING JUNGLE. YET YOU PREFER THE COMPANY OF WILD ANIMALS!
IT IS NO DOUBT A JUNGLE, BUT OUR FAMILY MADE IT! FROM THE JUDENGASSE GHETTO TO THE HIGH SOCIETY OF EUROPE!
DON'T LISTEN TO THEM, WALTER. NOT EVERYBODY CAN BE A BANKER!
MAY I ADD THAT NOT **EVERY ROTHSCHILD** CAN BE A BANKER.
YOUR GRAND-MOTHER GUTLE IS RIGHT.
I'M **ALWAYS** RIGHT, MAYER AMSCHEL!
UN... UNCLE WALTER? ARE YOU ALL RIGHT?
OH, GOOD HEAVENS! NOT AGAIN!

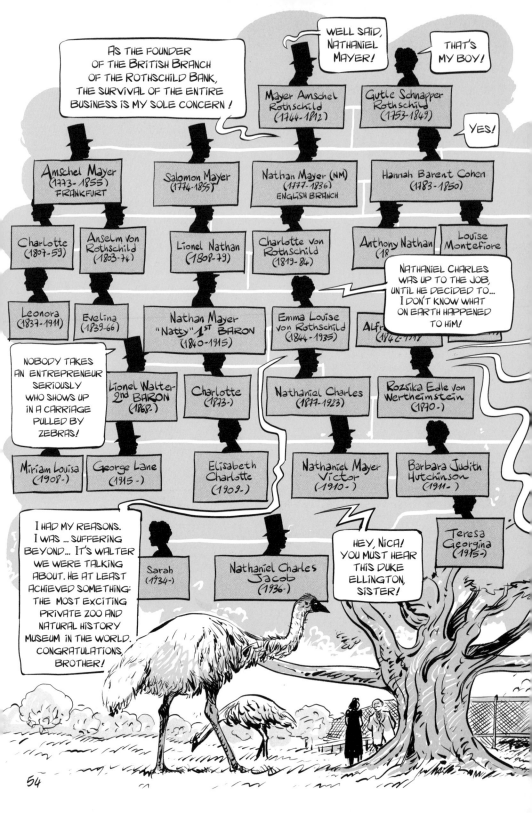

AS THE FOUNDER OF THE BRITISH BRANCH OF THE ROTHSCHILD BANK, THE SURVIVAL OF THE ENTIRE BUSINESS IS MY SOLE CONCERN!

WELL SAID, NATHANIEL MAYER!

THAT'S MY BOY!

Mayer Amschel Rothschild (1744-1812)

Gutle Schnapper Rothschild (1753-1849)

YES!

Amschel Mayer (1773-1855) FRANKFURT

Salomon Mayer (1774-1855)

Nathan Mayer (NM) (1777-1836) ENGLISH BRANCH

Hannah Barent Cohen (1783-1850)

Charlotte (1807-59)

Anselm von Rothschild (1803-74)

Lionel Nathan (1808-79)

Charlotte von Rothschild (1819-84)

Anthony Nathan (18

Louise Montefiore

NATHANIEL CHARLES WAS UP TO THE JOB, UNTIL HE DECIDED TO... I DON'T KNOW WHAT ON EARTH HAPPENED TO HIM!

Leonora (1837-1911)

Evelina (1839-66)

Nathan Mayer "Natty" 1st BARON (1840-1915)

Emma Louise von Rothschild (1844-1935)

Alfr (1842-

NOBODY TAKES AN ENTREPRENEUR SERIOUSLY WHO SHOWS UP IN A CARRIAGE PULLED BY ZEBRAS!

Lionel Walter 2nd BARON (1868-)

Charlotte (1873-)

Nathaniel Charles (1877-1923)

Rozsika Edle von Wertheimstein (1870-)

Miriam Louisa (1908-)

George Lane (1915-)

Elisabeth Charlotte (1909-)

Nathaniel Mayer Victor (1910-)

Barbara Judith Hutchinson (1911-)

I HAD MY REASONS. I WAS ... SUFFERING BEYOND... IT'S WALTER WE WERE TALKING ABOUT. HE AT LEAST ACHIEVED SOMETHING: THE MOST EXCITING PRIVATE ZOO AND NATURAL HISTORY MUSEUM IN THE WORLD. CONGRATULATIONS, BROTHER!

Sarah (1934-)

Nathaniel Charles Jacob (1936-)

HEY, NICA! YOU MUST HEAR THIS DUKE ELLINGTON, SISTER!

Teresa Georgina (1915-)

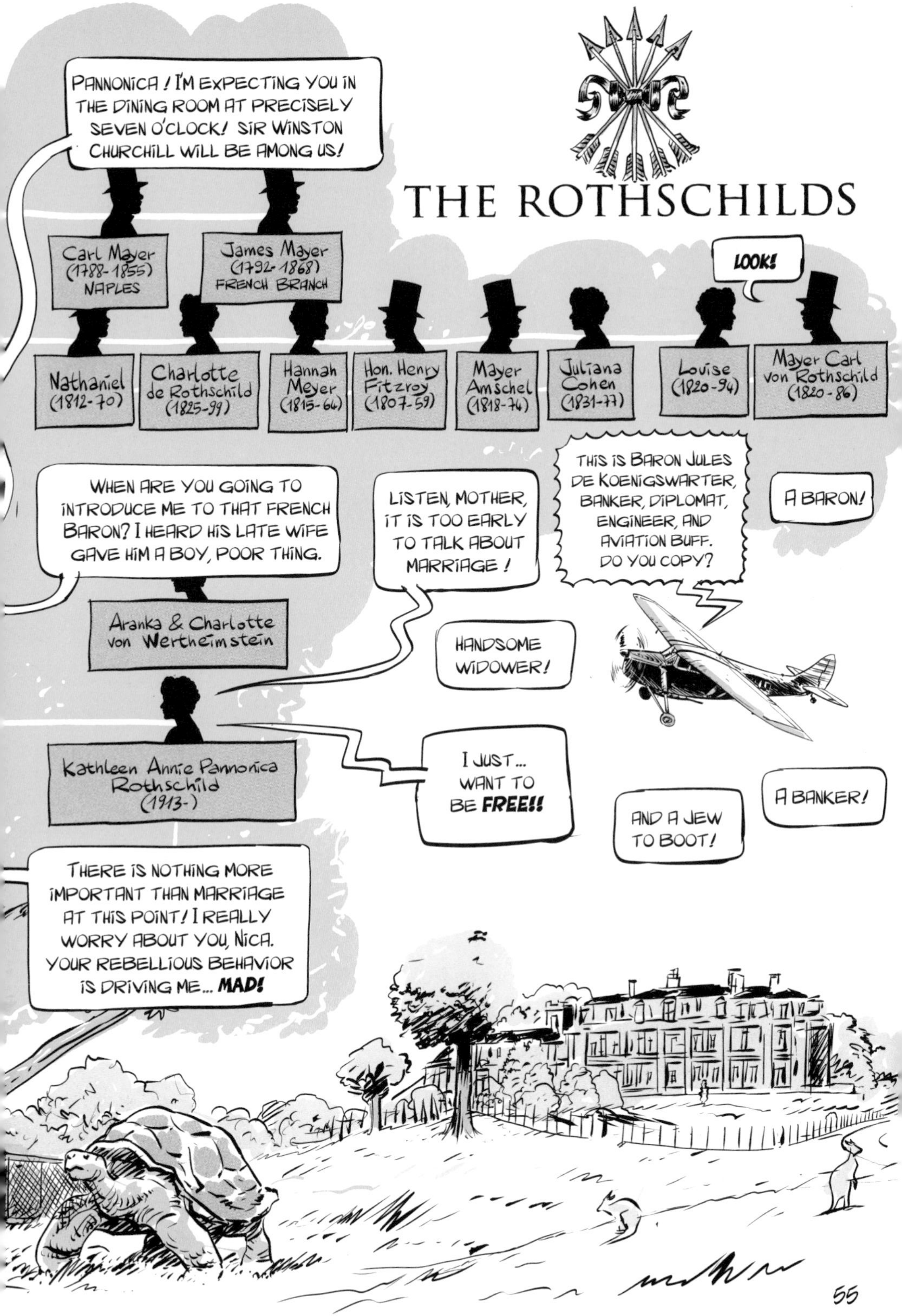

PANNONICA! I'M EXPECTING YOU IN THE DINING ROOM AT PRECISELY SEVEN O'CLOCK! SIR WINSTON CHURCHILL WILL BE AMONG US!
THE ROTHSCHILDS
Carl Mayer (1788-1855) NAPLES
James Mayer (1792-1868) FRENCH BRANCH
LOOK!
Nathaniel (1812-70)
Charlotte de Rothschild (1825-99)
Hannah Meyer (1815-64)
Hon. Henry Fitzroy (1807-59)
Mayer Amschel (1818-74)
Juliana Cohen (1831-77)
Louise (1820-94)
Mayer Carl von Rothschild (1820-86)
WHEN ARE YOU GOING TO INTRODUCE ME TO THAT FRENCH BARON? I HEARD HIS LATE WIFE GAVE HIM A BOY, POOR THING.
LISTEN, MOTHER, IT IS TOO EARLY TO TALK ABOUT MARRIAGE!
THIS IS BARON JULES DE KOENIGSWARTER, BANKER, DIPLOMAT, ENGINEER, AND AVIATION BUFF. DO YOU COPY?
A BARON!
Aranka & Charlotte von Wertheimstein
HANDSOME WIDOWER!
Kathleen Annie Pannonica Rothschild (1913-)
I JUST... WANT TO BE **FREE!!**
A BANKER!
AND A JEW TO BOOT!
THERE IS NOTHING MORE IMPORTANT THAN MARRIAGE AT THIS POINT! I REALLY WORRY ABOUT YOU, NICA. YOUR REBELLIOUS BEHAVIOR IS DRIVING ME... **MAD!**

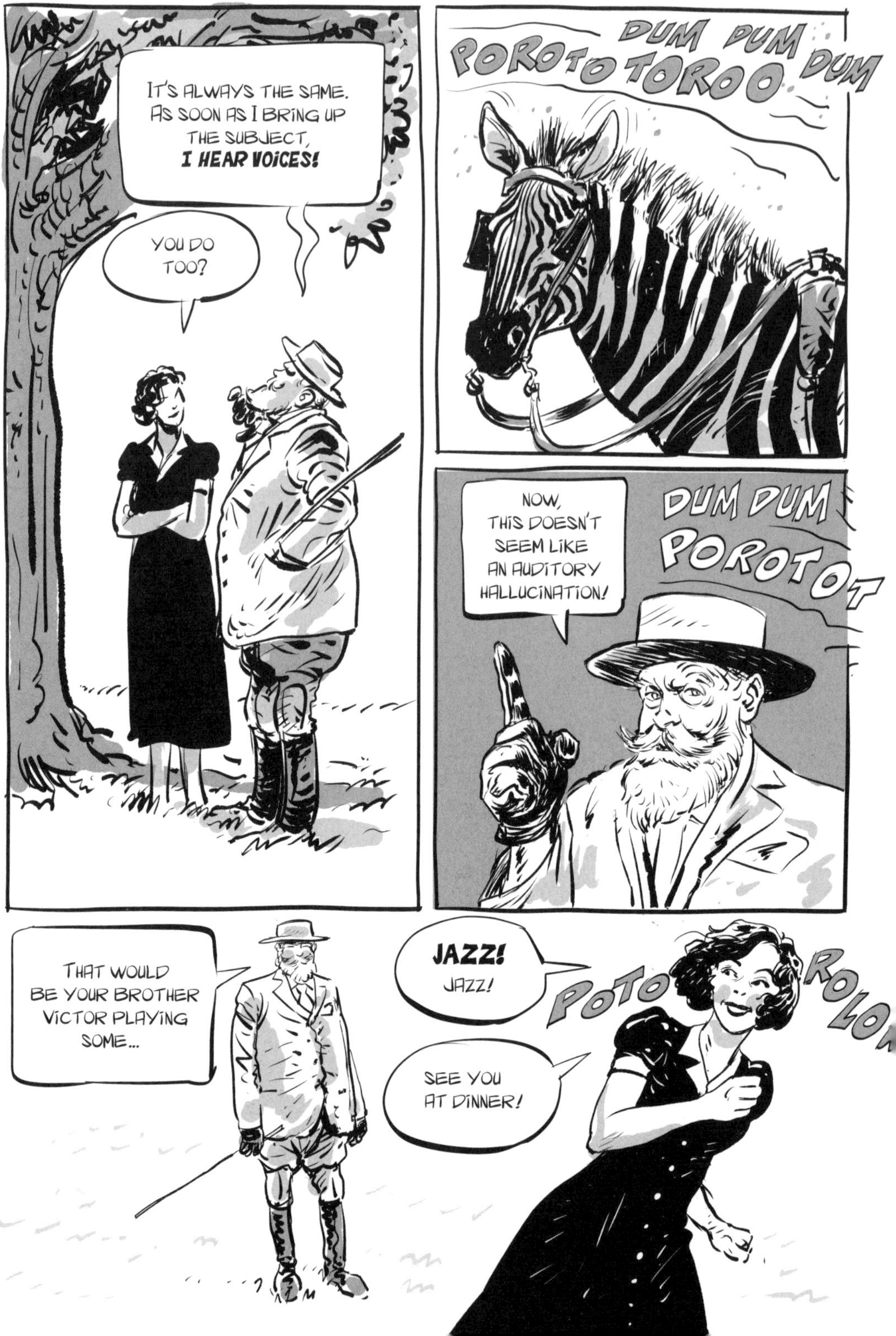
IT'S ALWAYS THE SAME. AS SOON AS I BRING UP THE SUBJECT, **I HEAR VOICES!**
YOU DO TOO?
POROTOTOTOROO DUM DUM DUM
NOW, THIS DOESN'T SEEM LIKE AN AUDITORY HALLUCINATION!
DUM DUM POROTOT
THAT WOULD BE YOUR BROTHER VICTOR PLAYING SOME...
JAZZ! JAZZ!
POTO ROLO
SEE YOU AT DINNER!

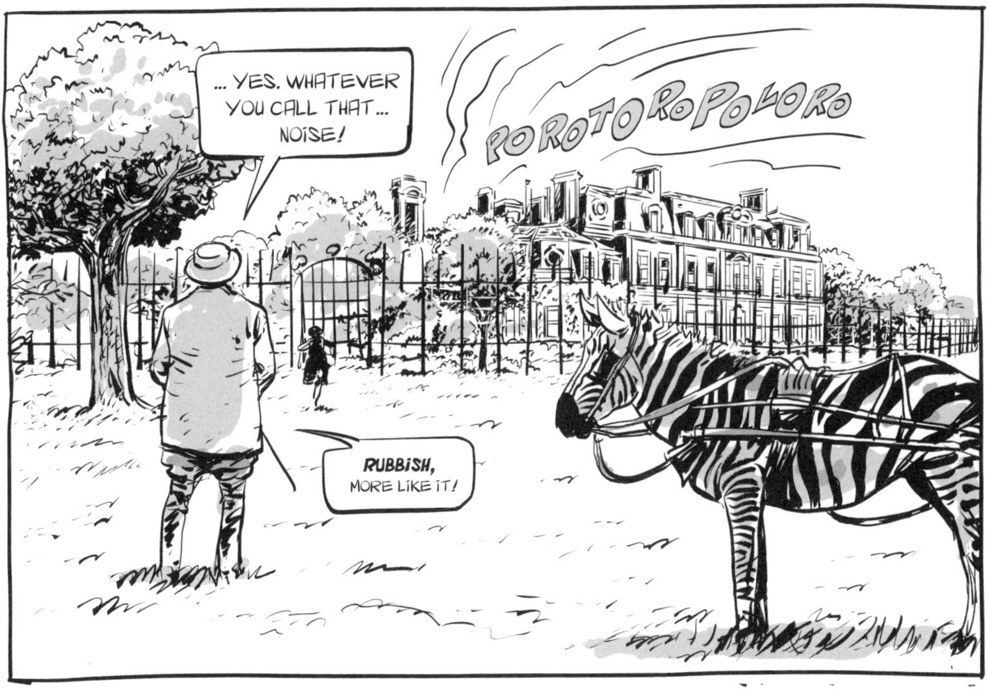
... YES. WHATEVER YOU CALL THAT... NOISE!
POROTOROPOLORO
RUBBiSH, MORE LiKE iT!

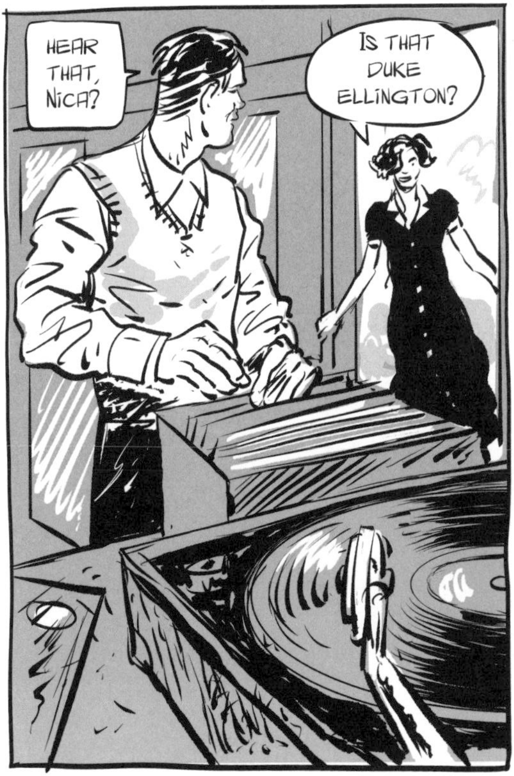
HEAR THAT, NiCA?
IS THAT DUKE ELLiNGTON?

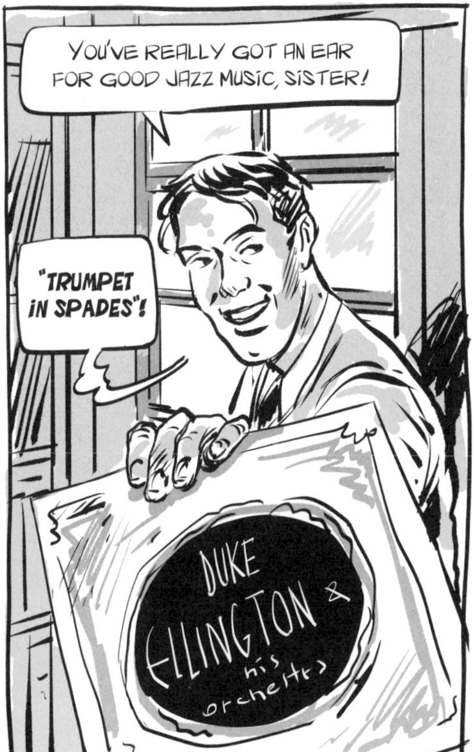
YOU'VE REALLY GOT AN EAR FOR GOOD JAZZ MUSIC, SiSTER!
"TRUMPET iN SPADES"!
DUKE ELLINGTON & his orchestra

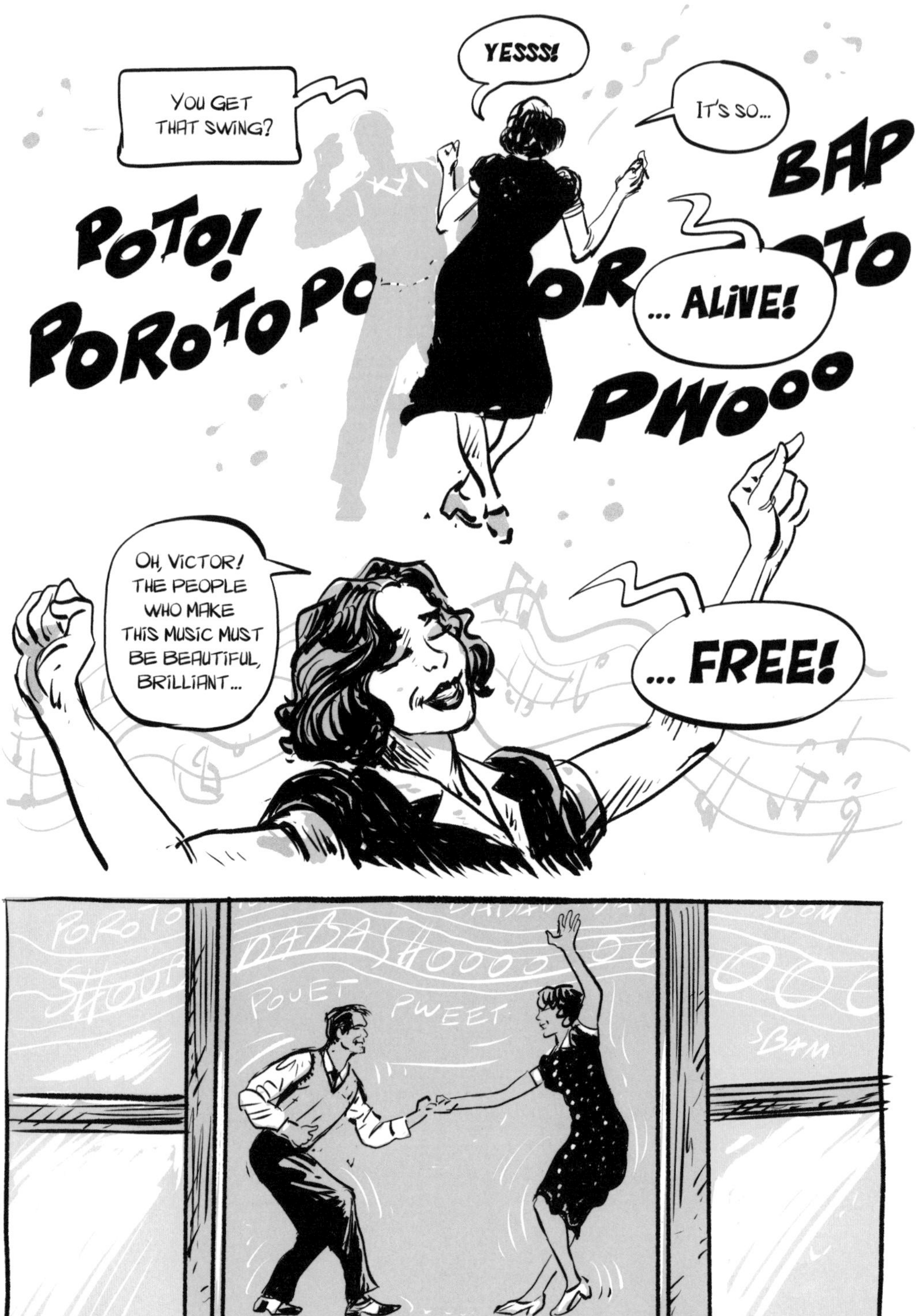
YOU GET THAT SWING?
YESSS!
IT'S SO...
POTO!
POROTOPO
OR
BAP
...ALIVE!
PWOOO
OH, VICTOR! THE PEOPLE WHO MAKE THIS MUSIC MUST BE BEAUTIFUL, BRILLIANT...
... FREE!
POUET
PWEET
SBAM

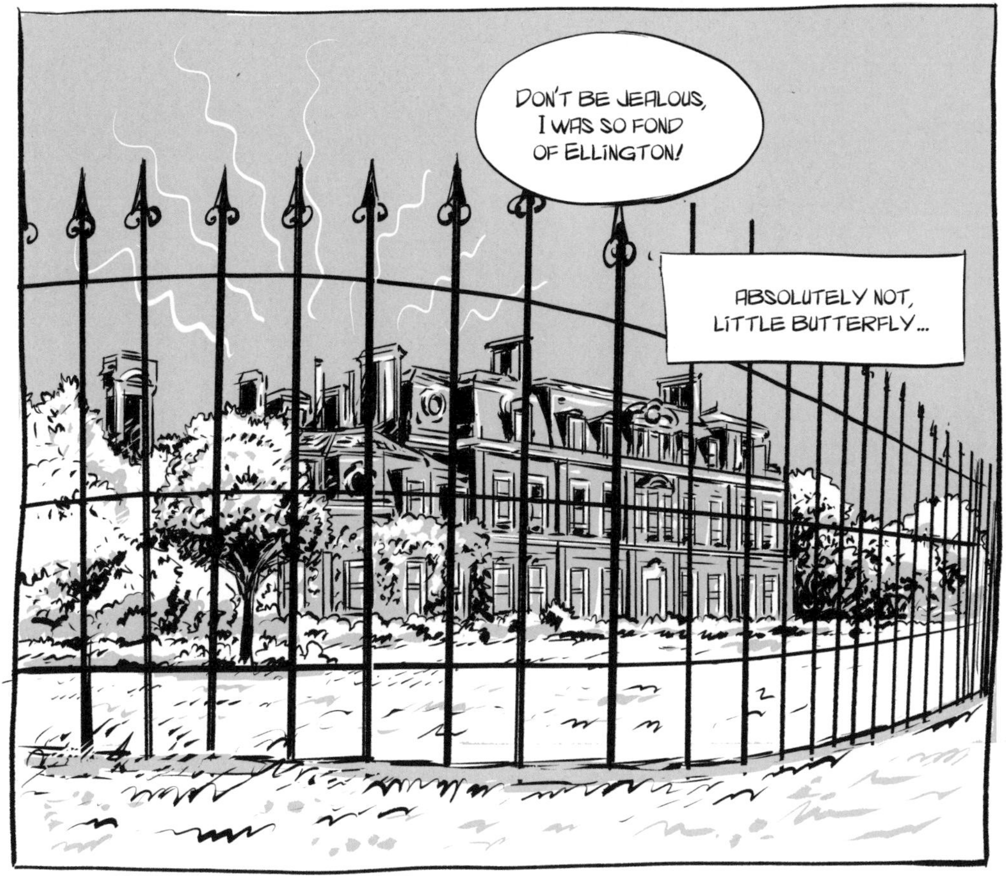
DON'T BE JEALOUS,
I WAS SO FOND
OF ELLINGTON!
ABSOLUTELY NOT,
LITTLE BUTTERFLY...

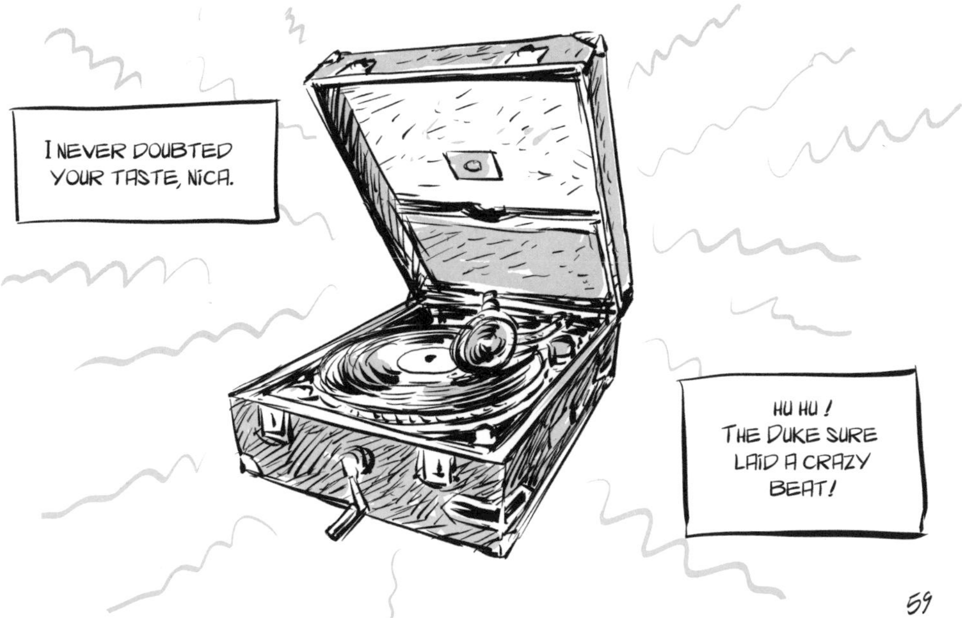
I NEVER DOUBTED
YOUR TASTE, NICA.
HU HU!
THE DUKE SURE
LAID A CRAZY
BEAT!

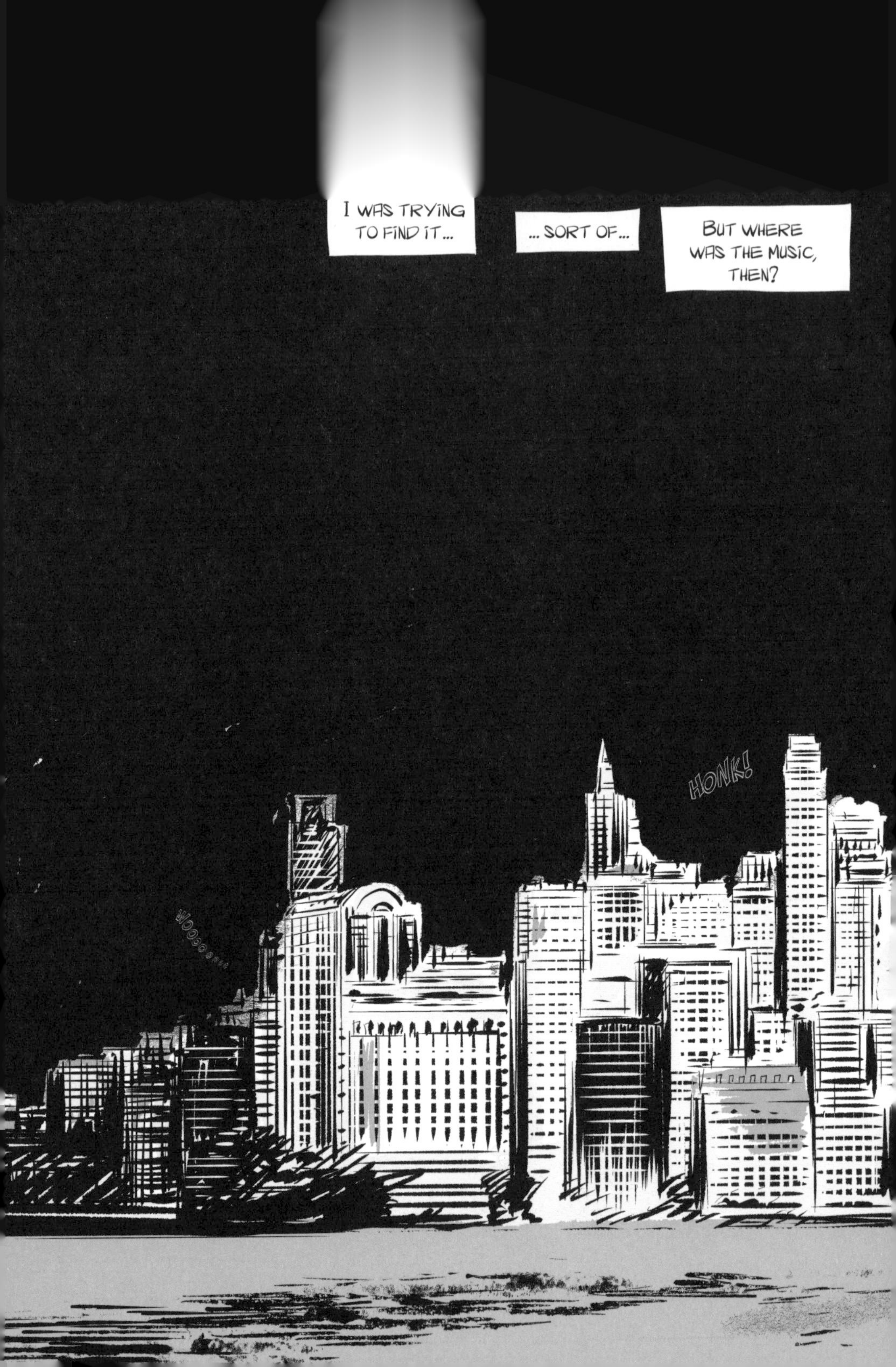
I WAS TRYING TO FIND IT...
...SORT OF...
BUT WHERE WAS THE MUSIC, THEN?
WOOOOO
HONK!

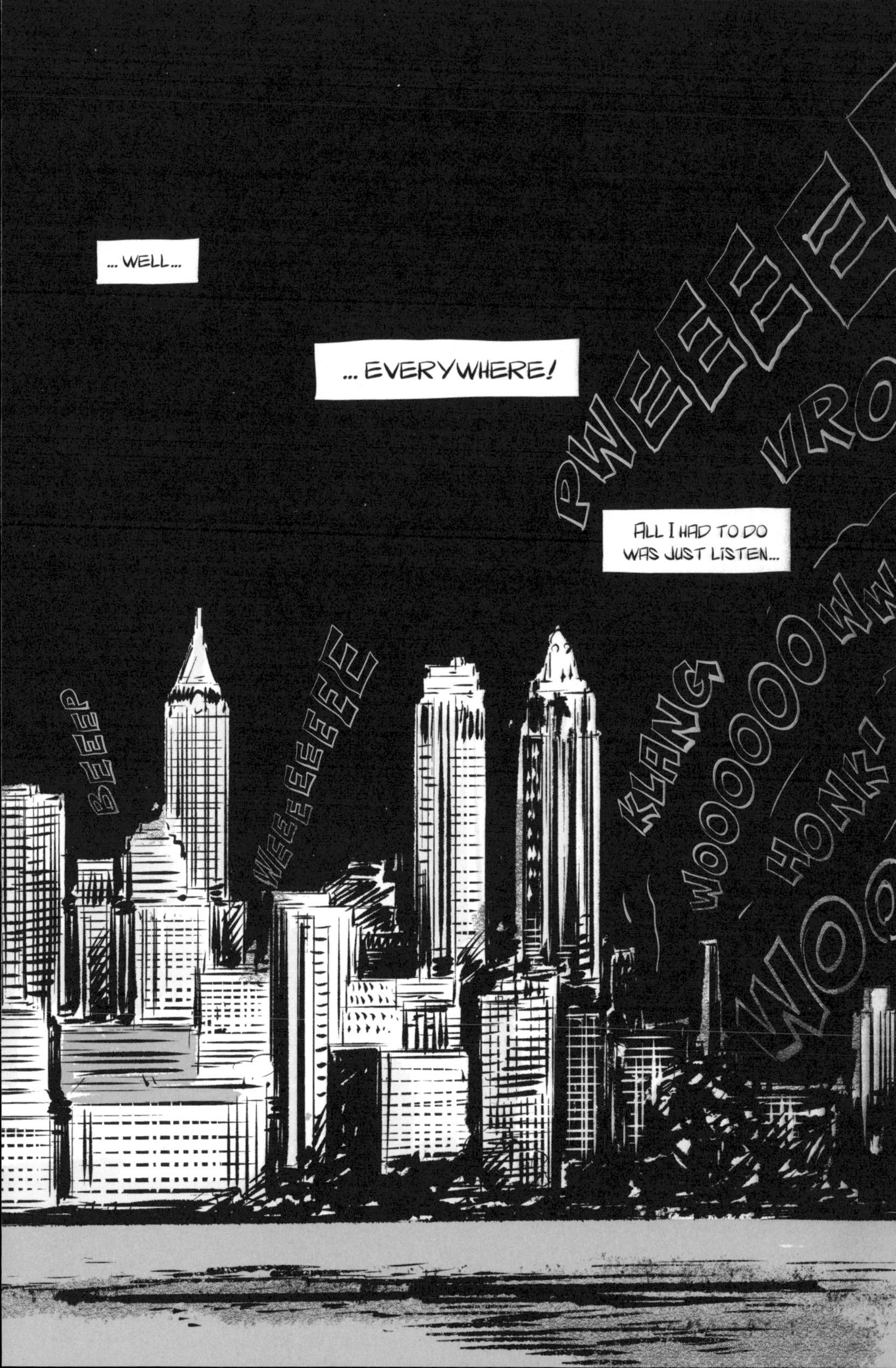
... WELL...
... EVERYWHERE!
ALL I HAD TO DO WAS JUST LISTEN...
BEEEEP
KLANG
HONK!

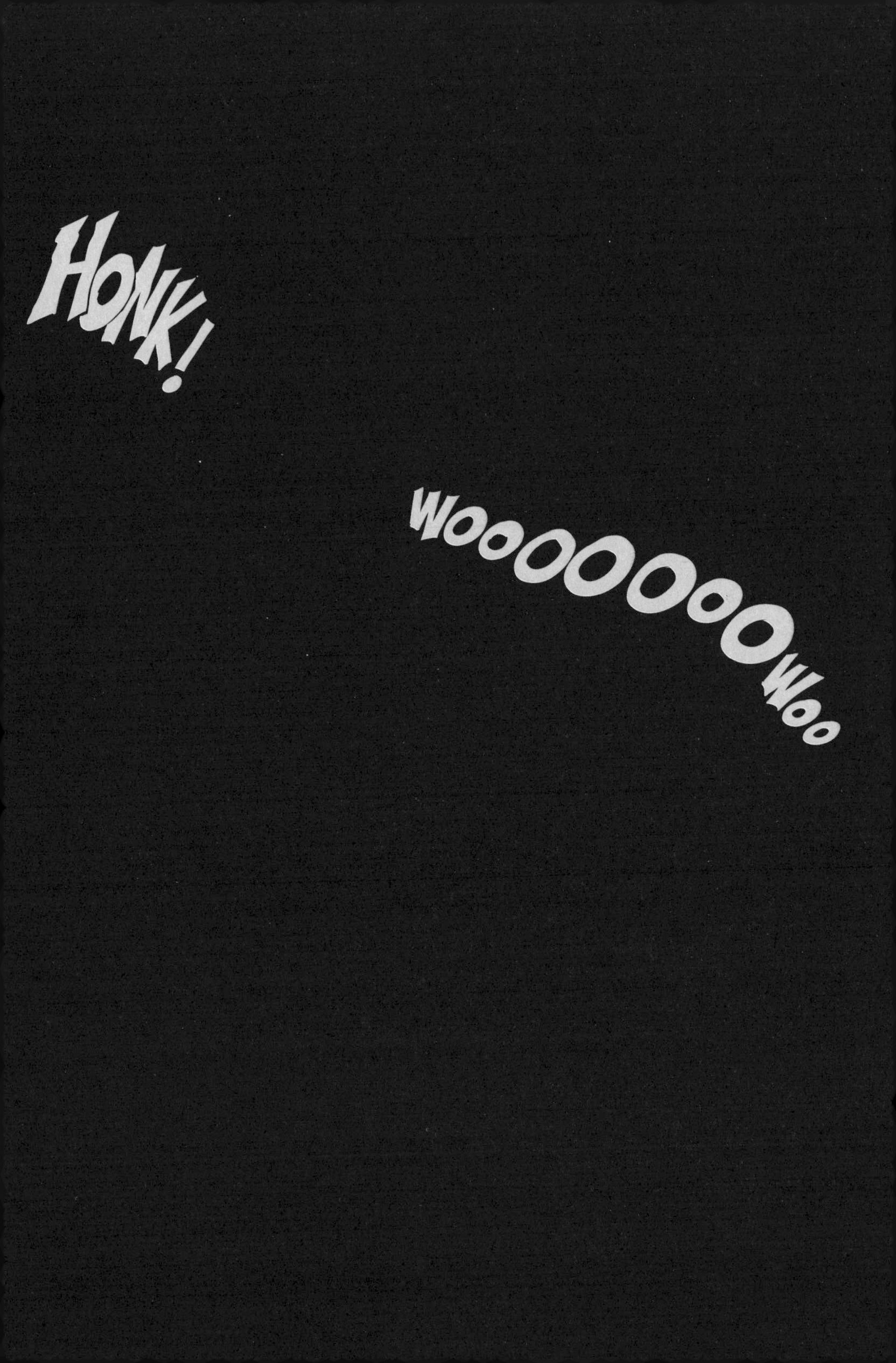

HONK!
WooOOOoOWoo

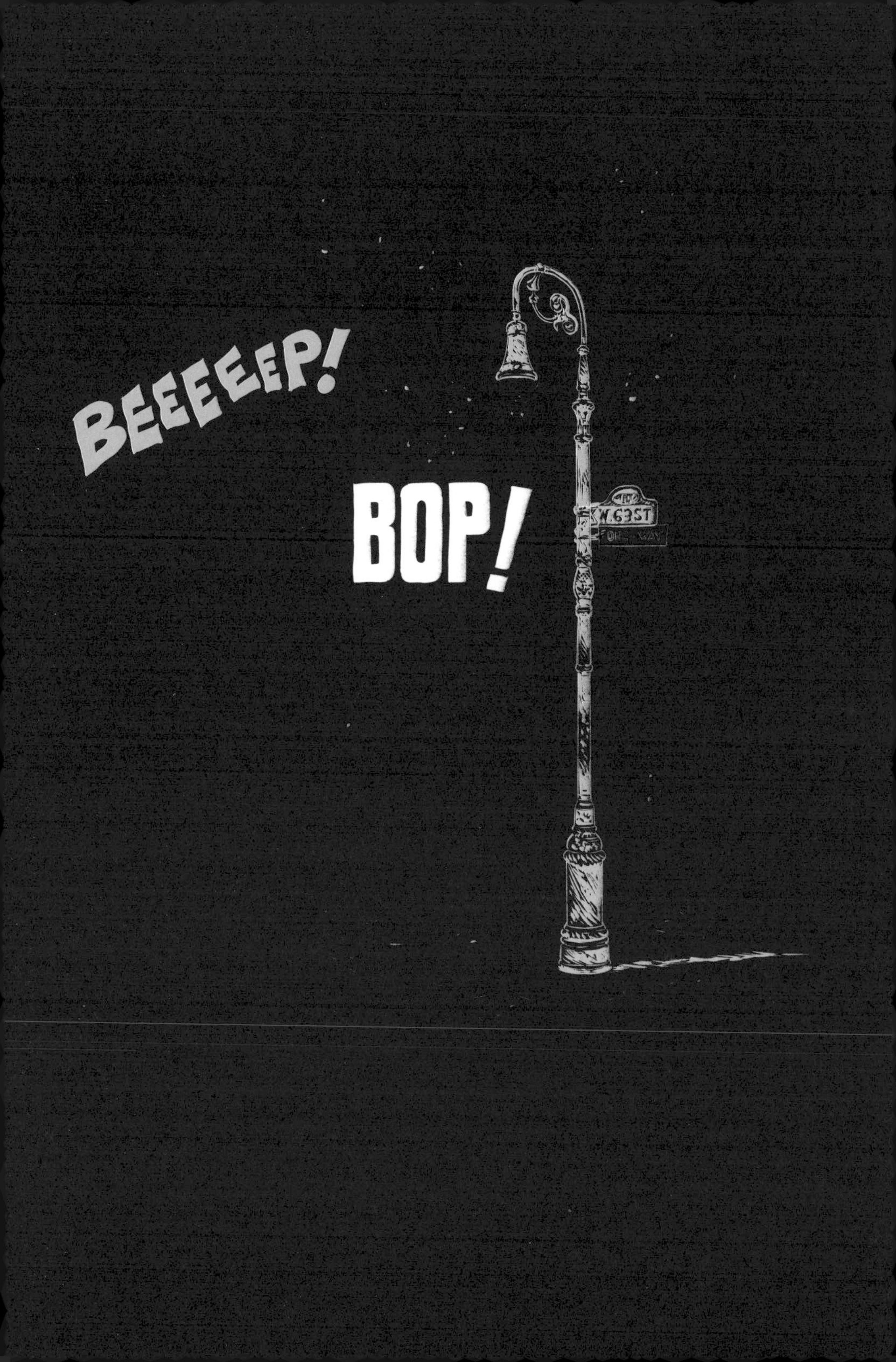
BEEEEEP!
BOP!
W. 63 ST

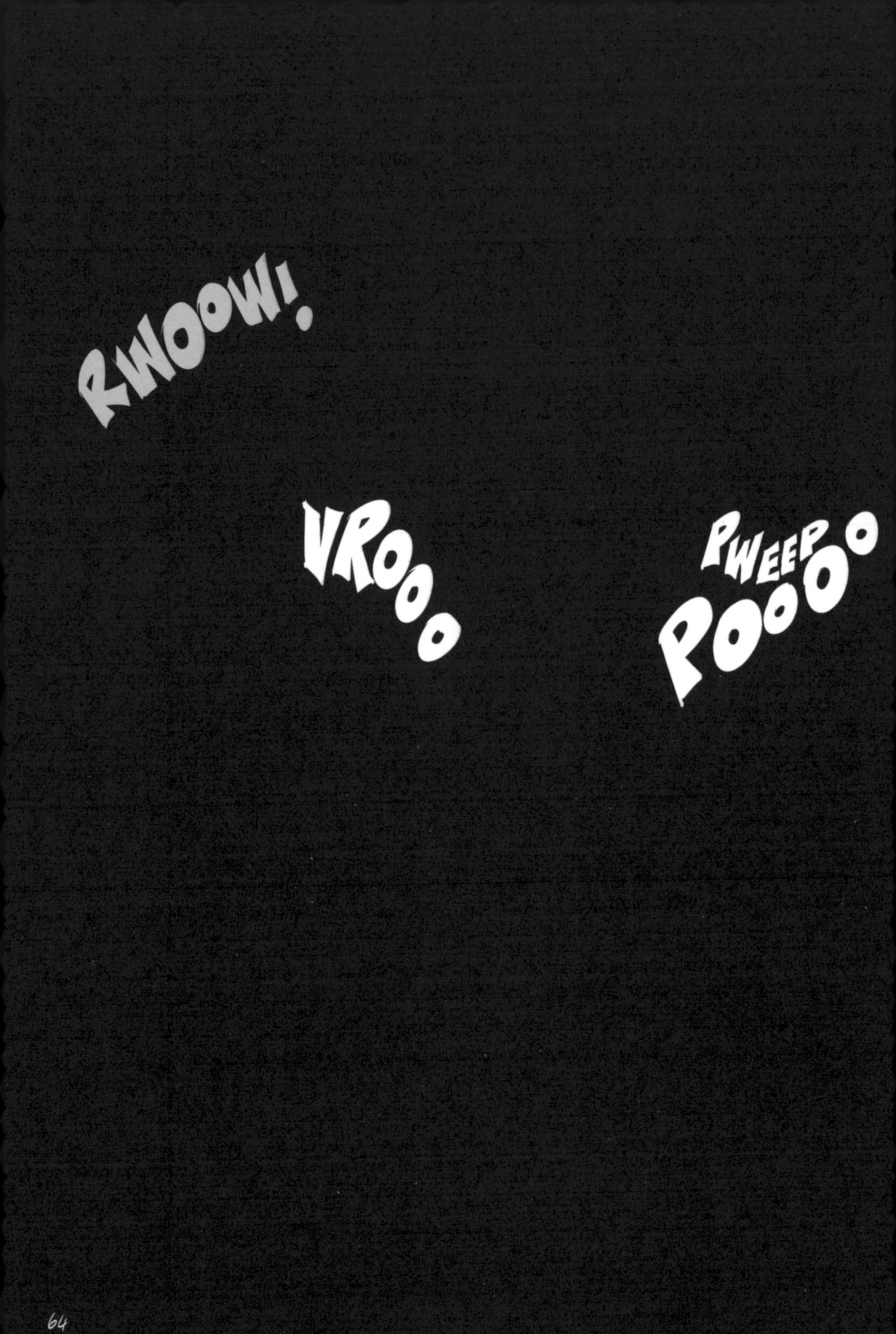
RWOOW!
VROOOO
PWEEP
POOOOO

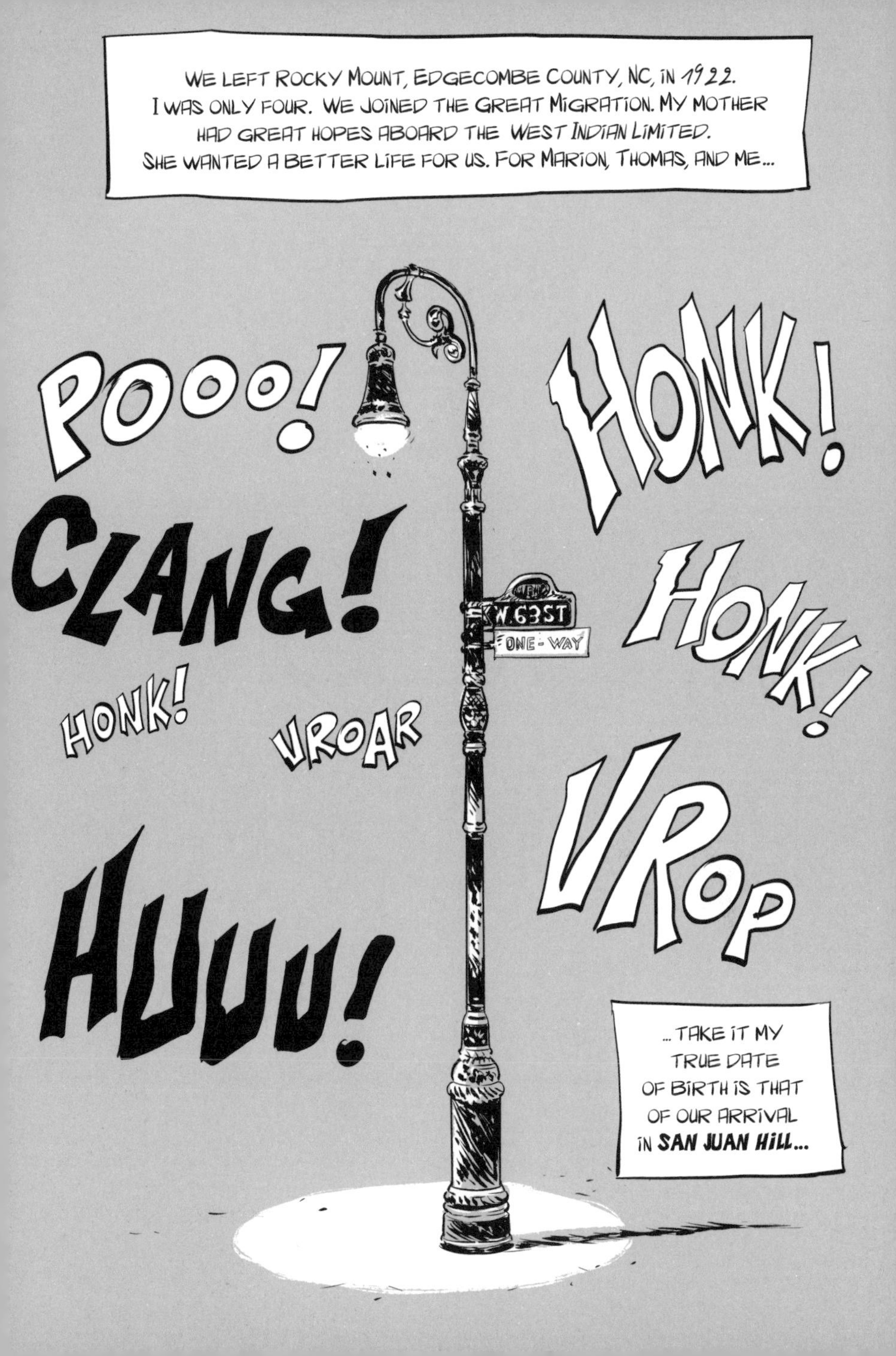
WE LEFT ROCKY MOUNT, EDGECOMBE COUNTY, NC, IN 1922. I WAS ONLY FOUR. WE JOINED THE GREAT MIGRATION. MY MOTHER HAD GREAT HOPES ABOARD THE WEST INDIAN LIMITED. SHE WANTED A BETTER LIFE FOR US. FOR MARION, THOMAS, AND ME...
POOO!
HONK!
CLANG!
W. 63ST
ONE-WAY
HONK!
HONK!
VROAR
HUUUU!
VROP
...TAKE IT MY TRUE DATE OF BIRTH IS THAT OF OUR ARRIVAL IN **SAN JUAN HILL...**

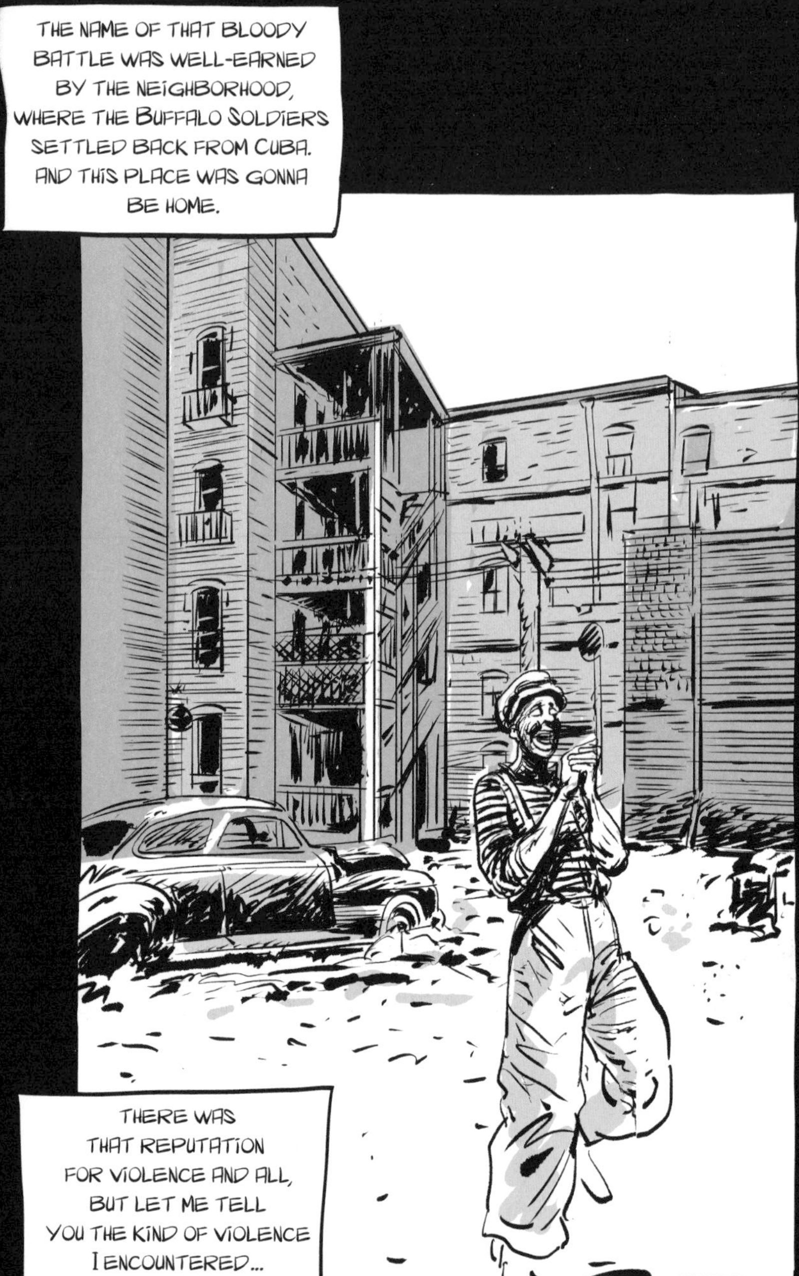
THE NAME OF THAT BLOODY BATTLE WAS WELL-EARNED BY THE NEIGHBORHOOD, WHERE THE BUFFALO SOLDIERS SETTLED BACK FROM CUBA. AND THIS PLACE WAS GONNA BE HOME.
THERE WAS THAT REPUTATION FOR VIOLENCE AND ALL, BUT LET ME TELL YOU THE KIND OF VIOLENCE I ENCOUNTERED...

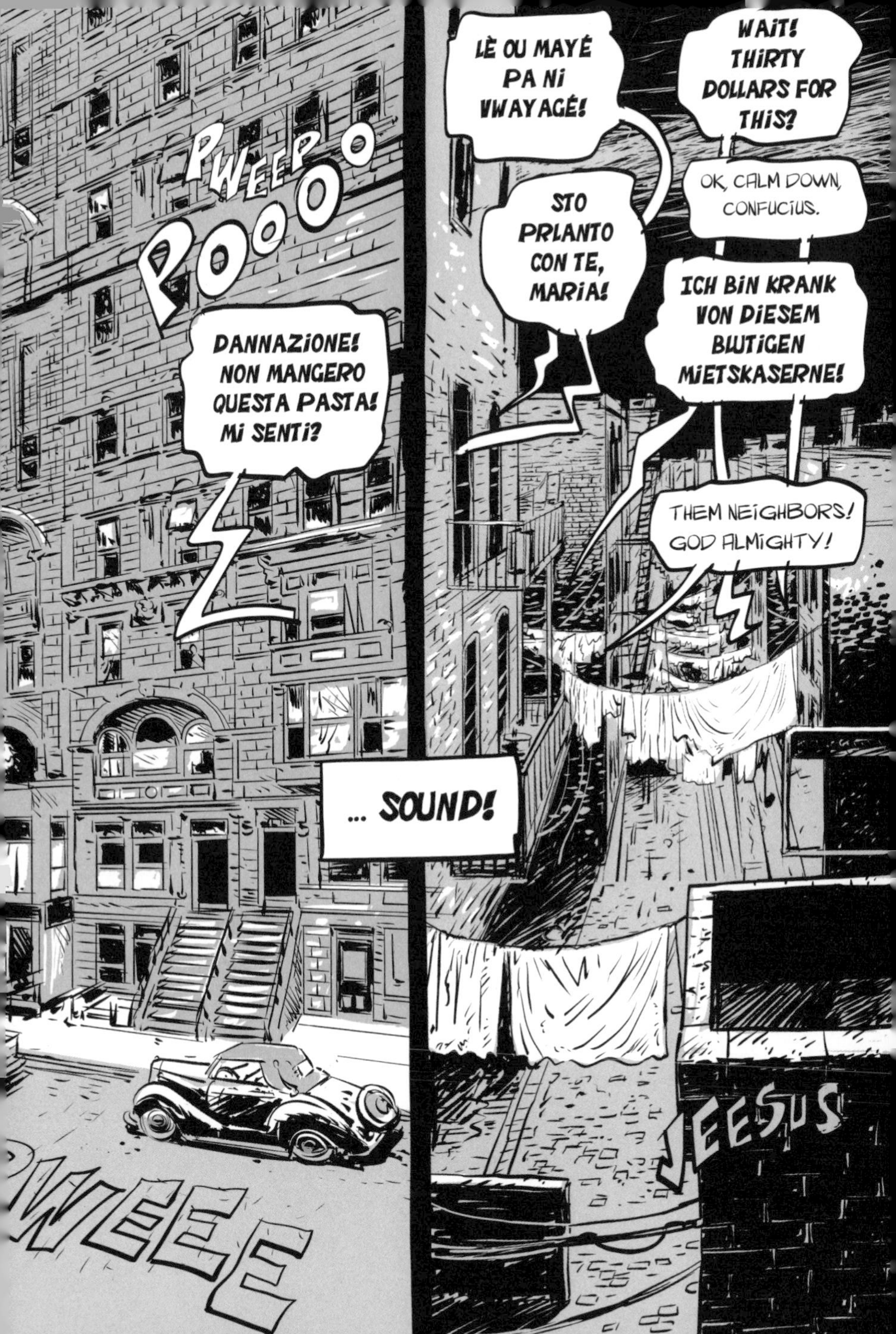
PWEEP O
POOOO
DANNAZIONE! NON MANGERO QUESTA PASTA! MI SENTI?
PWEEE
... SOUND!
LÈ OU MAYÉ PA NI VWAYAGÉ!
STO PRLANTO CON TE, MARIA!
WAIT! THIRTY DOLLARS FOR THIS?
OK, CALM DOWN, CONFUCIUS.
ICH BIN KRANK VON DIESEM BLUTIGEN MIETSKASERNE!
THEM NEIGHBORS! GOD ALMIGHTY!
JEESUS

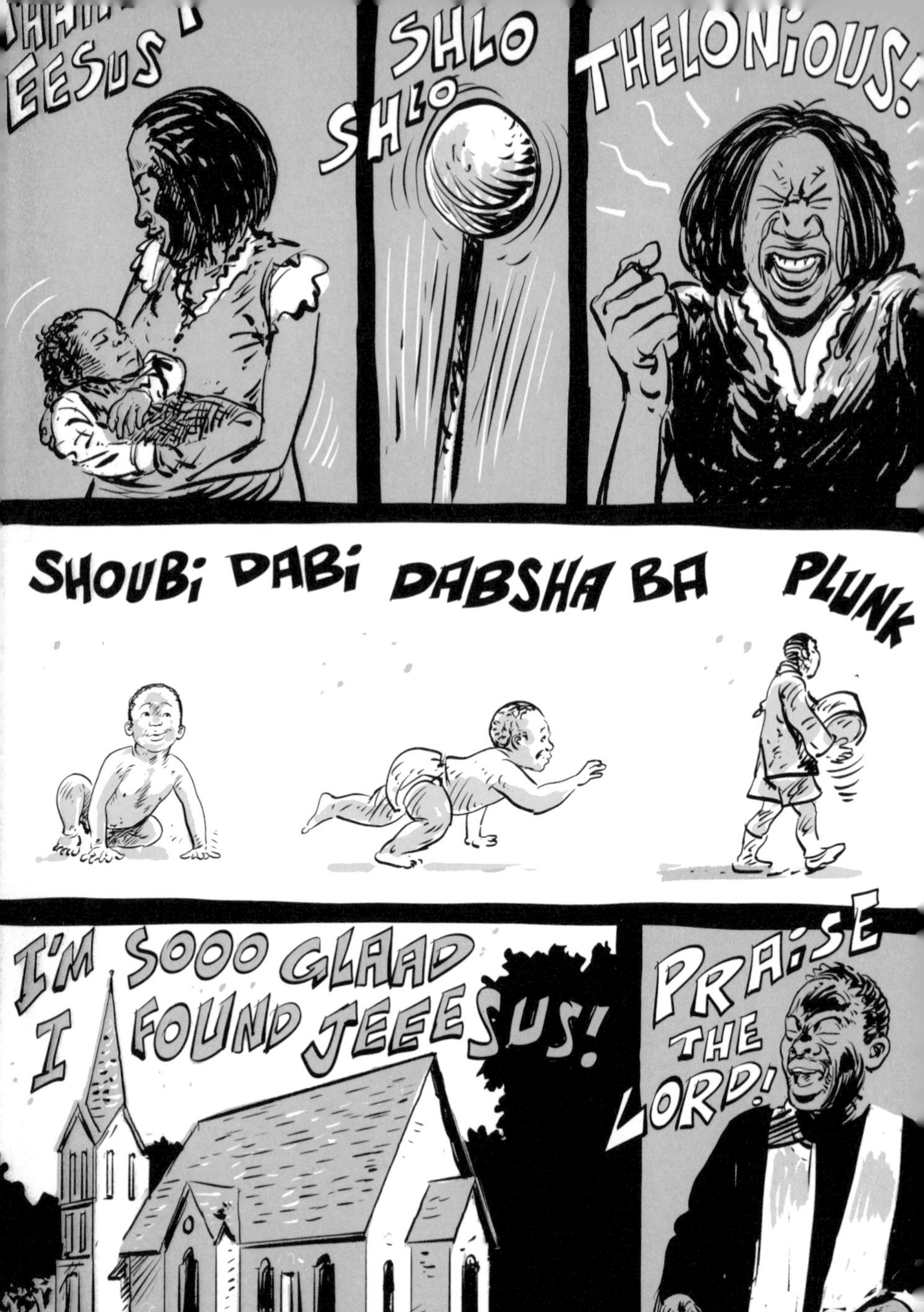
SHLO
SHLO
THELONIOUS!
SHOUBI DABI DABSHA BA
PLUNK
I'M SOOO GLAAD I FOUND JEEESUS!
PRAISE THE LORD!

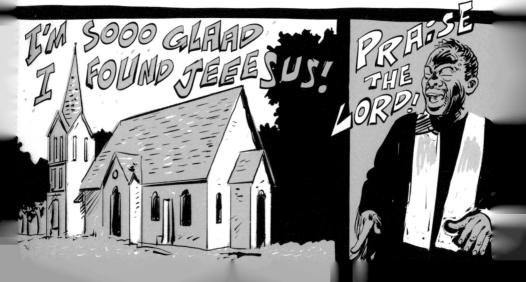

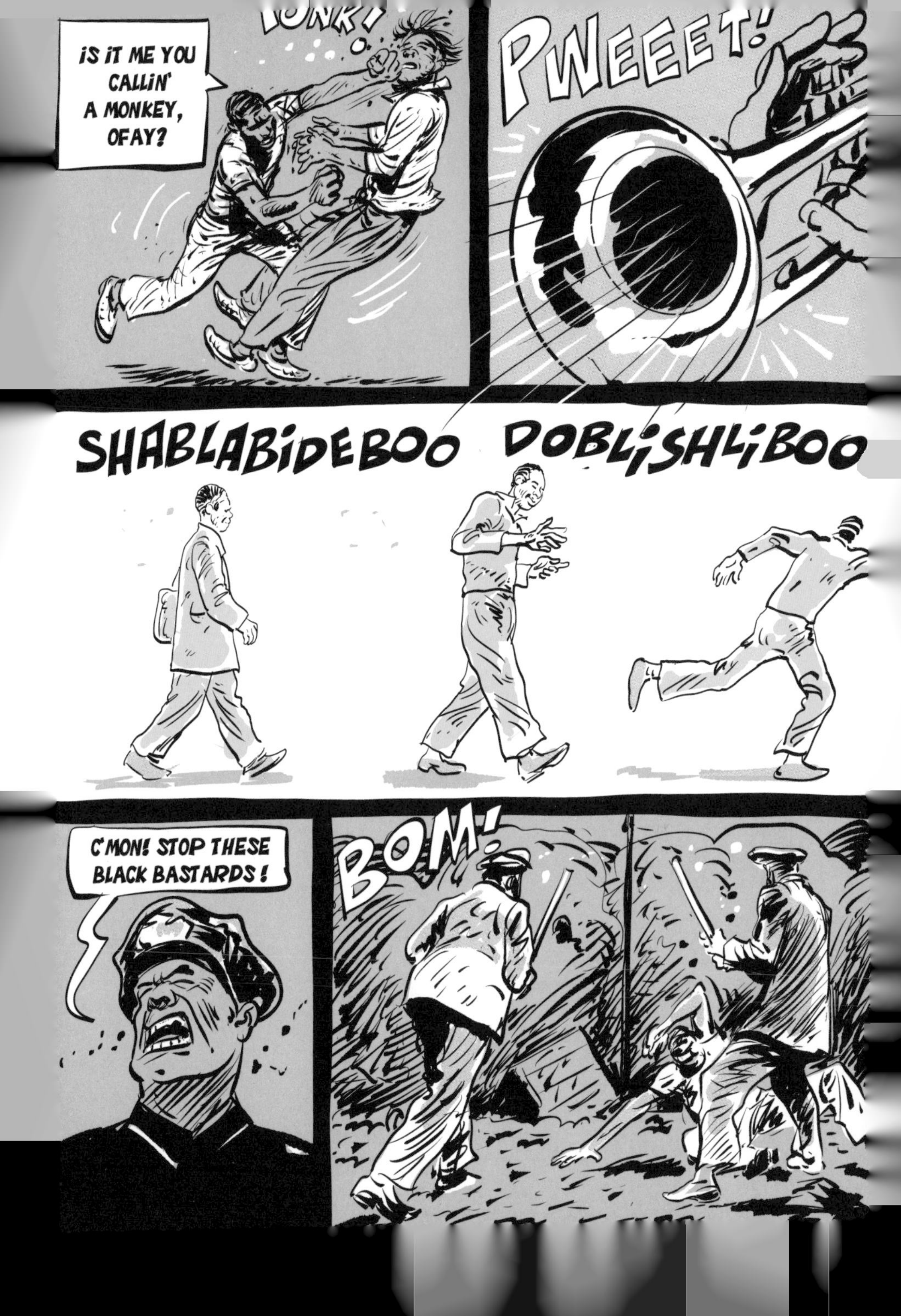
IS IT ME YOU CALLIN' A MONKEY, OFAY?
PWEEET!
SHABLABIDEBOO DOBLISHLIBOO
C'MON! STOP THESE BLACK BASTARDS!
BOM!

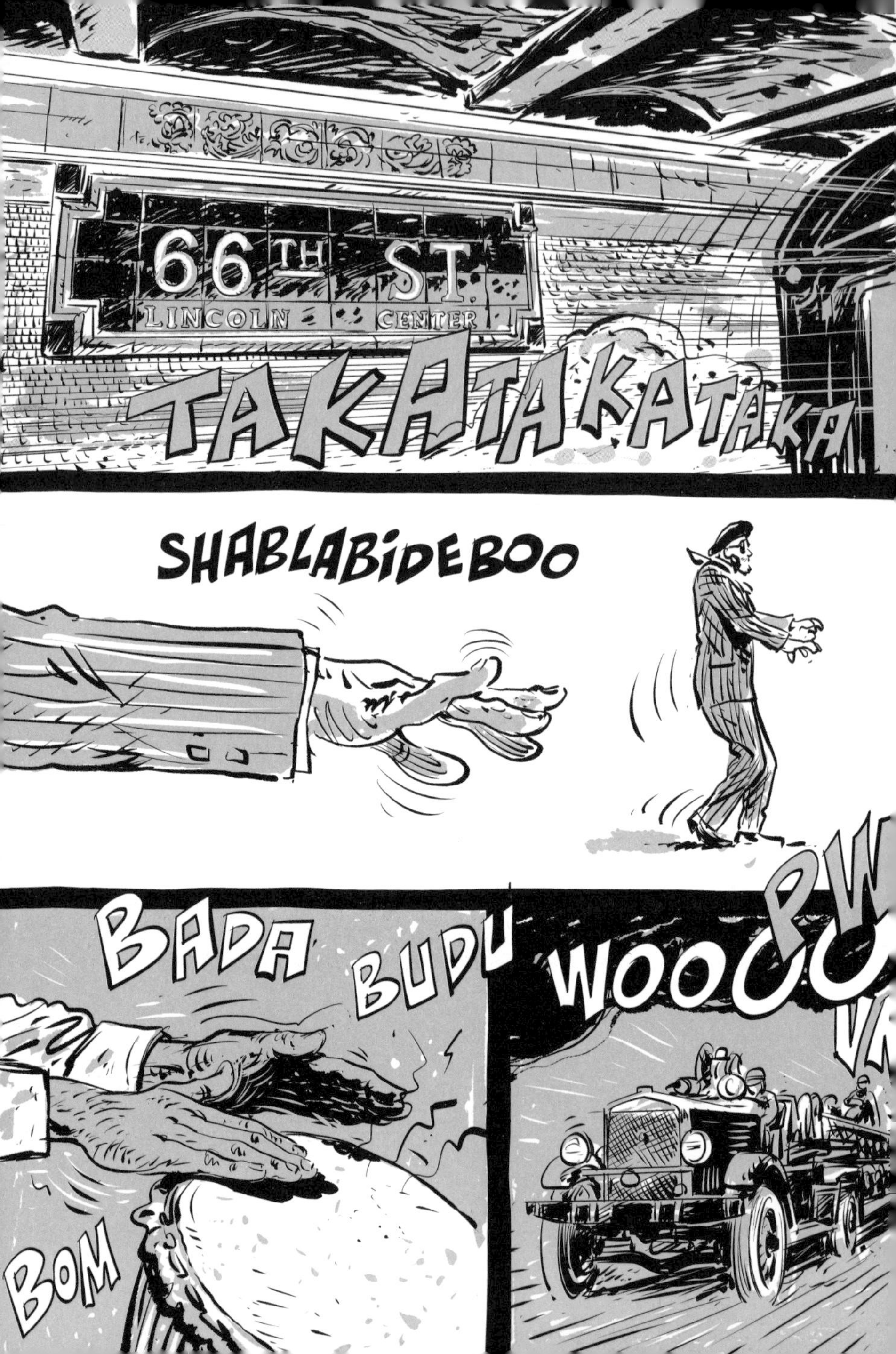
66TH ST.
LINCOLN CENTER
TAKATAKATAKA
SHABLABIDEBOO
BADA
BUDU
BOM
WOOO
PW
VR

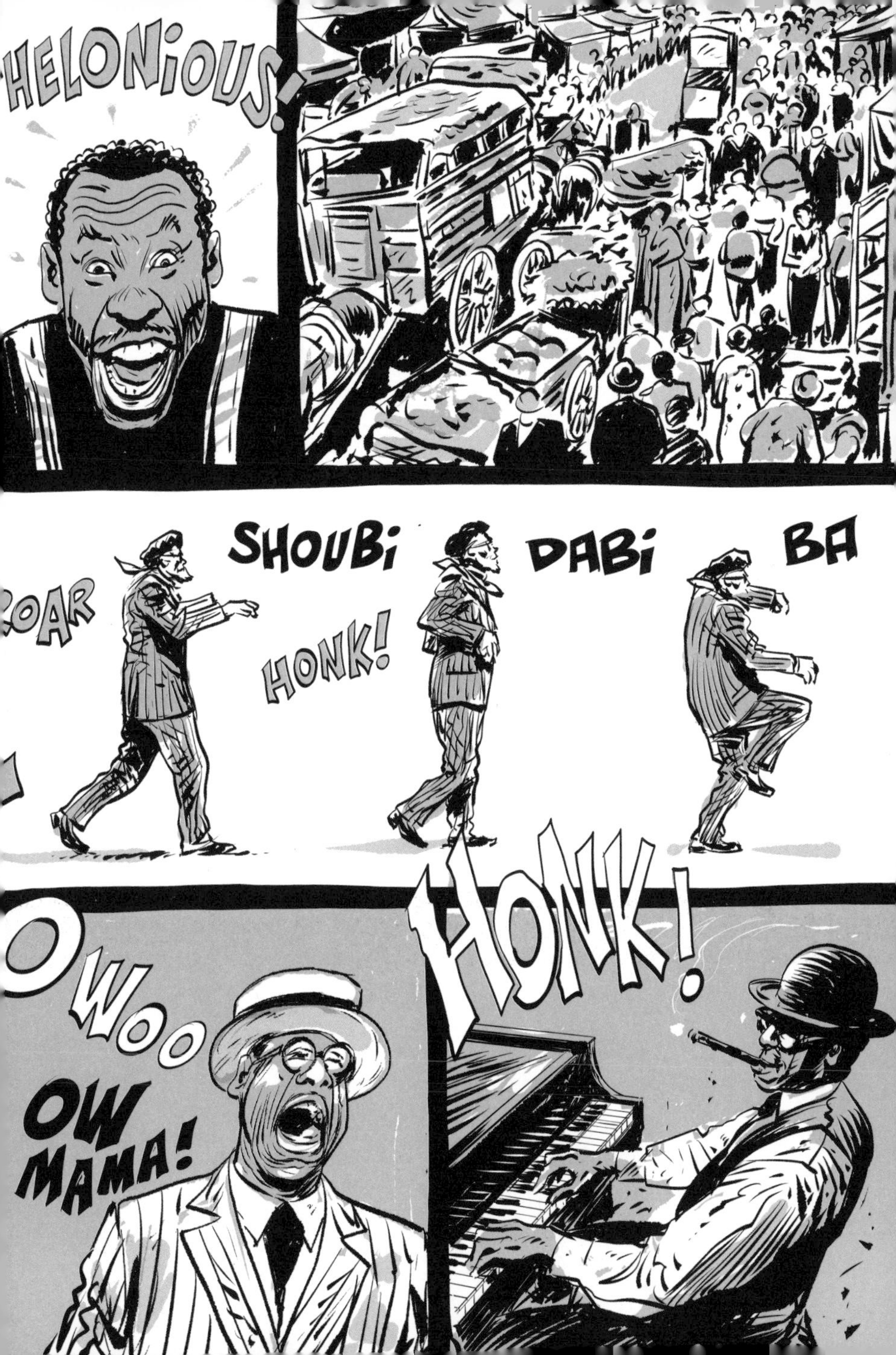
HELONiOUS!
ROAR
SHOUBi
HONK!
DABi
BA
OWOO
OW
MAMA!
HONK!

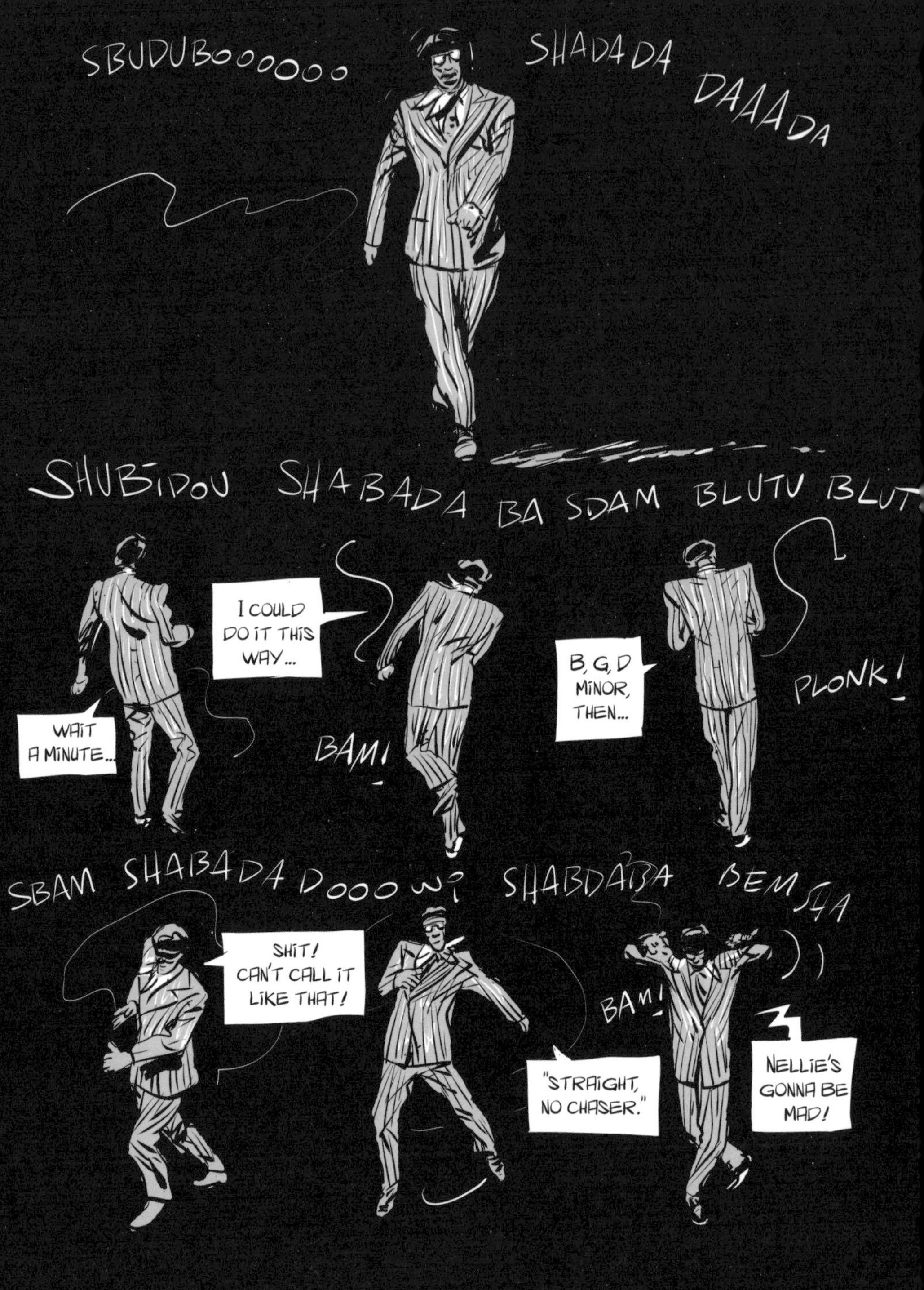
SBUDUBOOOOOOO
SHADADA DAAAADA
SHUBIDOU SHABADA BA SDAM BLUTU BLUT
WAIT A MINUTE...
I COULD DO IT THIS WAY...
BAM!
B, G, D MINOR, THEN...
PLONK!
SBAM SHABADA DOOOW! SHABDABA BEM SHA
SHIT! CAN'T CALL IT LIKE THAT!
"STRAIGHT, NO CHASER."
BAM!
NELLIE'S GONNA BE MAD!

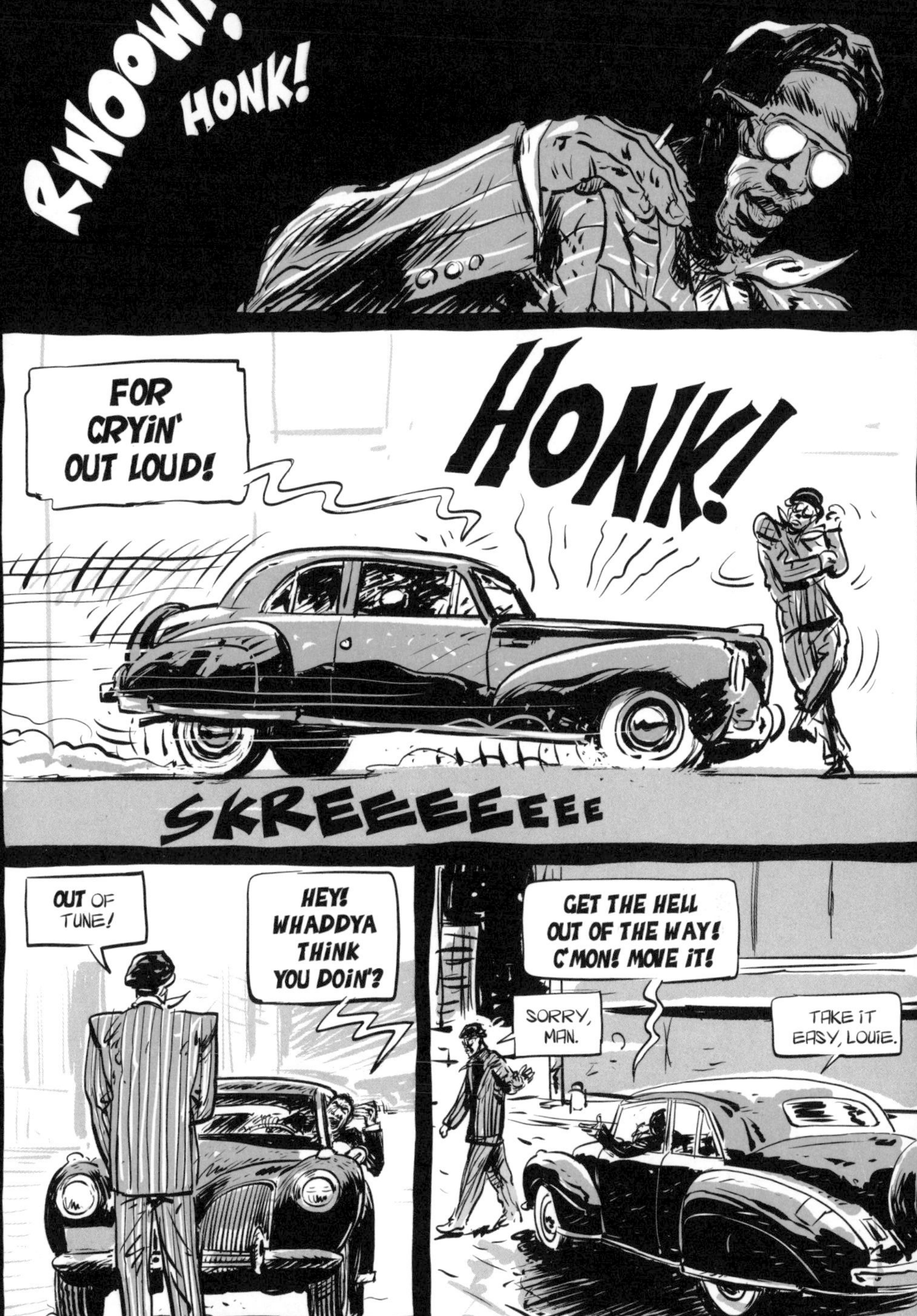
RWOOW!
HONK!
FOR CRYIN' OUT LOUD!
HONK!
SKREEEEEEEE
OUT OF TUNE!
HEY! WHADDYA THINK YOU DOIN'?
GET THE HELL OUT OF THE WAY! C'MON! MOVE IT!
SORRY, MAN.
TAKE IT EASY, LOUIE.

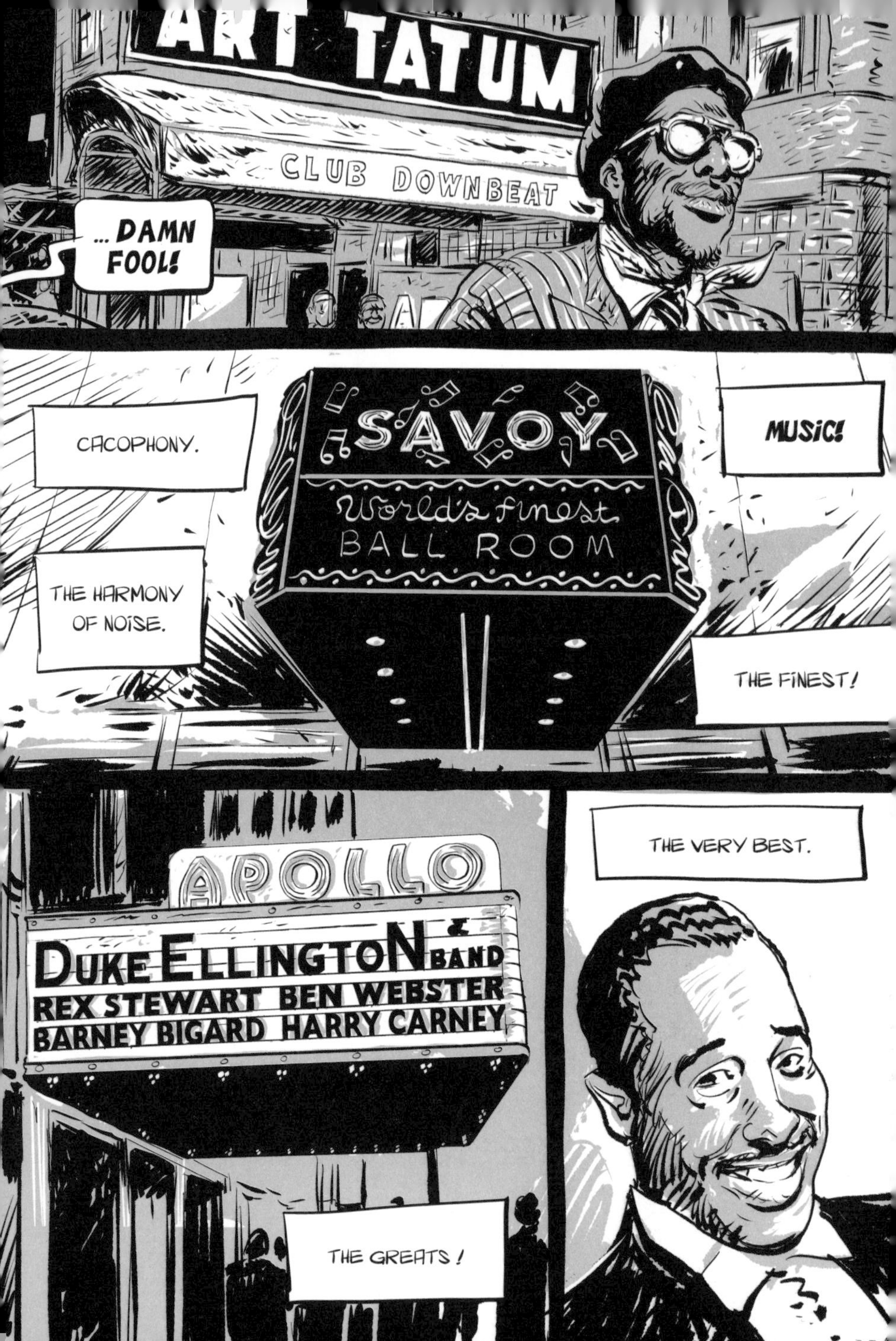
ART TATUM
CLUB DOWNBEAT
...DAMN FOOL!
SAVOY
World's finest BALL ROOM
CACOPHONY.
MUSIC!
THE HARMONY OF NOISE.
THE FINEST!
APOLLO
DUKE ELLINGTON & BAND
REX STEWART BEN WEBSTER
BARNEY BIGARD HARRY CARNEY
THE GREATS!
THE VERY BEST.

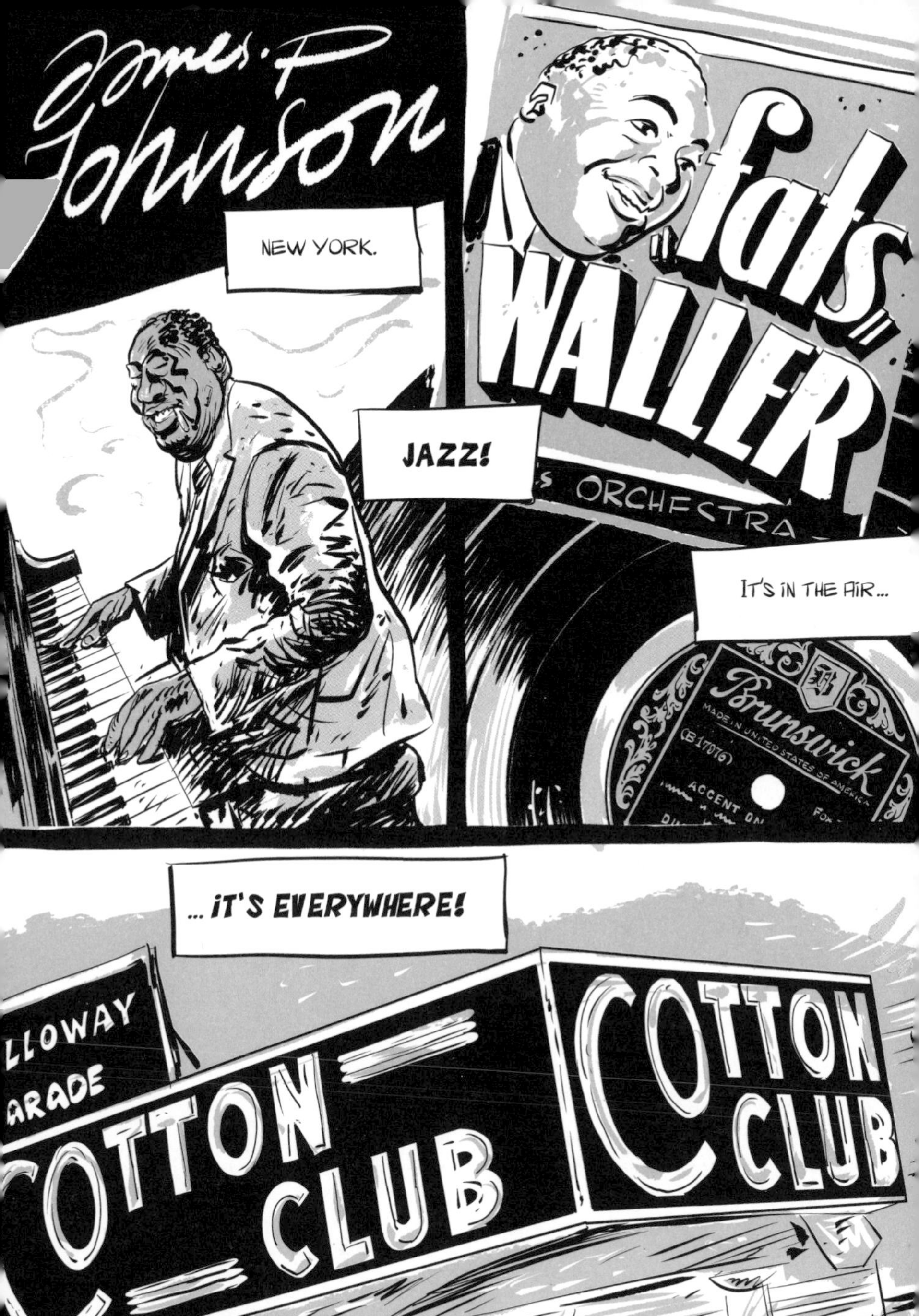

James P. Johnson
NEW YORK.
JAZZ!
"Fats" WALLER
S ORCHESTRA
IT'S IN THE AIR...
Brunswick
MADE IN UNITED STATES OF AMERICA
(B 17076)
ACCENT ON
...IT'S EVERYWHERE!
LLOWAY
ARADE
COTTON CLUB
COTTON CLUB

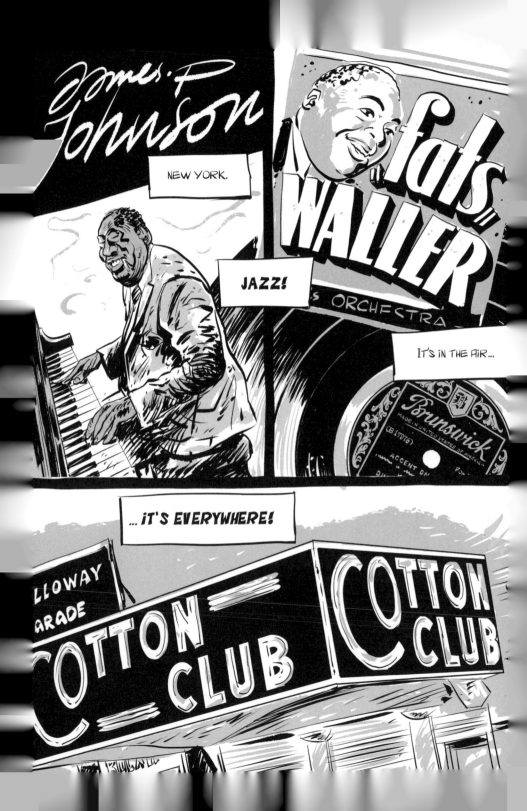

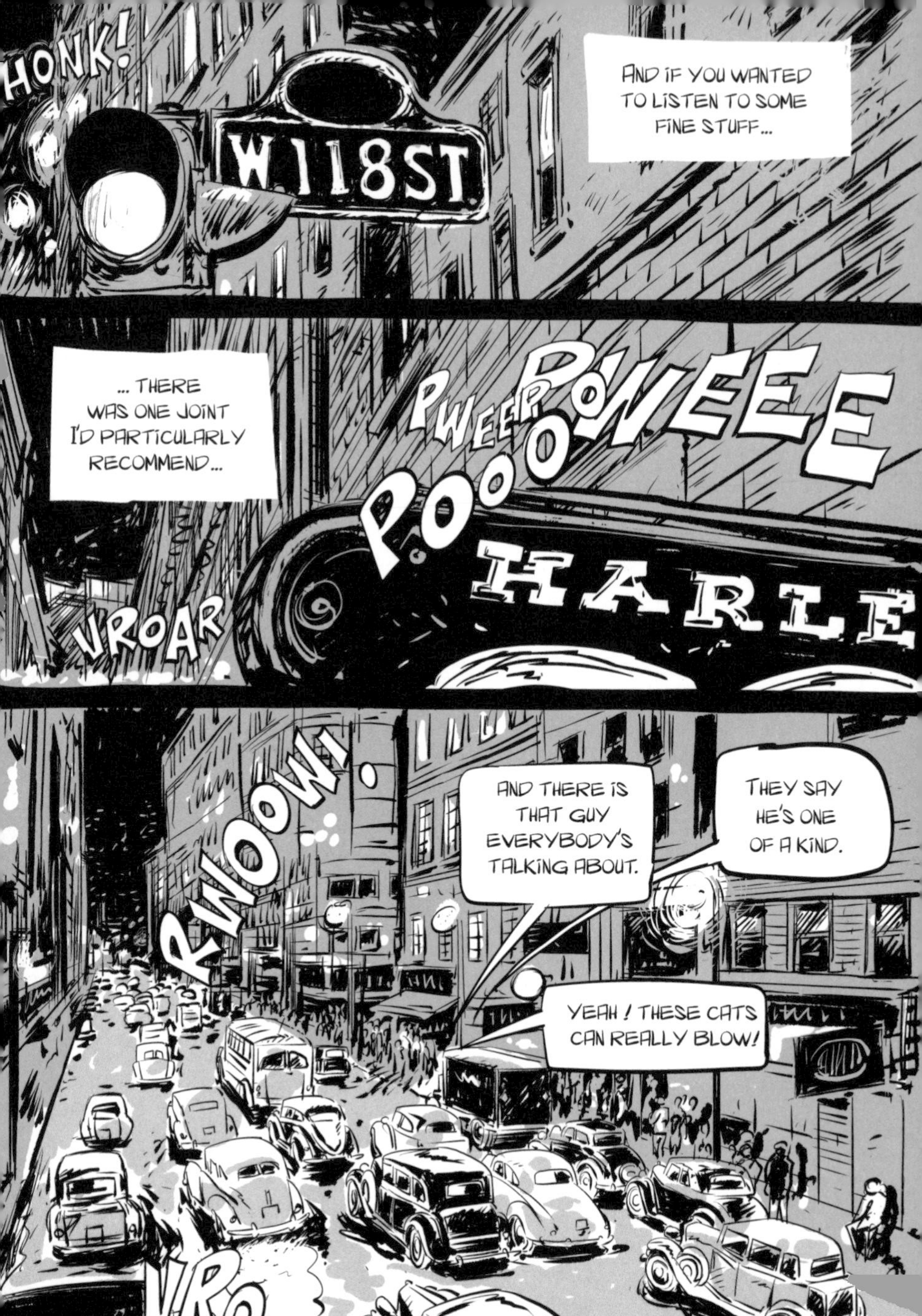
HONK!
W 118 ST
AND IF YOU WANTED TO LISTEN TO SOME FINE STUFF...
... THERE WAS ONE JOINT I'D PARTICULARLY RECOMMEND...
PWEEP
POWEEE
POOOO
HARLE
VROAR
RWOOOW!
AND THERE IS THAT GUY EVERYBODY'S TALKING ABOUT.
THEY SAY HE'S ONE OF A KIND.
YEAH! THESE CATS CAN REALLY BLOW!
VROOO

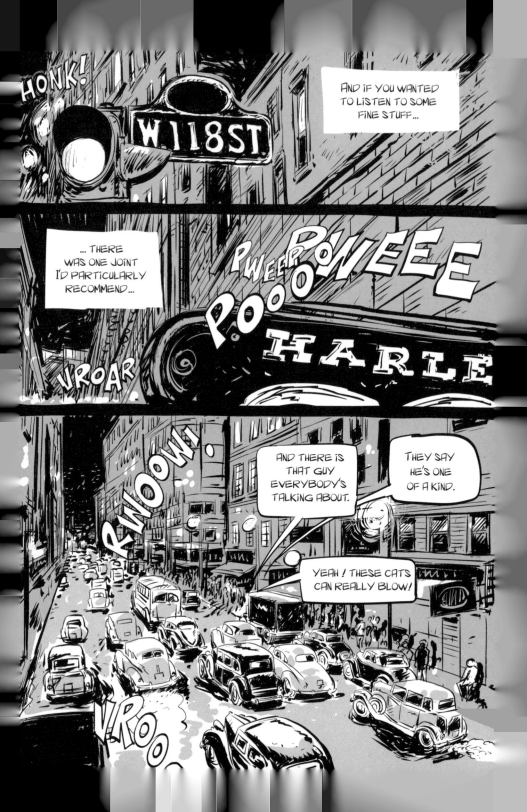

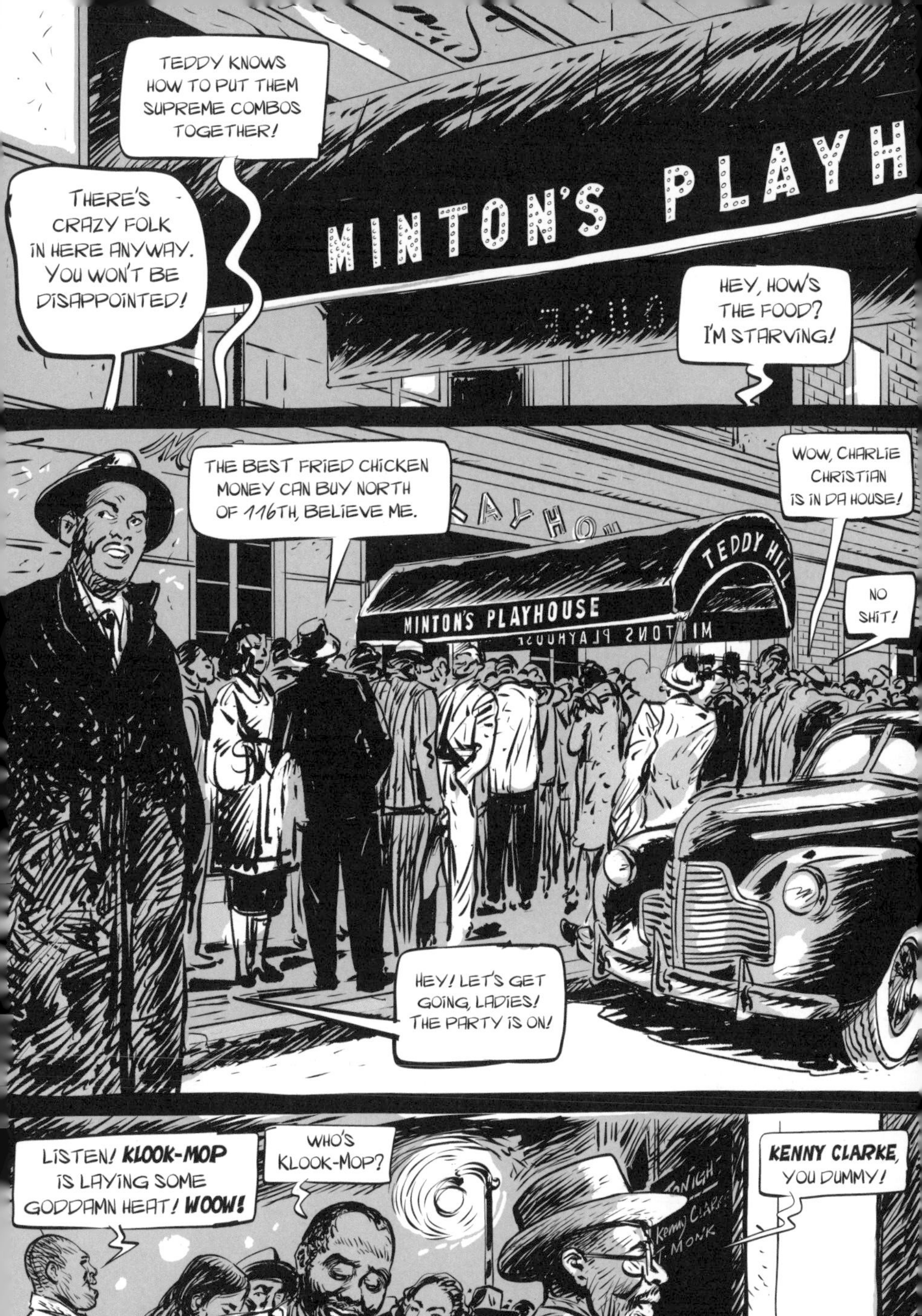

TEDDY KNOWS HOW TO PUT THEM SUPREME COMBOS TOGETHER!
THERE'S CRAZY FOLK IN HERE ANYWAY. YOU WON'T BE DISAPPOINTED!
MINTON'S PLAYH
HEY, HOW'S THE FOOD? I'M STARVING!
THE BEST FRIED CHICKEN MONEY CAN BUY NORTH OF 116TH, BELIEVE ME.
WOW, CHARLIE CHRISTIAN IS IN DA HOUSE!
NO SHIT!
TEDDY HILL
MINTON'S PLAYHOUSE
HEY! LET'S GET GOING, LADIES! THE PARTY IS ON!
LISTEN! KLOOK-MOP IS LAYING SOME GODDAMN HEAT! WOOW!
WHO'S KLOOK-MOP?
KENNY CLARKE, YOU DUMMY!

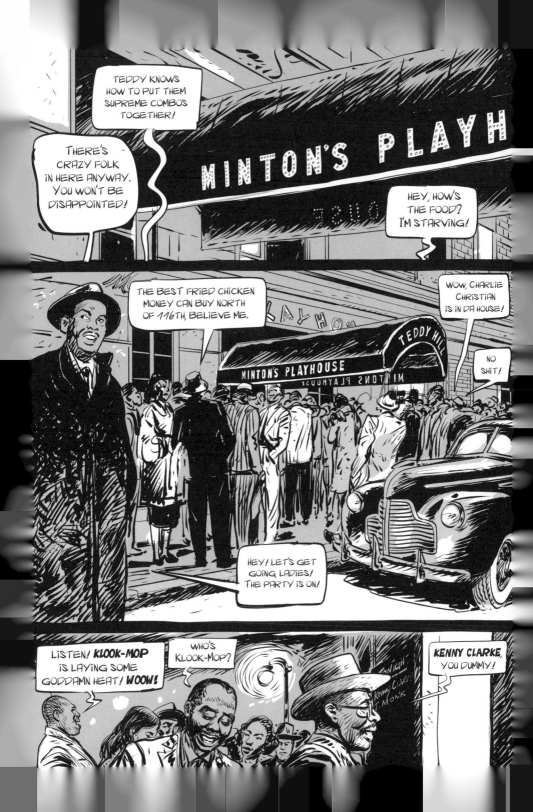

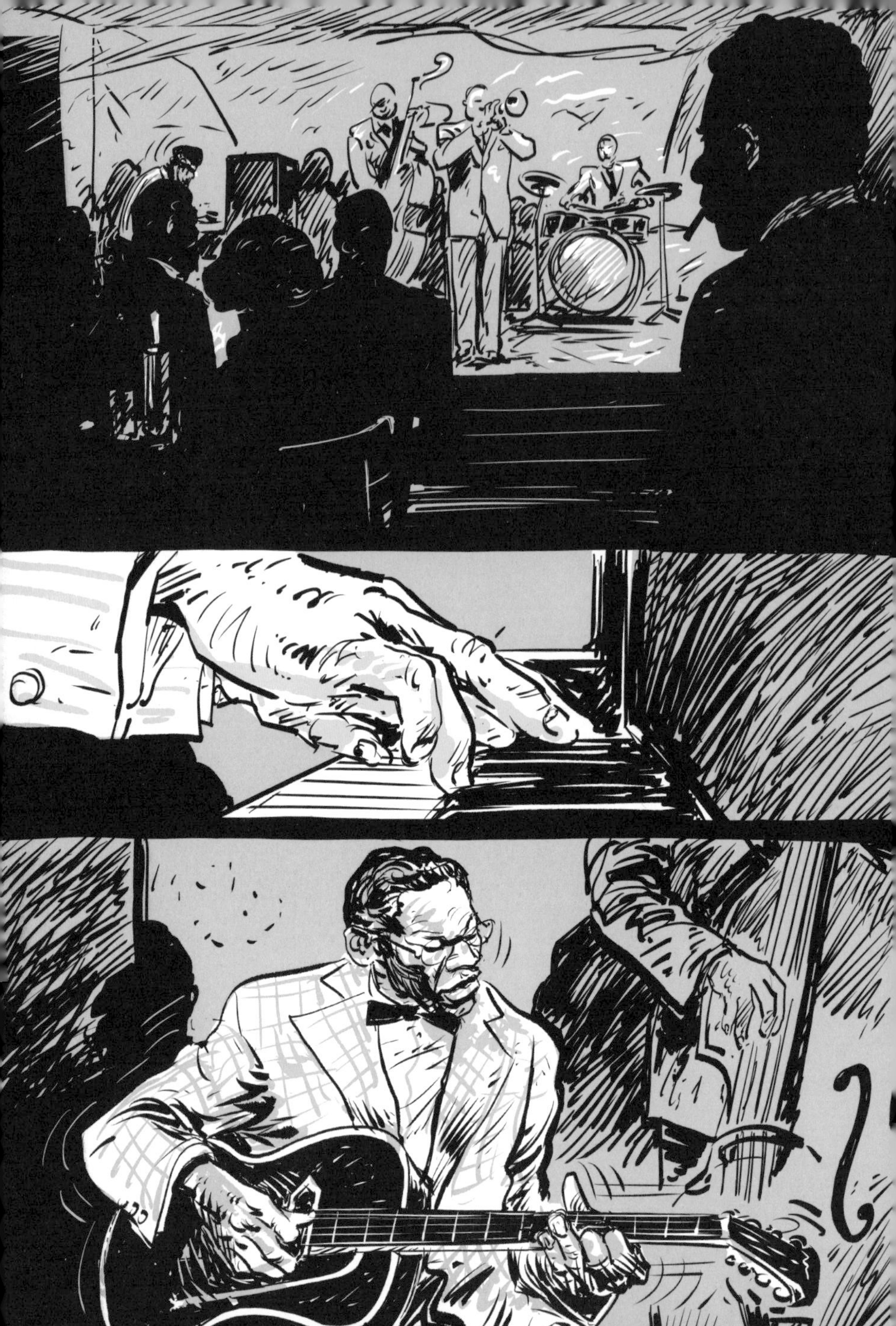

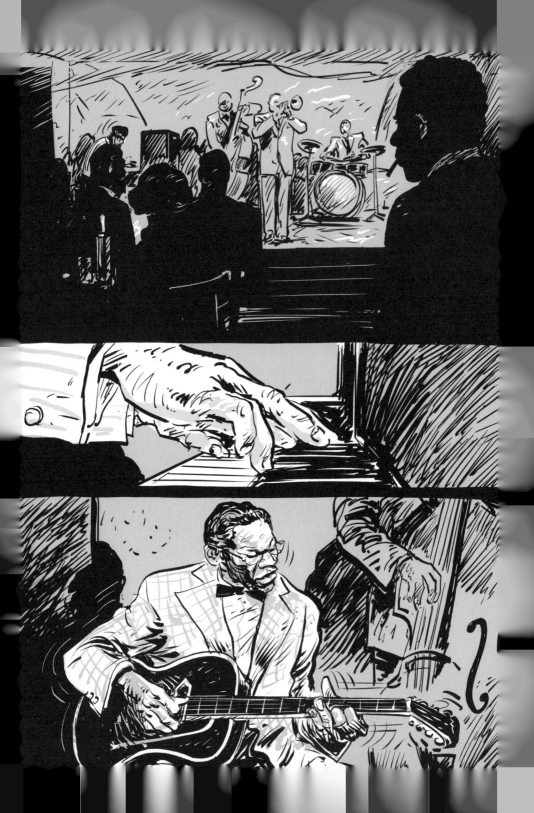

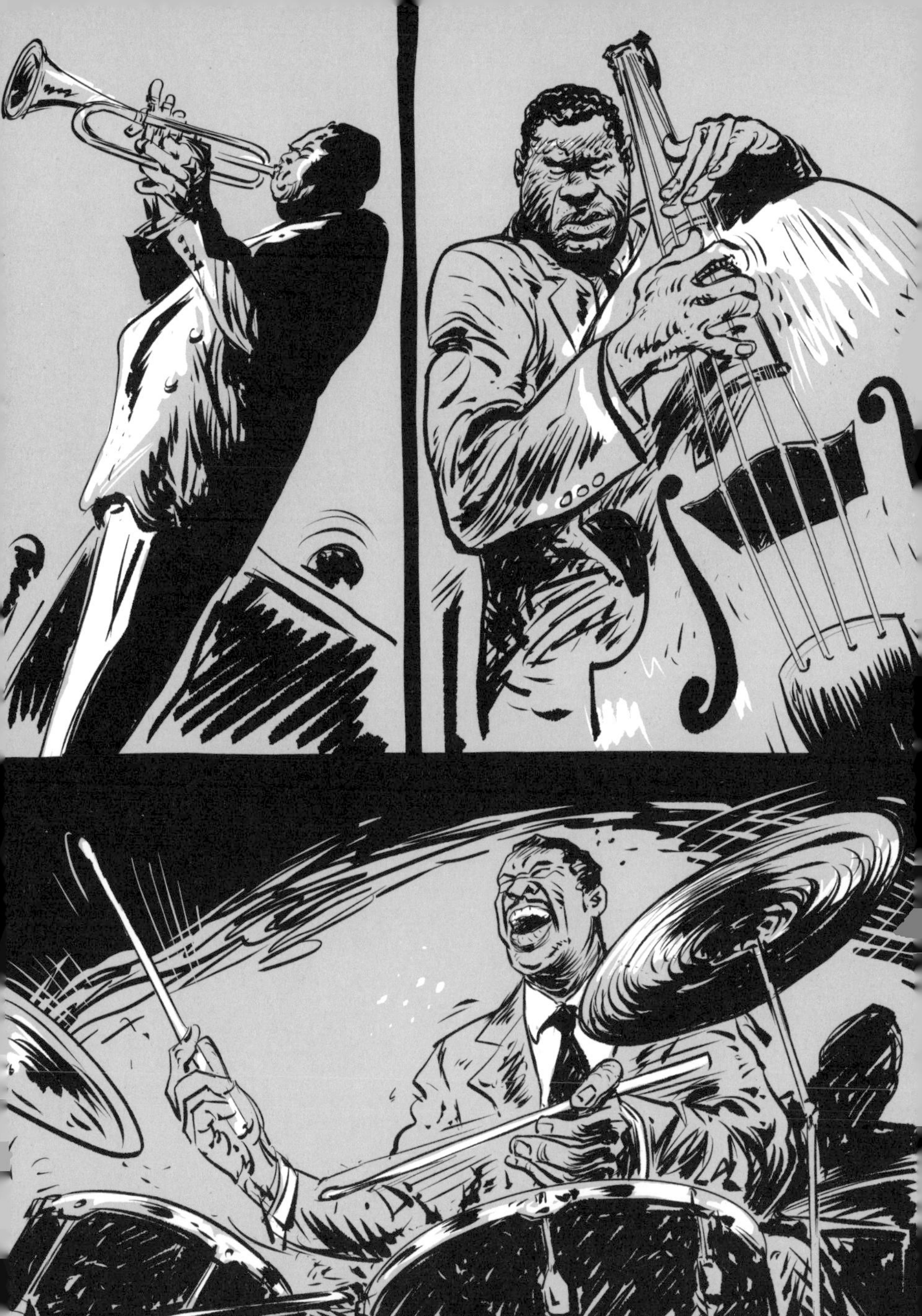

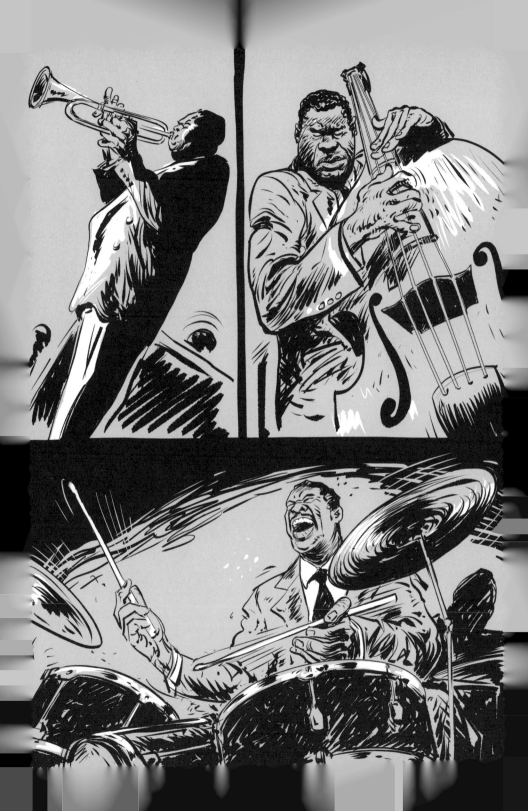

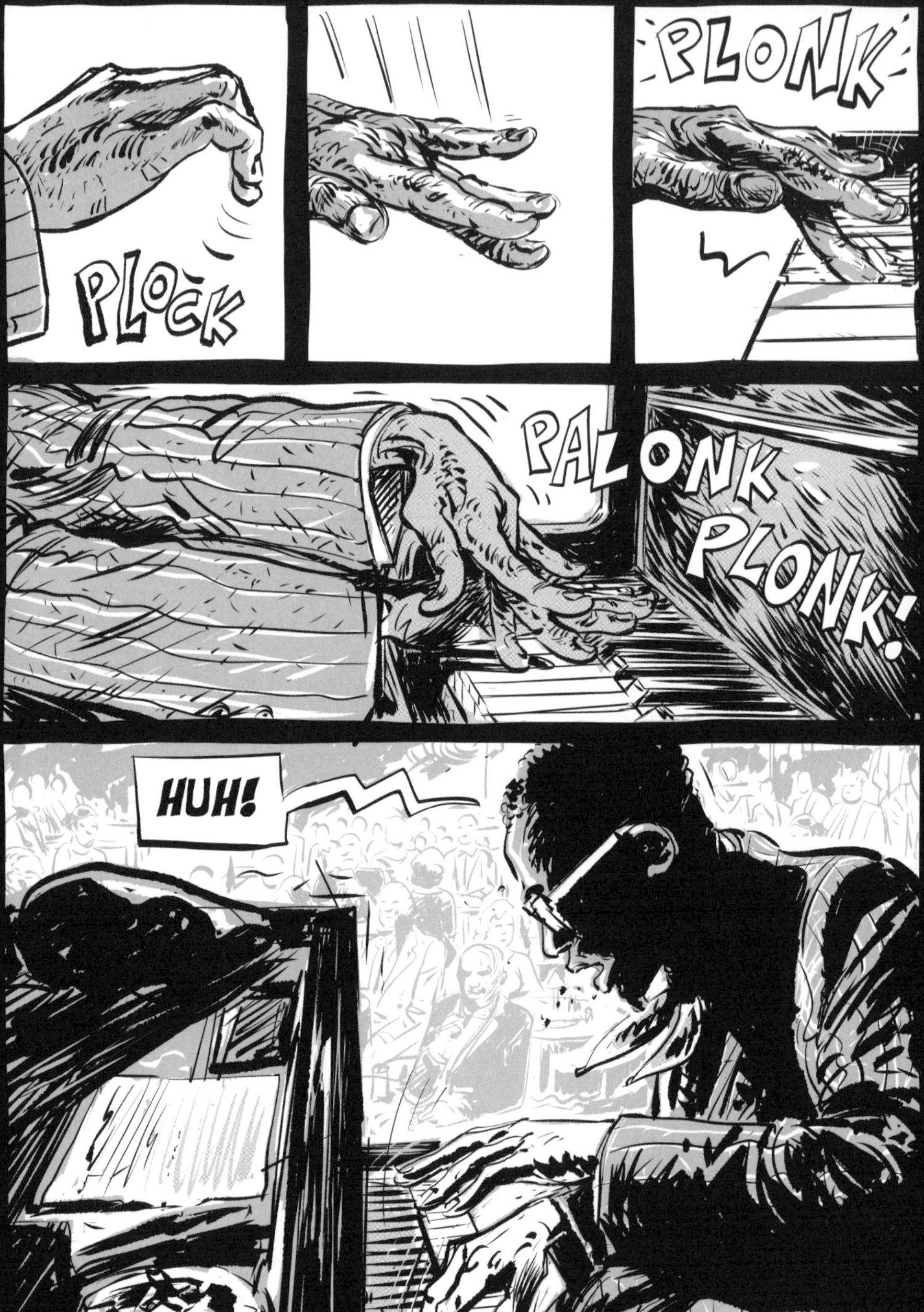
PLOCK
PLONK
PALONK
PLONK PLONK!
HUH!

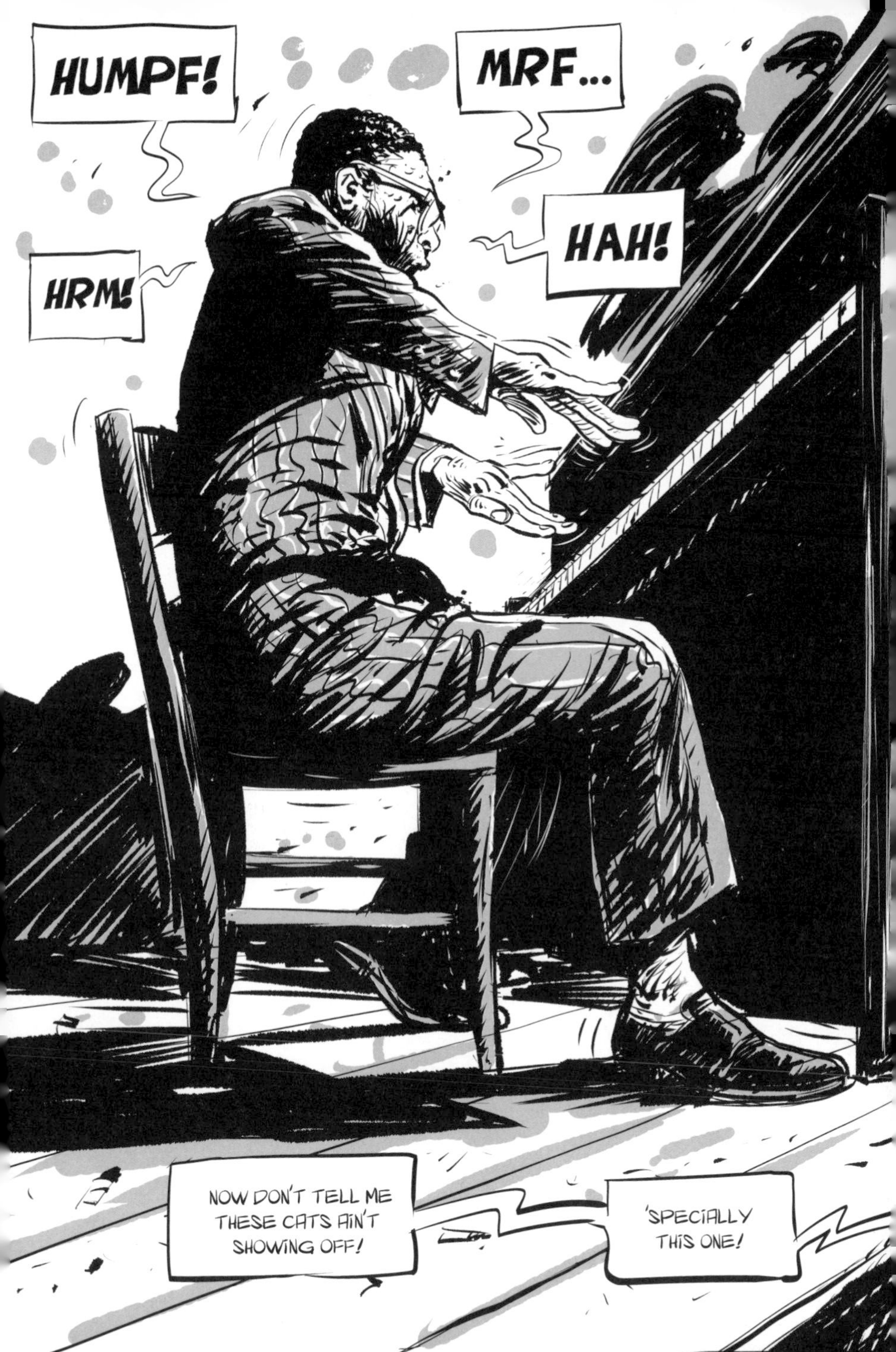
HUMPF!
MRF...
HRM!
HAH!
NOW DON'T TELL ME THESE CATS AIN'T SHOWING OFF!
'SPECIALLY THIS ONE!

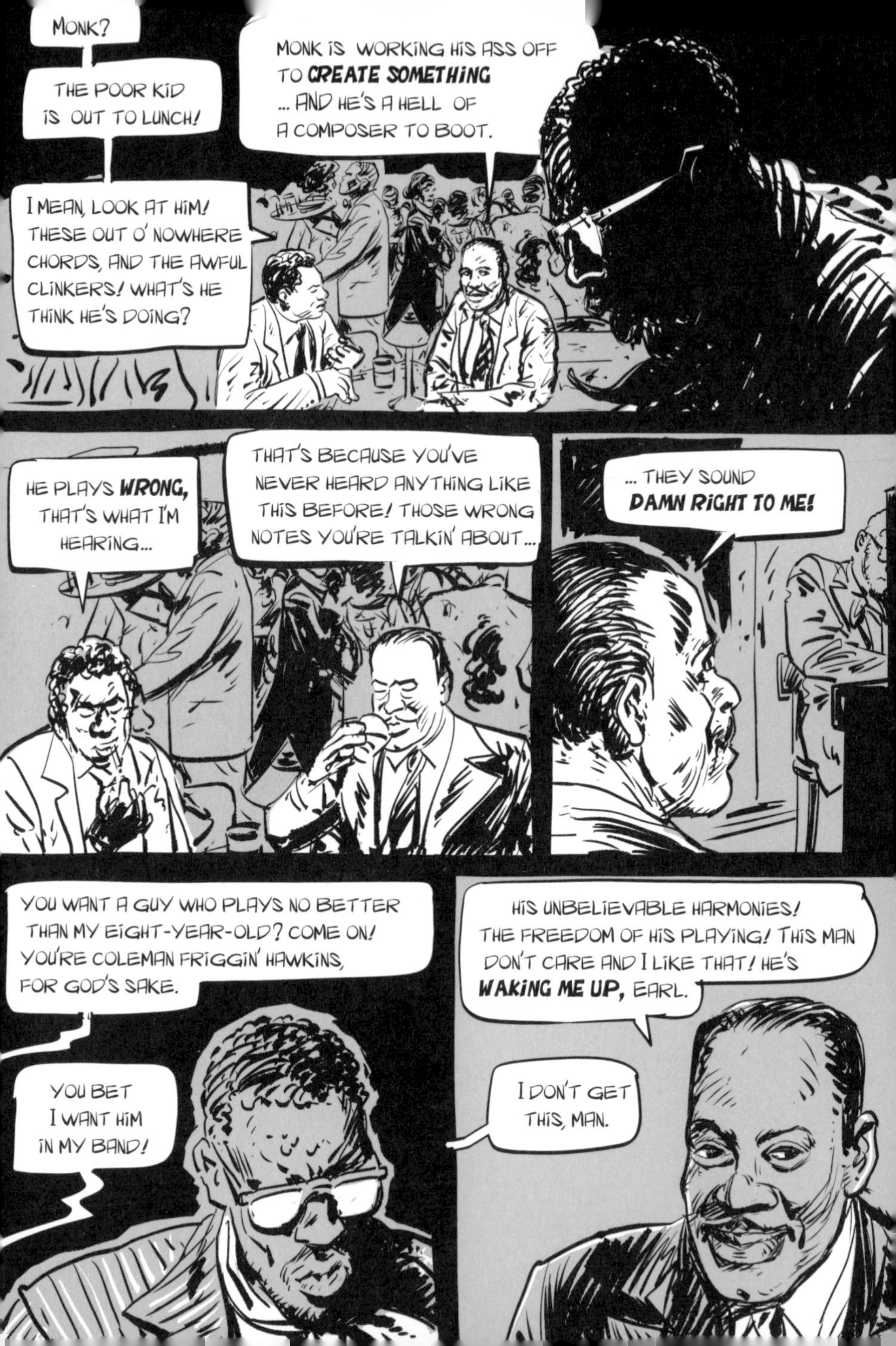
MONK?
THE POOR KID IS OUT TO LUNCH!
I MEAN, LOOK AT HIM! THESE OUT O' NOWHERE CHORDS, AND THE AWFUL CLINKERS! WHAT'S HE THINK HE'S DOING?
MONK IS WORKING HIS ASS OFF TO **CREATE SOMETHING** ... AND HE'S A HELL OF A COMPOSER TO BOOT.
HE PLAYS **WRONG,** THAT'S WHAT I'M HEARING...
THAT'S BECAUSE YOU'VE NEVER HEARD ANYTHING LIKE THIS BEFORE! THOSE WRONG NOTES YOU'RE TALKIN' ABOUT...
... THEY SOUND **DAMN RIGHT TO ME!**
YOU WANT A GUY WHO PLAYS NO BETTER THAN MY EIGHT-YEAR-OLD? COME ON! YOU'RE COLEMAN FRIGGIN' HAWKINS, FOR GOD'S SAKE.
YOU BET I WANT HIM IN MY BAND!
HIS UNBELIEVABLE HARMONIES! THE FREEDOM OF HIS PLAYING! THIS MAN DON'T CARE AND I LIKE THAT! HE'S **WAKING ME UP,** EARL.
I DON'T GET THIS, MAN.

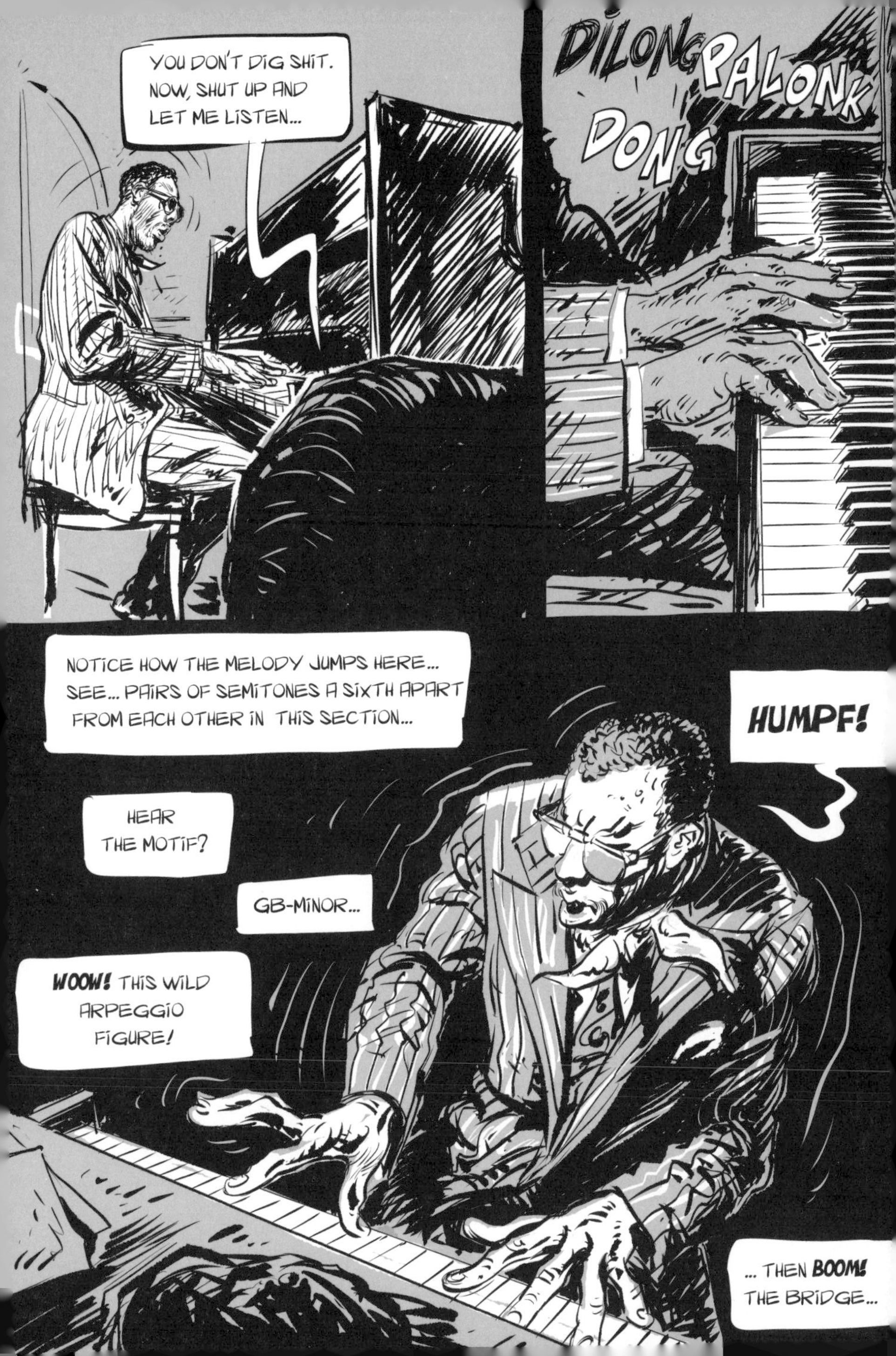
YOU DON'T DIG SHIT. NOW, SHUT UP AND LET ME LISTEN...
DILONG
PALONK
DONG
NOTICE HOW THE MELODY JUMPS HERE... SEE... PAIRS OF SEMITONES A SIXTH APART FROM EACH OTHER IN THIS SECTION...
HUMPF!
HEAR THE MOTIF?
GB-MINOR...
WOOW! THIS WILD ARPEGGIO FIGURE!
... THEN BOOM! THE BRIDGE...

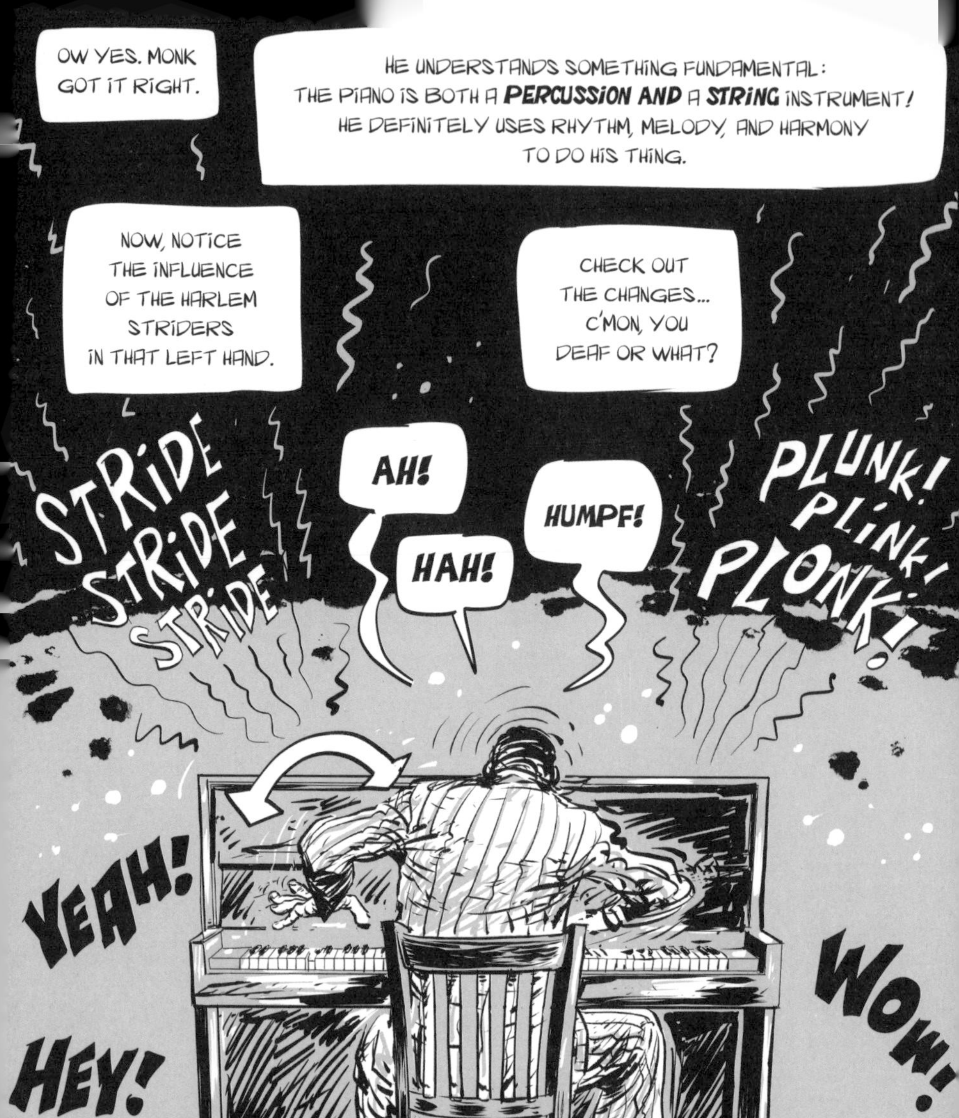
OW YES. MONK GOT IT RIGHT.
HE UNDERSTANDS SOMETHING FUNDAMENTAL: THE PIANO IS BOTH A **PERCUSSION AND** A **STRING** INSTRUMENT! HE DEFINITELY USES RHYTHM, MELODY, AND HARMONY TO DO HIS THING.
NOW, NOTICE THE INFLUENCE OF THE HARLEM STRIDERS IN THAT LEFT HAND.
CHECK OUT THE CHANGES... C'MON, YOU DEAF OR WHAT?
STRIDE STRIDE STRIDE
AH!
HAH!
HUMPF!
PLUNK! PLINK! PLONK!
YEAH!
HEY!
WOW!
MAN

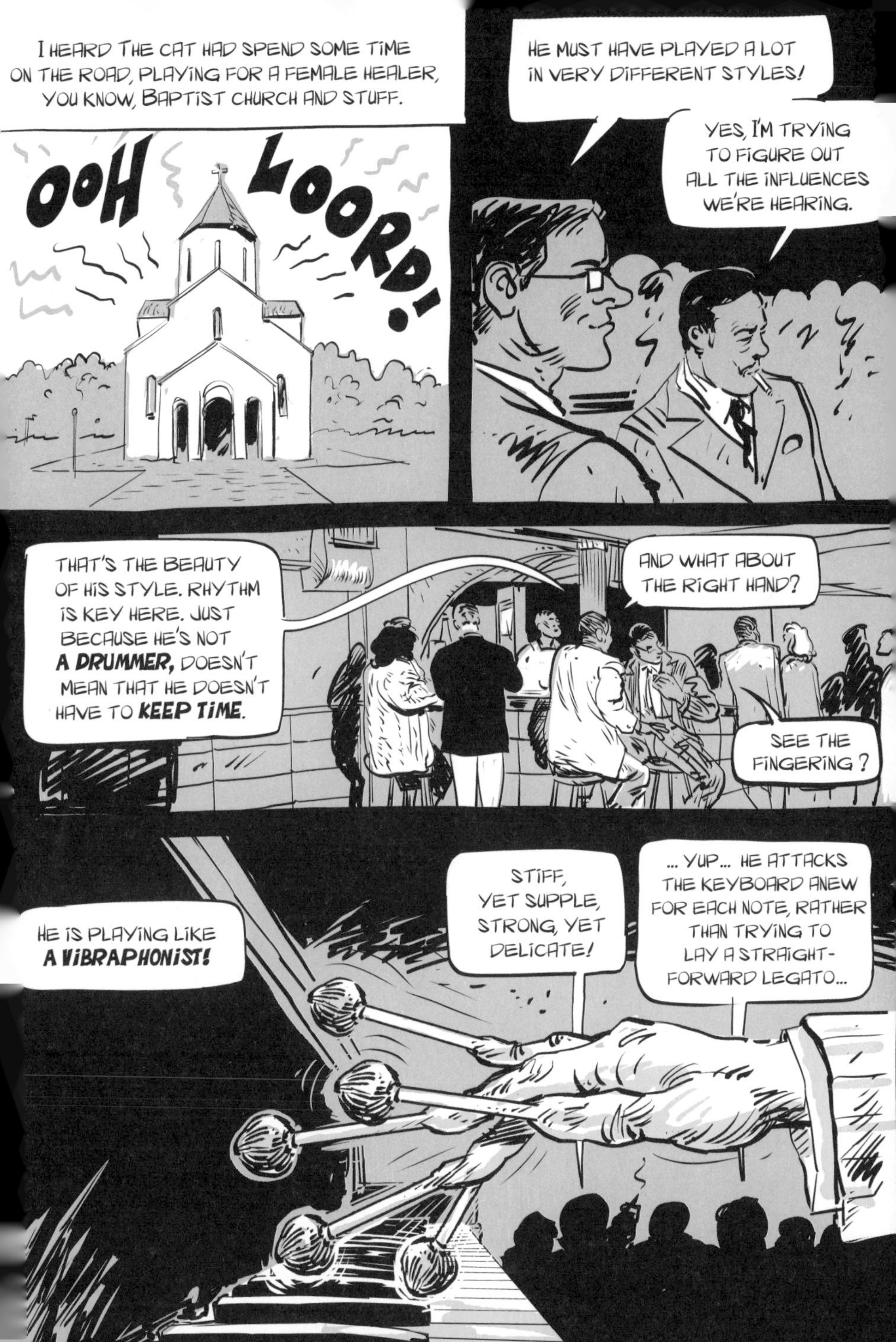
I HEARD THE CAT HAD SPEND SOME TIME ON THE ROAD, PLAYING FOR A FEMALE HEALER, YOU KNOW, BAPTIST CHURCH AND STUFF.
OOH LOORD!
HE MUST HAVE PLAYED A LOT IN VERY DIFFERENT STYLES!
YES, I'M TRYING TO FIGURE OUT ALL THE INFLUENCES WE'RE HEARING.
THAT'S THE BEAUTY OF HIS STYLE. RHYTHM IS KEY HERE. JUST BECAUSE HE'S NOT **A DRUMMER,** DOESN'T MEAN THAT HE DOESN'T HAVE TO **KEEP TIME**.
AND WHAT ABOUT THE RIGHT HAND?
SEE THE FINGERING?
HE IS PLAYING LIKE **A VIBRAPHONIST!**
STIFF, YET SUPPLE, STRONG, YET DELICATE!
... YUP... HE ATTACKS THE KEYBOARD ANEW FOR EACH NOTE, RATHER THAN TRYING TO LAY A STRAIGHT-FORWARD LEGATO...

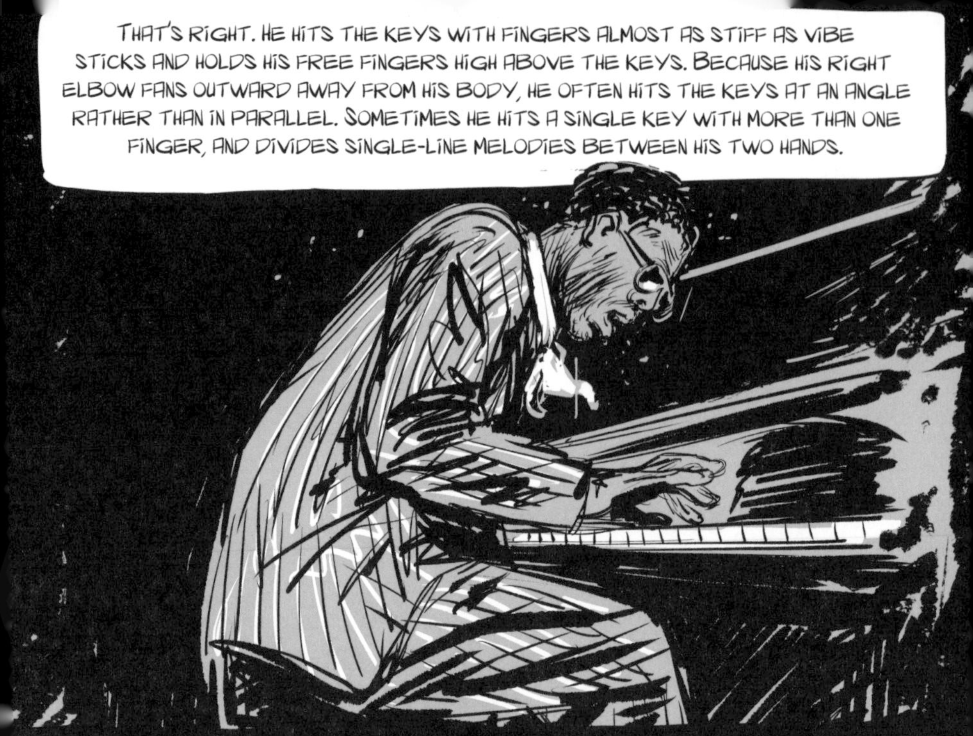
THAT'S RIGHT. HE HITS THE KEYS WITH FINGERS ALMOST AS STIFF AS VIBE STICKS AND HOLDS HIS FREE FINGERS HIGH ABOVE THE KEYS. BECAUSE HIS RIGHT ELBOW FANS OUTWARD AWAY FROM HIS BODY, HE OFTEN HITS THE KEYS AT AN ANGLE RATHER THAN IN PARALLEL. SOMETIMES HE HITS A SINGLE KEY WITH MORE THAN ONE FINGER, AND DIVIDES SINGLE-LINE MELODIES BETWEEN HIS TWO HANDS.

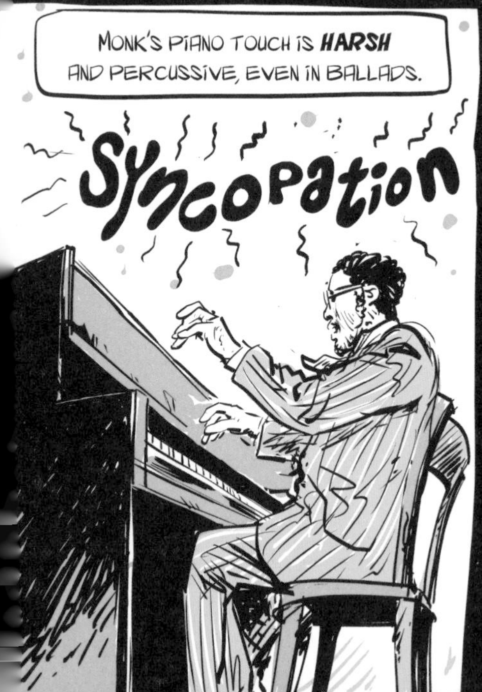
MONK'S PIANO TOUCH IS **HARSH** AND PERCUSSIVE, EVEN IN BALLADS.
SYNCOPATION

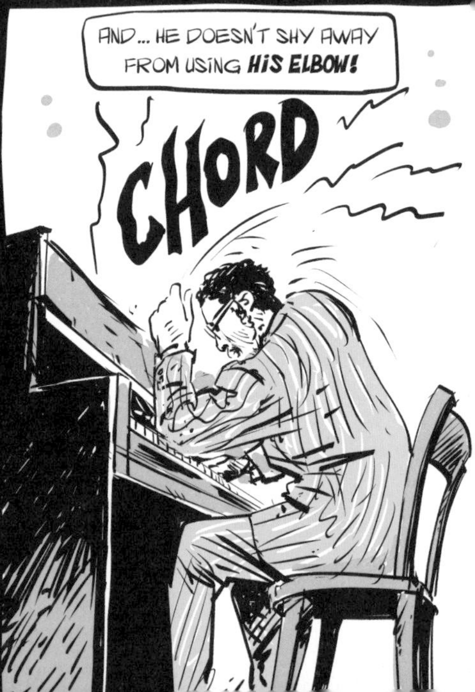
AND... HE DOESN'T SHY AWAY FROM USING **HIS ELBOW!**
CHORD

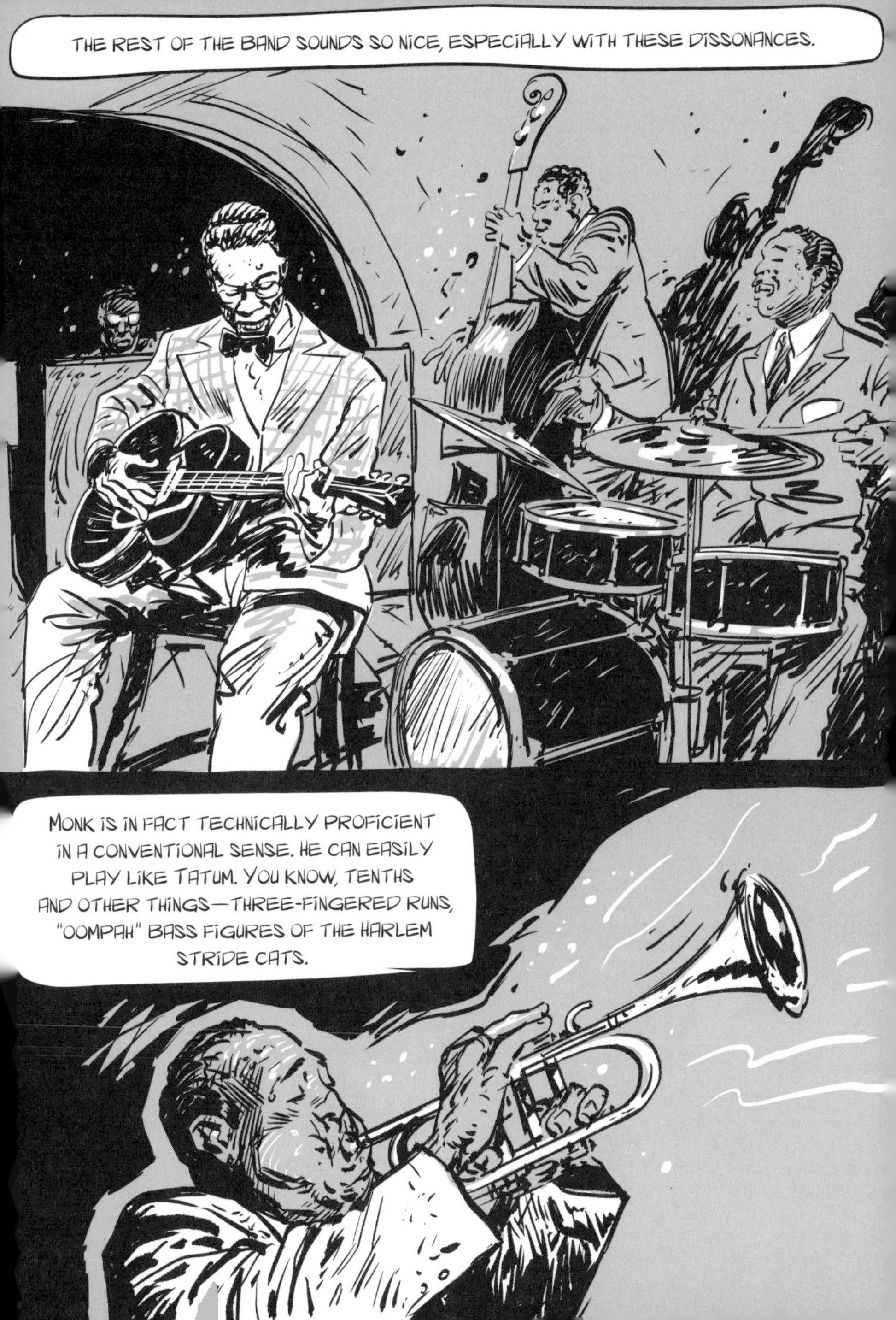
THE REST OF THE BAND SOUNDS SO NICE, ESPECIALLY WITH THESE DISSONANCES.
MONK IS IN FACT TECHNICALLY PROFICIENT IN A CONVENTIONAL SENSE. HE CAN EASILY PLAY LIKE TATUM. YOU KNOW, TENTHS AND OTHER THINGS—THREE-FINGERED RUNS, "OOMPAH" BASS FIGURES OF THE HARLEM STRIDE CATS.

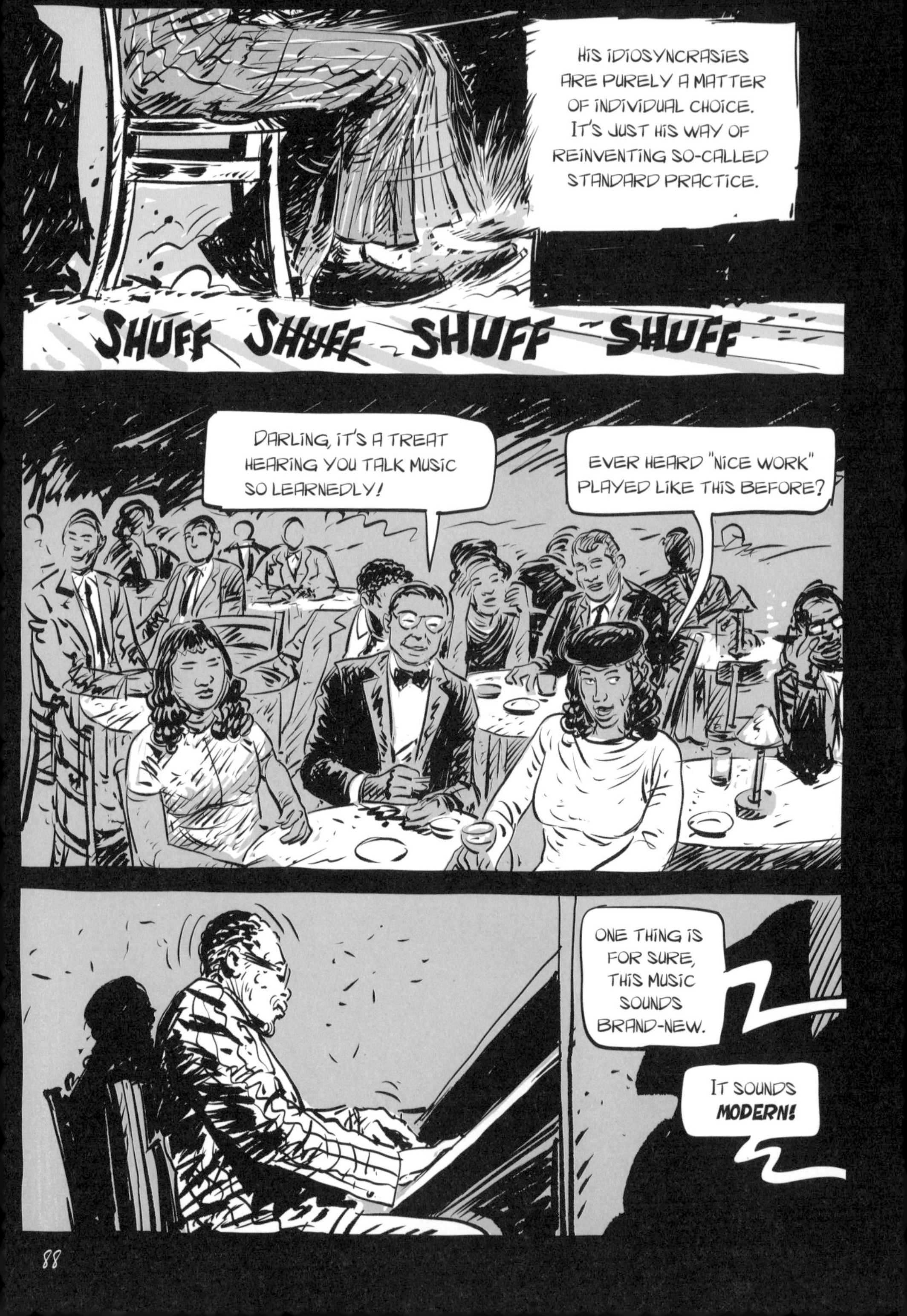
HIS IDIOSYNCRASIES ARE PURELY A MATTER OF INDIVIDUAL CHOICE. IT'S JUST HIS WAY OF REINVENTING SO-CALLED STANDARD PRACTICE.
SHUFF SHUFF SHUFF SHUFF
DARLING, IT'S A TREAT HEARING YOU TALK MUSIC SO LEARNEDLY!
EVER HEARD "NICE WORK" PLAYED LIKE THIS BEFORE?
ONE THING IS FOR SURE, THIS MUSIC SOUNDS BRAND-NEW.
IT SOUNDS **MODERN!**

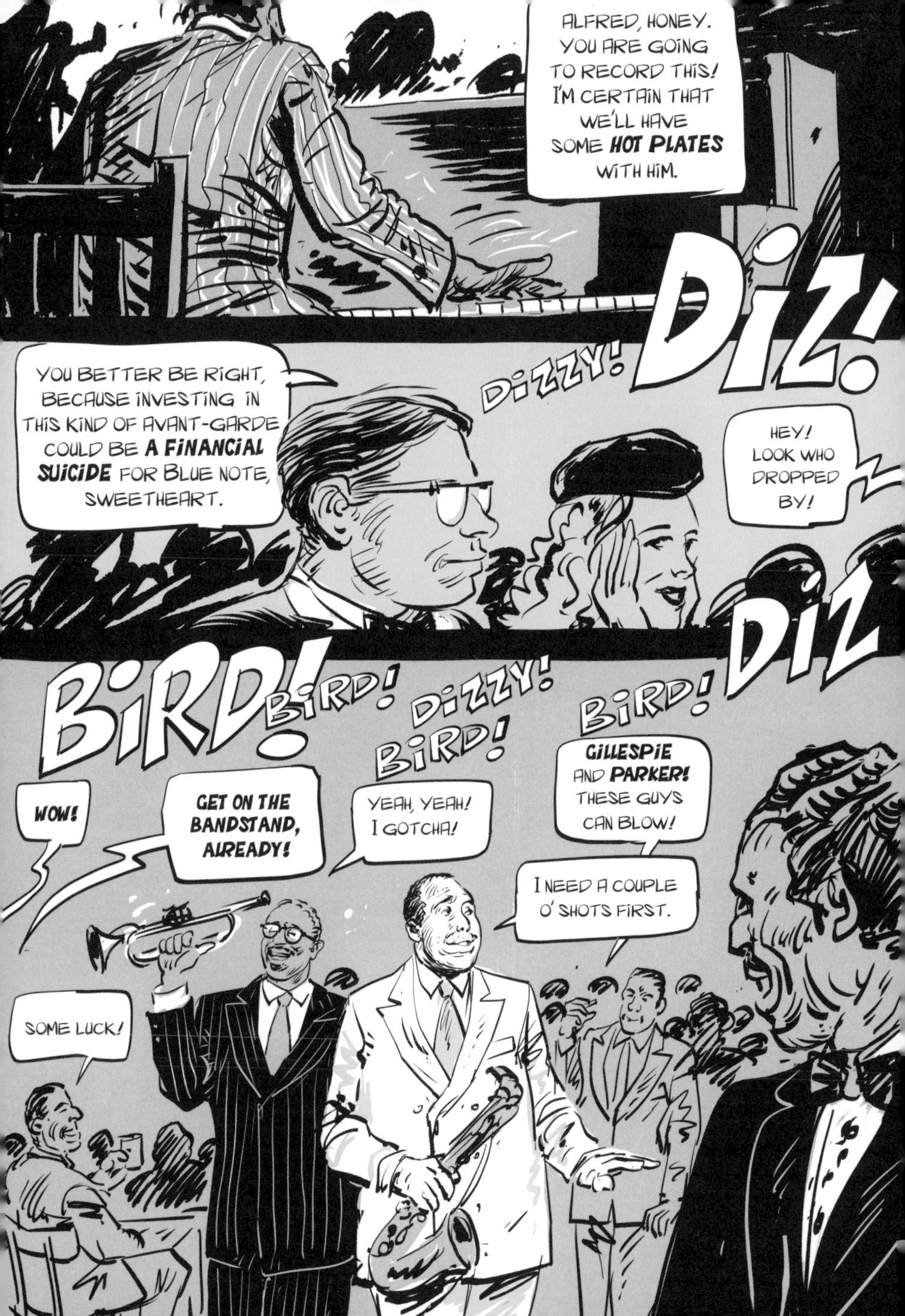
ALFRED, HONEY. YOU ARE GOING TO RECORD THIS! I'M CERTAIN THAT WE'LL HAVE SOME **HOT PLATES** WITH HIM.
YOU BETTER BE RIGHT, BECAUSE INVESTING IN THIS KIND OF AVANT-GARDE COULD BE **A FINANCIAL SUICIDE** FOR BLUE NOTE, SWEETHEART.
DIZZY!
DIZ!
HEY! LOOK WHO DROPPED BY!
BIRD!
BIRD!
DIZZY!
BIRD!
BIRD!
DIZ
WOW!
GET ON THE BANDSTAND, ALREADY!
YEAH, YEAH! I GOTCHA!
GILLESPIE AND **PARKER!** THESE GUYS CAN BLOW!
I NEED A COUPLE O' SHOTS FIRST.
SOME LUCK!

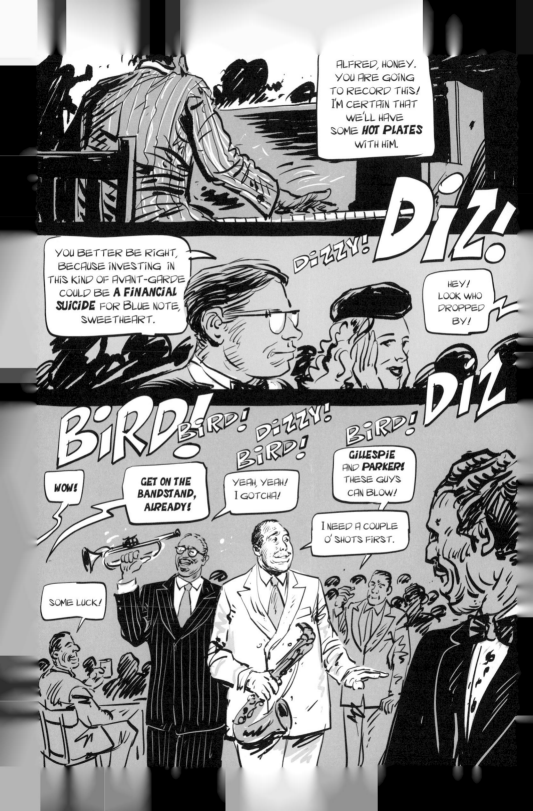

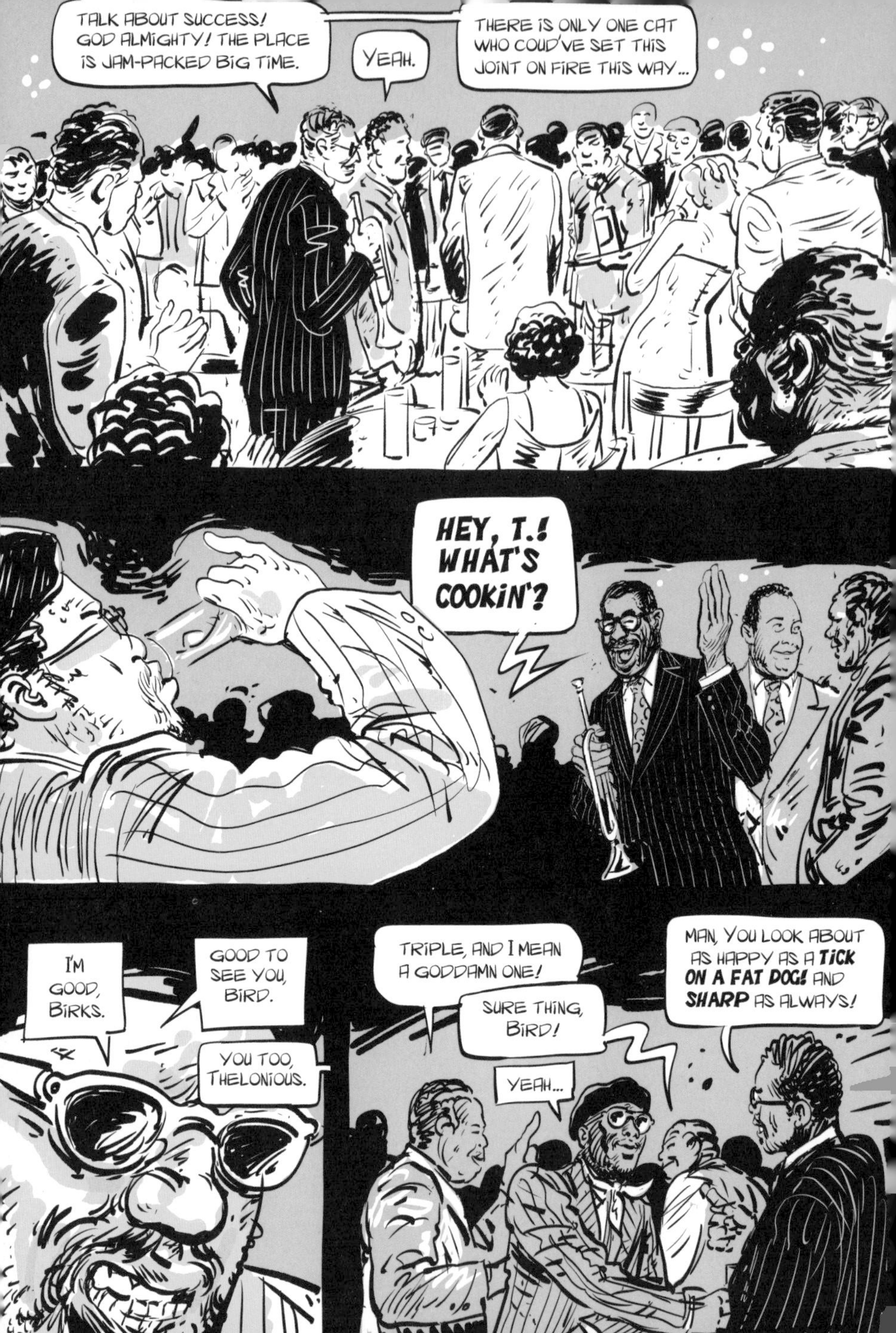
TALK ABOUT SUCCESS! GOD ALMIGHTY! THE PLACE IS JAM-PACKED BIG TIME.
YEAH.
THERE IS ONLY ONE CAT WHO COUD'VE SET THIS JOINT ON FIRE THIS WAY...
HEY, T.! WHAT'S COOKIN'?
I'M GOOD, BIRKS.
GOOD TO SEE YOU, BIRD.
YOU TOO, THELONIOUS.
TRIPLE, AND I MEAN A GODDAMN ONE!
SURE THING, BIRD!
YEAH...
MAN, YOU LOOK ABOUT AS HAPPY AS A TICK ON A FAT DOG! AND SHARP AS ALWAYS!

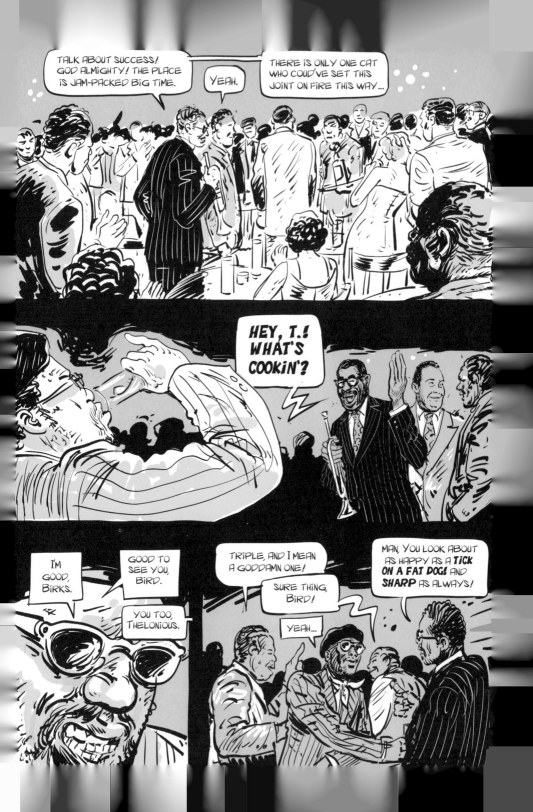

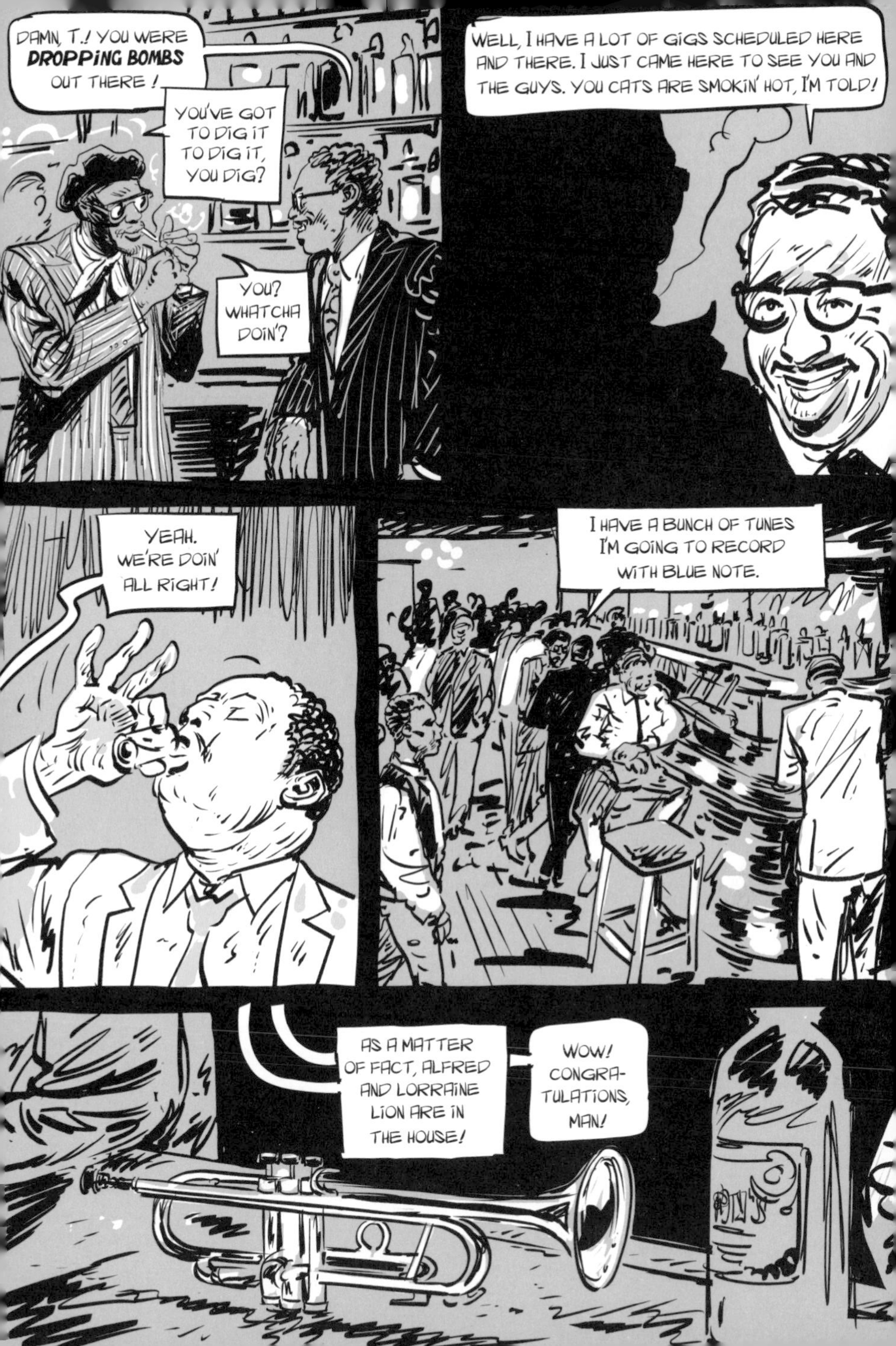
DAMN, T.! YOU WERE **DROPPING BOMBS** OUT THERE!
YOU'VE GOT TO DIG IT TO DIG IT, YOU DIG?
YOU? WHATCHA DOIN'?
WELL, I HAVE A LOT OF GIGS SCHEDULED HERE AND THERE. I JUST CAME HERE TO SEE YOU AND THE GUYS. YOU CATS ARE SMOKIN' HOT, I'M TOLD!
YEAH. WE'RE DOIN' ALL RIGHT!
I HAVE A BUNCH OF TUNES I'M GOING TO RECORD WITH BLUE NOTE.
AS A MATTER OF FACT, ALFRED AND LORRAINE LION ARE IN THE HOUSE!
WOW! CONGRA-TULATIONS, MAN!

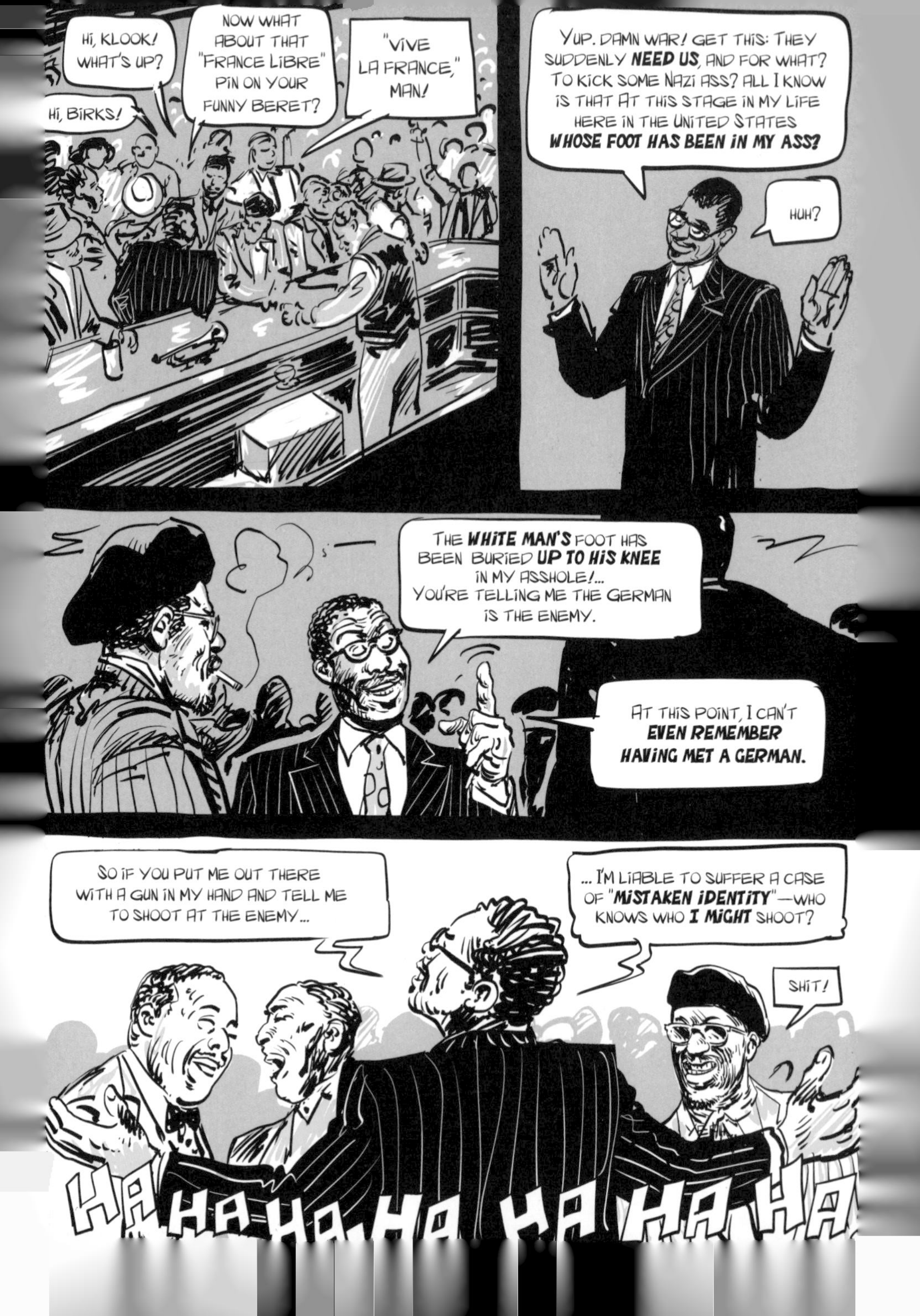
HI, KLOOK! WHAT'S UP?
HI, BIRKS!
NOW WHAT ABOUT THAT "FRANCE LIBRE" PIN ON YOUR FUNNY BERET?
"VIVE LA FRANCE," MAN!
YUP. DAMN WAR! GET THIS: THEY SUDDENLY **NEED US**, AND FOR WHAT? TO KICK SOME NAZI ASS? ALL I KNOW IS THAT AT THIS STAGE IN MY LIFE HERE IN THE UNITED STATES **WHOSE FOOT HAS BEEN IN MY ASS?**
HUH?
THE **WHITE MAN'S** FOOT HAS BEEN BURIED **UP TO HIS KNEE** IN MY ASSHOLE!... YOU'RE TELLING ME THE GERMAN IS THE ENEMY.
AT THIS POINT, I CAN'T **EVEN REMEMBER HAVING MET A GERMAN.**
SO IF YOU PUT ME OUT THERE WITH A GUN IN MY HAND AND TELL ME TO SHOOT AT THE ENEMY...
... I'M LIABLE TO SUFFER A CASE OF "**MISTAKEN IDENTITY**"—WHO KNOWS WHO **I MIGHT** SHOOT?
SHIT!
HA HA HA HA HA HA HA HA

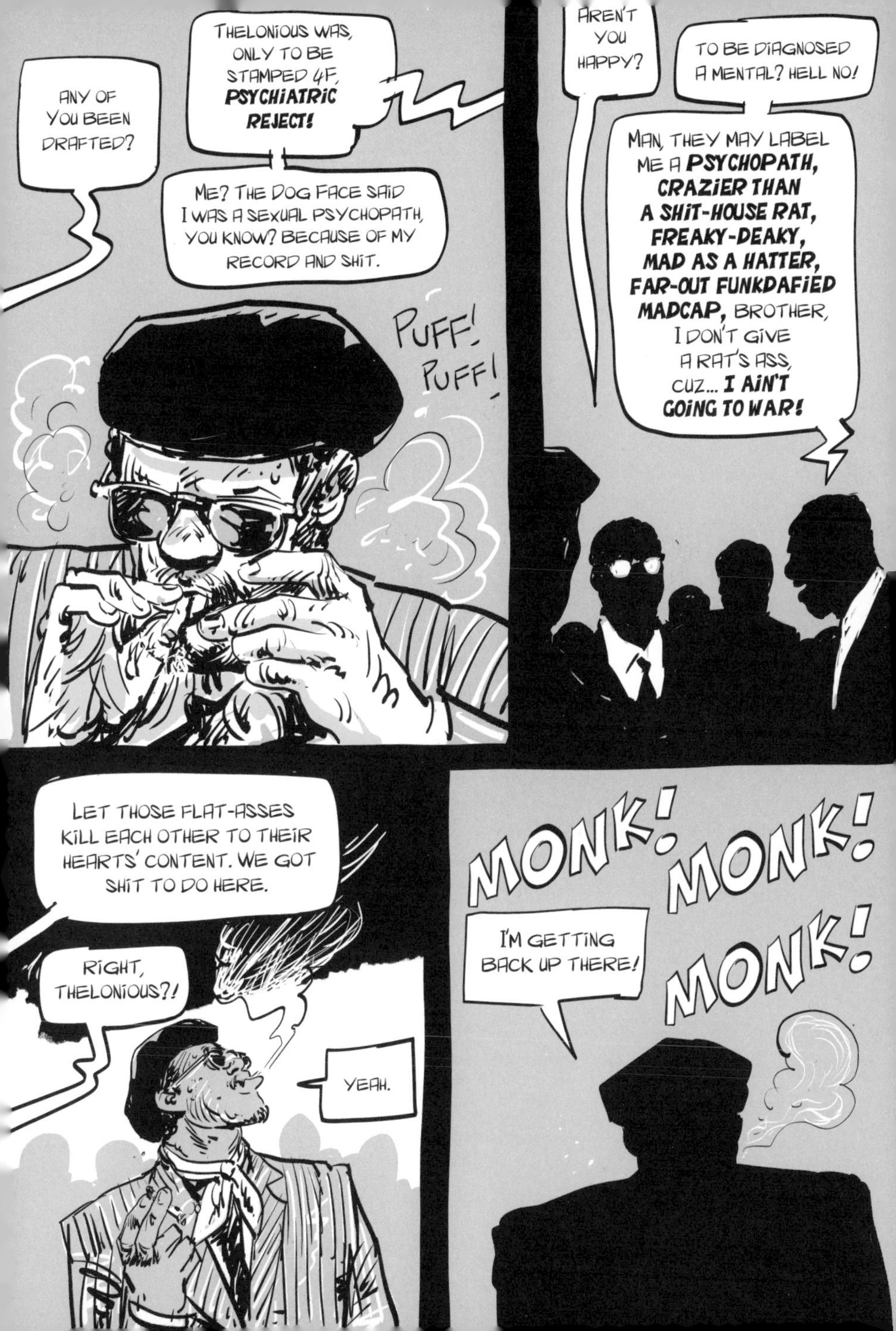
ANY OF YOU BEEN DRAFTED?
THELONIOUS WAS, ONLY TO BE STAMPED 4F, PSYCHIATRIC REJECT!
ME? THE DOG FACE SAID I WAS A SEXUAL PSYCHOPATH, YOU KNOW? BECAUSE OF MY RECORD AND SHIT.
PUFF! PUFF!
AREN'T YOU HAPPY?
TO BE DIAGNOSED A MENTAL? HELL NO!
MAN, THEY MAY LABEL ME A PSYCHOPATH, CRAZIER THAN A SHIT-HOUSE RAT, FREAKY-DEAKY, MAD AS A HATTER, FAR-OUT FUNKDAFIED MADCAP, BROTHER, I DON'T GIVE A RAT'S ASS, CUZ... I AIN'T GOING TO WAR!
LET THOSE FLAT-ASSES KILL EACH OTHER TO THEIR HEARTS' CONTENT. WE GOT SHIT TO DO HERE.
RIGHT, THELONIOUS?!
YEAH.
MONK! MONK! MONK!
I'M GETTING BACK UP THERE!

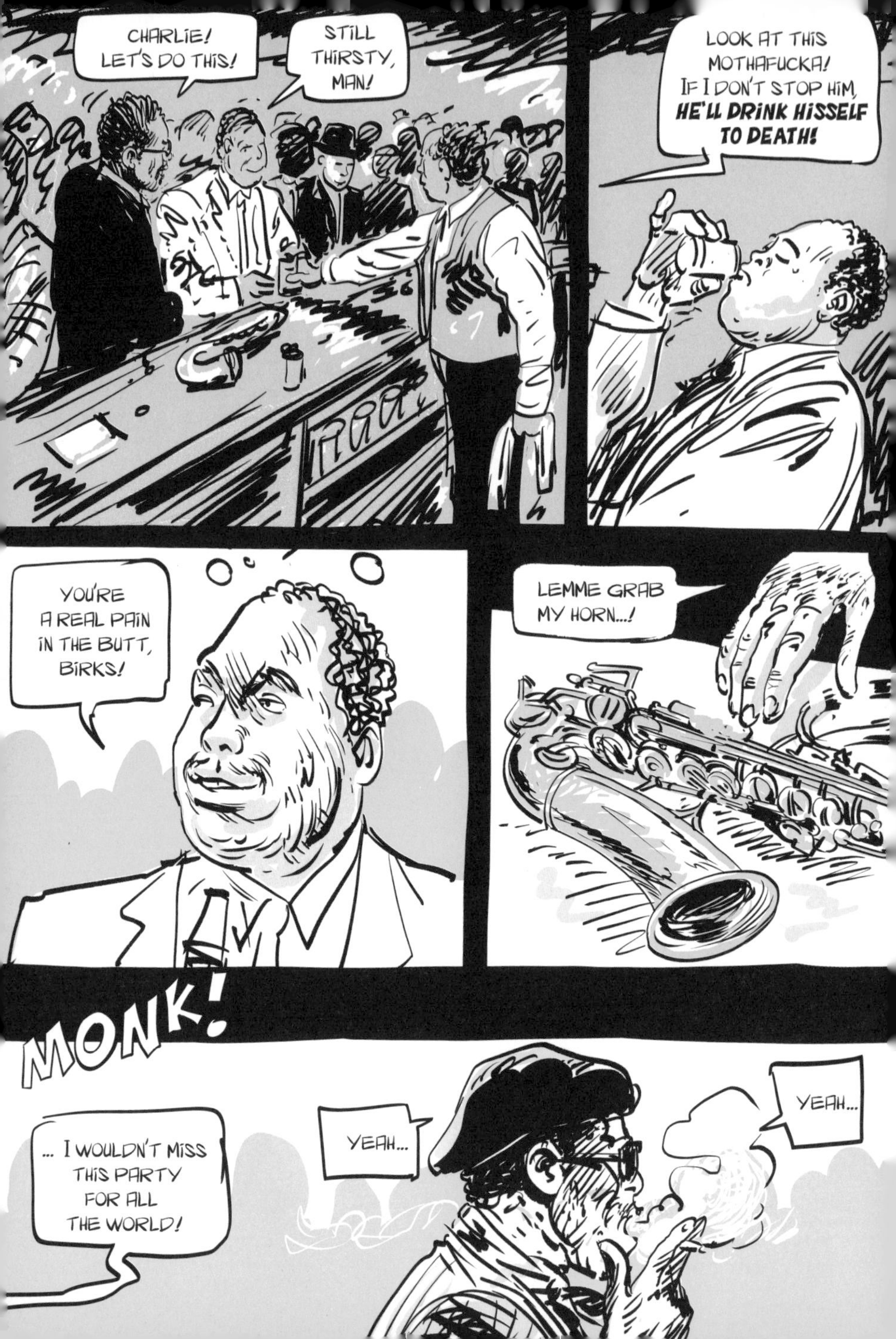
CHARLIE! LET'S DO THIS!
STILL THIRSTY, MAN!
LOOK AT THIS MOTHAFUCKA! IF I DON'T STOP HIM, HE'LL DRINK HISSELF TO DEATH!
YOU'RE A REAL PAIN IN THE BUTT, BIRKS!
LEMME GRAB MY HORN...!
MONK!
... I WOULDN'T MISS THIS PARTY FOR ALL THE WORLD!
YEAH...
YEAH...

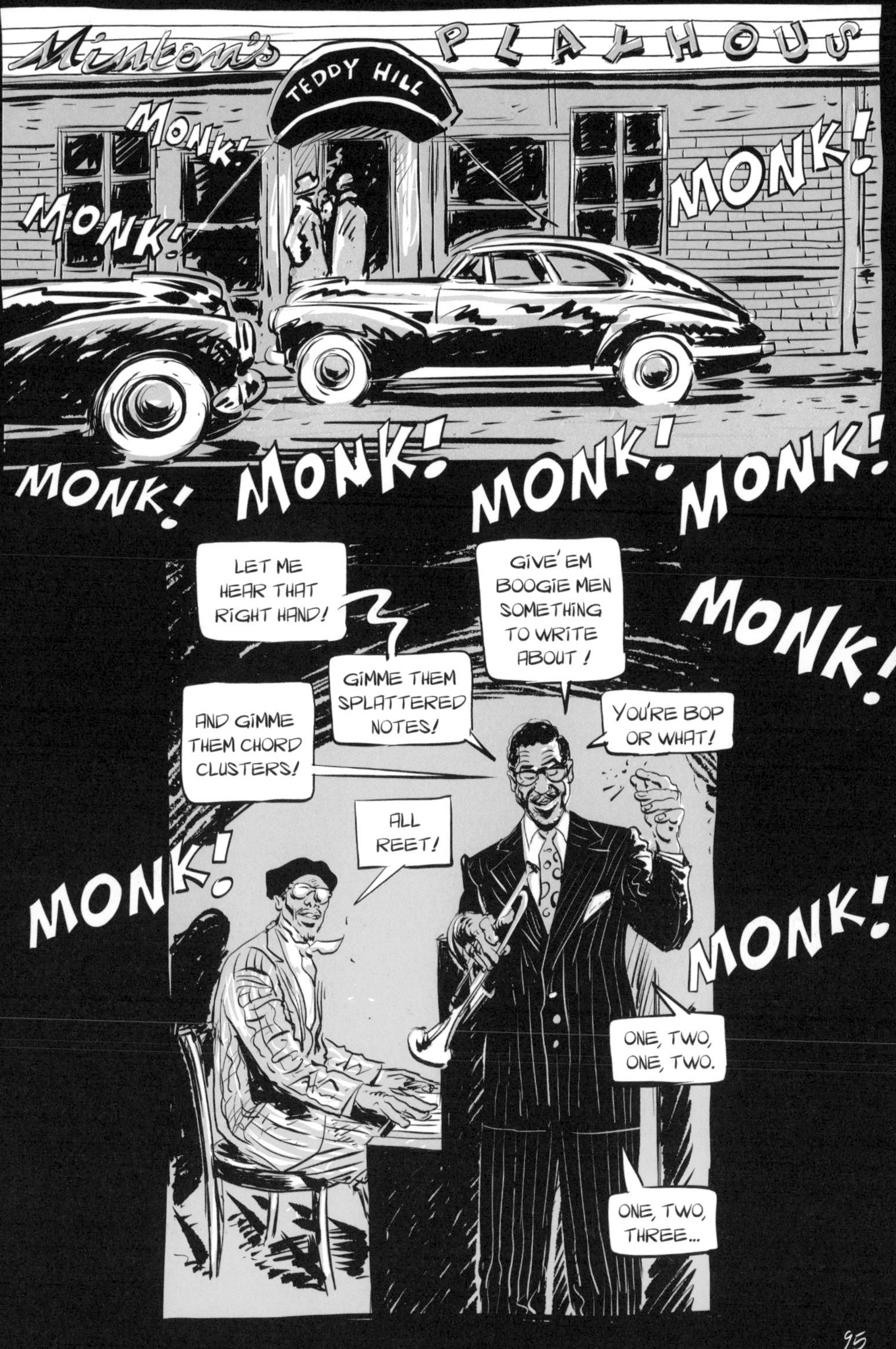
Minton's PLAYHOUS
TEDDY HILL
MONK!
MONK!
MONK!
MONK! MONK! MONK! MONK!
LET ME HEAR THAT RIGHT HAND!
GIMME THEM SPLATTERED NOTES!
AND GIMME THEM CHORD CLUSTERS!
GIVE' EM BOOGIE MEN SOMETHING TO WRITE ABOUT!
YOU'RE BOP OR WHAT!
MONK!
MONK!
ALL REET!
MONK!
ONE, TWO, ONE, TWO.
ONE, TWO, THREE...

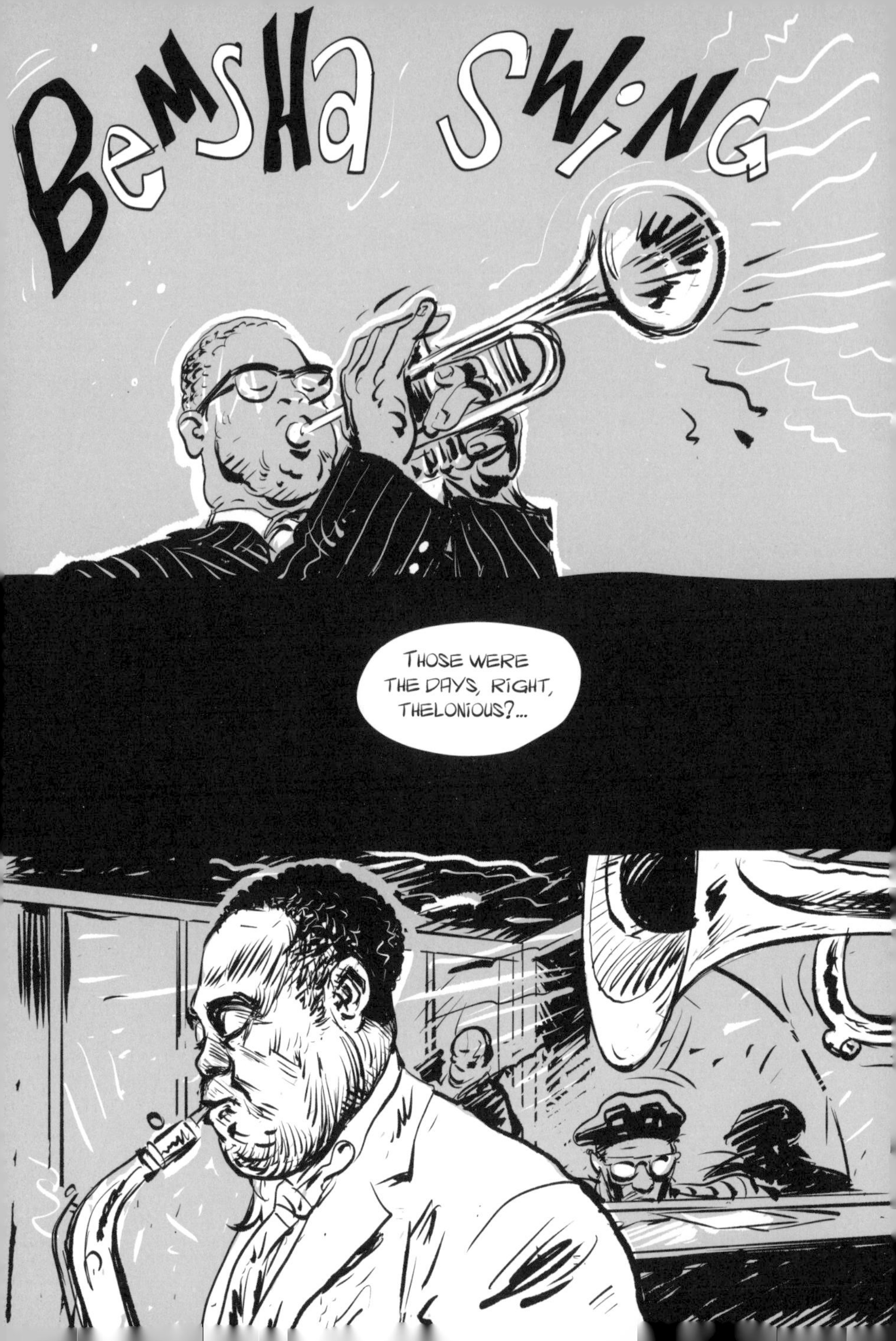
BEMSHA SWING
THOSE WERE THE DAYS, RIGHT, THELONIOUS?...

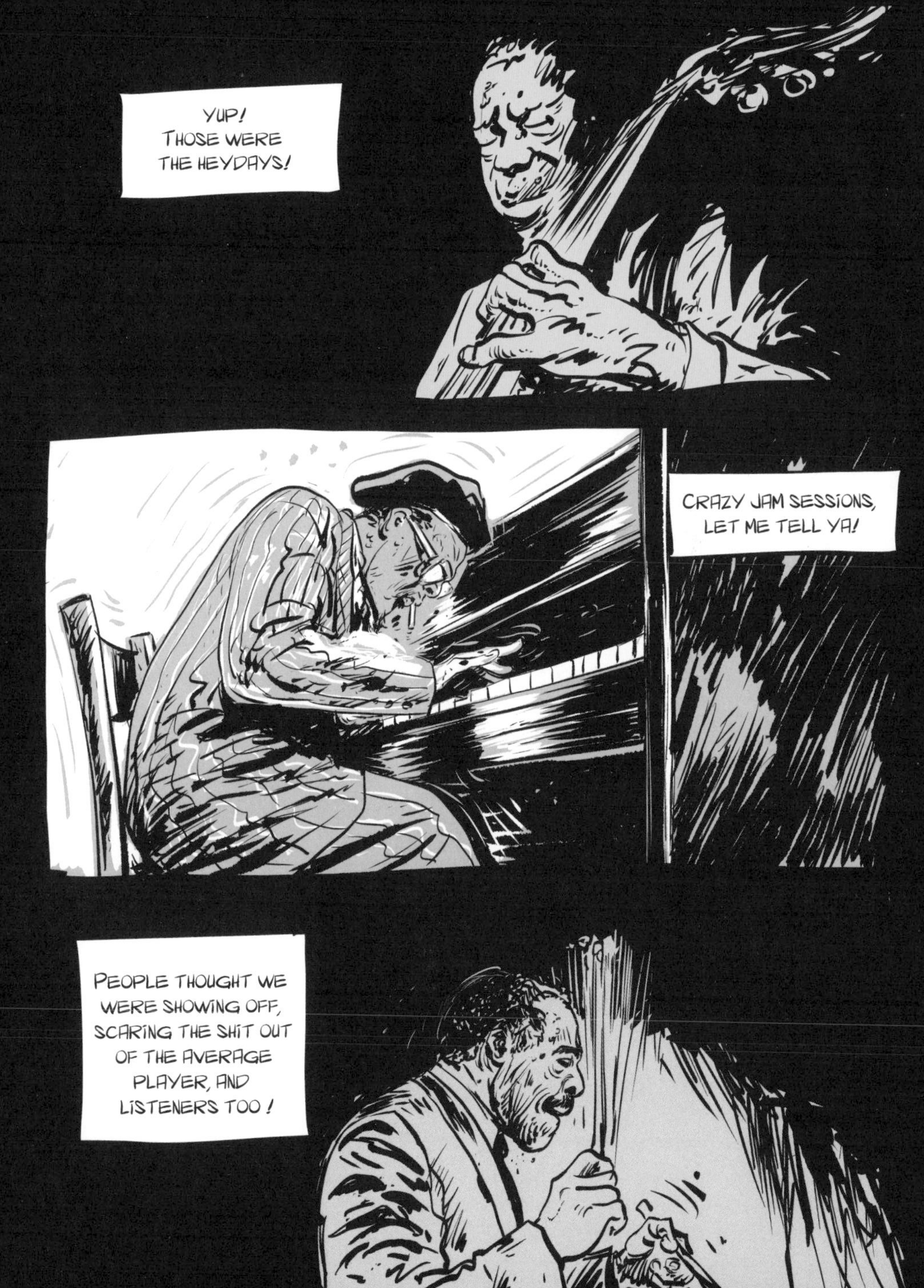
YUP!
THOSE WERE
THE HEYDAYS!
CRAZY JAM SESSIONS,
LET ME TELL YA!
PEOPLE THOUGHT WE
WERE SHOWING OFF,
SCARING THE SHIT OUT
OF THE AVERAGE
PLAYER, AND
LISTENERS TOO!

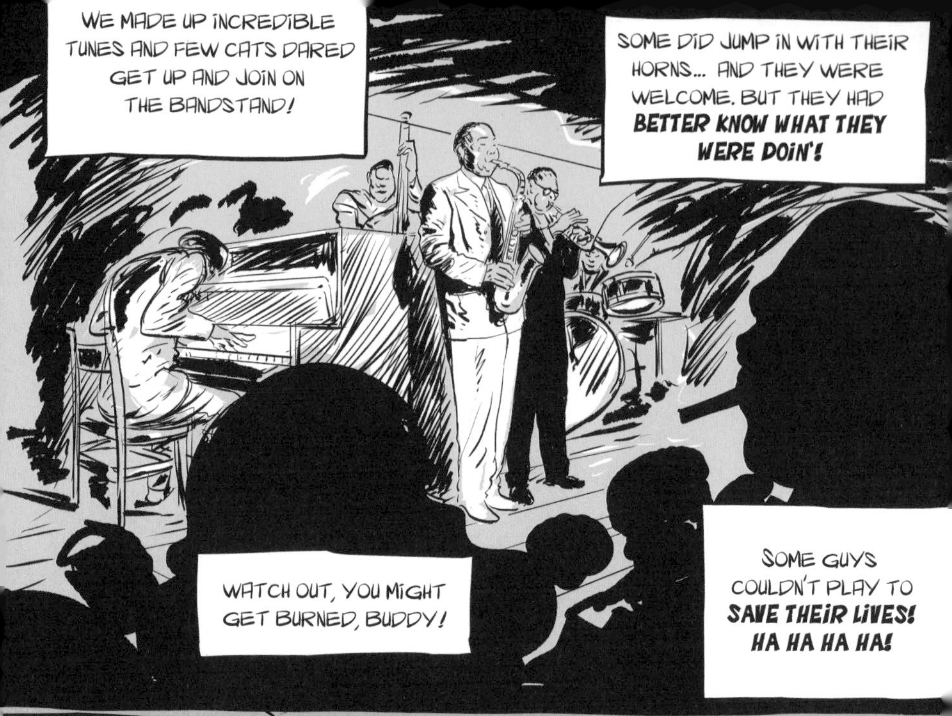
WE MADE UP INCREDIBLE TUNES AND FEW CATS DARED GET UP AND JOIN ON THE BANDSTAND!
SOME DID JUMP IN WITH THEIR HORNS... AND THEY WERE WELCOME. BUT THEY HAD **BETTER KNOW WHAT THEY WERE DOIN'!**
WATCH OUT, YOU MIGHT GET BURNED, BUDDY!
SOME GUYS COULDN'T PLAY TO **SAVE THEIR LIVES! HA HA HA HA!**

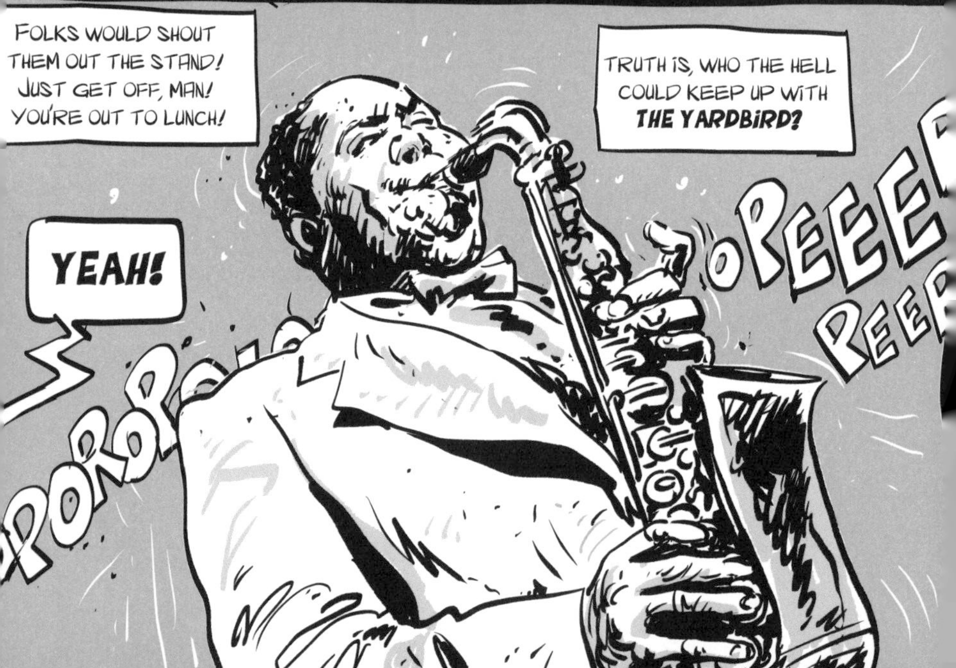
FOLKS WOULD SHOUT THEM OUT THE STAND! JUST GET OFF, MAN! YOU'RE OUT TO LUNCH!
TRUTH IS, WHO THE HELL COULD KEEP UP WITH **THE YARDBIRD?**
YEAH!
POROPO
OPEEE
REE

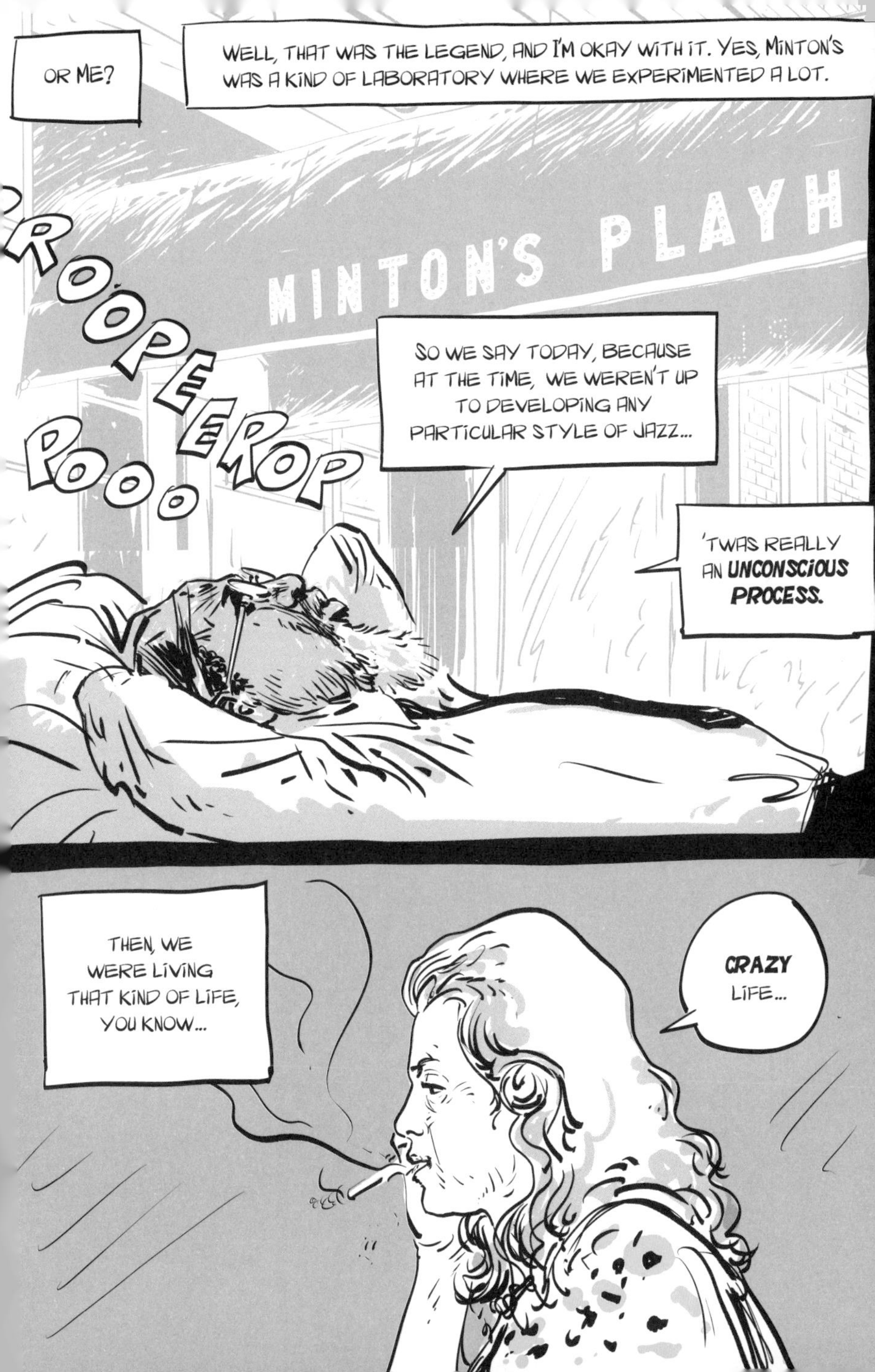

OR ME?
WELL, THAT WAS THE LEGEND, AND I'M OKAY WITH IT. YES, MINTON'S WAS A KIND OF LABORATORY WHERE WE EXPERIMENTED A LOT.
ROOPEEROP
POOOO
MINTON'S PLAYH
SO WE SAY TODAY, BECAUSE AT THE TIME, WE WEREN'T UP TO DEVELOPING ANY PARTICULAR STYLE OF JAZZ...
'TWAS REALLY AN **UNCONSCIOUS PROCESS.**
THEN, WE WERE LIVING THAT KIND OF LIFE, YOU KNOW...
CRAZY LIFE...

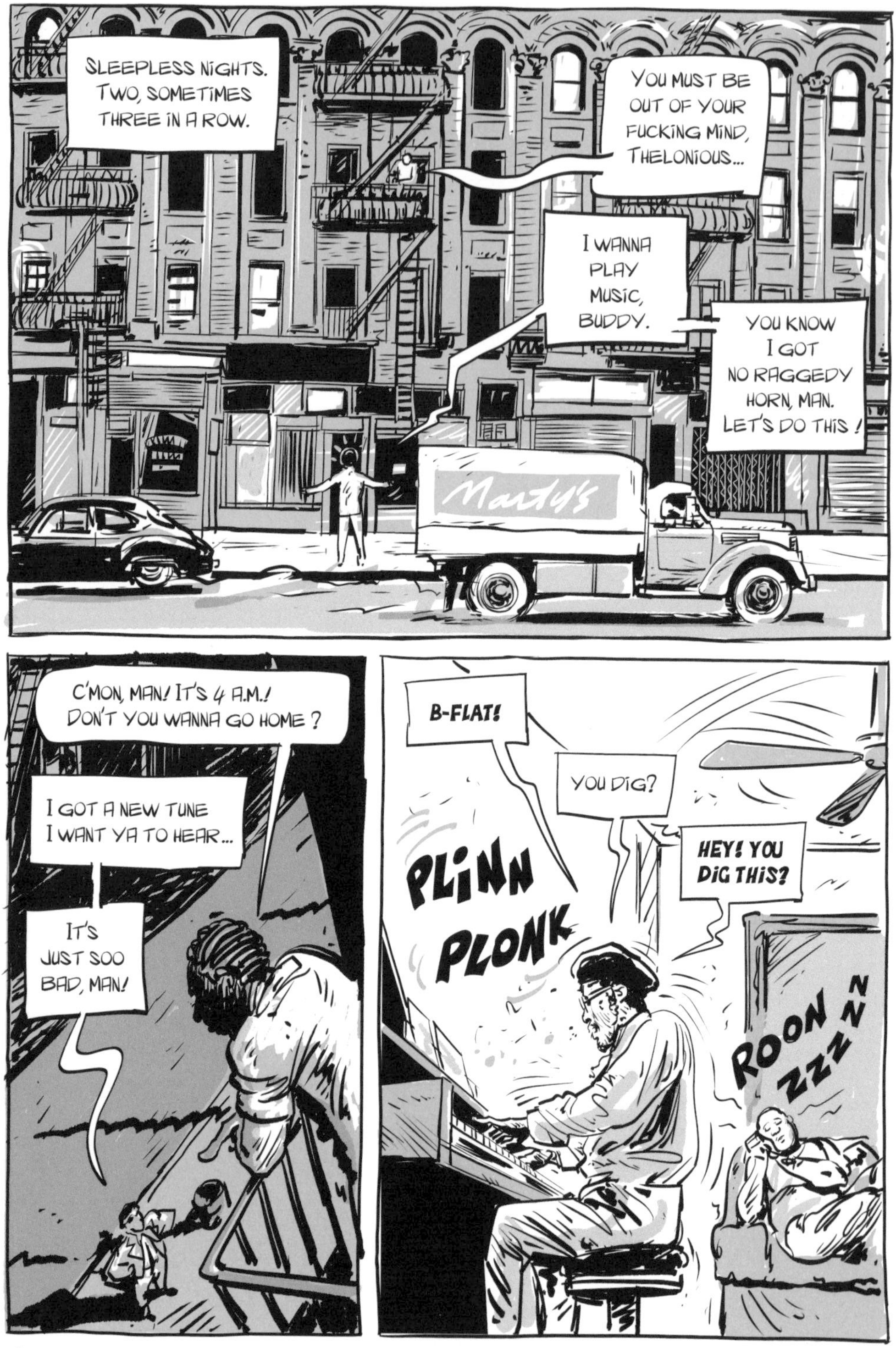
SLEEPLESS NIGHTS. TWO, SOMETIMES THREE IN A ROW.
YOU MUST BE OUT OF YOUR FUCKING MIND, THELONIOUS...
I WANNA PLAY MUSIC, BUDDY.
YOU KNOW I GOT NO RAGGEDY HORN, MAN. LET'S DO THIS!
Marty's
C'MON, MAN! IT'S 4 A.M.! DON'T YOU WANNA GO HOME?
I GOT A NEW TUNE I WANT YA TO HEAR...
IT'S JUST SOO BAD, MAN!
B-FLAT!
YOU DIG?
HEY! YOU DIG THIS?
PLINN
PLONK
ROON
ZZZNNN

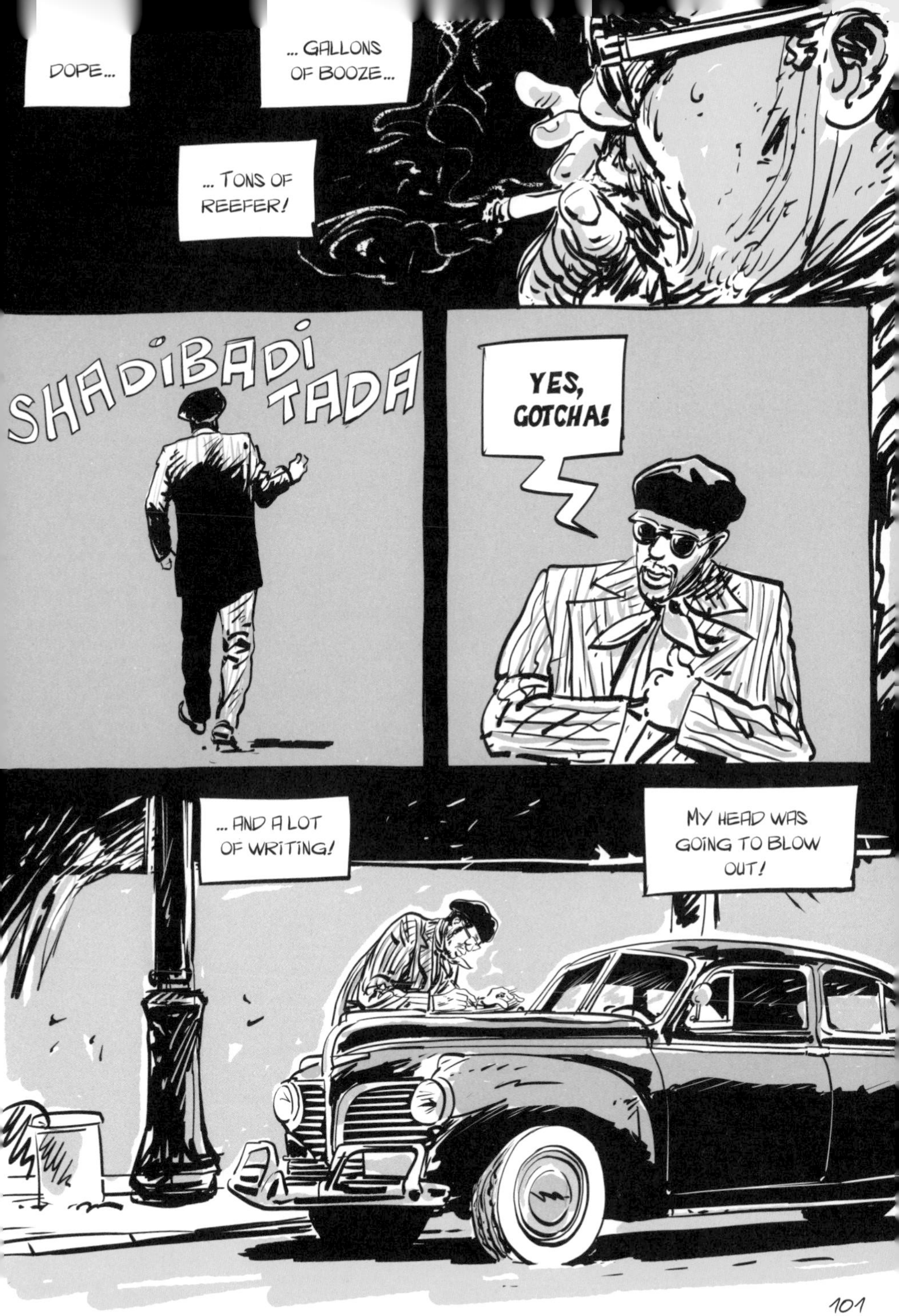
DOPE...
... GALLONS OF BOOZE...
... TONS OF REEFER!
SHADIBADI TADA
YES, GOTCHA!
... AND A LOT OF WRITING!
MY HEAD WAS GOING TO BLOW OUT!

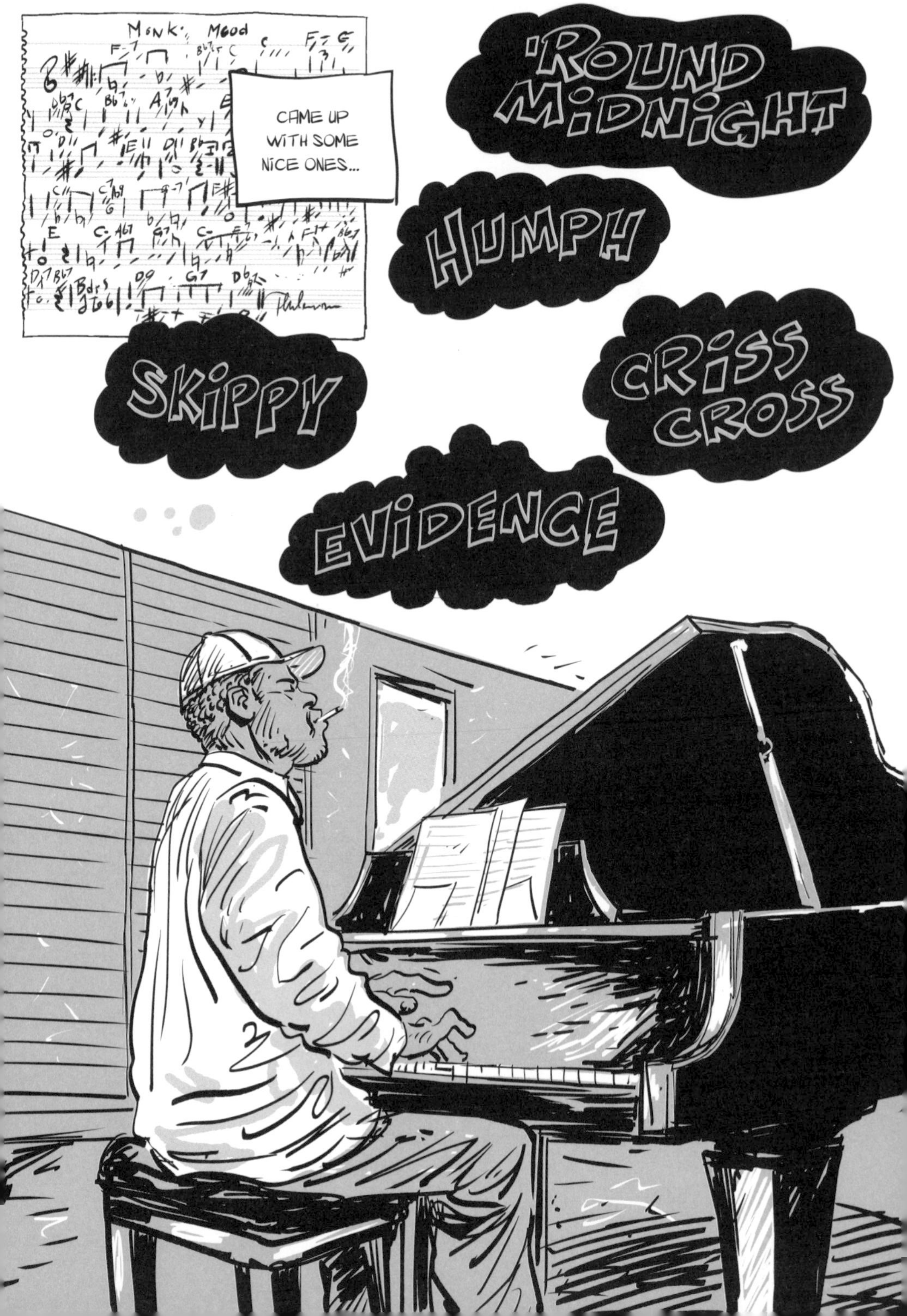

Monk's Mood
CAME UP WITH SOME NICE ONES...
'ROUND MIDNIGHT
HUMPH
SKIPPY
CRISS CROSS
EVIDENCE

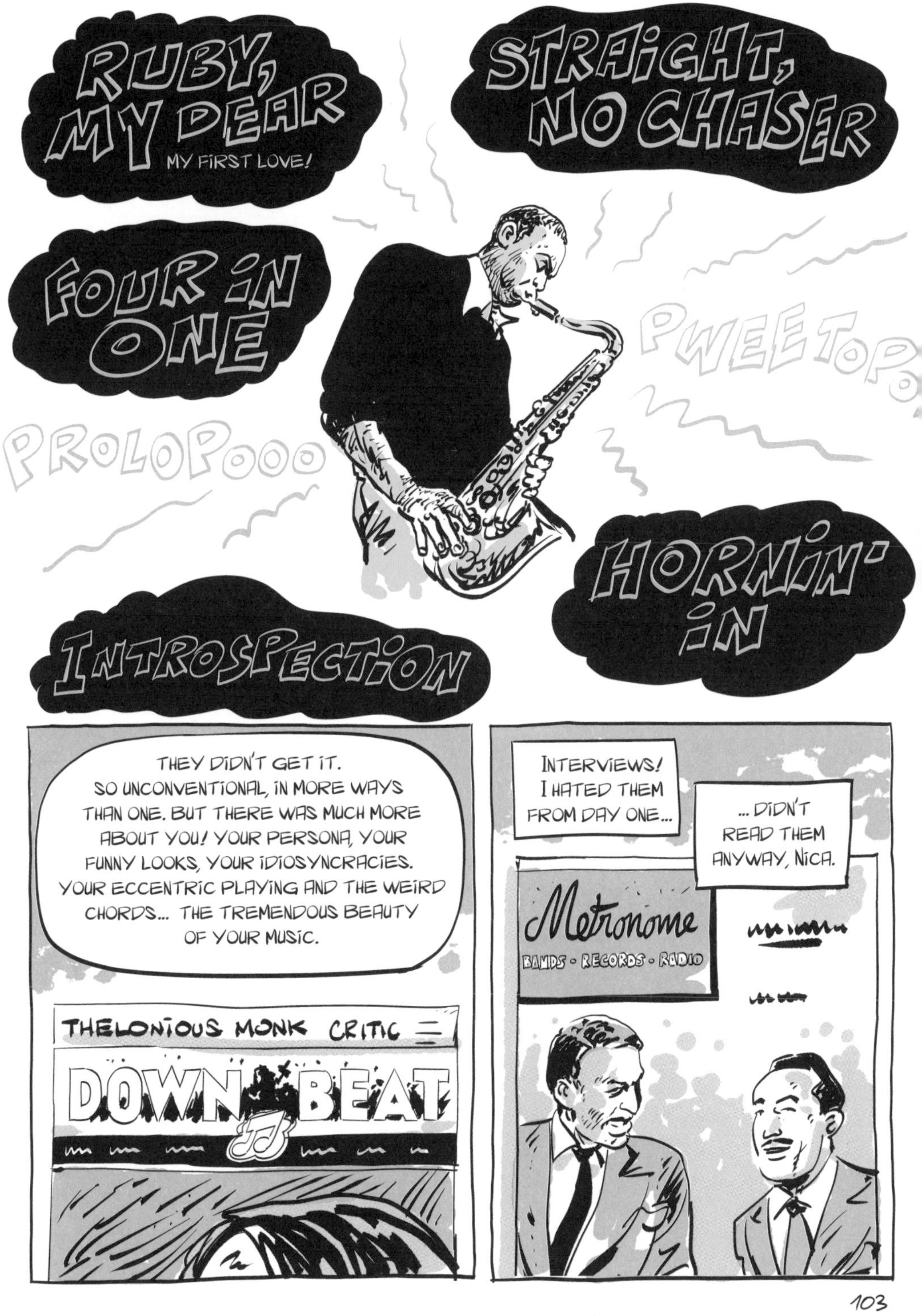
RUBY, MY DEAR
MY FIRST LOVE!
STRAIGHT, NO CHASER
FOUR IN ONE
PWEETOPO
PROLOPOOO
HORNIN' IN
INTROSPECTION
THEY DIDN'T GET IT. SO UNCONVENTIONAL, IN MORE WAYS THAN ONE. BUT THERE WAS MUCH MORE ABOUT YOU! YOUR PERSONA, YOUR FUNNY LOOKS, YOUR IDIOSYNCRACIES. YOUR ECCENTRIC PLAYING AND THE WEIRD CHORDS... THE TREMENDOUS BEAUTY OF YOUR MUSIC.
THELONIOUS MONK CRITIC
DOWN BEAT
INTERVIEWS! I HATED THEM FROM DAY ONE...
... DIDN'T READ THEM ANYWAY, NICA.
Metronome
BANDS • RECORDS • RADIO

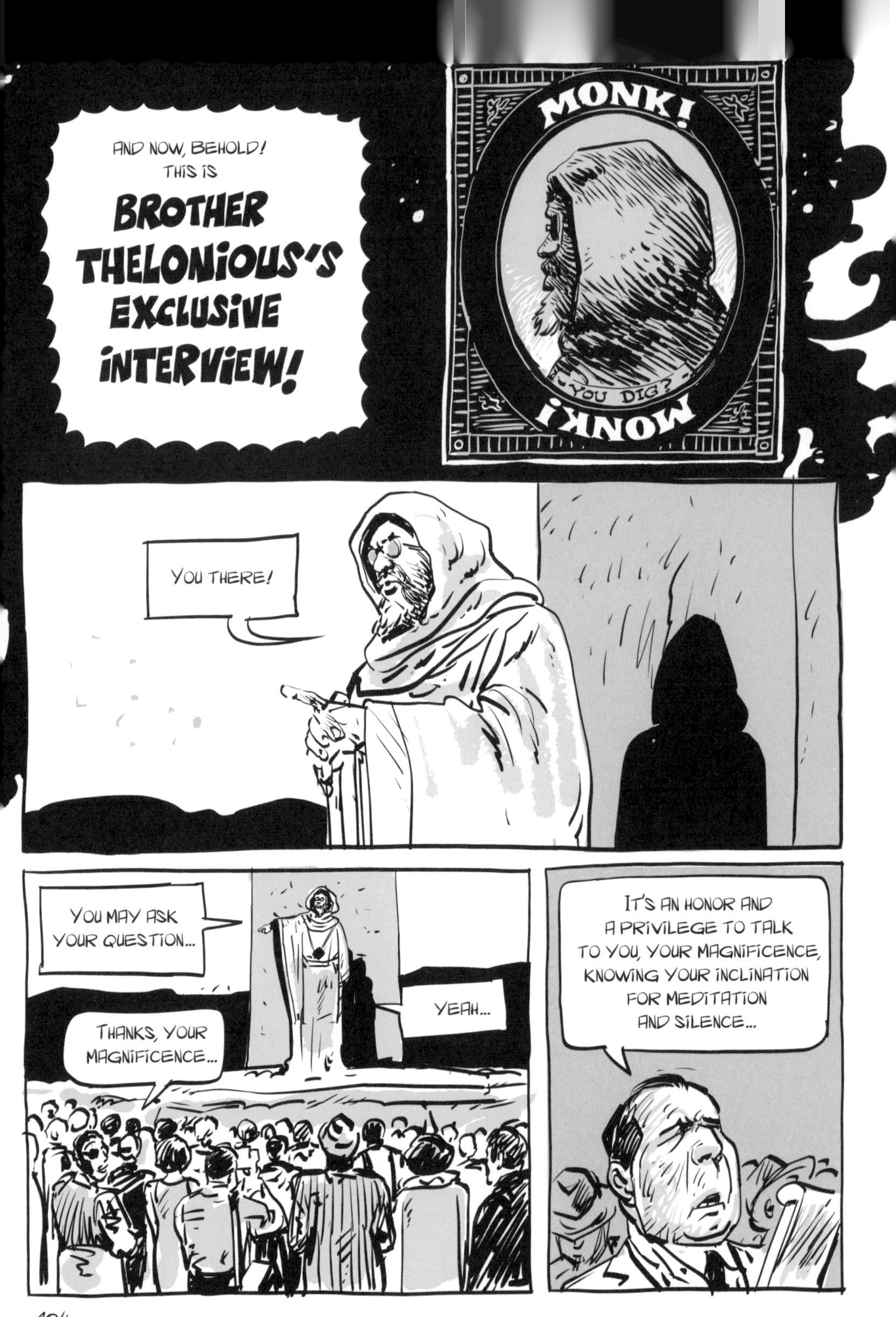

AND NOW, BEHOLD!
THIS IS
BROTHER THELONIOUS'S EXCLUSIVE INTERVIEW!
MONK!
YOU DIG?
MONK!
YOU THERE!
YOU MAY ASK YOUR QUESTION...
THANKS, YOUR MAGNIFICENCE...
YEAH...
IT'S AN HONOR AND A PRIVILEGE TO TALK TO YOU, YOUR MAGNIFICENCE, KNOWING YOUR INCLINATION FOR MEDITATION AND SILENCE...

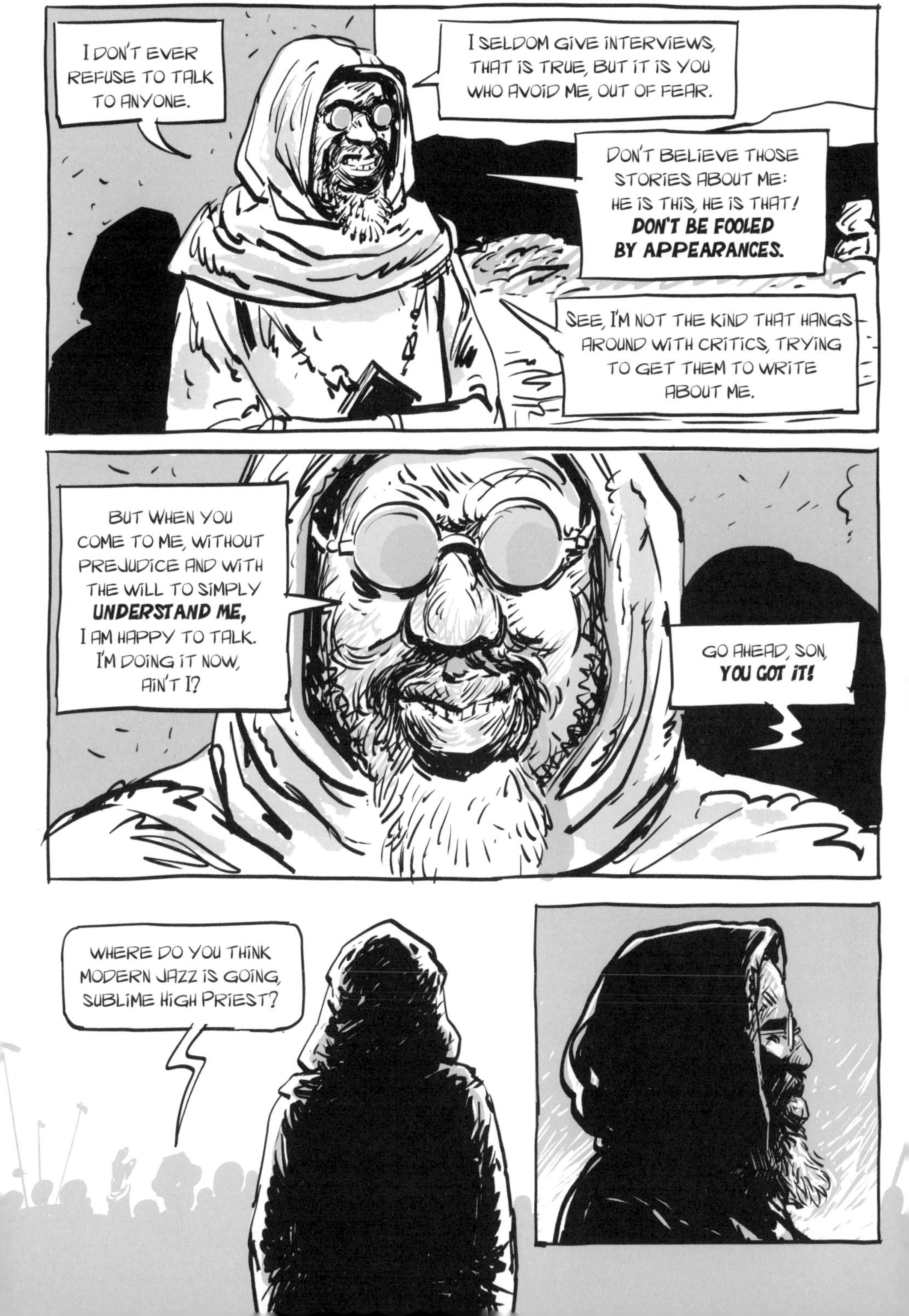
I DON'T EVER REFUSE TO TALK TO ANYONE.
I SELDOM GIVE INTERVIEWS, THAT IS TRUE, BUT IT IS YOU WHO AVOID ME, OUT OF FEAR.
DON'T BELIEVE THOSE STORIES ABOUT ME: HE IS THIS, HE IS THAT! DON'T BE FOOLED BY APPEARANCES.
SEE, I'M NOT THE KIND THAT HANGS AROUND WITH CRITICS, TRYING TO GET THEM TO WRITE ABOUT ME.
BUT WHEN YOU COME TO ME, WITHOUT PREJUDICE AND WITH THE WILL TO SIMPLY UNDERSTAND ME, I AM HAPPY TO TALK. I'M DOING IT NOW, AIN'T I?
GO AHEAD, SON, YOU GOT IT!
WHERE DO YOU THINK MODERN JAZZ IS GOING, SUBLIME HIGH PRIEST?

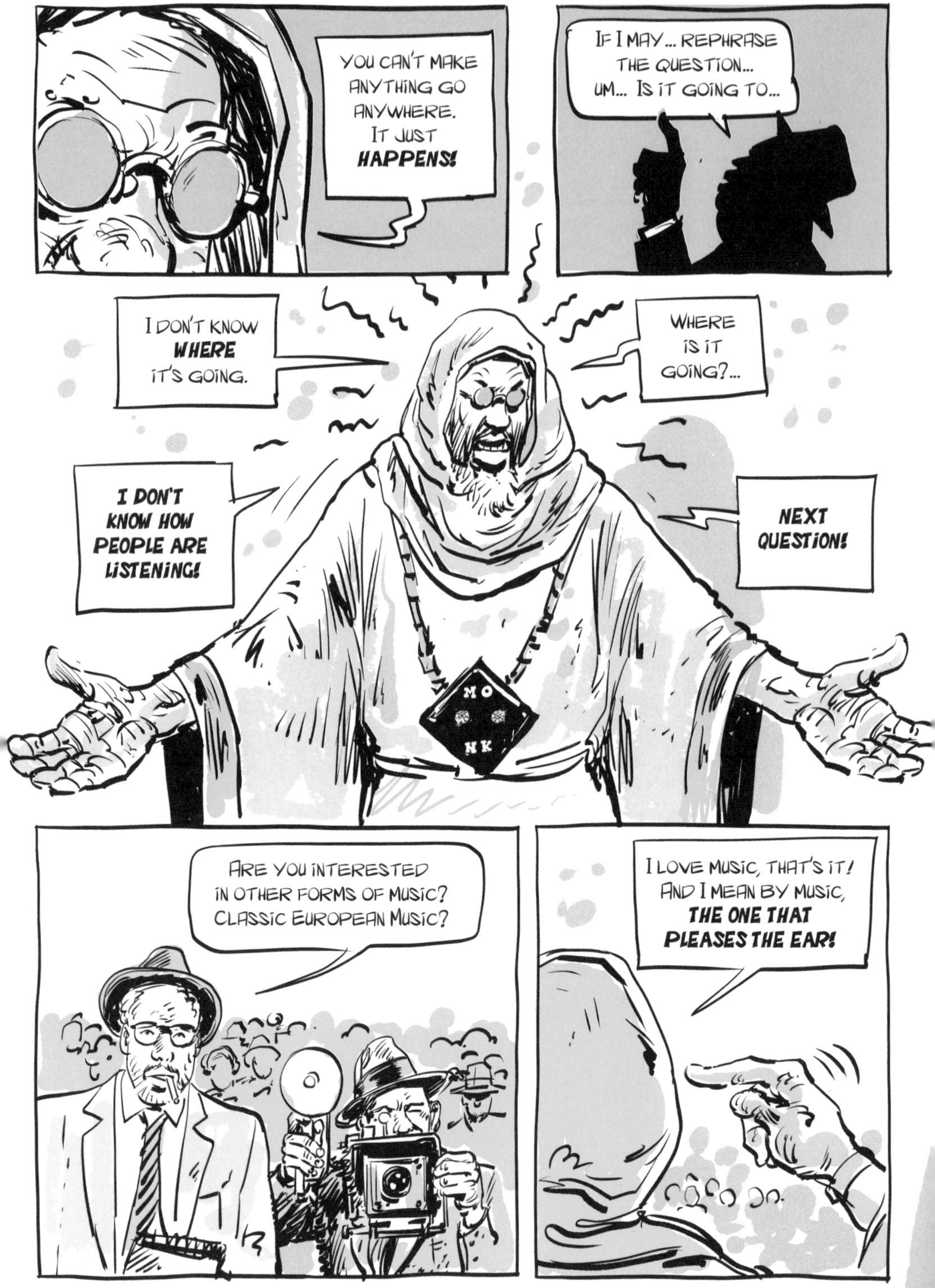
YOU CAN'T MAKE ANYTHING GO ANYWHERE. IT JUST **HAPPENS!**
IF I MAY... REPHRASE THE QUESTION... UM... IS IT GOING TO...
I DON'T KNOW **WHERE** IT'S GOING.
WHERE IS IT GOING?...
I DON'T KNOW HOW PEOPLE ARE LISTENING!
NEXT QUESTION!
MO NK
ARE YOU INTERESTED IN OTHER FORMS OF MUSIC? CLASSIC EUROPEAN MUSIC?
I LOVE MUSIC, THAT'S IT! AND I MEAN BY MUSIC, **THE ONE THAT PLEASES THE EAR!**

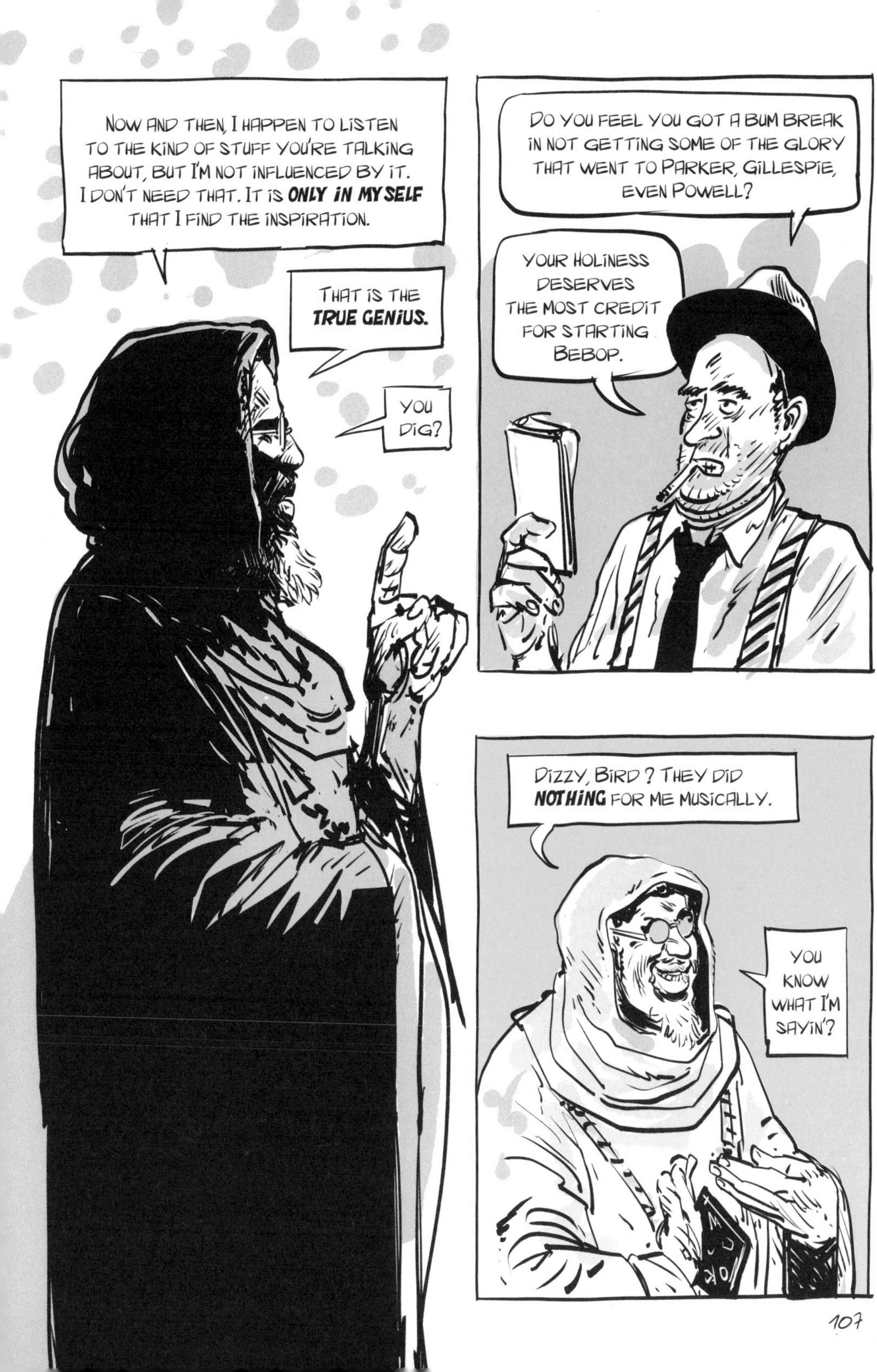
NOW AND THEN, I HAPPEN TO LISTEN TO THE KIND OF STUFF YOU'RE TALKING ABOUT, BUT I'M NOT INFLUENCED BY IT. I DON'T NEED THAT. IT IS **ONLY IN MY SELF** THAT I FIND THE INSPIRATION.
THAT IS THE **TRUE GENIUS.**
YOU DIG?
DO YOU FEEL YOU GOT A BUM BREAK IN NOT GETTING SOME OF THE GLORY THAT WENT TO PARKER, GILLESPIE, EVEN POWELL?
YOUR HOLINESS DESERVES THE MOST CREDIT FOR STARTING BEBOP.
DIZZY, BIRD? THEY DID **NOTHING** FOR ME MUSICALLY.
YOU KNOW WHAT I'M SAYIN'?

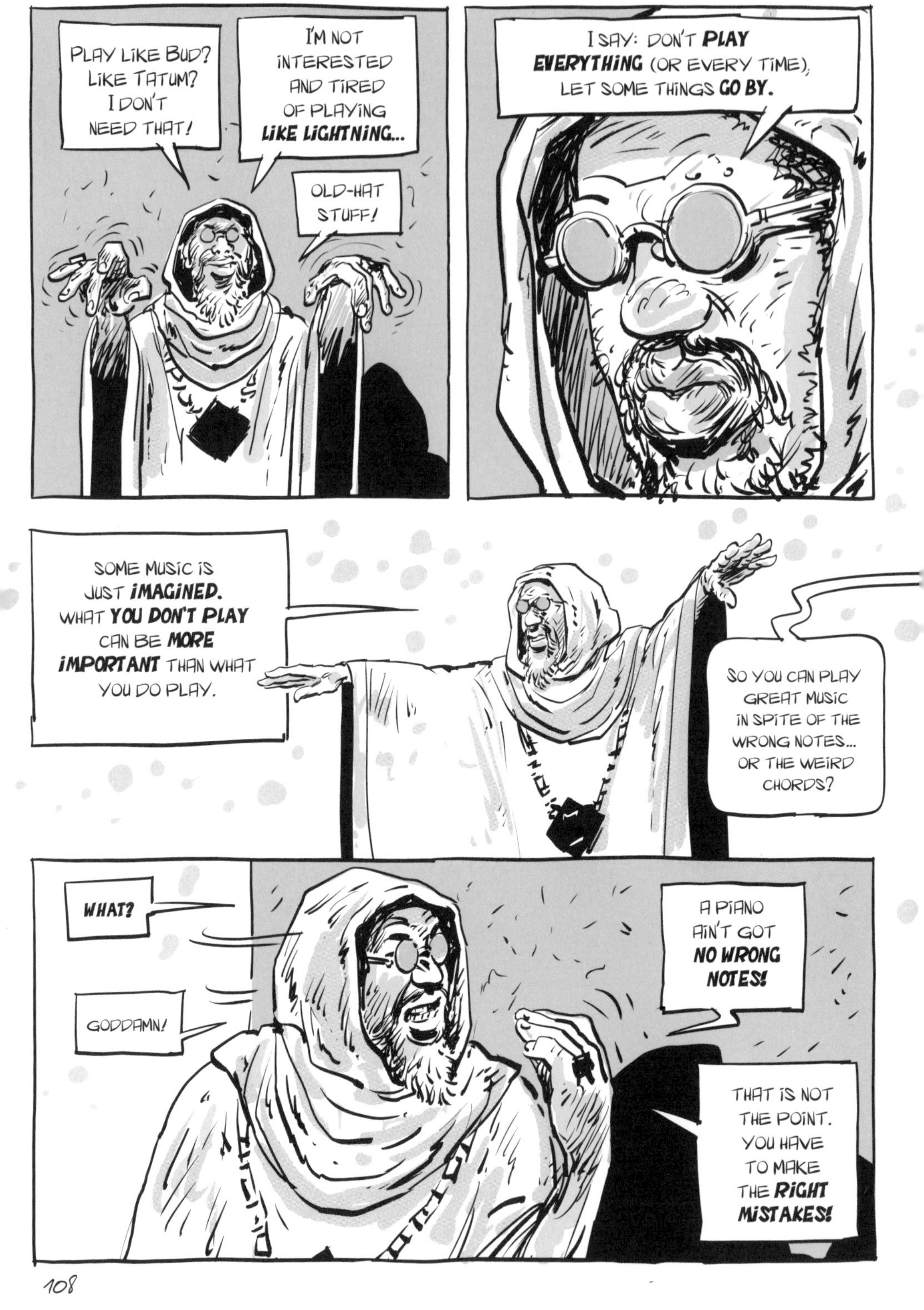
PLAY LIKE BUD? LIKE TATUM? I DON'T NEED THAT!
I'M NOT INTERESTED AND TIRED OF PLAYING **LIKE LIGHTNING...**
OLD-HAT STUFF!
I SAY: DON'T **PLAY EVERYTHING** (OR EVERY TIME); LET SOME THINGS **GO BY.**
SOME MUSIC IS JUST **IMAGINED.** WHAT **YOU DON'T PLAY** CAN BE **MORE IMPORTANT** THAN WHAT YOU DO PLAY.
SO YOU CAN PLAY GREAT MUSIC IN SPITE OF THE WRONG NOTES... OR THE WEIRD CHORDS?
WHAT?
GODDAMN!
A PIANO AIN'T GOT **NO WRONG NOTES!**
THAT IS NOT THE POINT. YOU HAVE TO MAKE THE **RIGHT MISTAKES!**

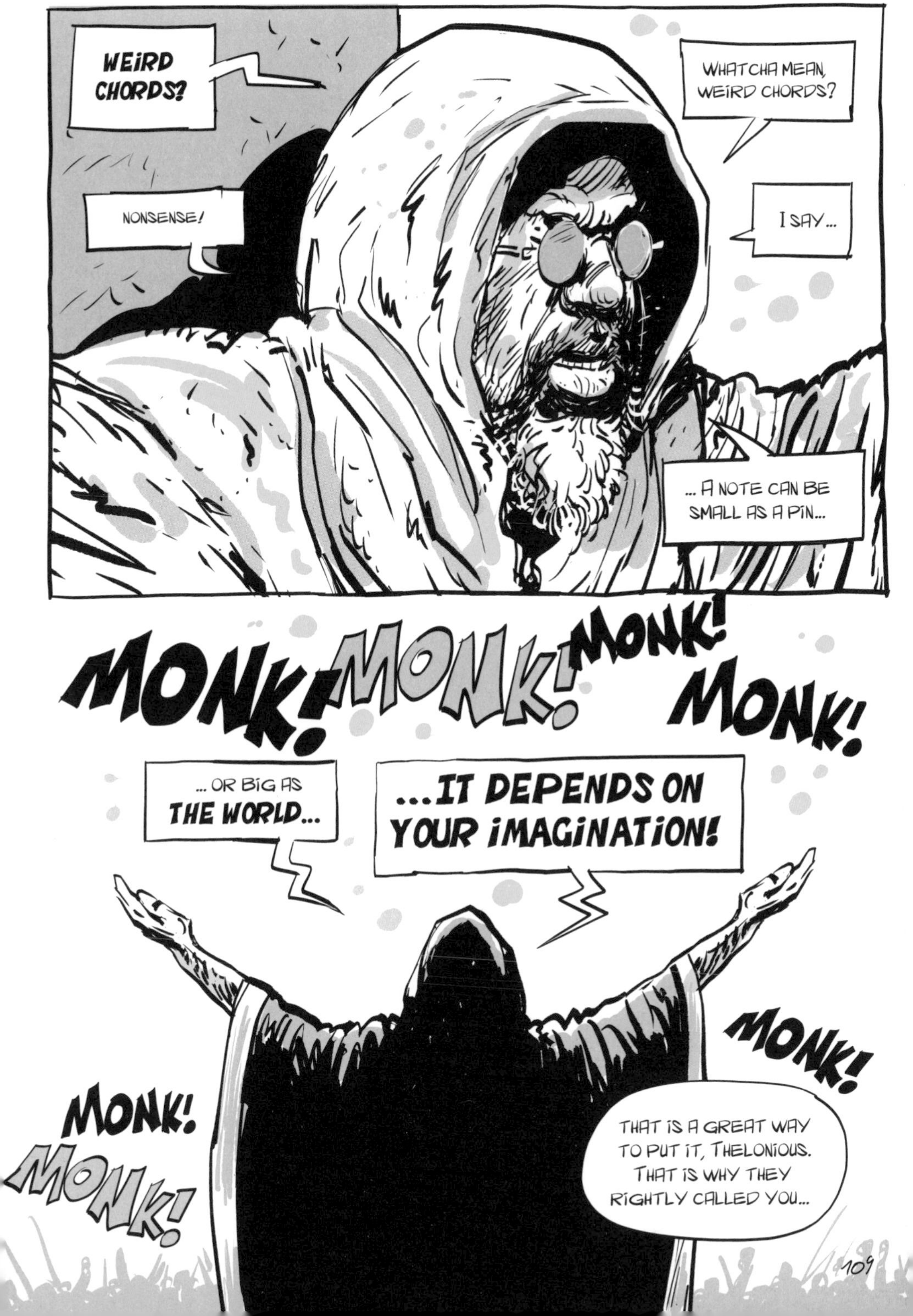
WEIRD CHORDS?
WHATCHA MEAN, WEIRD CHORDS?
NONSENSE!
I SAY...
... A NOTE CAN BE SMALL AS A PIN...
MONK! MONK! MONK! MONK!
... OR BIG AS THE WORLD...
...IT DEPENDS ON YOUR IMAGINATION!
MONK!
MONK! MONK!
THAT IS A GREAT WAY TO PUT IT, THELONIOUS. THAT IS WHY THEY RIGHTLY CALLED YOU...

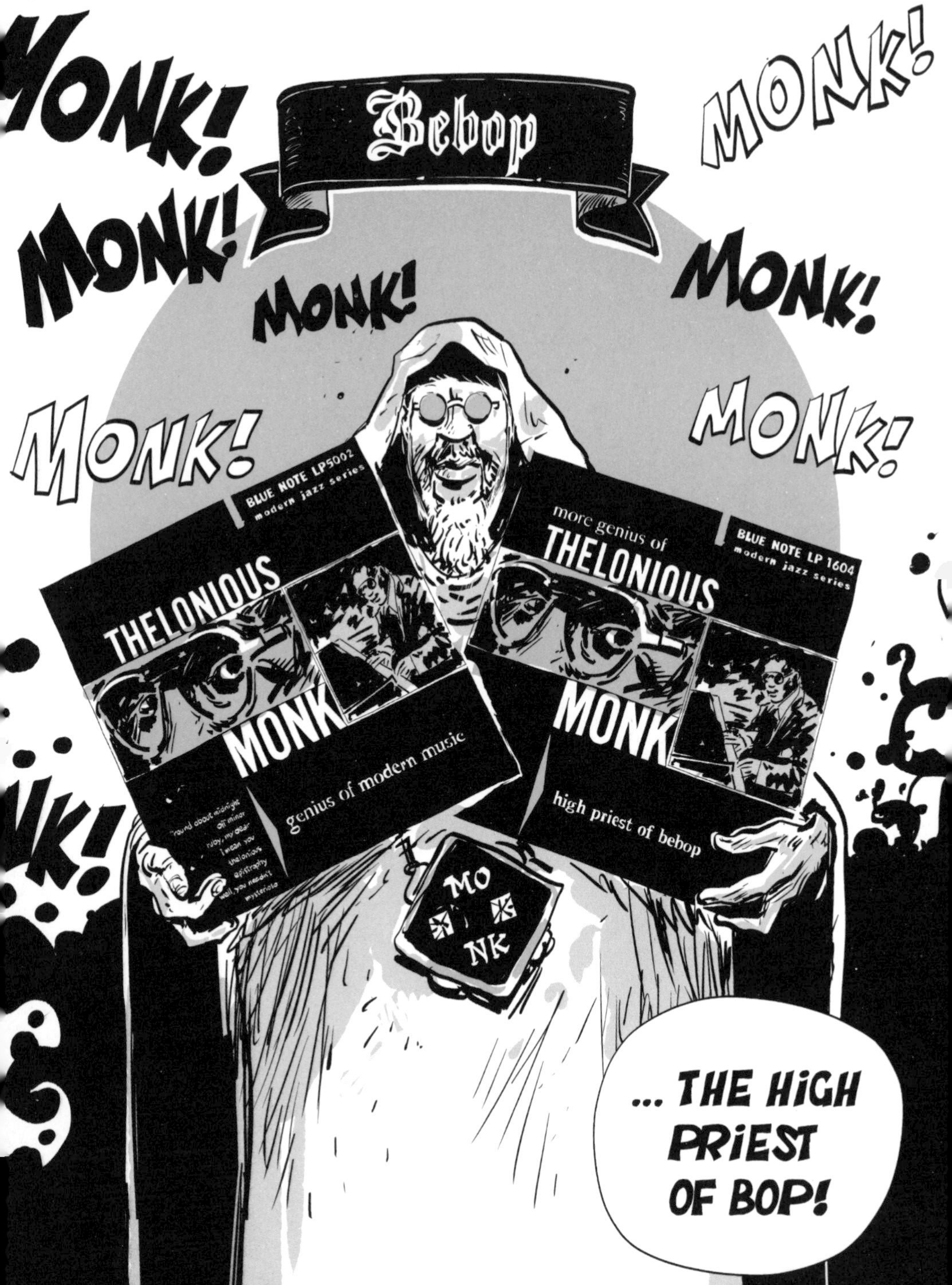
Bebop
MONK!
MONK!
MONK!
MONK!
MONK!
MONK!
MONK!
NK!
BLUE NOTE LP5002
modern jazz series
THELONIOUS
MONK
genius of modern music
more genius of
THELONIOUS
MONK
BLUE NOTE LP 1604
modern jazz series
high priest of bebop
MO
NK
... THE HIGH PRIEST OF BOP!

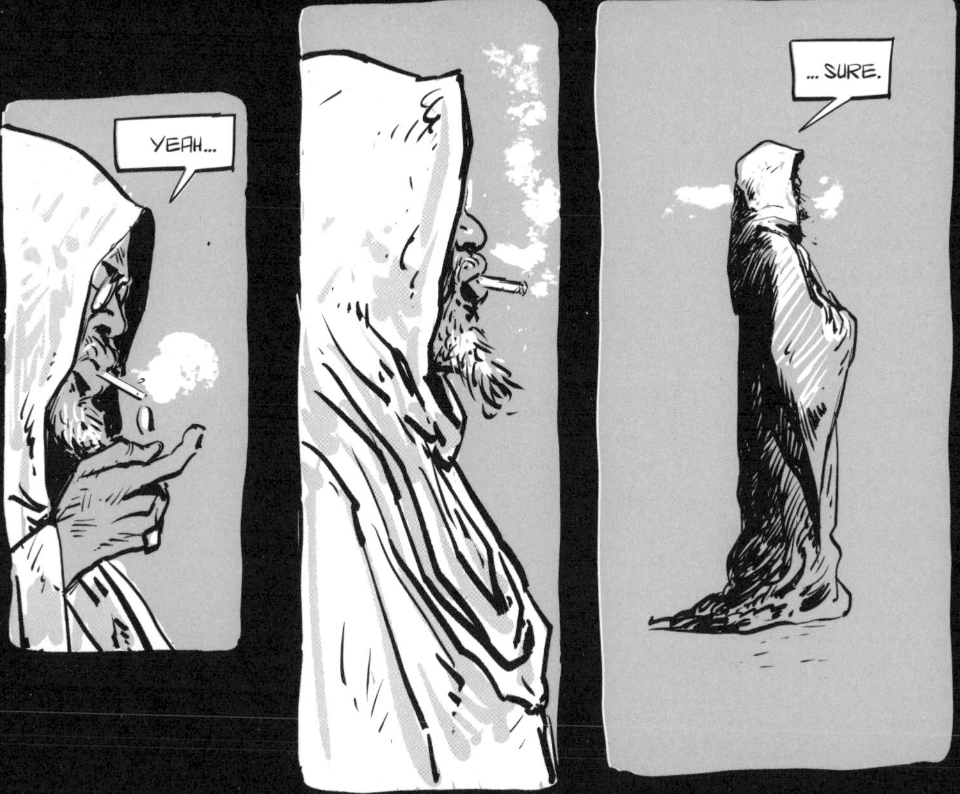
YEAH...
... SURE.

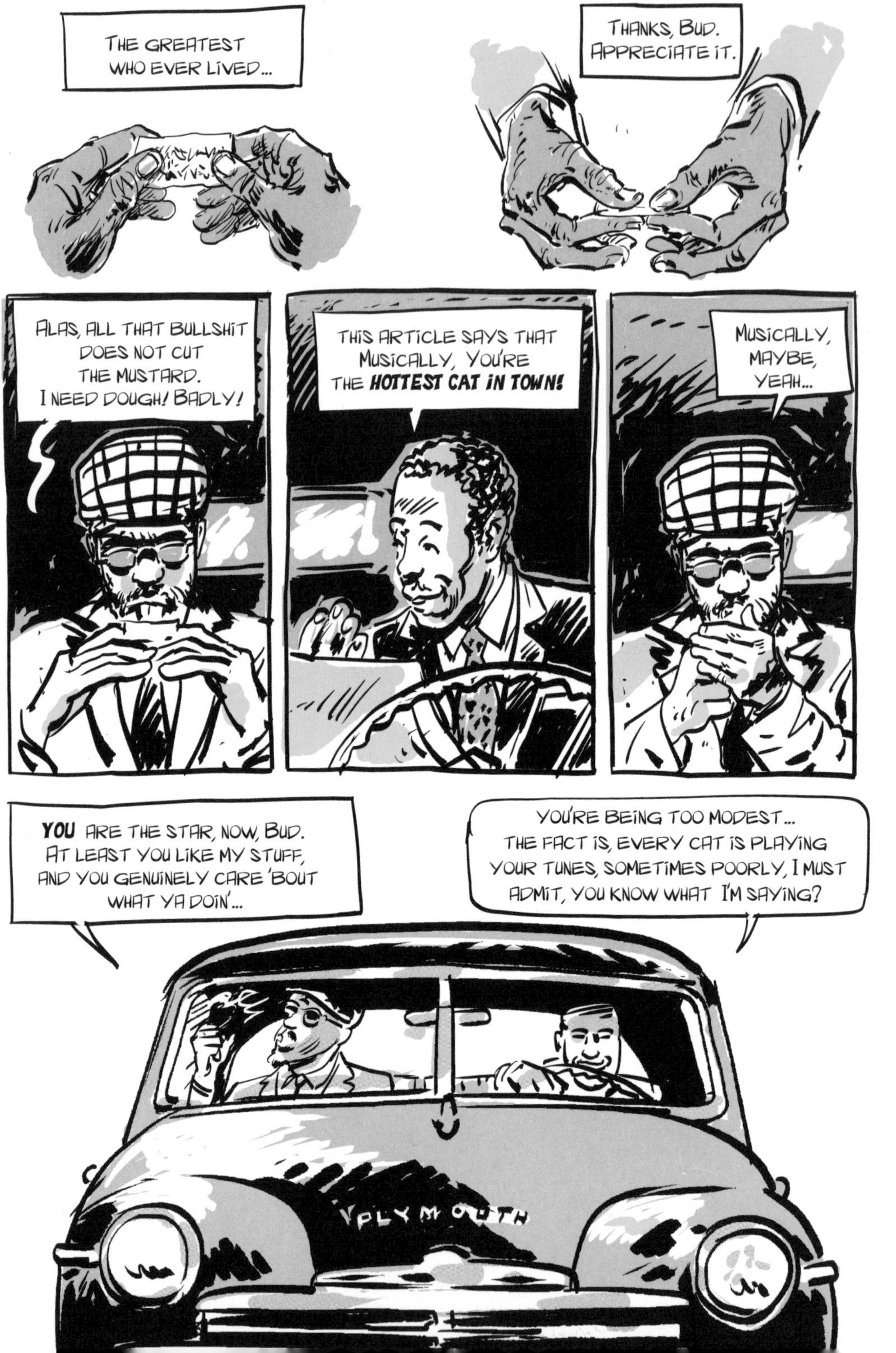
THE GREATEST WHO EVER LIVED...
THANKS, BUD. APPRECIATE IT.
ALAS, ALL THAT BULLSHIT DOES NOT CUT THE MUSTARD. I NEED DOUGH! BADLY!
THIS ARTICLE SAYS THAT MUSICALLY, YOU'RE THE **HOTTEST CAT IN TOWN!**
MUSICALLY, MAYBE, YEAH...
YOU ARE THE STAR, NOW, BUD. AT LEAST YOU LIKE MY STUFF, AND YOU GENUINELY CARE 'BOUT WHAT YA DOIN'...
YOU'RE BEING TOO MODEST... THE FACT IS, EVERY CAT IS PLAYING YOUR TUNES, SOMETIMES POORLY, I MUST ADMIT, YOU KNOW WHAT I'M SAYING?
PLYMOUTH

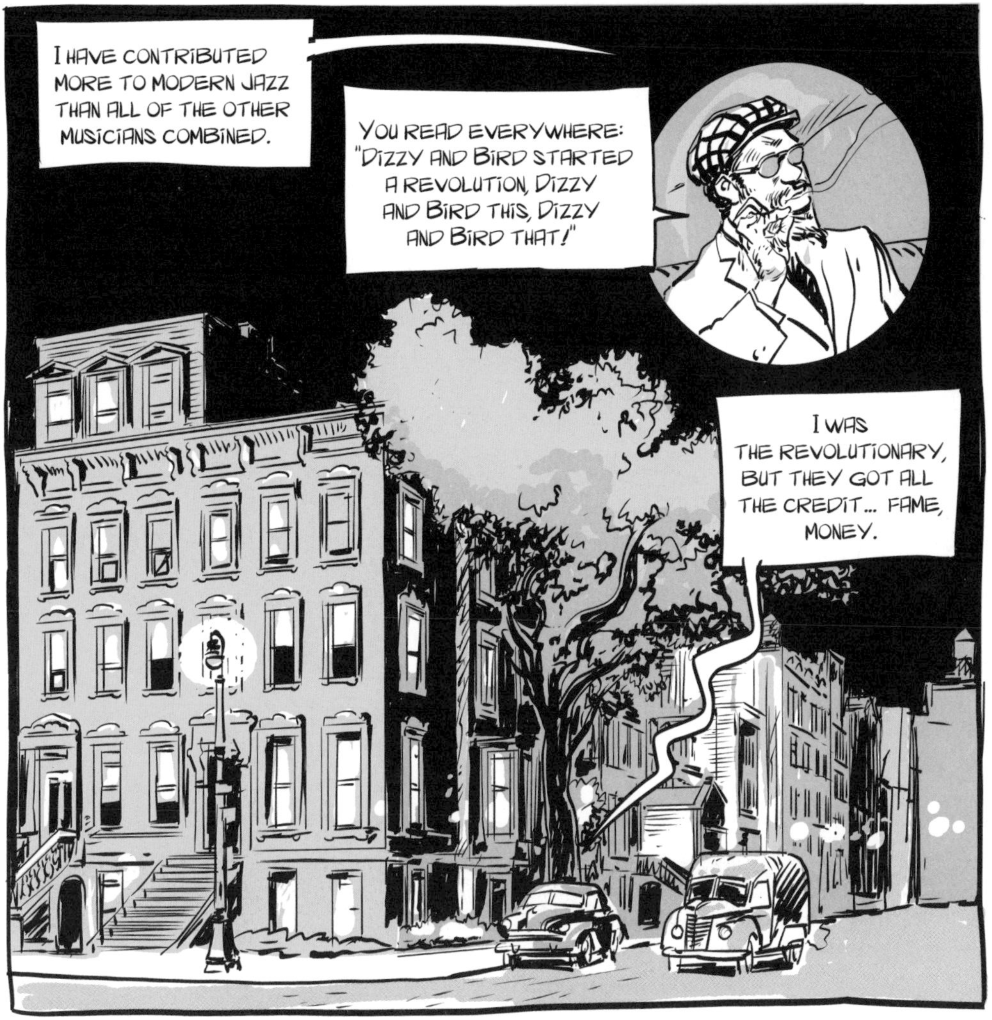
I HAVE CONTRIBUTED MORE TO MODERN JAZZ THAN ALL OF THE OTHER MUSICIANS COMBINED.
YOU READ EVERYWHERE: "DIZZY AND BIRD STARTED A REVOLUTION, DIZZY AND BIRD THIS, DIZZY AND BIRD THAT!"
I WAS THE REVOLUTIONARY, BUT THEY GOT ALL THE CREDIT... FAME, MONEY.

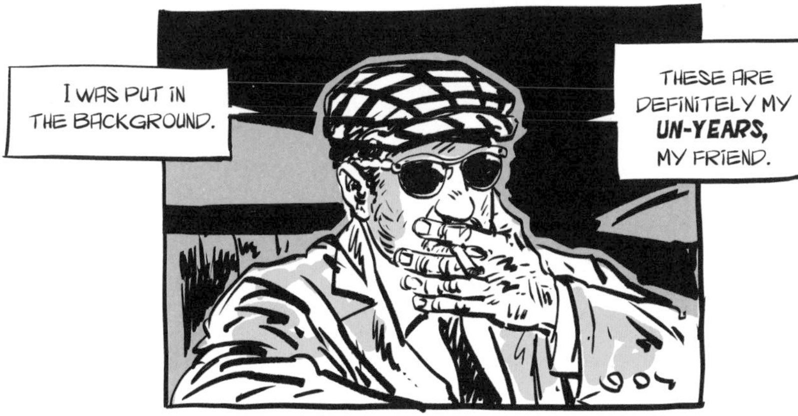
I WAS PUT IN THE BACKGROUND.
THESE ARE DEFINITELY MY **UN-YEARS,** MY FRIEND.

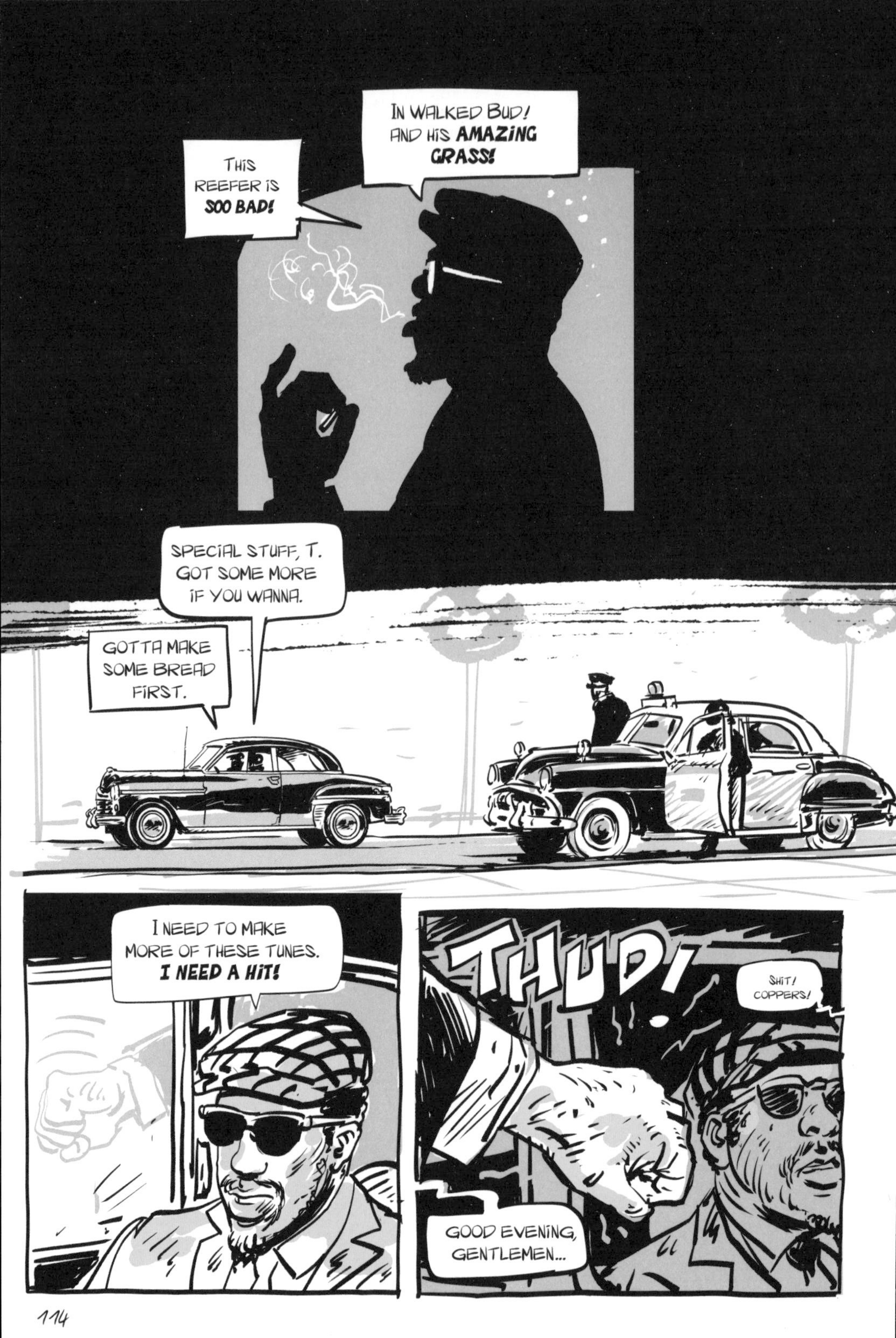
THIS REEFER IS SOO BAD!
IN WALKED BUD! AND HIS AMAZING GRASS!
SPECIAL STUFF, T. GOT SOME MORE IF YOU WANNA.
GOTTA MAKE SOME BREAD FIRST.
I NEED TO MAKE MORE OF THESE TUNES. I NEED A HIT!
THUD!
SHIT! COPPERS!
GOOD EVENING, GENTLEMEN...

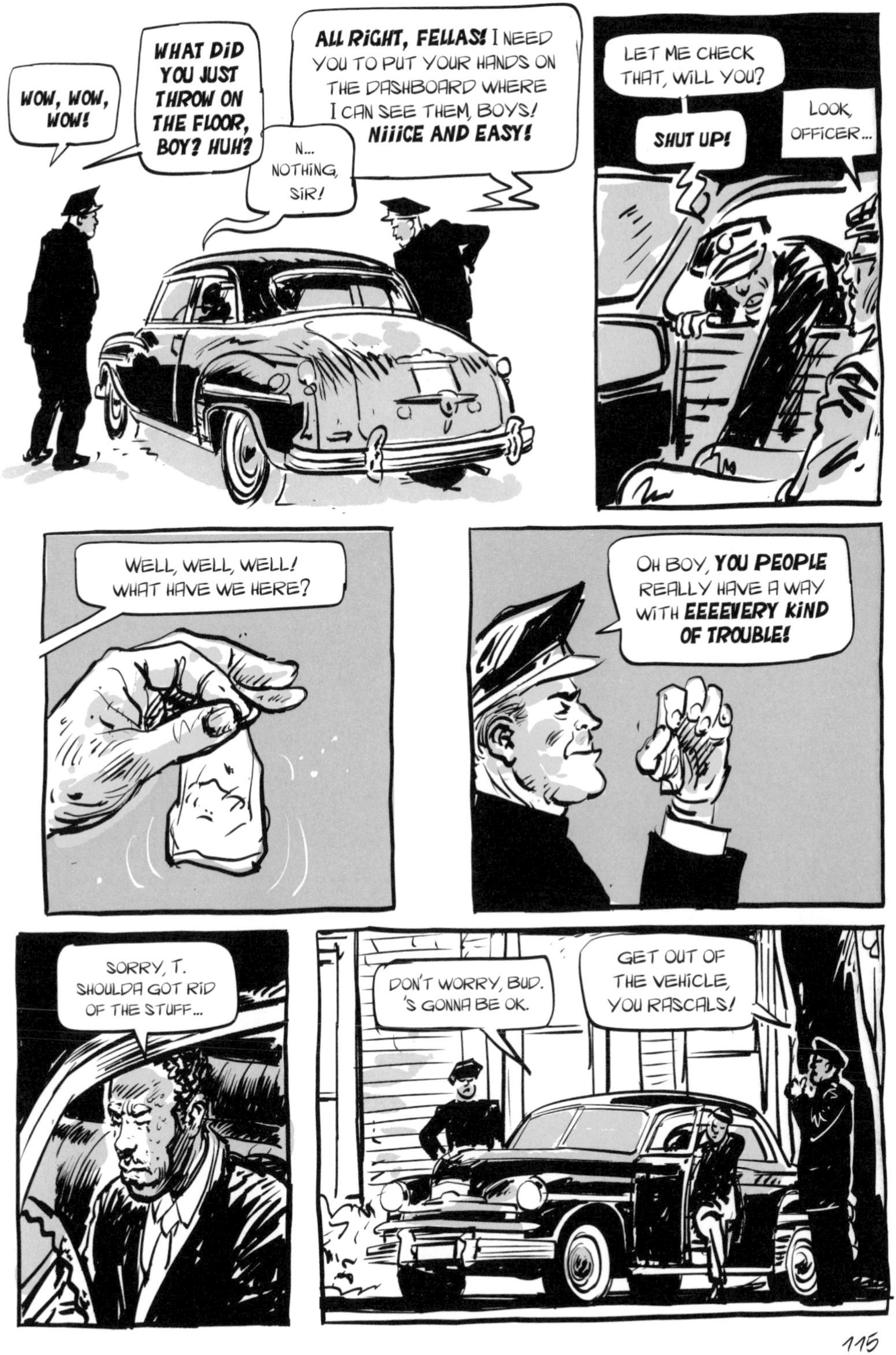
WOW, WOW, WOW!
WHAT DID YOU JUST THROW ON THE FLOOR, BOY? HUH?
N... NOTHING, SIR!
ALL RIGHT, FELLAS! I NEED YOU TO PUT YOUR HANDS ON THE DASHBOARD WHERE I CAN SEE THEM, BOYS! NIIICE AND EASY!
LET ME CHECK THAT, WILL YOU?
SHUT UP!
LOOK, OFFICER...
WELL, WELL, WELL! WHAT HAVE WE HERE?
OH BOY, YOU PEOPLE REALLY HAVE A WAY WITH EEEEVERY KIND OF TROUBLE!
SORRY, T. SHOULDA GOT RID OF THE STUFF...
DON'T WORRY, BUD. 'S GONNA BE OK.
GET OUT OF THE VEHICLE, YOU RASCALS!

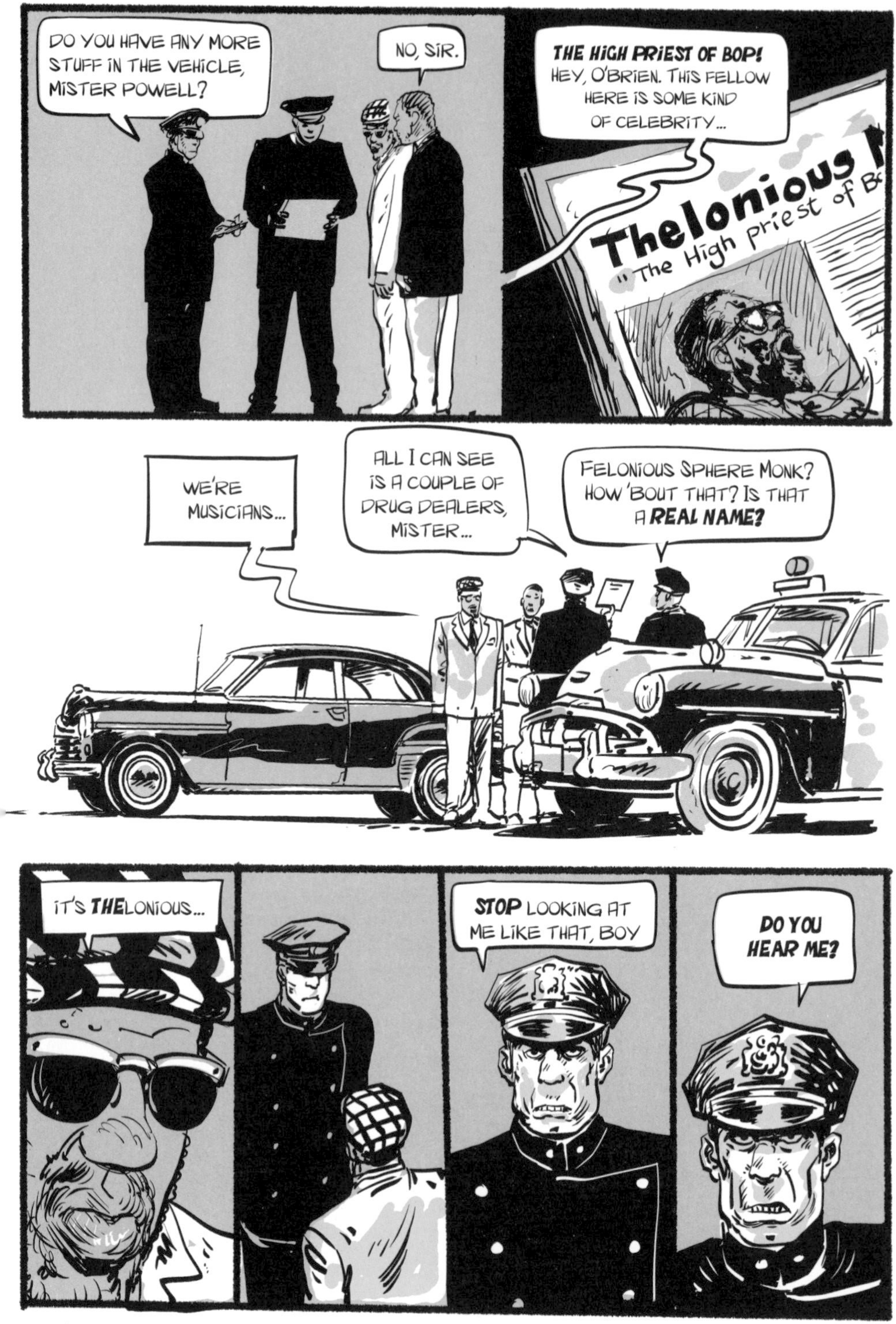
DO YOU HAVE ANY MORE STUFF IN THE VEHICLE, MISTER POWELL?
NO, SIR.
THE HIGH PRIEST OF BOP! HEY, O'BRIEN. THIS FELLOW HERE IS SOME KIND OF CELEBRITY...
Thelonious M
"The High priest of Bo
WE'RE MUSICIANS...
ALL I CAN SEE IS A COUPLE OF DRUG DEALERS, MISTER...
FELONIOUS SPHERE MONK? HOW 'BOUT THAT? IS THAT A REAL NAME?
IT'S THELONIOUS...
STOP LOOKING AT ME LIKE THAT, BOY
DO YOU HEAR ME?

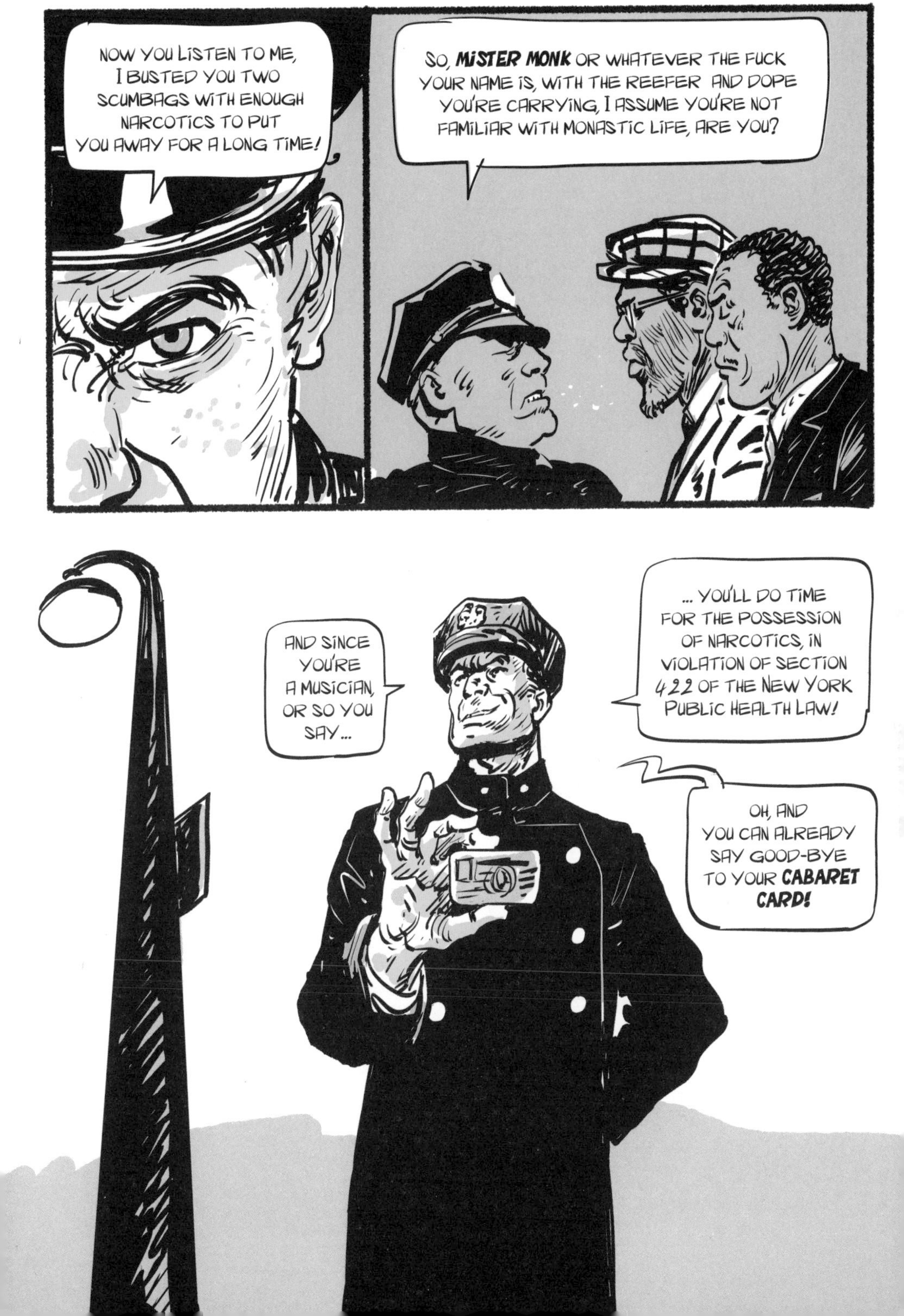
NOW YOU LISTEN TO ME, I BUSTED YOU TWO SCUMBAGS WITH ENOUGH NARCOTICS TO PUT YOU AWAY FOR A LONG TIME!
SO, **MISTER MONK** OR WHATEVER THE FUCK YOUR NAME IS, WITH THE REEFER AND DOPE YOU'RE CARRYING, I ASSUME YOU'RE NOT FAMILIAR WITH MONASTIC LIFE, ARE YOU?
AND SINCE YOU'RE A MUSICIAN, OR SO YOU SAY...
... YOU'LL DO TIME FOR THE POSSESSION OF NARCOTICS, IN VIOLATION OF SECTION 422 OF THE NEW YORK PUBLIC HEALTH LAW!
OH, AND YOU CAN ALREADY SAY GOOD-BYE TO YOUR **CABARET CARD!**

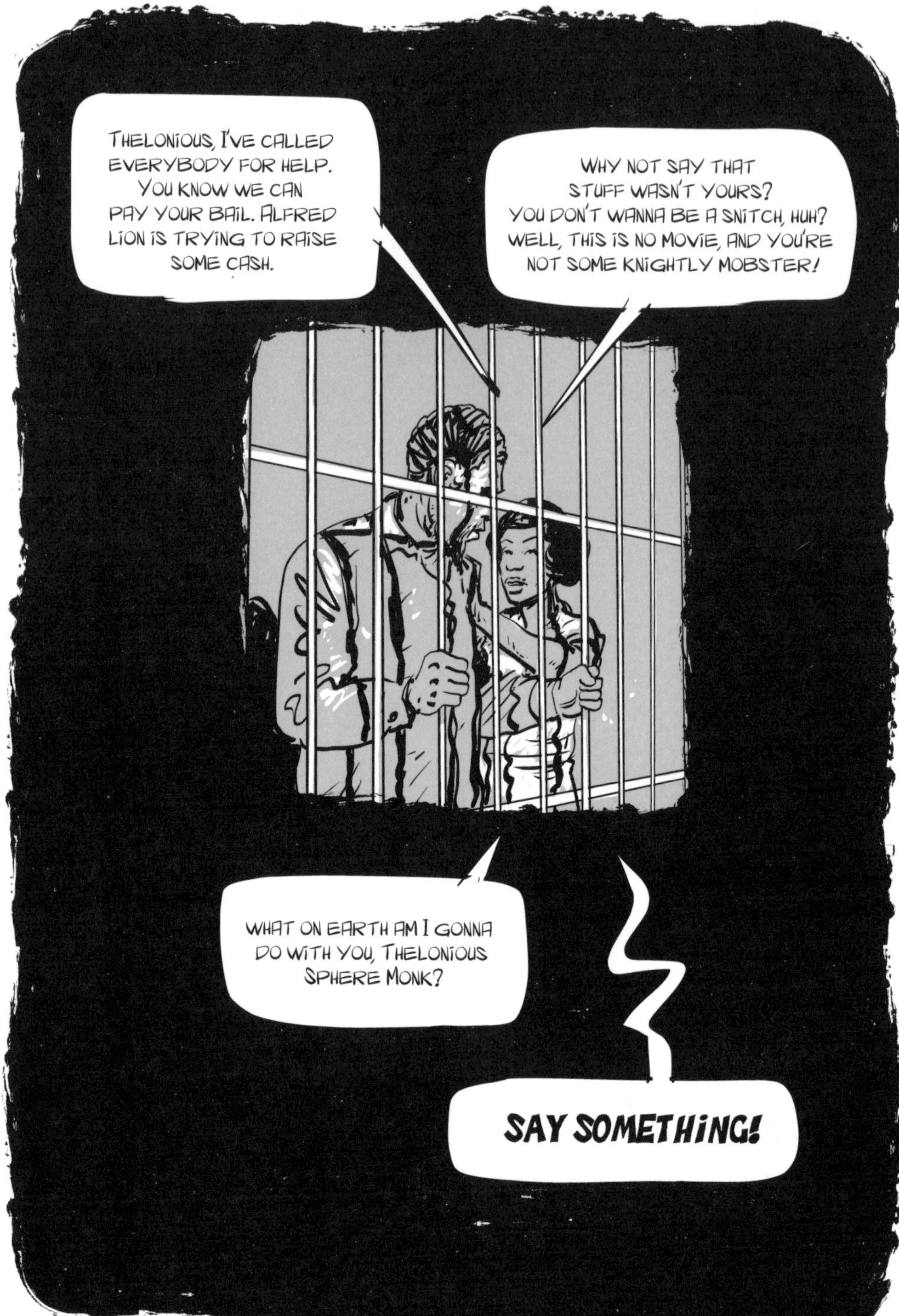
THELONIOUS, I'VE CALLED EVERYBODY FOR HELP. YOU KNOW WE CAN PAY YOUR BAIL. ALFRED LION IS TRYING TO RAISE SOME CASH.
WHY NOT SAY THAT STUFF WASN'T YOURS? YOU DON'T WANNA BE A SNITCH, HUH? WELL, THIS IS NO MOVIE, AND YOU'RE NOT SOME KNIGHTLY MOBSTER!
WHAT ON EARTH AM I GONNA DO WITH YOU, THELONIOUS SPHERE MONK?
SAY SOMETHING!

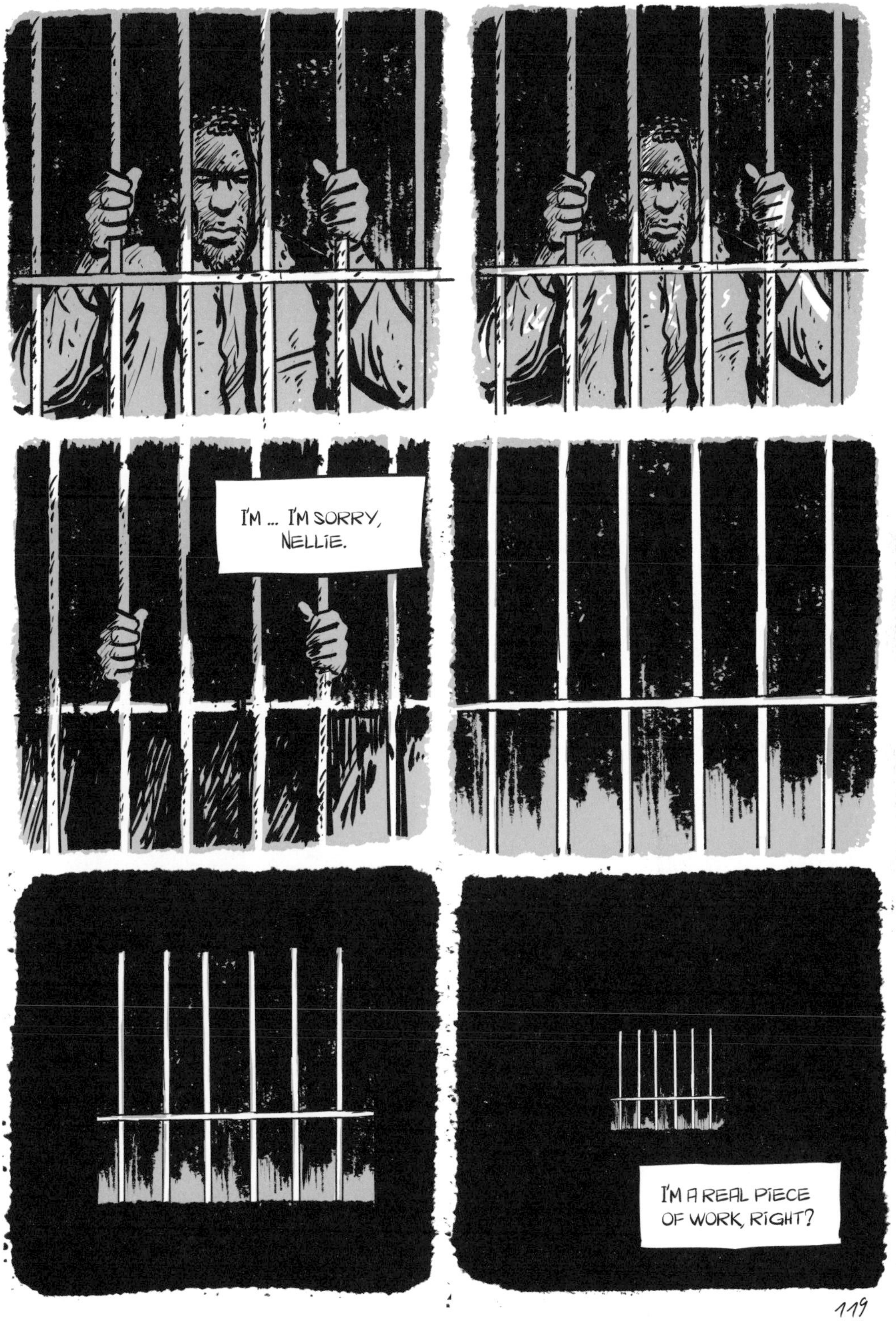
I'M ... I'M SORRY, NELLIE.
I'M A REAL PIECE OF WORK, RIGHT?

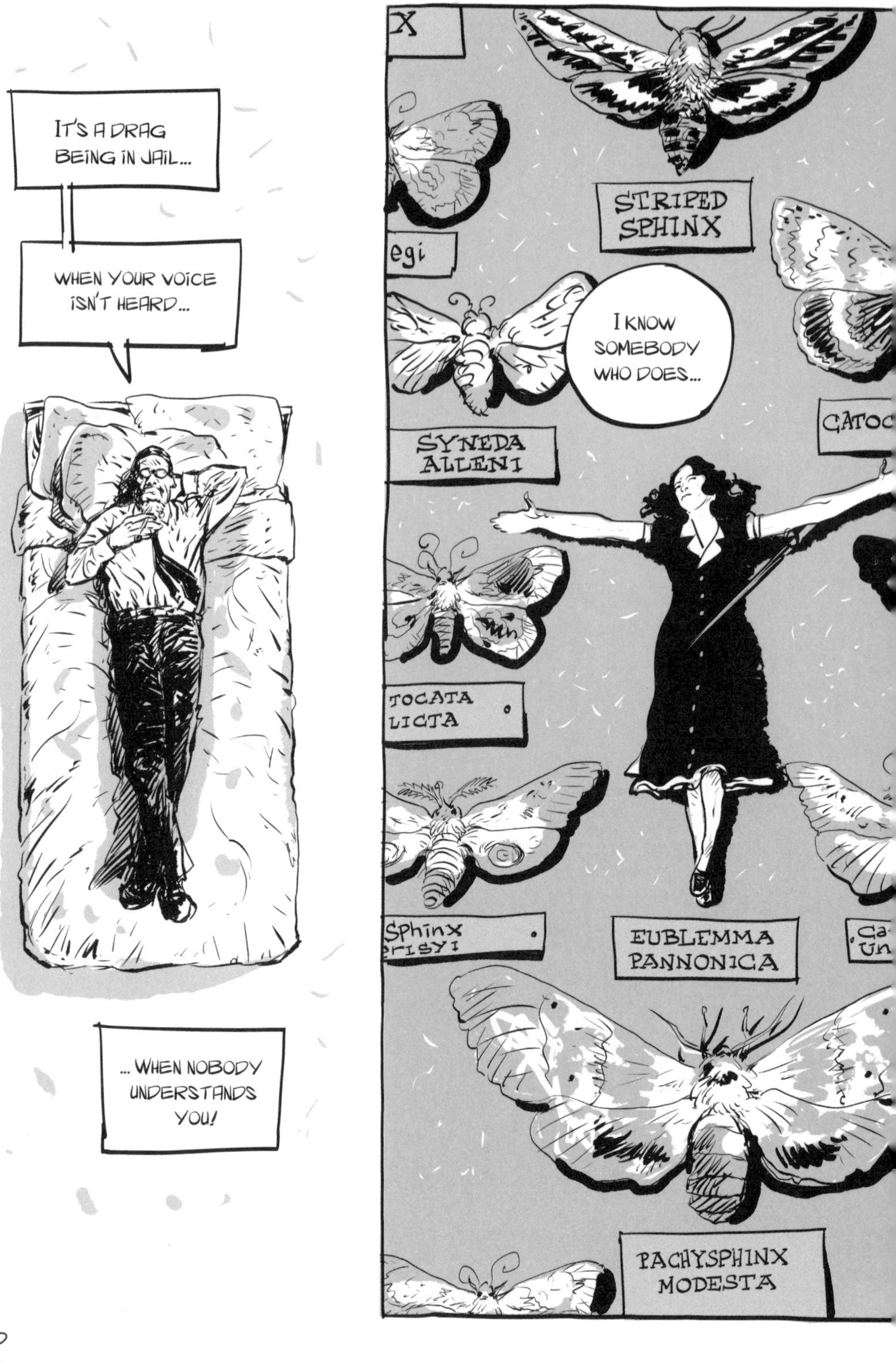

IT'S A DRAG BEING IN JAIL...
WHEN YOUR VOICE ISN'T HEARD...
...WHEN NOBODY UNDERSTANDS YOU!
STRIPED SPHINX
SYNEDA ALLENI
I KNOW SOMEBODY WHO DOES...
EUBLEMMA PANNONICA
PACHYSPHINX MODESTA

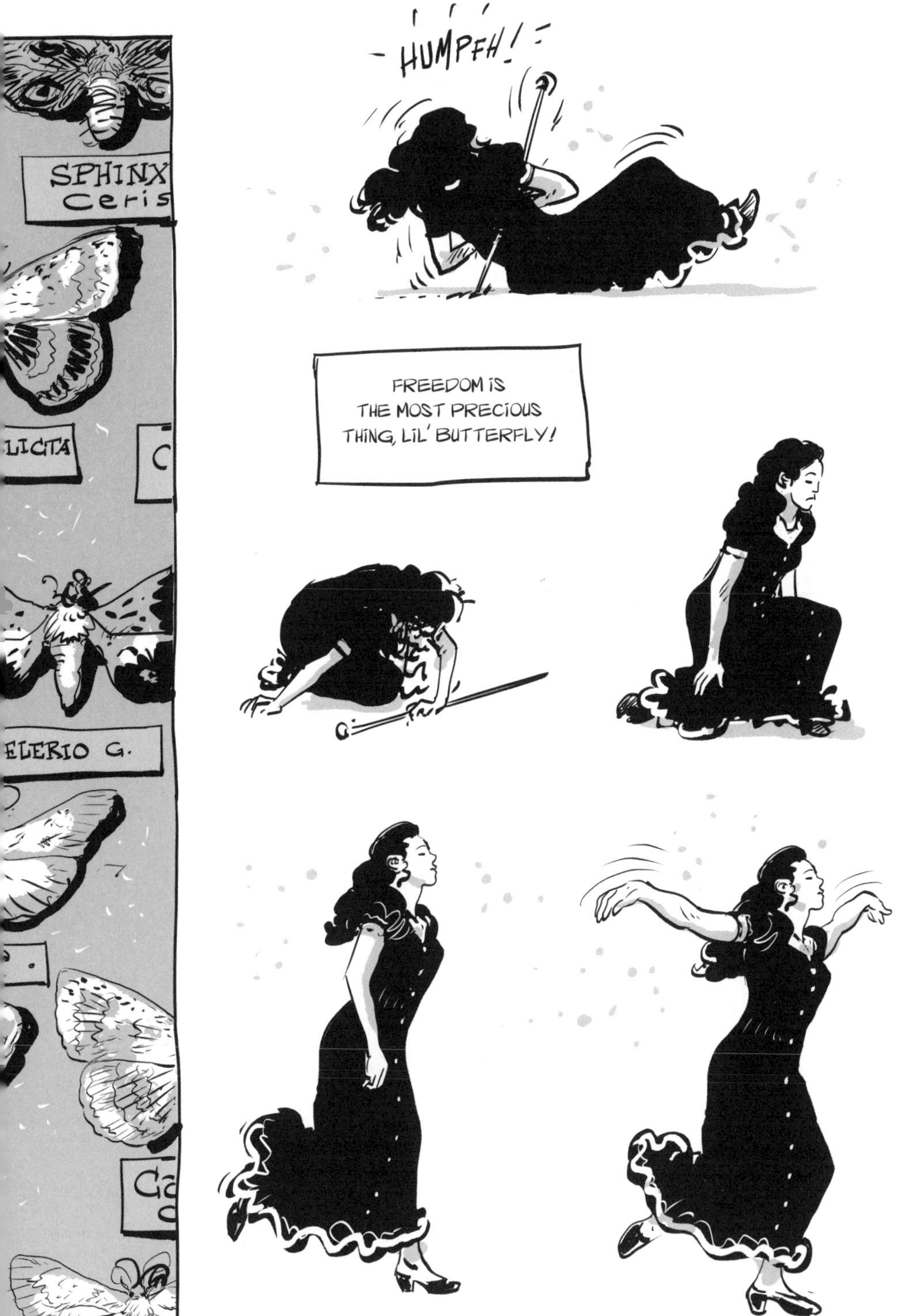
HUMPFH!
SPHINX
Ceris
LICITA
ELERIO G.
FREEDOM IS THE MOST PRECIOUS THING, LIL' BUTTERFLY!

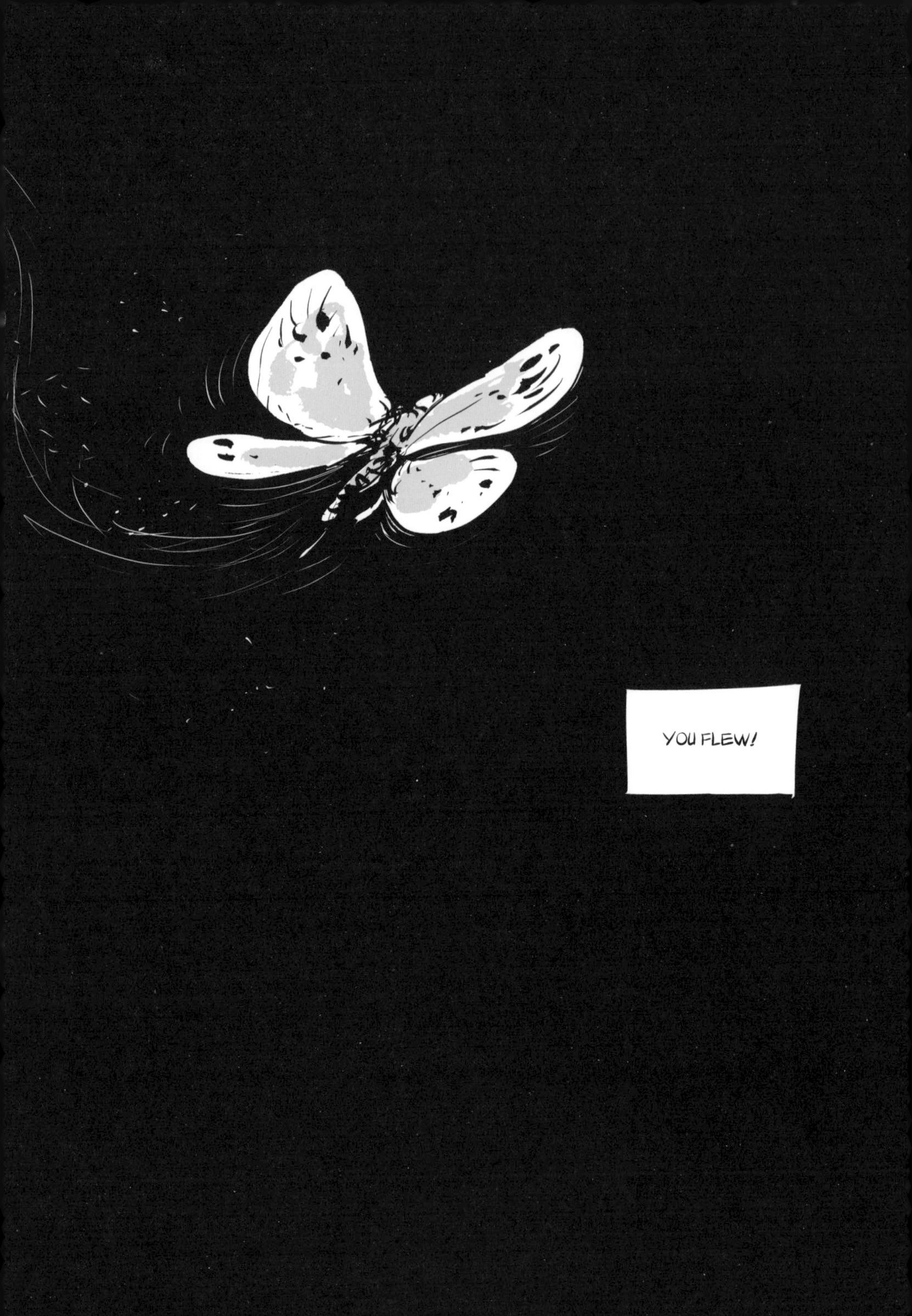
YOU FLEW!

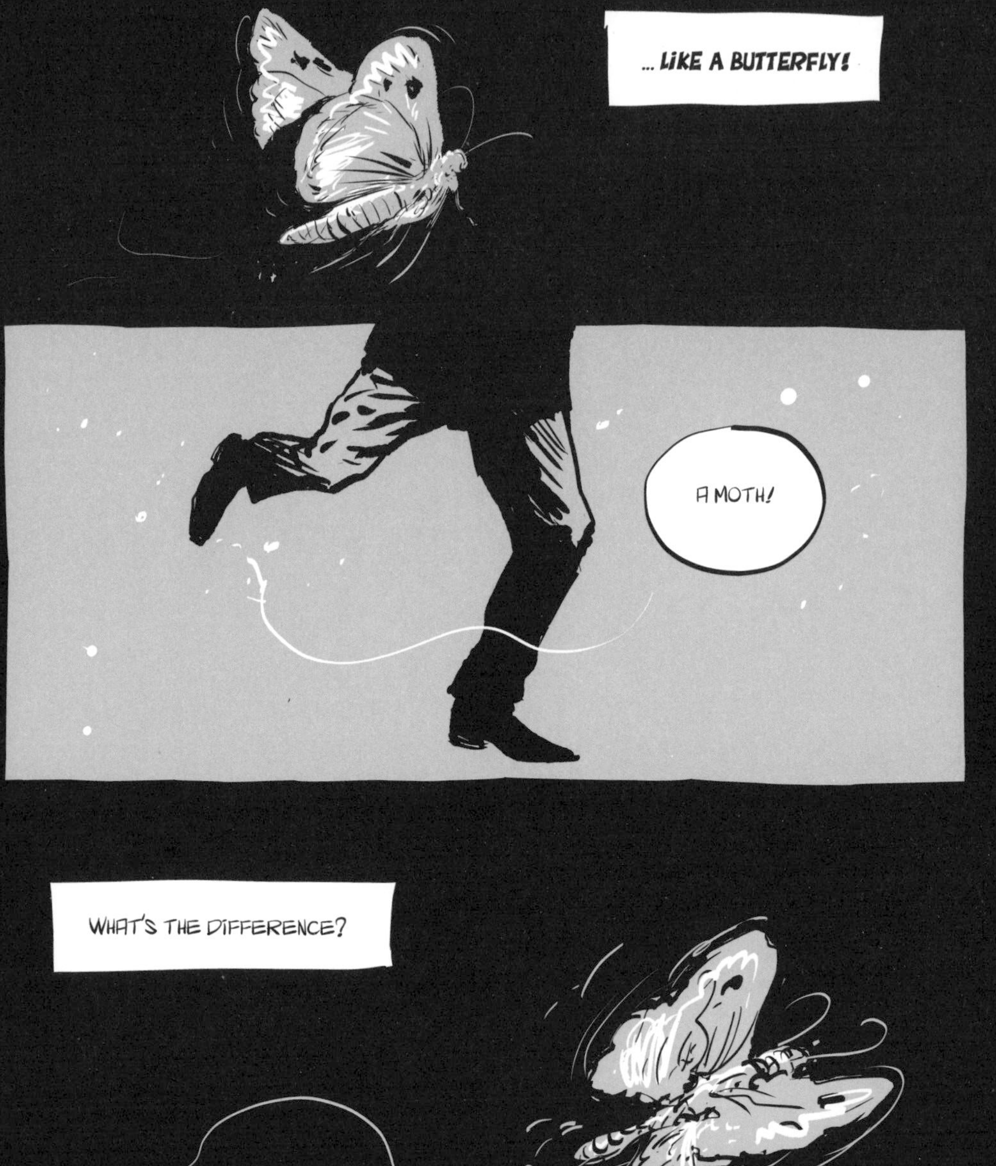
... LIKE A BUTTERFLY!
A MOTH!
WHAT'S THE DIFFERENCE?

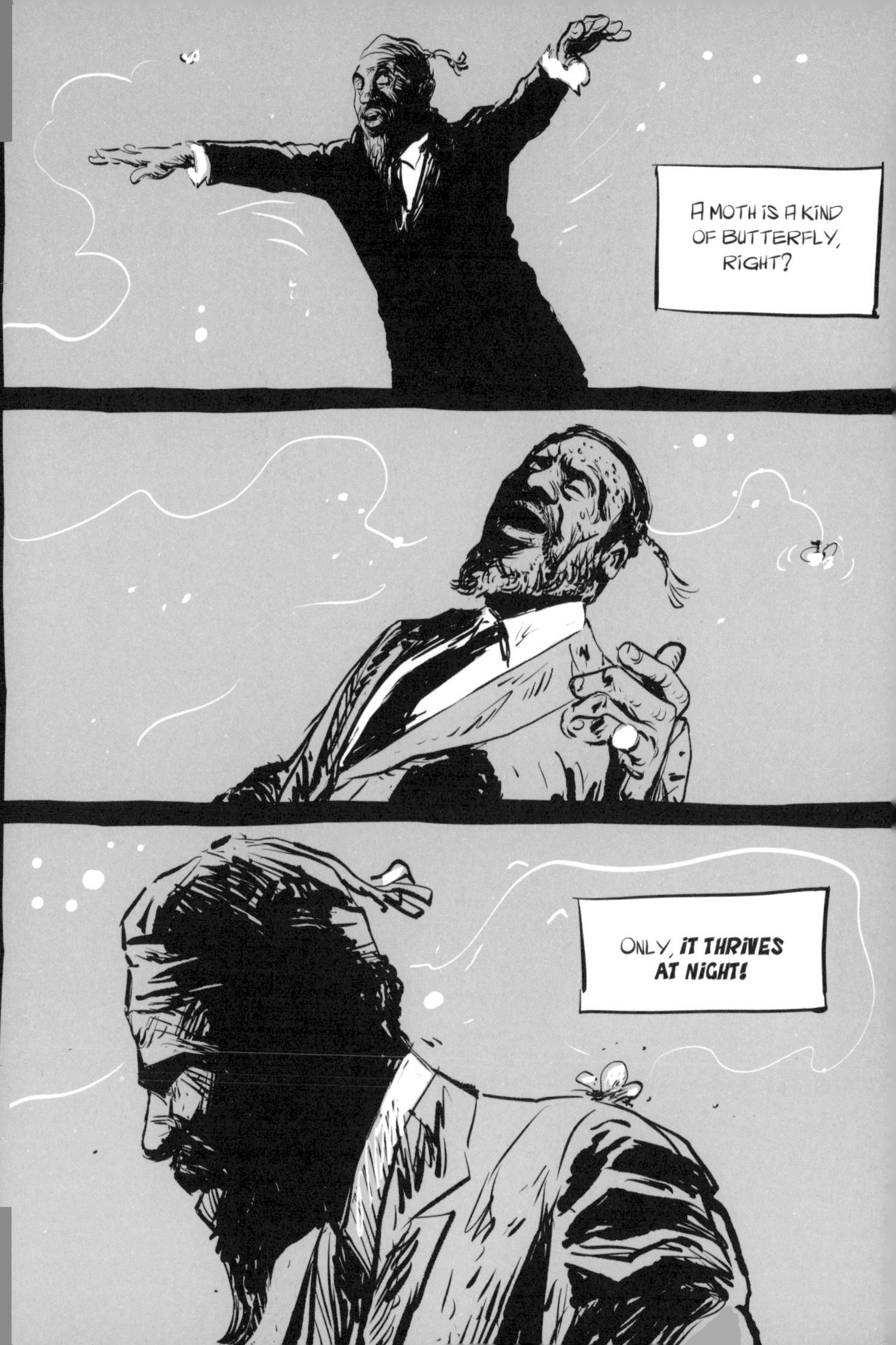
A MOTH IS A KIND OF BUTTERFLY, RIGHT?
ONLY, IT THRIVES AT NIGHT!

THELONIOUS

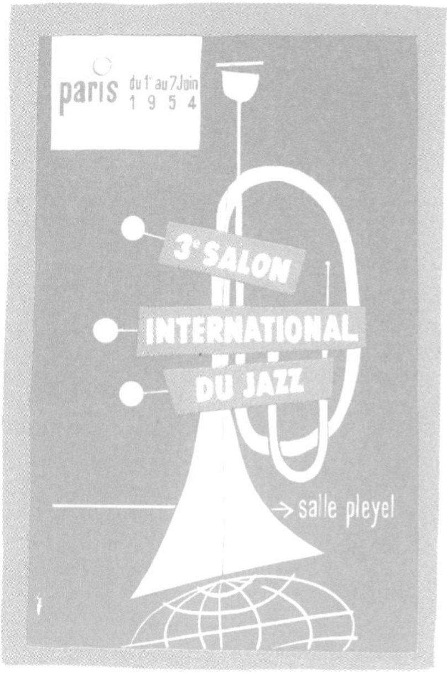
paris
du 1er au 7 Juin
1 9 5 4
3e SALON
INTERNATIONAL
DU JAZZ
→ salle pleyel

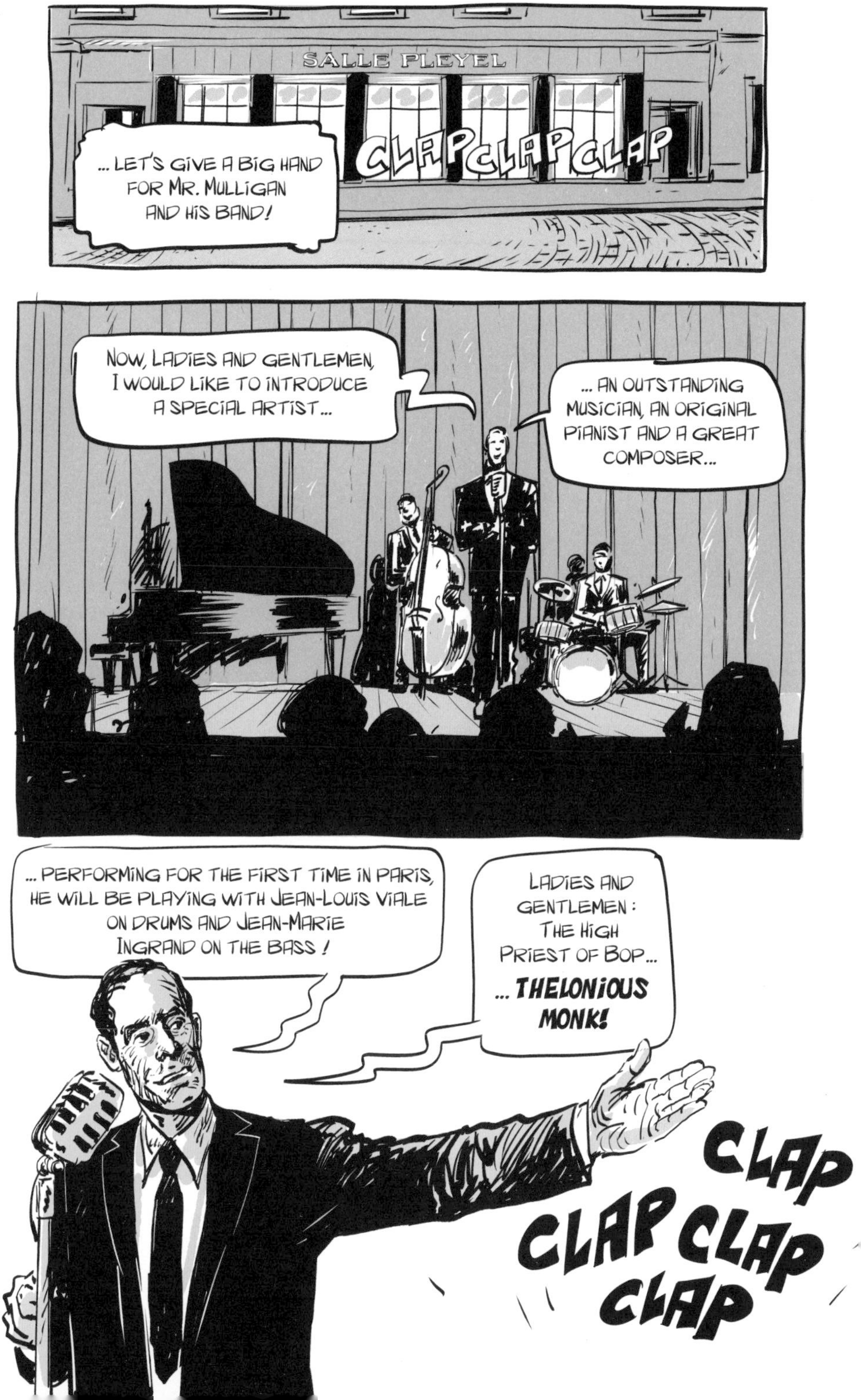
SALLE PLEYEL
... LET'S GIVE A BIG HAND FOR MR. MULLIGAN AND HIS BAND!
CLAP CLAP CLAP
NOW, LADIES AND GENTLEMEN, I WOULD LIKE TO INTRODUCE A SPECIAL ARTIST...
... AN OUTSTANDING MUSICIAN, AN ORIGINAL PIANIST AND A GREAT COMPOSER...
... PERFORMING FOR THE FIRST TIME IN PARIS, HE WILL BE PLAYING WITH JEAN-LOUIS VIALE ON DRUMS AND JEAN-MARIE INGRAND ON THE BASS !
LADIES AND GENTLEMEN : THE HIGH PRIEST OF BOP... ... THELONIOUS MONK!
CLAP CLAP CLAP CLAP

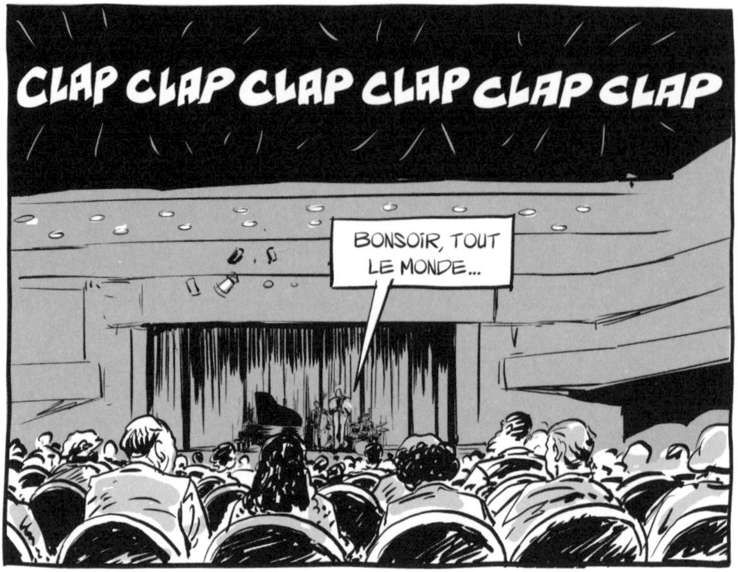
CLAP CLAP CLAP CLAP CLAP CLAP
BONSOIR, TOUT LE MONDE...

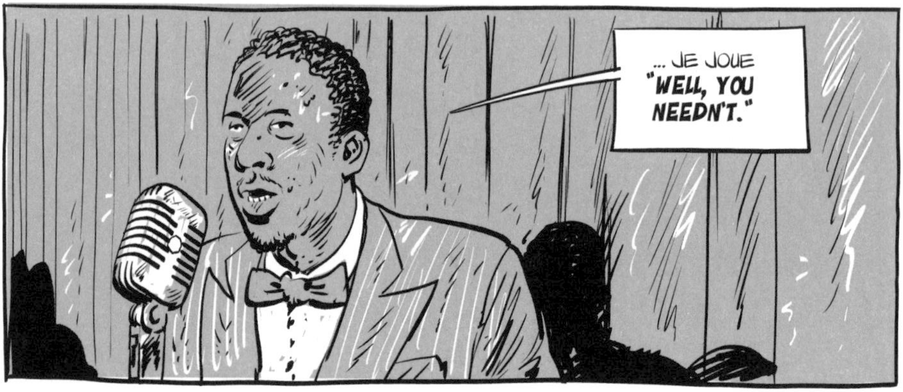
... JE JOUE "WELL, YOU NEEDN'T."

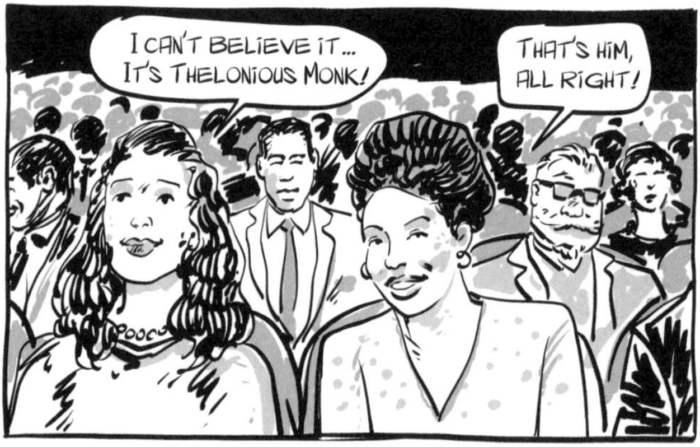
I CAN'T BELIEVE IT... IT'S THELONIOUS MONK!
THAT'S HIM, ALL RIGHT!

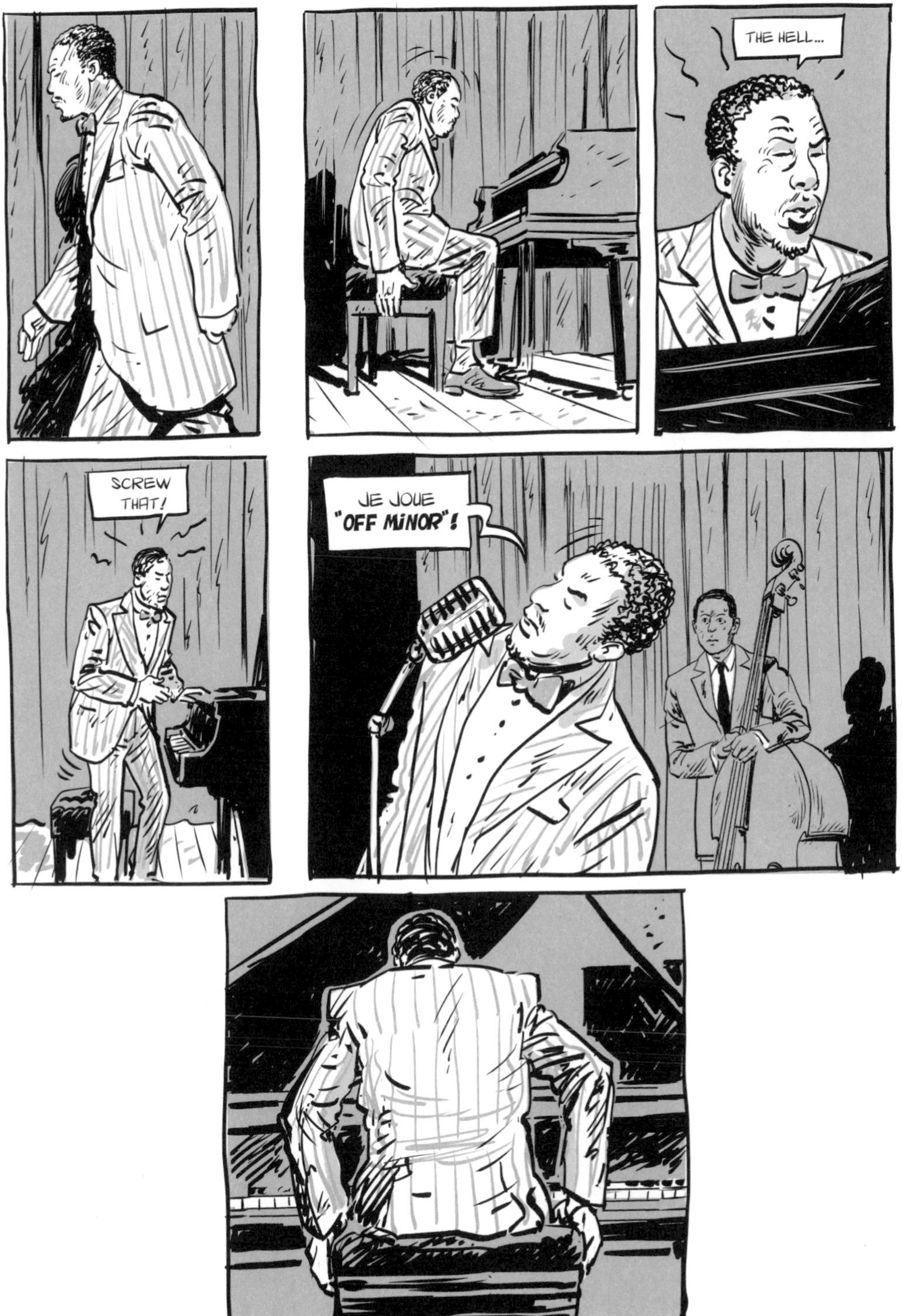
THE HELL...
SCREW THAT!
JE JOUE "OFF MINOR"!

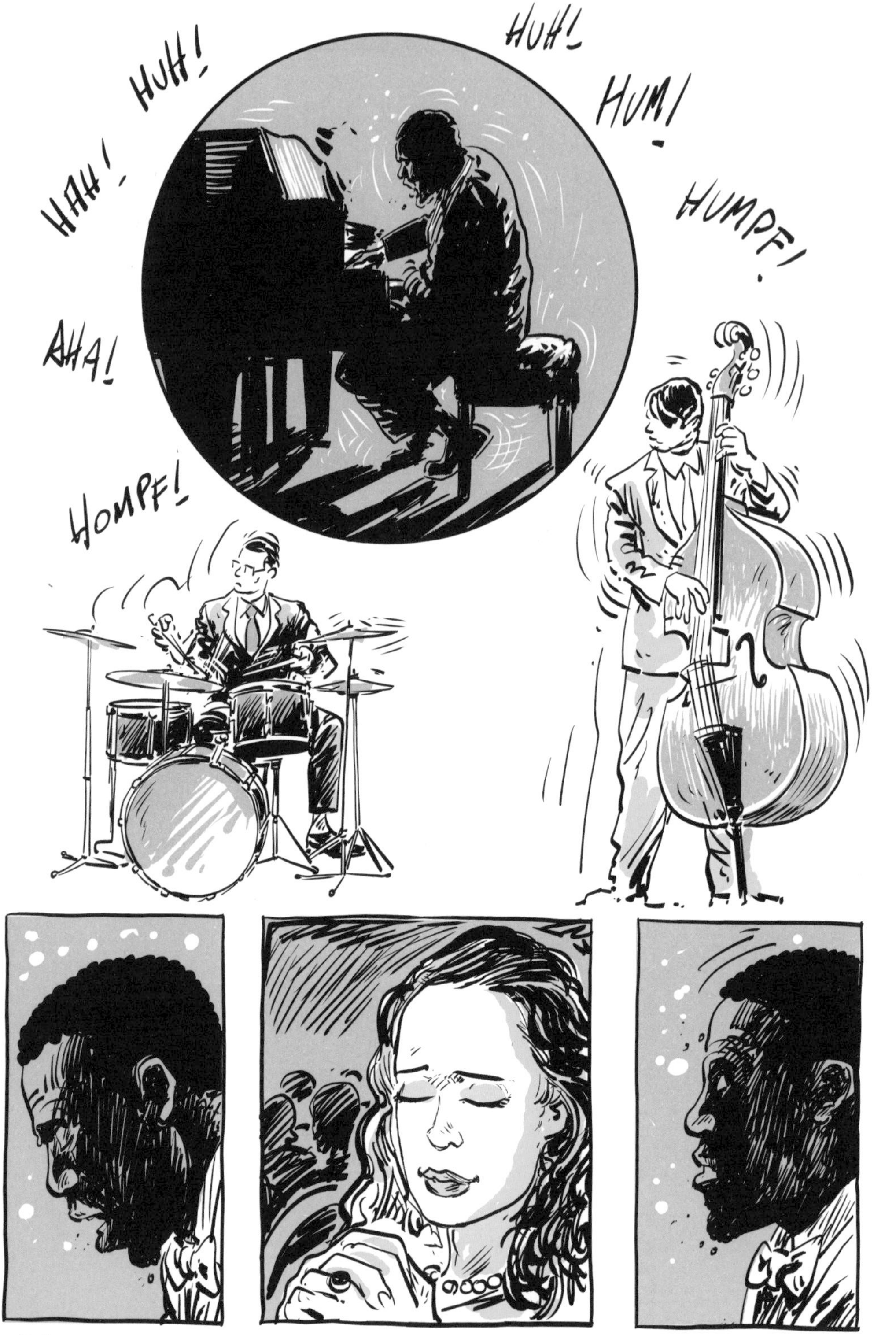
HAH!
HUH!
HUH!
HUM!
HUMPF!
AHA!
HOMPF!

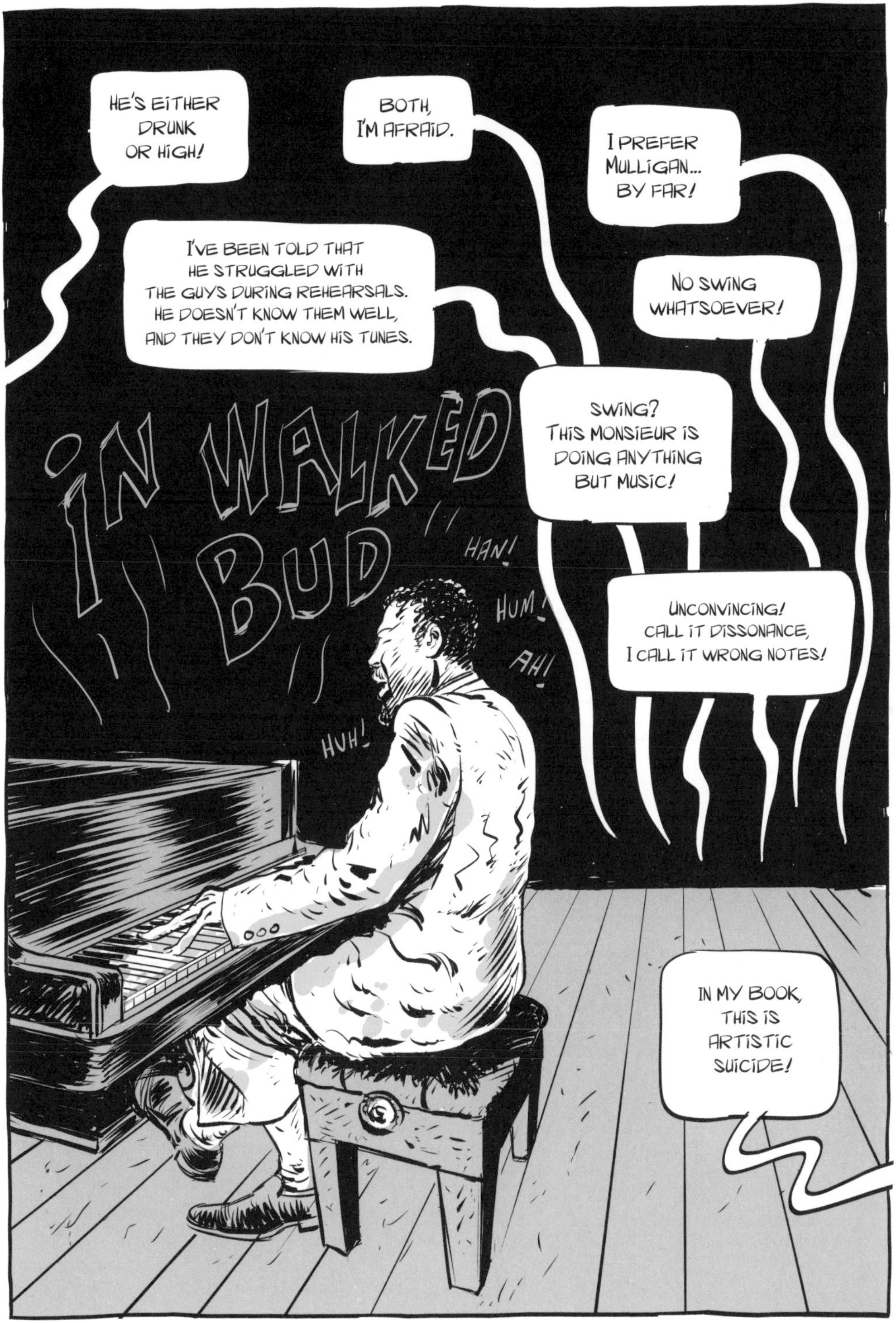
HE'S EITHER DRUNK OR HIGH!
BOTH, I'M AFRAID.
I PREFER MULLIGAN... BY FAR!
I'VE BEEN TOLD THAT HE STRUGGLED WITH THE GUYS DURING REHEARSALS. HE DOESN'T KNOW THEM WELL, AND THEY DON'T KNOW HIS TUNES.
NO SWING WHATSOEVER!
SWING? THIS MONSIEUR IS DOING ANYTHING BUT MUSIC!
IN WALKED BUD
HAN!
HUM!
AH!
HUH!
UNCONVINCING! CALL IT DISSONANCE, I CALL IT WRONG NOTES!
IN MY BOOK, THIS IS ARTISTIC SUICIDE!

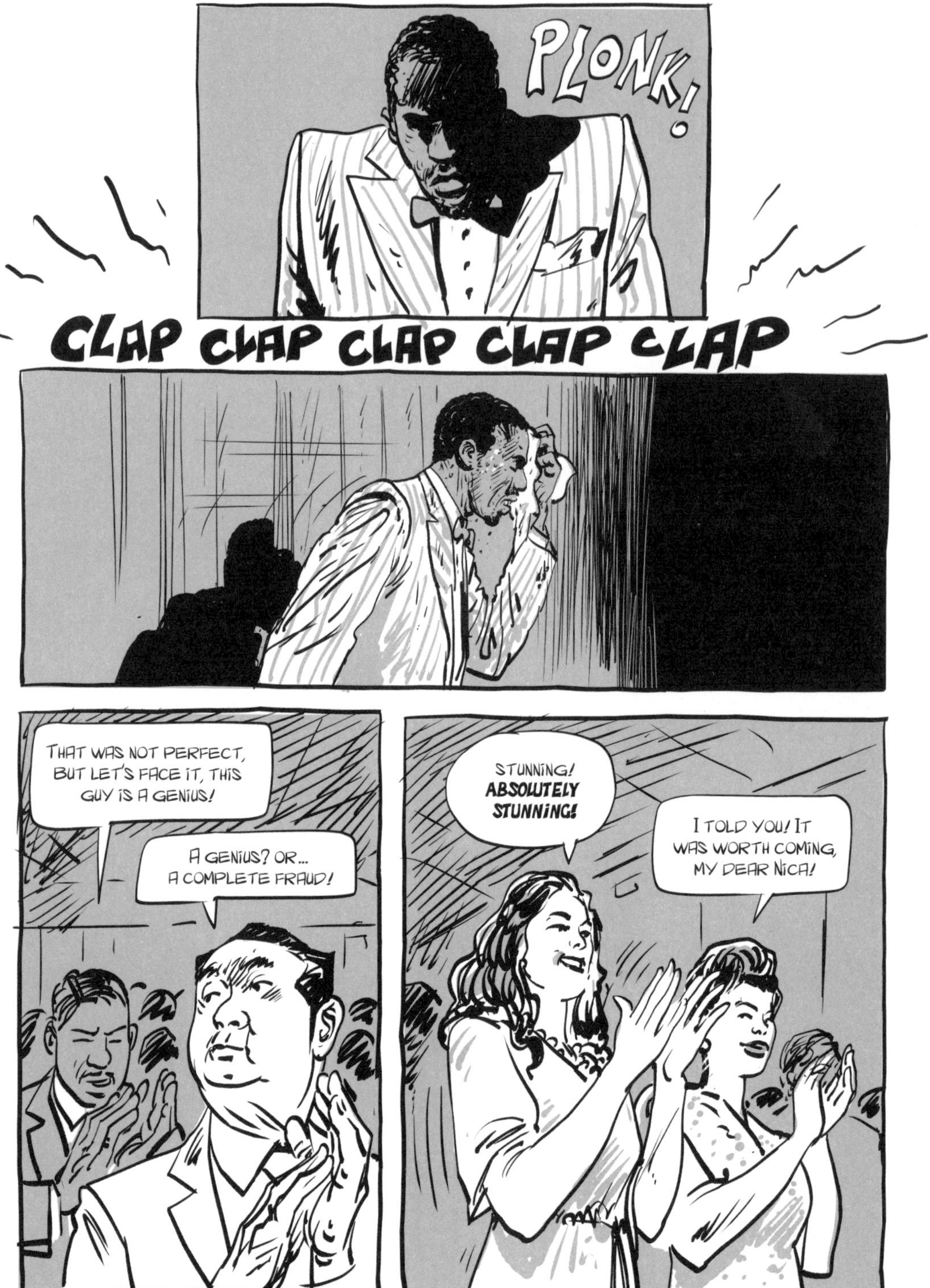
PLONK!
CLAP CLAP CLAP CLAP CLAP
THAT WAS NOT PERFECT, BUT LET'S FACE IT, THIS GUY IS A GENIUS!
A GENIUS? OR... A COMPLETE FRAUD!
STUNNING! ABSOLUTELY STUNNING!
I TOLD YOU! IT WAS WORTH COMING, MY DEAR NICA!

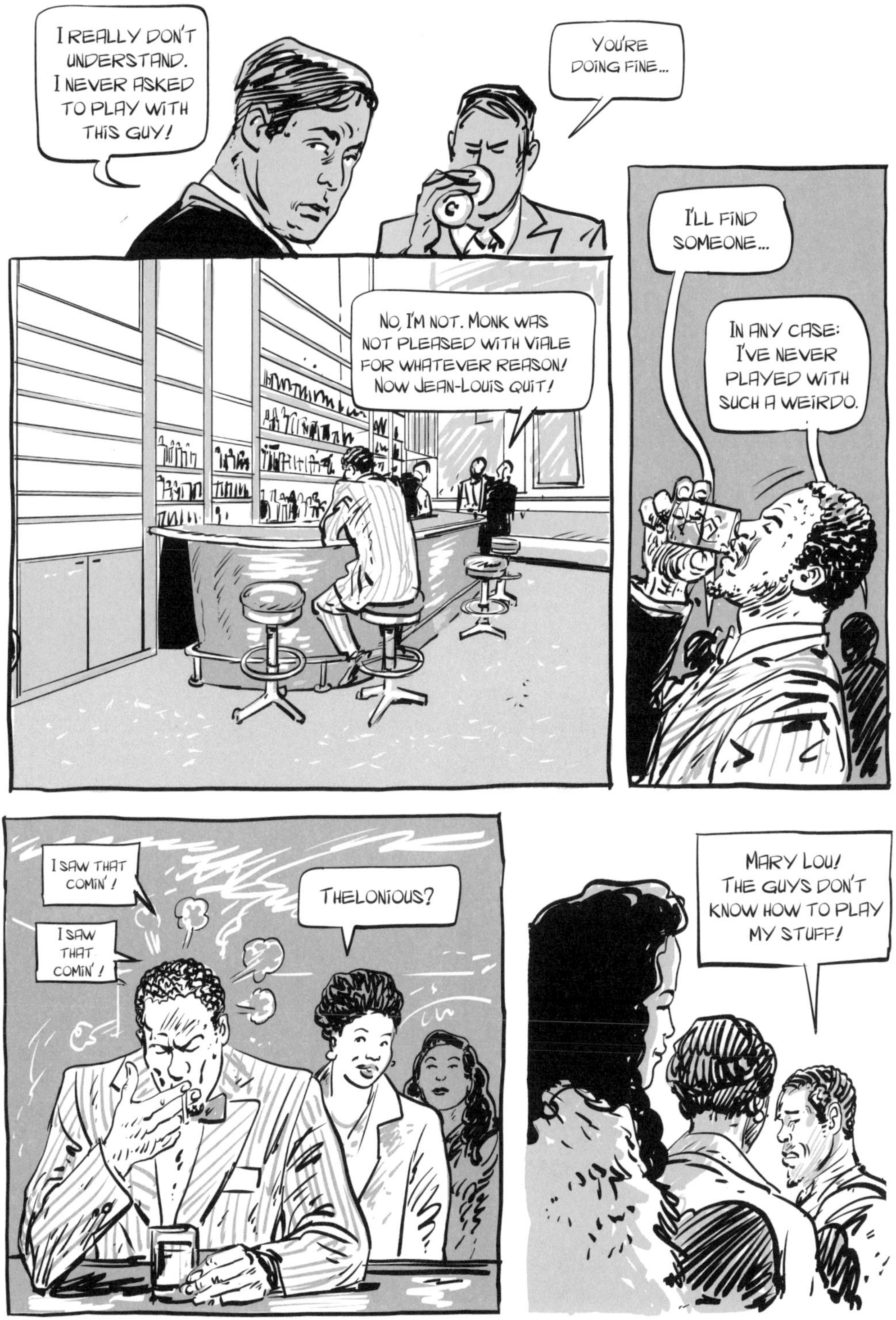
I REALLY DON'T UNDERSTAND. I NEVER ASKED TO PLAY WITH THIS GUY!
YOU'RE DOING FINE...
NO, I'M NOT. MONK WAS NOT PLEASED WITH VIALE FOR WHATEVER REASON! NOW JEAN-LOUIS QUIT!
I'LL FIND SOMEONE...
IN ANY CASE: I'VE NEVER PLAYED WITH SUCH A WEIRDO.
I SAW THAT COMIN'!
I SAW THAT COMIN'!
THELONIOUS?
MARY LOU! THE GUYS DON'T KNOW HOW TO PLAY MY STUFF!

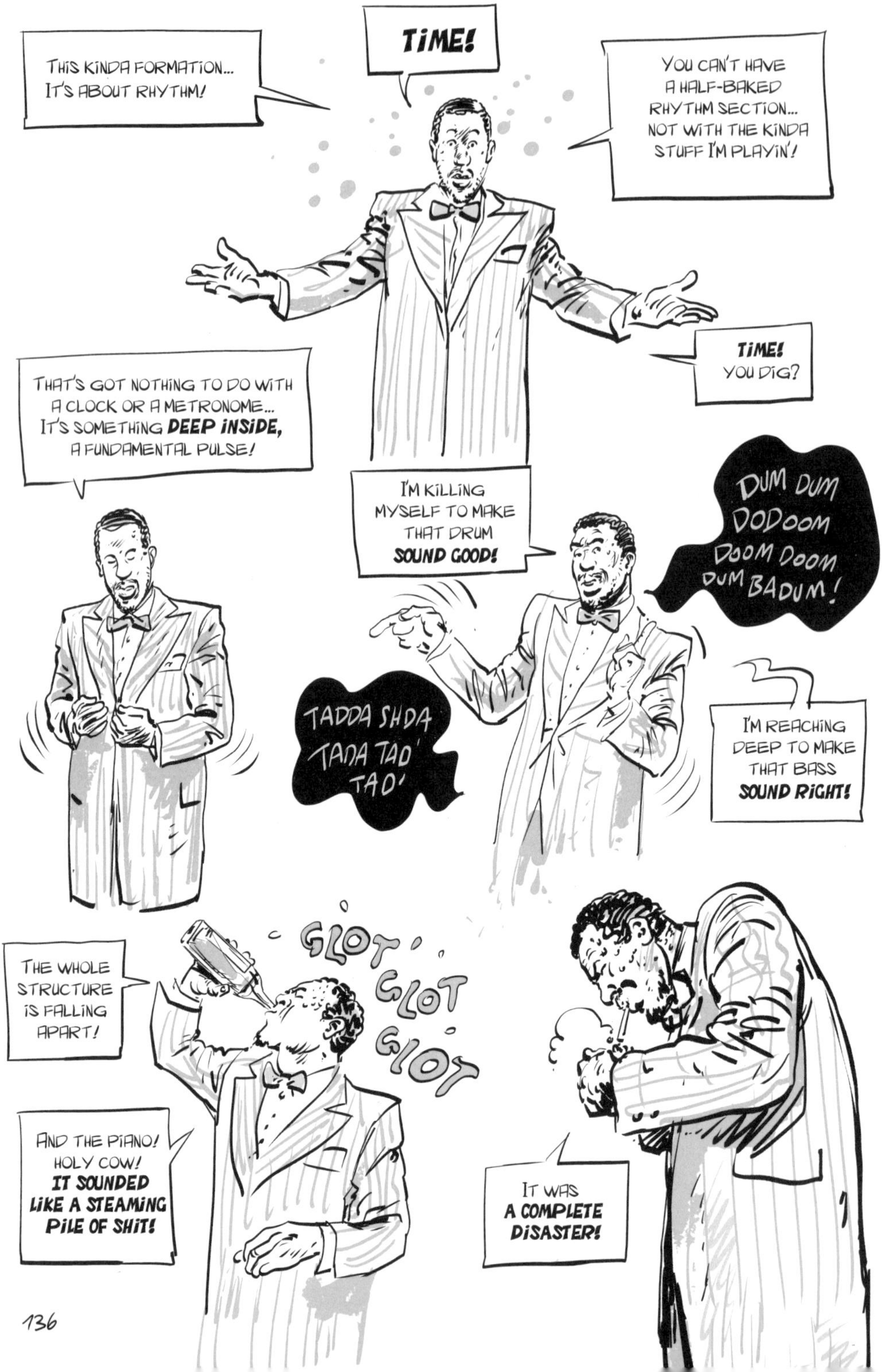
THIS KINDA FORMATION...
IT'S ABOUT RHYTHM!
TIME!
YOU CAN'T HAVE A HALF-BAKED RHYTHM SECTION... NOT WITH THE KINDA STUFF I'M PLAYIN'!
TIME! YOU DIG?
THAT'S GOT NOTHING TO DO WITH A CLOCK OR A METRONOME... IT'S SOMETHING DEEP INSIDE, A FUNDAMENTAL PULSE!
I'M KILLING MYSELF TO MAKE THAT DRUM SOUND GOOD!
DUM DUM DODOOM DOOM DOOM DUM BADUM!
TADDA SHDA TADA TAD' TAD'
I'M REACHING DEEP TO MAKE THAT BASS SOUND RIGHT!
THE WHOLE STRUCTURE IS FALLING APART!
GLOT GLOT GLOT
AND THE PIANO! HOLY COW! IT SOUNDED LIKE A STEAMING PILE OF SHIT!
IT WAS A COMPLETE DISASTER!

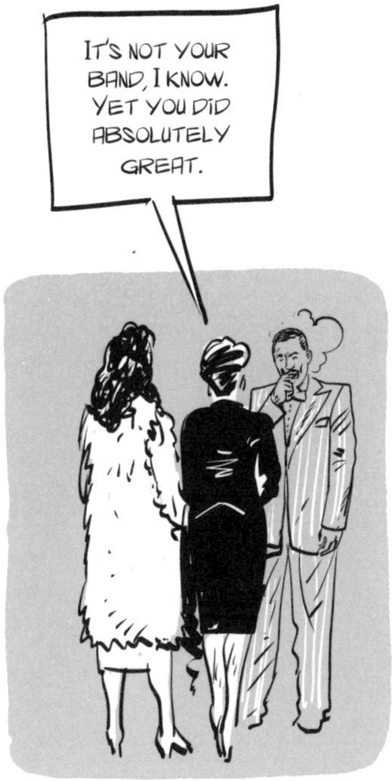
IT'S NOT YOUR BAND, I KNOW. YET YOU DID ABSOLUTELY GREAT.

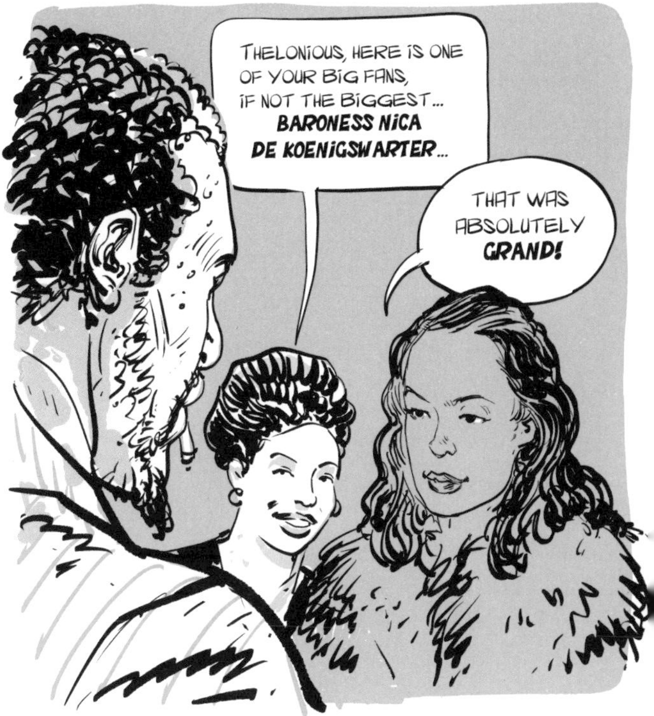
THELONIOUS, HERE IS ONE OF YOUR BIG FANS, IF NOT THE BIGGEST... BARONESS NICA DE KOENIGSWARTER...
THAT WAS ABSOLUTELY GRAND!

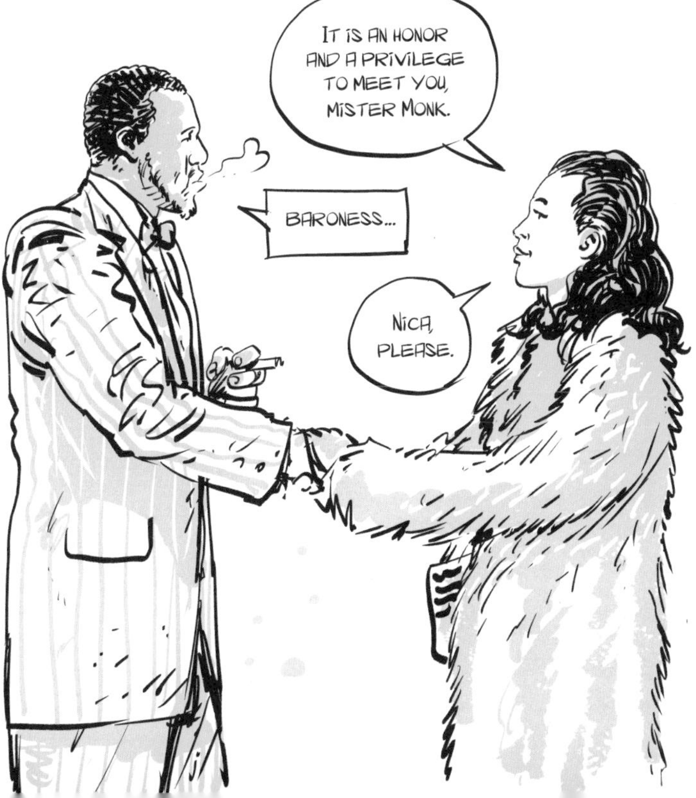
IT IS AN HONOR AND A PRIVILEGE TO MEET YOU, MISTER MONK.
BARONESS...
NICA, PLEASE.

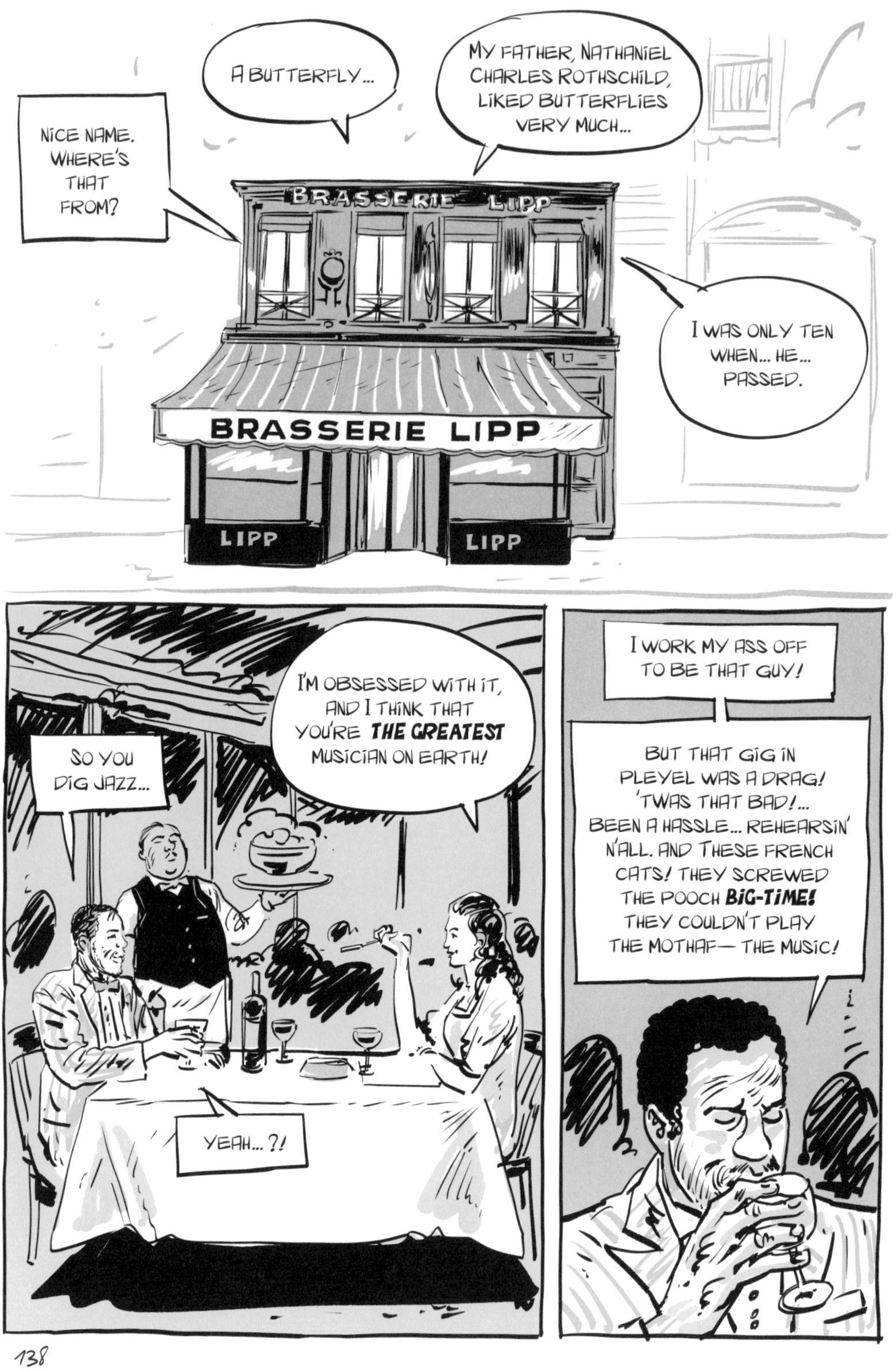
NICE NAME. WHERE'S THAT FROM?
A BUTTERFLY...
MY FATHER, NATHANIEL CHARLES ROTHSCHILD, LIKED BUTTERFLIES VERY MUCH...
BRASSERIE LIPP
BRASSERIE LIPP
LIPP
LIPP
I WAS ONLY TEN WHEN... HE... PASSED.
SO YOU DIG JAZZ...
I'M OBSESSED WITH IT, AND I THINK THAT YOU'RE **THE GREATEST** MUSICIAN ON EARTH!
YEAH...?!
I WORK MY ASS OFF TO BE THAT GUY!
BUT THAT GIG IN PLEYEL WAS A DRAG! 'TWAS THAT BAD!... BEEN A HASSLE... REHEARSIN' N'ALL. AND THESE FRENCH CATS! THEY SCREWED THE POOCH **BIG-TIME!** THEY COULDN'T PLAY THE MOTHAF— THE MUSIC!

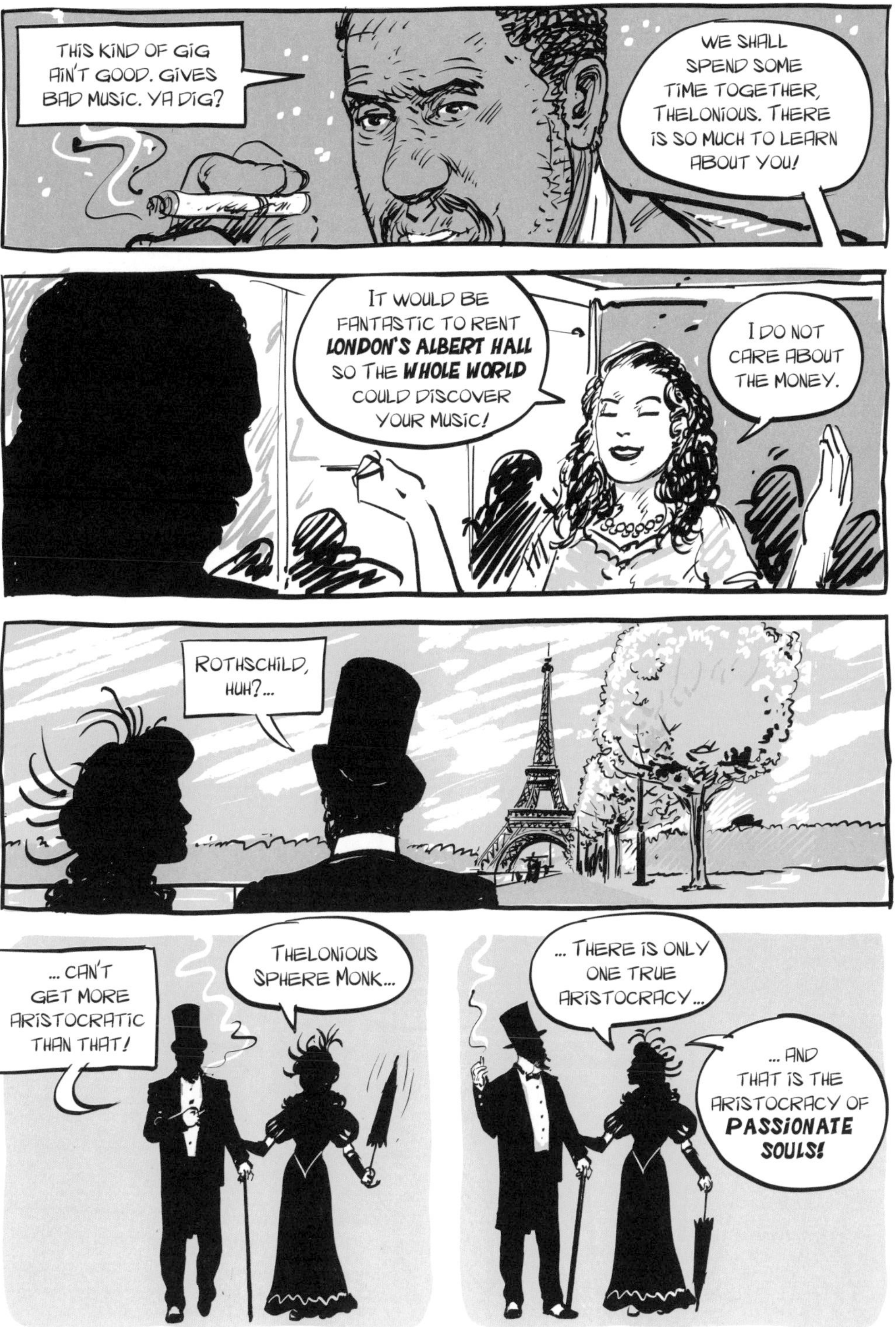
THIS KIND OF GIG AIN'T GOOD. GIVES BAD MUSIC. YA DIG?
WE SHALL SPEND SOME TIME TOGETHER, THELONIOUS. THERE IS SO MUCH TO LEARN ABOUT YOU!
IT WOULD BE FANTASTIC TO RENT **LONDON'S ALBERT HALL** SO THE **WHOLE WORLD** COULD DISCOVER YOUR MUSIC!
I DO NOT CARE ABOUT THE MONEY.
ROTHSCHILD, HUH?...
... CAN'T GET MORE ARISTOCRATIC THAN THAT!
THELONIOUS SPHERE MONK...
... THERE IS ONLY ONE TRUE ARISTOCRACY...
... AND THAT IS THE ARISTOCRACY OF **PASSIONATE SOULS!**

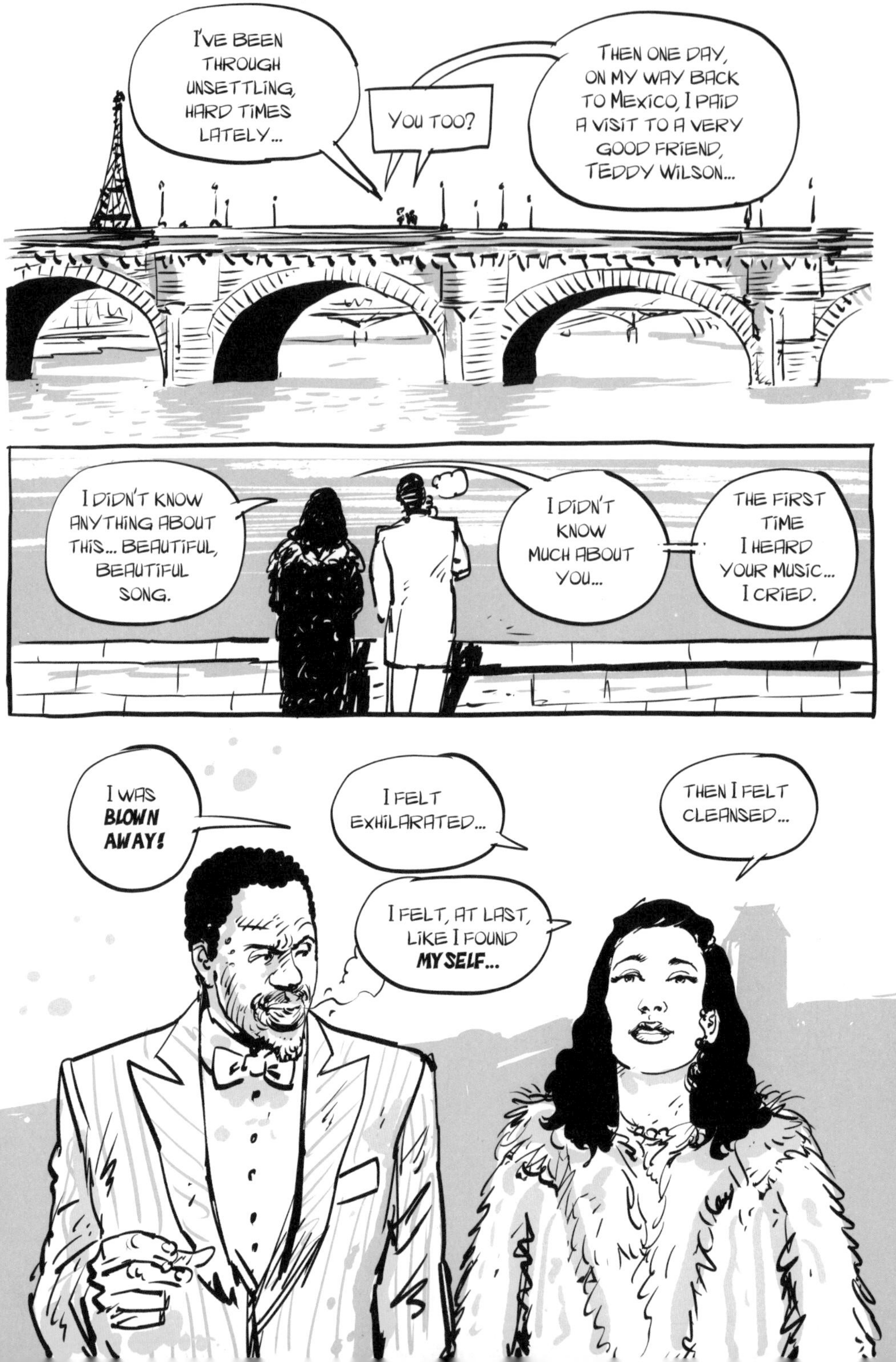
I'VE BEEN THROUGH UNSETTLING, HARD TIMES LATELY...
YOU TOO?
THEN ONE DAY, ON MY WAY BACK TO MEXICO, I PAID A VISIT TO A VERY GOOD FRIEND, TEDDY WILSON...
I DIDN'T KNOW ANYTHING ABOUT THIS... BEAUTIFUL, BEAUTIFUL SONG.
I DIDN'T KNOW MUCH ABOUT YOU...
THE FIRST TIME I HEARD YOUR MUSIC... I CRIED.
I WAS **BLOWN AWAY!**
I FELT EXHILARATED...
THEN I FELT CLEANSED...
I FELT, AT LAST, LIKE I FOUND **MYSELF...**

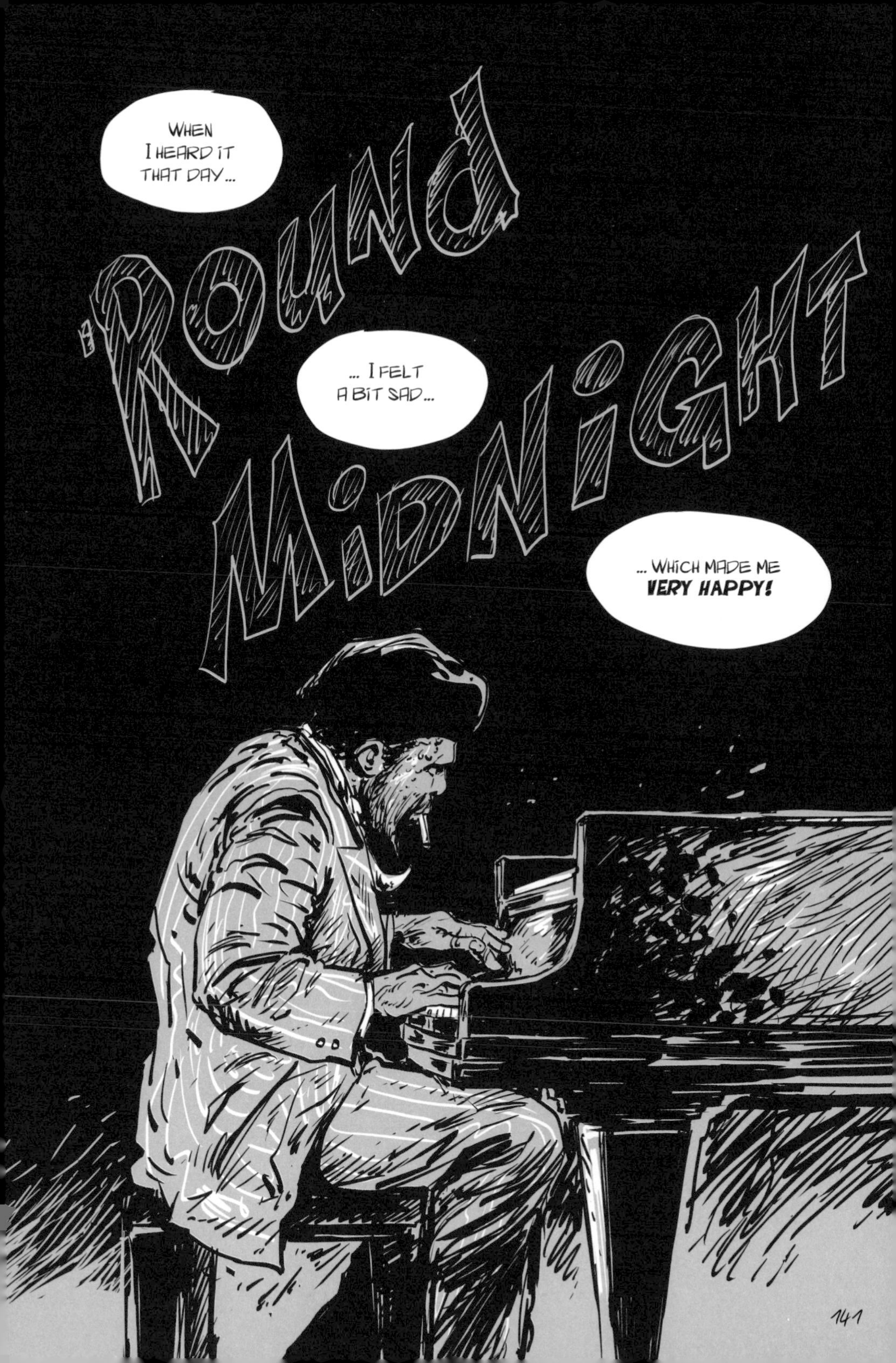
WHEN I HEARD IT THAT DAY...
'ROUND MIDNIGHT
... I FELT A BIT SAD...
... WHICH MADE ME VERY HAPPY!

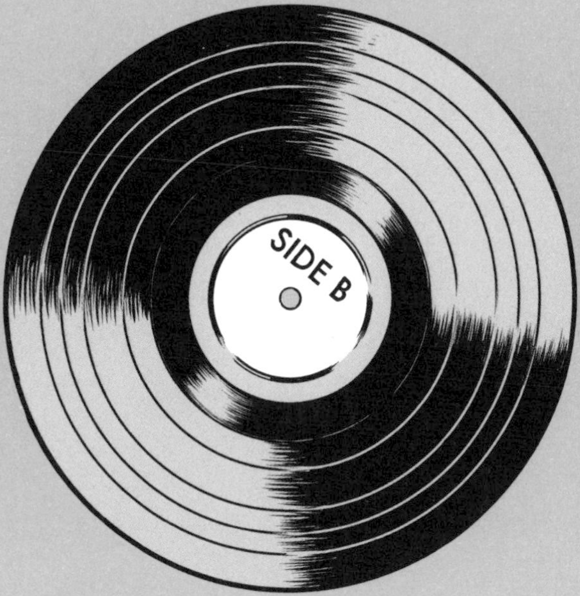
SIDE B

PANNONIOUS

Dear Mary Lou!

A **LOT OF THINGS** have been happening since I moved to New York.

I was thinking about it for a LOONG TIME! (In fact, as far as I can remember, I've pursued ABSOLUTE FREEDOM!!!), besides, I could no longer stand that French embassy in Mexico, the palm trees, the heat, **EVERYTHING** about it! This was such an easy move to make!

As Thelonious. put it: **I FLEW!**

Years later, my life was a real **MESS**. (My marriage, that is.) The whole business went sour since Jules and I got back from the war. We won it together, but I guess we've lost **THE MOST IMPORTANT BATTLE!**!!!

I was **STIFLED** // by the conventions of diplomatic life. Jules always found **TOTAL FULFILLMENT** in public service; where everything was meticulously well ordered, strictly scheduled. He kept acting like a **COMMANDING OFFICER!!!** I tried to get along for the sake of the kids...

You know what **SAVED ME?**??

MUSIC !!!

147

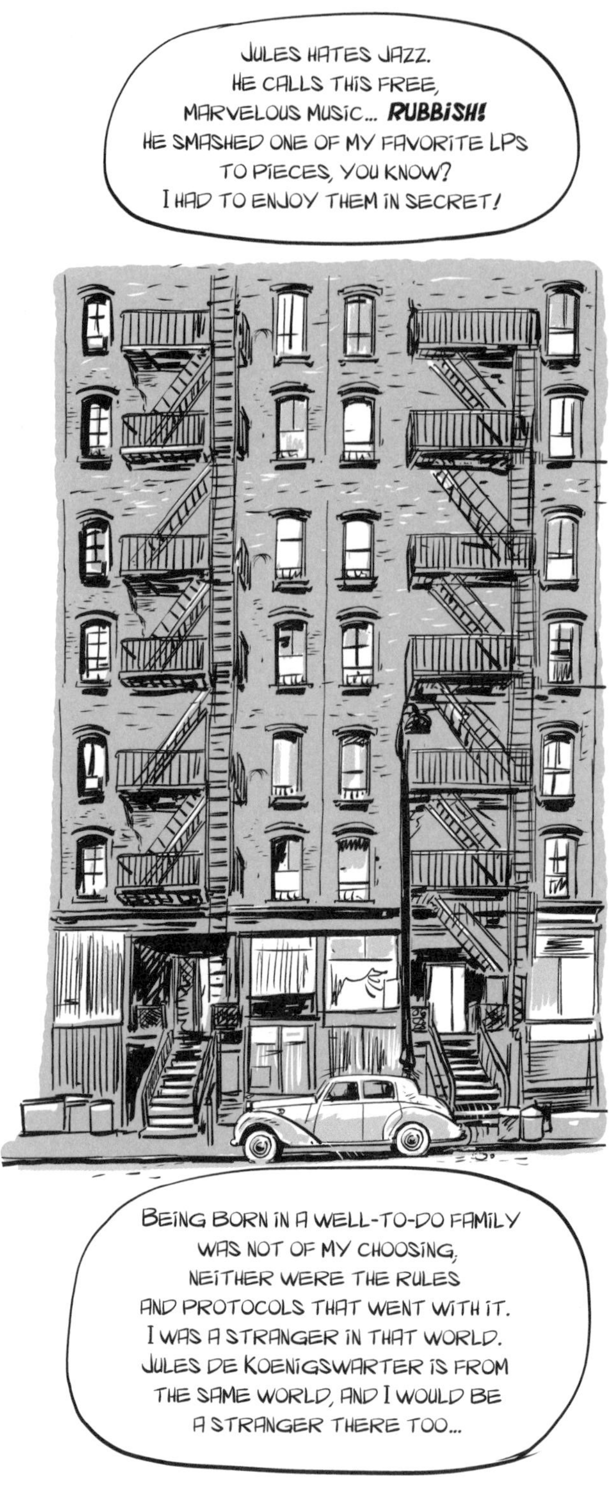
JULES HATES JAZZ. HE CALLS THIS FREE, MARVELOUS MUSIC... **RUBBISH!** HE SMASHED ONE OF MY FAVORITE LPS TO PIECES, YOU KNOW? I HAD TO ENJOY THEM IN SECRET!
BEING BORN IN A WELL-TO-DO FAMILY WAS NOT OF MY CHOOSING, NEITHER WERE THE RULES AND PROTOCOLS THAT WENT WITH IT. I WAS A STRANGER IN THAT WORLD. JULES DE KOENIGSWARTER IS FROM THE SAME WORLD, AND I WOULD BE A STRANGER THERE TOO...

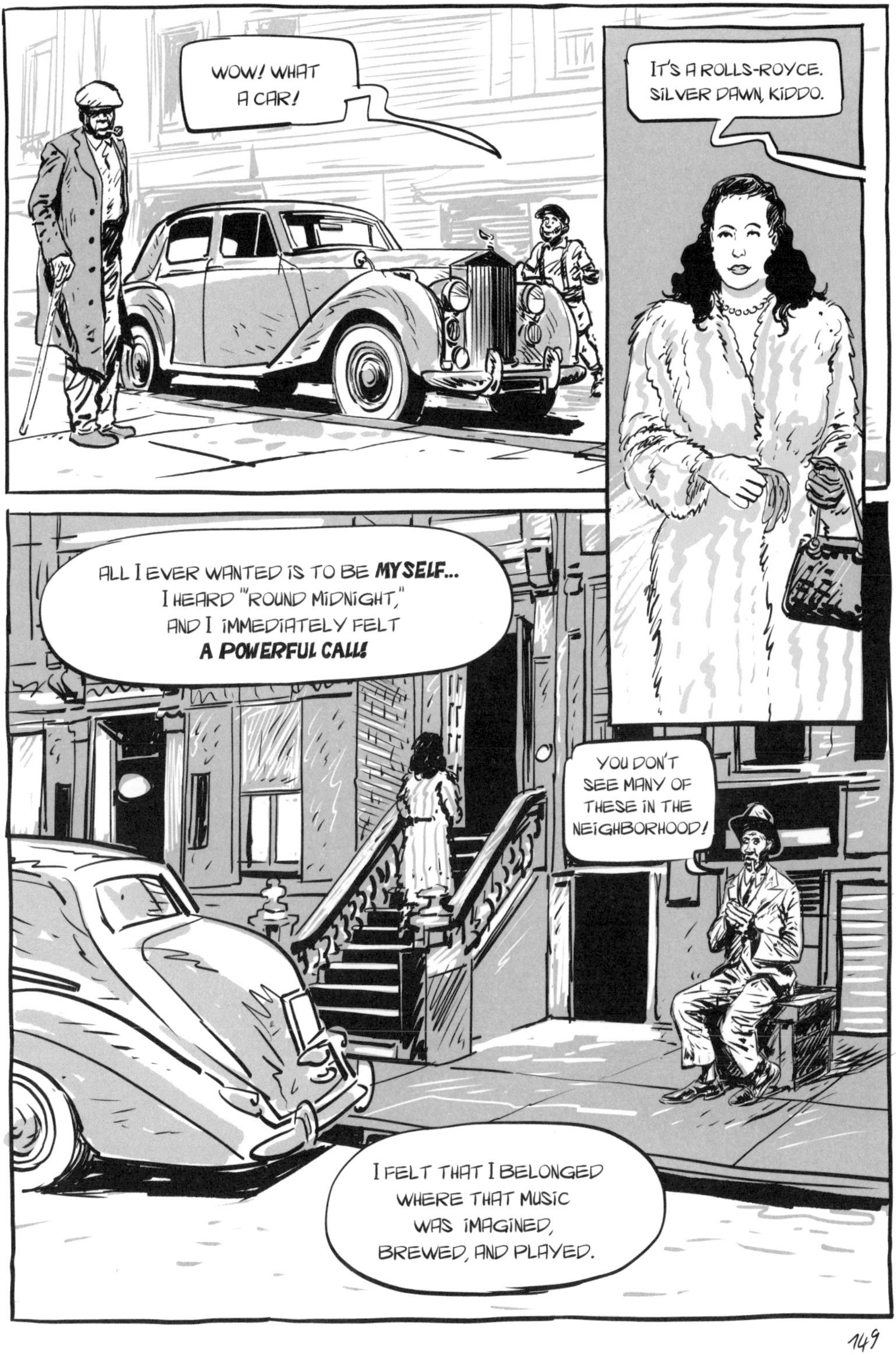
WOW! WHAT A CAR!
IT'S A ROLLS-ROYCE. SILVER DAWN, KIDDO.
ALL I EVER WANTED IS TO BE **MYSELF...** I HEARD "ROUND MIDNIGHT," AND I IMMEDIATELY FELT **A POWERFUL CALL!**
YOU DON'T SEE MANY OF THESE IN THE NEIGHBORHOOD!
I FELT THAT I BELONGED WHERE THAT MUSIC WAS IMAGINED, BREWED, AND PLAYED.

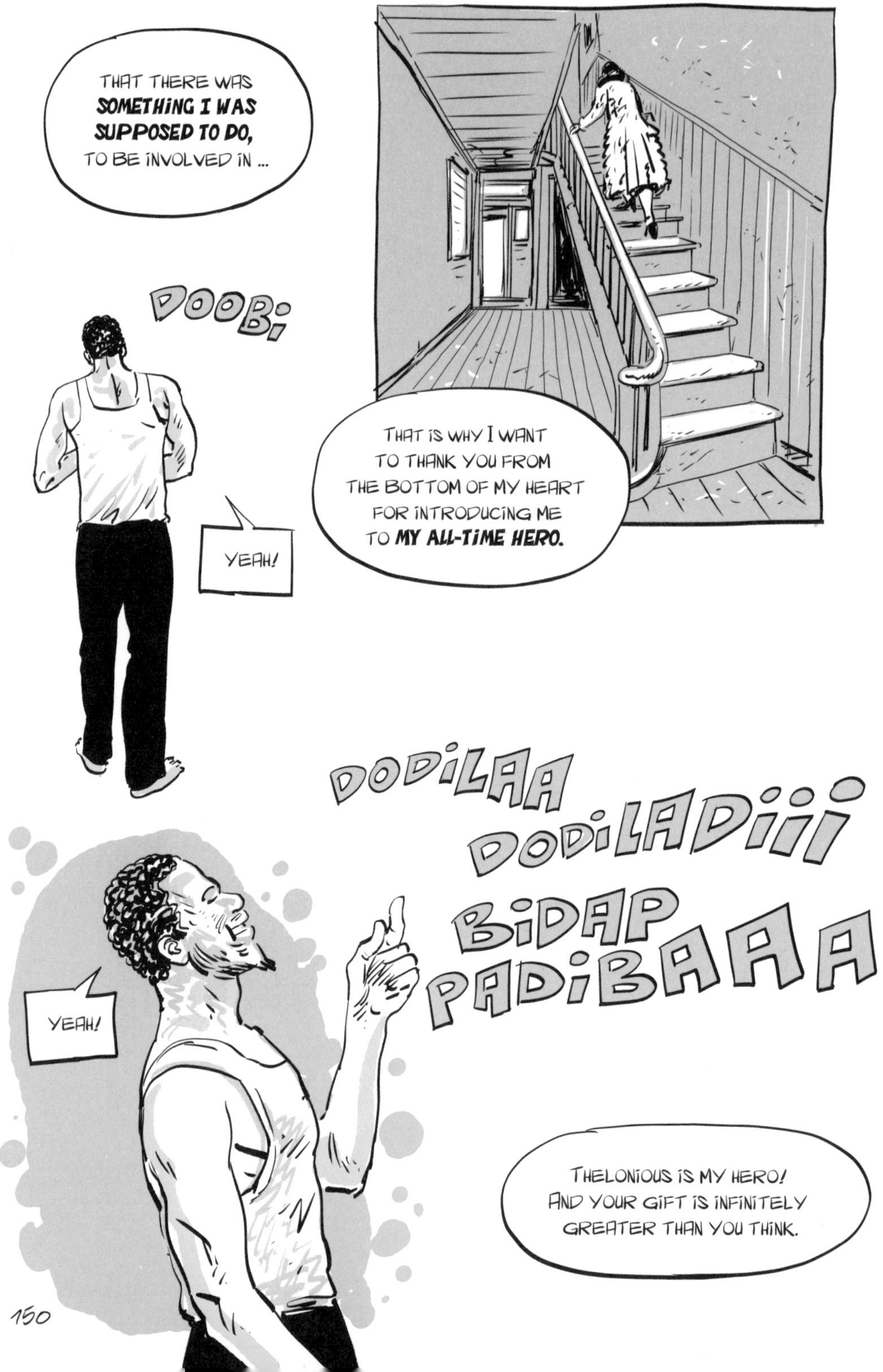
THAT THERE WAS **SOMETHING I WAS SUPPOSED TO DO,** TO BE INVOLVED IN ...
DOOBi
THAT IS WHY I WANT TO THANK YOU FROM THE BOTTOM OF MY HEART FOR INTRODUCING ME TO **MY ALL-TIME HERO.**
YEAH!
DODiLAA DODiLADiii BiDAP PADiBAAA
YEAH!
THELONIOUS IS MY HERO! AND YOUR GIFT IS INFINITELY GREATER THAN YOU THINK.

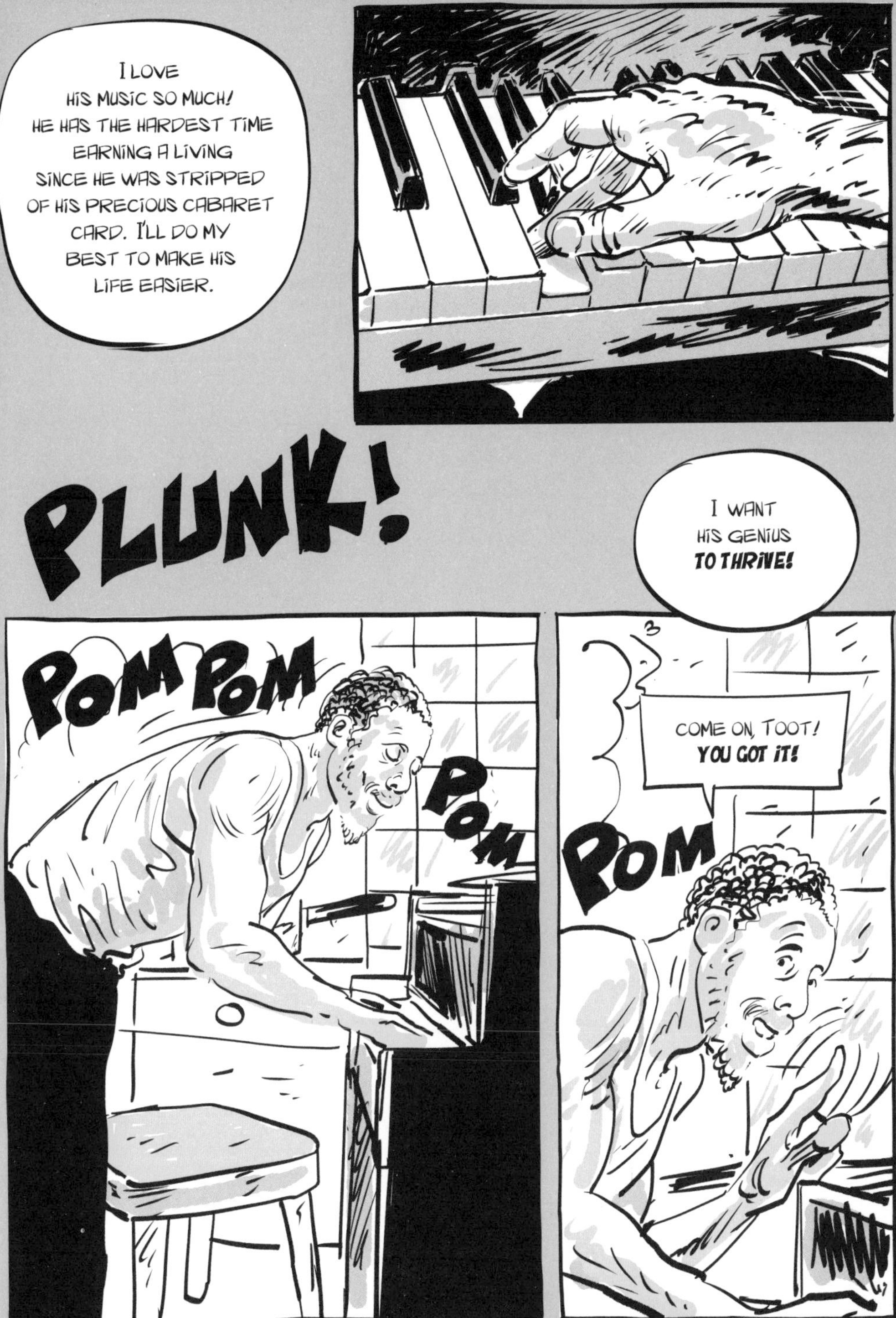
I LOVE HIS MUSIC SO MUCH! HE HAS THE HARDEST TIME EARNING A LIVING SINCE HE WAS STRIPPED OF HIS PRECIOUS CABARET CARD. I'LL DO MY BEST TO MAKE HIS LIFE EASIER.
PLUNK!
I WANT HIS GENIUS TO THRIVE!
POM POM
POM
POM
COME ON, TOOT! YOU GOT IT!
POM

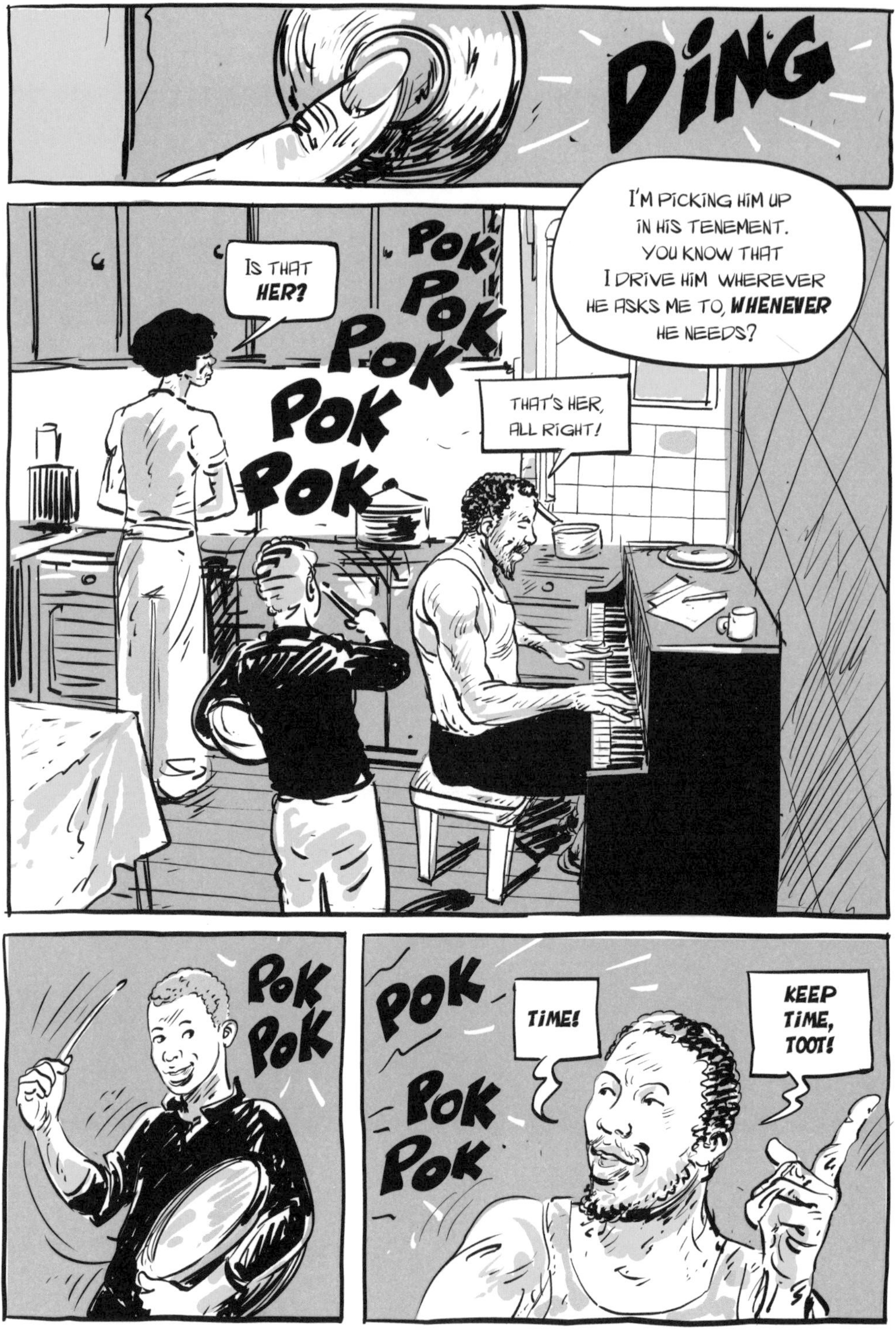
DING
IS THAT **HER?**
POK POK POK POK POK
I'M PICKING HIM UP IN HIS TENEMENT. YOU KNOW THAT I DRIVE HIM WHEREVER HE ASKS ME TO, **WHENEVER** HE NEEDS?
THAT'S HER, ALL RIGHT!
POK POK
POK POK POK
TIME!
KEEP TIME, TOOT!

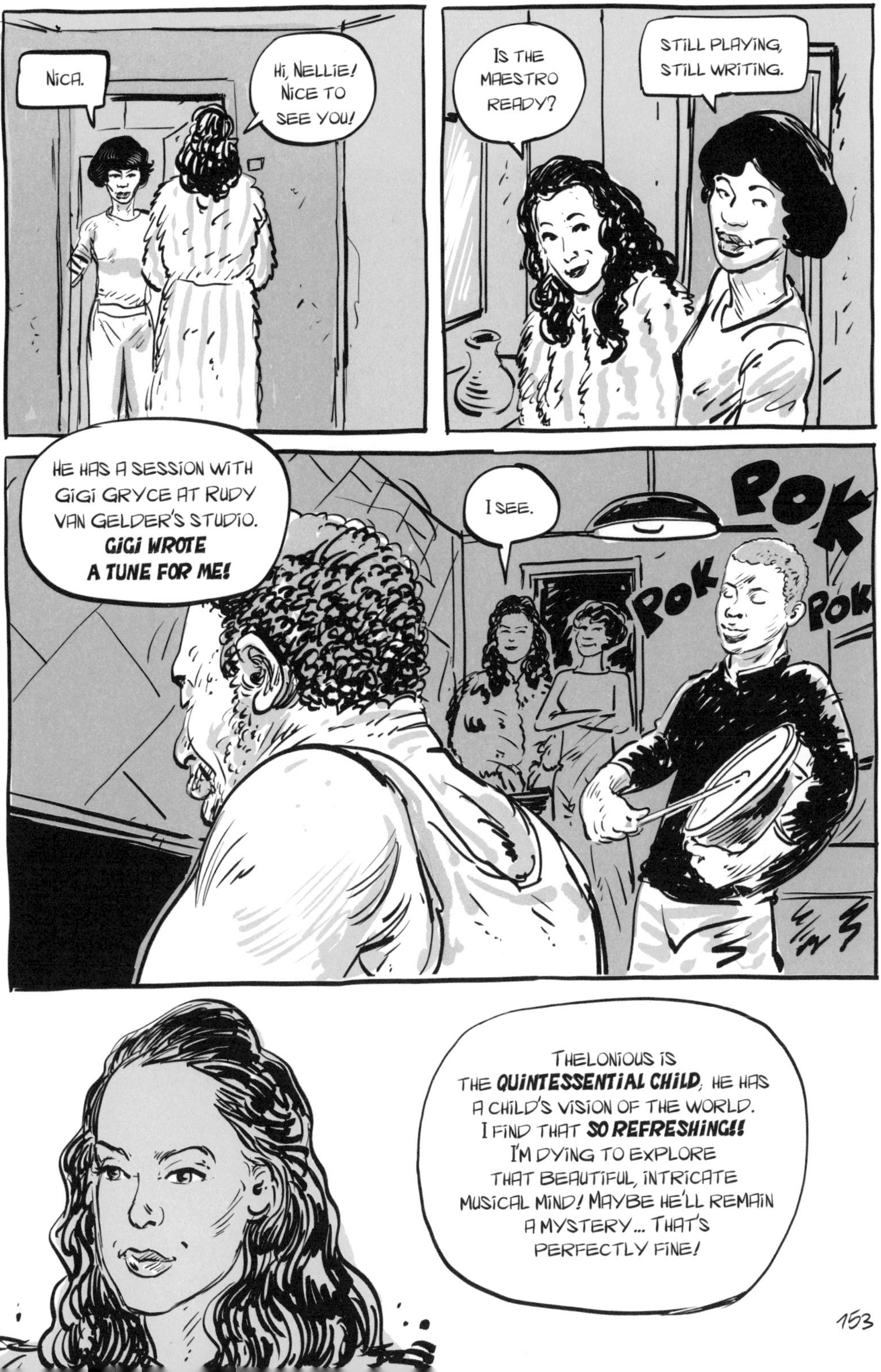
Nica.
Hi, Nellie! Nice to see you!
Is the maestro ready?
Still playing, still writing.
He has a session with Gigi Gryce at Rudy Van Gelder's studio. **Gigi wrote a tune for me!**
I see.
POK
POK
POK
Thelonious is the **QUINTESSENTIAL CHILD**; he has a child's vision of the world. I find that **SO REFRESHING!!** I'm dying to explore that beautiful, intricate musical mind! Maybe he'll remain a mystery... That's perfectly fine!

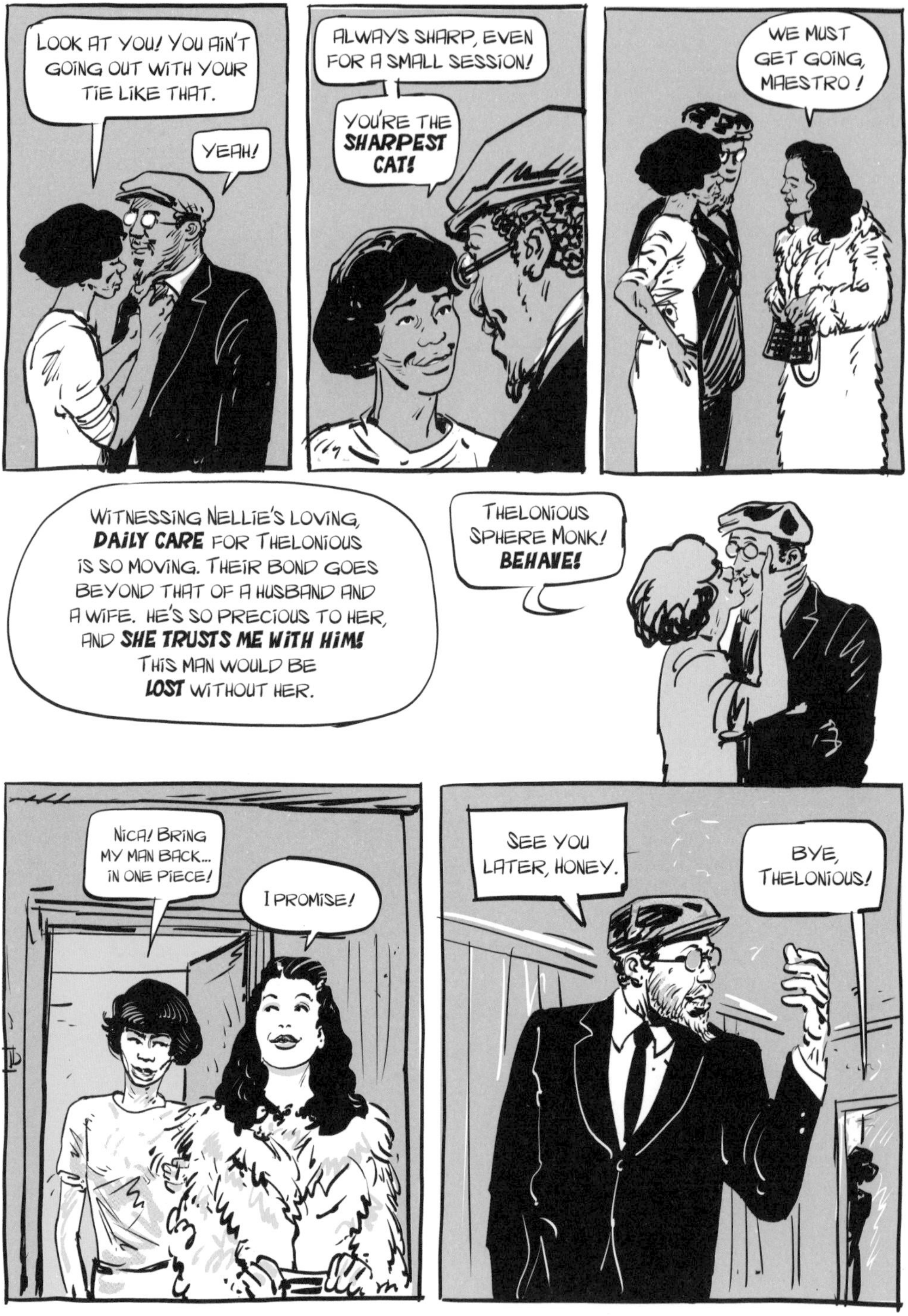

LOOK AT YOU! YOU AIN'T GOING OUT WITH YOUR TIE LIKE THAT.
YEAH!
ALWAYS SHARP, EVEN FOR A SMALL SESSION!
YOU'RE THE **SHARPEST CAT!**
WE MUST GET GOING, MAESTRO!
WITNESSING NELLIE'S LOVING, **DAILY CARE** FOR THELONIOUS IS SO MOVING. THEIR BOND GOES BEYOND THAT OF A HUSBAND AND A WIFE. HE'S SO PRECIOUS TO HER, AND **SHE TRUSTS ME WITH HIM!** THIS MAN WOULD BE **LOST** WITHOUT HER.
THELONIOUS SPHERE MONK! **BEHAVE!**
NICA! BRING MY MAN BACK... IN ONE PIECE!
I PROMISE!
SEE YOU LATER, HONEY.
BYE, THELONIOUS!

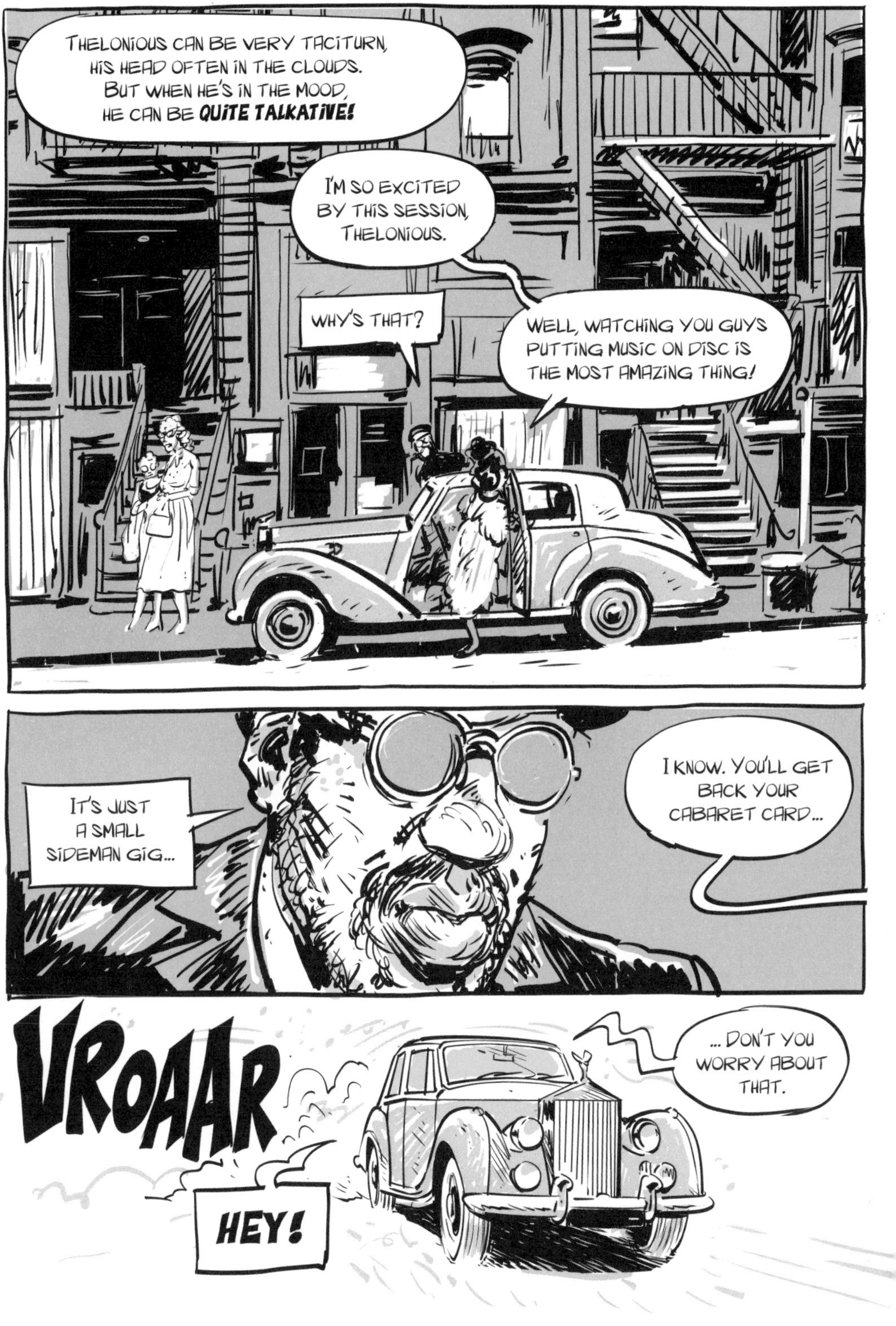
THELONIOUS CAN BE VERY TACITURN, HIS HEAD OFTEN IN THE CLOUDS. BUT WHEN HE'S IN THE MOOD, HE CAN BE **QUITE TALKATIVE!**
I'M SO EXCITED BY THIS SESSION, THELONIOUS.
WHY'S THAT?
WELL, WATCHING YOU GUYS PUTTING MUSIC ON DISC IS THE MOST AMAZING THING!
IT'S JUST A SMALL SIDEMAN GIG...
I KNOW. YOU'LL GET BACK YOUR CABARET CARD...
VROAAR
...DON'T YOU WORRY ABOUT THAT.
HEY!

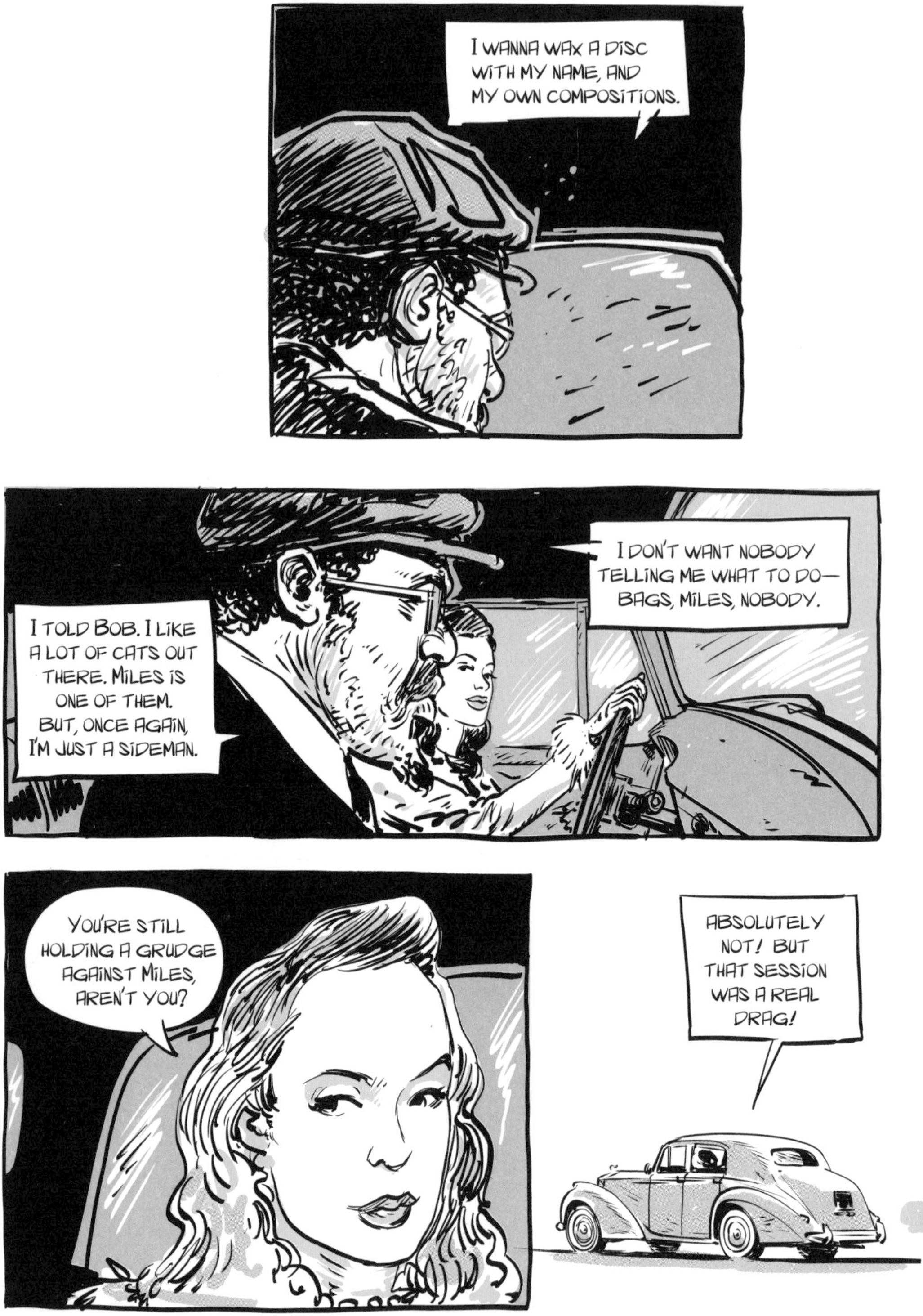
I WANNA WAX A DISC WITH MY NAME, AND MY OWN COMPOSITIONS.
I DON'T WANT NOBODY TELLING ME WHAT TO DO—BAGS, MILES, NOBODY.
I TOLD BOB. I LIKE A LOT OF CATS OUT THERE. MILES IS ONE OF THEM. BUT, ONCE AGAIN, I'M JUST A SIDEMAN.
YOU'RE STILL HOLDING A GRUDGE AGAINST MILES, AREN'T YOU?
ABSOLUTELY NOT! BUT THAT SESSION WAS A REAL DRAG!

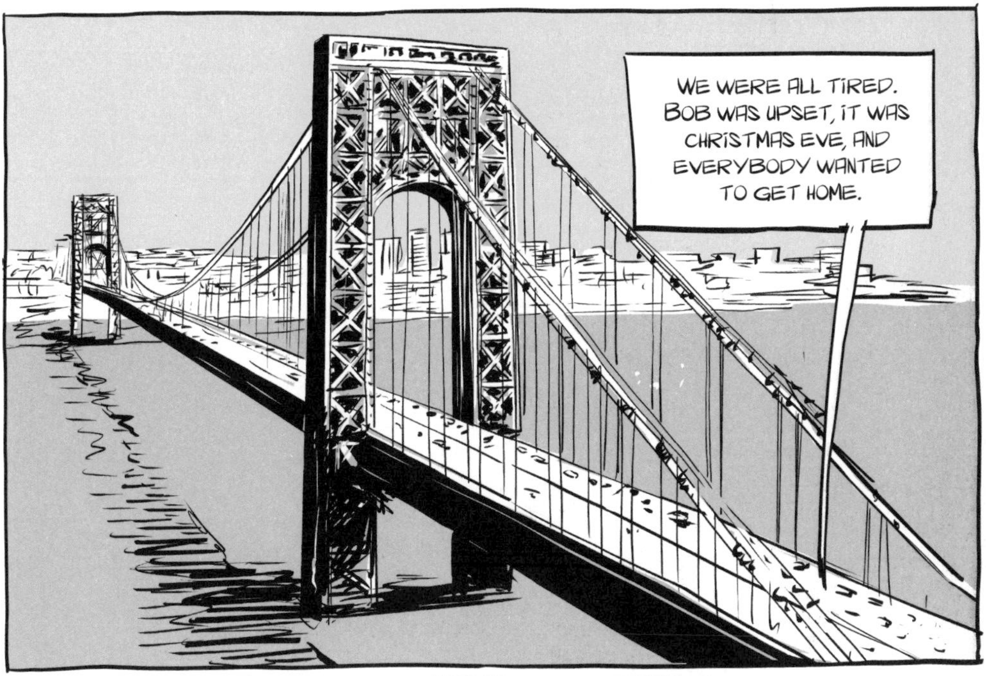
WE WERE ALL TIRED. BOB WAS UPSET, IT WAS CHRISTMAS EVE, AND EVERYBODY WANTED TO GET HOME.

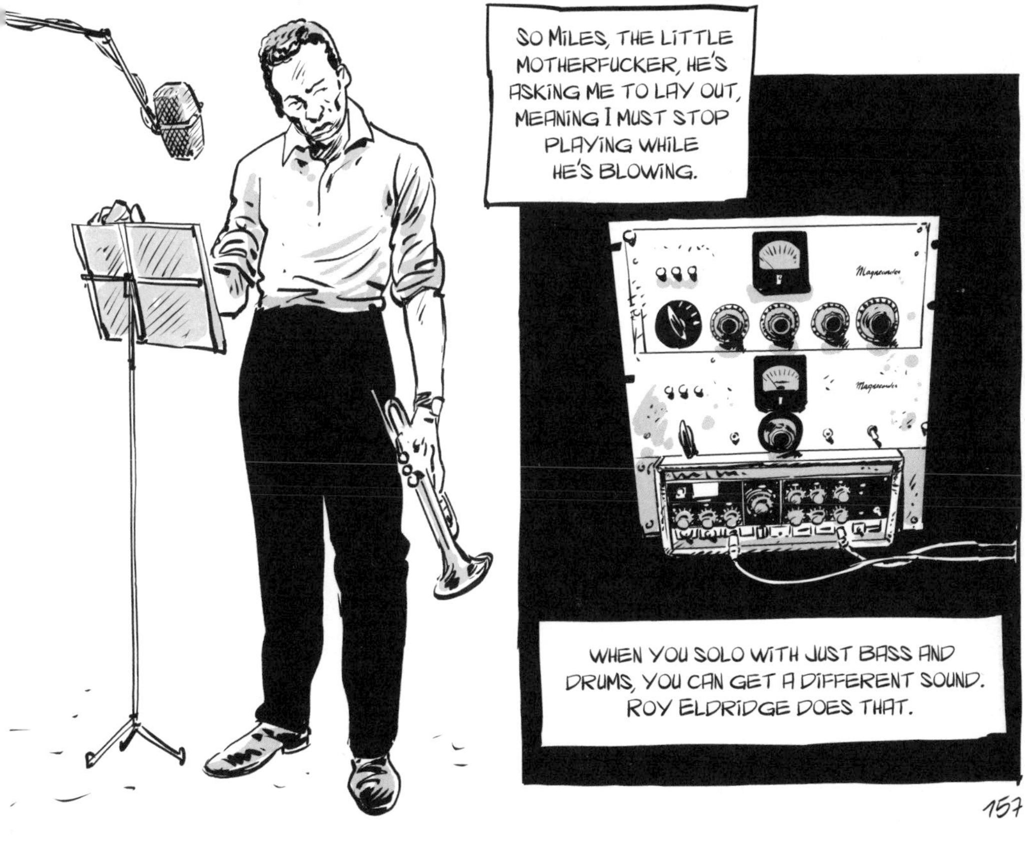
SO MILES, THE LITTLE MOTHERFUCKER, HE'S ASKING ME TO LAY OUT, MEANING I MUST STOP PLAYING WHILE HE'S BLOWING.
WHEN YOU SOLO WITH JUST BASS AND DRUMS, YOU CAN GET A DIFFERENT SOUND. ROY ELDRIDGE DOES THAT.

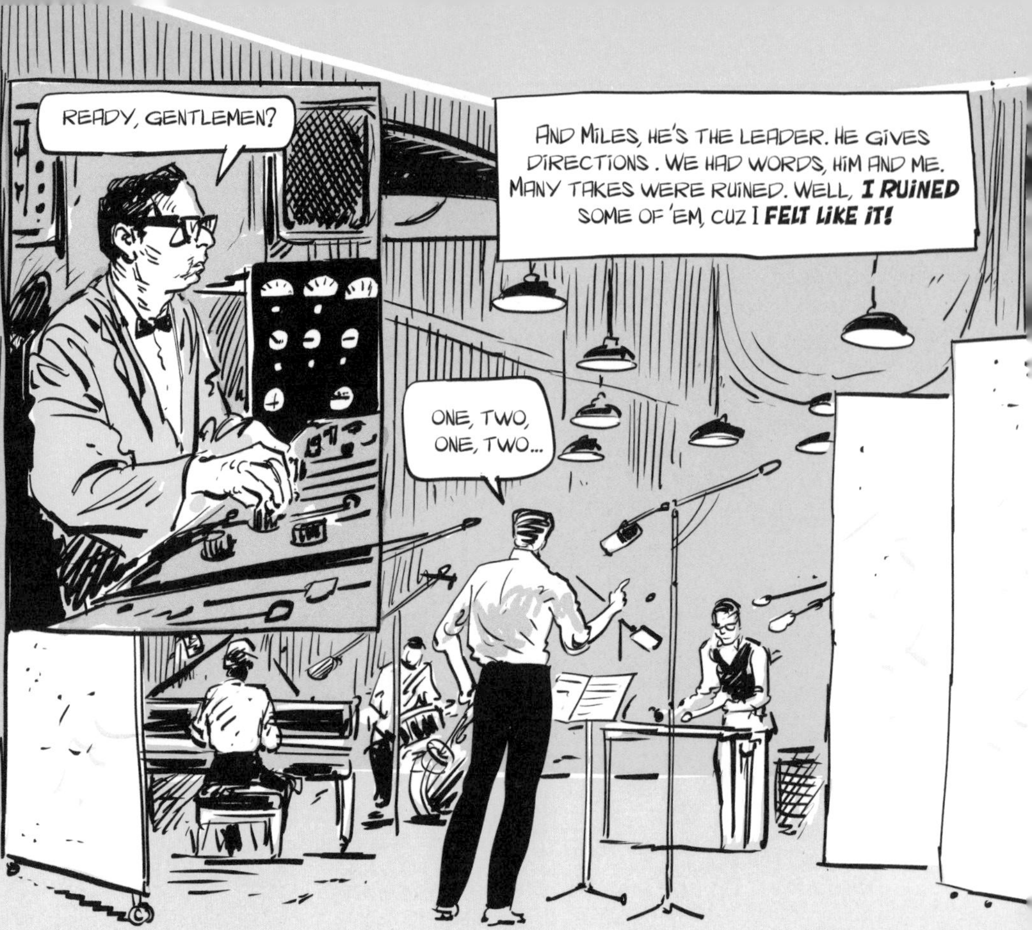
READY, GENTLEMEN?
AND MILES, HE'S THE LEADER. HE GIVES DIRECTIONS . WE HAD WORDS, HIM AND ME. MANY TAKES WERE RUINED. WELL, **I RUINED** SOME OF 'EM, CUZ I **FELT LIKE IT!**
ONE, TWO, ONE, TWO...

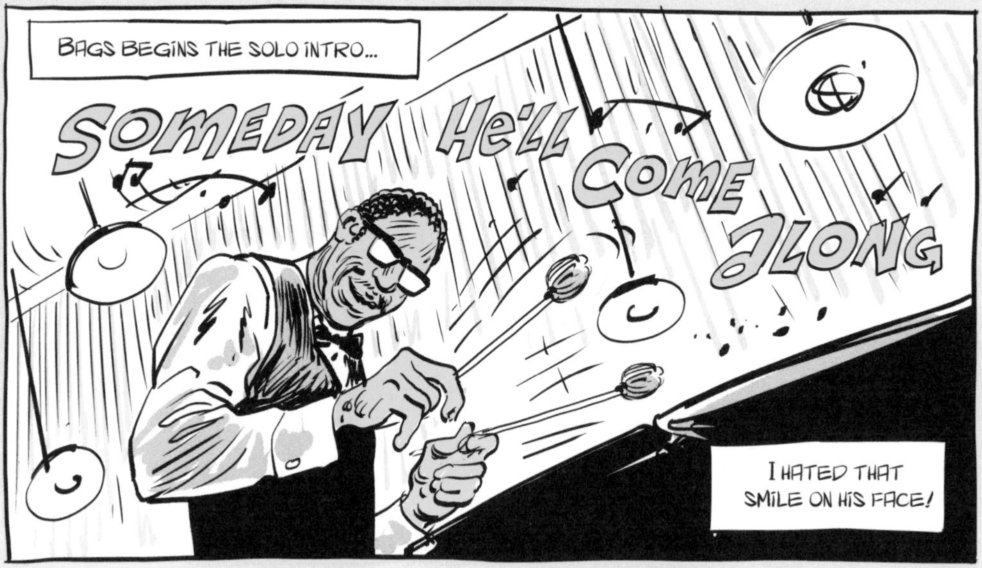
BAGS BEGINS THE SOLO INTRO...
SOMEDAY HE'LL COME ALONG
I HATED THAT SMILE ON HIS FACE!

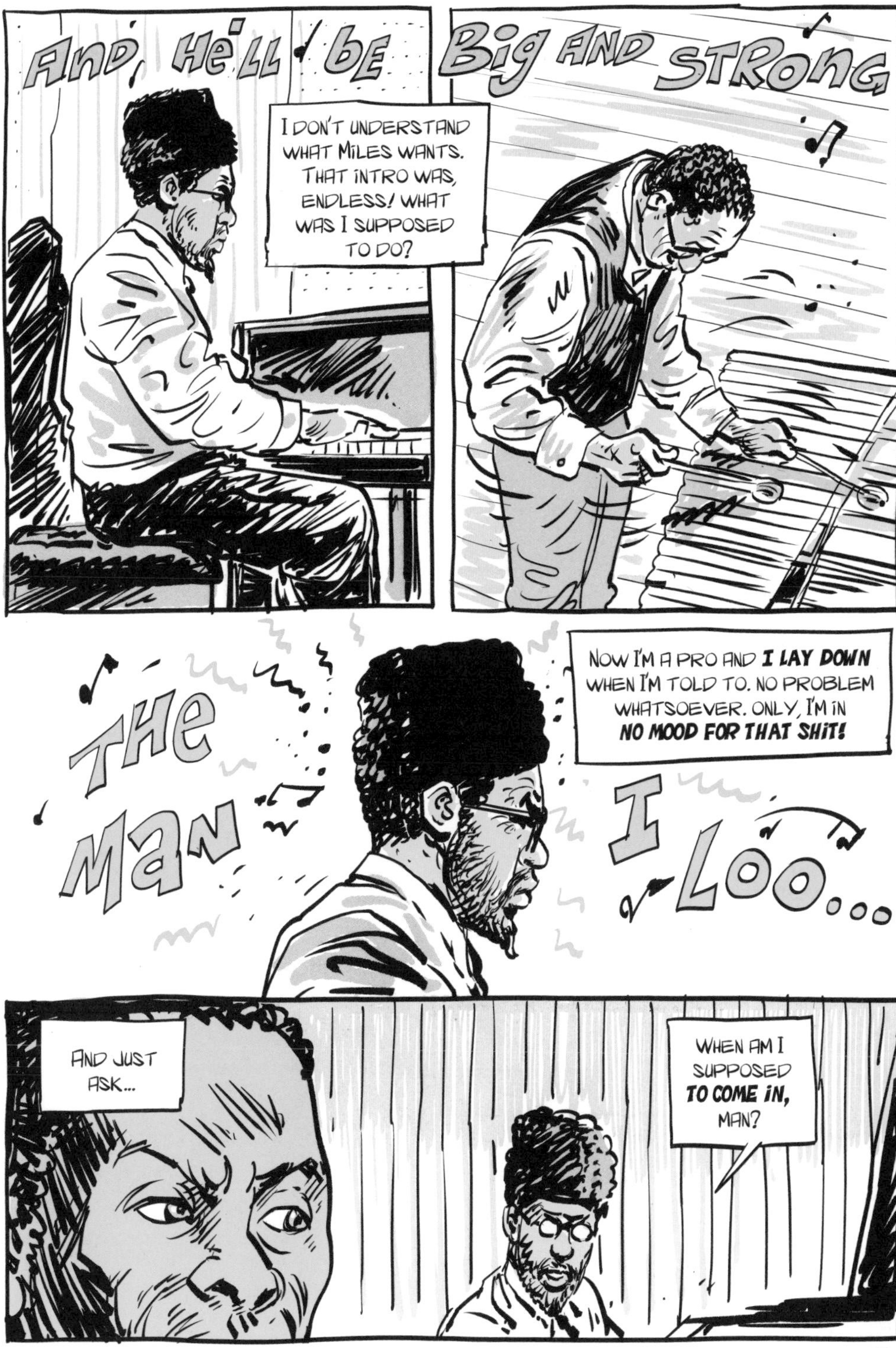

AND, HE'LL BE
I DON'T UNDERSTAND WHAT MILES WANTS. THAT INTRO WAS, ENDLESS! WHAT WAS I SUPPOSED TO DO?
BIG AND STRONG
THE MAN
NOW I'M A PRO AND **I LAY DOWN** WHEN I'M TOLD TO. NO PROBLEM WHATSOEVER. ONLY, I'M IN **NO MOOD FOR THAT SHIT!**
I LOO...
AND JUST ASK...
WHEN AM I SUPPOSED **TO COME IN,** MAN?

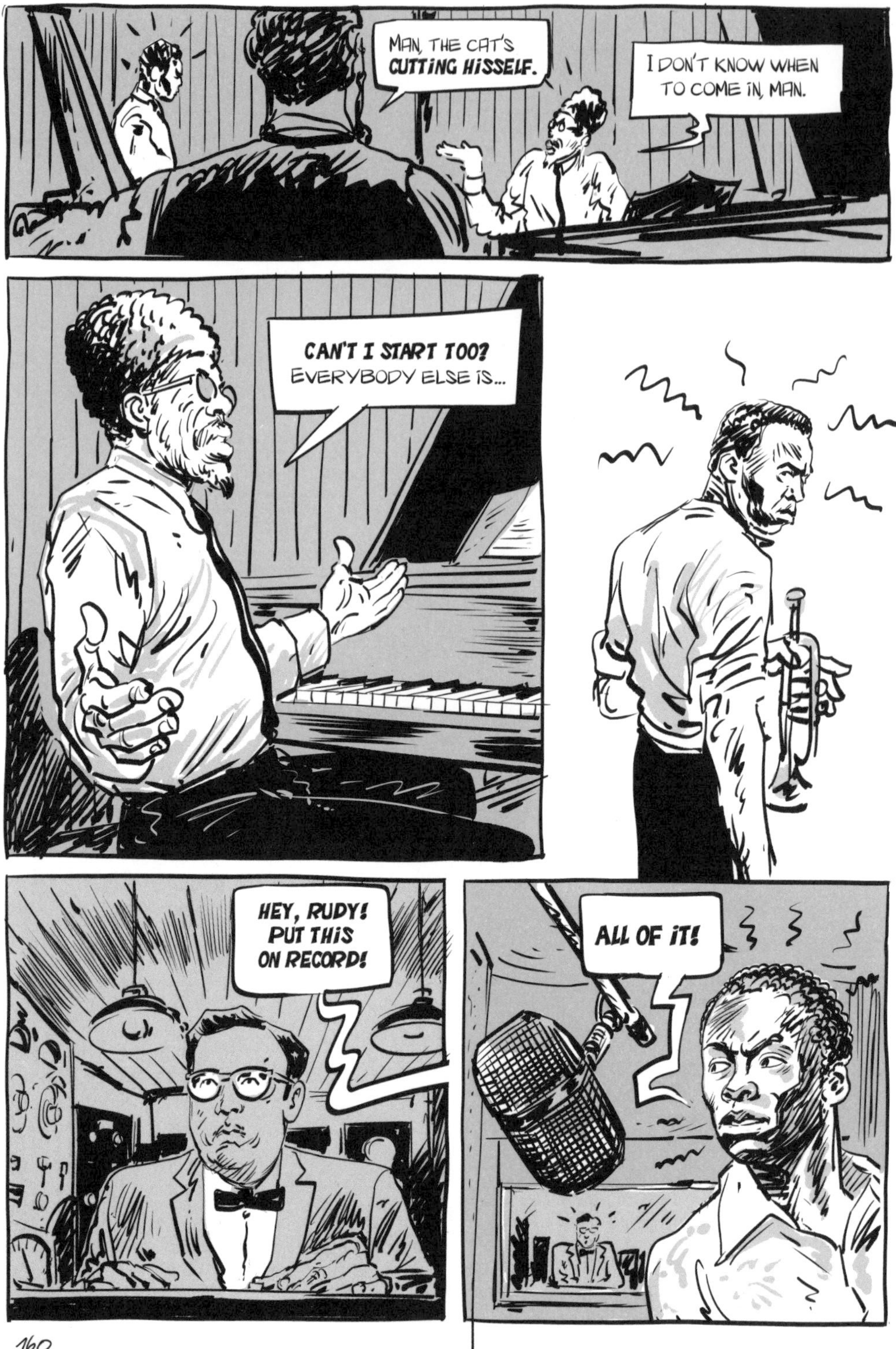
MAN, THE CAT'S CUTTING HISSELF.
I DON'T KNOW WHEN TO COME IN, MAN.
CAN'T I START TOO? EVERYBODY ELSE IS...
HEY, RUDY! PUT THIS ON RECORD!
ALL OF IT!

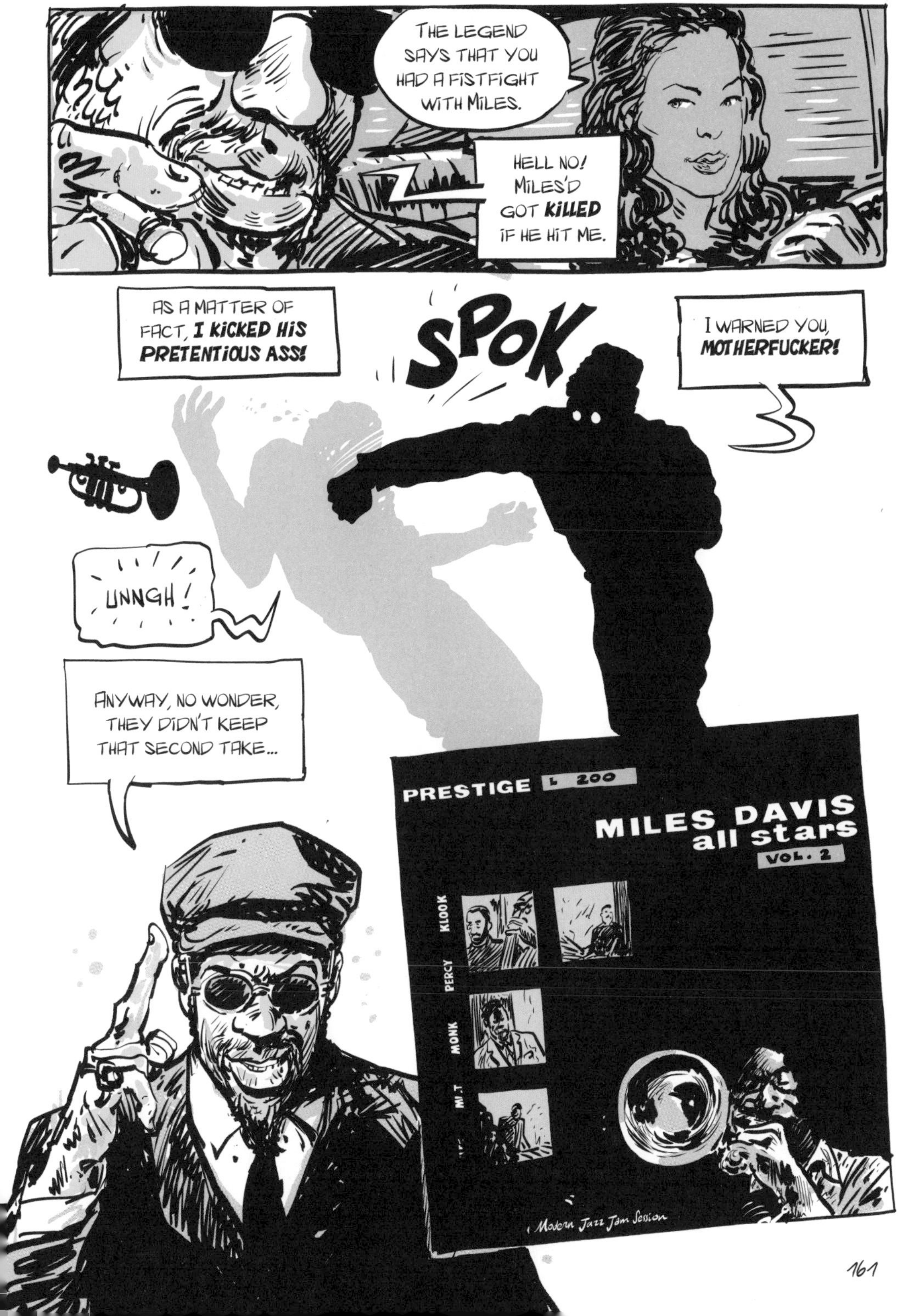

THE LEGEND SAYS THAT YOU HAD A FISTFIGHT WITH MILES.
HELL NO! MILES'D GOT KILLED IF HE HIT ME.
AS A MATTER OF FACT, I KICKED HIS PRETENTIOUS ASS!
SPOK
I WARNED YOU, MOTHERFUCKER!
UNNGH!
ANYWAY, NO WONDER, THEY DIDN'T KEEP THAT SECOND TAKE...
PRESTIGE L 200
MILES DAVIS all stars
VOL. 2
KLOOK
PERCY
MONK
MILT
Modern Jazz Jam Session

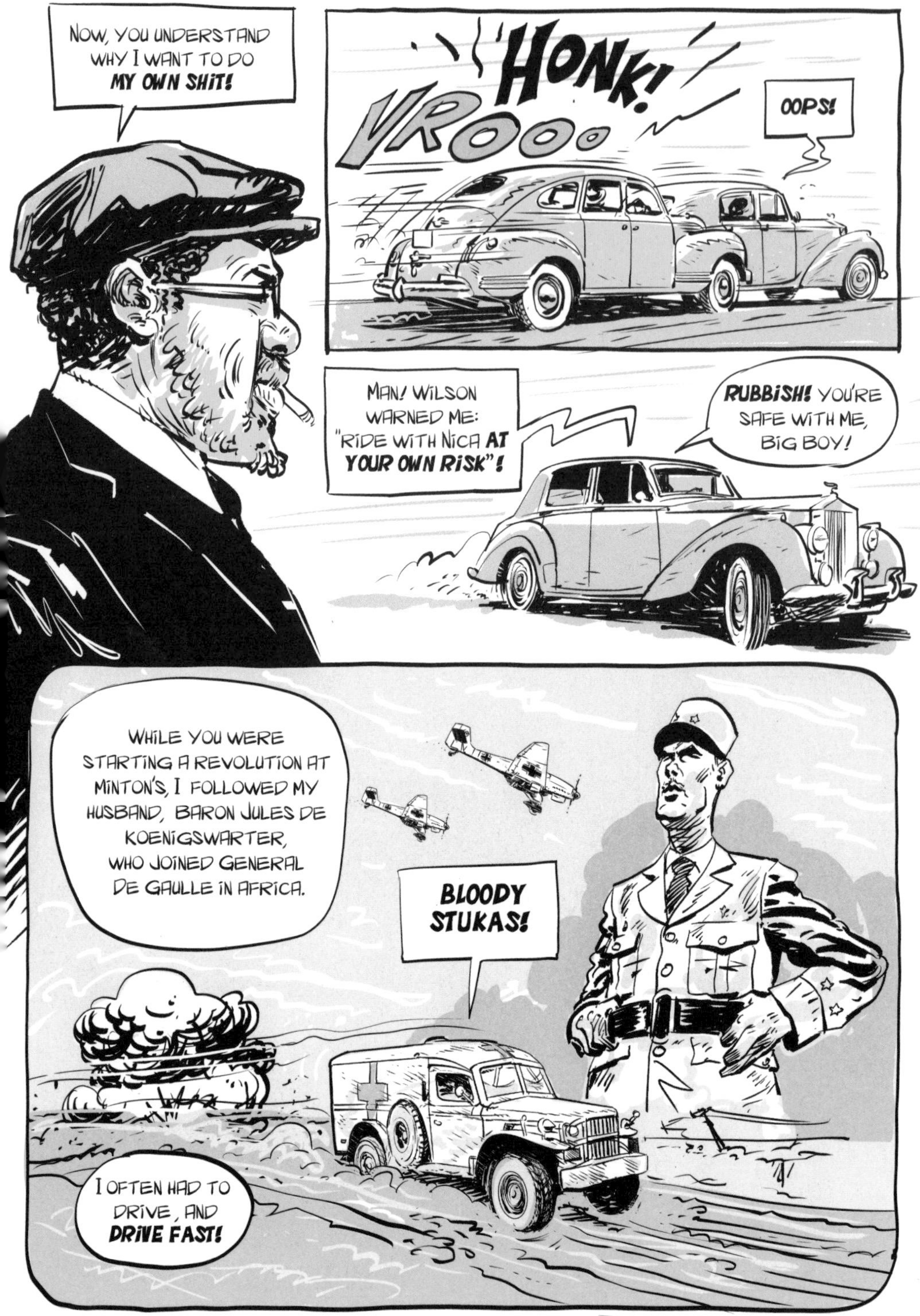
NOW, YOU UNDERSTAND WHY I WANT TO DO MY OWN SHIT!
HONK!
VROOoo
OOPS!
MAN! WILSON WARNED ME: "RIDE WITH NICA AT YOUR OWN RISK"!
RUBBISH! YOU'RE SAFE WITH ME, BIG BOY!
WHILE YOU WERE STARTING A REVOLUTION AT MINTON'S, I FOLLOWED MY HUSBAND, BARON JULES DE KOENIGSWARTER, WHO JOINED GENERAL DE GAULLE IN AFRICA.
BLOODY STUKAS!
I OFTEN HAD TO DRIVE, AND DRIVE FAST!

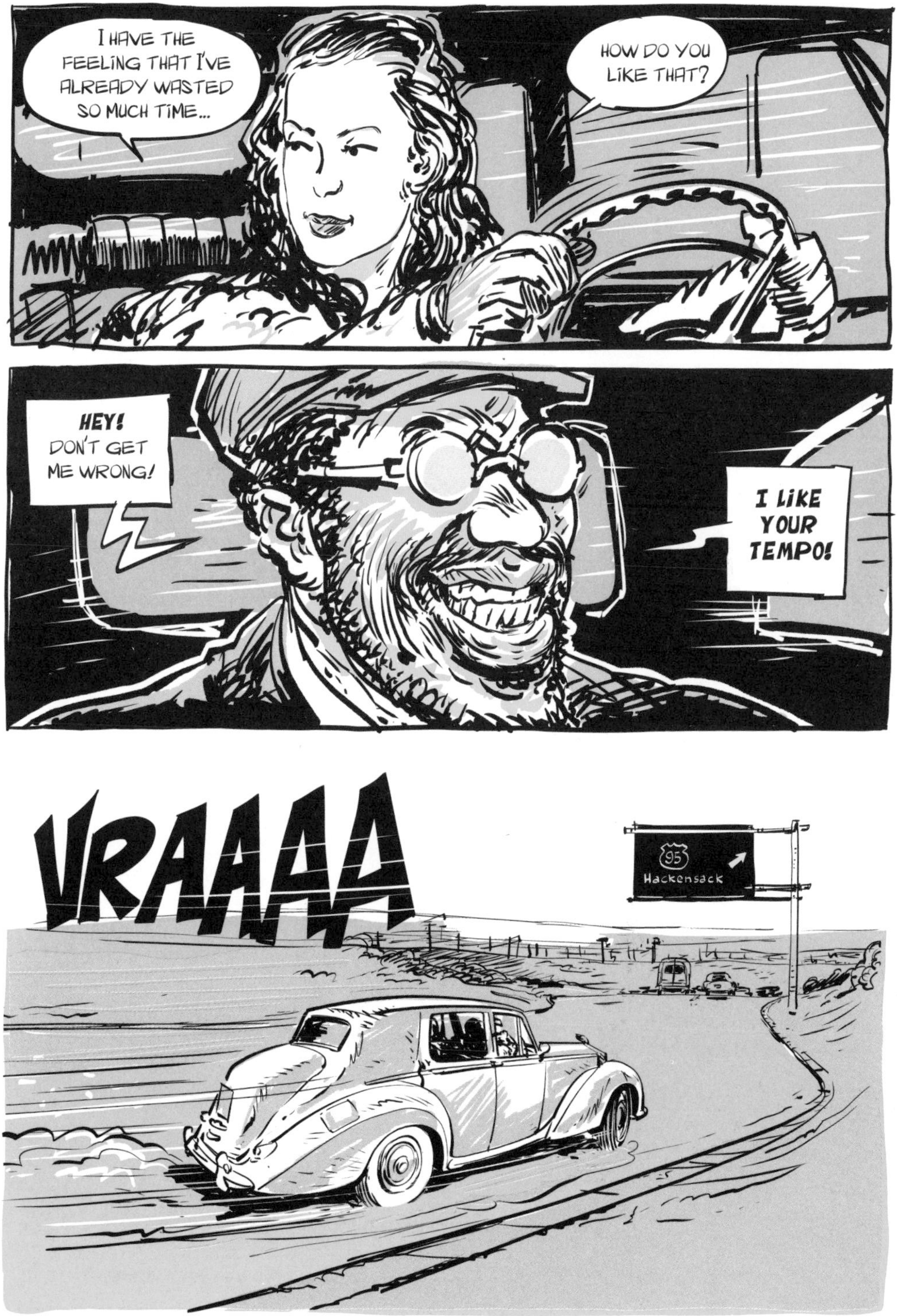
I HAVE THE FEELING THAT I'VE ALREADY WASTED SO MUCH TIME...
HOW DO YOU LIKE THAT?
HEY! DON'T GET ME WRONG!
I LIKE YOUR TEMPO!
VRAAAA
95
Hackensack

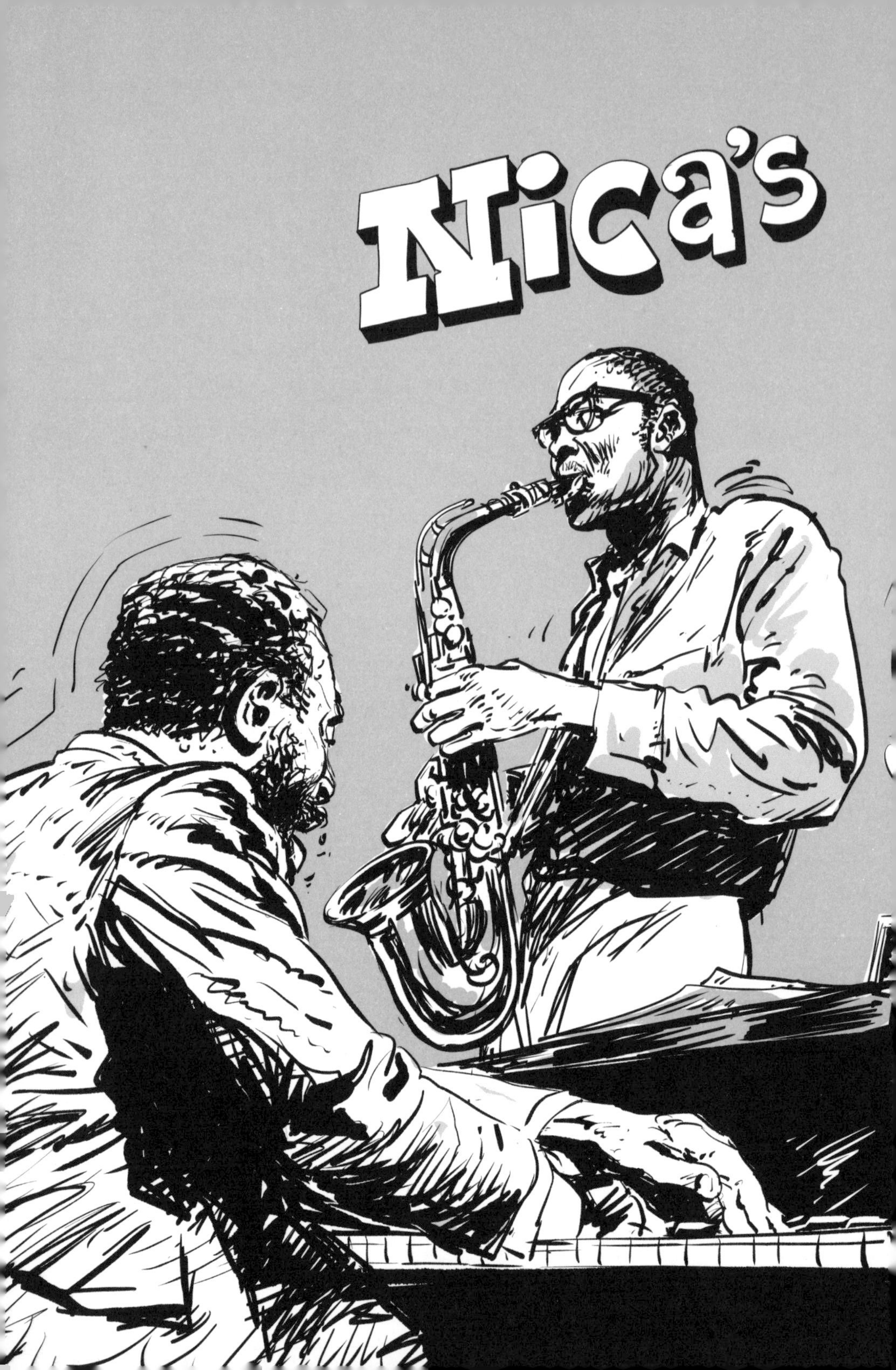
Nica's

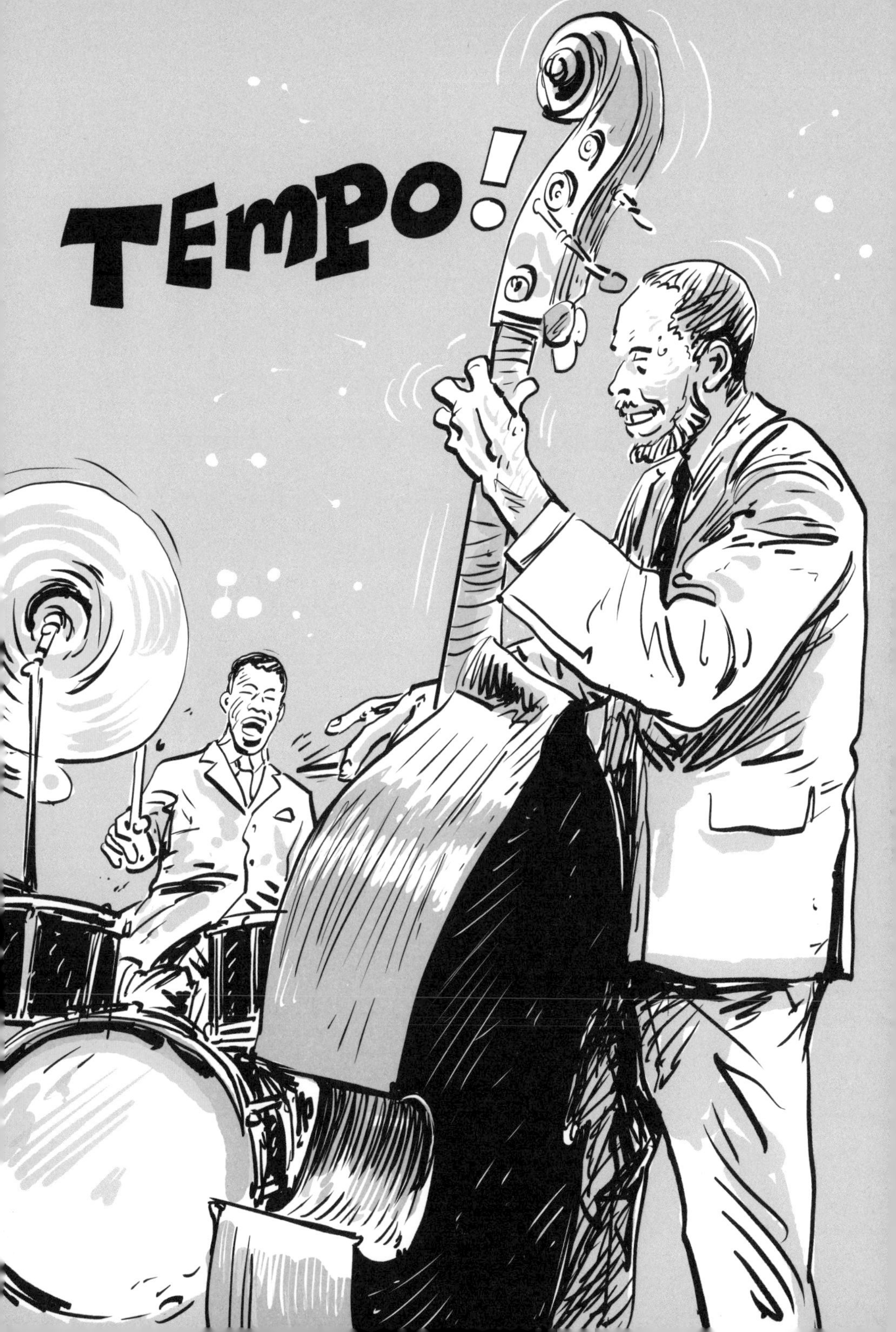
TEMPO!

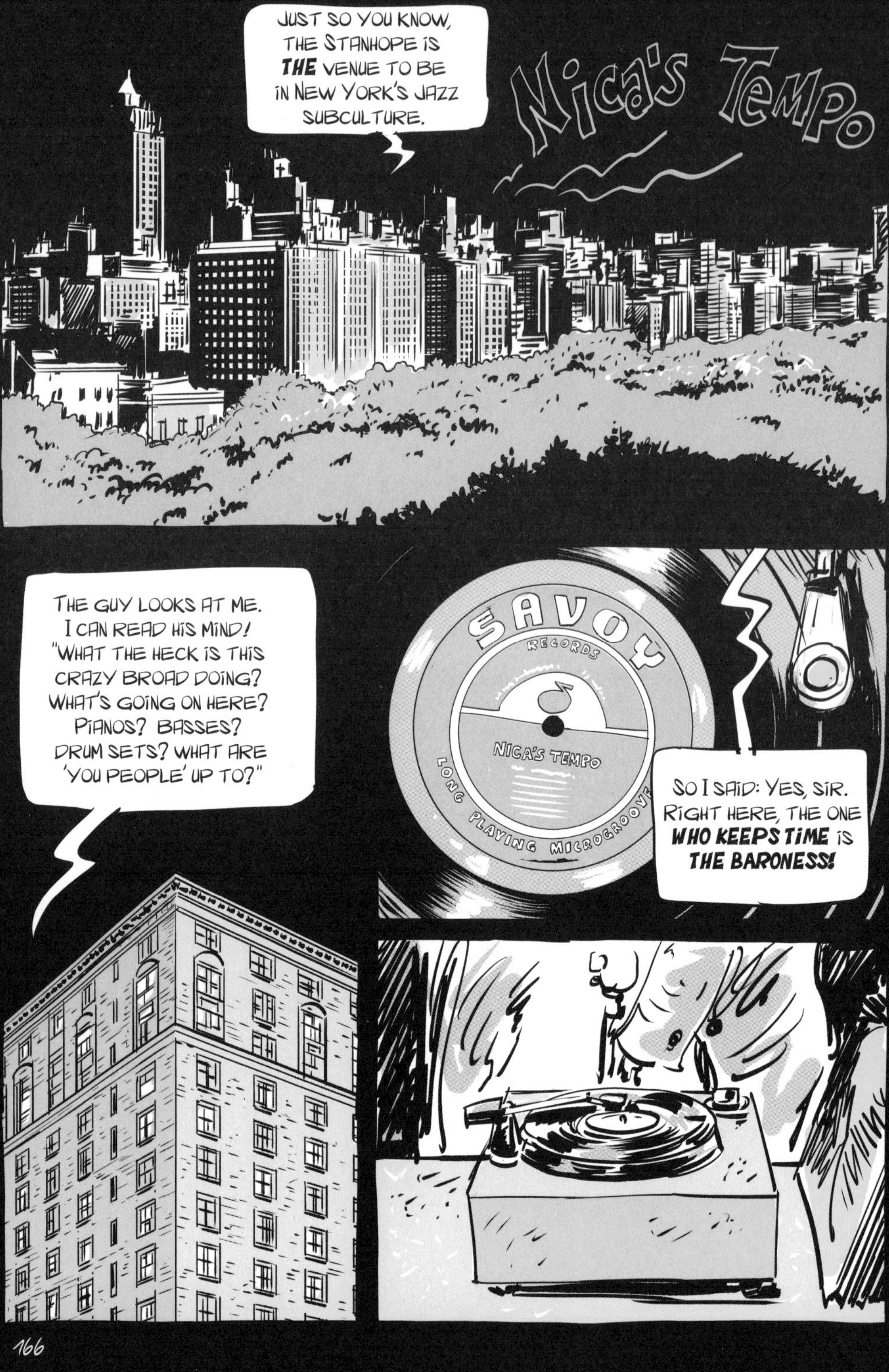
JUST SO YOU KNOW, THE STANHOPE IS **THE** VENUE TO BE IN NEW YORK'S JAZZ SUBCULTURE.
Nica's Tempo
THE GUY LOOKS AT ME. I CAN READ HIS MIND! "WHAT THE HECK IS THIS CRAZY BROAD DOING? WHAT'S GOING ON HERE? PIANOS? BASSES? DRUM SETS? WHAT ARE 'YOU PEOPLE' UP TO?"
SAVOY RECORDS
NICA'S TEMPO
LONG PLAYING MICROGROOVE
SO I SAID: YES, SIR. RIGHT HERE, THE ONE **WHO KEEPS TIME** IS **THE BARONESS!**

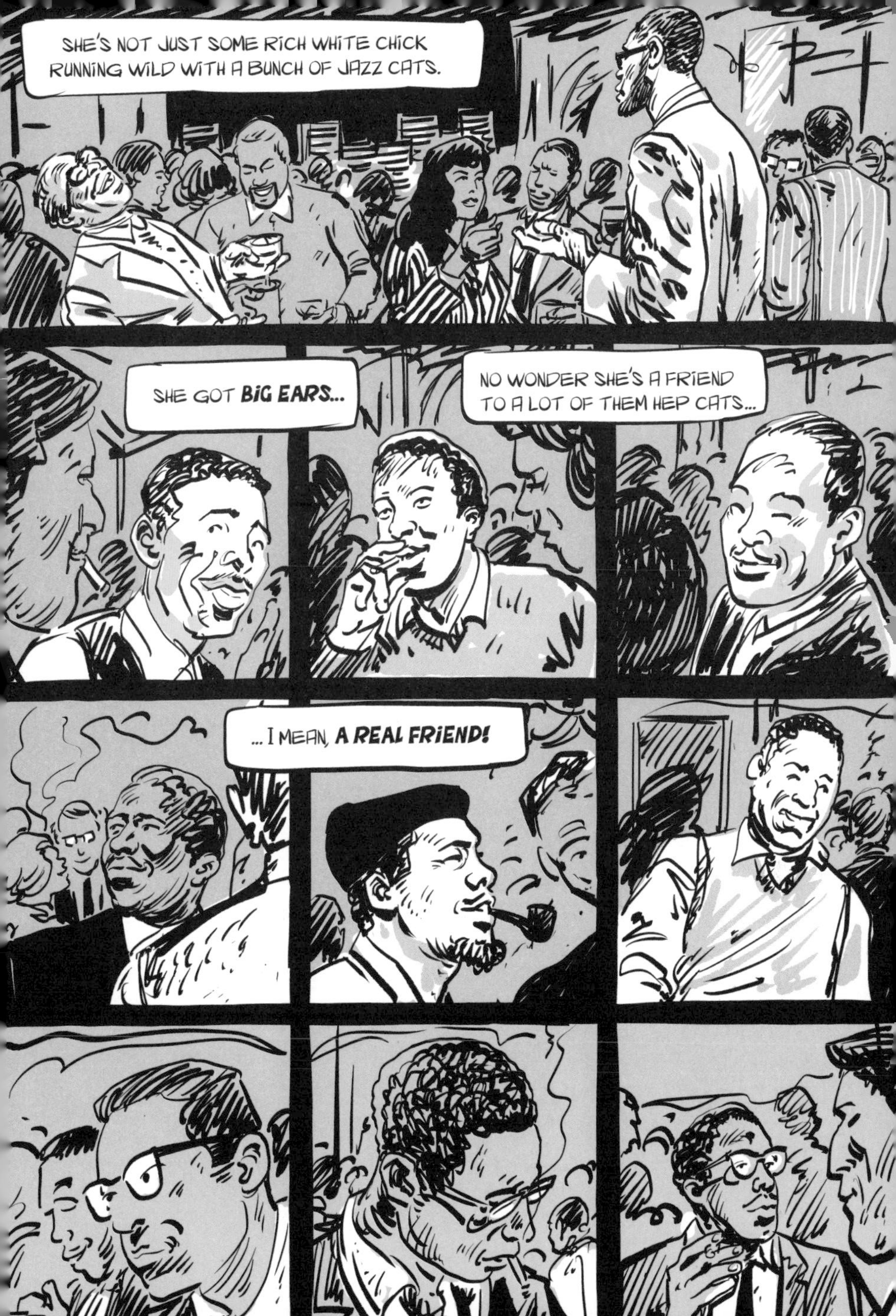
SHE'S NOT JUST SOME RICH WHITE CHICK RUNNING WILD WITH A BUNCH OF JAZZ CATS.
SHE GOT **BIG EARS...**
NO WONDER SHE'S A FRIEND TO A LOT OF THEM HEP CATS...
... I MEAN, **A REAL FRIEND!**

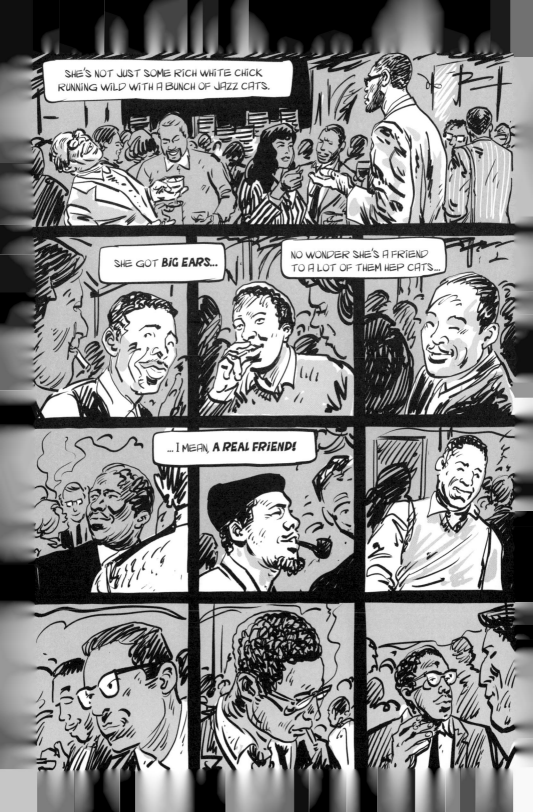

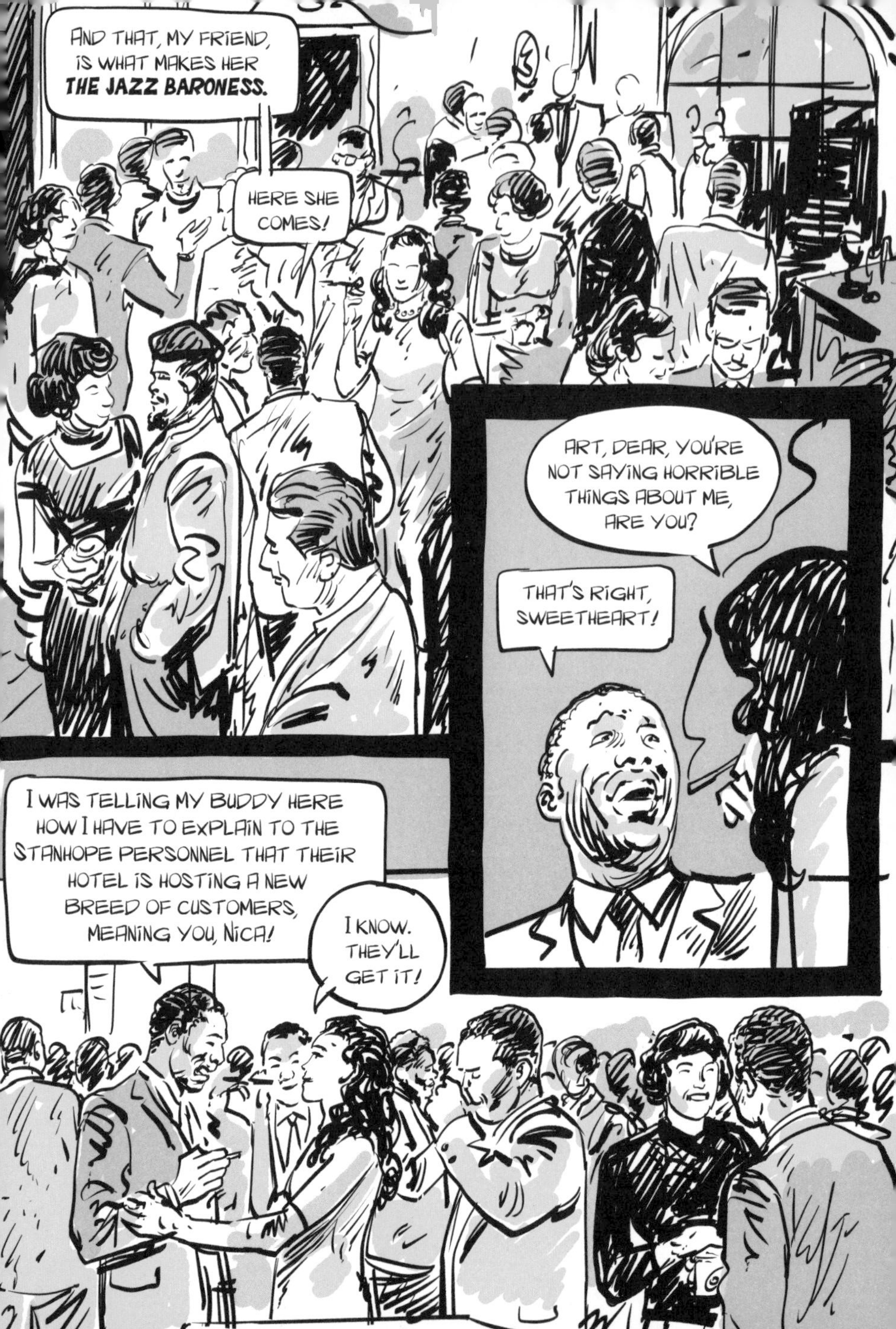
AND THAT, MY FRIEND, IS WHAT MAKES HER THE JAZZ BARONESS.
HERE SHE COMES!
ART, DEAR, YOU'RE NOT SAYING HORRIBLE THINGS ABOUT ME, ARE YOU?
THAT'S RIGHT, SWEETHEART!
I WAS TELLING MY BUDDY HERE HOW I HAVE TO EXPLAIN TO THE STANHOPE PERSONNEL THAT THEIR HOTEL IS HOSTING A NEW BREED OF CUSTOMERS, MEANING YOU, NICA!
I KNOW. THEY'LL GET IT!

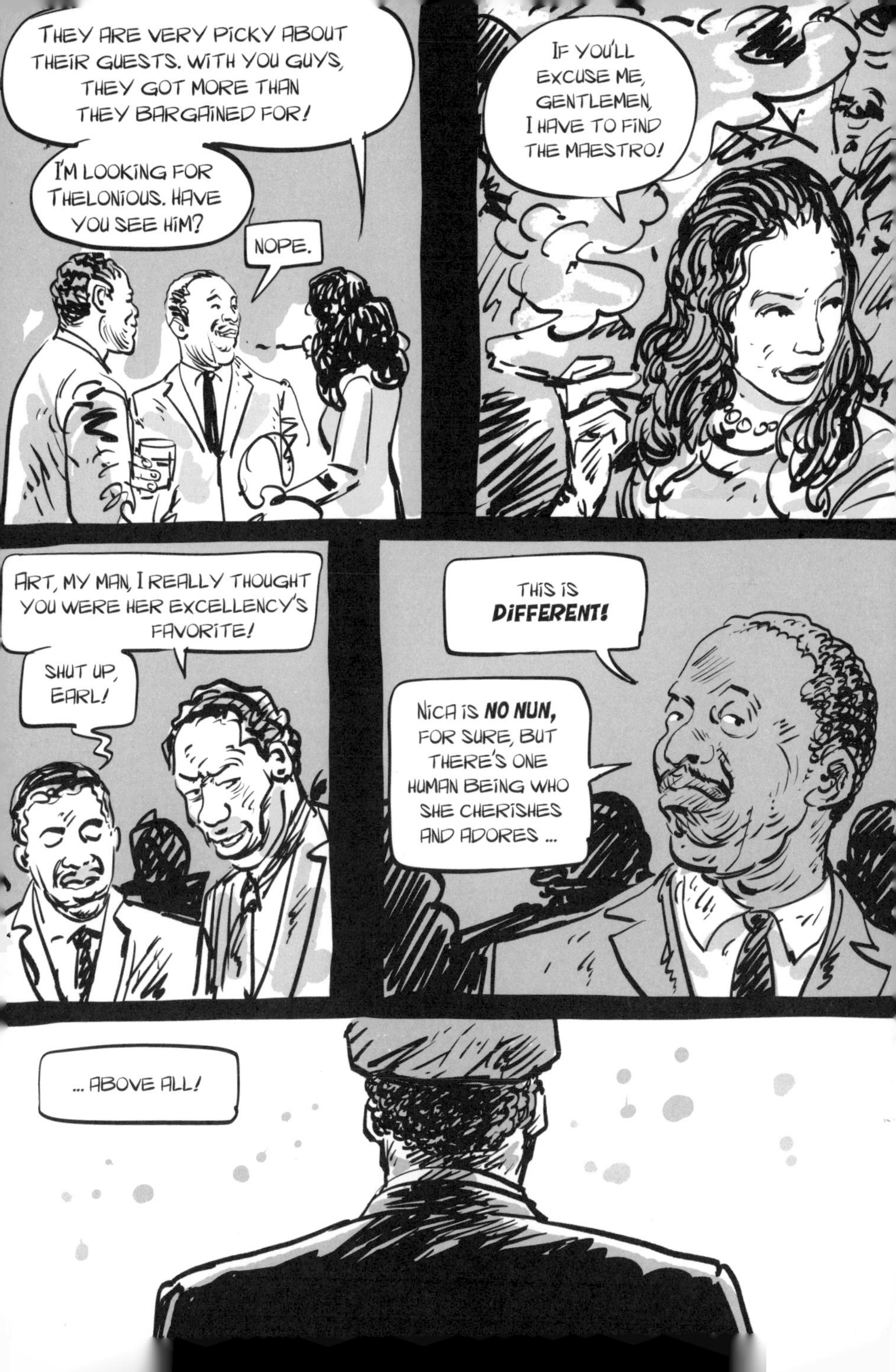
THEY ARE VERY PICKY ABOUT THEIR GUESTS. WITH YOU GUYS, THEY GOT MORE THAN THEY BARGAINED FOR!
I'M LOOKING FOR THELONIOUS. HAVE YOU SEE HIM?
NOPE.
IF YOU'LL EXCUSE ME, GENTLEMEN, I HAVE TO FIND THE MAESTRO!
ART, MY MAN, I REALLY THOUGHT YOU WERE HER EXCELLENCY'S FAVORITE!
SHUT UP, EARL!
THIS IS **DIFFERENT!**
NICA IS **NO NUN,** FOR SURE, BUT THERE'S ONE HUMAN BEING WHO SHE CHERISHES AND ADORES ...
... ABOVE ALL!

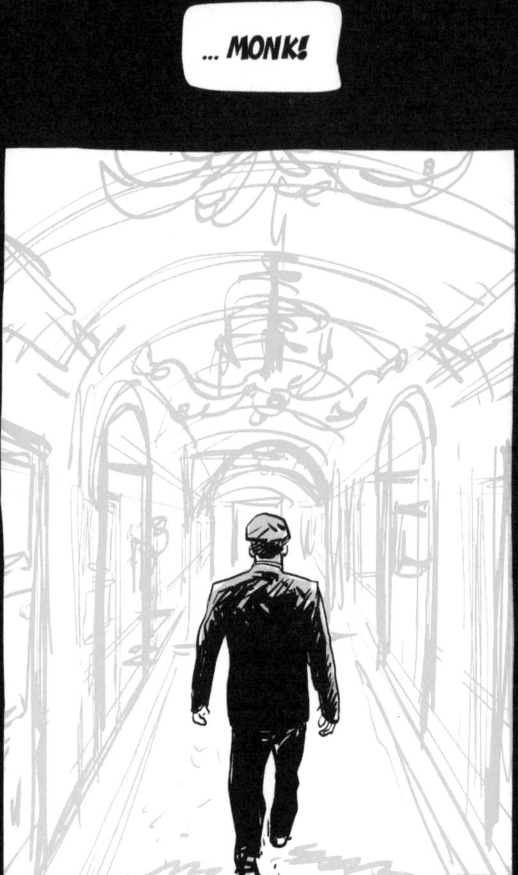
... MONK!

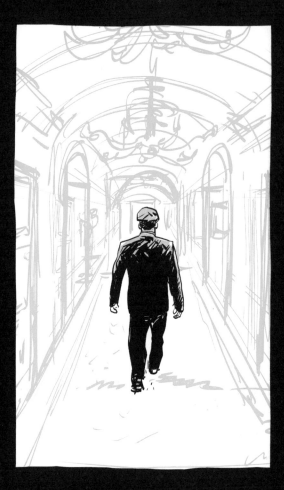

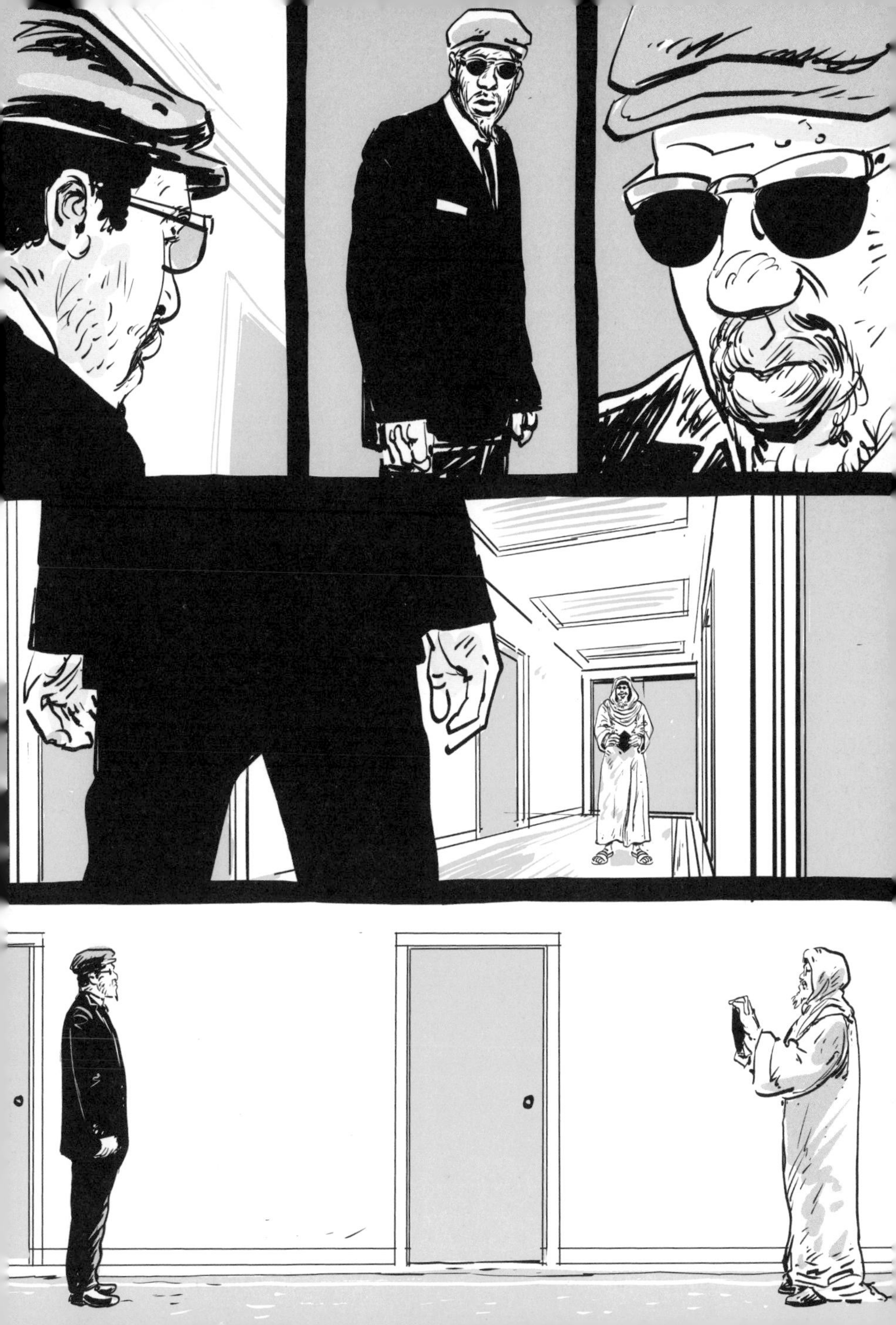

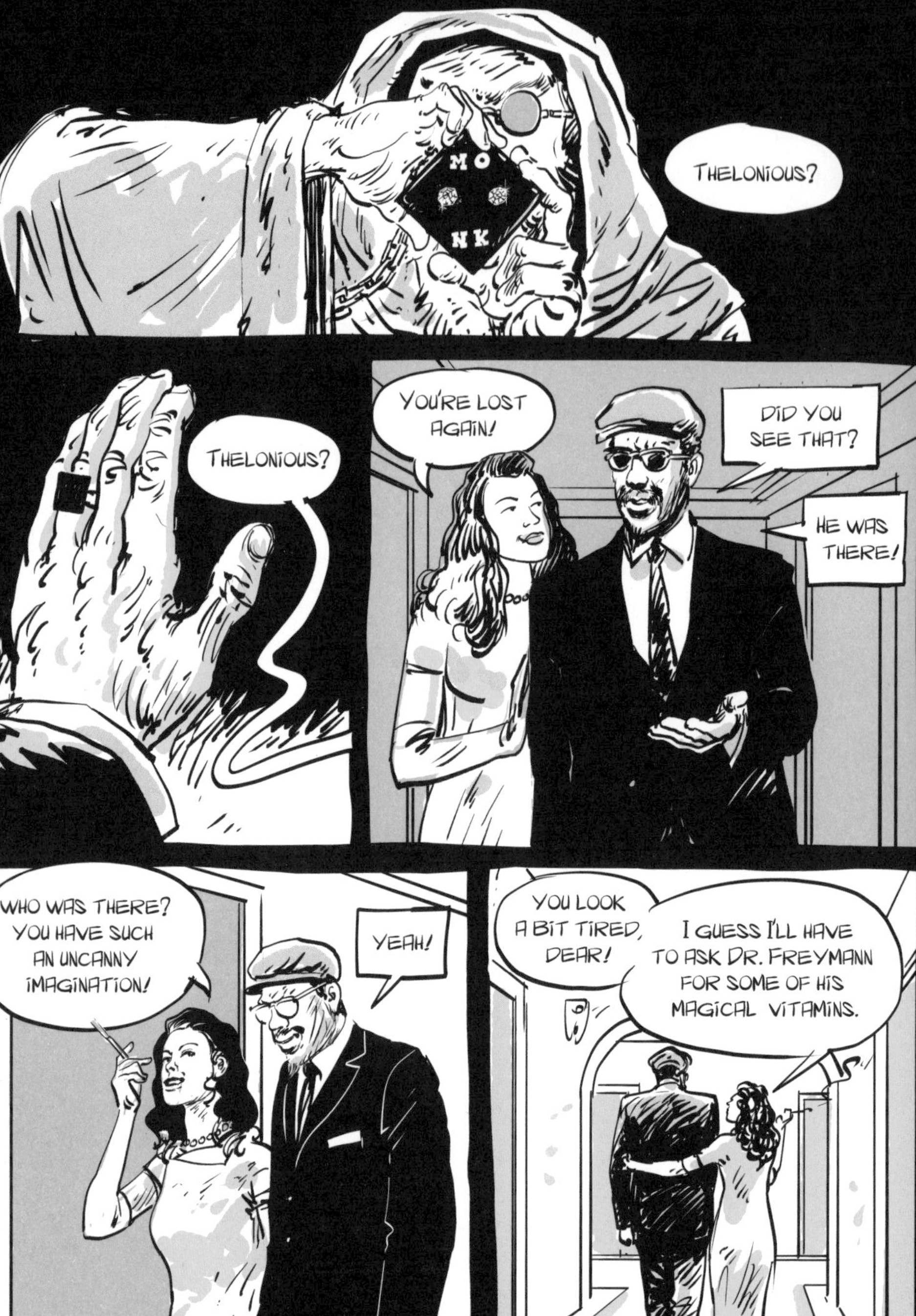

MO
NK
THELONIOUS?
THELONIOUS?
YOU'RE LOST AGAIN!
DID YOU SEE THAT?
HE WAS THERE!
WHO WAS THERE? YOU HAVE SUCH AN UNCANNY IMAGINATION!
YEAH!
YOU LOOK A BIT TIRED, DEAR!
I GUESS I'LL HAVE TO ASK DR. FREYMANN FOR SOME OF HIS MAGICAL VITAMINS.

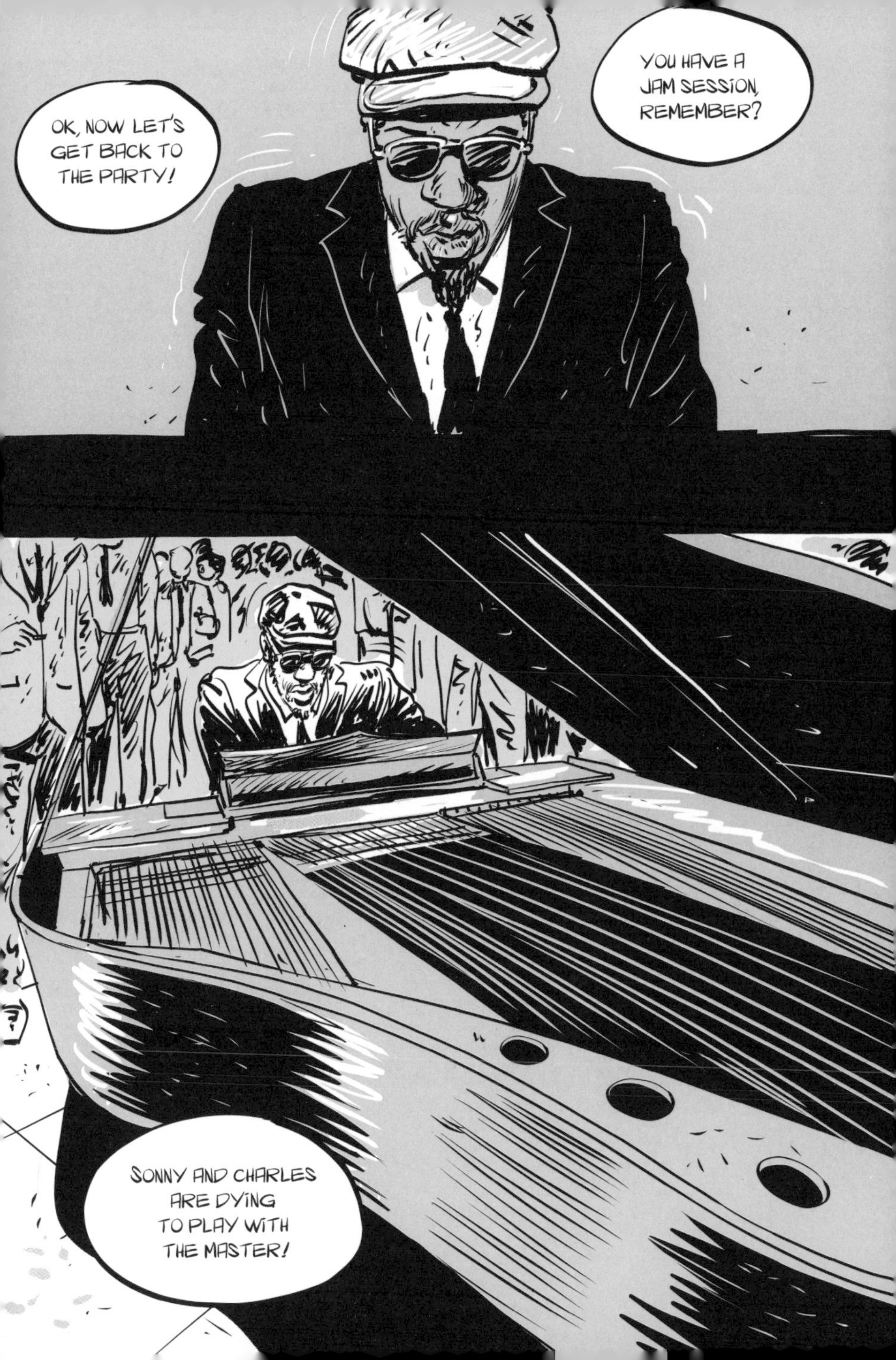
OK, NOW LET'S GET BACK TO THE PARTY!
YOU HAVE A JAM SESSION, REMEMBER?
SONNY AND CHARLES ARE DYING TO PLAY WITH THE MASTER!

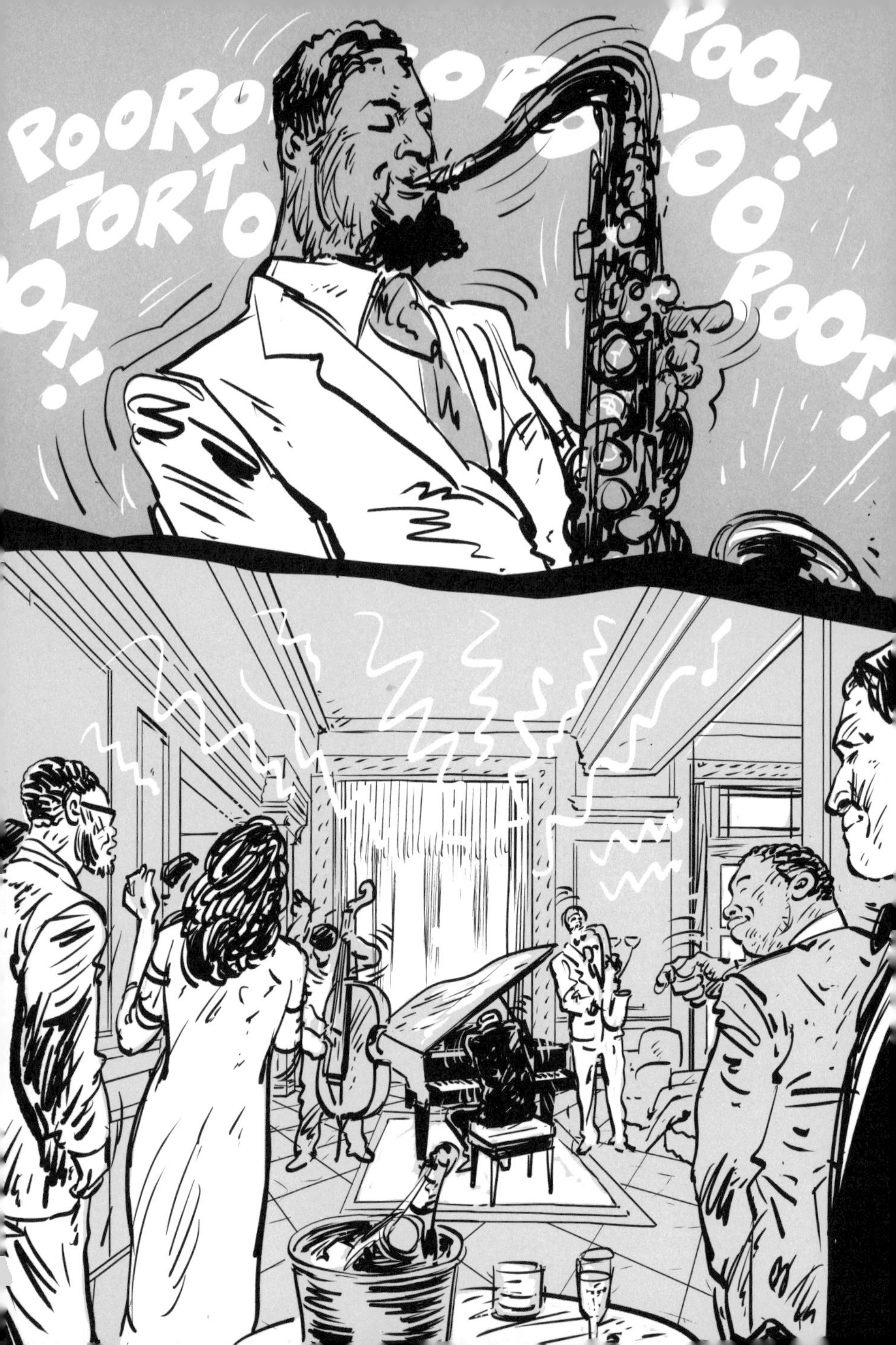
ROORO
TORTO
OT!!
KOOT!!
POOT!!

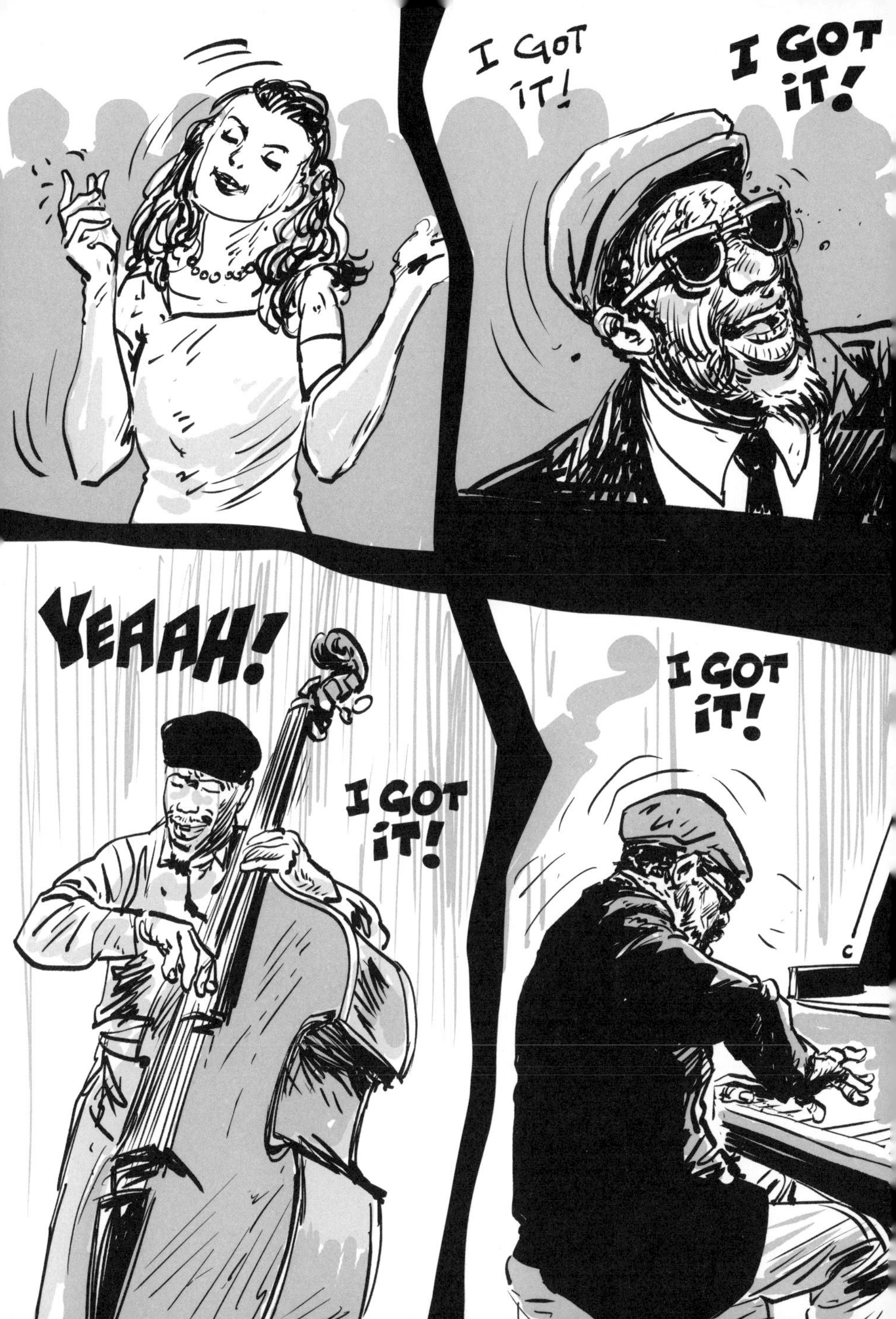
I GOT IT!
I GOT IT!
YEAAH!
I GOT IT!
I GOT IT!

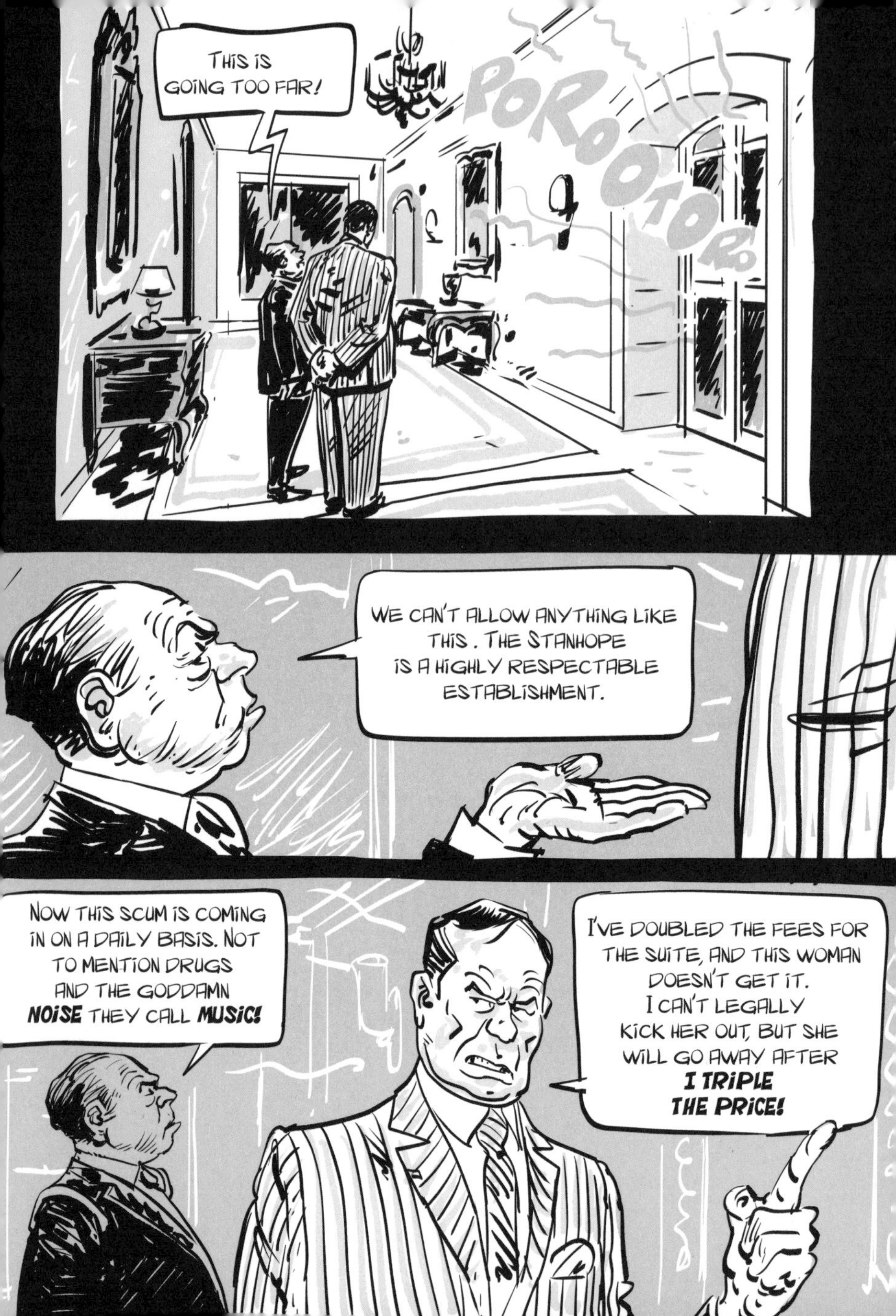
THIS IS GOING TOO FAR!
POROOOTORO
WE CAN'T ALLOW ANYTHING LIKE THIS. THE STANHOPE IS A HIGHLY RESPECTABLE ESTABLISHMENT.
NOW THIS SCUM IS COMING IN ON A DAILY BASIS. NOT TO MENTION DRUGS AND THE GODDAMN **NOISE** THEY CALL **MUSIC!**
I'VE DOUBLED THE FEES FOR THE SUITE, AND THIS WOMAN DOESN'T GET IT. I CAN'T LEGALLY KICK HER OUT, BUT SHE WILL GO AWAY AFTER **I TRIPLE THE PRICE!**

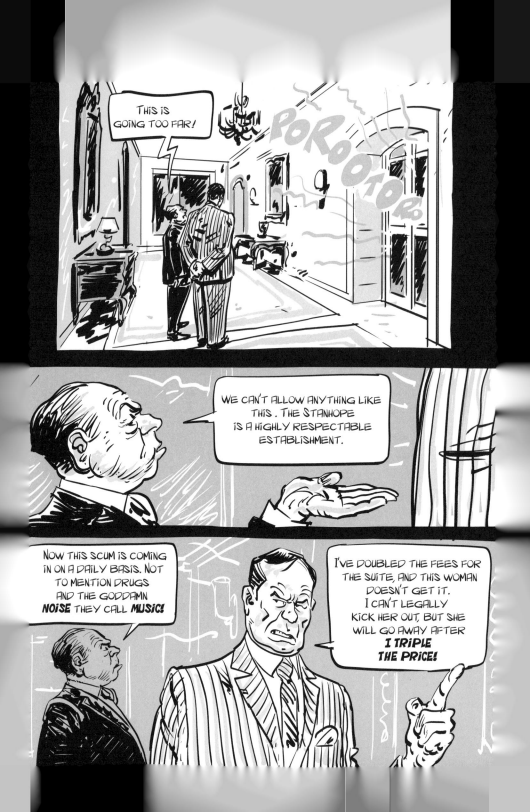

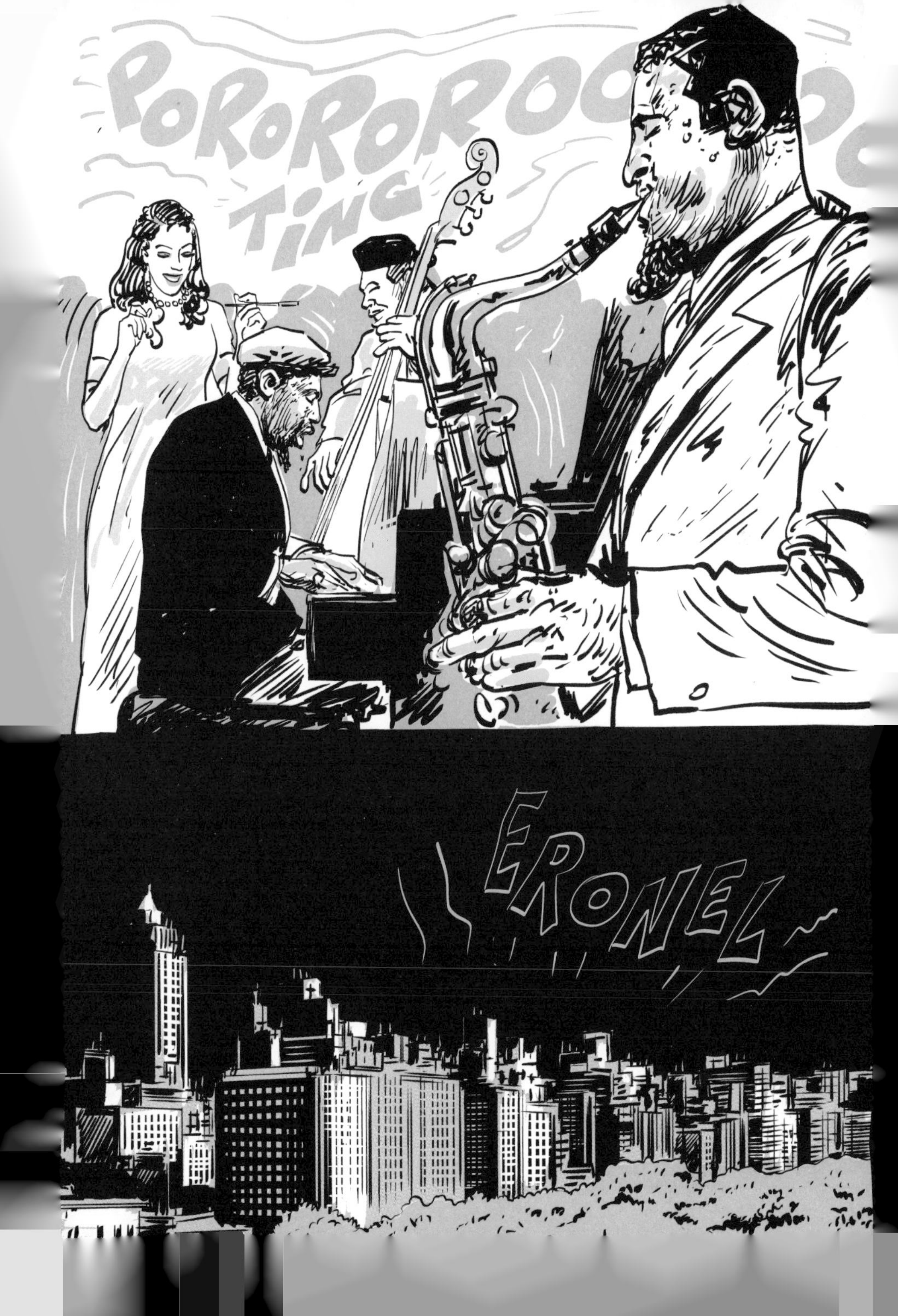
POROROROO
TING
ERONEL

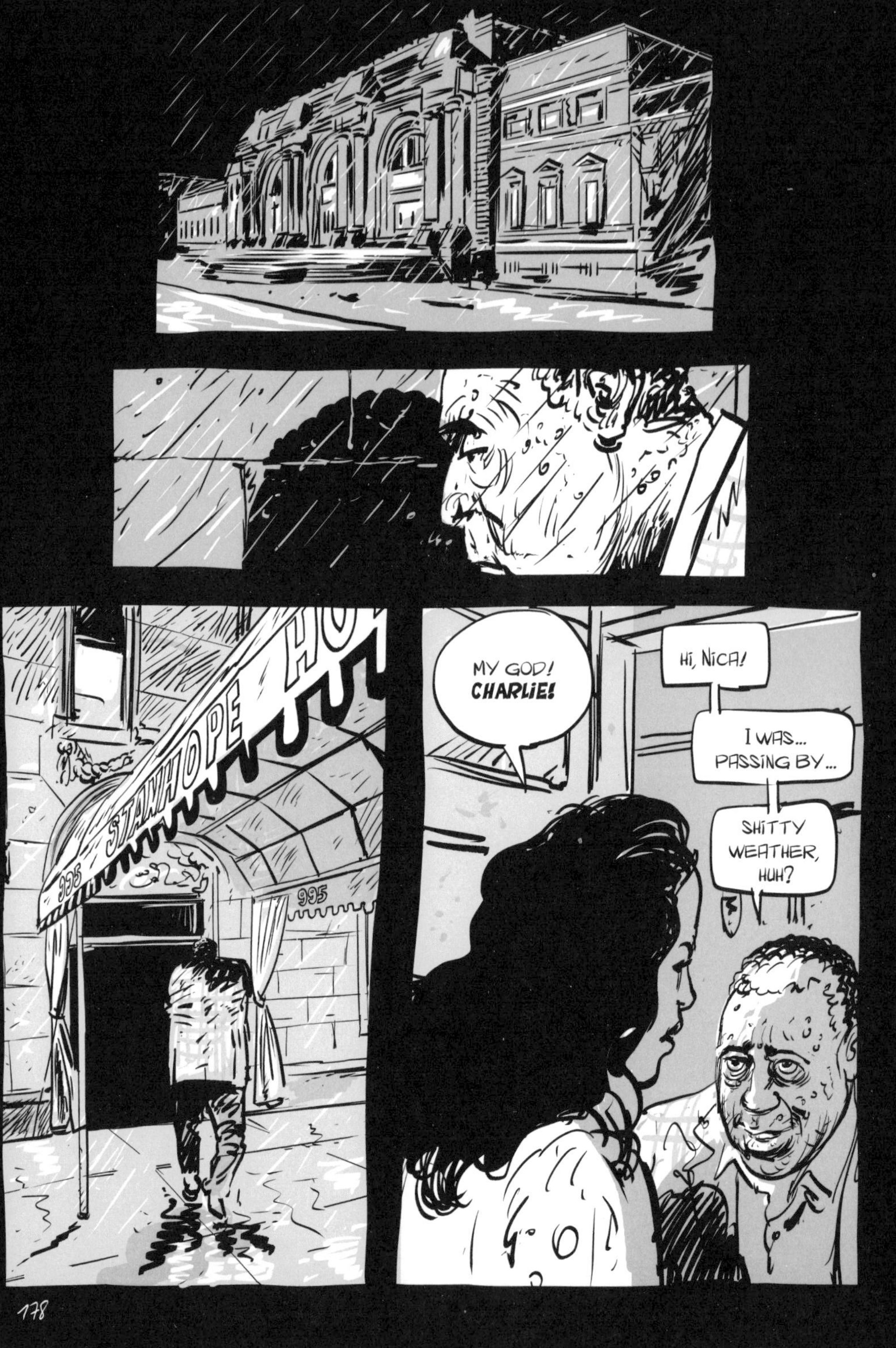
STANHOPE
995
995
MY GOD! CHARLIE!
HI, NICA!
I WAS... PASSING BY...
SHITTY WEATHER, HUH?

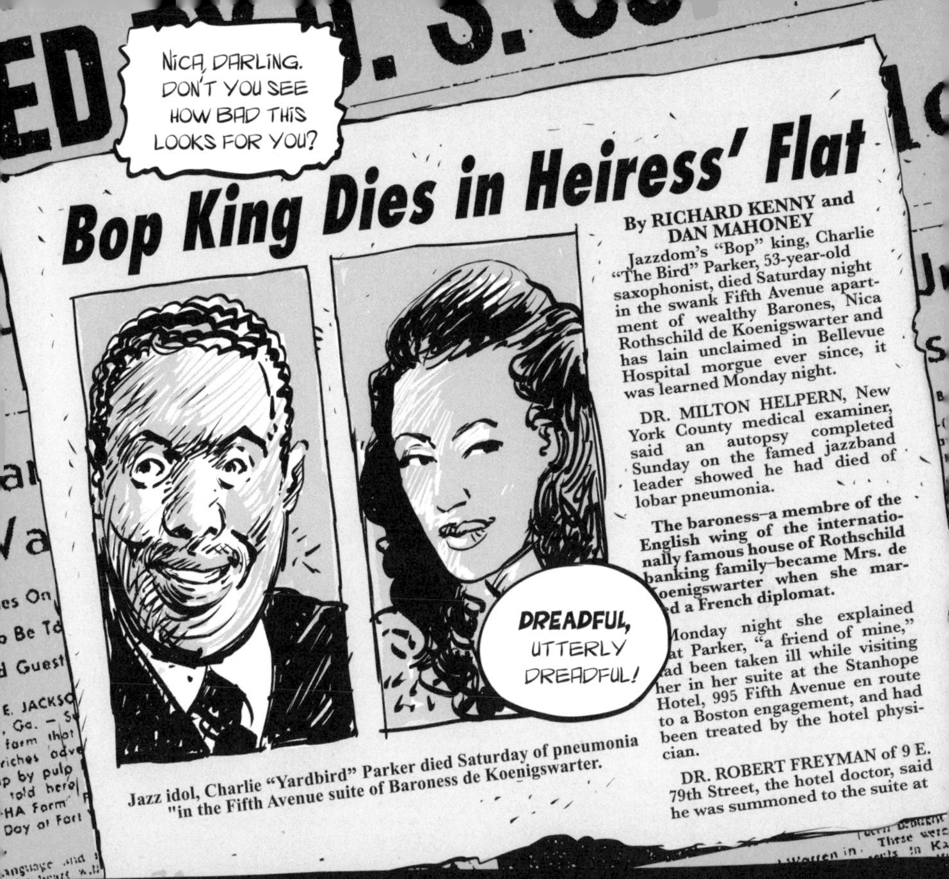
NICA, DARLING. DON'T YOU SEE HOW BAD THIS LOOKS FOR YOU?
Bop King Dies in Heiress' Flat
By RICHARD KENNY and DAN MAHONEY
Jazzdom's "Bop" king, Charlie "The Bird" Parker, 53-year-old saxophonist, died Saturday night in the swank Fifth Avenue apartment of wealthy Barones, Nica Rothschild de Koenigswarter and has lain unclaimed in Bellevue Hospital morgue ever since, it was learned Monday night.
DR. MILTON HELPERN, New York County medical examiner, said an autopsy completed Sunday on the famed jazzband leader showed he had died of lobar pneumonia.
The baroness–a membre of the English wing of the internationally famous house of Rothschild banking family–became Mrs. de Koenigswarter when she married a French diplomat.
Monday night she explained that Parker, "a friend of mine," had been taken ill while visiting her in her suite at the Stanhope Hotel, 995 Fifth Avenue en route to a Boston engagement, and had been treated by the hotel physician.
DR. ROBERT FREYMAN of 9 E. 79th Street, the hotel doctor, said he was summoned to the suite at
Jazz idol, Charlie "Yardbird" Parker died Saturday of pneumonia "in the Fifth Avenue suite of Baroness de Koenigswarter.
DREADFUL, UTTERLY DREADFUL!

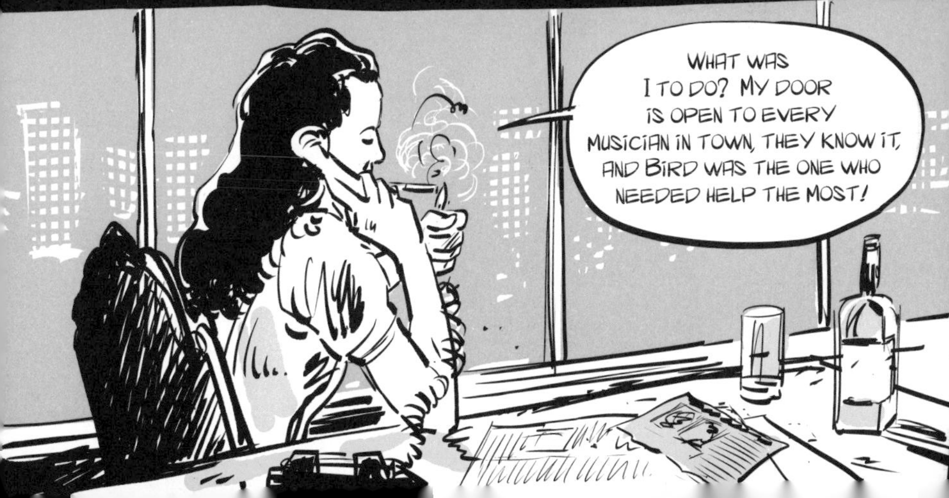
WHAT WAS I TO DO? MY DOOR IS OPEN TO EVERY MUSICIAN IN TOWN, THEY KNOW IT, AND BIRD WAS THE ONE WHO NEEDED HELP THE MOST!

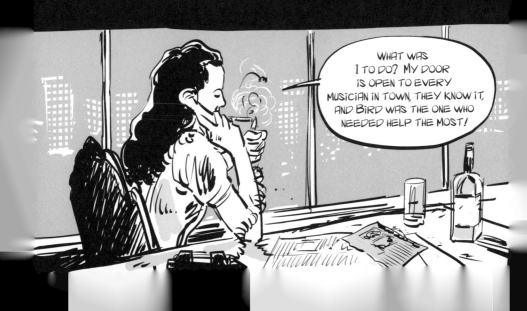

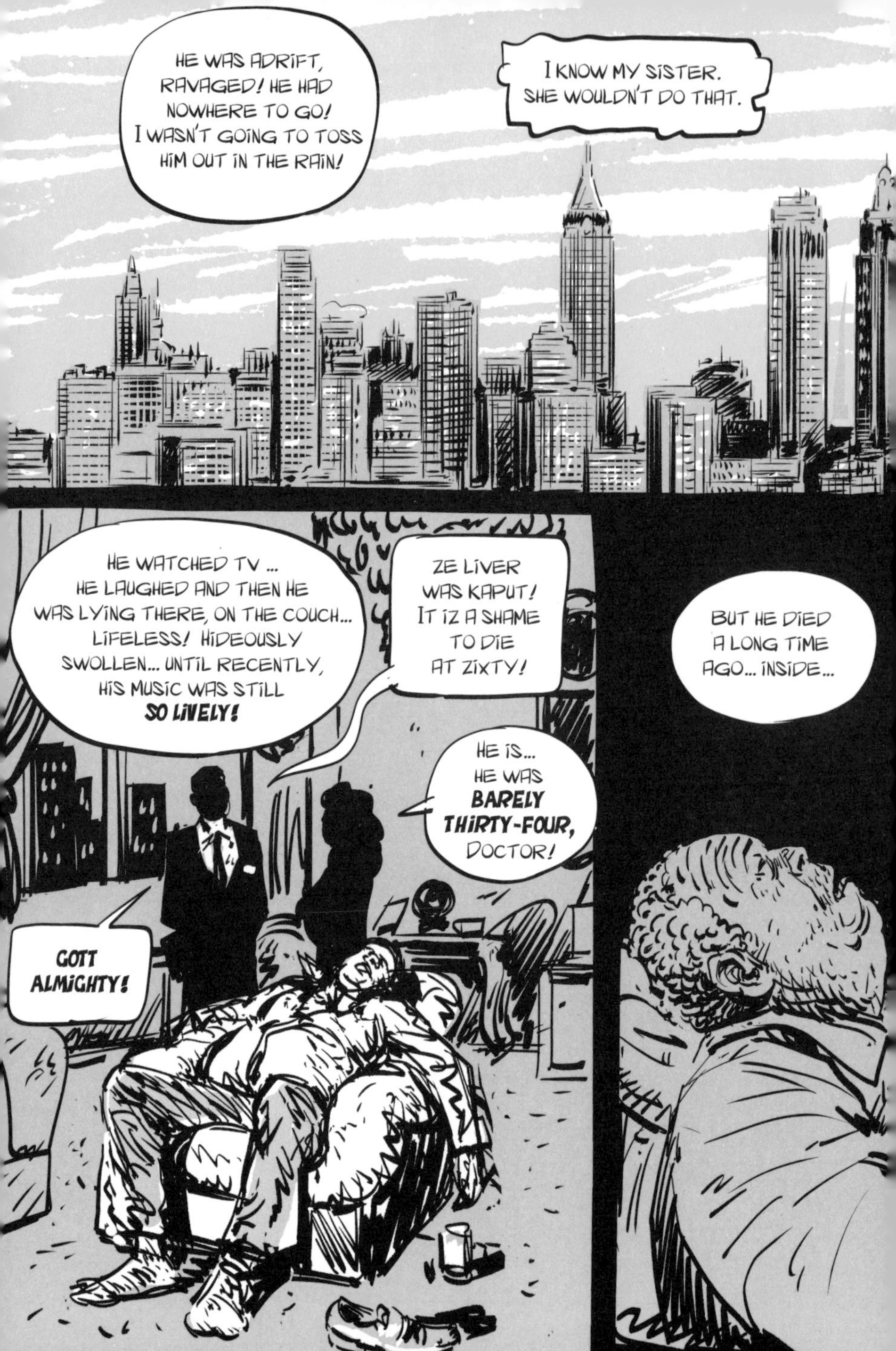
HE WAS ADRIFT, RAVAGED! HE HAD NOWHERE TO GO! I WASN'T GOING TO TOSS HIM OUT IN THE RAIN!
I KNOW MY SISTER. SHE WOULDN'T DO THAT.
HE WATCHED TV ... HE LAUGHED AND THEN HE WAS LYING THERE, ON THE COUCH... LIFELESS! HIDEOUSLY SWOLLEN... UNTIL RECENTLY, HIS MUSIC WAS STILL **SO LIVELY!**
ZE LIVER WAS KAPUT! IT IZ A SHAME TO DIE AT ZIXTY!
HE IS... HE WAS **BARELY THIRTY-FOUR,** DOCTOR!
GOTT ALMIGHTY!
BUT HE DIED A LONG TIME AGO... INSIDE...

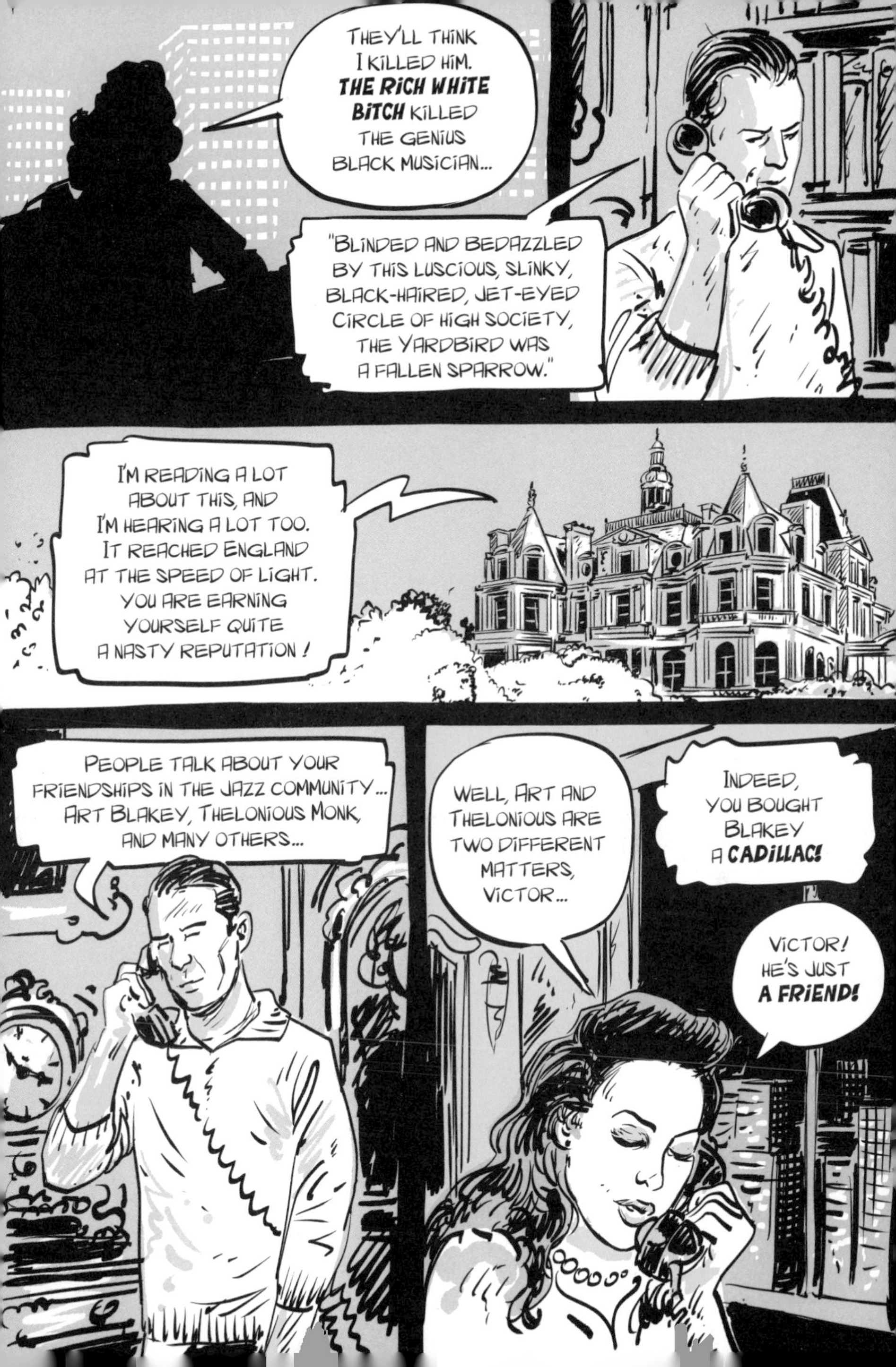
THEY'LL THINK I KILLED HIM. **THE RICH WHITE BITCH** KILLED THE GENIUS BLACK MUSICIAN...
"BLINDED AND BEDAZZLED BY THIS LUSCIOUS, SLINKY, BLACK-HAIRED, JET-EYED CIRCLE OF HIGH SOCIETY, THE YARDBIRD WAS A FALLEN SPARROW."
I'M READING A LOT ABOUT THIS, AND I'M HEARING A LOT TOO. IT REACHED ENGLAND AT THE SPEED OF LIGHT. YOU ARE EARNING YOURSELF QUITE A NASTY REPUTATION!
PEOPLE TALK ABOUT YOUR FRIENDSHIPS IN THE JAZZ COMMUNITY... ART BLAKEY, THELONIOUS MONK, AND MANY OTHERS...
WELL, ART AND THELONIOUS ARE TWO DIFFERENT MATTERS, VICTOR...
INDEED, YOU BOUGHT BLAKEY A **CADILLAC!**
VICTOR! HE'S JUST **A FRIEND!**

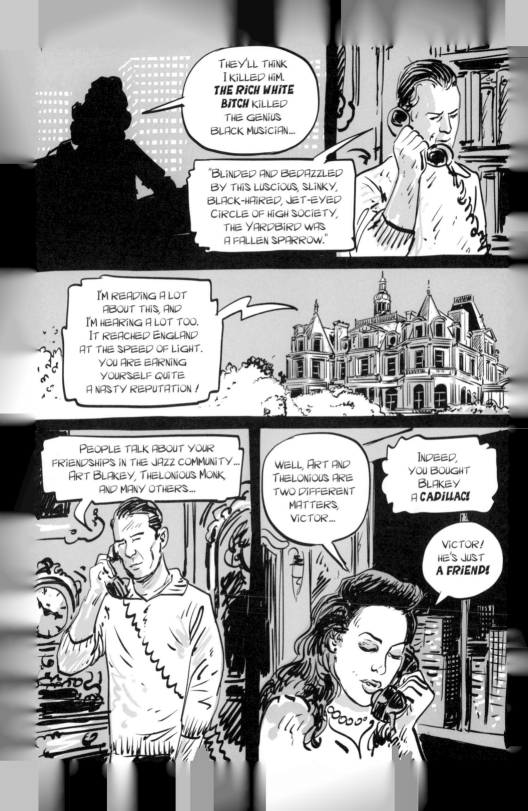

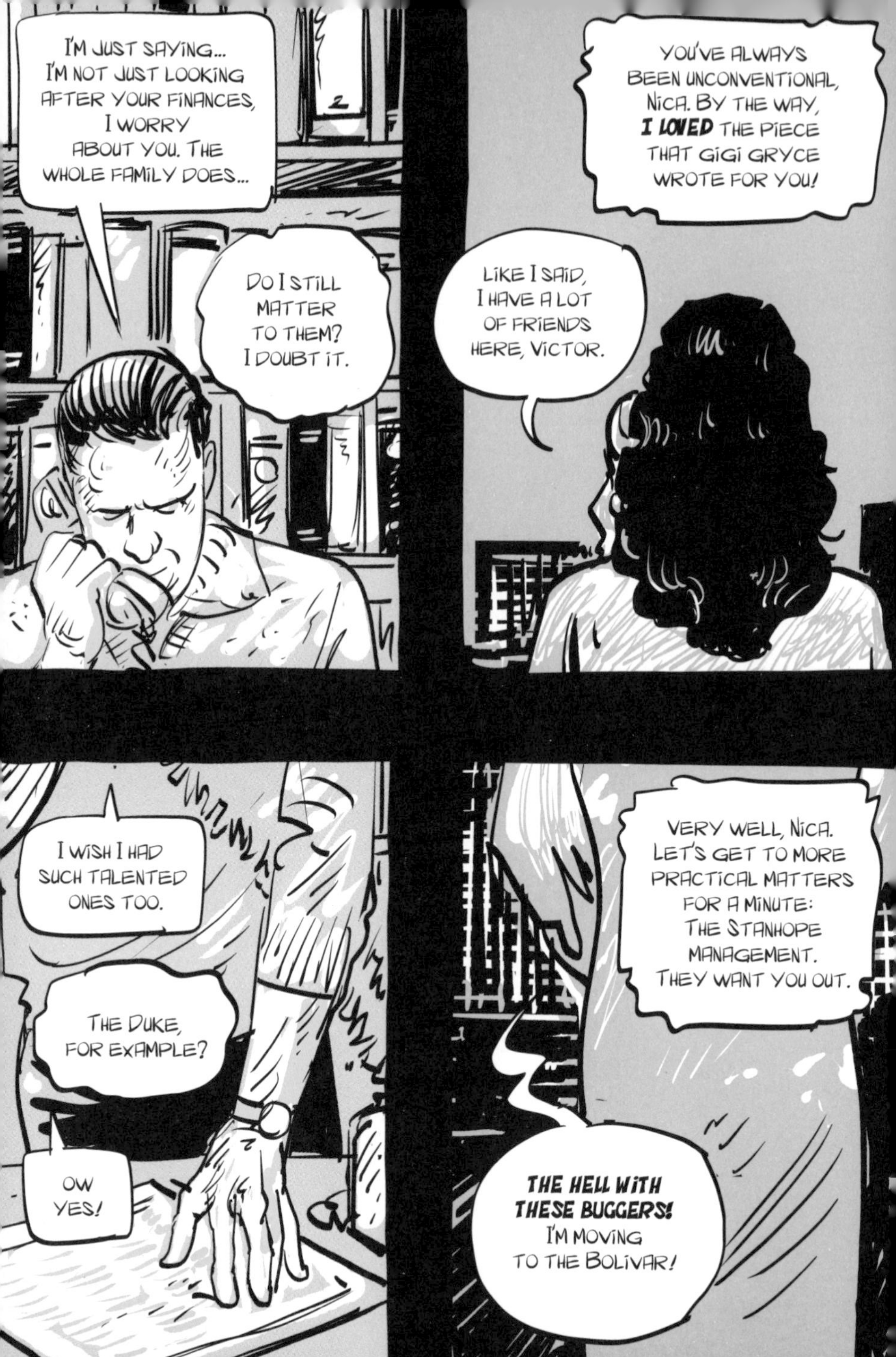
I'M JUST SAYING...
I'M NOT JUST LOOKING AFTER YOUR FINANCES, I WORRY ABOUT YOU. THE WHOLE FAMILY DOES...
DO I STILL MATTER TO THEM? I DOUBT IT.
YOU'VE ALWAYS BEEN UNCONVENTIONAL, NICA. BY THE WAY, **I LOVED** THE PIECE THAT GIGI GRYCE WROTE FOR YOU!
LIKE I SAID, I HAVE A LOT OF FRIENDS HERE, VICTOR.
I WISH I HAD SUCH TALENTED ONES TOO.
THE DUKE, FOR EXAMPLE?
OW YES!
VERY WELL, NICA. LET'S GET TO MORE PRACTICAL MATTERS FOR A MINUTE: THE STANHOPE MANAGEMENT. THEY WANT YOU OUT.
THE HELL WITH THESE BUGGERS! I'M MOVING TO THE BOLIVAR!

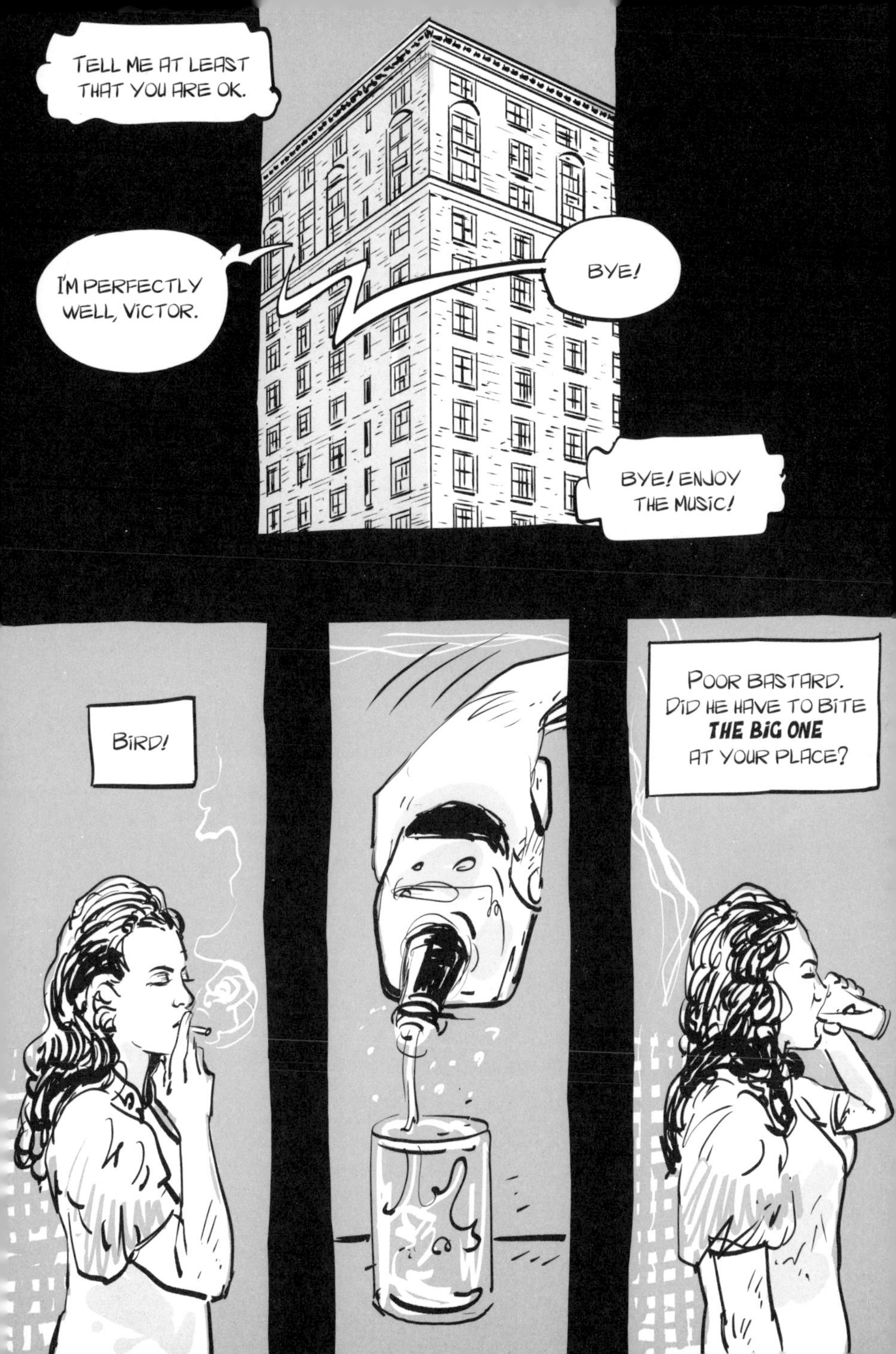
TELL ME AT LEAST THAT YOU ARE OK.
I'M PERFECTLY WELL, VICTOR.
BYE!
BYE! ENJOY THE MUSIC!
BIRD!
POOR BASTARD. DID HE HAVE TO BITE **THE BIG ONE** AT YOUR PLACE?

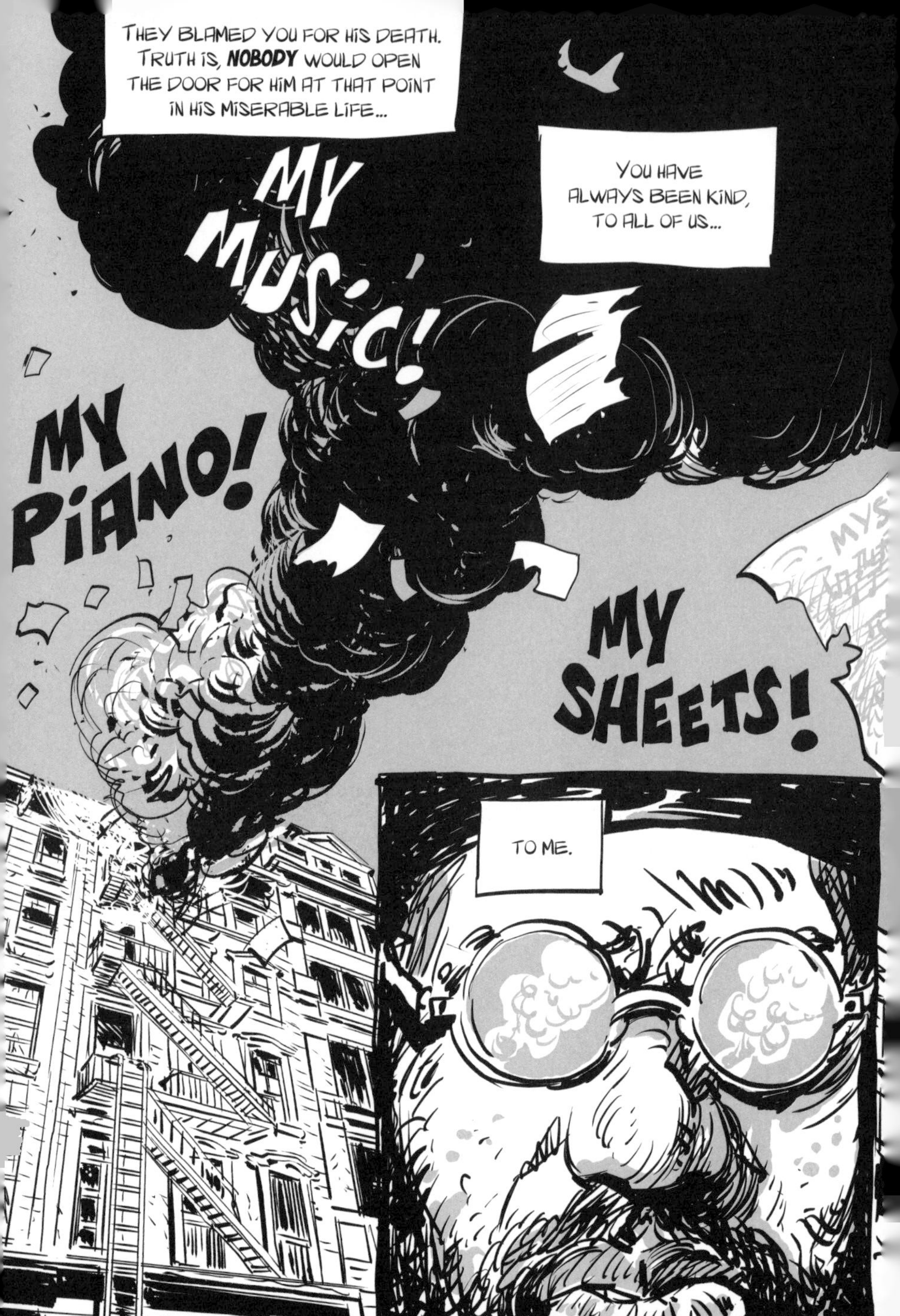
THEY BLAMED YOU FOR HIS DEATH. TRUTH IS, NOBODY WOULD OPEN THE DOOR FOR HIM AT THAT POINT IN HIS MISERABLE LIFE...
YOU HAVE ALWAYS BEEN KIND, TO ALL OF US...
MY MUSIC!
MY PIANO!
MY SHEETS!
TO ME.

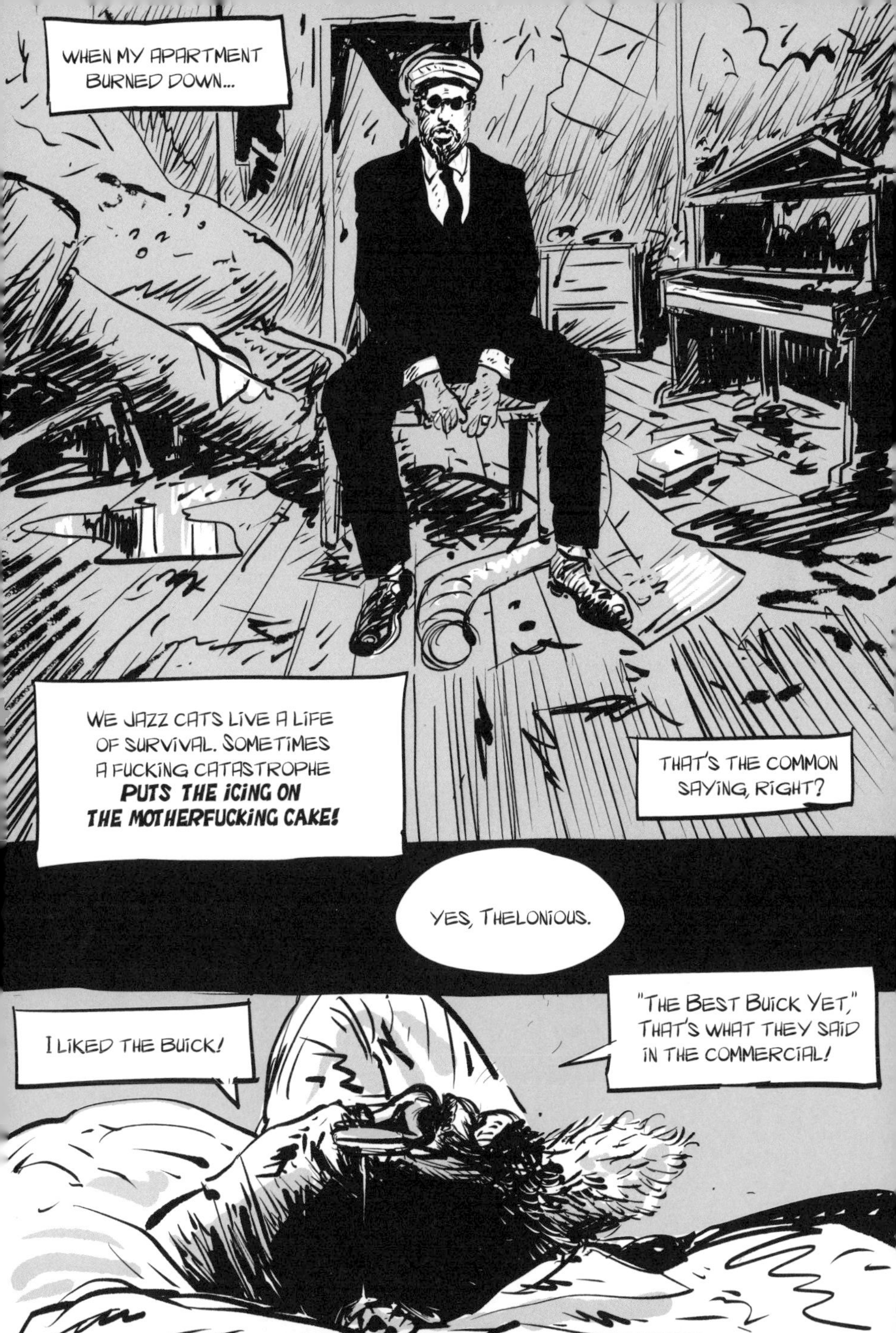
WHEN MY APARTMENT BURNED DOWN...
WE JAZZ CATS LIVE A LIFE OF SURVIVAL. SOMETIMES A FUCKING CATASTROPHE **PUTS THE ICING ON THE MOTHERFUCKING CAKE!**
THAT'S THE COMMON SAYING, RIGHT?
YES, THELONIOUS.
I LIKED THE BUICK!
"THE BEST BUICK YET," THAT'S WHAT THEY SAID IN THE COMMERCIAL!

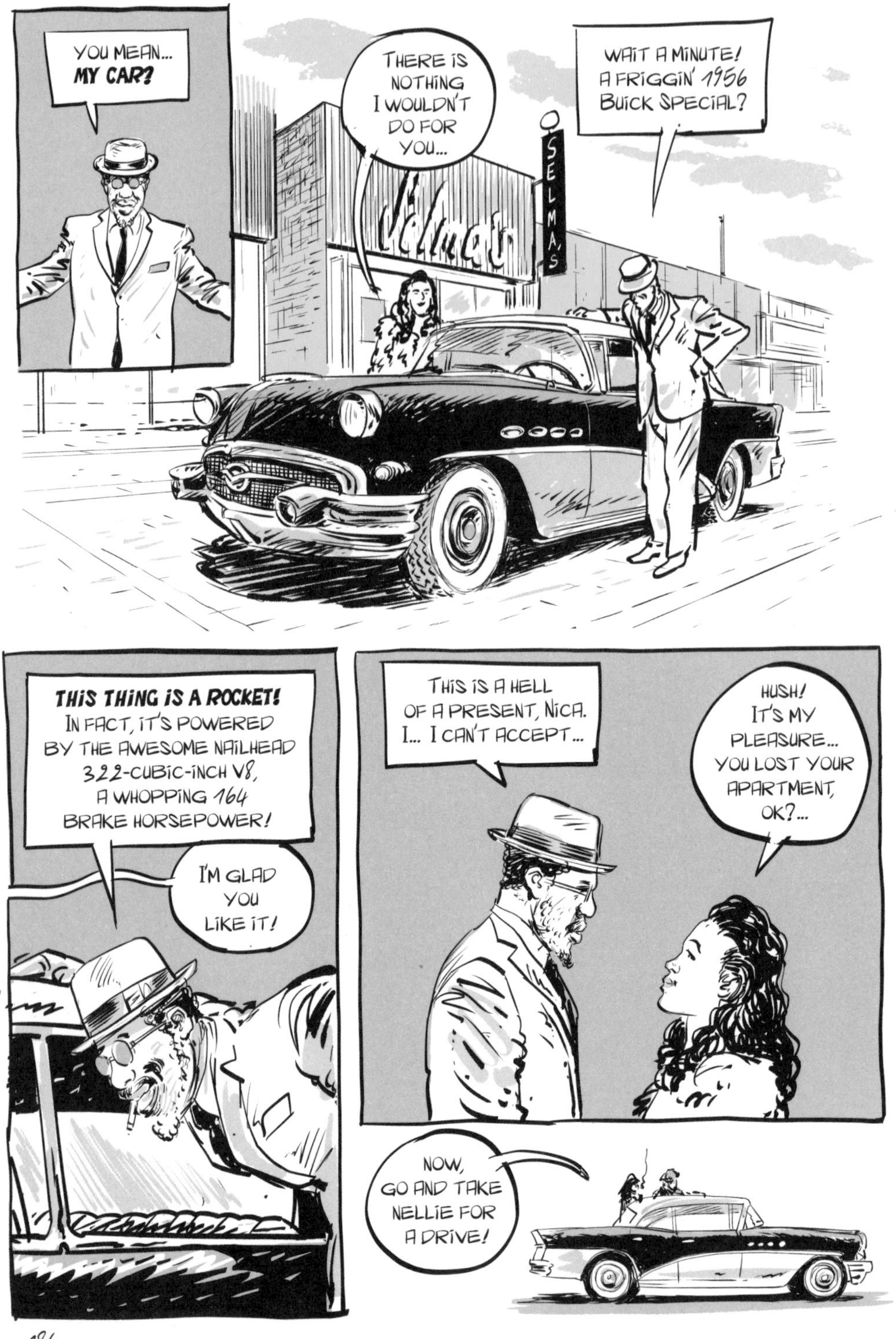

YOU MEAN... **MY CAR?**
THERE IS NOTHING I WOULDN'T DO FOR YOU...
WAIT A MINUTE! A FRIGGIN' 1956 BUICK SPECIAL?
SELMA'S
THIS THING IS A ROCKET! IN FACT, IT'S POWERED BY THE AWESOME NAILHEAD 322-CUBIC-INCH V8, A WHOPPING 164 BRAKE HORSEPOWER!
I'M GLAD YOU LIKE IT!
THIS IS A HELL OF A PRESENT, NICA. I... I CAN'T ACCEPT...
HUSH! IT'S MY PLEASURE... YOU LOST YOUR APARTMENT, OK?...
NOW, GO AND TAKE NELLIE FOR A DRIVE!

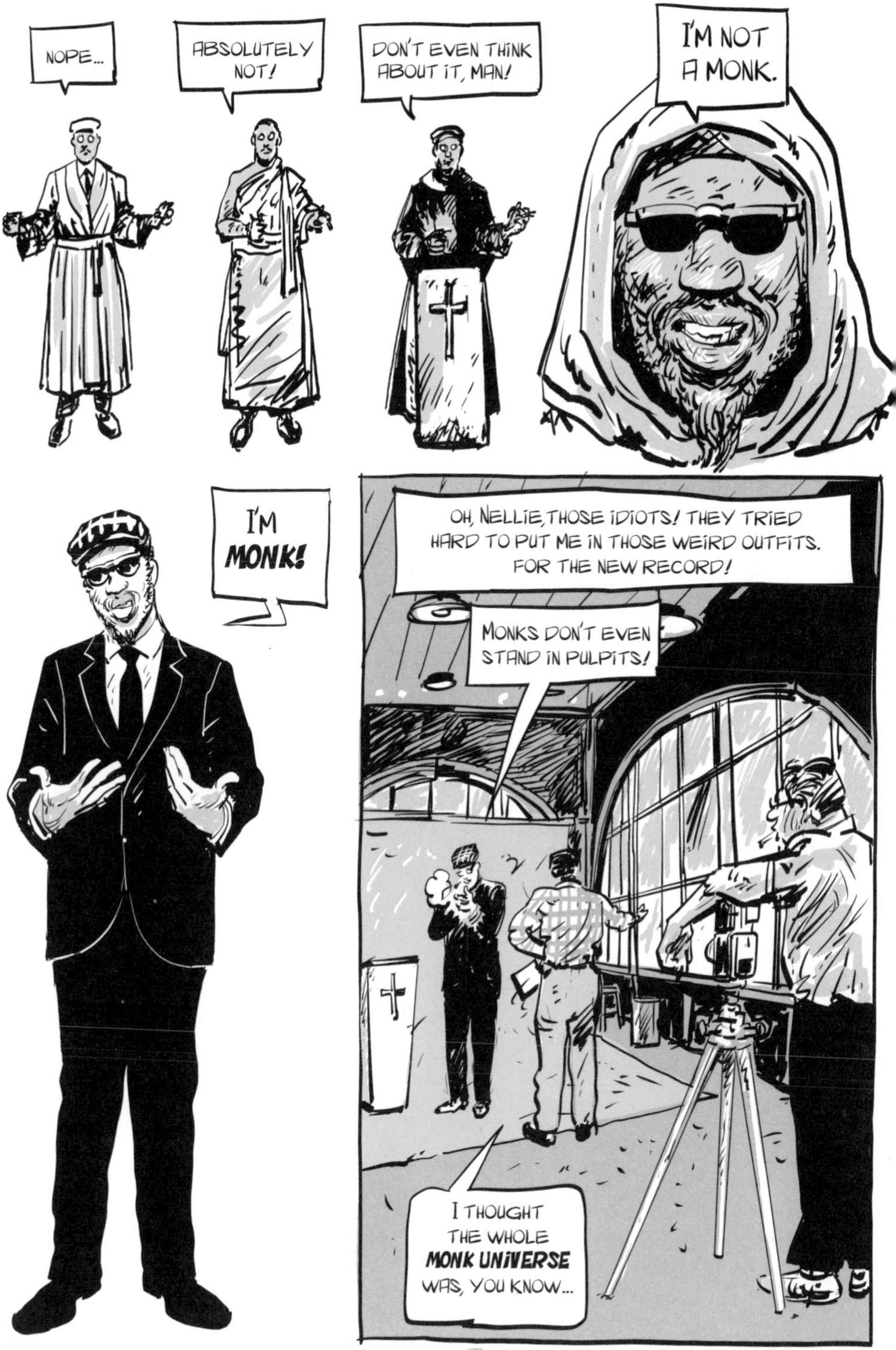
NOPE...
ABSOLUTELY NOT!
DON'T EVEN THINK ABOUT IT, MAN!
I'M NOT A MONK.
I'M MONK!
OH, NELLIE, THOSE IDIOTS! THEY TRIED HARD TO PUT ME IN THOSE WEIRD OUTFITS. FOR THE NEW RECORD!
MONKS DON'T EVEN STAND IN PULPITS!
I THOUGHT THE WHOLE MONK UNIVERSE WAS, YOU KNOW...

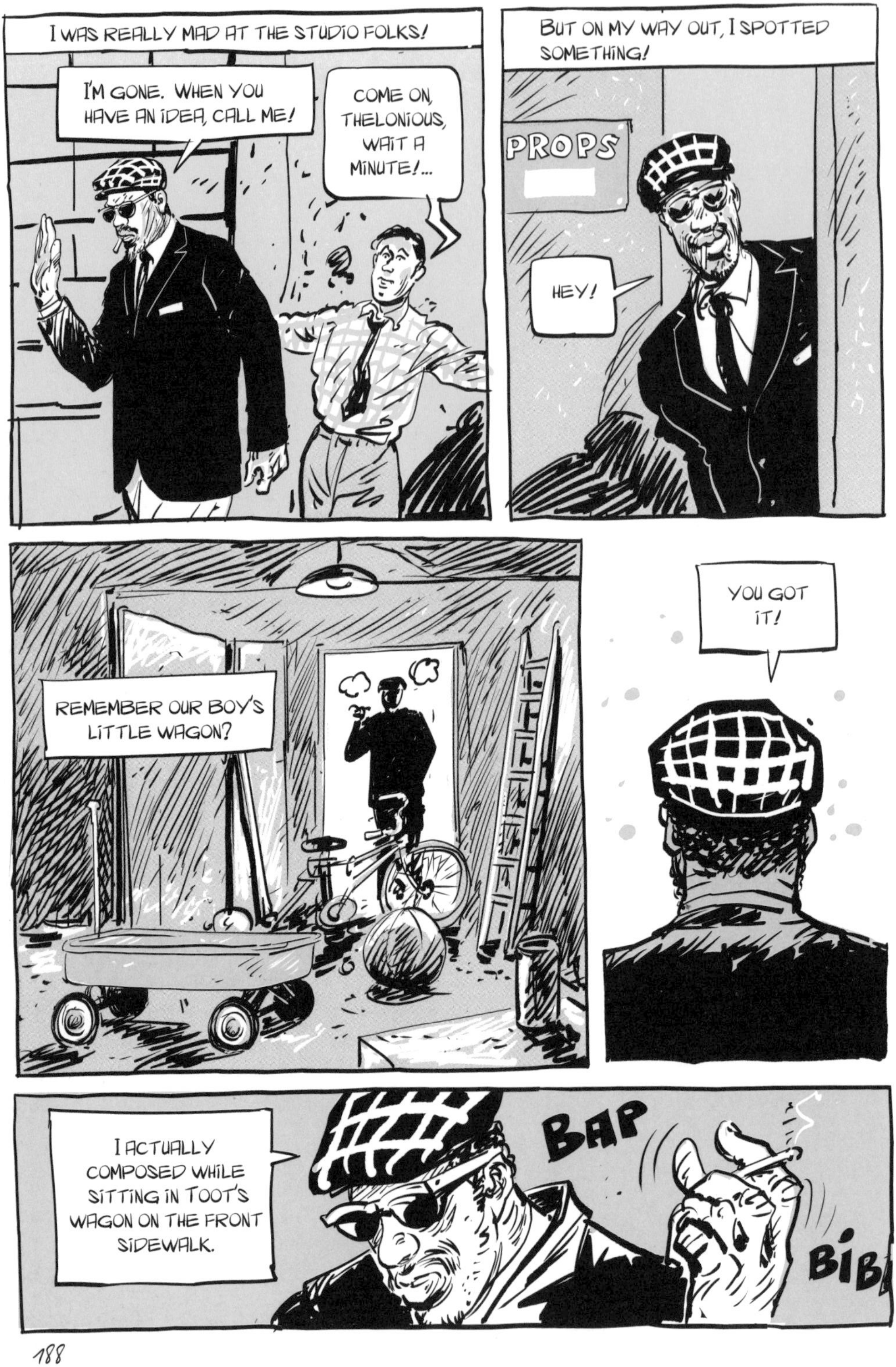
I WAS REALLY MAD AT THE STUDIO FOLKS!
I'M GONE. WHEN YOU HAVE AN IDEA, CALL ME!
COME ON, THELONIOUS, WAIT A MINUTE!...
BUT ON MY WAY OUT, I SPOTTED SOMETHING!
PROPS
HEY!
REMEMBER OUR BOY'S LITTLE WAGON?
YOU GOT IT!
I ACTUALLY COMPOSED WHILE SITTING IN TOOT'S WAGON ON THE FRONT SIDEWALK.
BAP
BIB

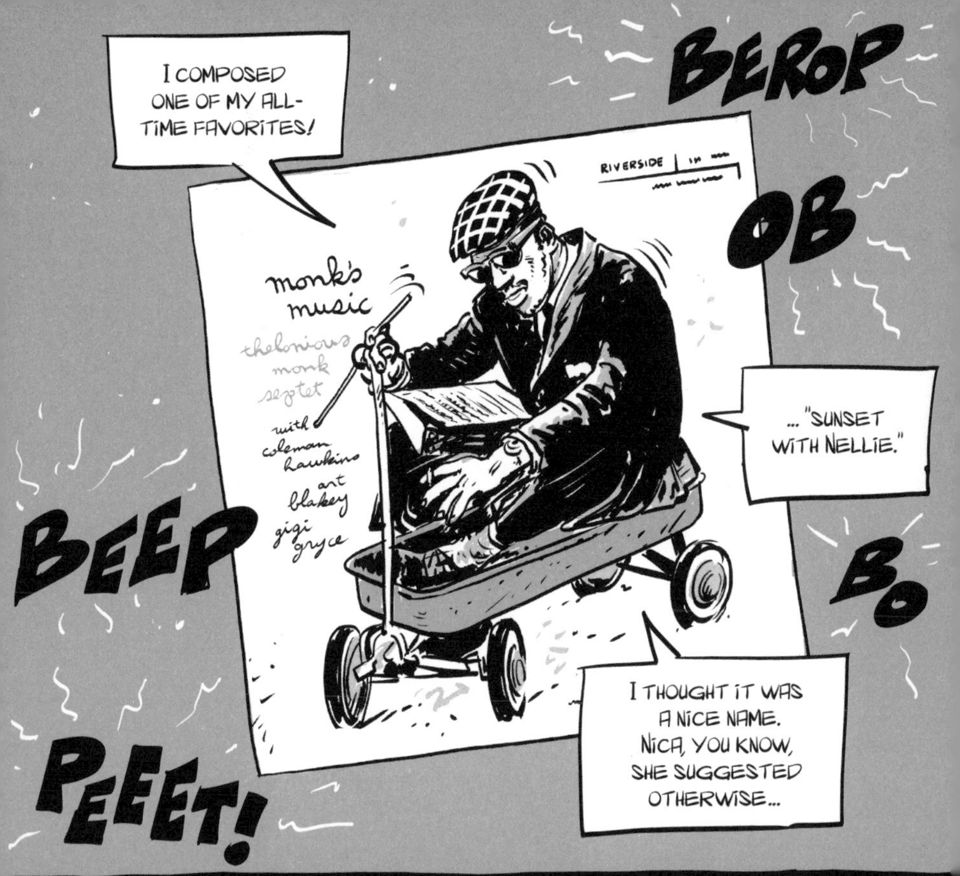

I COMPOSED ONE OF MY ALL-TIME FAVORITES!
BEROP
OB
RIVERSIDE
monk's music
thelonious monk septet
with coleman hawkins
art blakey
gigi gryce
... "SUNSET WITH NELLIE."
BEEP
BO
PEEET!
I THOUGHT IT WAS A NICE NAME. NICA, YOU KNOW, SHE SUGGESTED OTHERWISE...

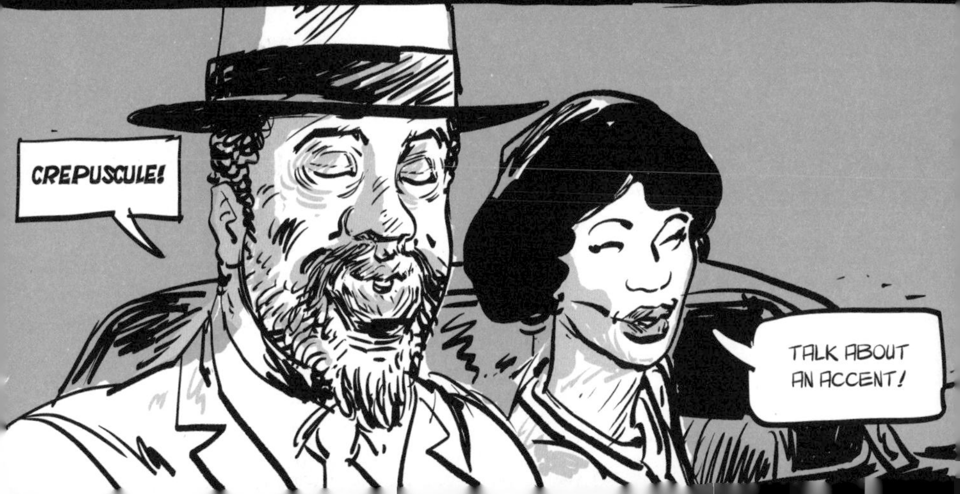

CREPUSCULE!
TALK ABOUT AN ACCENT!

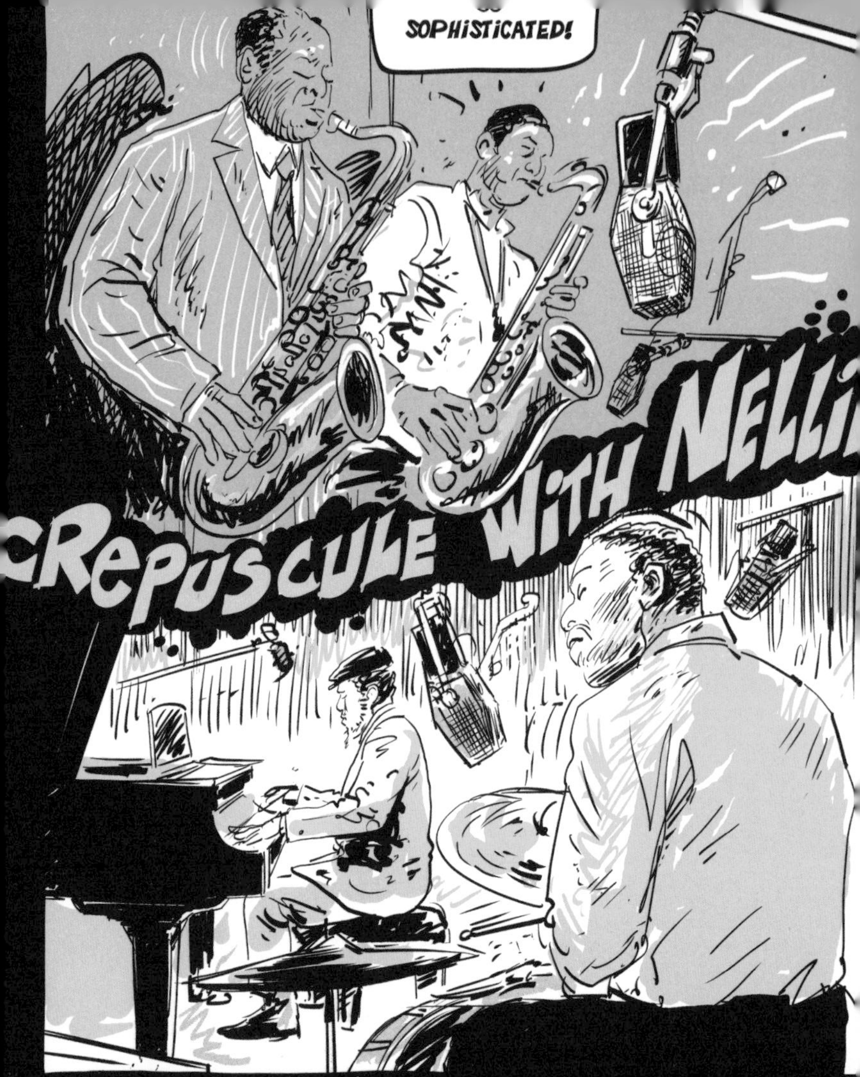
SOPHISTICATED!
CREPUSCULE WITH NELLI

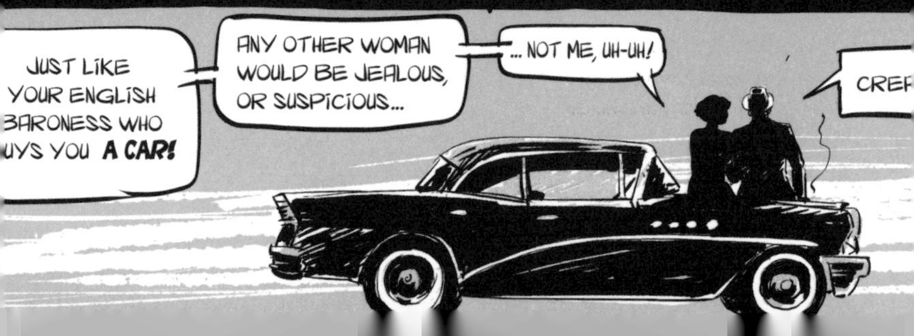
JUST LIKE YOUR ENGLISH BARONESS WHO UYS YOU A CAR!
ANY OTHER WOMAN WOULD BE JEALOUS, OR SUSPICIOUS...
... NOT ME, UH-UH!
CREF

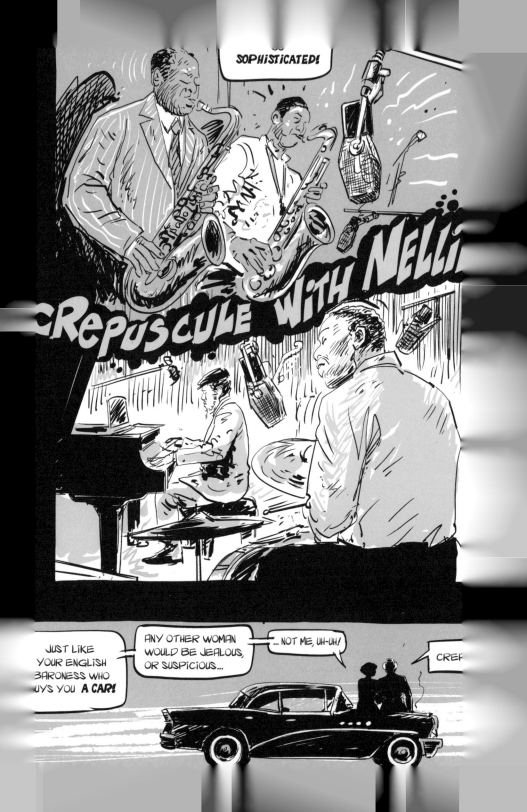

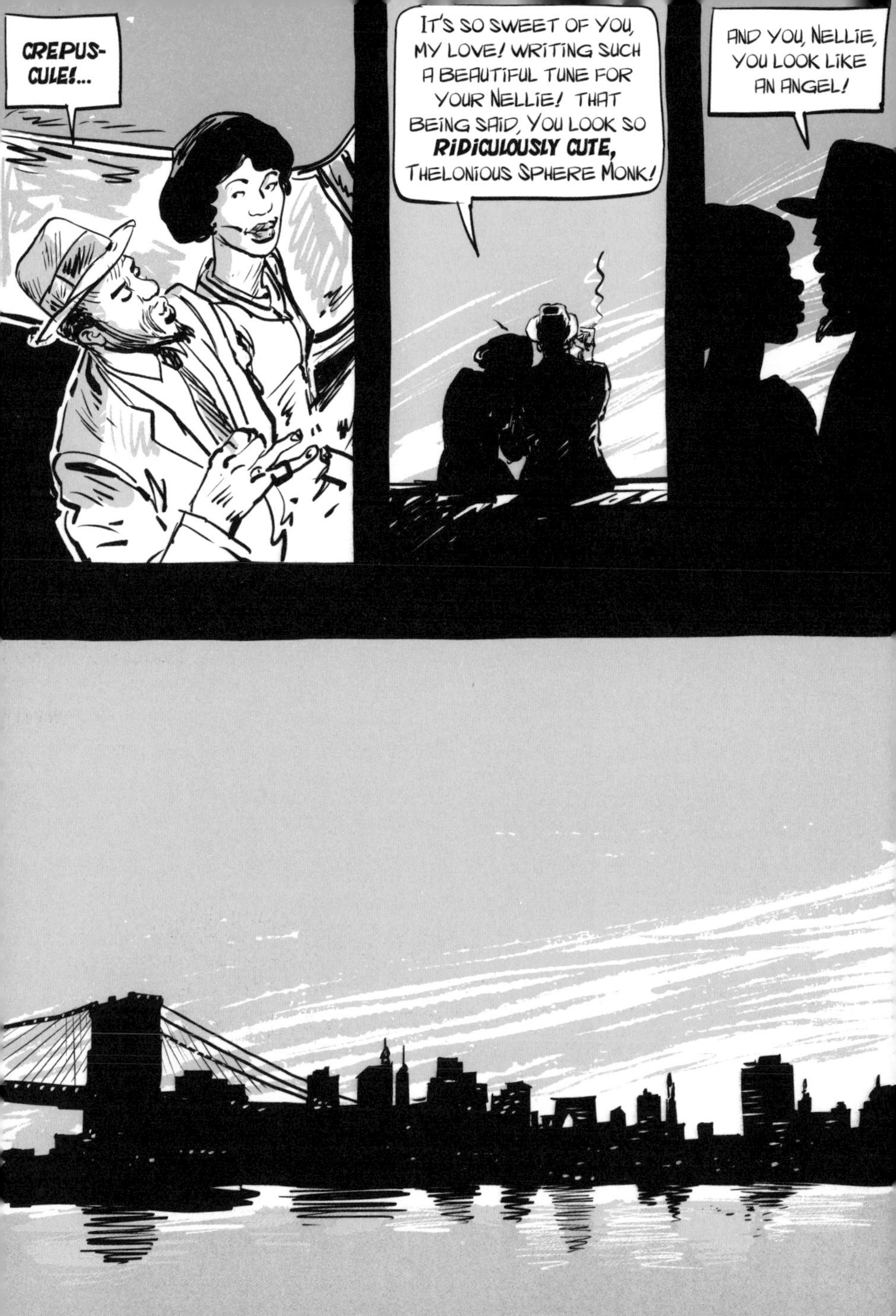
CREPUS-
CULE!...
IT'S SO SWEET OF YOU, MY LOVE! WRITING SUCH A BEAUTIFUL TUNE FOR YOUR NELLIE! THAT BEING SAID, YOU LOOK SO **RIDICULOUSLY CUTE,** THELONIOUS SPHERE MONK!
AND YOU, NELLIE, YOU LOOK LIKE AN ANGEL!

THE SCIENCE OF
IMPROVISATION

EVER NOTICE
A STRANGE
BEHAVIOR?

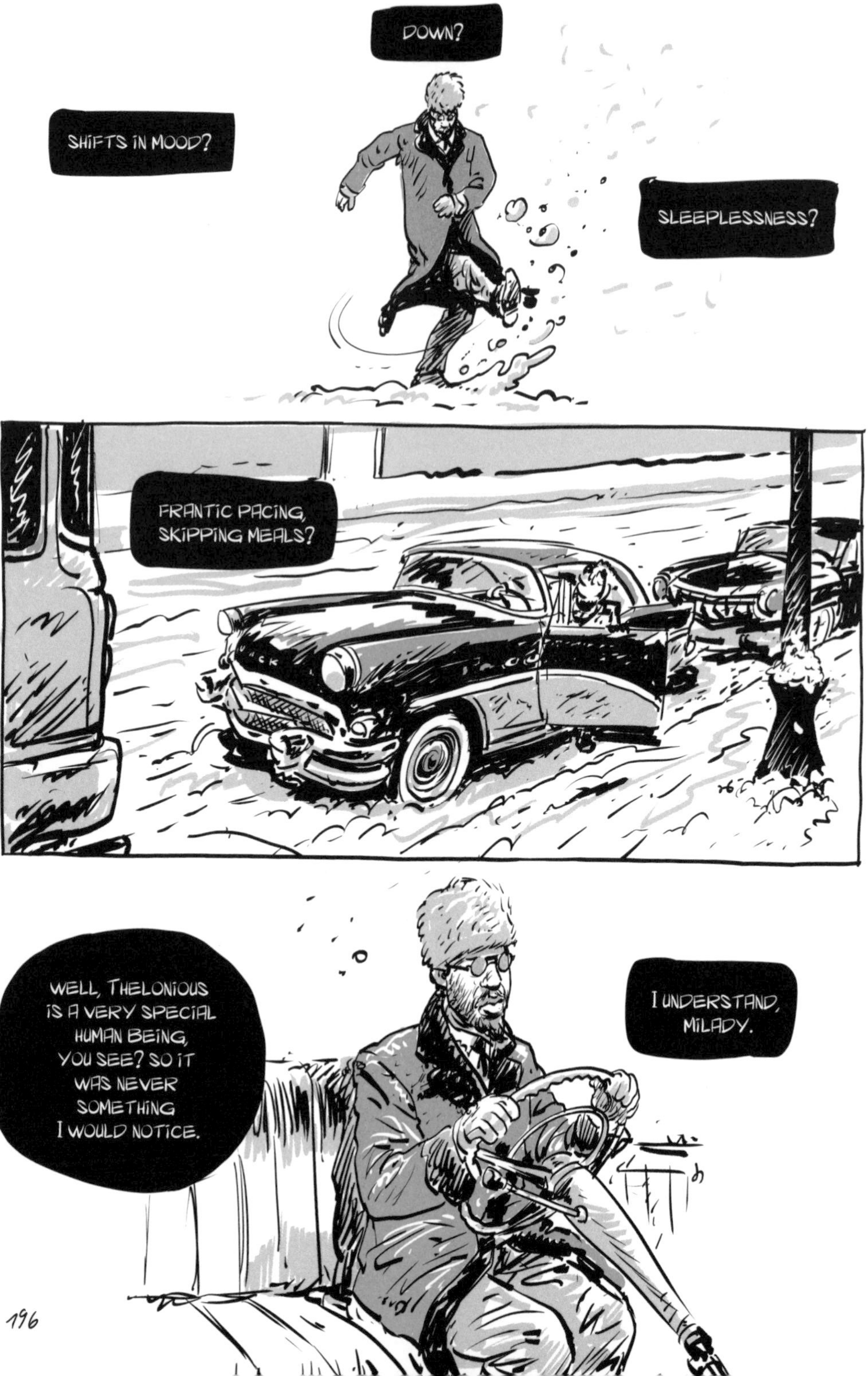
DOWN?
SHIFTS IN MOOD?
SLEEPLESSNESS?
FRANTIC PACING, SKIPPING MEALS?
WELL, THELONIOUS IS A VERY SPECIAL HUMAN BEING, YOU SEE? SO IT WAS NEVER SOMETHING I WOULD NOTICE.
I UNDERSTAND, MILADY.

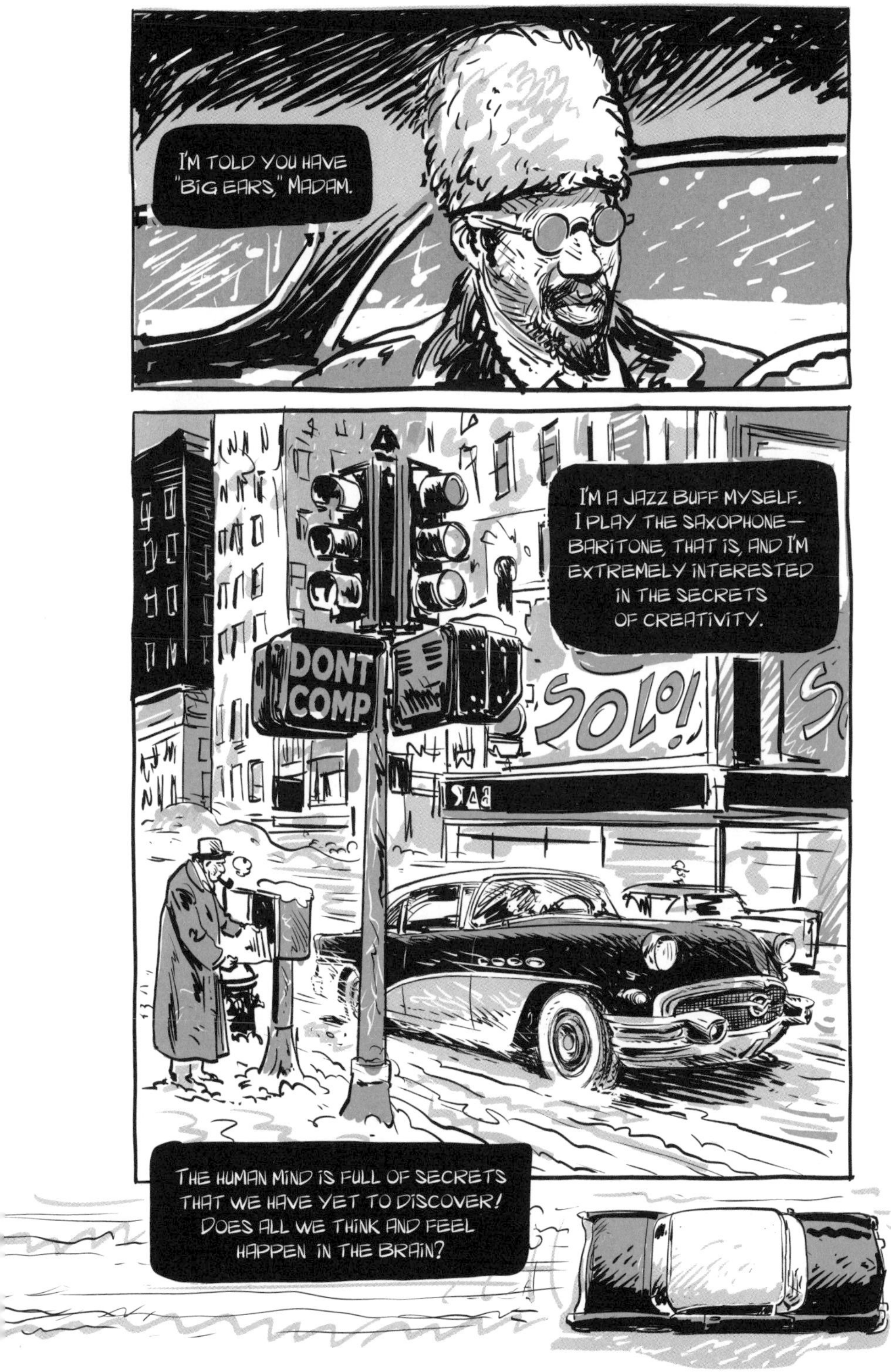
I'M TOLD YOU HAVE "BIG EARS," MADAM.
I'M A JAZZ BUFF MYSELF. I PLAY THE SAXOPHONE— BARITONE, THAT IS, AND I'M EXTREMELY INTERESTED IN THE SECRETS OF CREATIVITY.
DONT COMP
SOLO!
THE HUMAN MIND IS FULL OF SECRETS THAT WE HAVE YET TO DISCOVER! DOES ALL WE THINK AND FEEL HAPPEN IN THE BRAIN?

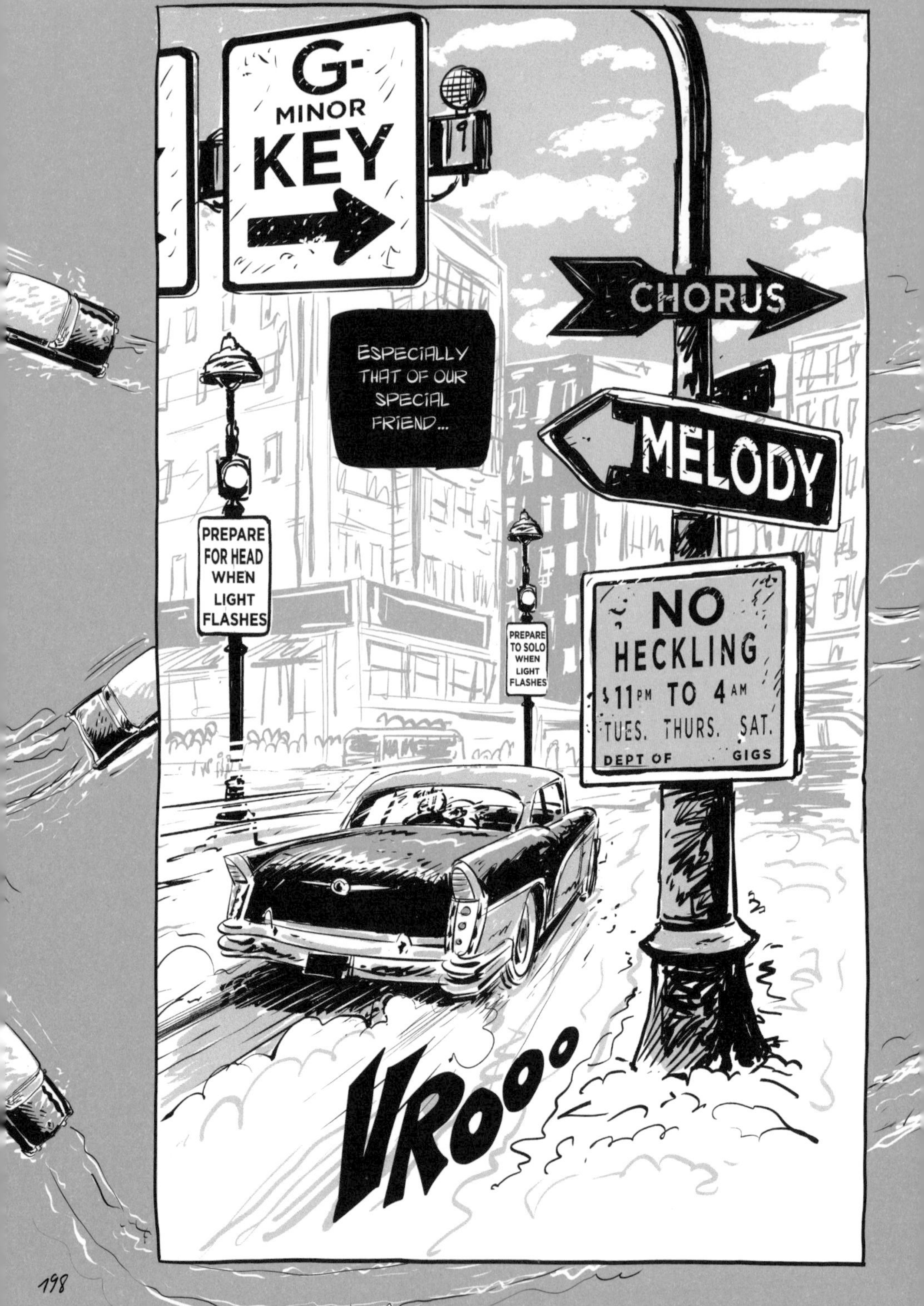
G-
MINOR
KEY
ESPECIALLY THAT OF OUR SPECIAL FRIEND...
CHORUS
MELODY
PREPARE FOR HEAD WHEN LIGHT FLASHES
PREPARE TO SOLO WHEN LIGHT FLASHES
NO HECKLING
$11PM TO 4AM
TUES. THURS. SAT.
DEPT OF GIGS
VROOO

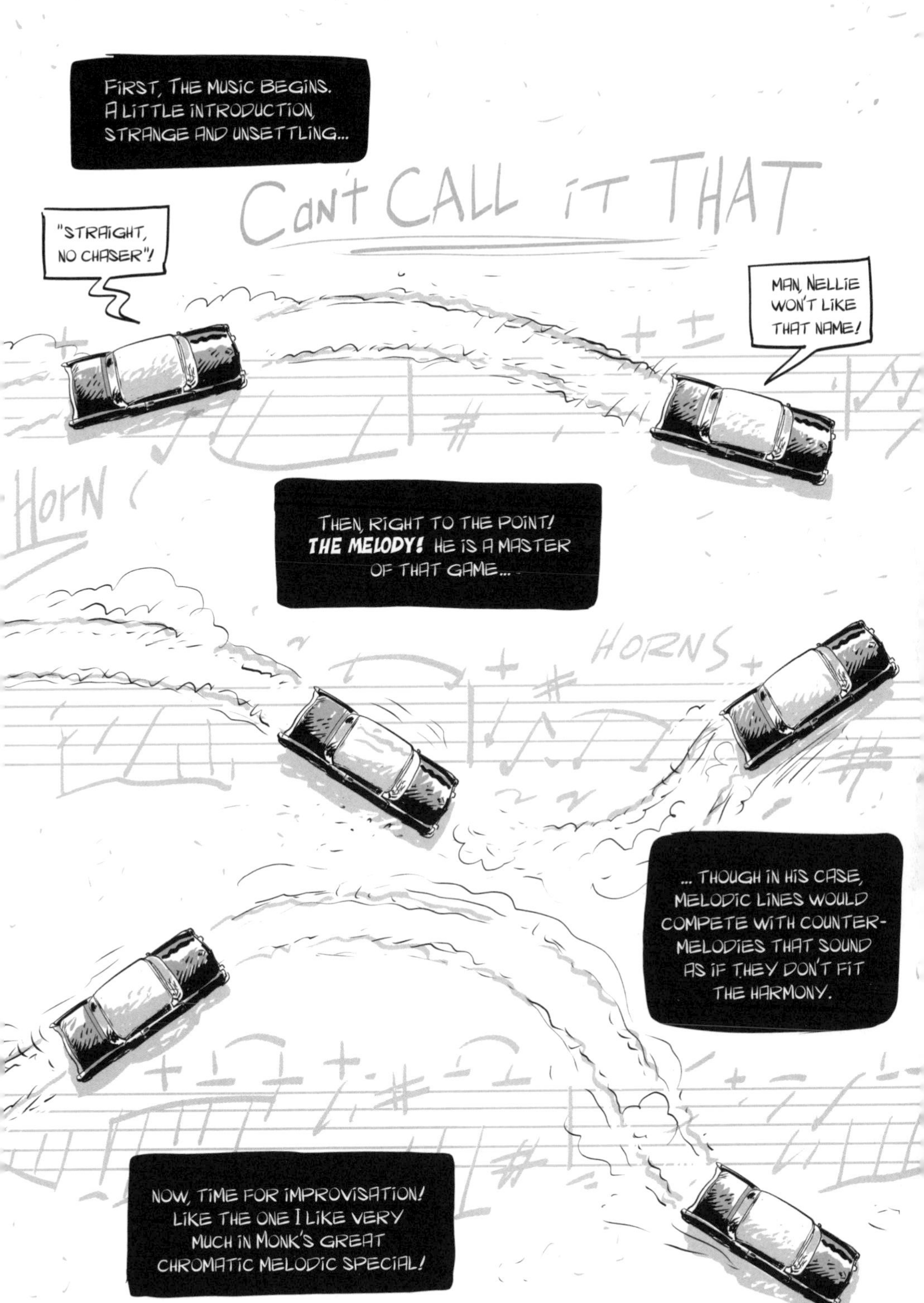
FIRST, THE MUSIC BEGINS. A LITTLE INTRODUCTION, STRANGE AND UNSETTLING...
Can't CALL it THAT
"STRAIGHT, NO CHASER"!
MAN, NELLIE WON'T LIKE THAT NAME!
Horn
THEN, RIGHT TO THE POINT! **THE MELODY!** HE IS A MASTER OF THAT GAME...
HORNS
... THOUGH IN HIS CASE, MELODIC LINES WOULD COMPETE WITH COUNTER-MELODIES THAT SOUND AS IF THEY DON'T FIT THE HARMONY.
NOW, TIME FOR IMPROVISATION! LIKE THE ONE I LIKE VERY MUCH IN MONK'S GREAT CHROMATIC MELODIC SPECIAL!

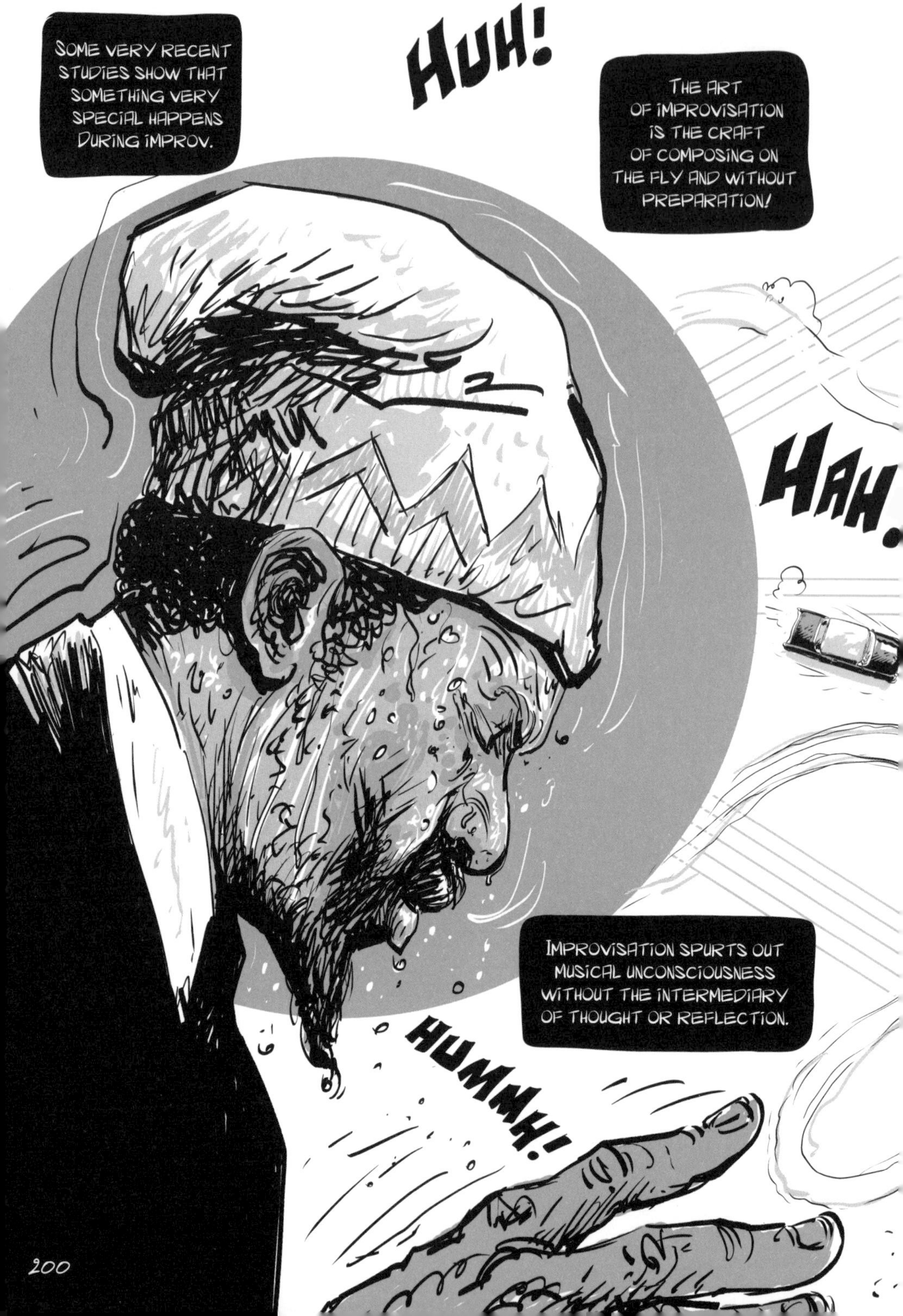
SOME VERY RECENT STUDIES SHOW THAT SOMETHING VERY SPECIAL HAPPENS DURING IMPROV.
HUH!
THE ART OF IMPROVISATION IS THE CRAFT OF COMPOSING ON THE FLY AND WITHOUT PREPARATION!
HAH.
IMPROVISATION SPURTS OUT MUSICAL UNCONSCIOUSNESS WITHOUT THE INTERMEDIARY OF THOUGHT OR REFLECTION.
HUMMH!

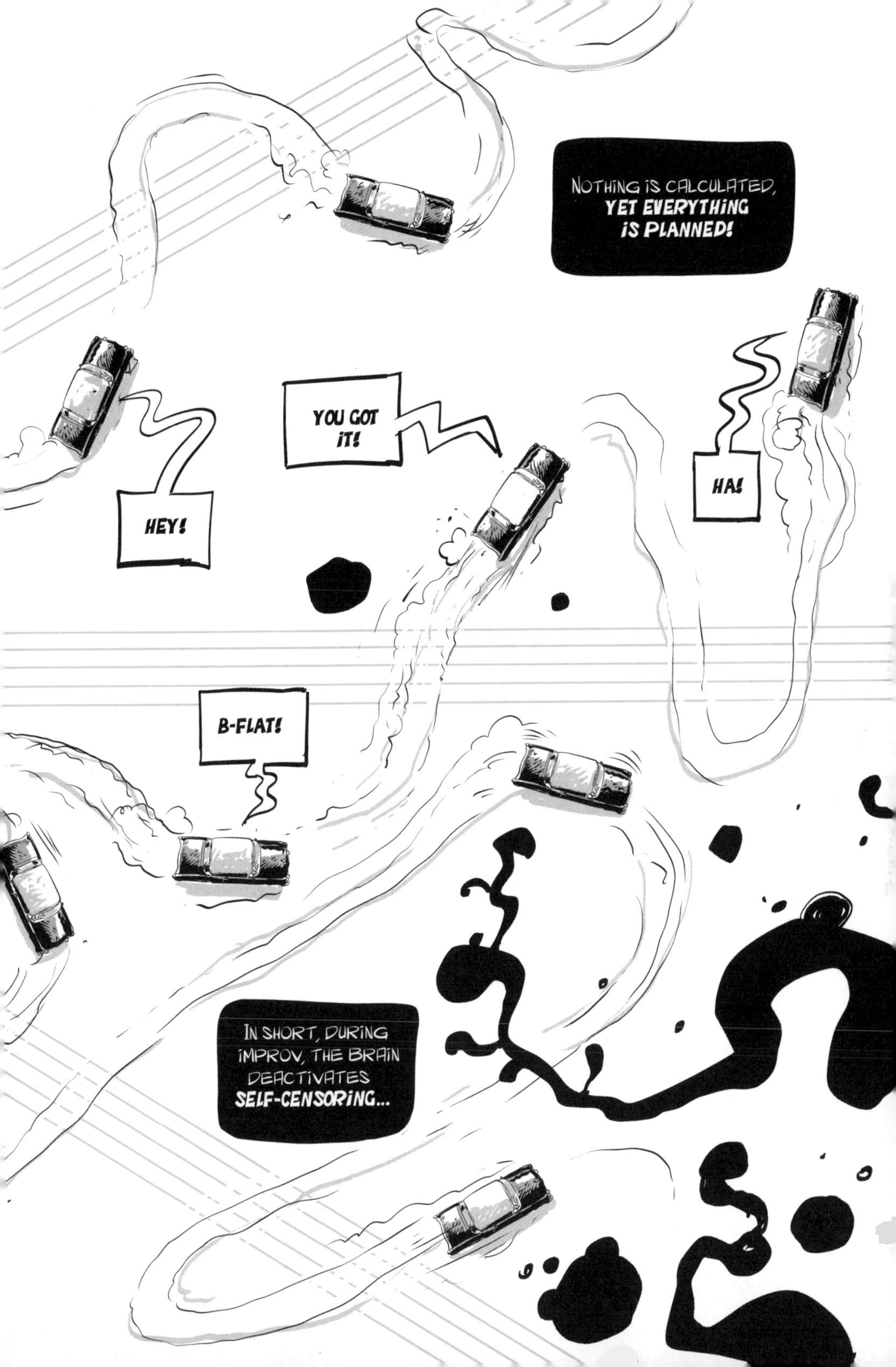
NOTHING IS CALCULATED, YET EVERYTHING IS PLANNED!
YOU GOT IT!
HEY!
HA!
B-FLAT!
IN SHORT, DURING IMPROV, THE BRAIN DEACTIVATES SELF-CENSORING...

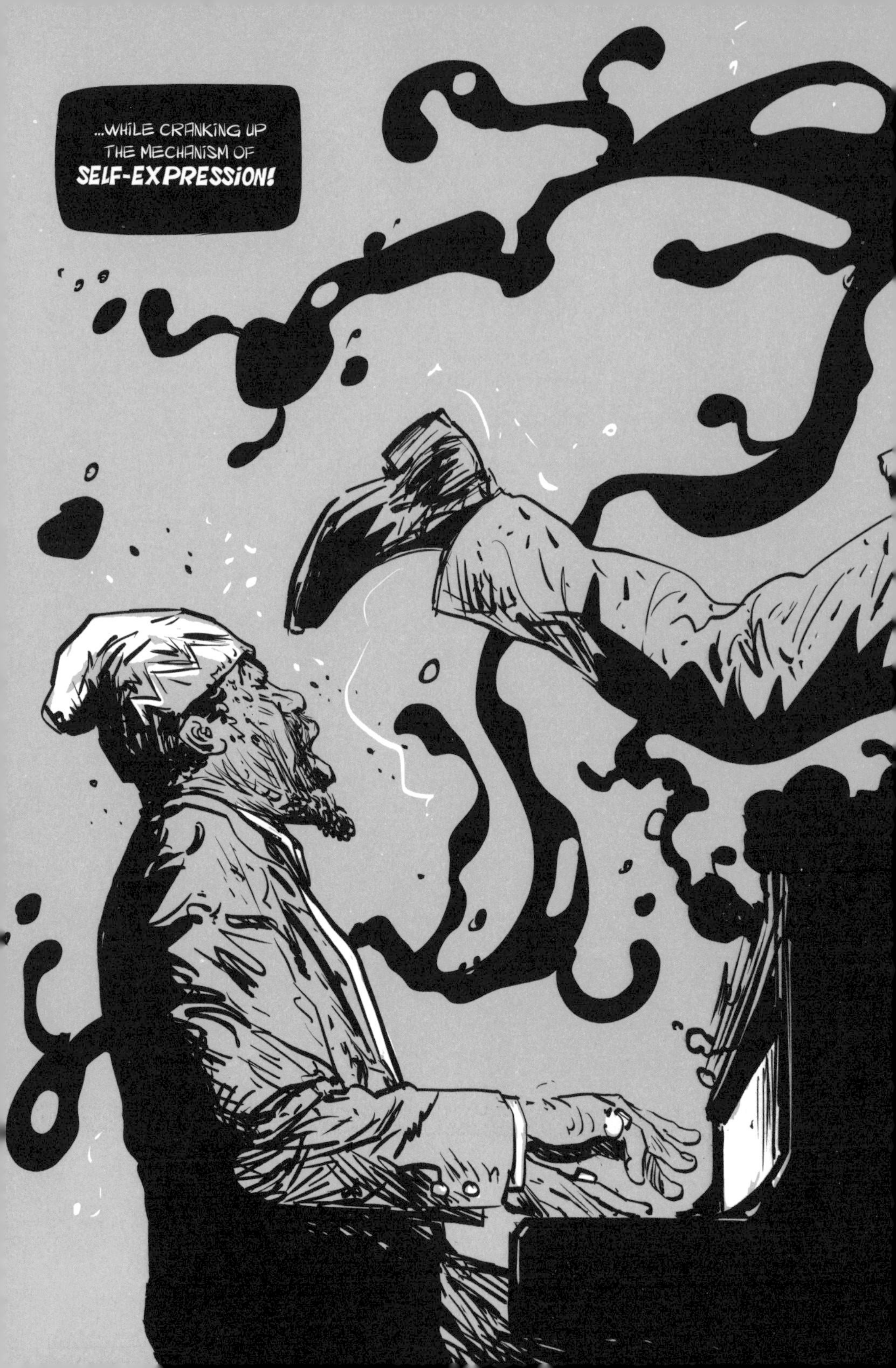
...WHILE CRANKING UP THE MECHANISM OF SELF-EXPRESSION!

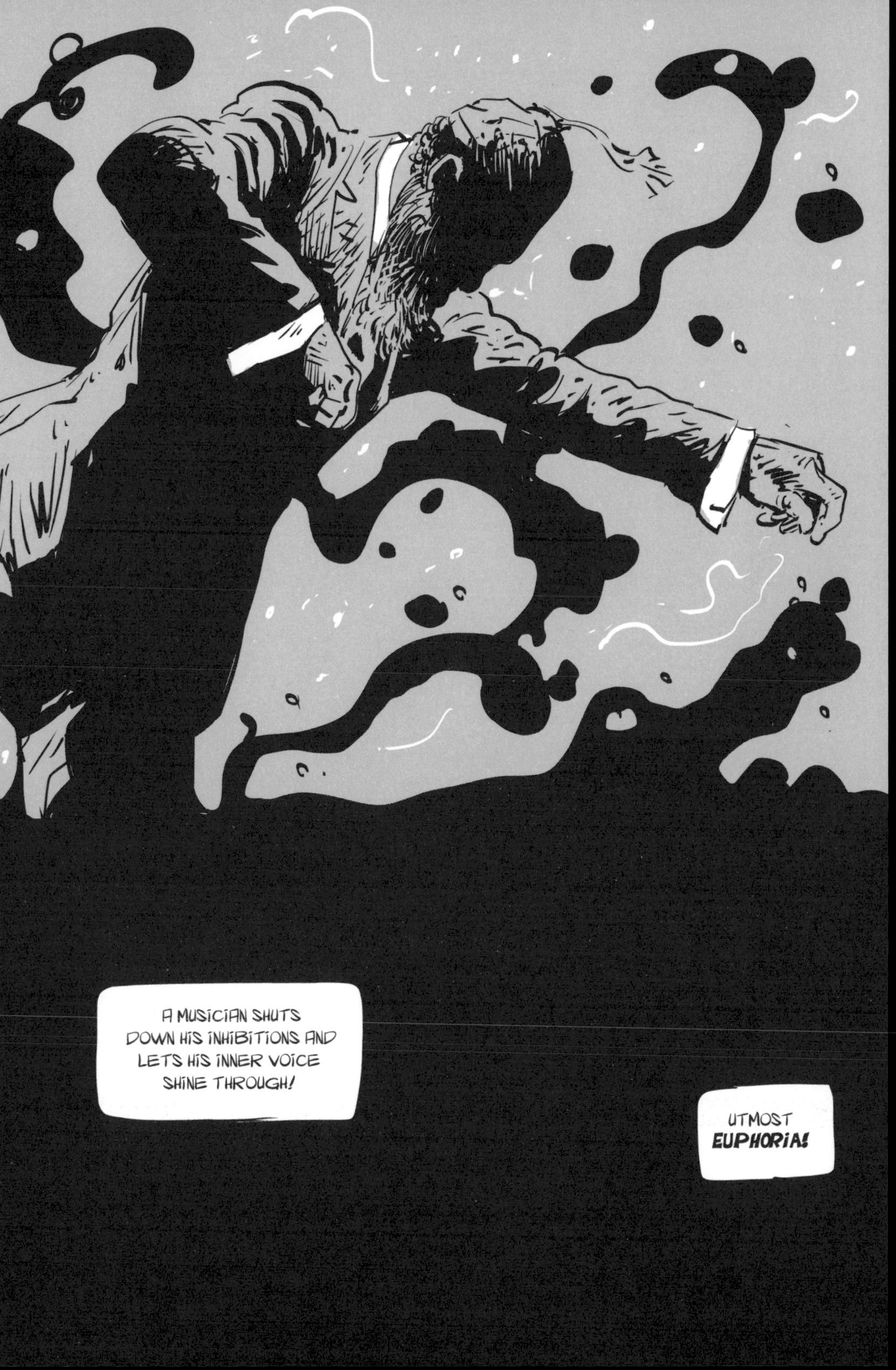
A MUSICIAN SHUTS DOWN HIS INHIBITIONS AND LETS HIS INNER VOICE SHINE THROUGH!
UTMOST **EUPHORIA!**

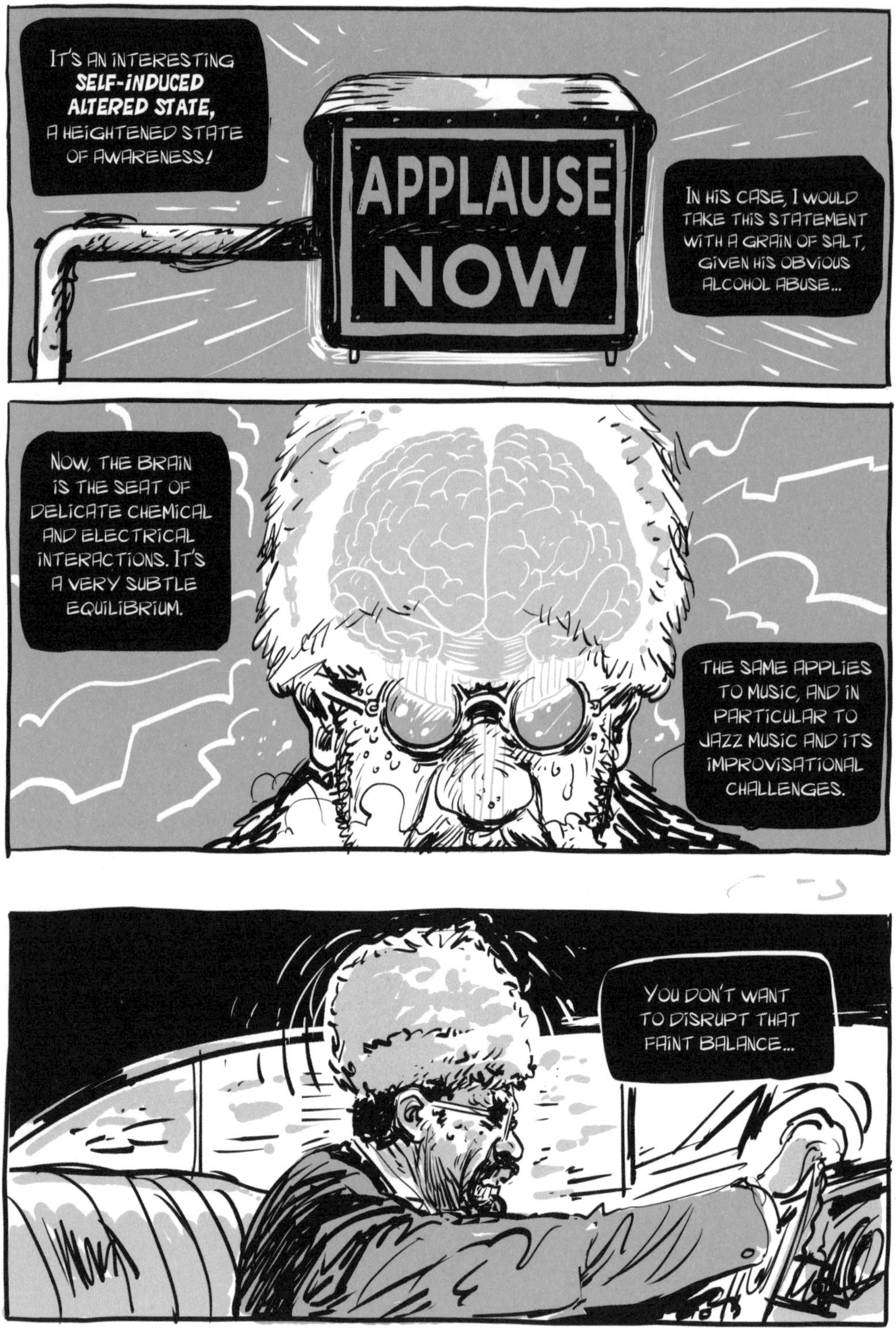

IT'S AN INTERESTING **SELF-INDUCED ALTERED STATE,** A HEIGHTENED STATE OF AWARENESS!
APPLAUSE NOW
IN HIS CASE, I WOULD TAKE THIS STATEMENT WITH A GRAIN OF SALT, GIVEN HIS OBVIOUS ALCOHOL ABUSE...
NOW, THE BRAIN IS THE SEAT OF DELICATE CHEMICAL AND ELECTRICAL INTERACTIONS. IT'S A VERY SUBTLE EQUILIBRIUM.
THE SAME APPLIES TO MUSIC, AND IN PARTICULAR TO JAZZ MUSIC AND ITS IMPROVISATIONAL CHALLENGES.
YOU DON'T WANT TO DISRUPT THAT FAINT BALANCE...

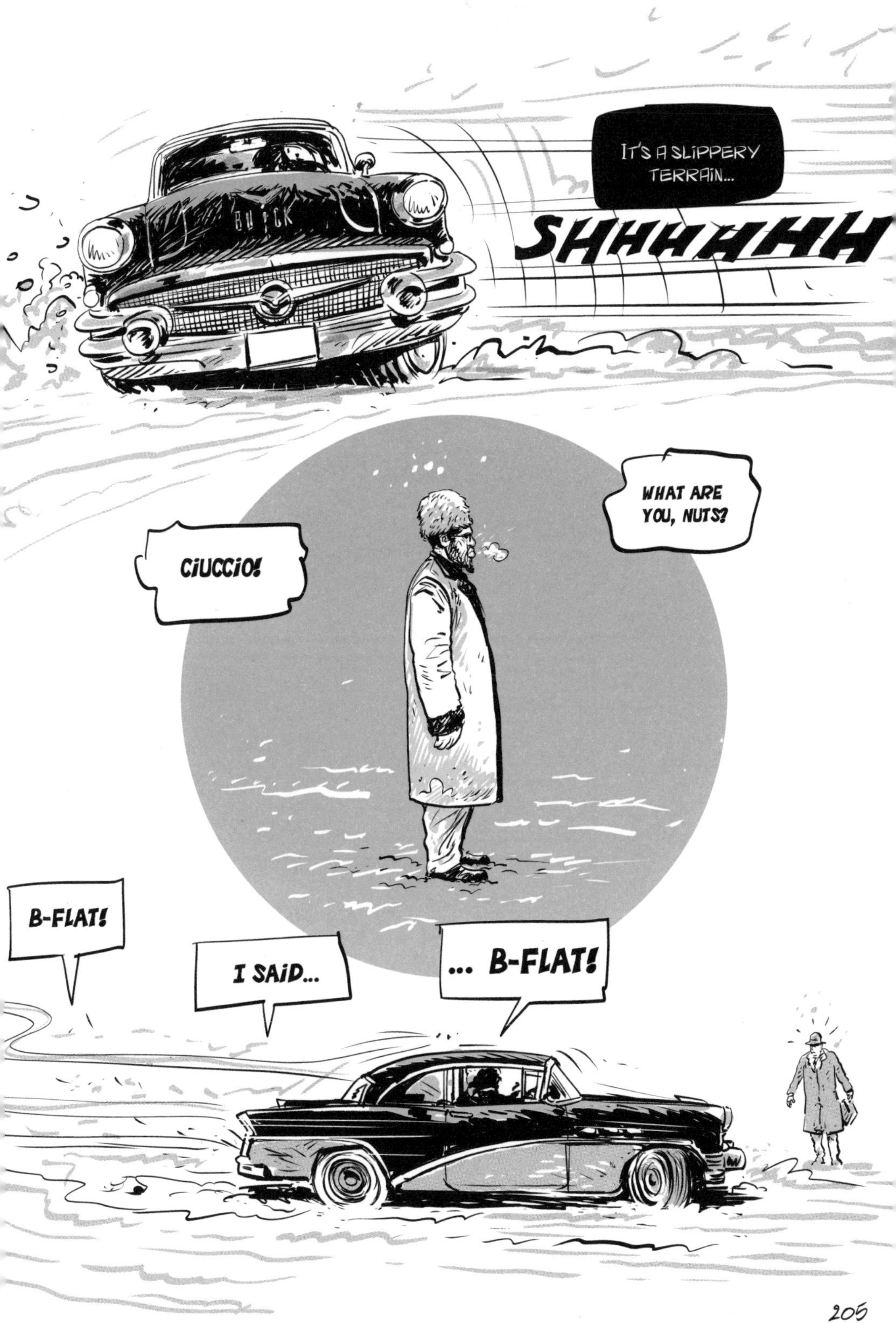

IT'S A SLIPPERY TERRAIN...
SHHHHHH
WHAT ARE YOU, NUTS?
CIUCCIO!
B-FLAT!
I SAID...
... B-FLAT!

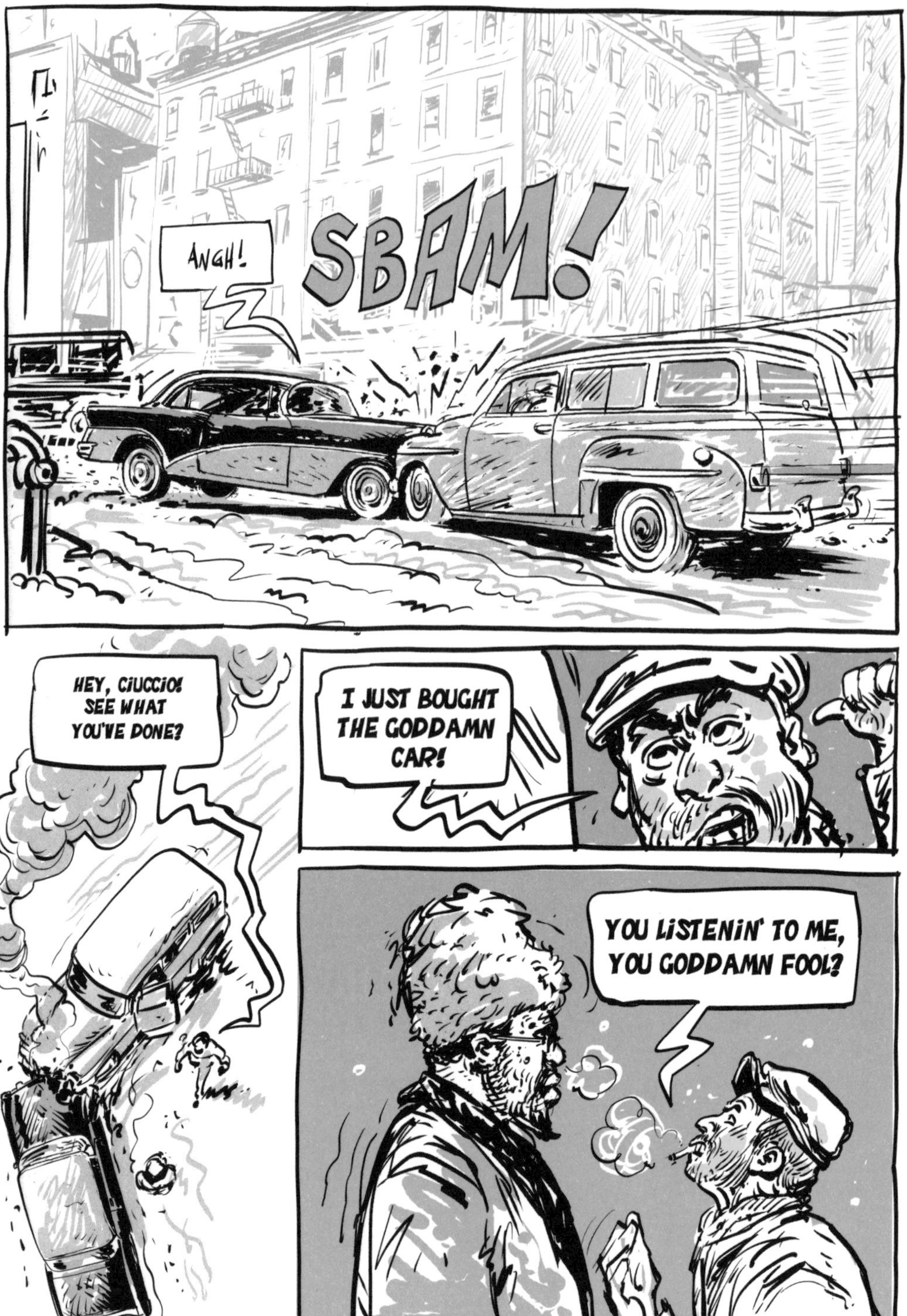
ANGH!
SBAM!
HEY, CIUCCIO! SEE WHAT YOU'VE DONE?
I JUST BOUGHT THE GODDAMN CAR!
YOU LISTENIN' TO ME, YOU GODDAMN FOOL?

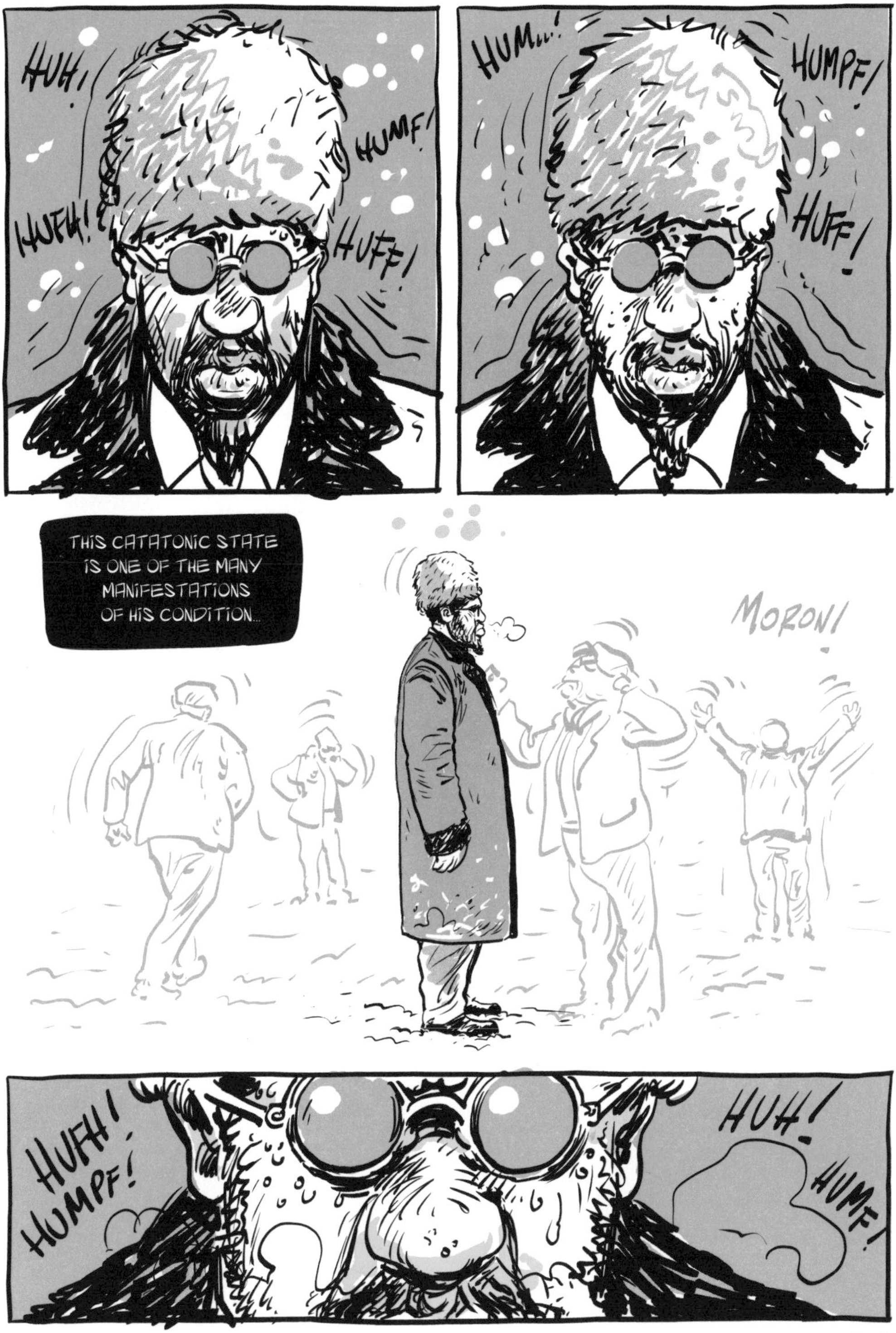
HUH!
HUMF!
HUFH!
HUFF!
HUM...!
HUMPF!
HUFF!
THIS CATATONIC STATE IS ONE OF THE MANY MANIFESTATIONS OF HIS CONDITION...
MORON!
HUFH!
HUMPF!
HUH!
HUMF!

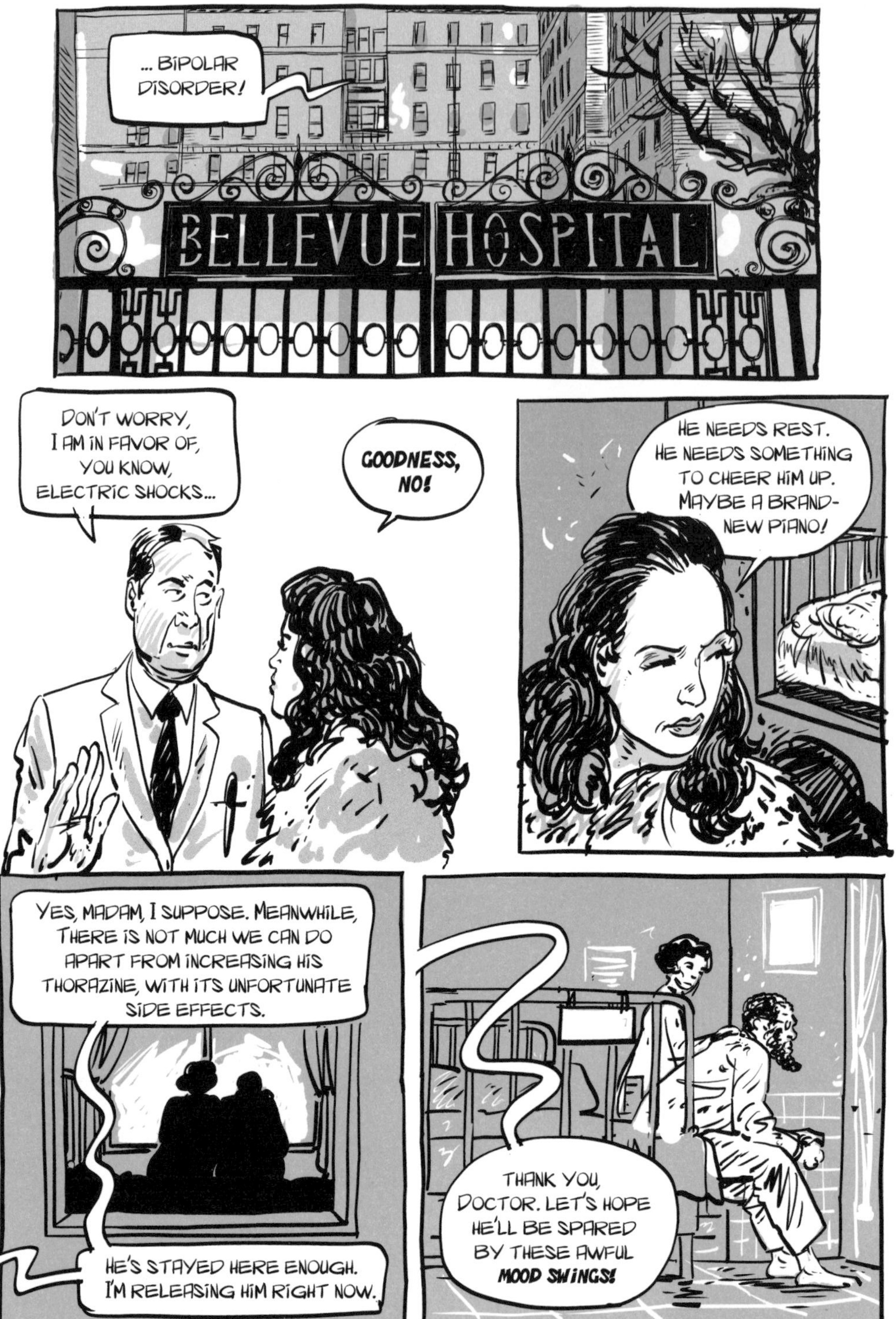
... BIPOLAR DISORDER!
BELLEVUE HOSPITAL
DON'T WORRY, I AM IN FAVOR OF, YOU KNOW, ELECTRIC SHOCKS...
GOODNESS, NO!
HE NEEDS REST. HE NEEDS SOMETHING TO CHEER HIM UP. MAYBE A BRAND-NEW PIANO!
YES, MADAM, I SUPPOSE. MEANWHILE, THERE IS NOT MUCH WE CAN DO APART FROM INCREASING HIS THORAZINE, WITH ITS UNFORTUNATE SIDE EFFECTS.
HE'S STAYED HERE ENOUGH. I'M RELEASING HIM RIGHT NOW.
THANK YOU, DOCTOR. LET'S HOPE HE'LL BE SPARED BY THESE AWFUL MOOD SWINGS!

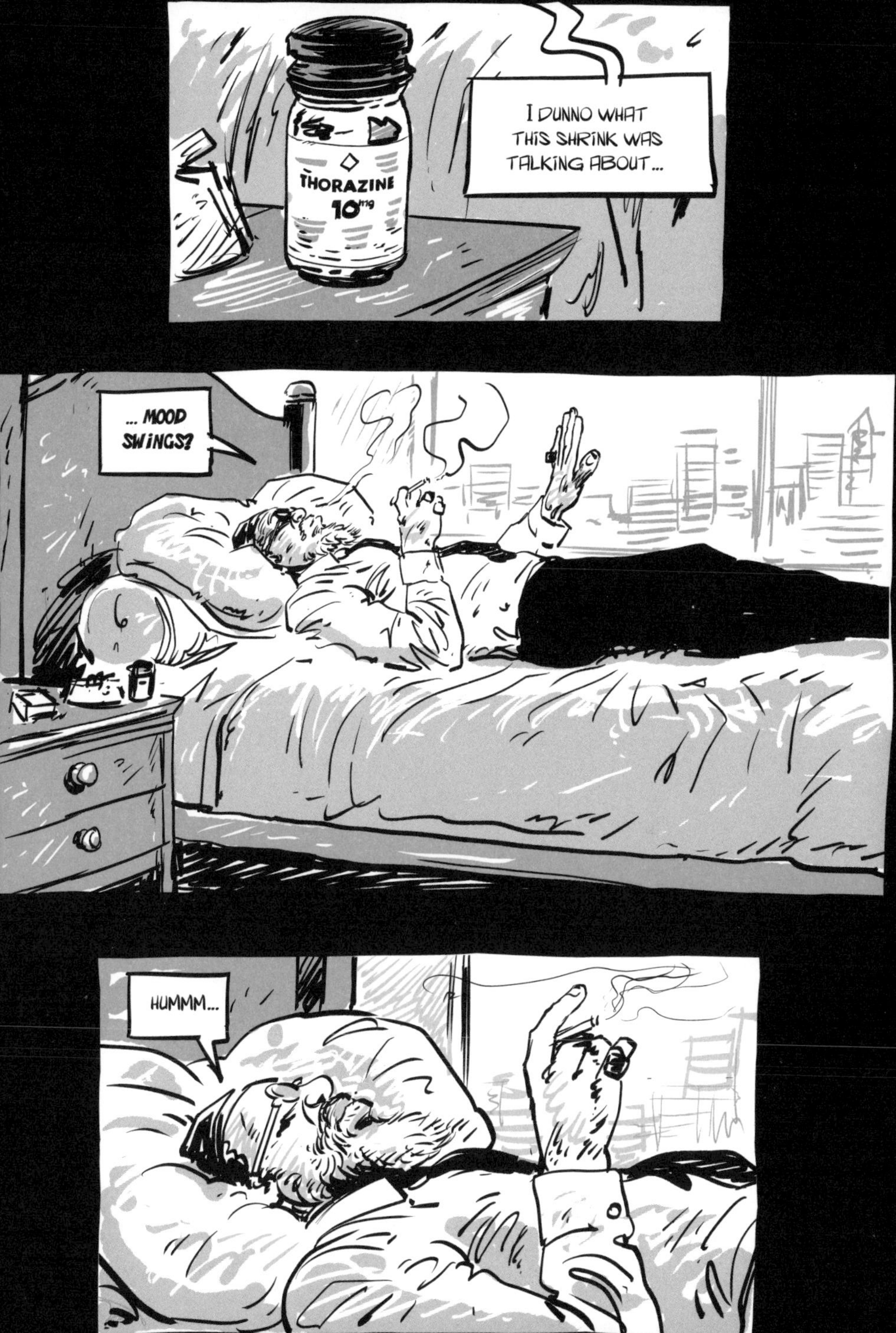
THORAZINE
10mg
I DUNNO WHAT THIS SHRINK WAS TALKING ABOUT...
... MOOD SWINGS?
HUMMM...

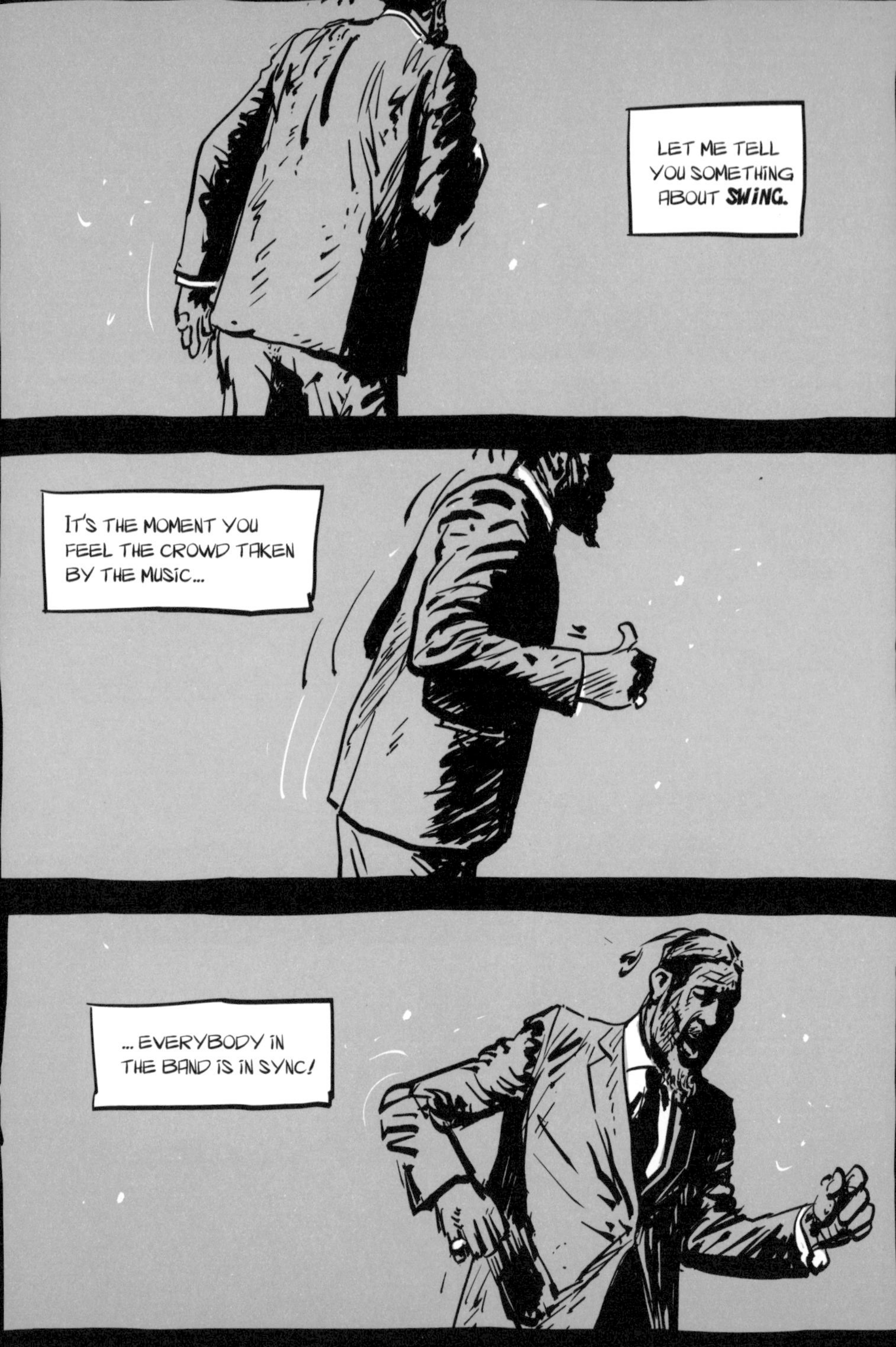
LET ME TELL YOU SOMETHING ABOUT SWING.
IT'S THE MOMENT YOU FEEL THE CROWD TAKEN BY THE MUSIC...
... EVERYBODY IN THE BAND IS IN SYNC!

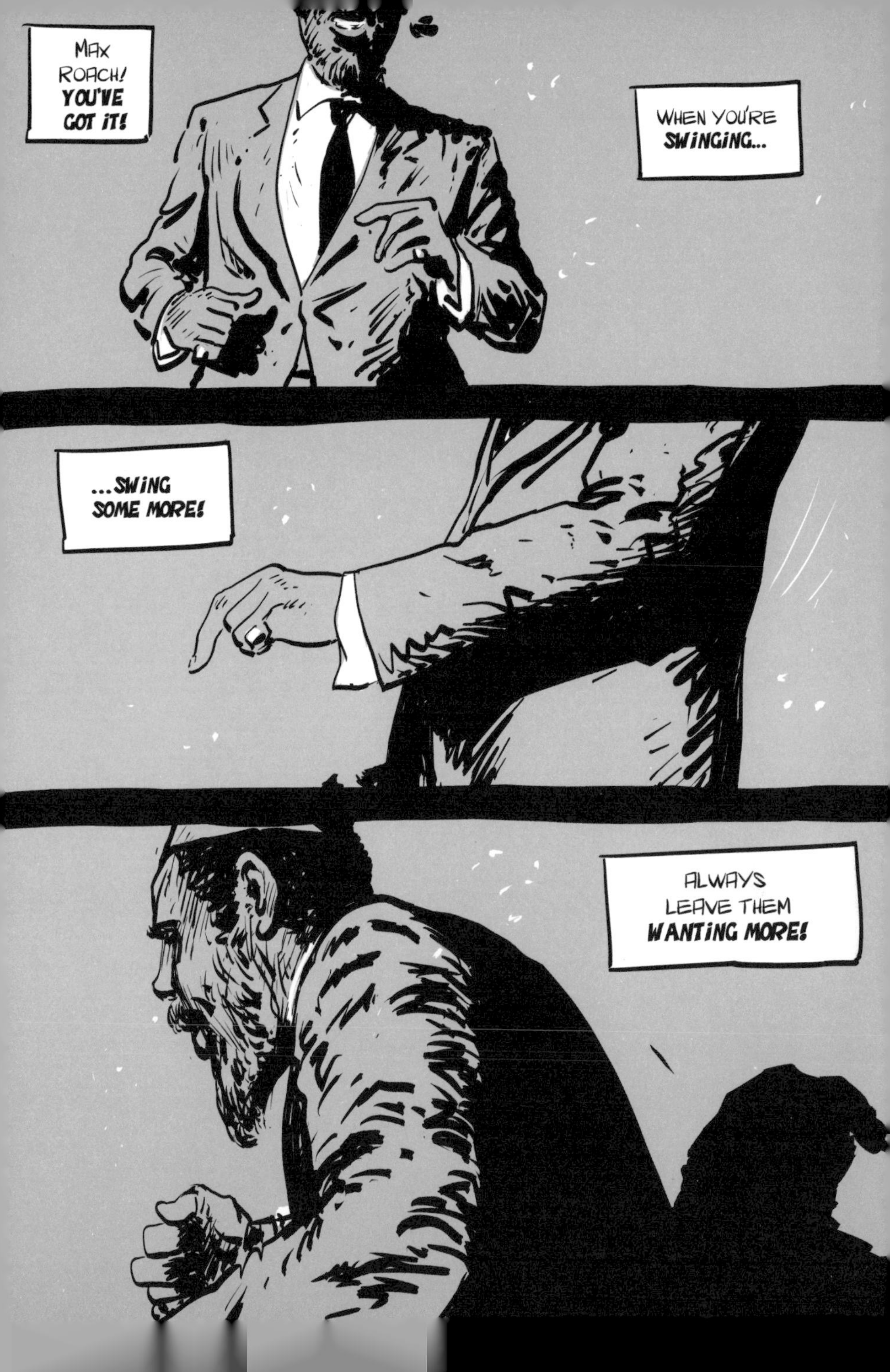
MAX ROACH! YOU'VE GOT IT!
WHEN YOU'RE SWINGING...
...SWING SOME MORE!
ALWAYS LEAVE THEM WANTING MORE!

GIGS

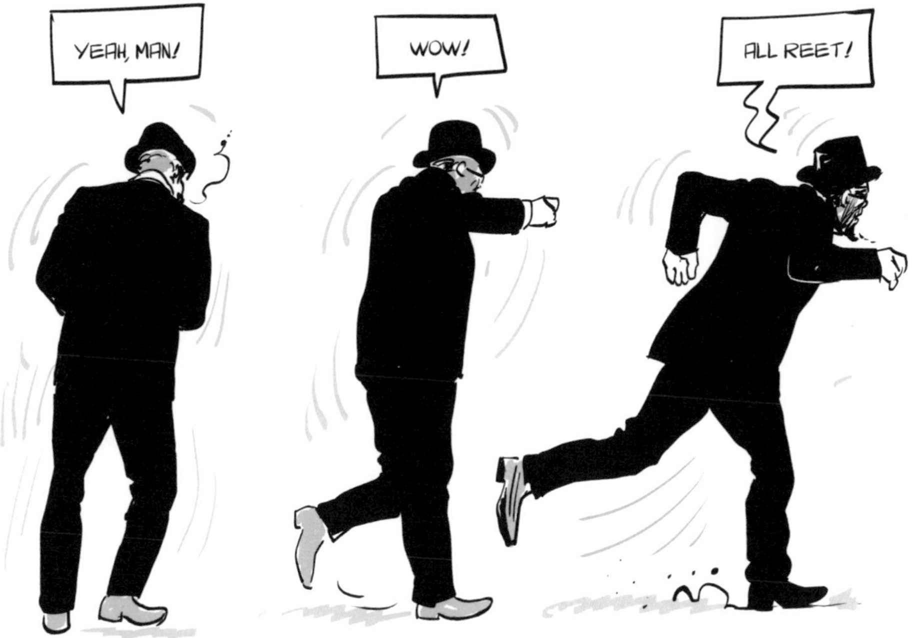
YEAH, MAN!
WOW!
ALL REET!

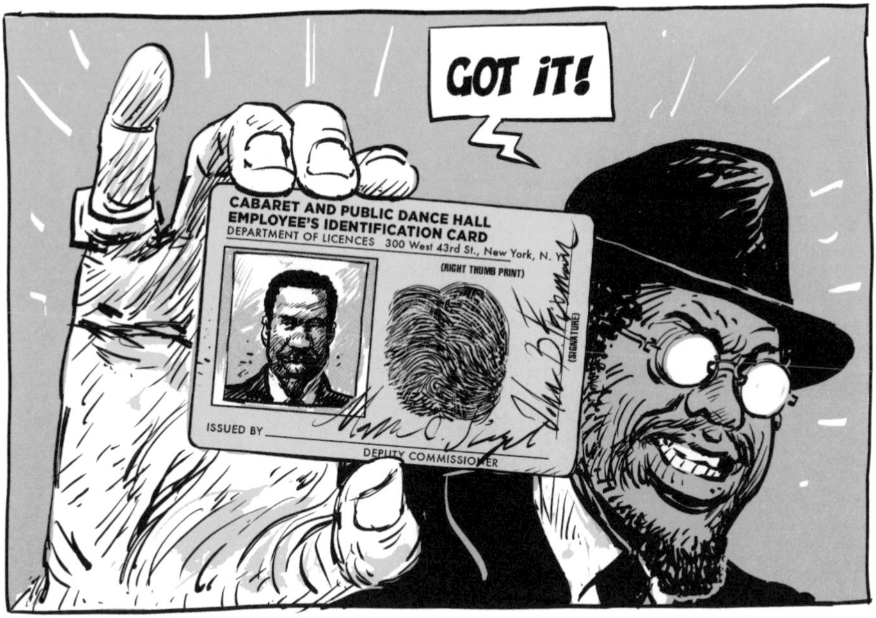
GOT IT!
CABARET AND PUBLIC DANCE HALL
EMPLOYEE'S IDENTIFICATION CARD
DEPARTMENT OF LICENCES 300 West 43rd St., New York, N. Y.
(RIGHT THUMB PRINT)
(SIGNATURE)
ISSUED BY
DEPUTY COMMISSIONER

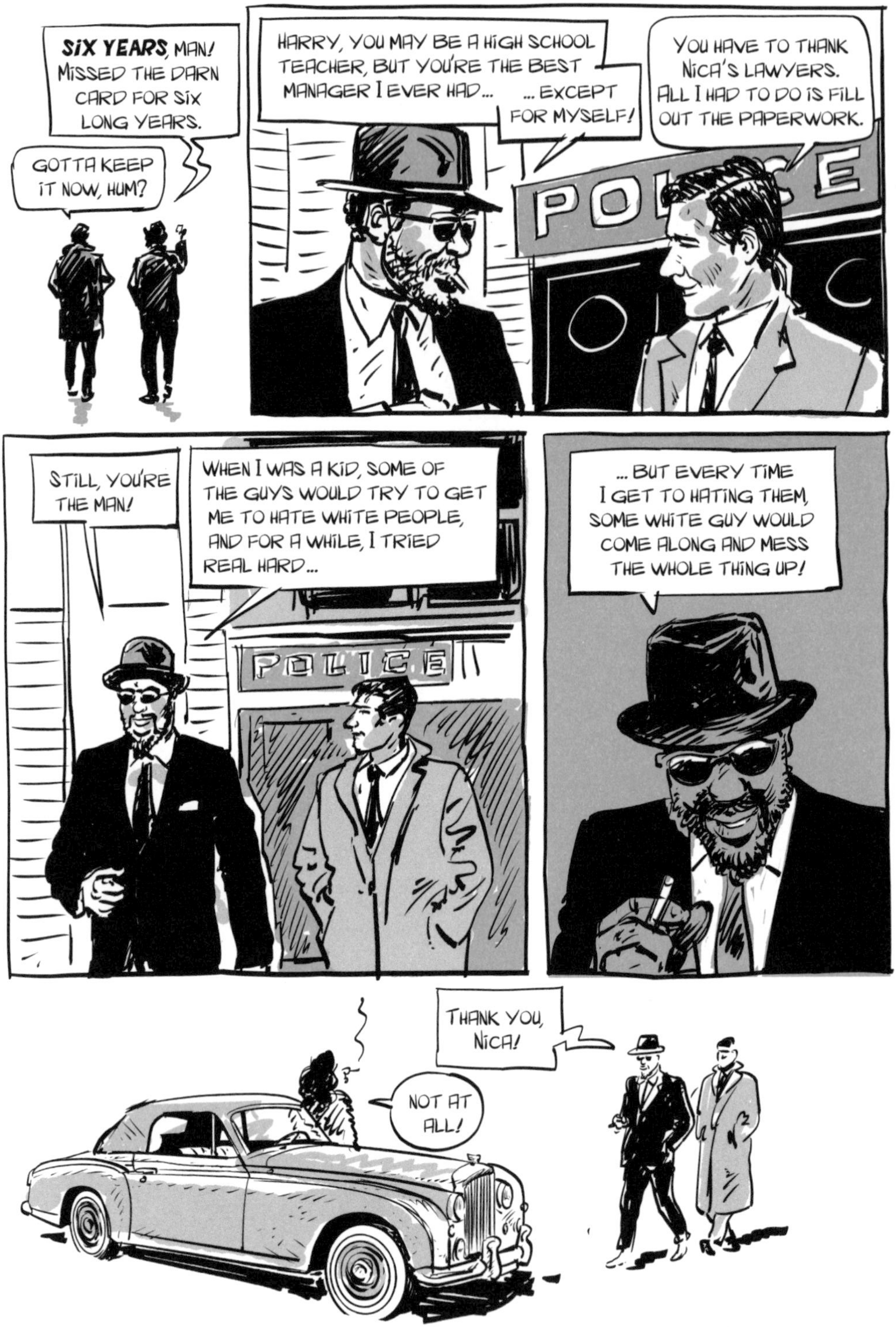
SIX YEARS, MAN! MISSED THE DARN CARD FOR SIX LONG YEARS.
GOTTA KEEP IT NOW, HUM?
HARRY, YOU MAY BE A HIGH SCHOOL TEACHER, BUT YOU'RE THE BEST MANAGER I EVER HAD...
... EXCEPT FOR MYSELF!
YOU HAVE TO THANK NICA'S LAWYERS. ALL I HAD TO DO IS FILL OUT THE PAPERWORK.
POLICE
STILL, YOU'RE THE MAN!
WHEN I WAS A KID, SOME OF THE GUYS WOULD TRY TO GET ME TO HATE WHITE PEOPLE, AND FOR A WHILE, I TRIED REAL HARD...
POLICE
... BUT EVERY TIME I GET TO HATING THEM, SOME WHITE GUY WOULD COME ALONG AND MESS THE WHOLE THING UP!
THANK YOU, NICA!
NOT AT ALL!

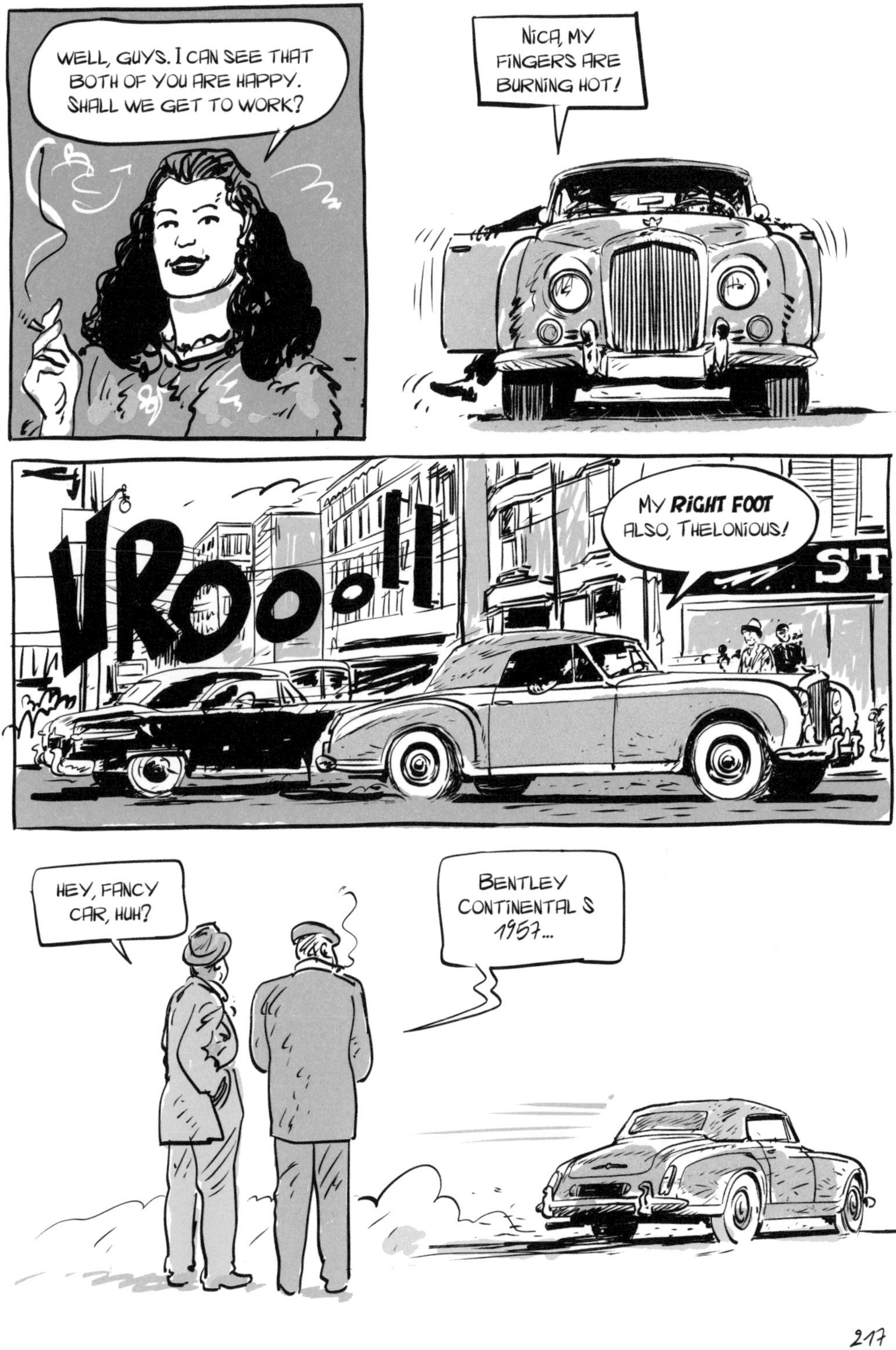
WELL, GUYS. I CAN SEE THAT BOTH OF YOU ARE HAPPY. SHALL WE GET TO WORK?
NICA, MY FINGERS ARE BURNING HOT!
VROOOII
MY **RIGHT FOOT** ALSO, THELONIOUS!
ST
HEY, FANCY CAR, HUH?
BENTLEY CONTINENTAL S 1957...

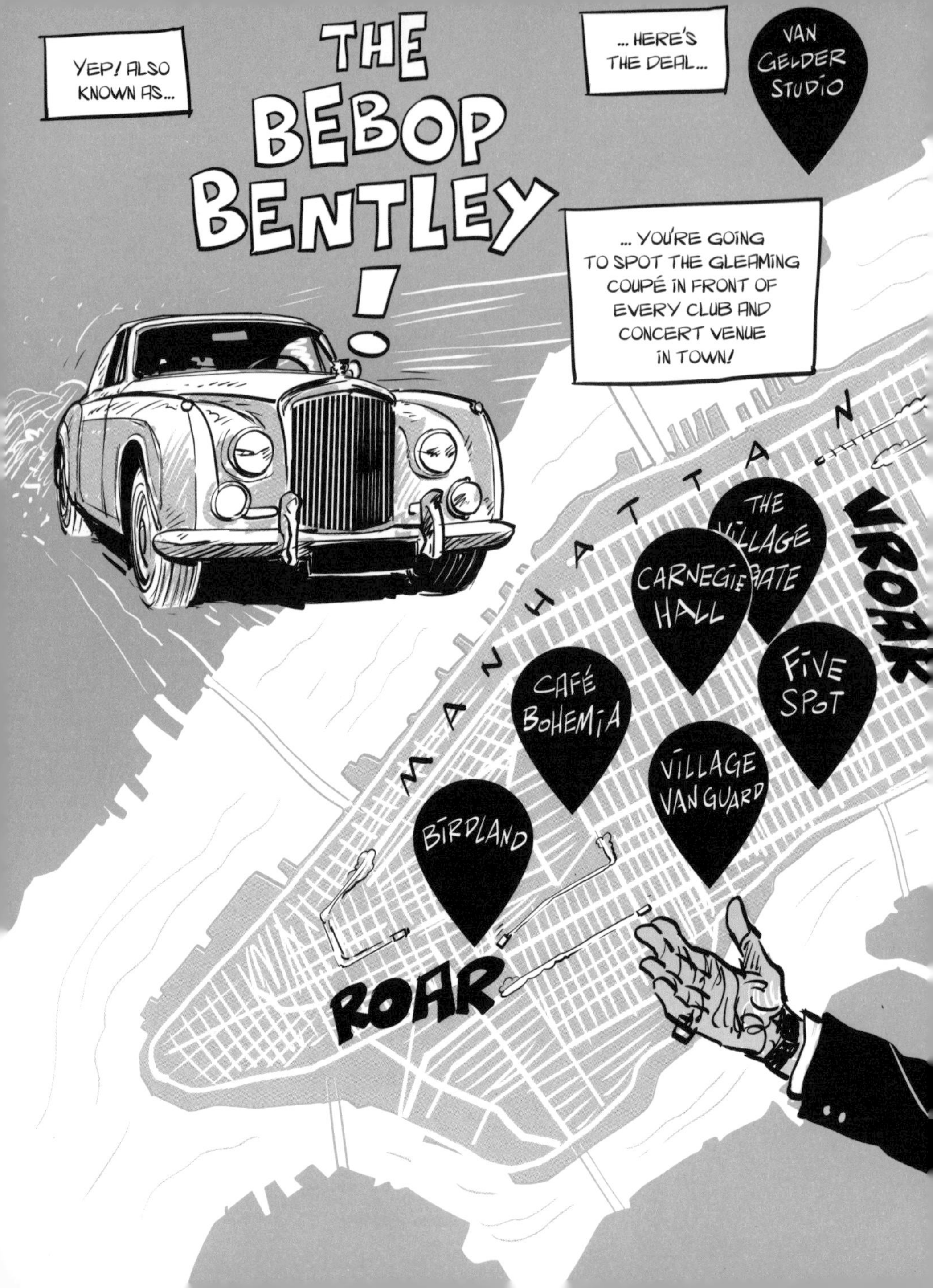
YEP! ALSO KNOWN AS...
THE BEBOP BENTLEY!
... HERE'S THE DEAL...
VAN GELDER STUDIO
... YOU'RE GOING TO SPOT THE GLEAMING COUPÉ IN FRONT OF EVERY CLUB AND CONCERT VENUE IN TOWN!
MANHATTAN
THE VILLAGE GATE
CARNEGIE HALL
VROAR
FIVE SPOT
CAFÉ BOHEMIA
VILLAGE VANGUARD
BIRDLAND
ROAR

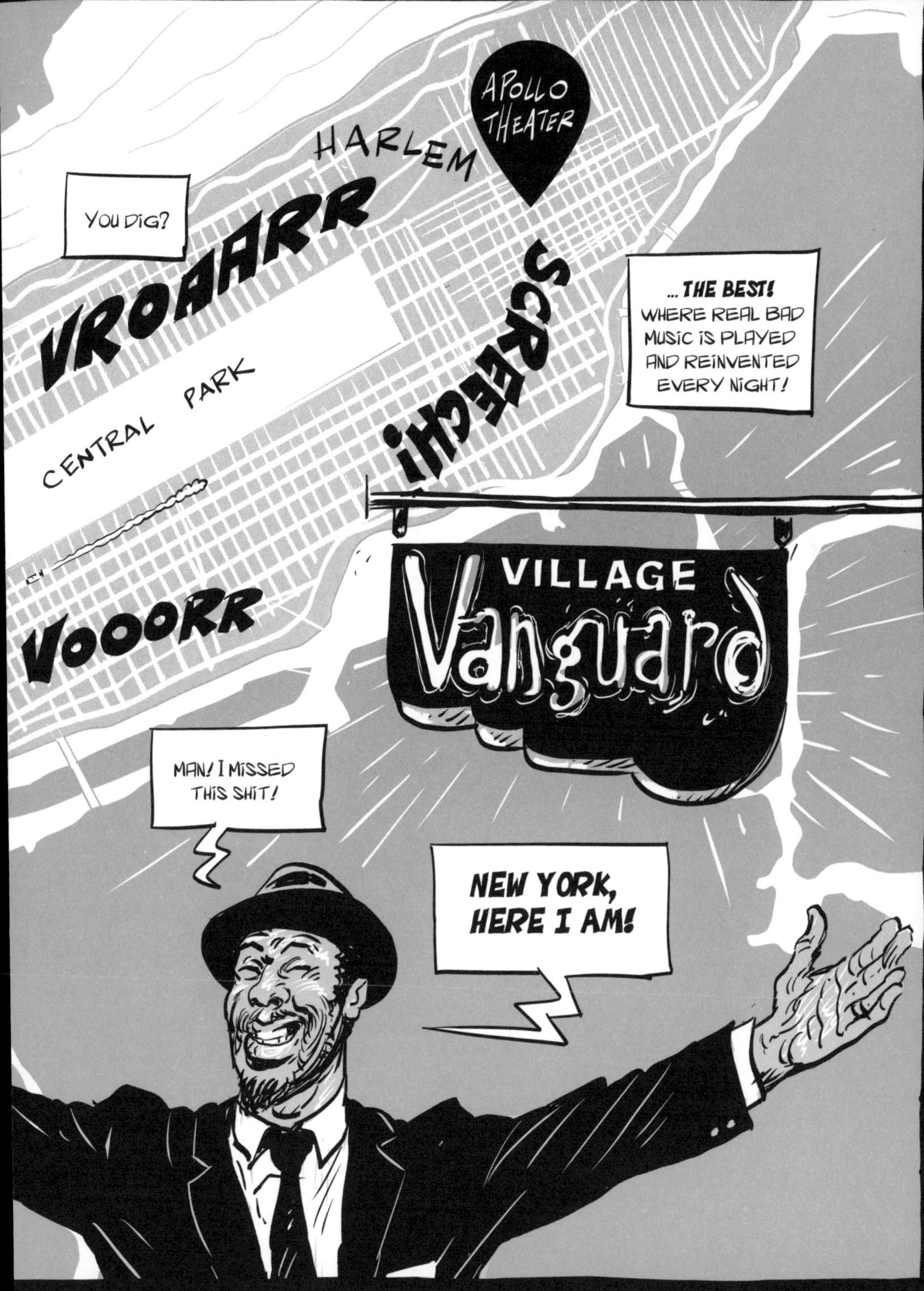
YOU DIG?
VROAARR
HARLEM
APOLLO THEATER
SCREECH!
...THE BEST! WHERE REAL BAD MUSIC IS PLAYED AND REINVENTED EVERY NIGHT!
CENTRAL PARK
VOOORR
VILLAGE Vanguard
MAN! I MISSED THIS SHIT!
NEW YORK, HERE I AM!

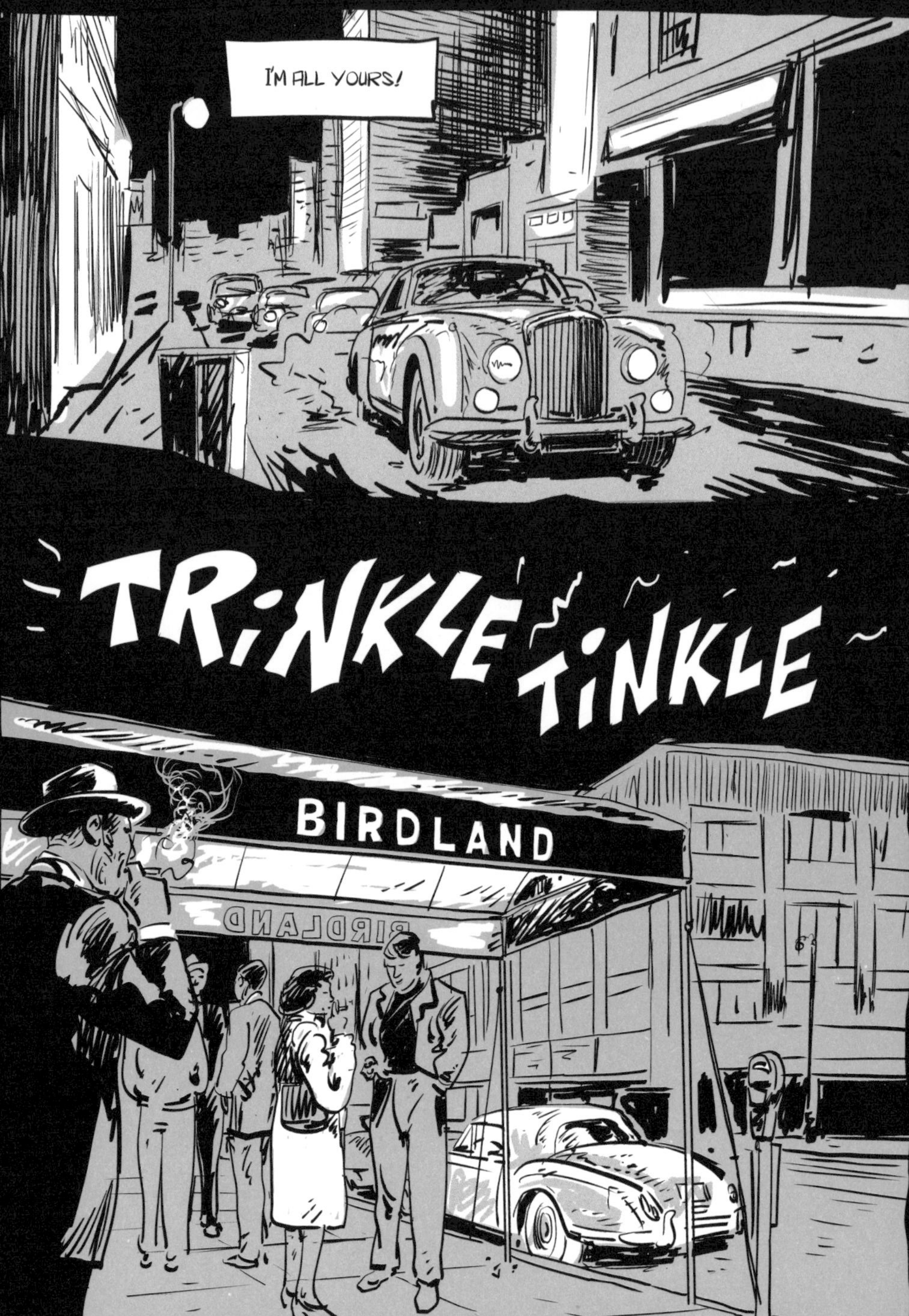
I'M ALL YOURS!
TRINKLE TINKLE
BIRDLAND
BIRDLAND

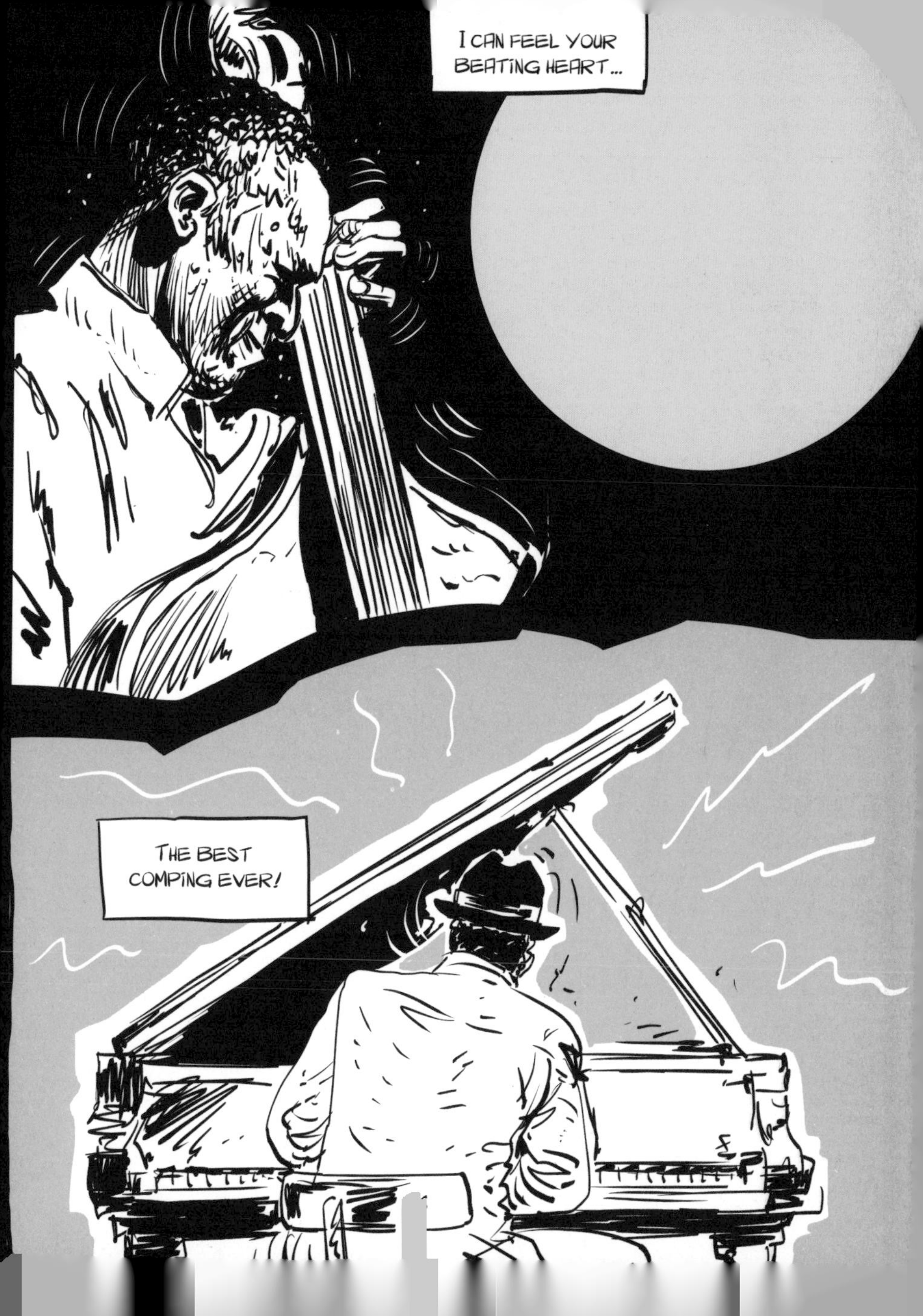
I CAN FEEL YOUR BEATING HEART...
THE BEST COMPING EVER!

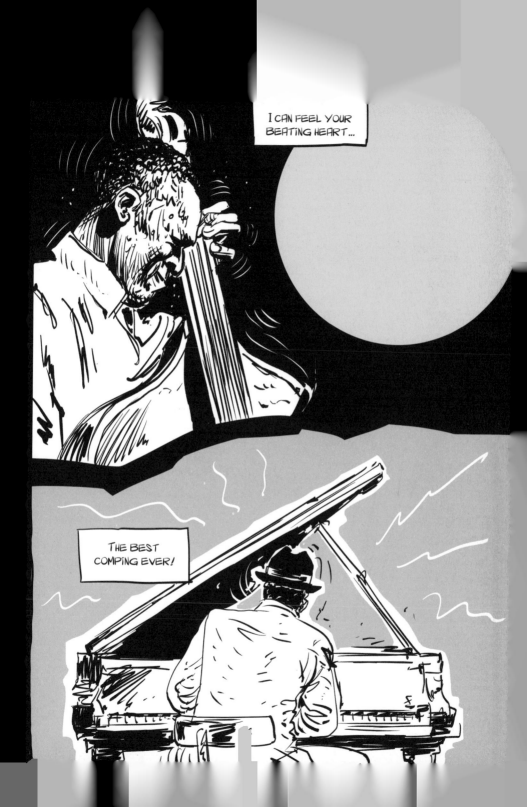

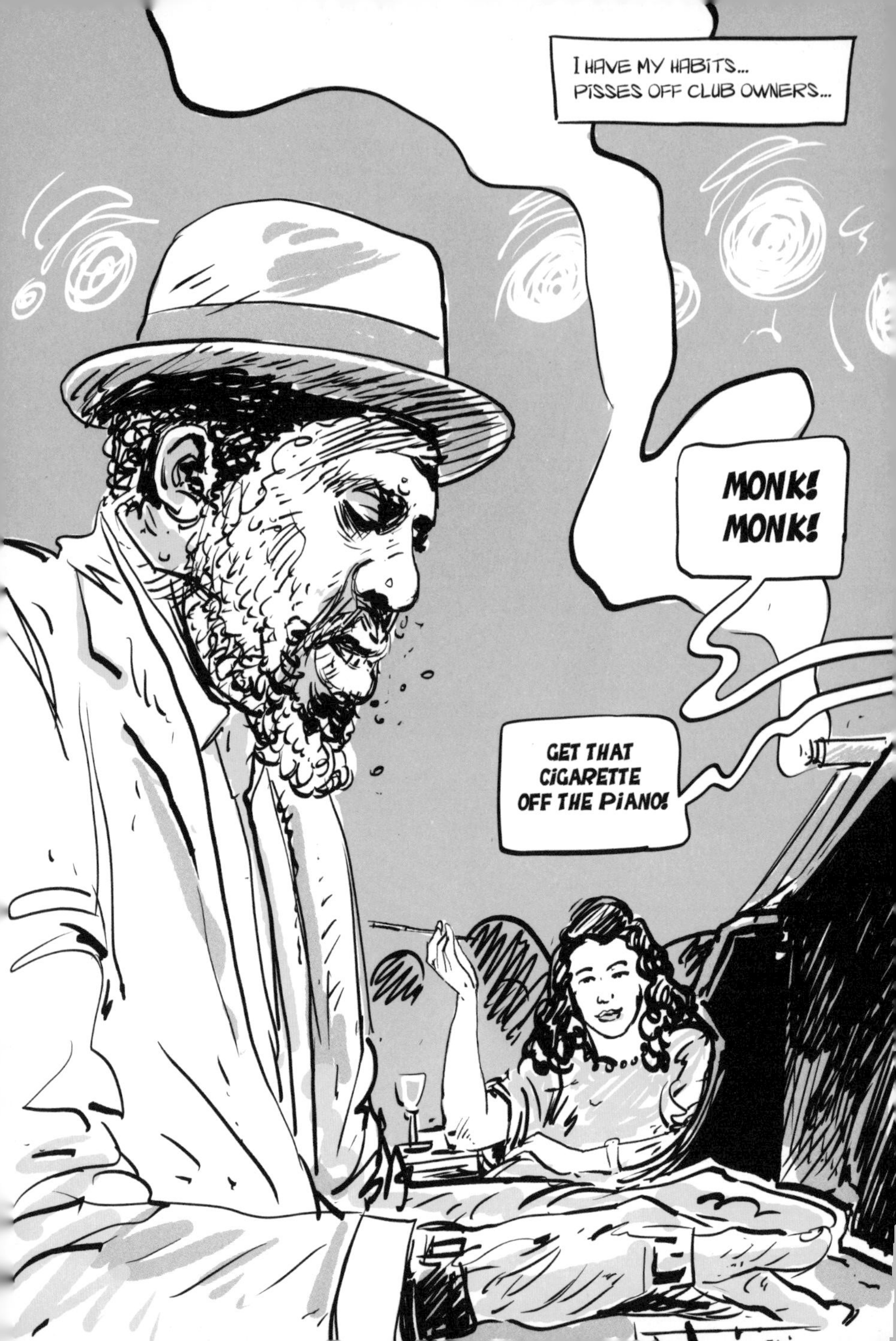
I HAVE MY HABITS...
PISSES OFF CLUB OWNERS...
MONK! MONK!
GET THAT CIGARETTE OFF THE PIANO!

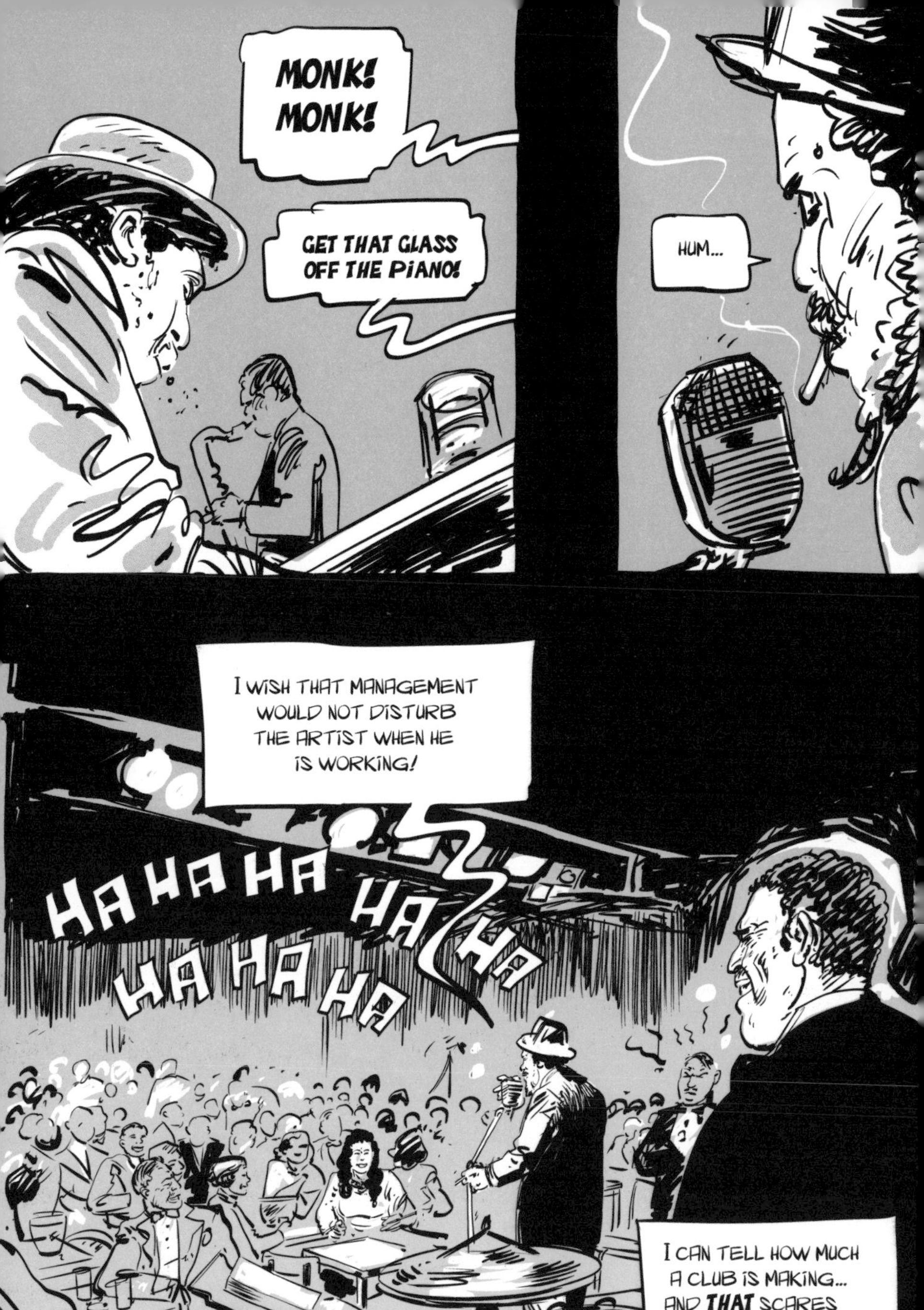
MONK! MONK!
GET THAT GLASS OFF THE PIANO!
HUM...
I WISH THAT MANAGEMENT WOULD NOT DISTURB THE ARTIST WHEN HE IS WORKING!
HA HA HA HA HA HA HA HA HA HA
I CAN TELL HOW MUCH A CLUB IS MAKING... AND **THAT** SCARES THE SHIT OUT OF THEM...

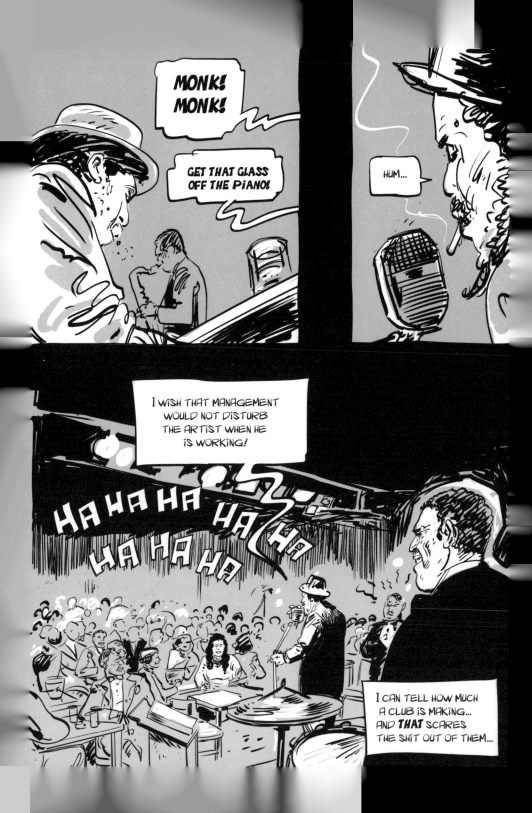

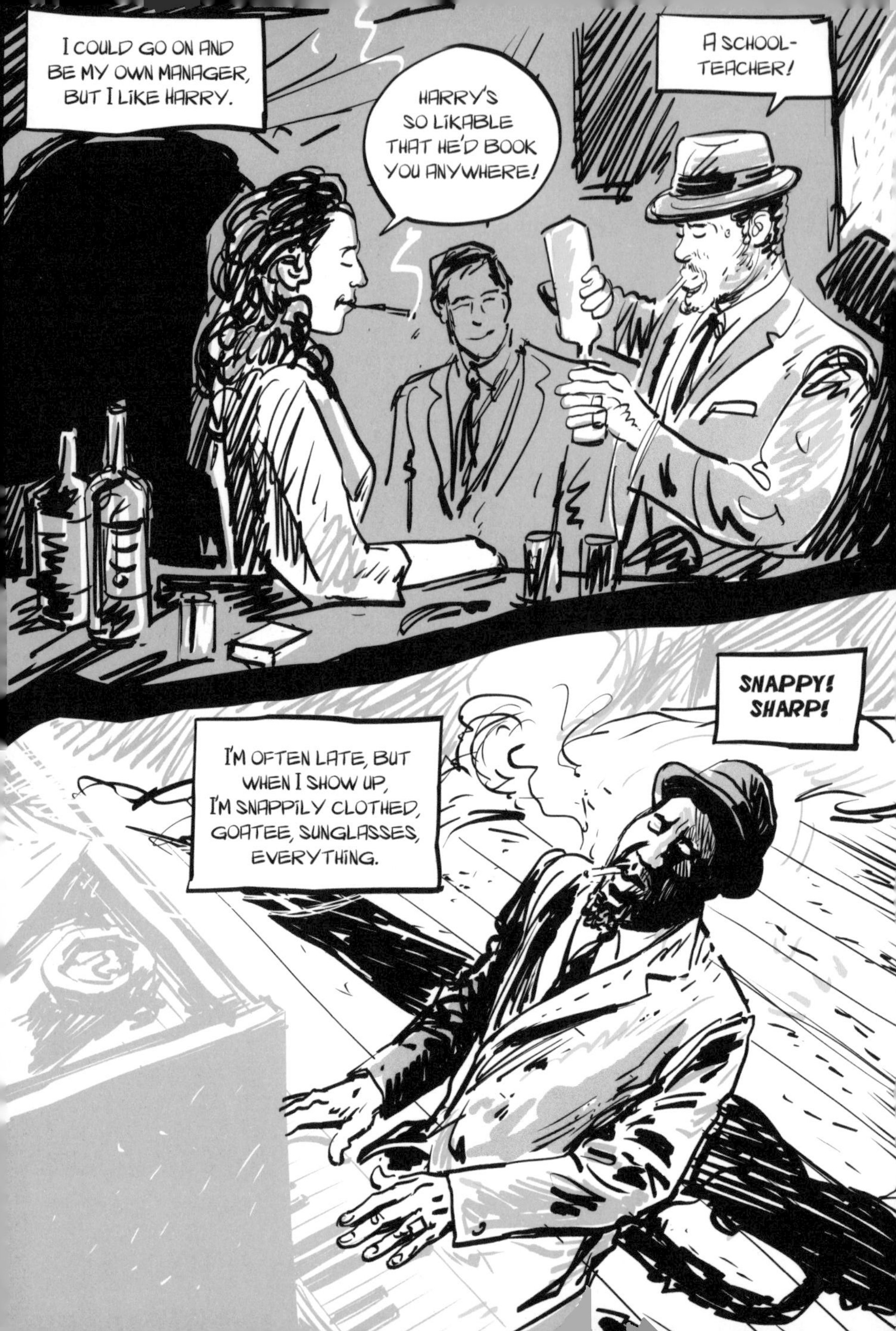
I COULD GO ON AND BE MY OWN MANAGER, BUT I LIKE HARRY.
HARRY'S SO LIKABLE THAT HE'D BOOK YOU ANYWHERE!
A SCHOOL-TEACHER!
SNAPPY! SHARP!
I'M OFTEN LATE, BUT WHEN I SHOW UP, I'M SNAPPILY CLOTHED, GOATEE, SUNGLASSES, EVERYTHING.

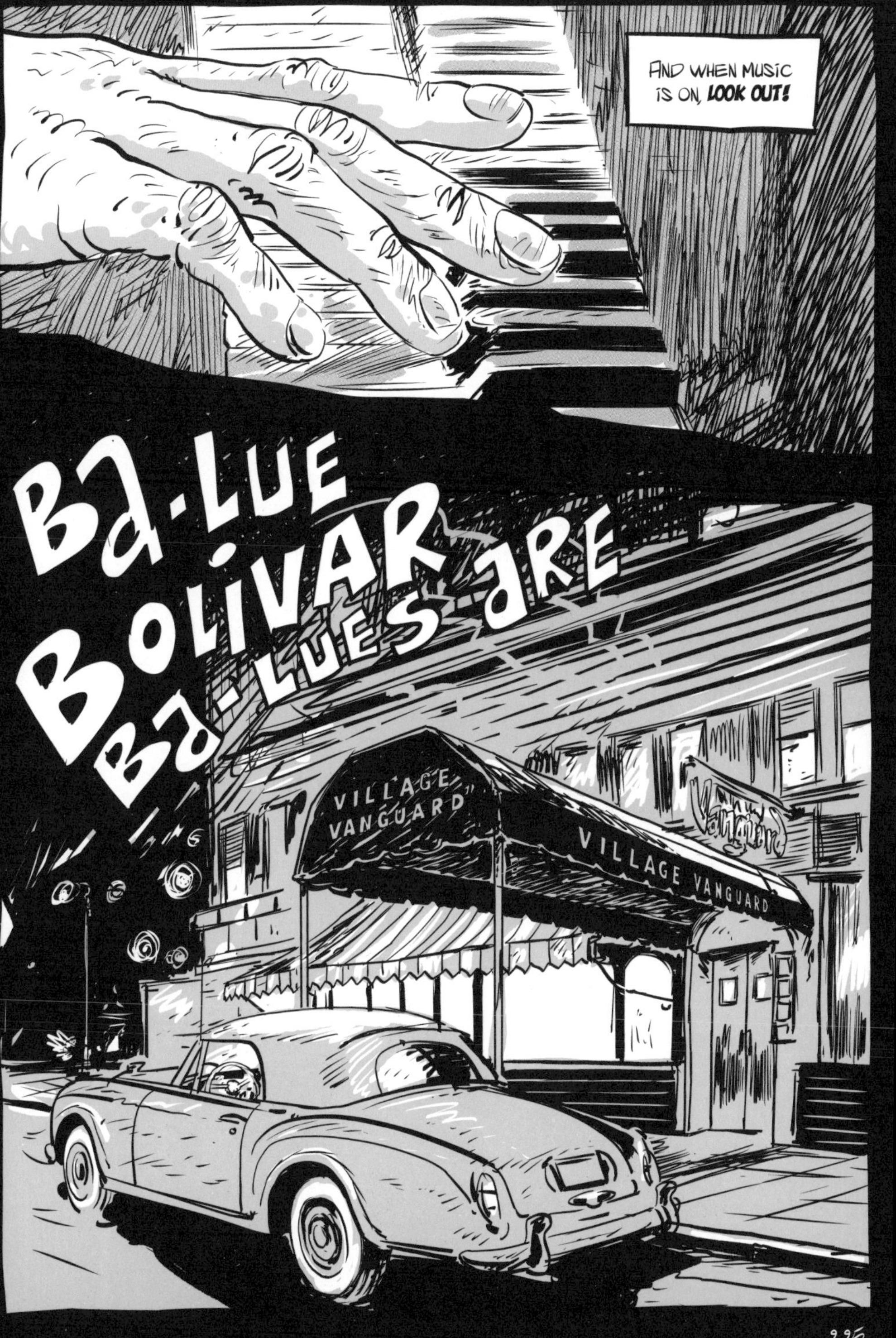
AND WHEN MUSIC IS ON, **LOOK OUT!**
BA-LUE BOLIVAR BA-LUES ARE
VILLAGE VANGUARD
VILLAGE VANGUARD
Vanguard

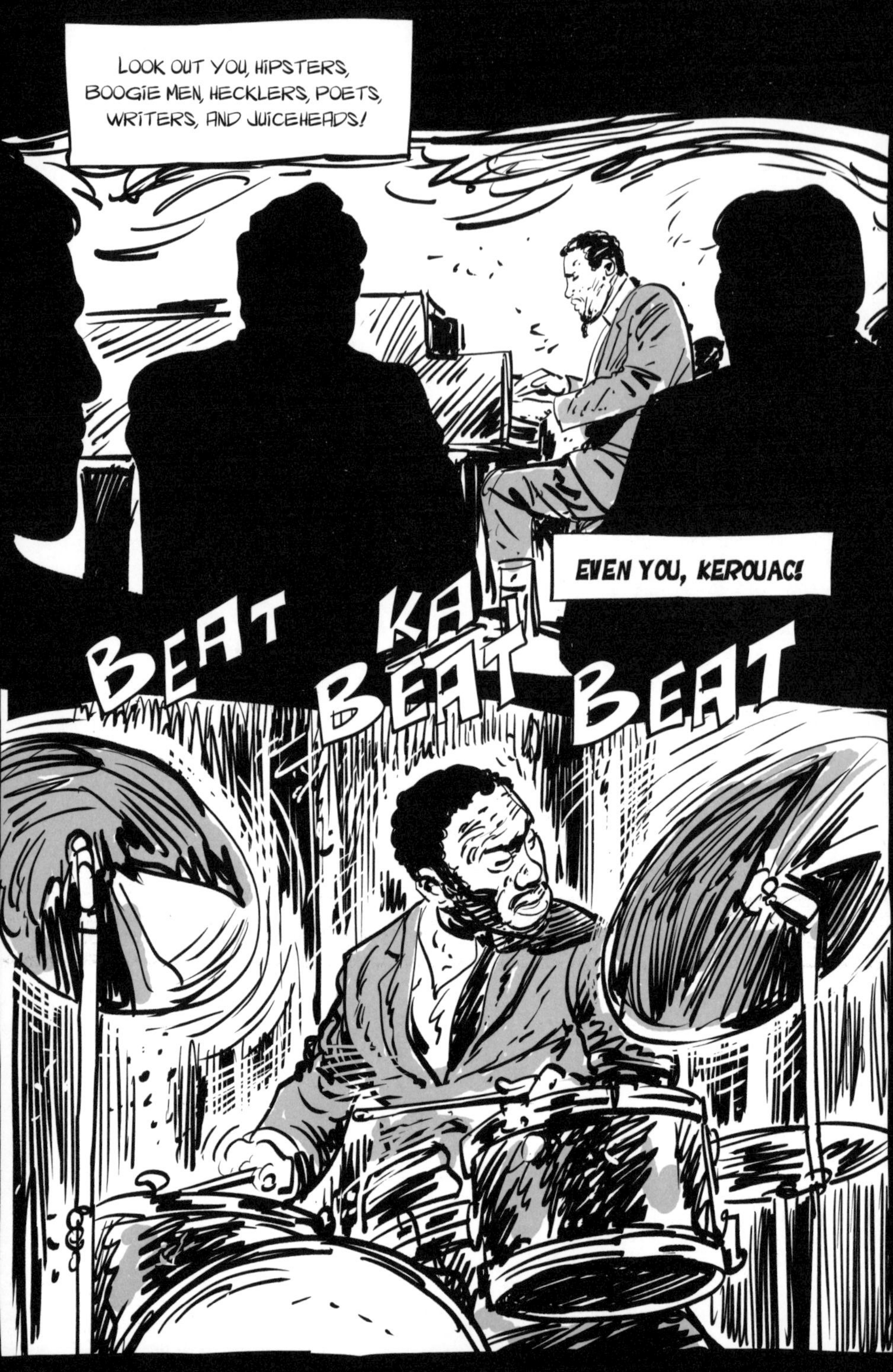
LOOK OUT YOU, HIPSTERS, BOOGIE MEN, HECKLERS, POETS, WRITERS, AND JUICEHEADS!
EVEN YOU, KEROUAC!
BEAT
KA
BEAT
BEAT

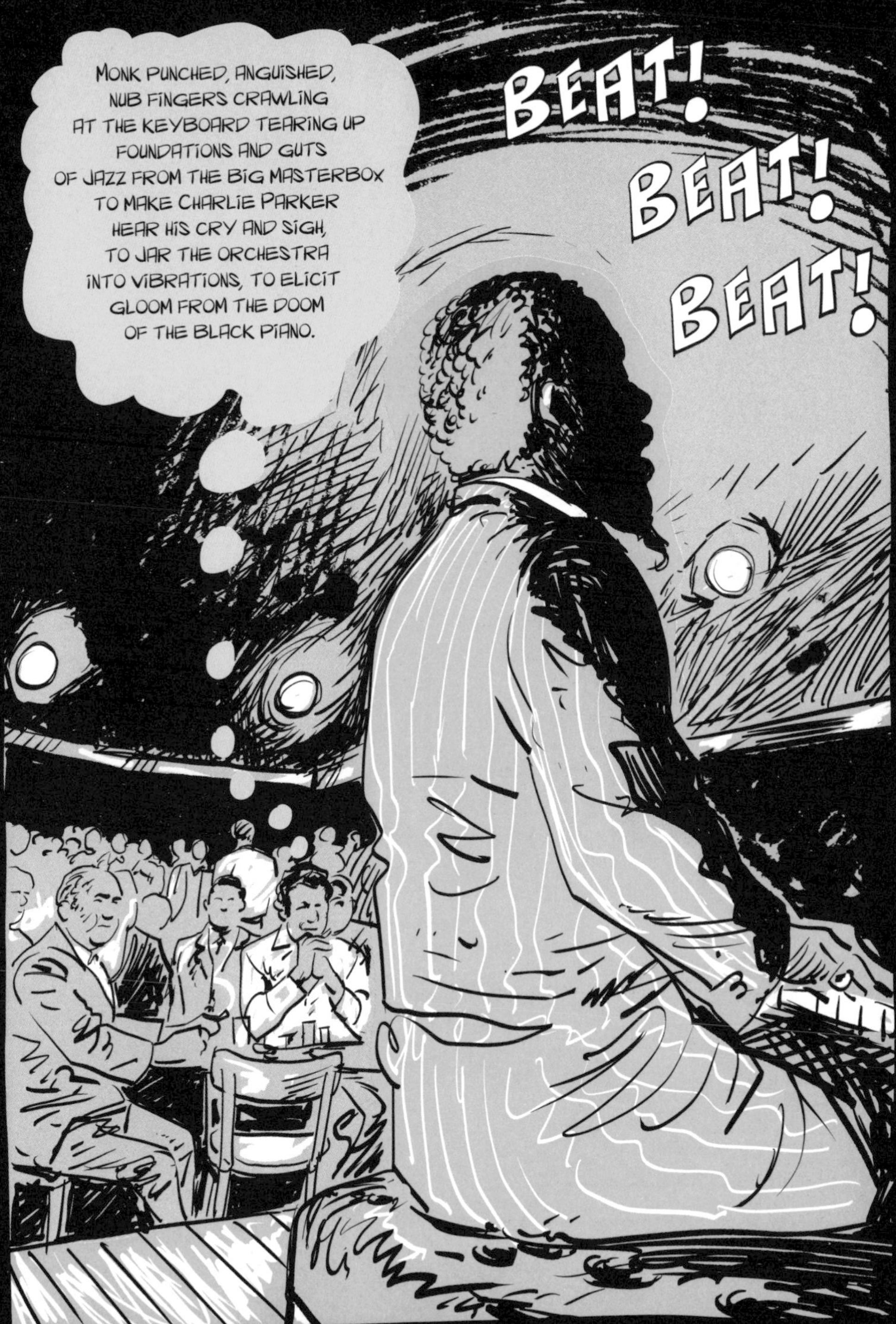
MONK PUNCHED, ANGUISHED, NUB FINGERS CRAWLING AT THE KEYBOARD TEARING UP FOUNDATIONS AND GUTS OF JAZZ FROM THE BIG MASTERBOX TO MAKE CHARLIE PARKER HEAR HIS CRY AND SIGH, TO JAR THE ORCHESTRA INTO VIBRATIONS, TO ELICIT GLOOM FROM THE DOOM OF THE BLACK PIANO.
BEAT!
BEAT!
BEAT!

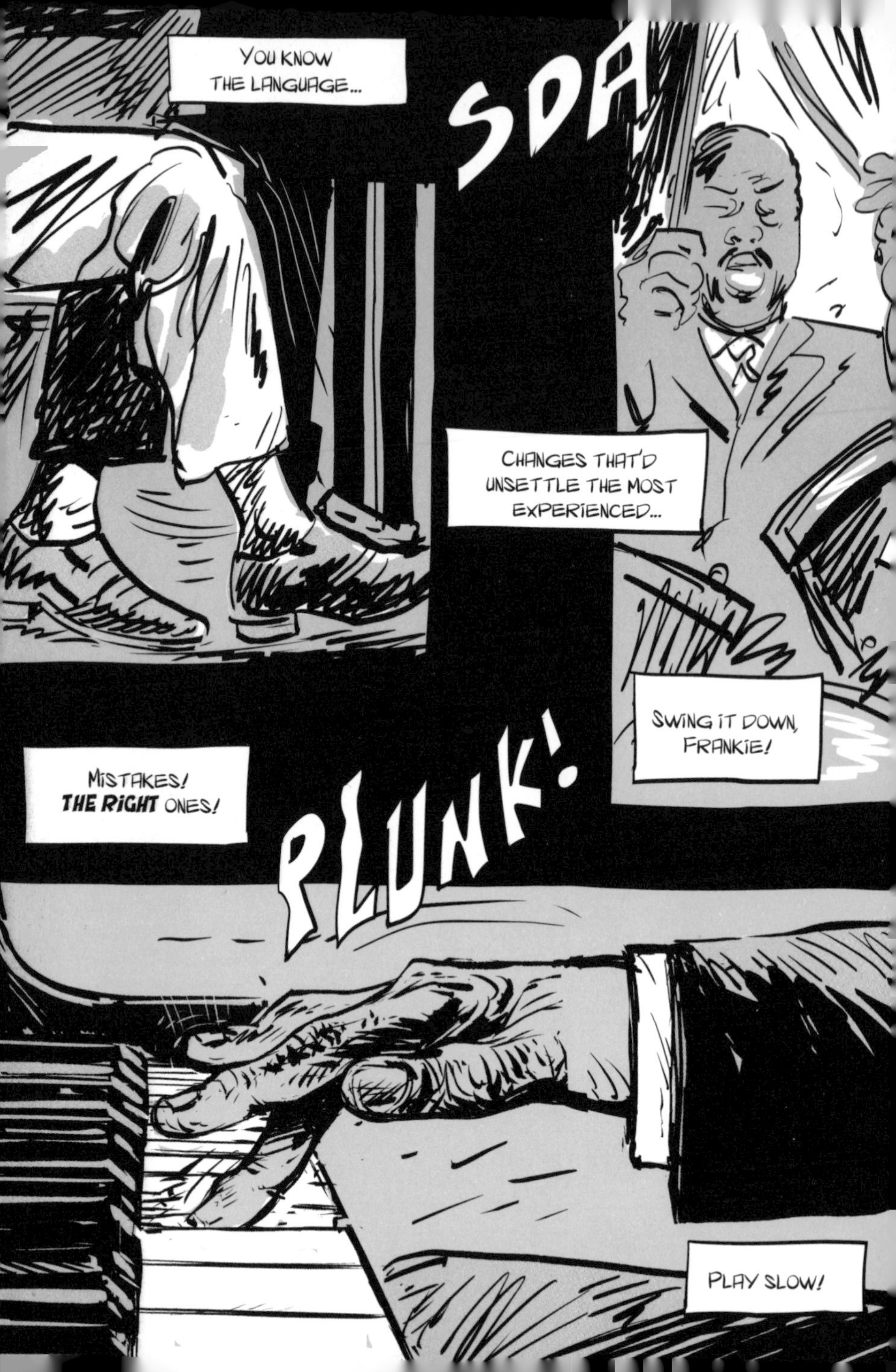

YOU KNOW THE LANGUAGE...
SDA
CHANGES THAT'D UNSETTLE THE MOST EXPERIENCED...
SWING IT DOWN, FRANKIE!
MISTAKES! THE RIGHT ONES!
PLUNK!
PLAY SLOW!

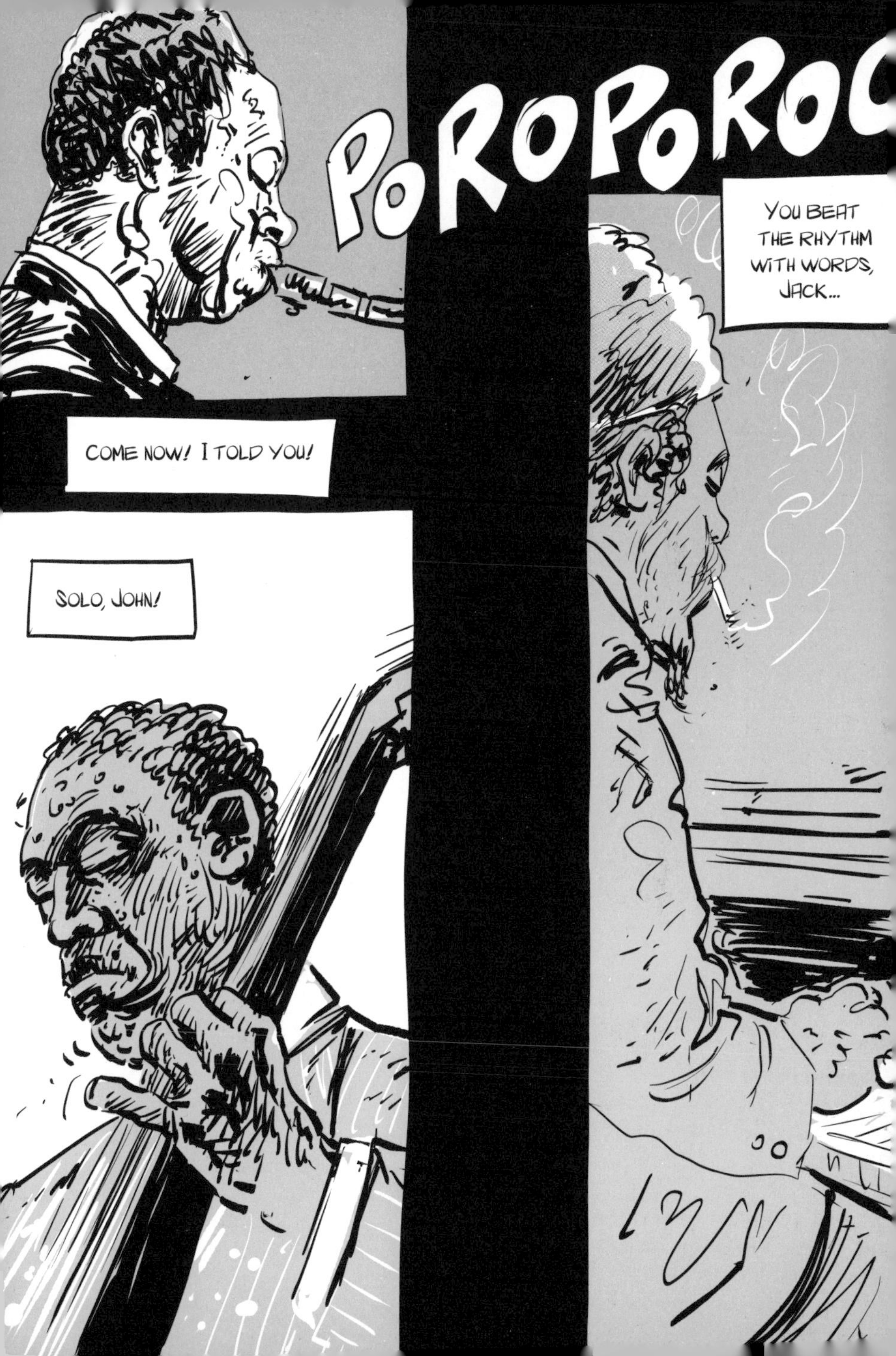
POROPOROC
YOU BEAT THE RHYTHM WITH WORDS, JACK...
COME NOW! I TOLD YOU!
SOLO, JOHN!

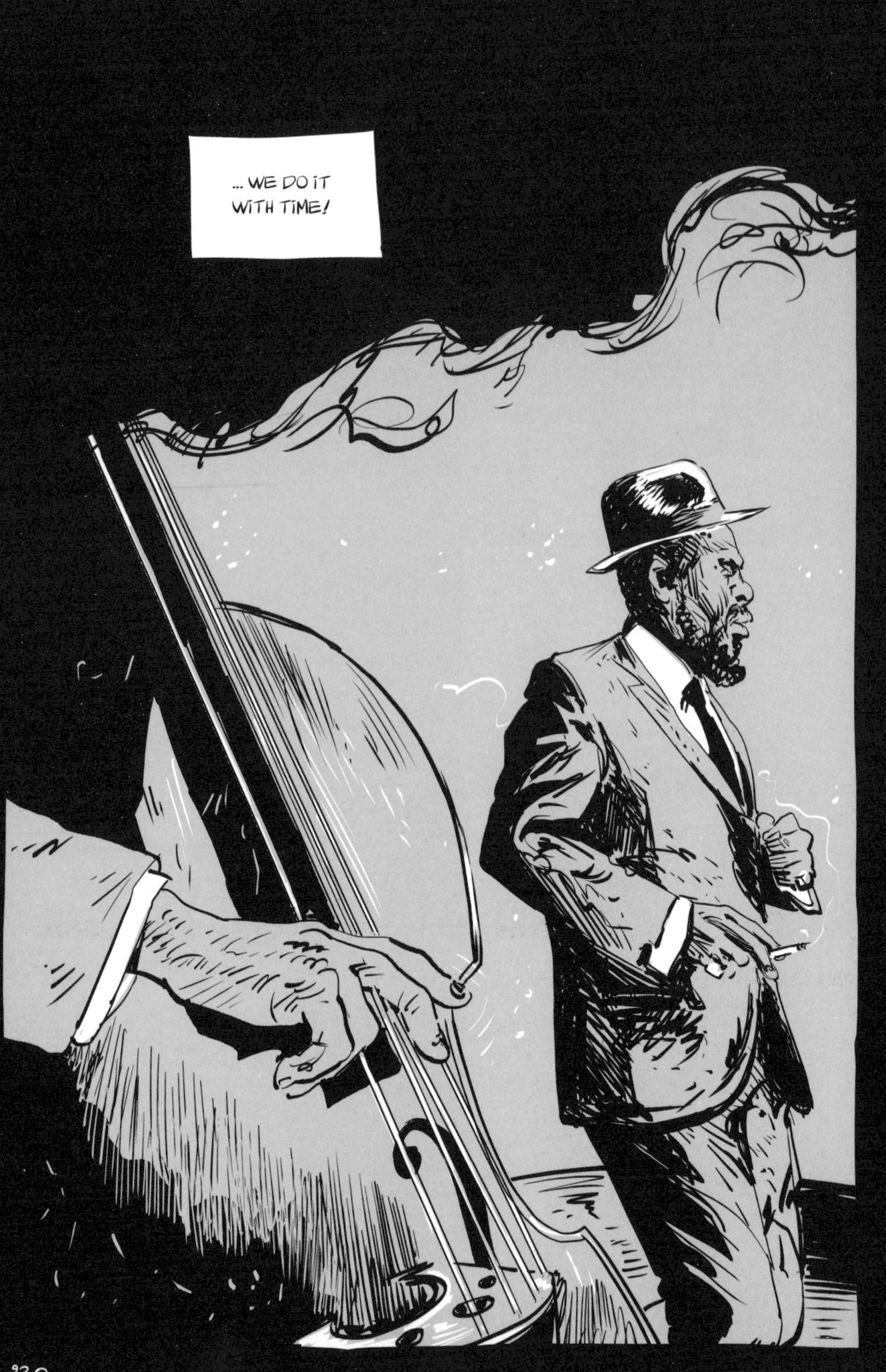
... WE DO IT
WITH TIME!

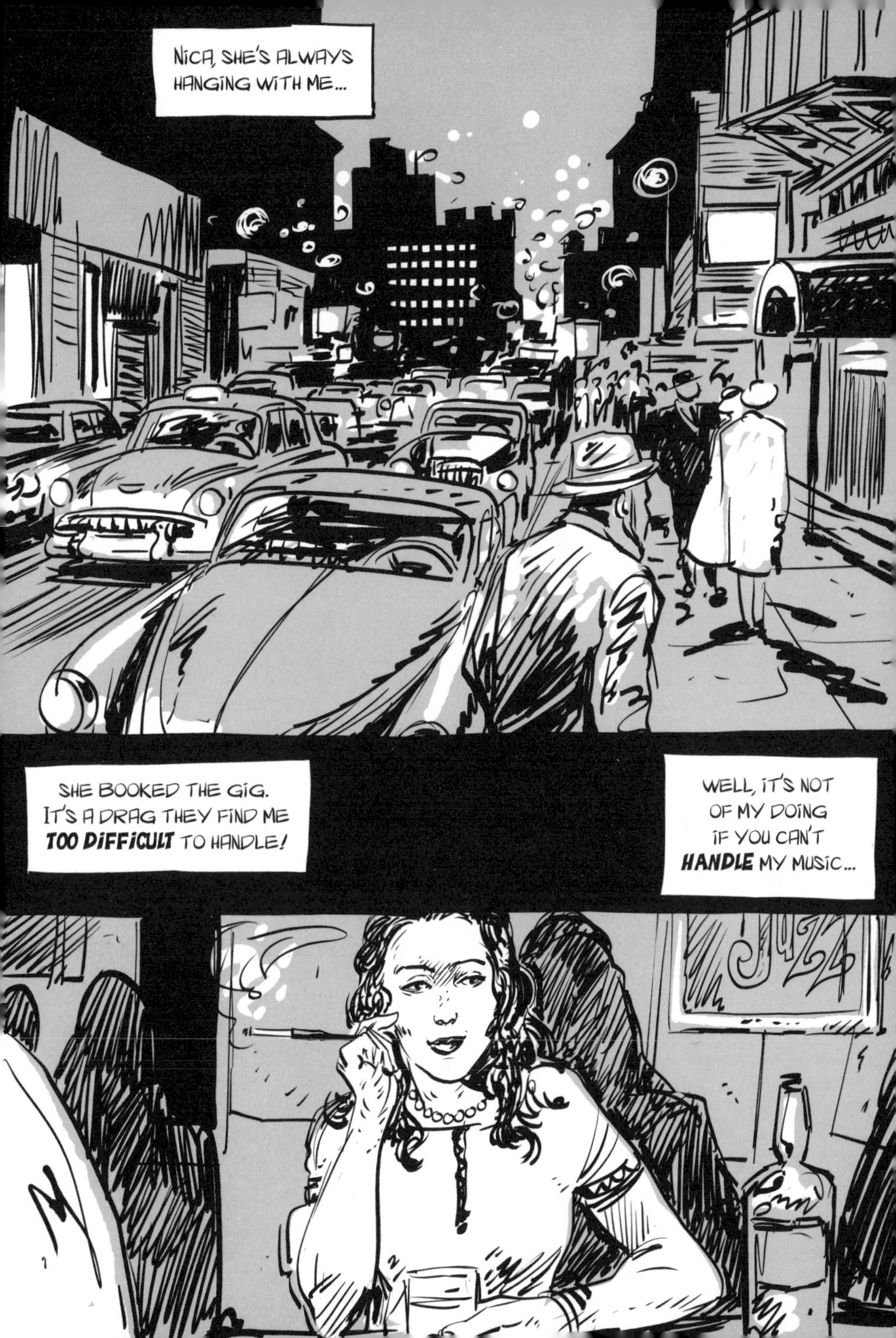
NICA, SHE'S ALWAYS HANGING WITH ME...
SHE BOOKED THE GIG. IT'S A DRAG THEY FIND ME **TOO DIFFICULT** TO HANDLE!
WELL, IT'S NOT OF MY DOING IF YOU CAN'T **HANDLE** MY MUSIC...
JAZZ

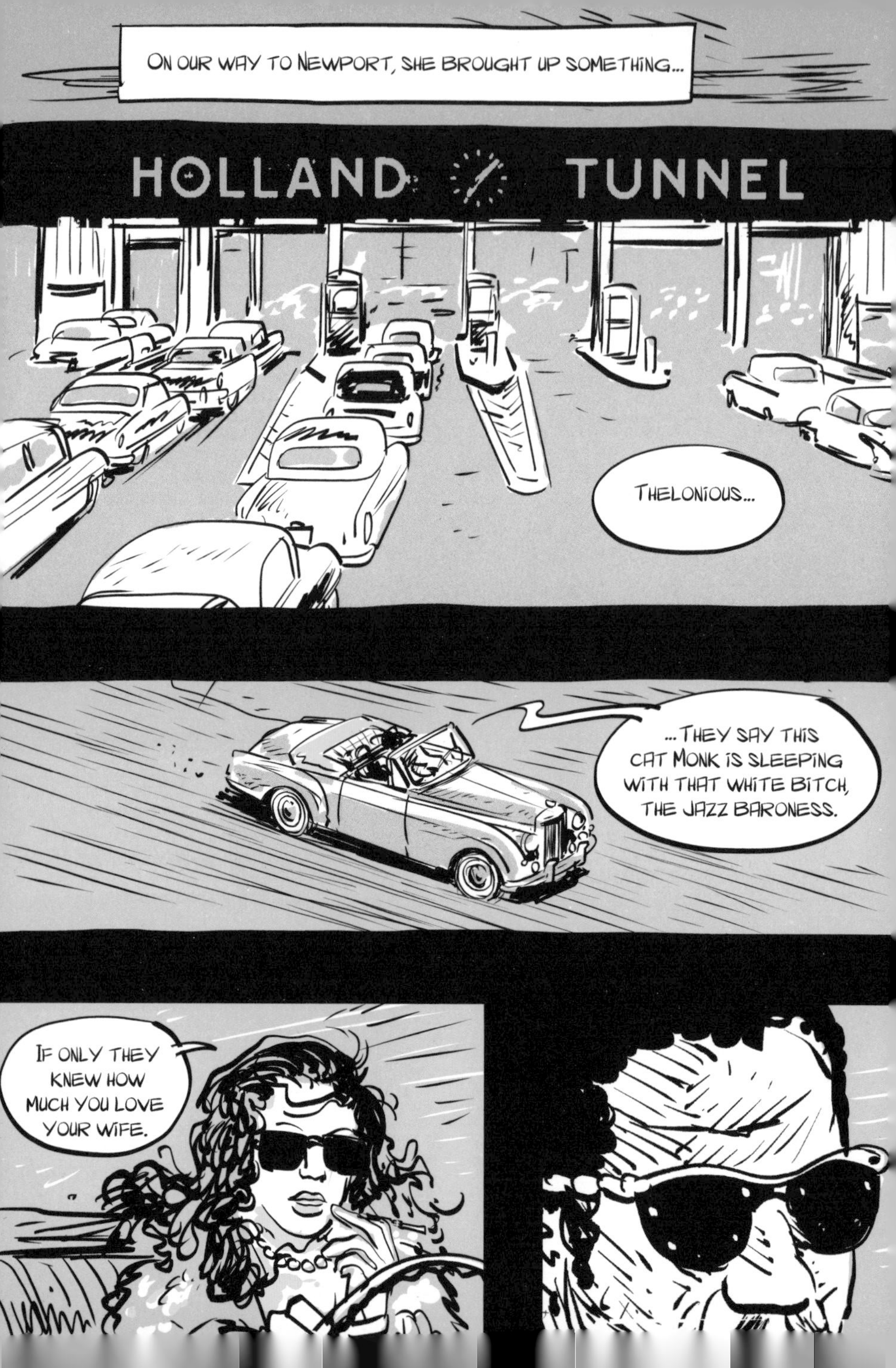

ON OUR WAY TO NEWPORT, SHE BROUGHT UP SOMETHING...
HOLLAND TUNNEL
THELONIOUS...
...THEY SAY THIS CAT MONK IS SLEEPING WITH THAT WHITE BITCH, THE JAZZ BARONESS.
IF ONLY THEY KNEW HOW MUCH YOU LOVE YOUR WIFE.

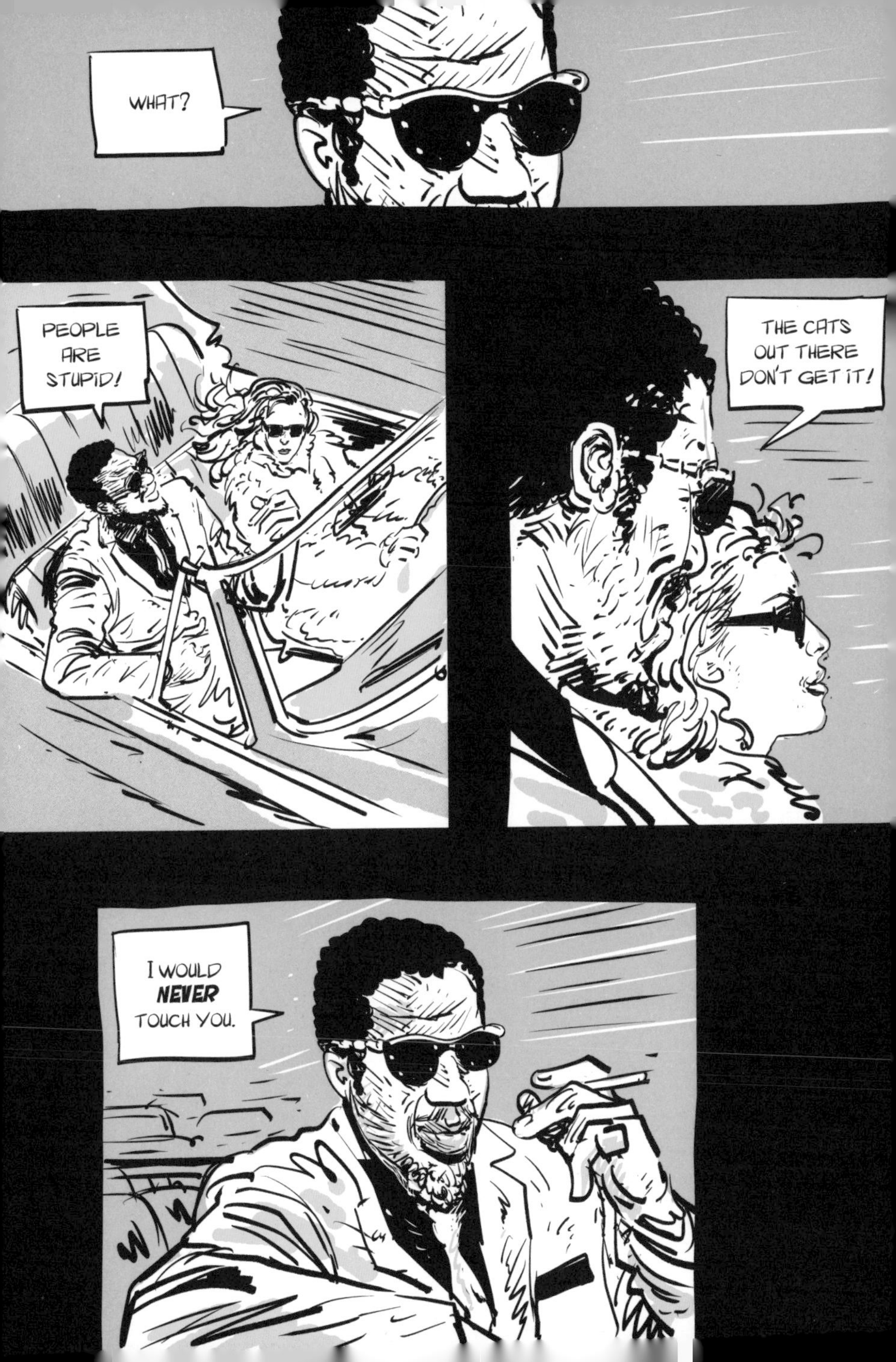
WHAT?
PEOPLE ARE STUPID!
THE CATS OUT THERE DON'T GET IT!
I WOULD **NEVER** TOUCH YOU.

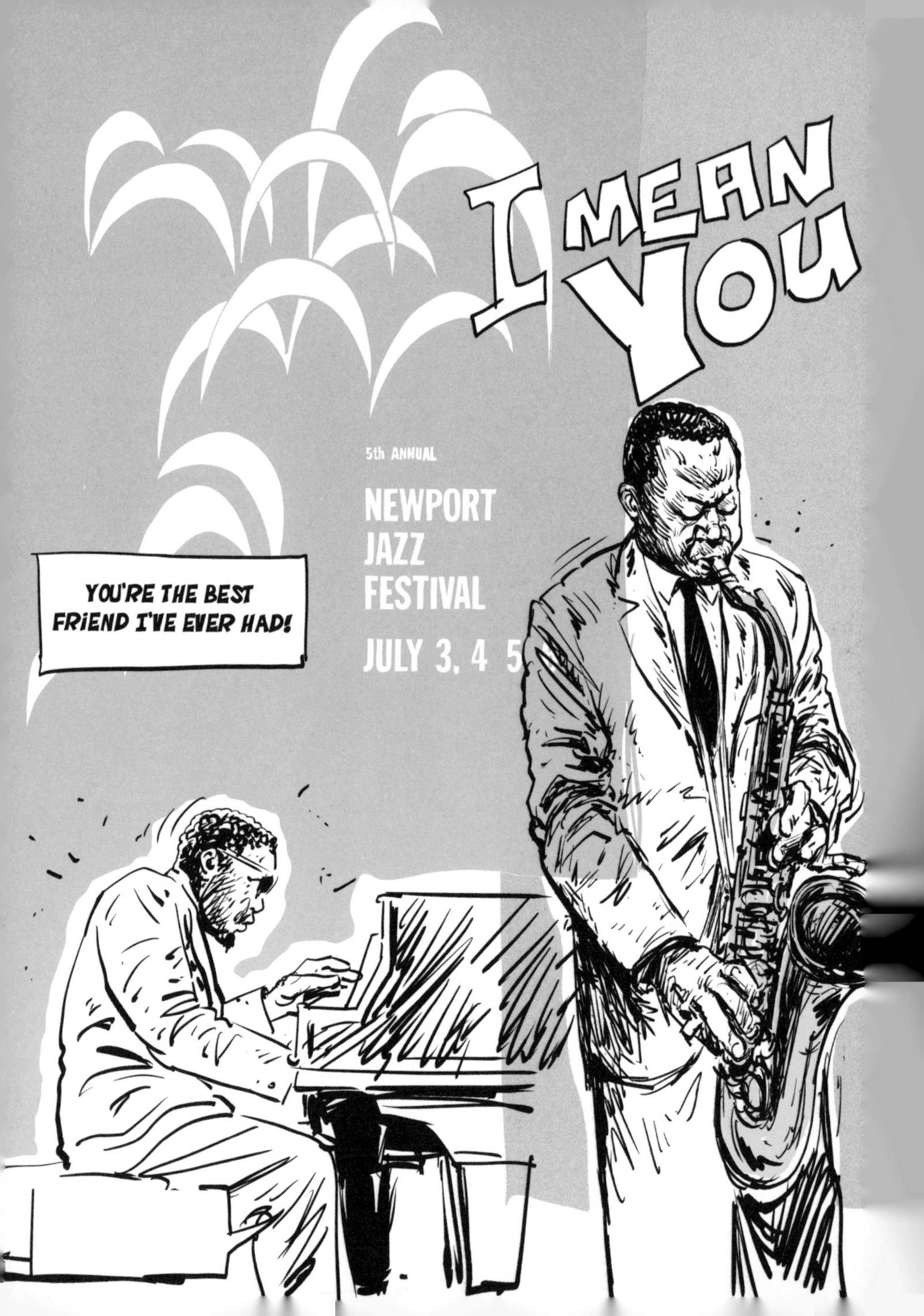
I MEAN YOU
5th ANNUAL
NEWPORT
JAZZ
FESTIVAL
JULY 3, 4 5
YOU'RE THE BEST
FRIEND I'VE EVER HAD!

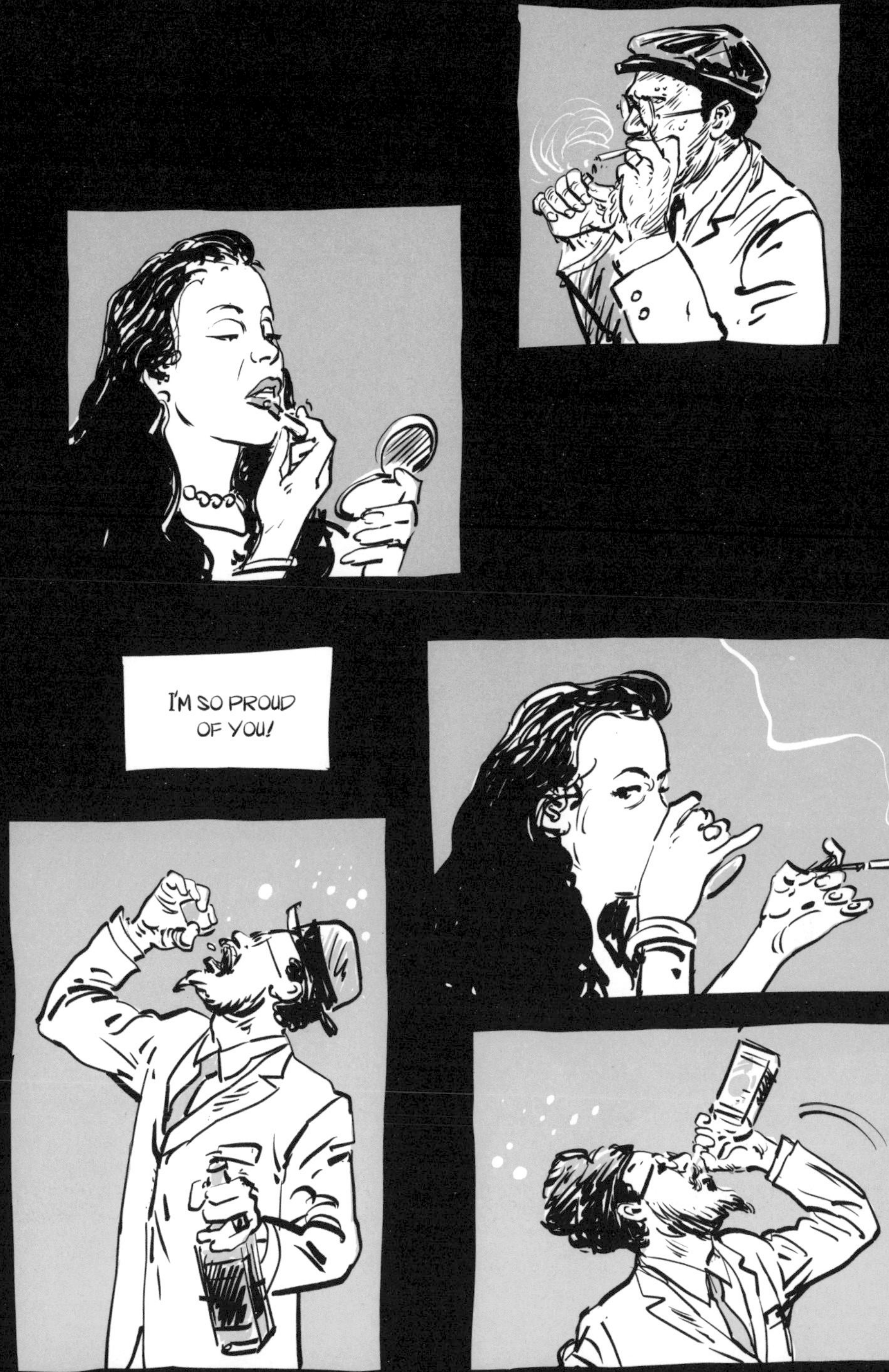
I'M SO PROUD
OF YOU!

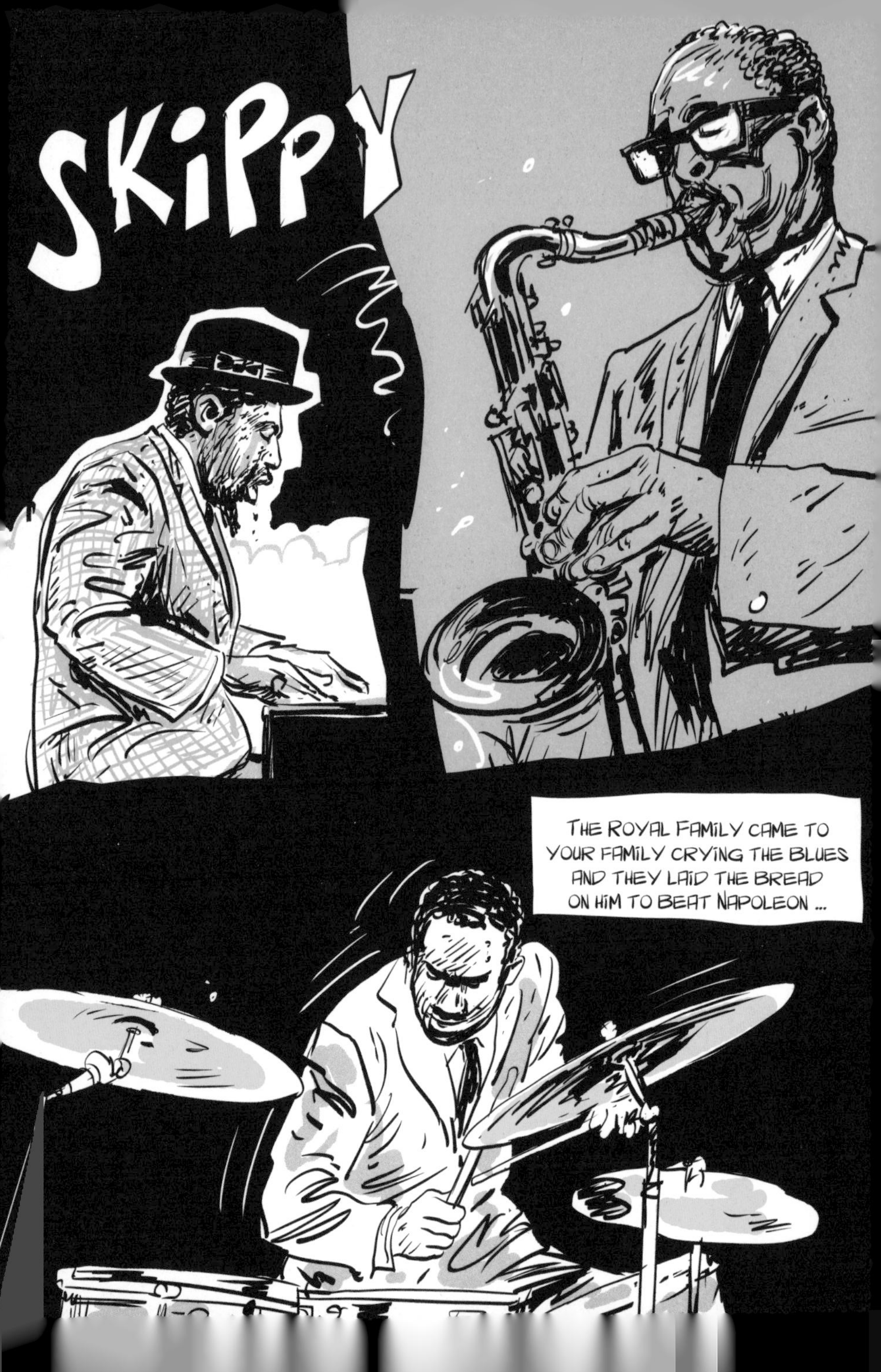
SKIPPY
THE ROYAL FAMILY CAME TO YOUR FAMILY CRYING THE BLUES AND THEY LAID THE BREAD ON HIM TO BEAT NAPOLEON ...

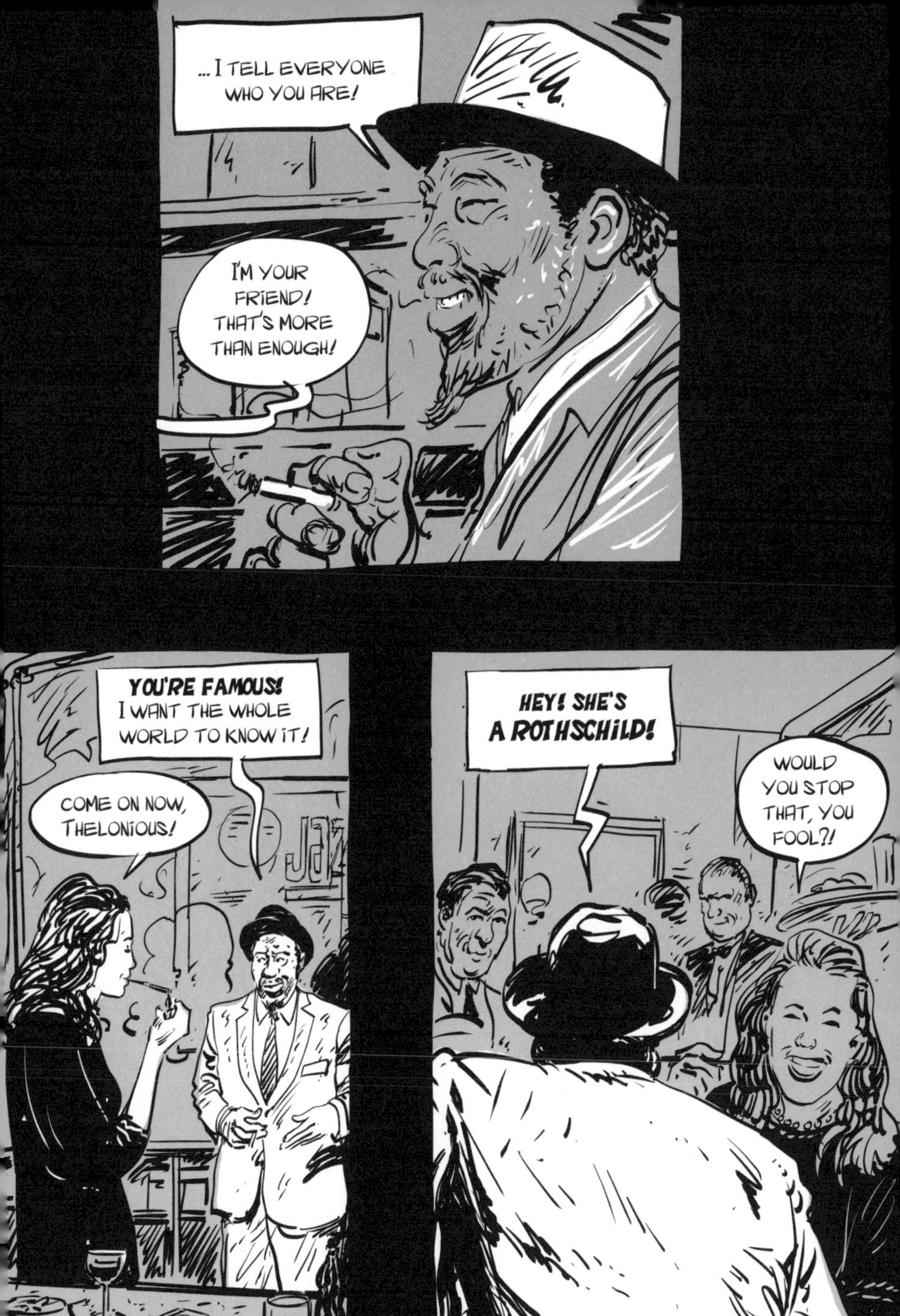

...I TELL EVERYONE WHO YOU ARE!
I'M YOUR FRIEND! THAT'S MORE THAN ENOUGH!
YOU'RE FAMOUS! I WANT THE WHOLE WORLD TO KNOW IT!
COME ON NOW, THELONIOUS!
HEY! SHE'S A ROTHSCHILD!
WOULD YOU STOP THAT, YOU FOOL?!

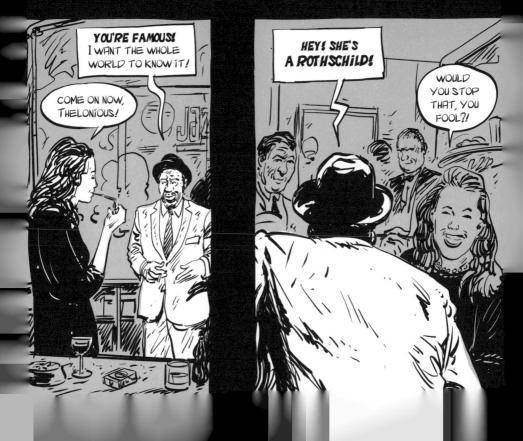

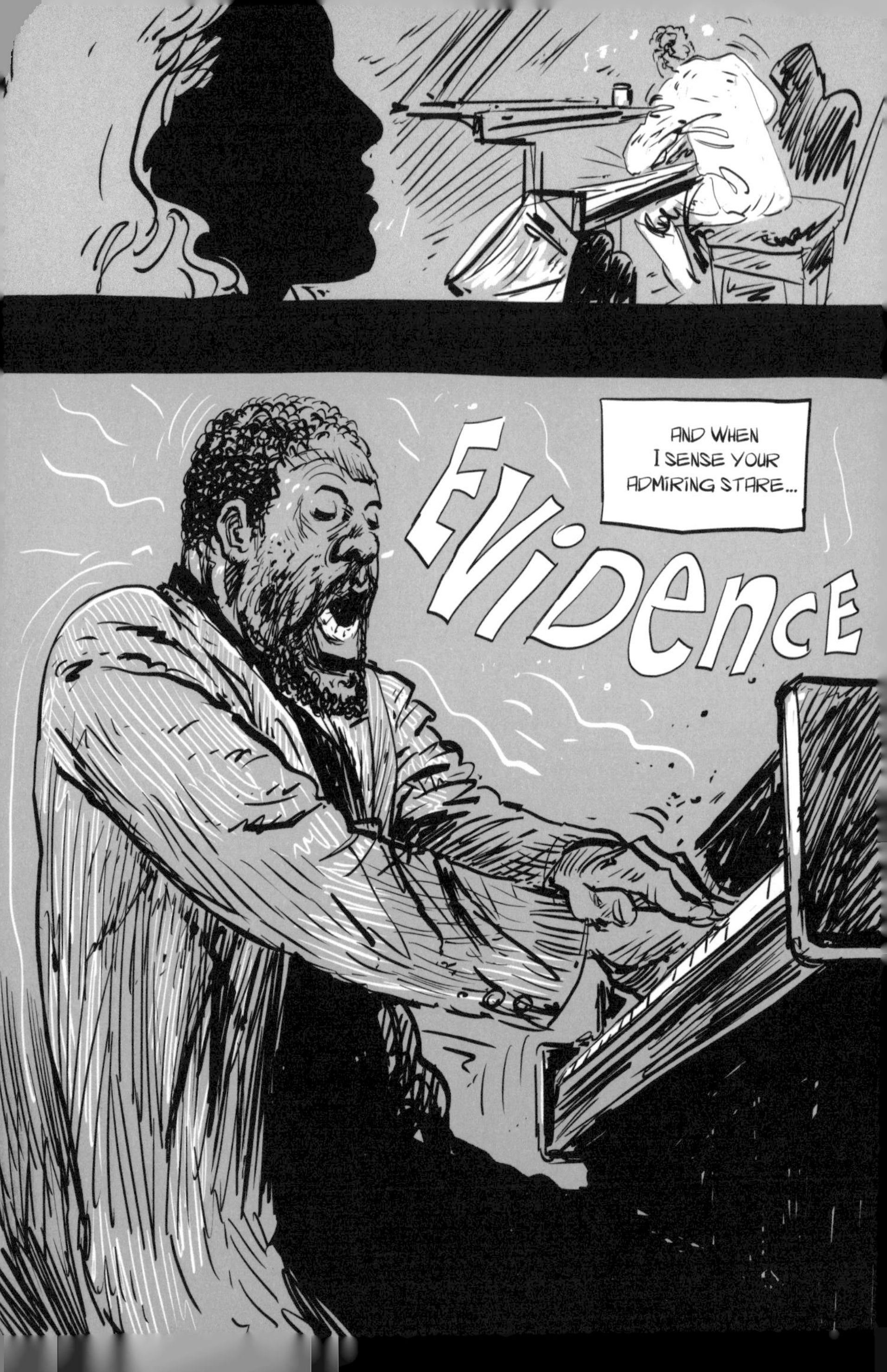
AND WHEN
I SENSE YOUR
ADMIRING STARE...
EVIDENCE

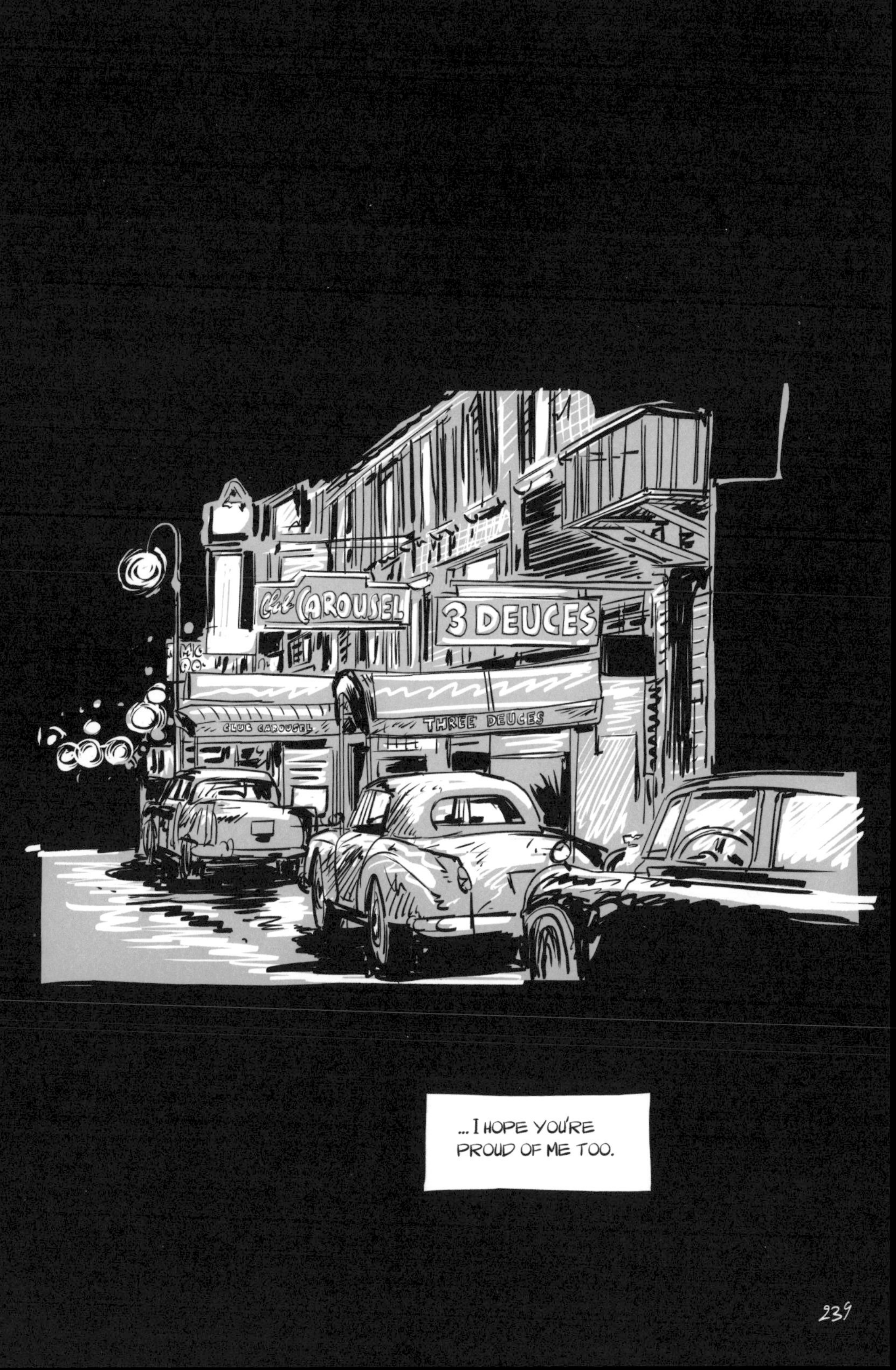
Club CAROUSEL
3 DEUCES
CLUB CAROUSEL
THREE DEUCES
...I HOPE YOU'RE PROUD OF ME TOO.

NICA'S DREAM

tuna
4
cats.
RED AND LIGHT MEAT TUNA
FOR CATS

NET WT.
6 OZ.

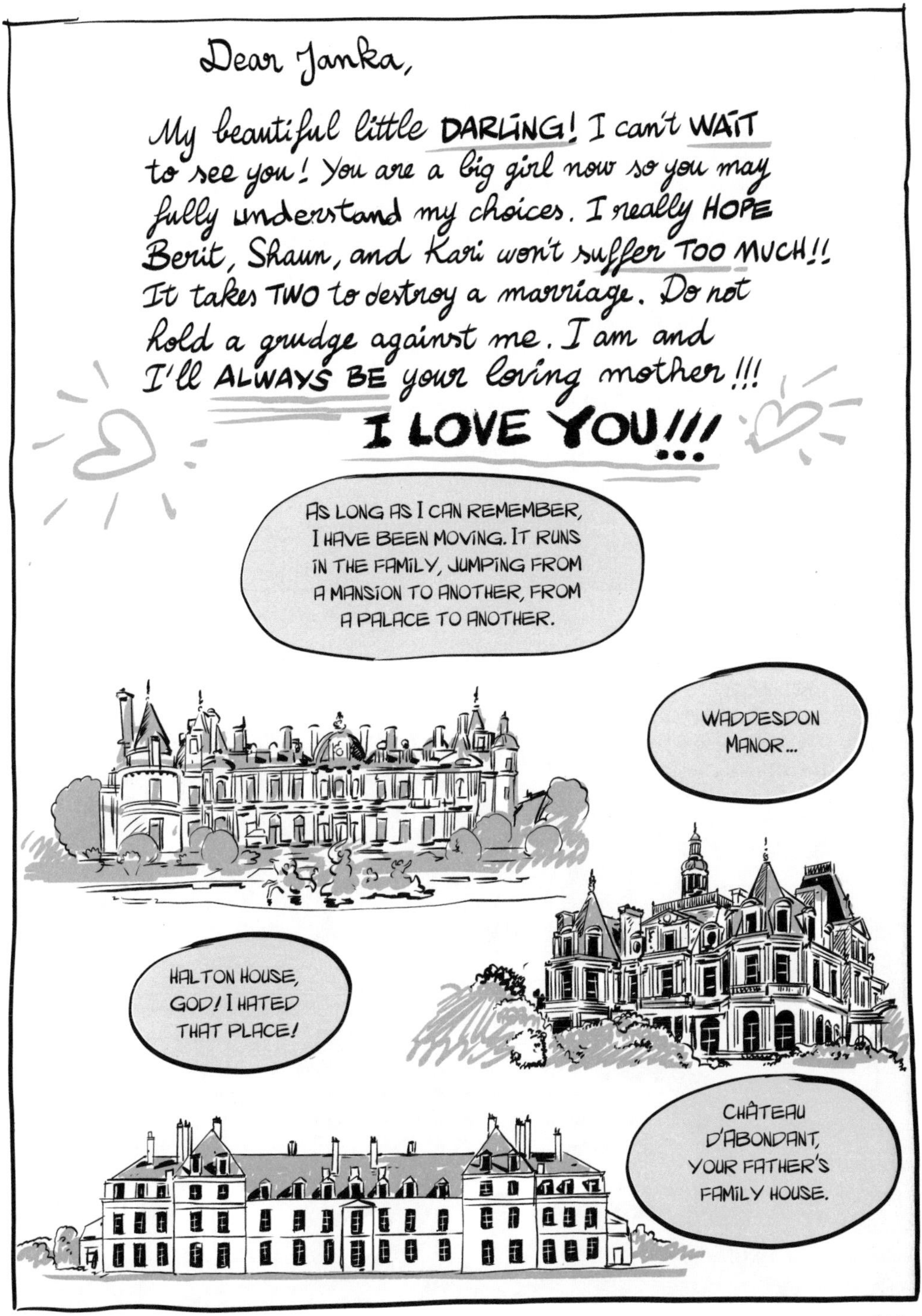
Dear Janka,
My beautiful little DARLING! I can't WAIT to see you! You are a big girl now so you may fully understand my choices. I really HOPE Berit, Shaun, and Kari won't suffer TOO MUCH!! It takes TWO to destroy a marriage. Do not hold a grudge against me. I am and I'll ALWAYS BE your loving mother!!!
I LOVE YOU!!!...
AS LONG AS I CAN REMEMBER, I HAVE BEEN MOVING. IT RUNS IN THE FAMILY, JUMPING FROM A MANSION TO ANOTHER, FROM A PALACE TO ANOTHER.
WADDESDON MANOR...
HALTON HOUSE, GOD! I HATED THAT PLACE!
CHÂTEAU D'ABONDANT, YOUR FATHER'S FAMILY HOUSE.

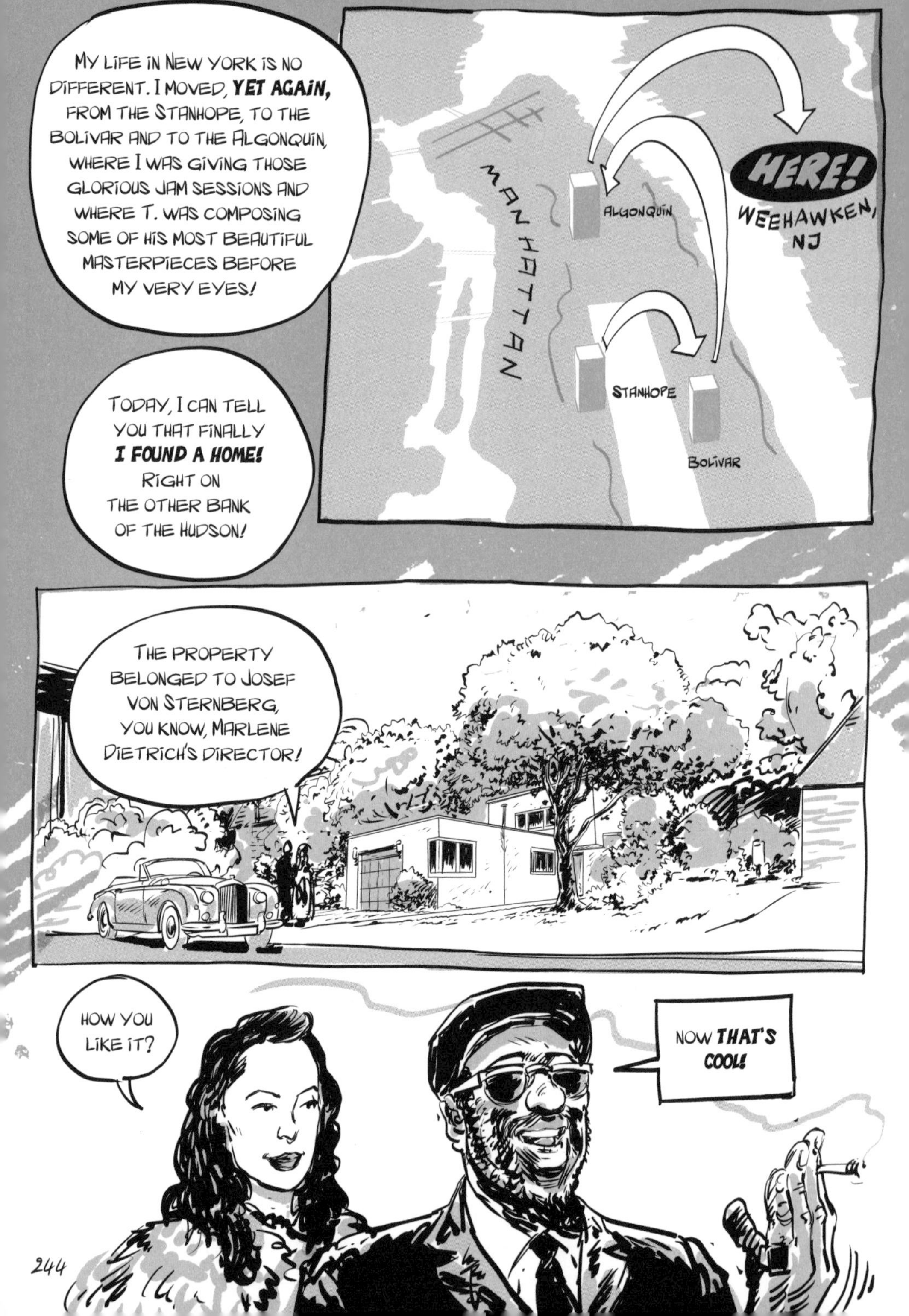
MY LIFE IN NEW YORK IS NO DIFFERENT. I MOVED, **YET AGAIN,** FROM THE STANHOPE, TO THE BOLIVAR AND TO THE ALGONQUIN, WHERE I WAS GIVING THOSE GLORIOUS JAM SESSIONS AND WHERE T. WAS COMPOSING SOME OF HIS MOST BEAUTIFUL MASTERPIECES BEFORE MY VERY EYES!
MANHATTAN
ALGONQUIN
STANHOPE
BOLIVAR
HERE!
WEEHAWKEN, NJ
TODAY, I CAN TELL YOU THAT FINALLY **I FOUND A HOME!** RIGHT ON THE OTHER BANK OF THE HUDSON!
THE PROPERTY BELONGED TO JOSEF VON STERNBERG, YOU KNOW, MARLENE DIETRICH'S DIRECTOR!
HOW YOU LIKE IT?
NOW **THAT'S COOL!**

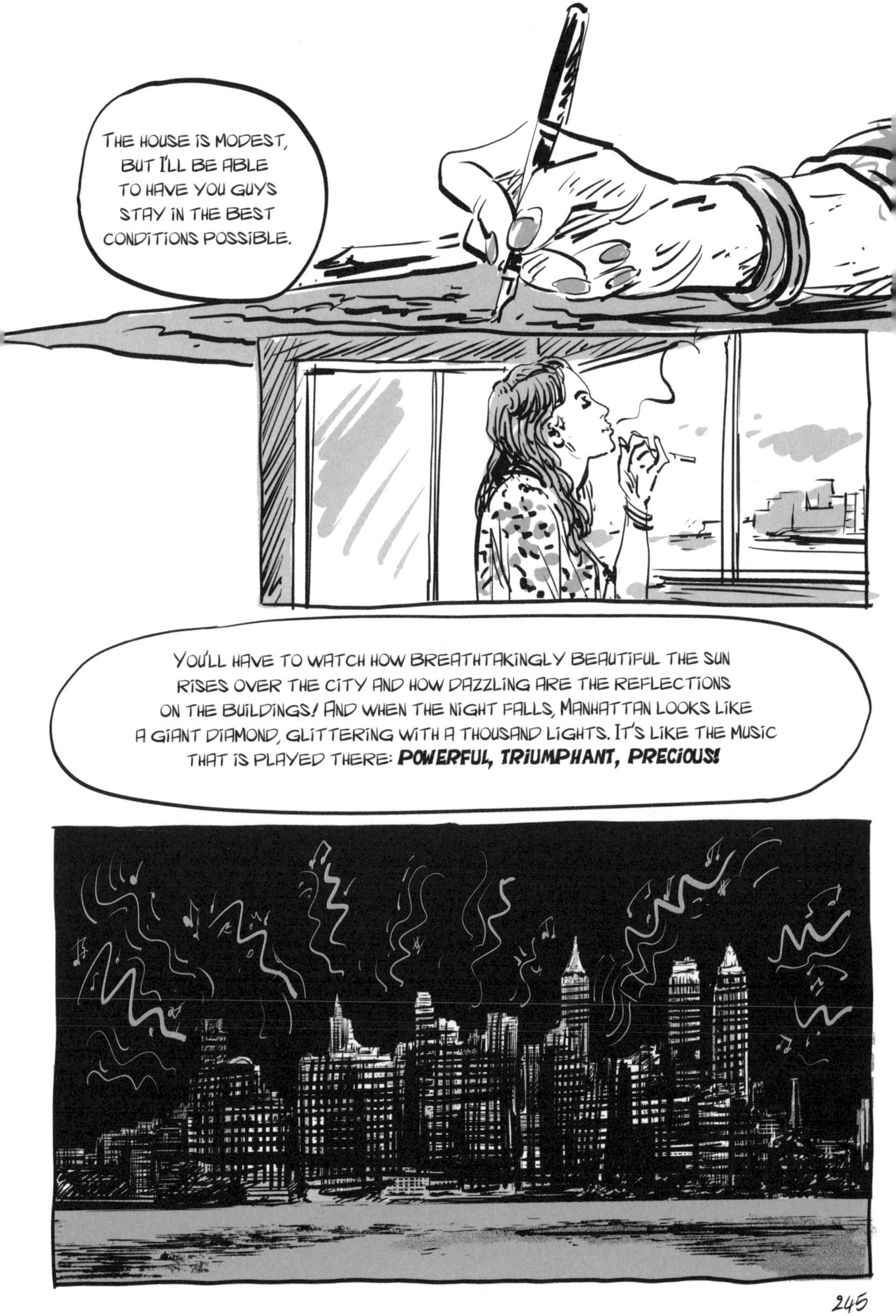
THE HOUSE IS MODEST, BUT I'LL BE ABLE TO HAVE YOU GUYS STAY IN THE BEST CONDITIONS POSSIBLE.
YOU'LL HAVE TO WATCH HOW BREATHTAKINGLY BEAUTIFUL THE SUN RISES OVER THE CITY AND HOW DAZZLING ARE THE REFLECTIONS ON THE BUILDINGS! AND WHEN THE NIGHT FALLS, MANHATTAN LOOKS LIKE A GIANT DIAMOND, GLITTERING WITH A THOUSAND LIGHTS. IT'S LIKE THE MUSIC THAT IS PLAYED THERE: **POWERFUL, TRIUMPHANT, PRECIOUS!**

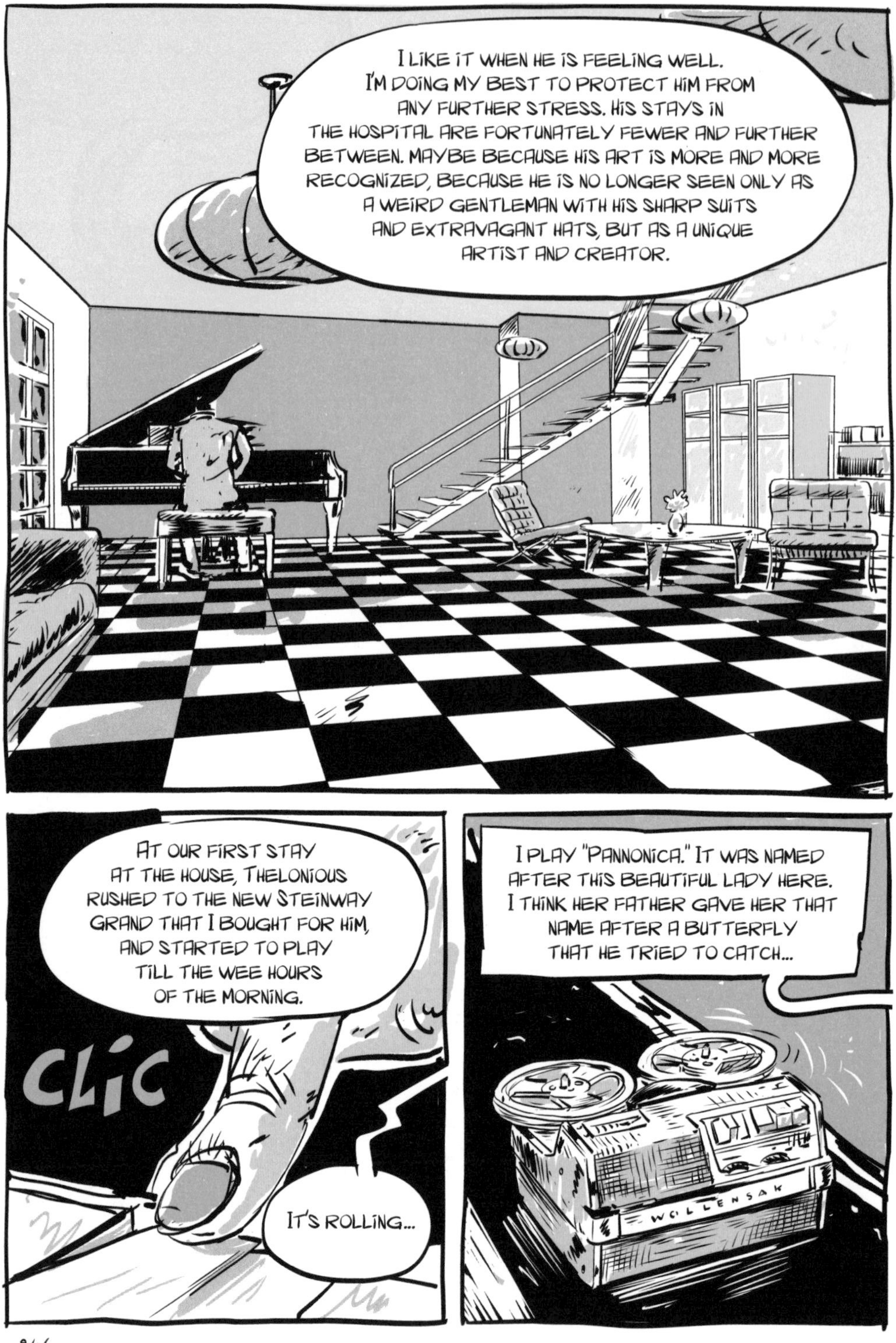
I LIKE IT WHEN HE IS FEELING WELL. I'M DOING MY BEST TO PROTECT HIM FROM ANY FURTHER STRESS. HIS STAYS IN THE HOSPITAL ARE FORTUNATELY FEWER AND FURTHER BETWEEN. MAYBE BECAUSE HIS ART IS MORE AND MORE RECOGNIZED, BECAUSE HE IS NO LONGER SEEN ONLY AS A WEIRD GENTLEMAN WITH HIS SHARP SUITS AND EXTRAVAGANT HATS, BUT AS A UNIQUE ARTIST AND CREATOR.
AT OUR FIRST STAY AT THE HOUSE, THELONIOUS RUSHED TO THE NEW STEINWAY GRAND THAT I BOUGHT FOR HIM, AND STARTED TO PLAY TILL THE WEE HOURS OF THE MORNING.
CLIC
IT'S ROLLING...
I PLAY "PANNONICA." IT WAS NAMED AFTER THIS BEAUTIFUL LADY HERE. I THINK HER FATHER GAVE HER THAT NAME AFTER A BUTTERFLY THAT HE TRIED TO CATCH...
WOLLENSAK

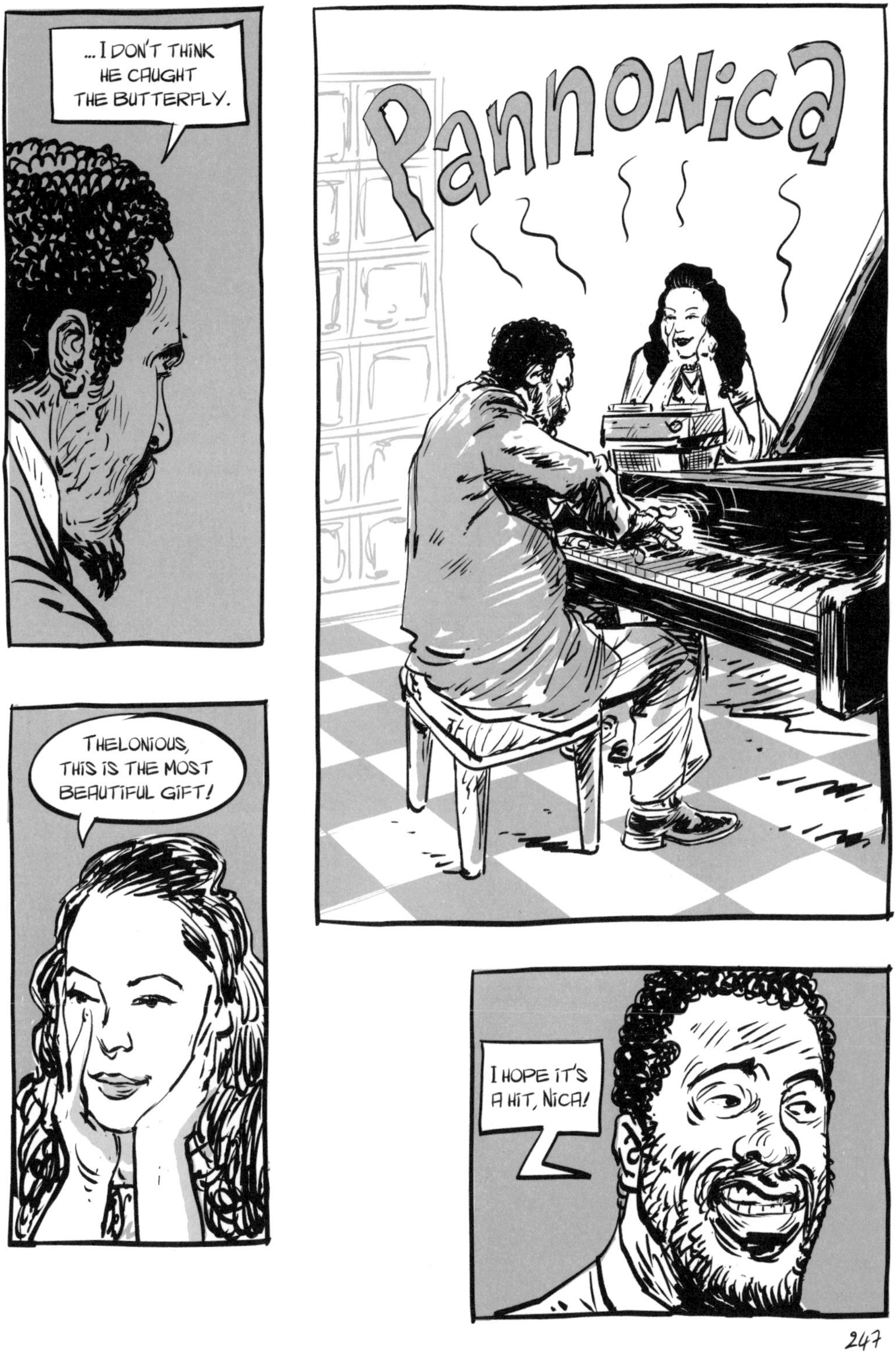
...I DON'T THINK HE CAUGHT THE BUTTERFLY.
PANNONICA
THELONIOUS, THIS IS THE MOST BEAUTIFUL GIFT!
I HOPE IT'S A HIT, NICA!

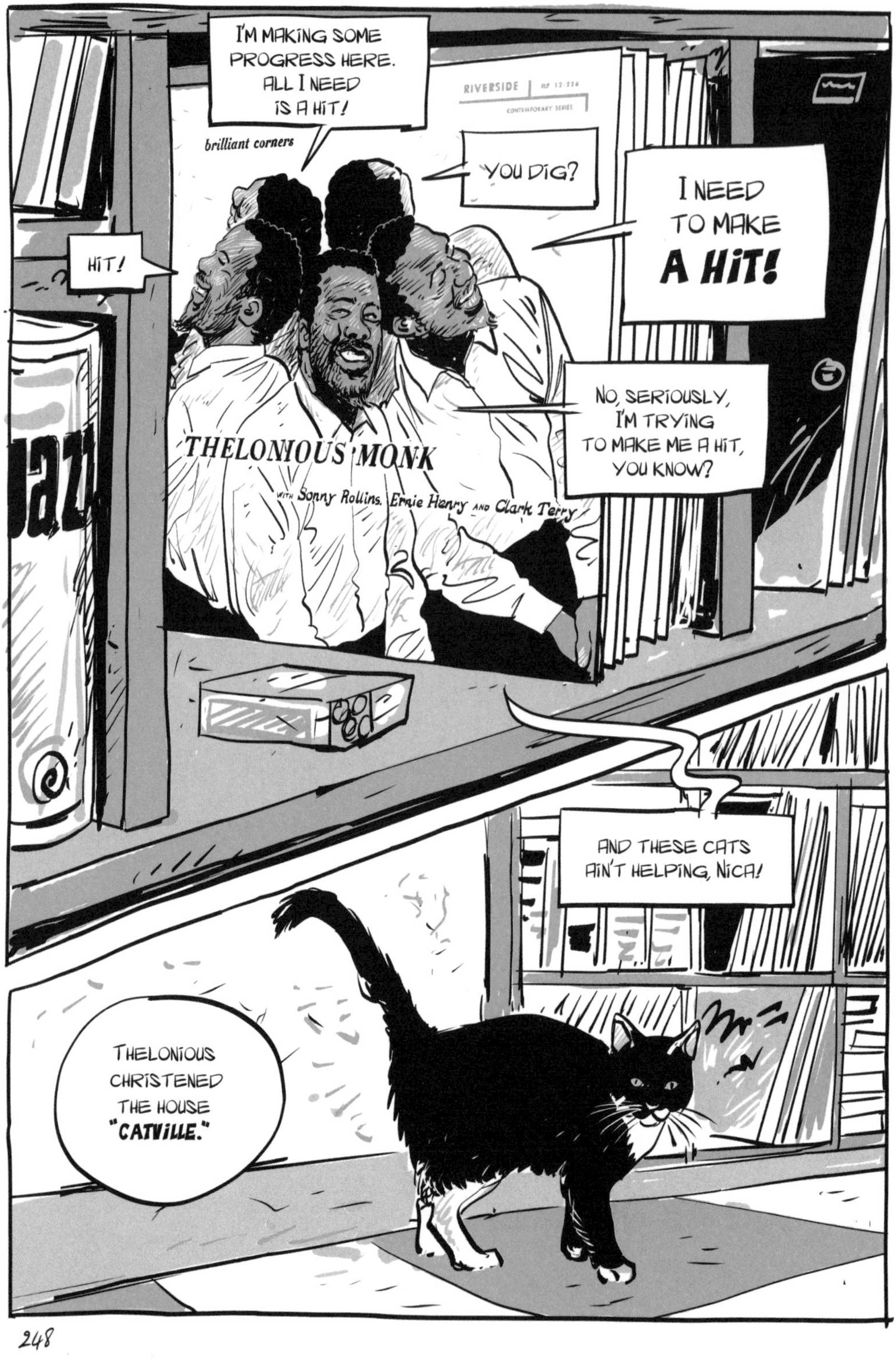

I'M MAKING SOME PROGRESS HERE. ALL I NEED IS A HIT!
RIVERSIDE RLP 12-226
CONTEMPORARY SERIES
brilliant corners
YOU DIG?
I NEED TO MAKE A HIT!
HIT!
NO, SERIOUSLY, I'M TRYING TO MAKE ME A HIT, YOU KNOW?
THELONIOUS MONK
WITH Sonny Rollins, Ernie Henry AND Clark Terry
AND THESE CATS AIN'T HELPING, NICA!
THELONIOUS CHRISTENED THE HOUSE "CATVILLE."

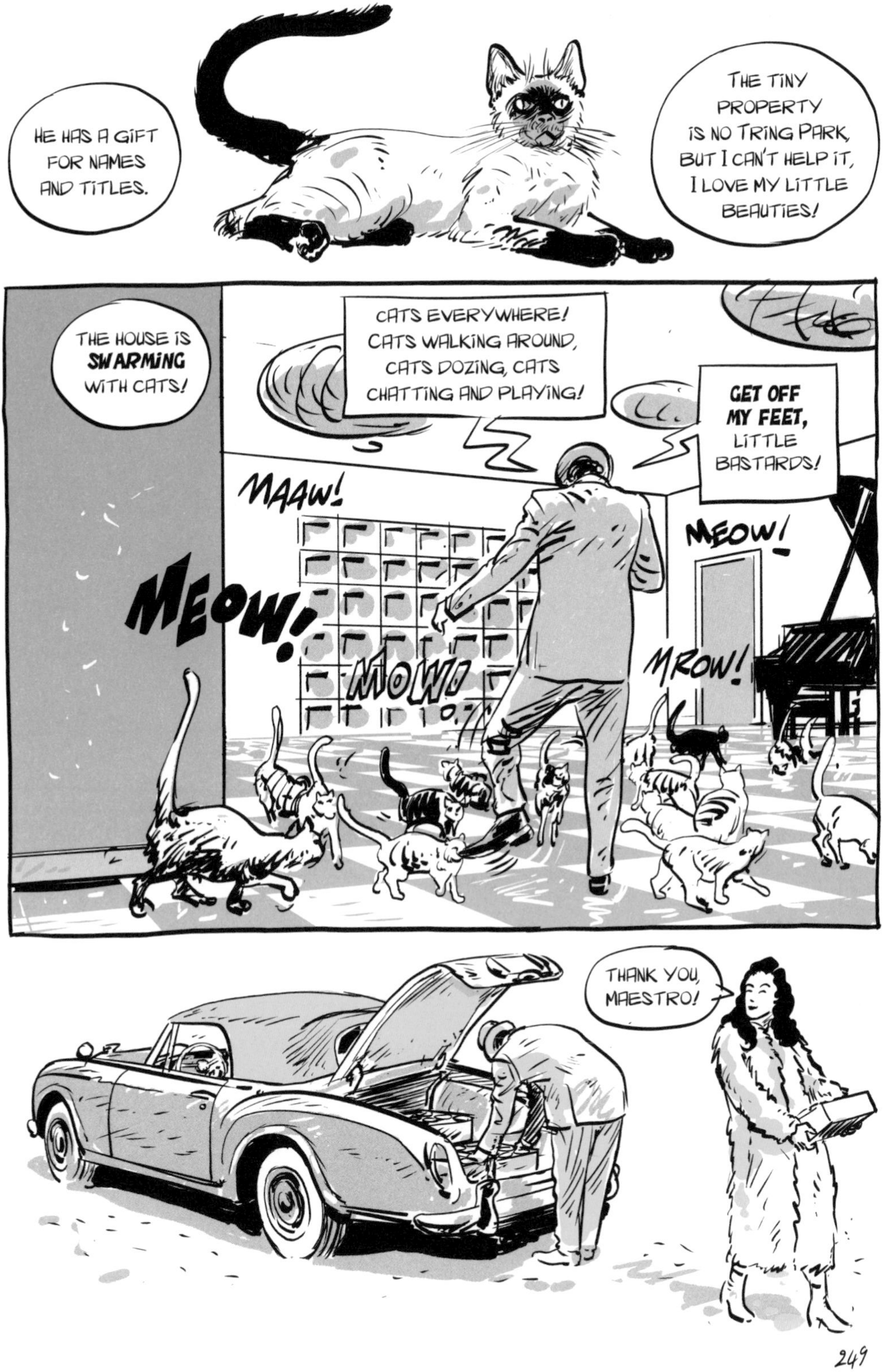
HE HAS A GIFT FOR NAMES AND TITLES.
THE TINY PROPERTY IS NO TRING PARK, BUT I CAN'T HELP IT, I LOVE MY LITTLE BEAUTIES!
THE HOUSE IS **SWARMING** WITH CATS!
CATS EVERYWHERE! CATS WALKING AROUND, CATS DOZING, CATS CHATTING AND PLAYING!
GET OFF MY FEET, LITTLE BASTARDS!
MAAW!
MEOW!
MEOW!
MOW!
MROW!
THANK YOU, MAESTRO!

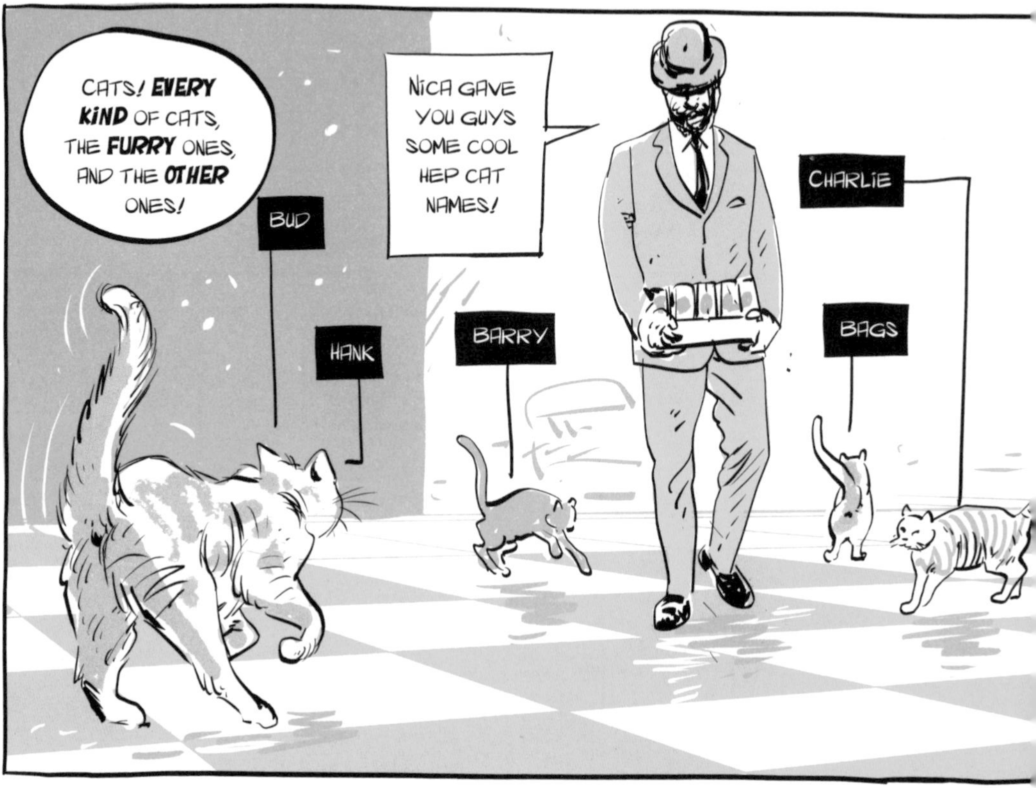
CATS! **EVERY KIND** OF CATS, THE **FURRY** ONES, AND THE **OTHER** ONES!
NICA GAVE YOU GUYS SOME COOL HEP CAT NAMES!
BUD
HANK
BARRY
CHARLIE
BAGS

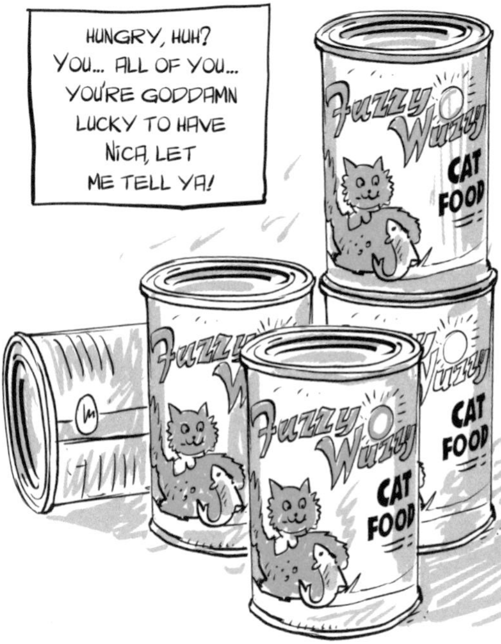
HUNGRY, HUH? YOU... ALL OF YOU... YOU'RE GODDAMN LUCKY TO HAVE NICA, LET ME TELL YA!
Fuzzy Wuzzy
CAT FOOD
Fuzzy Wuzzy
CAT FOOD
Fuzzy Wuzzy
CAT FOOD

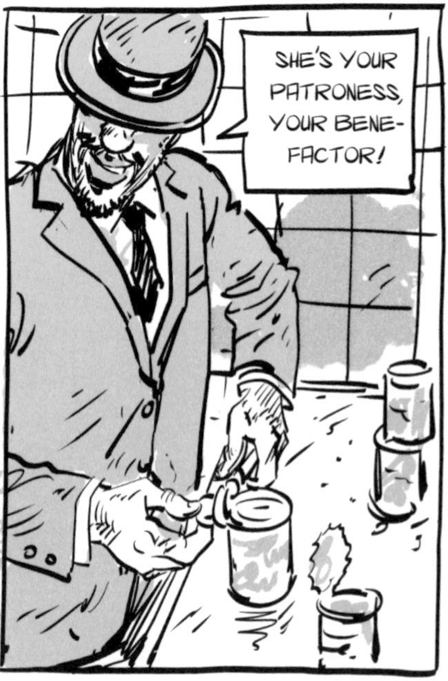
SHE'S YOUR PATRONESS, YOUR BENE-FACTOR!

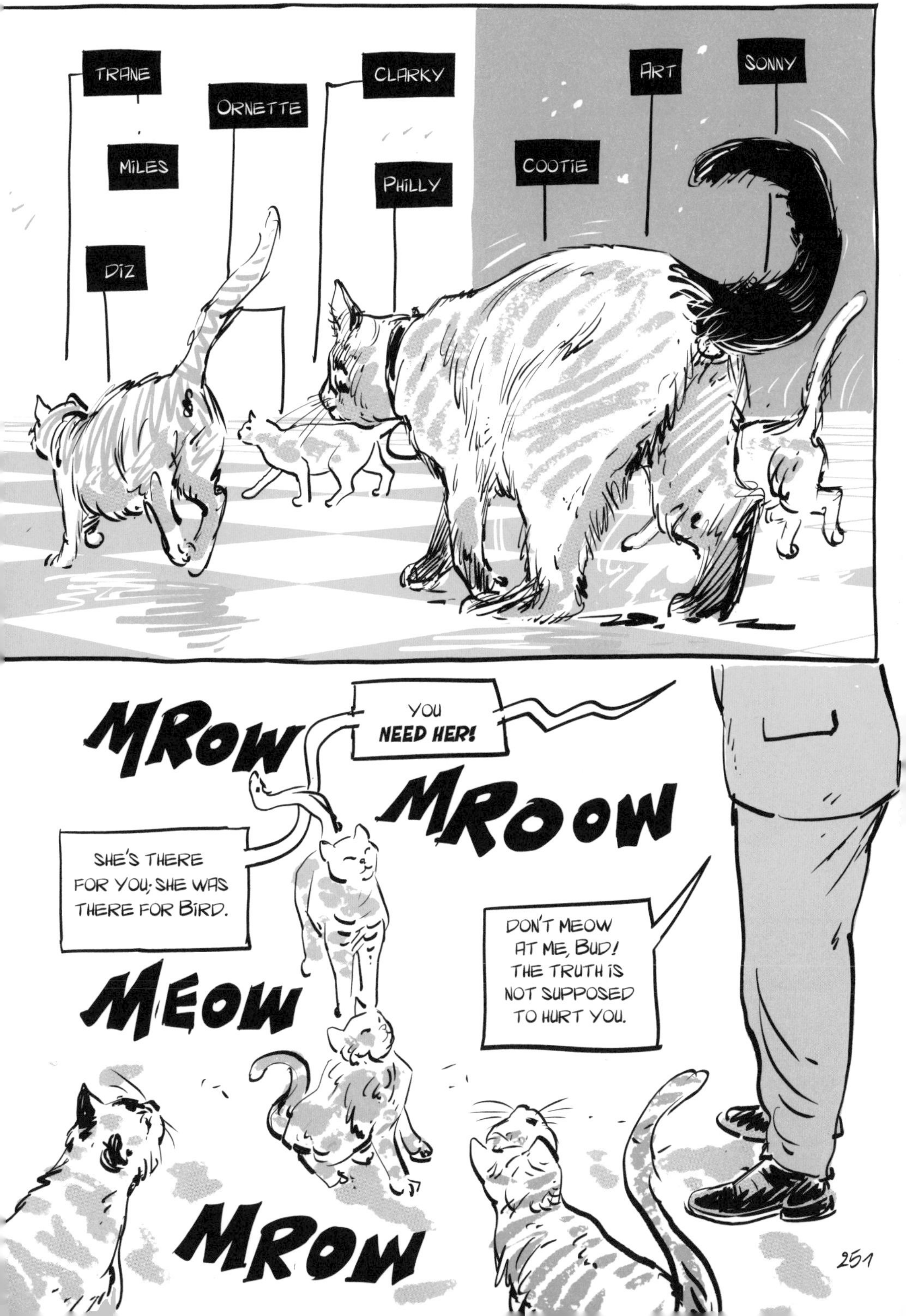
TRANE
MILES
DIZ
ORNETTE
CLARKY
PHILLY
COOTIE
ART
SONNY
MROW
YOU NEED HER!
MROOW
SHE'S THERE FOR YOU; SHE WAS THERE FOR BIRD.
DON'T MEOW AT ME, BUD! THE TRUTH IS NOT SUPPOSED TO HURT YOU.
MEOW
MROW

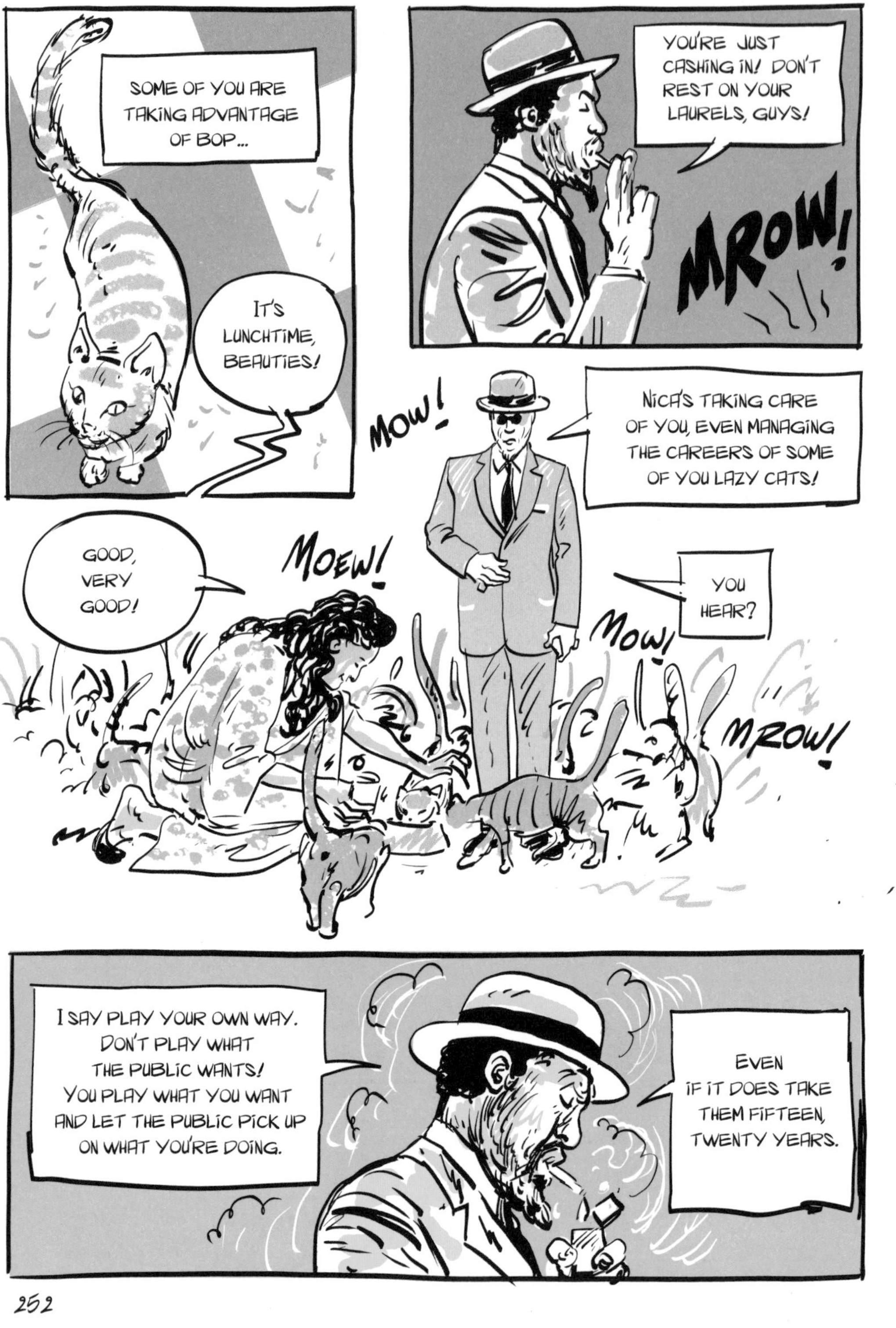
SOME OF YOU ARE TAKING ADVANTAGE OF BOP...
IT'S LUNCHTIME, BEAUTIES!
YOU'RE JUST CASHING IN! DON'T REST ON YOUR LAURELS, GUYS!
MROW!
MOW!
NICA'S TAKING CARE OF YOU, EVEN MANAGING THE CAREERS OF SOME OF YOU LAZY CATS!
GOOD, VERY GOOD!
MOEW!
YOU HEAR?
MOW!
MROW!
I SAY PLAY YOUR OWN WAY. DON'T PLAY WHAT THE PUBLIC WANTS! YOU PLAY WHAT YOU WANT AND LET THE PUBLIC PICK UP ON WHAT YOU'RE DOING.
EVEN IF IT DOES TAKE THEM FIFTEEN, TWENTY YEARS.

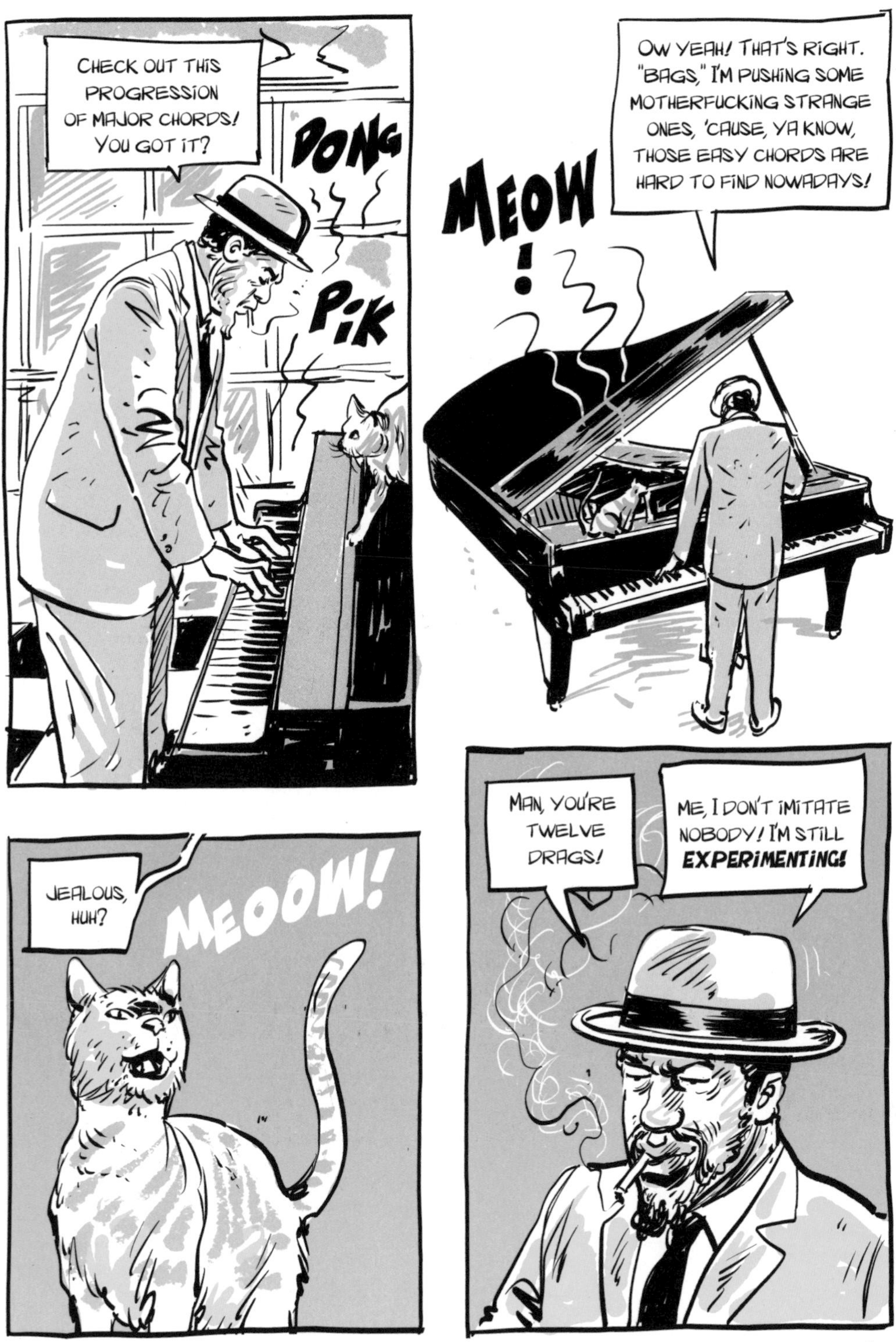
CHECK OUT THIS PROGRESSION OF MAJOR CHORDS! YOU GOT IT?
DONG
PIK
MEOW
!
OW YEAH! THAT'S RIGHT. "BAGS," I'M PUSHING SOME MOTHERFUCKING STRANGE ONES, 'CAUSE, YA KNOW, THOSE EASY CHORDS ARE HARD TO FIND NOWADAYS!
JEALOUS, HUH?
MEOOW!
MAN, YOU'RE TWELVE DRAGS!
ME, I DON'T IMITATE NOBODY! I'M STILL **EXPERIMENTING!**

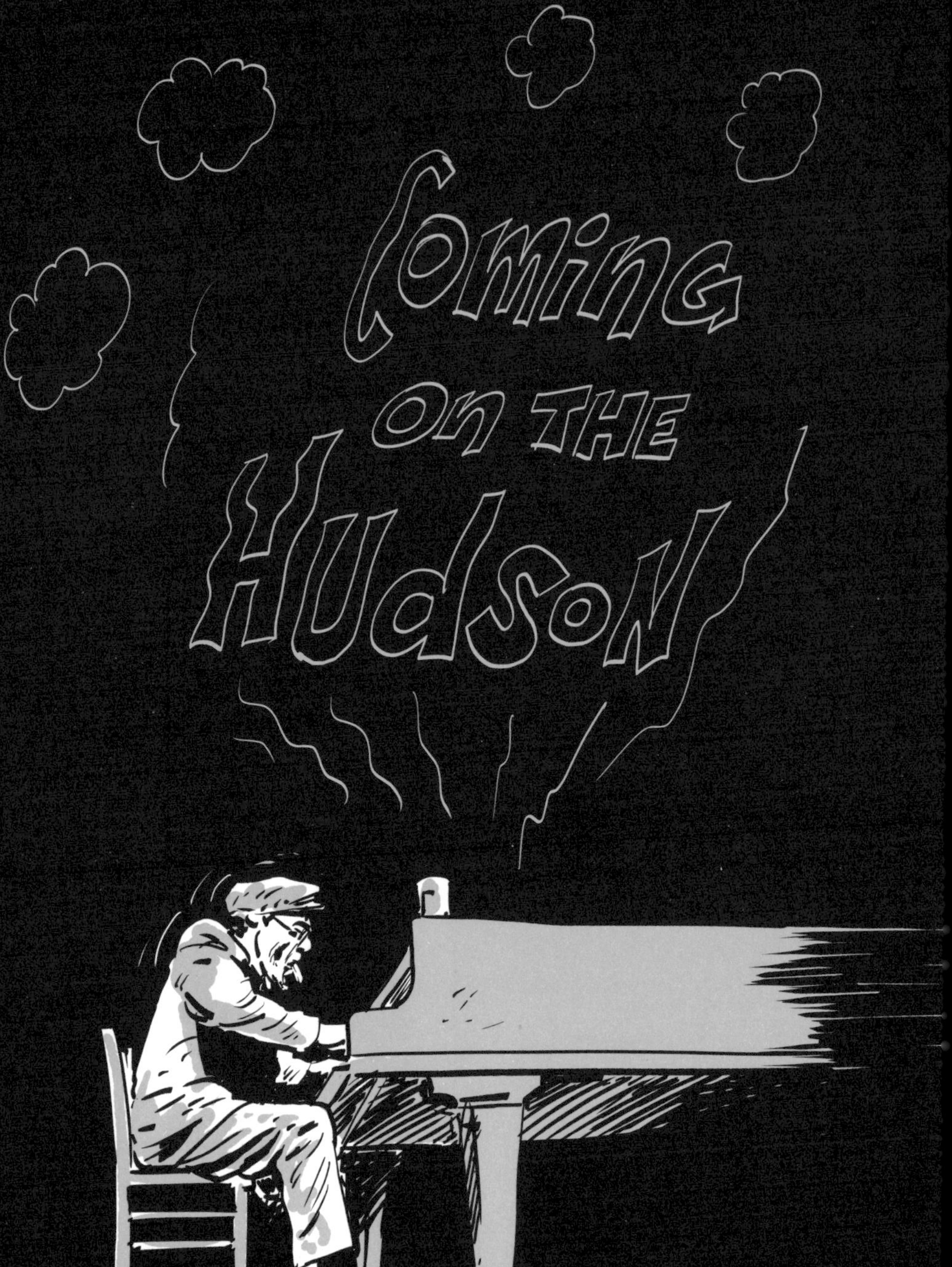
Coming on the Hudson

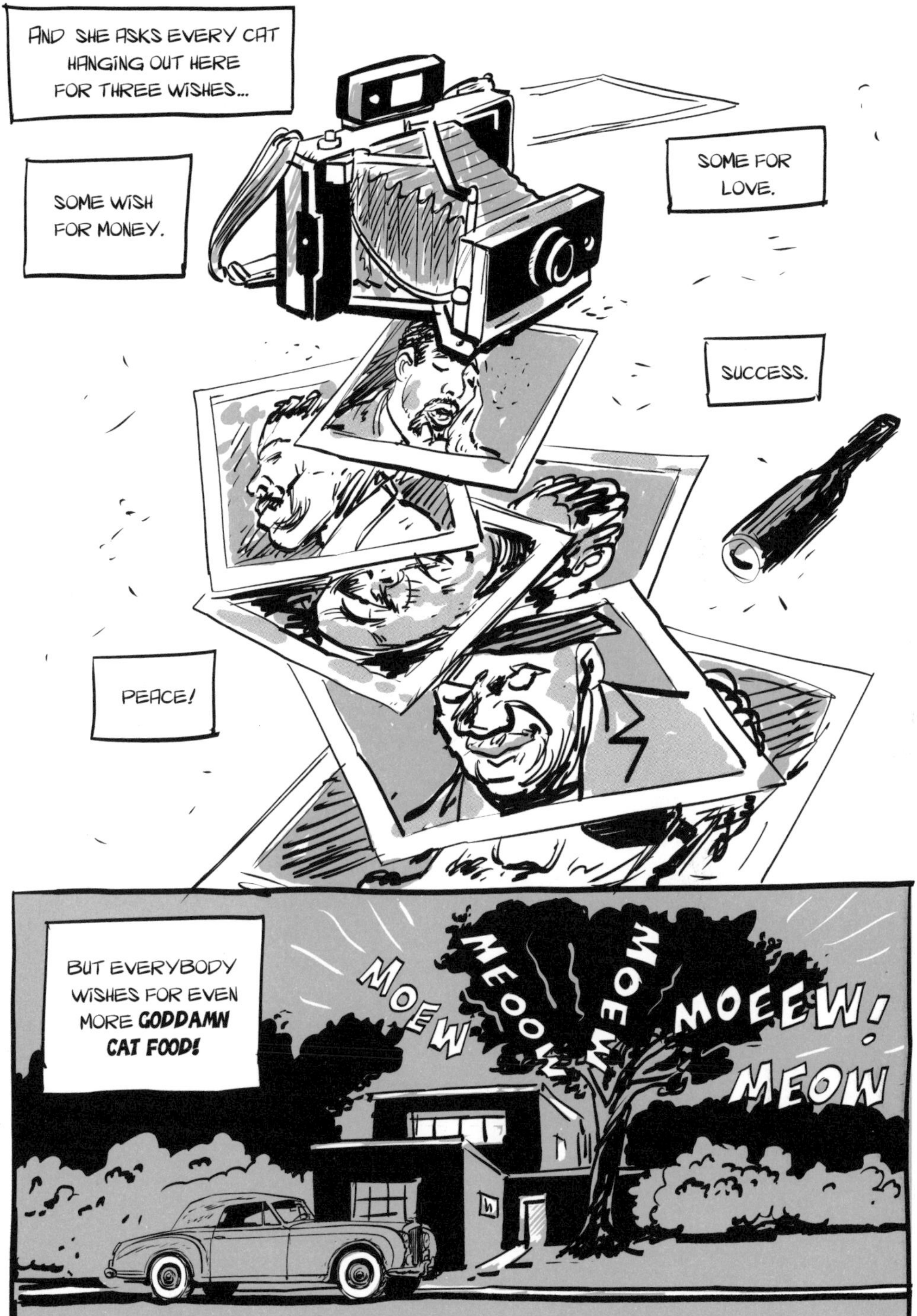
AND SHE ASKS EVERY CAT HANGING OUT HERE FOR THREE WISHES...
SOME WISH FOR MONEY.
SOME FOR LOVE.
SUCCESS.
PEACE!
BUT EVERYBODY WISHES FOR EVEN MORE **GODDAMN CAT FOOD!**
MOEW
MEOOW
MOEW
MOEEW!
MEOW

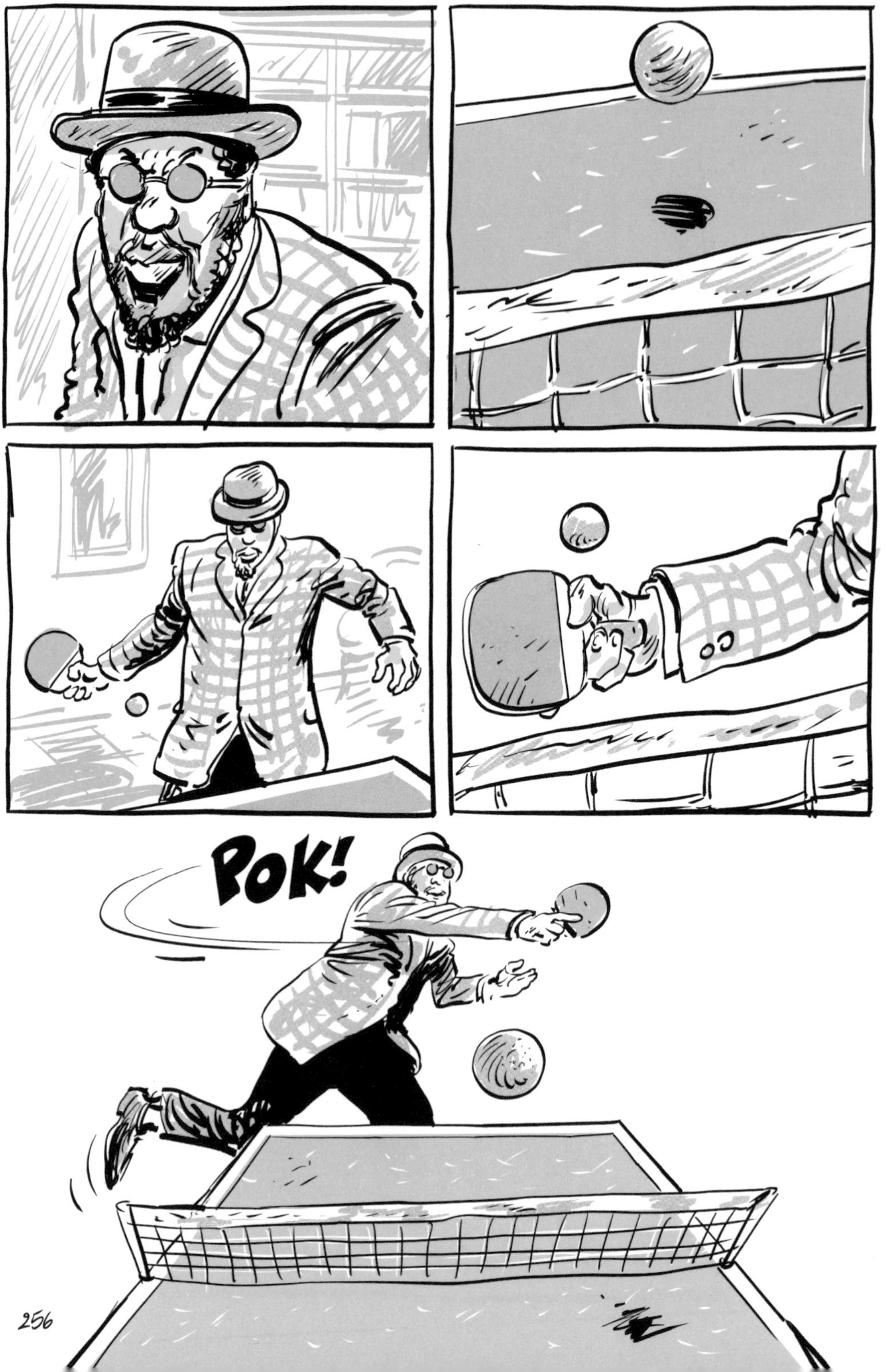
POK!

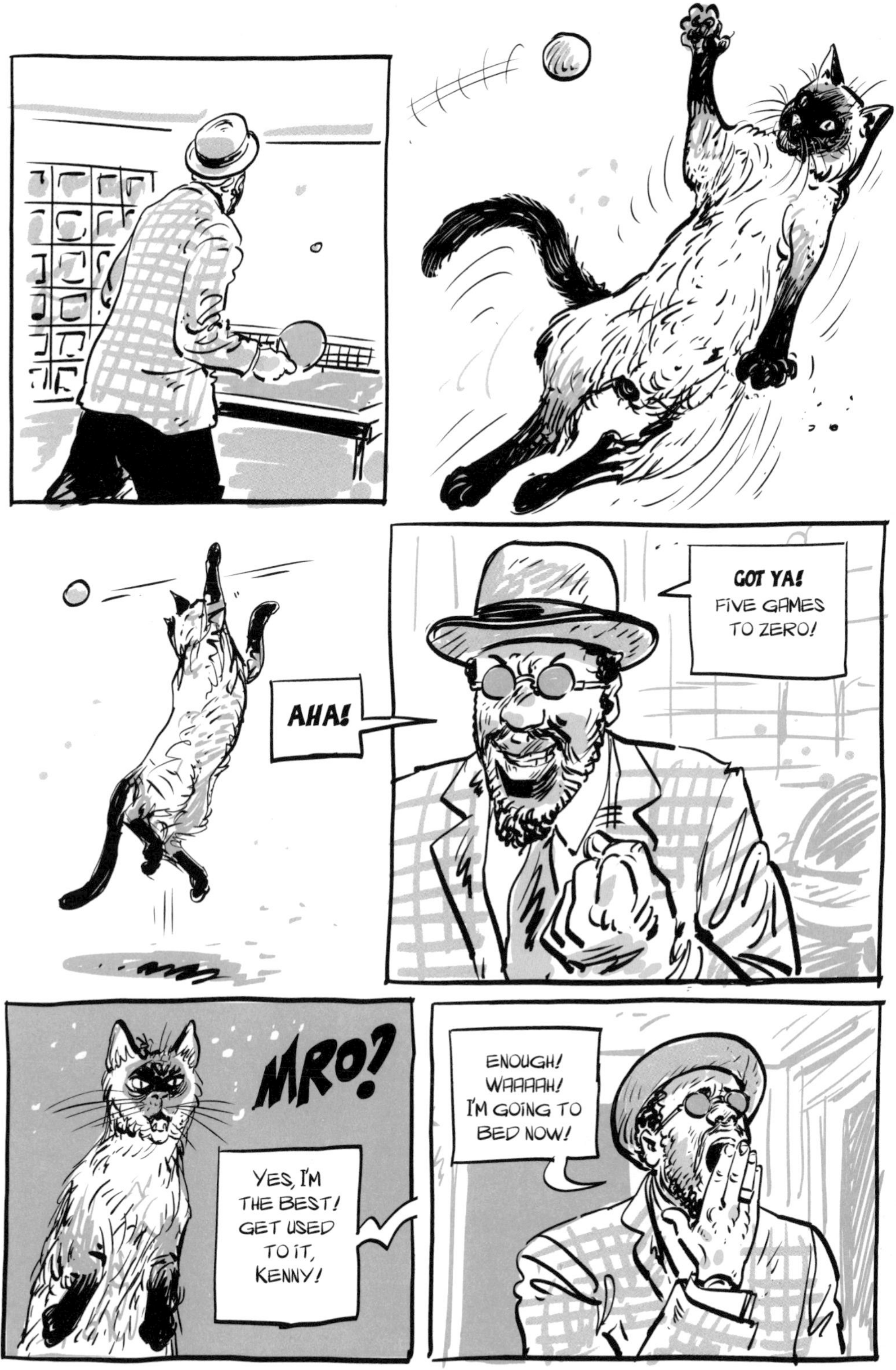
GOT YA!
FIVE GAMES TO ZERO!
AHA!
MRO?
YES, I'M THE BEST! GET USED TO IT, KENNY!
ENOUGH! WAAAAH! I'M GOING TO BED NOW!

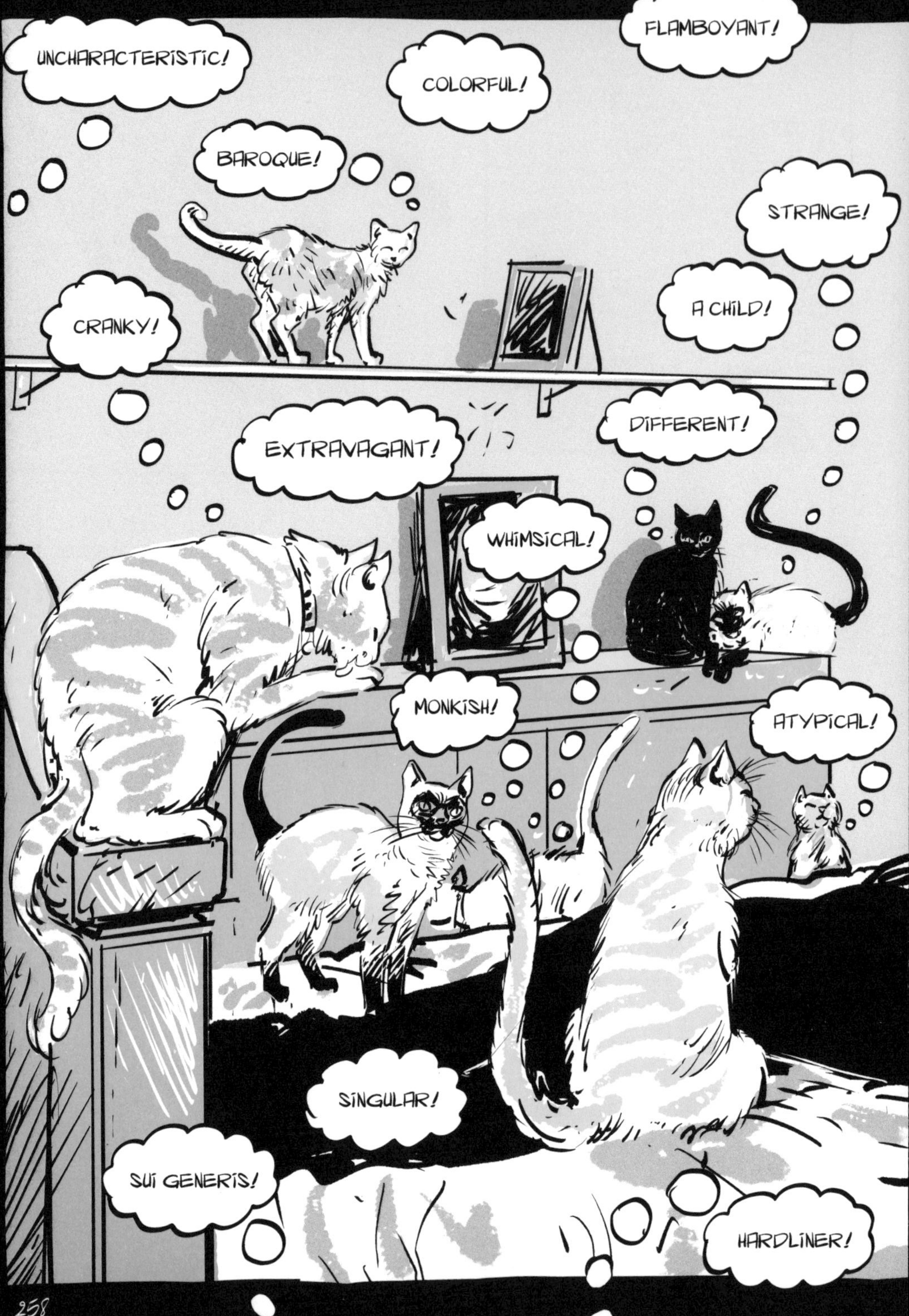
UNCHARACTERISTIC!
COLORFUL!
FLAMBOYANT!
BAROQUE!
STRANGE!
CRANKY!
A CHILD!
EXTRAVAGANT!
DIFFERENT!
WHIMSICAL!
MONKISH!
ATYPICAL!
SINGULAR!
SUI GENERIS!
HARDLINER!

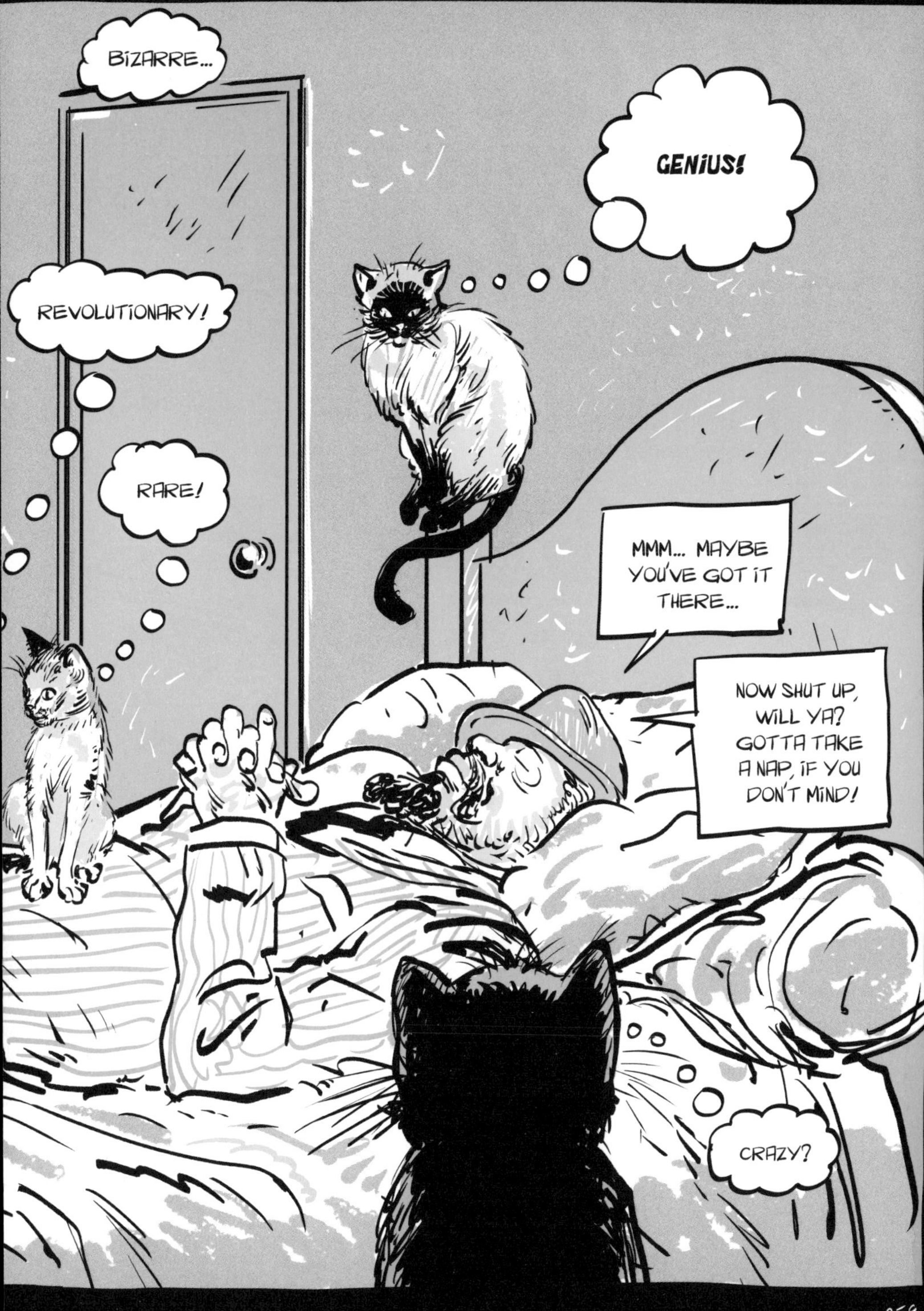
BIZARRE...
GENIUS!
REVOLUTIONARY!
RARE!
MMM... MAYBE YOU'VE GOT IT THERE...
NOW SHUT UP, WILL YA? GOTTA TAKE A NAP, IF YOU DON'T MIND!
CRAZY?

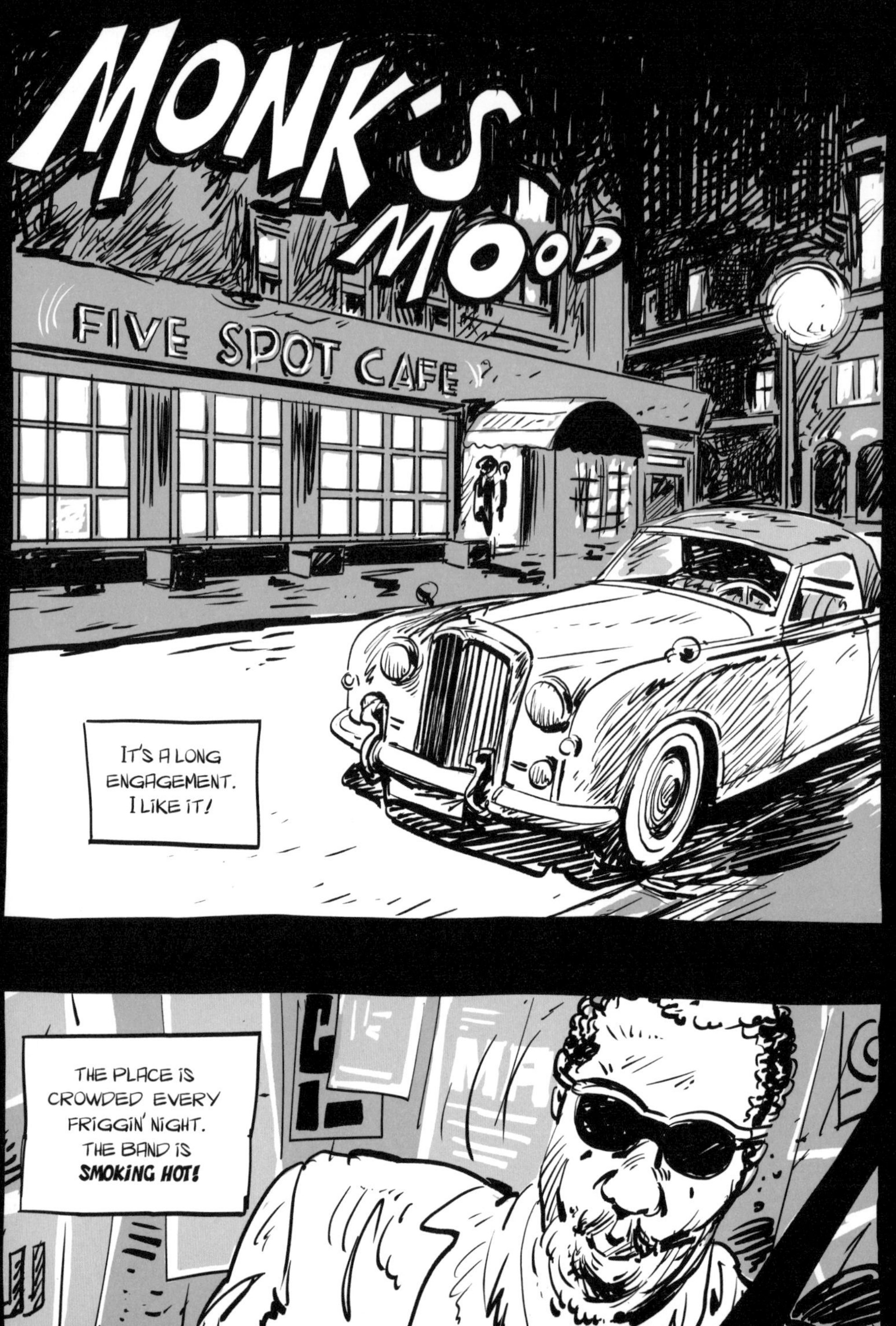
MONK'S MOOD
FIVE SPOT CAFE
IT'S A LONG ENGAGEMENT. I LIKE IT!
THE PLACE IS CROWDED EVERY FRIGGIN' NIGHT. THE BAND IS **SMOKING HOT!**

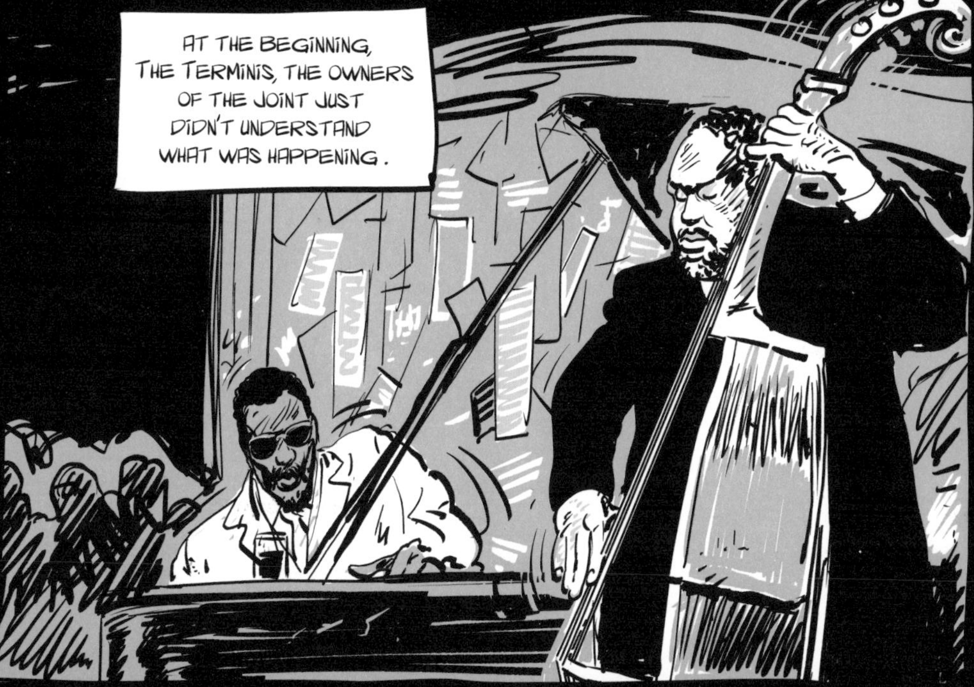
AT THE BEGINNING, THE TERMINIS, THE OWNERS OF THE JOINT JUST DIDN'T UNDERSTAND WHAT WAS HAPPENING.

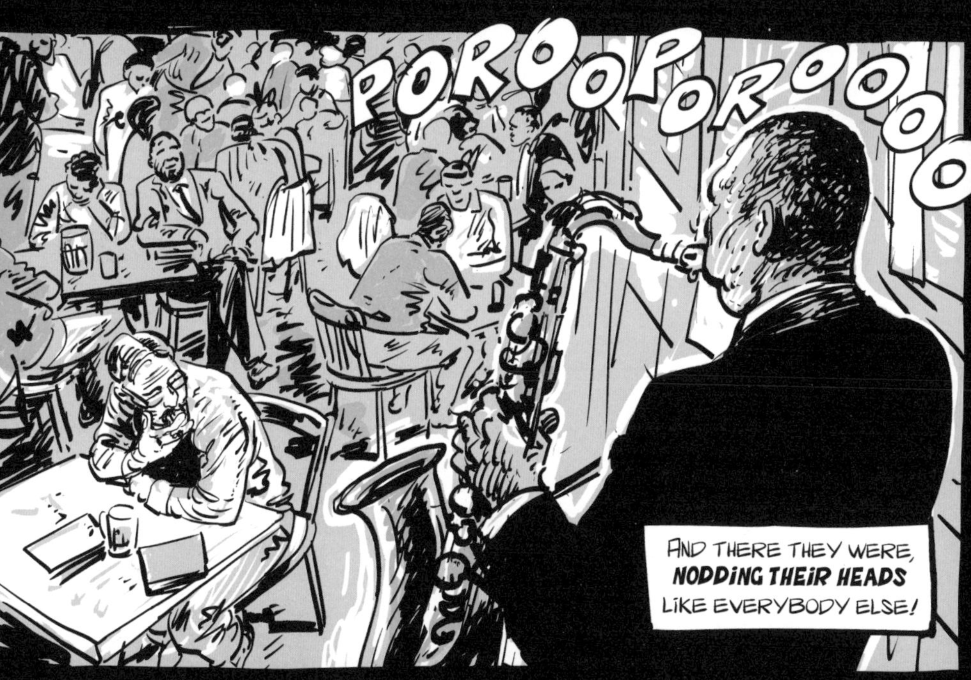
POROOPOROOOOO
AND THERE THEY WERE, **NODDING THEIR HEADS** LIKE EVERYBODY ELSE!

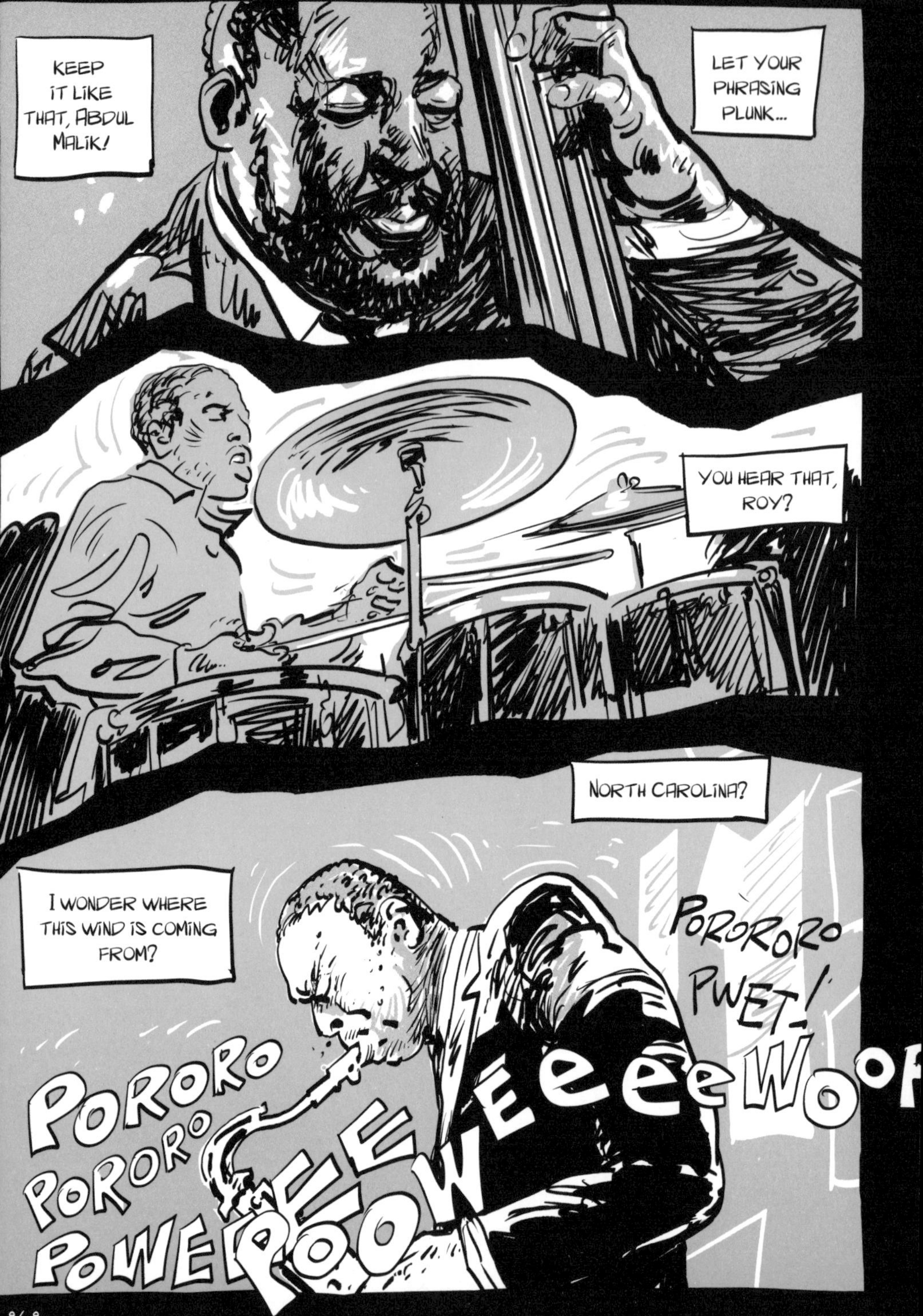
KEEP IT LIKE THAT, ABDUL MALIK!
LET YOUR PHRASING PLUNK...
YOU HEAR THAT, ROY?
NORTH CAROLINA?
I WONDER WHERE THIS WIND IS COMING FROM?
POROROPO PWET!
PORORO PORORO POWEEE
EEEWEEEEWOOF

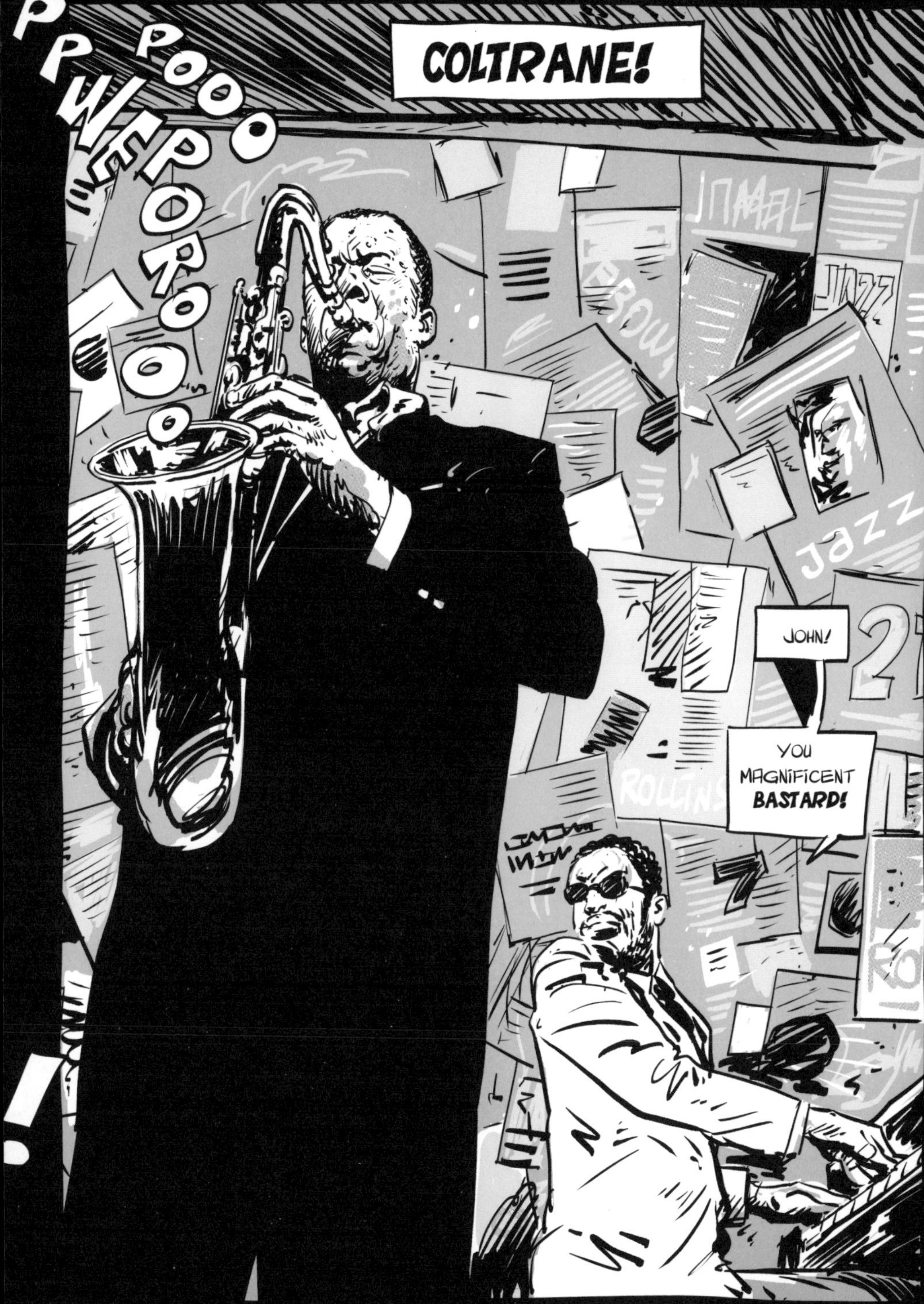
COLTRANE!
PPWEEPOOO
OROOROOOOOOO
JOHN!
YOU MAGNIFICENT BASTARD!
JAZZ
ROLLINS

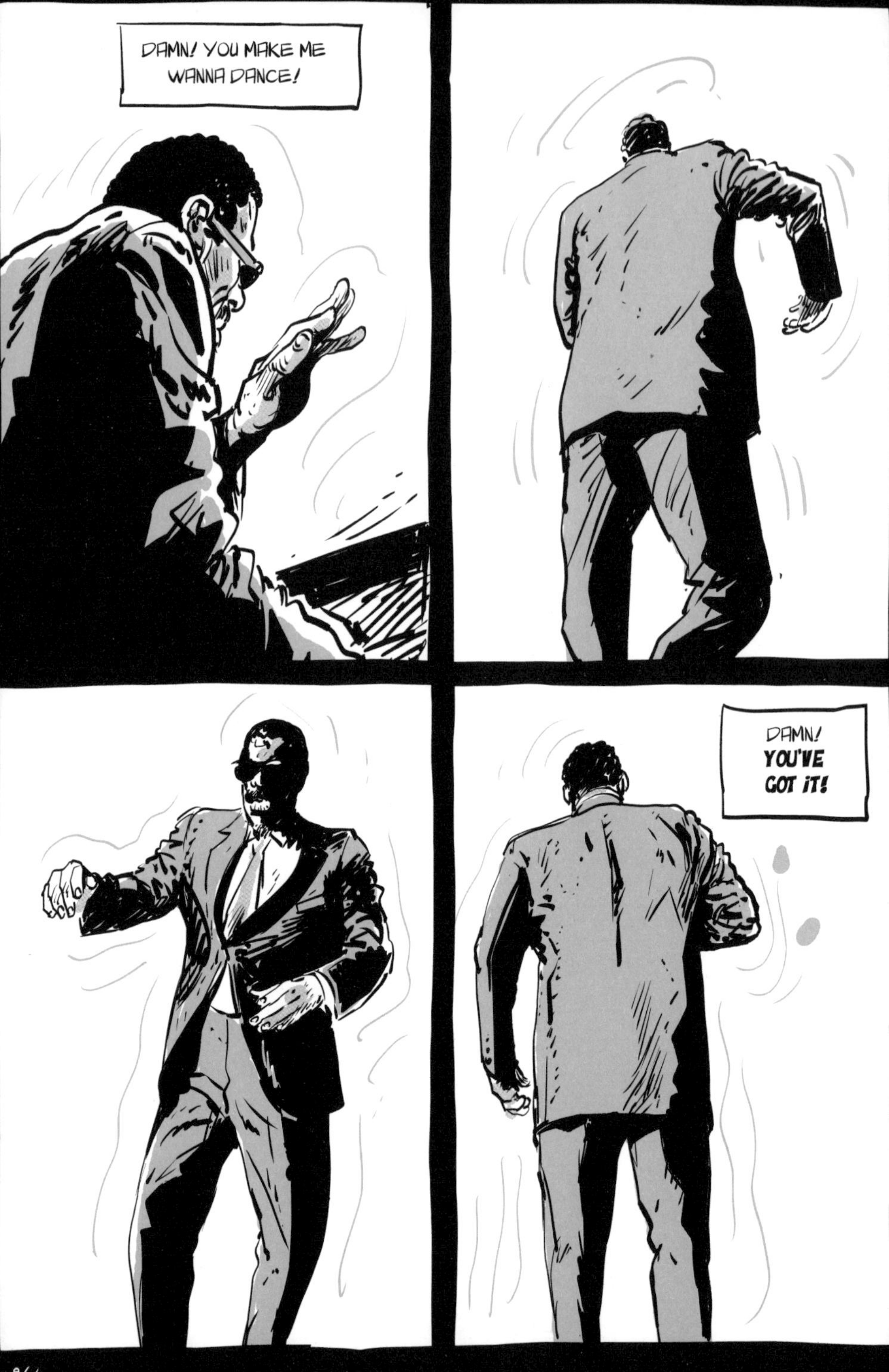
DAMN! YOU MAKE ME WANNA DANCE!
DAMN! YOU'VE GOT IT!

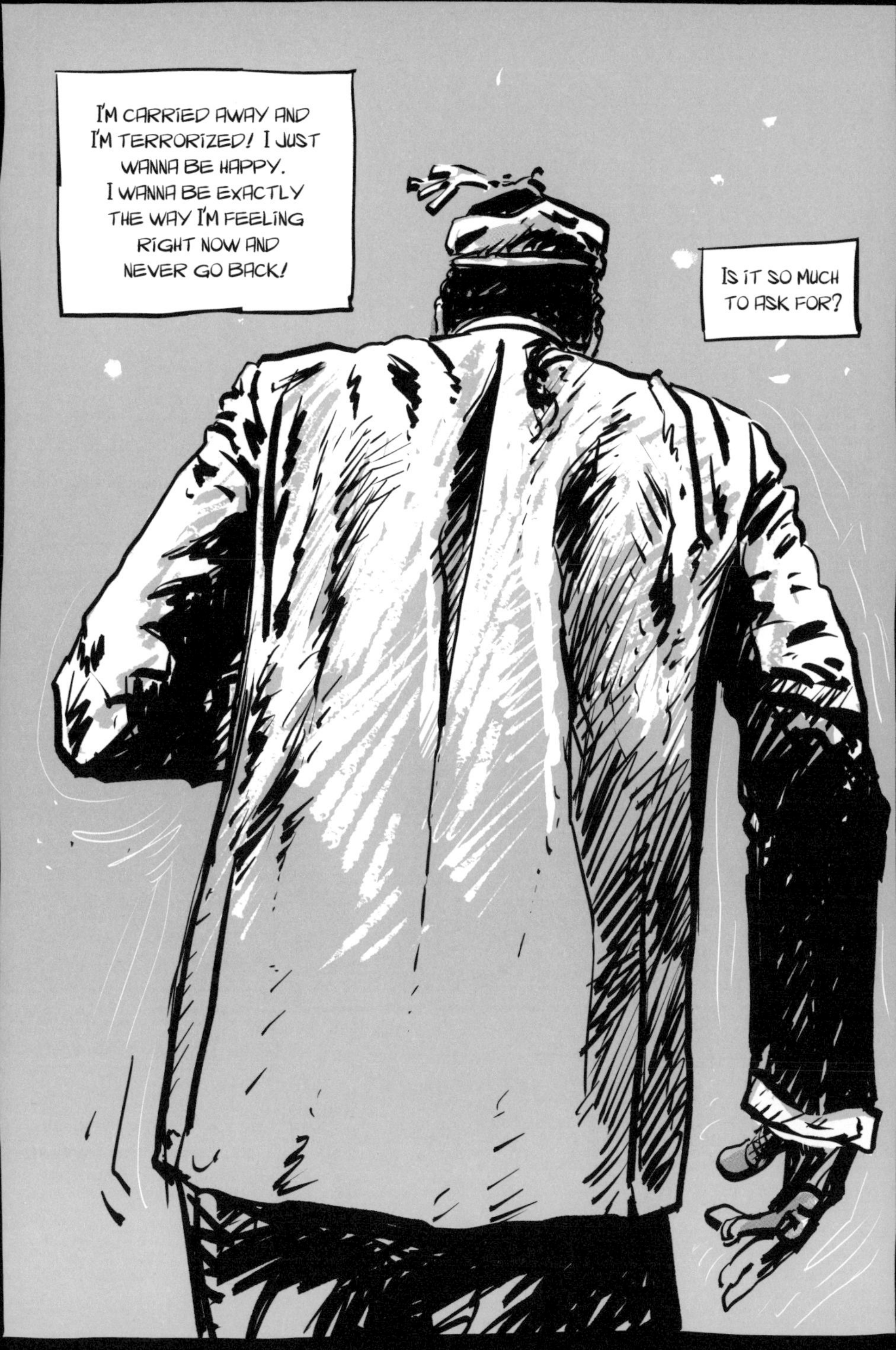
I'M CARRIED AWAY AND I'M TERRORIZED! I JUST WANNA BE HAPPY. I WANNA BE EXACTLY THE WAY I'M FEELING RIGHT NOW AND NEVER GO BACK!
IS IT SO MUCH TO ASK FOR?

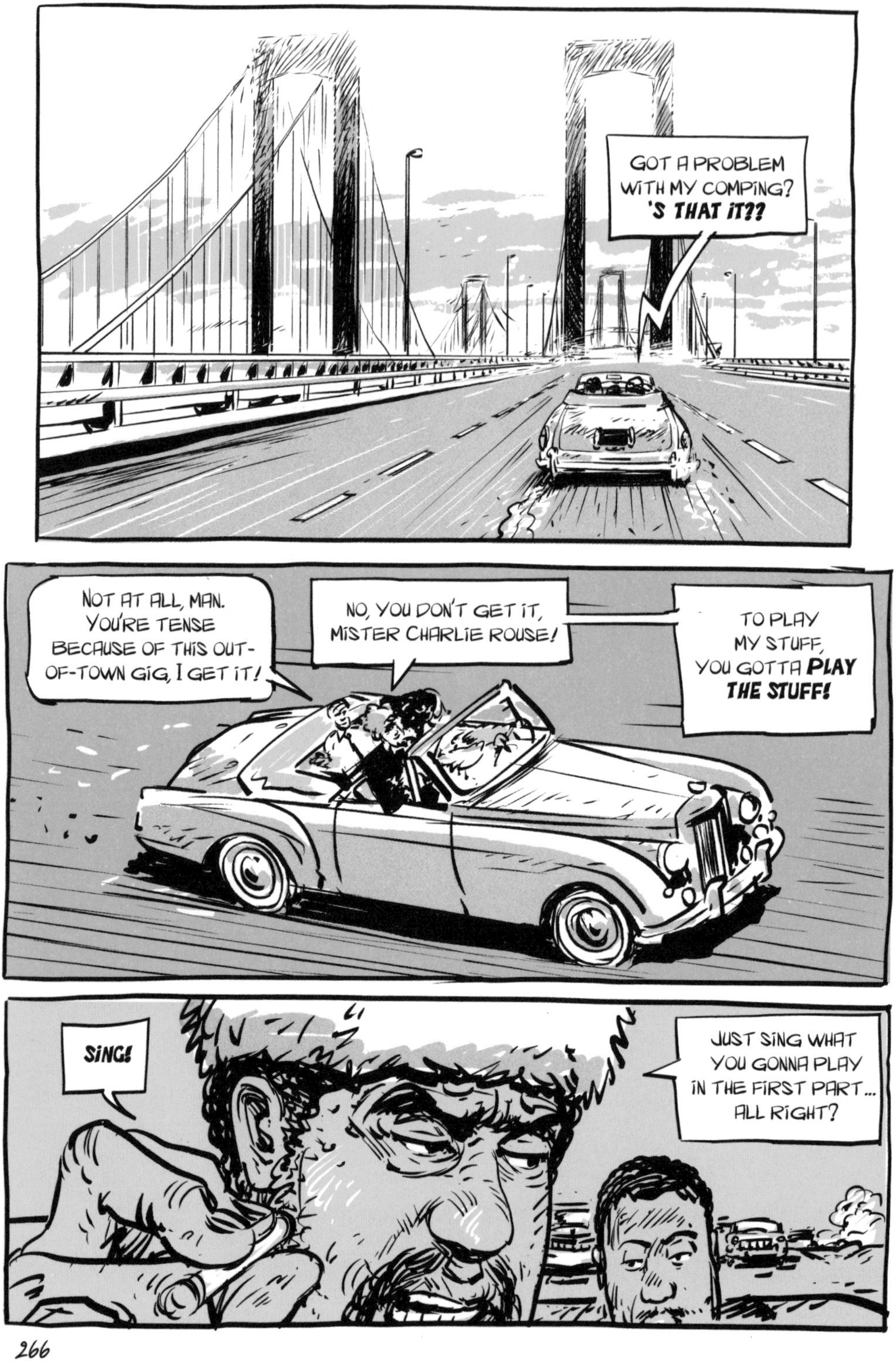
GOT A PROBLEM WITH MY COMPING? 'S THAT IT??
NOT AT ALL, MAN. YOU'RE TENSE BECAUSE OF THIS OUT-OF-TOWN GIG, I GET IT!
NO, YOU DON'T GET IT, MISTER CHARLIE ROUSE!
TO PLAY MY STUFF, YOU GOTTA PLAY THE STUFF!
SING!
JUST SING WHAT YOU GONNA PLAY IN THE FIRST PART... ALL RIGHT?

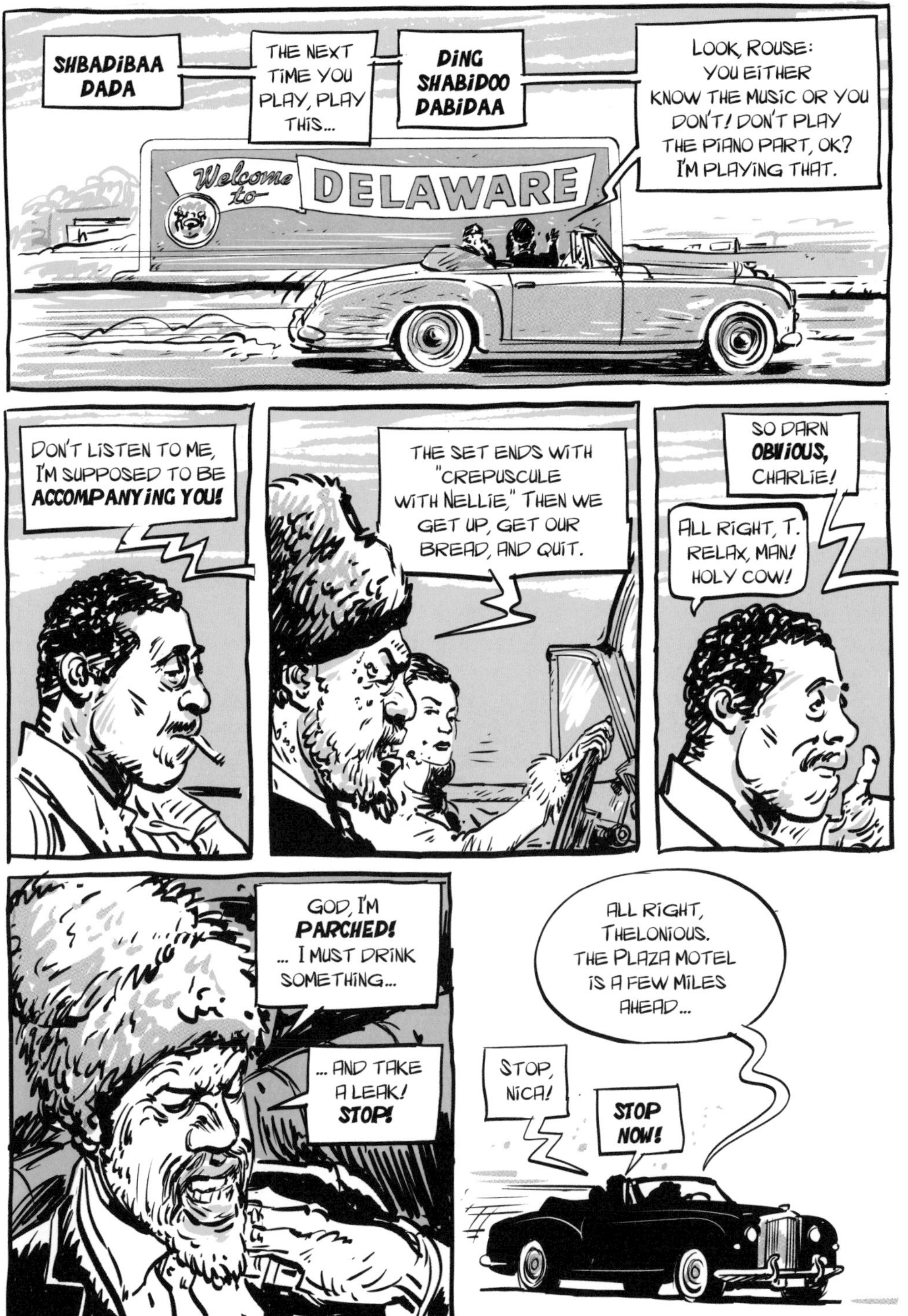
SHBADIBAA DADA
THE NEXT TIME YOU PLAY, PLAY THIS...
DING SHABIDOO DABIDAA
LOOK, ROUSE: YOU EITHER KNOW THE MUSIC OR YOU DON'T! DON'T PLAY THE PIANO PART, OK? I'M PLAYING THAT.
Welcome to DELAWARE
DON'T LISTEN TO ME, I'M SUPPOSED TO BE ACCOMPANYING YOU!
THE SET ENDS WITH "CREPUSCULE WITH NELLIE," THEN WE GET UP, GET OUR BREAD, AND QUIT.
SO DARN OBVIOUS, CHARLIE!
ALL RIGHT, T. RELAX, MAN! HOLY COW!
GOD, I'M PARCHED! ... I MUST DRINK SOMETHING...
... AND TAKE A LEAK! STOP!
ALL RIGHT, THELONIOUS. THE PLAZA MOTEL IS A FEW MILES AHEAD...
STOP, NICA!
STOP NOW!

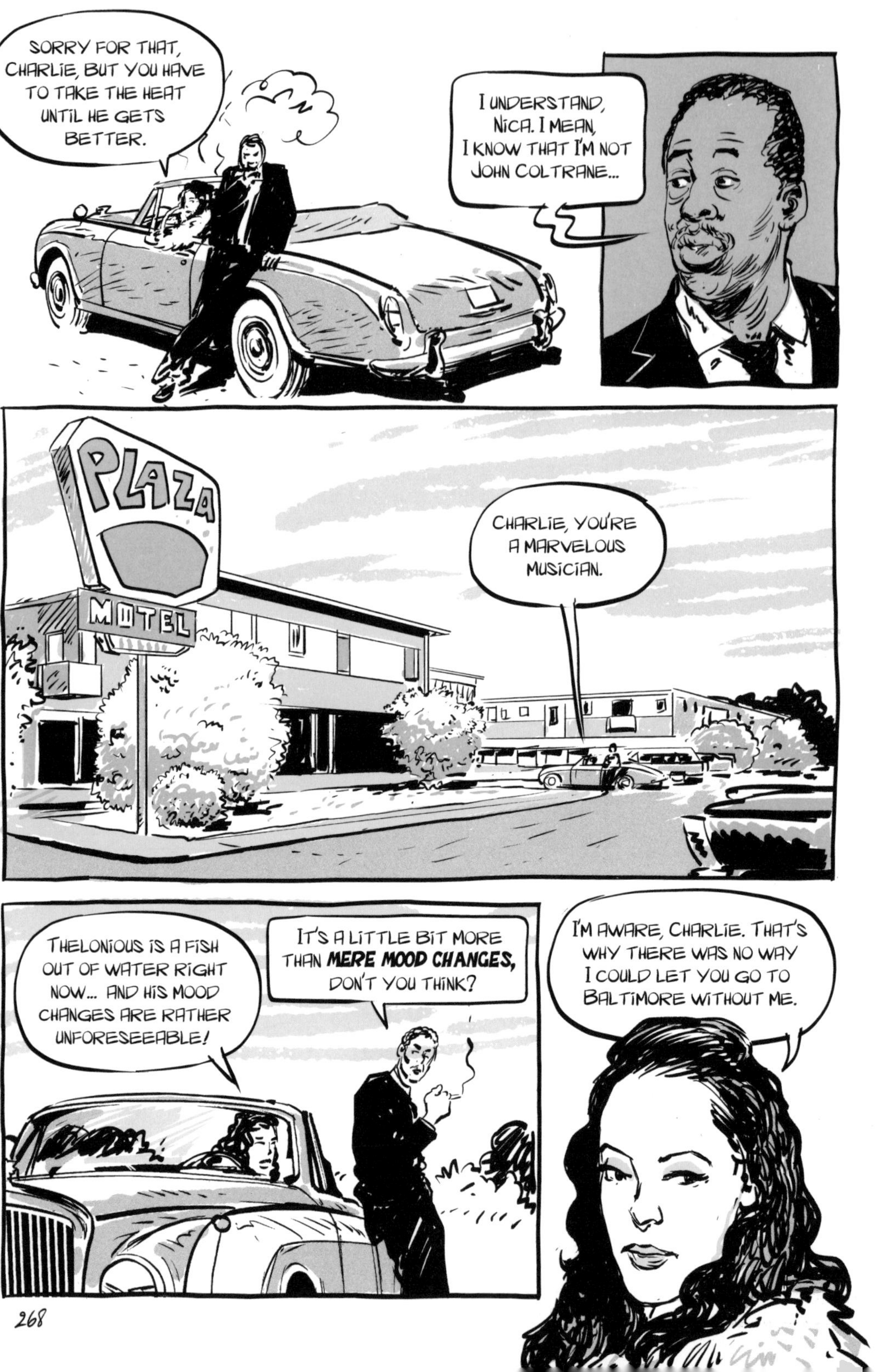
SORRY FOR THAT, CHARLIE, BUT YOU HAVE TO TAKE THE HEAT UNTIL HE GETS BETTER.
I UNDERSTAND, NICA. I MEAN, I KNOW THAT I'M NOT JOHN COLTRANE...
PLAZA
MOTEL
CHARLIE, YOU'RE A MARVELOUS MUSICIAN.
THELONIOUS IS A FISH OUT OF WATER RIGHT NOW... AND HIS MOOD CHANGES ARE RATHER UNFORESEEABLE!
IT'S A LITTLE BIT MORE THAN **MERE MOOD CHANGES,** DON'T YOU THINK?
I'M AWARE, CHARLIE. THAT'S WHY THERE WAS NO WAY I COULD LET YOU GO TO BALTIMORE WITHOUT ME.

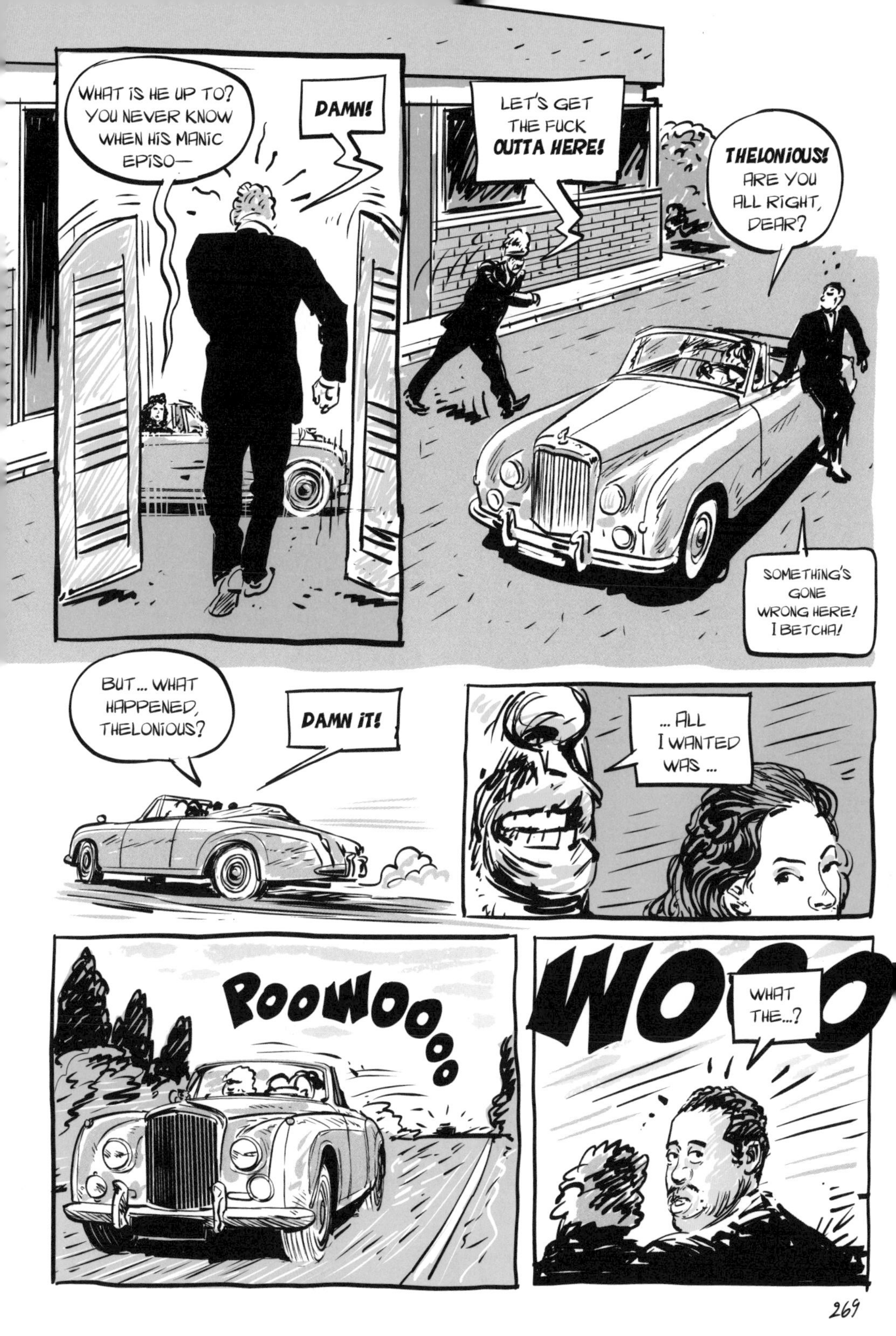
WHAT IS HE UP TO? YOU NEVER KNOW WHEN HIS MANIC EPISO—
DAMN!
LET'S GET THE FUCK OUTTA HERE!
THELONIOUS! ARE YOU ALL RIGHT, DEAR?
SOMETHING'S GONE WRONG HERE! I BETCHA!
BUT... WHAT HAPPENED, THELONIOUS?
DAMN IT!
... ALL I WANTED WAS ...
POOWOOOOO
WOO
WHAT THE...?

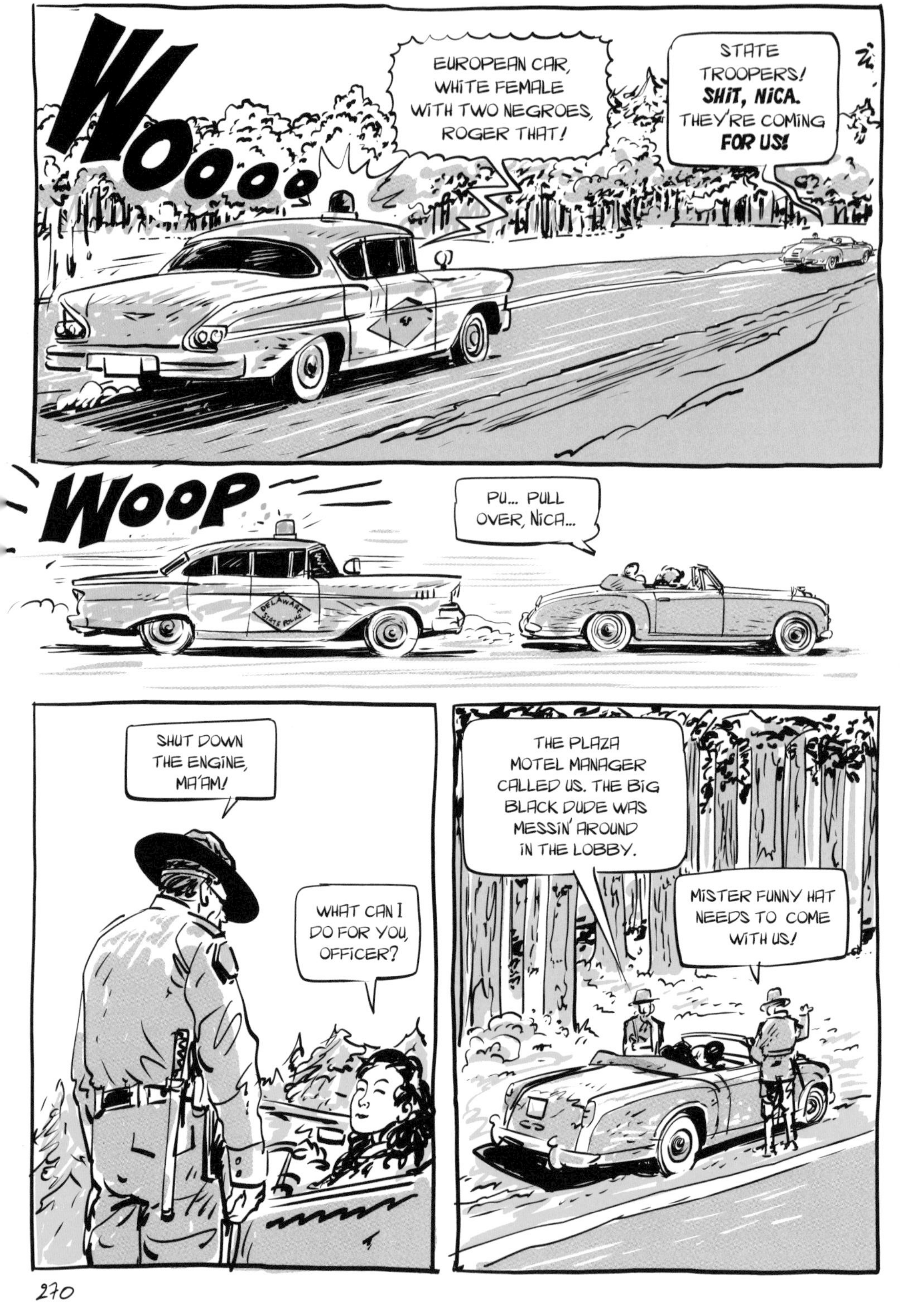
WOOOOO
EUROPEAN CAR, WHITE FEMALE WITH TWO NEGROES, ROGER THAT!
STATE TROOPERS! SHIT, NICA. THEY'RE COMING FOR US!
WOOP
PU... PULL OVER, NICA...
SHUT DOWN THE ENGINE, MA'AM!
WHAT CAN I DO FOR YOU, OFFICER?
THE PLAZA MOTEL MANAGER CALLED US. THE BIG BLACK DUDE WAS MESSIN' AROUND IN THE LOBBY.
MISTER FUNNY HAT NEEDS TO COME WITH US!

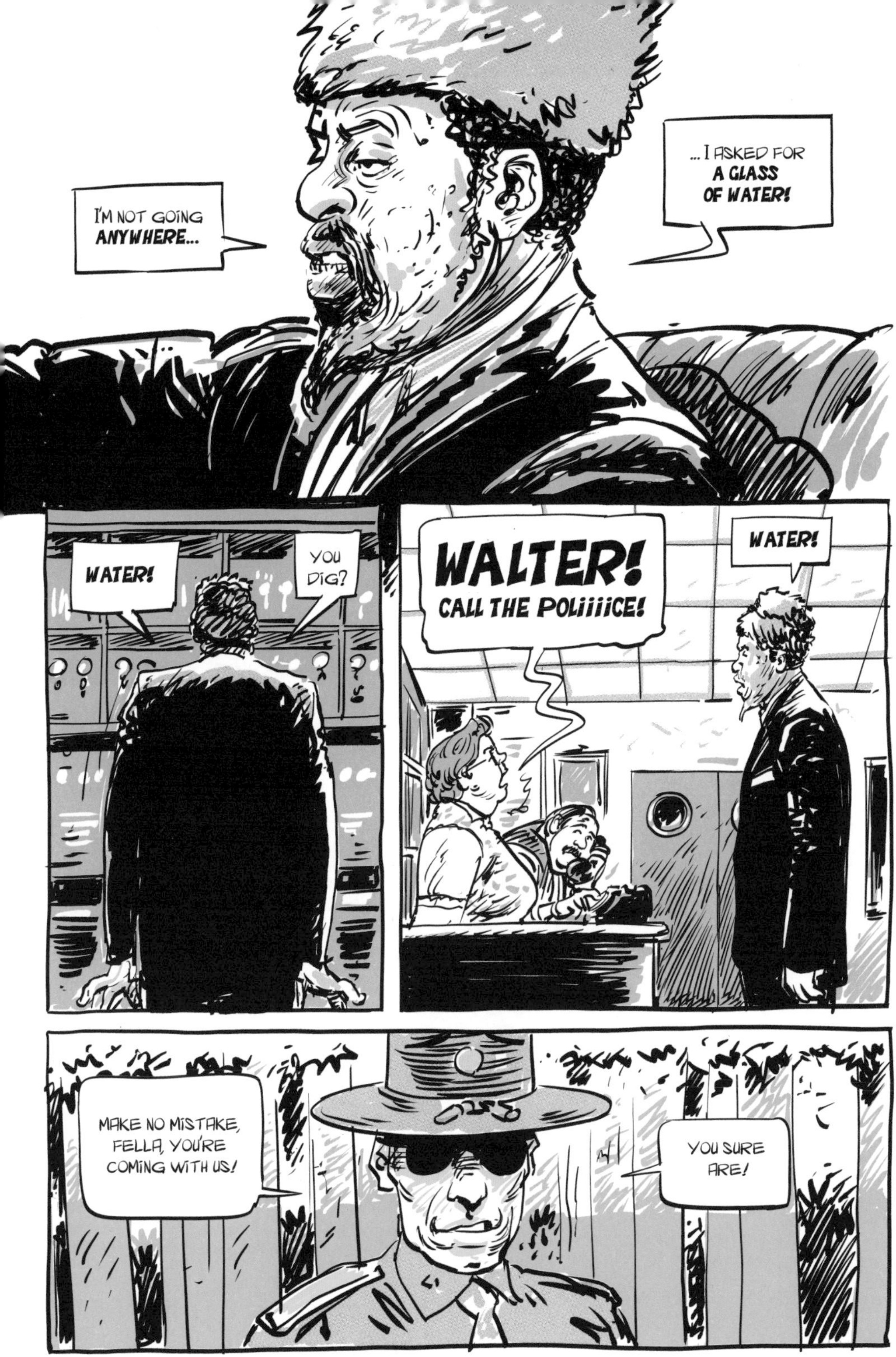
I'M NOT GOING ANYWHERE...
...I ASKED FOR A GLASS OF WATER!
WATER!
YOU DIG?
WALTER! CALL THE POLiiiiiCE!
WATER!
MAKE NO MISTAKE, FELLA, YOU'RE COMING WITH US!
YOU SURE ARE!

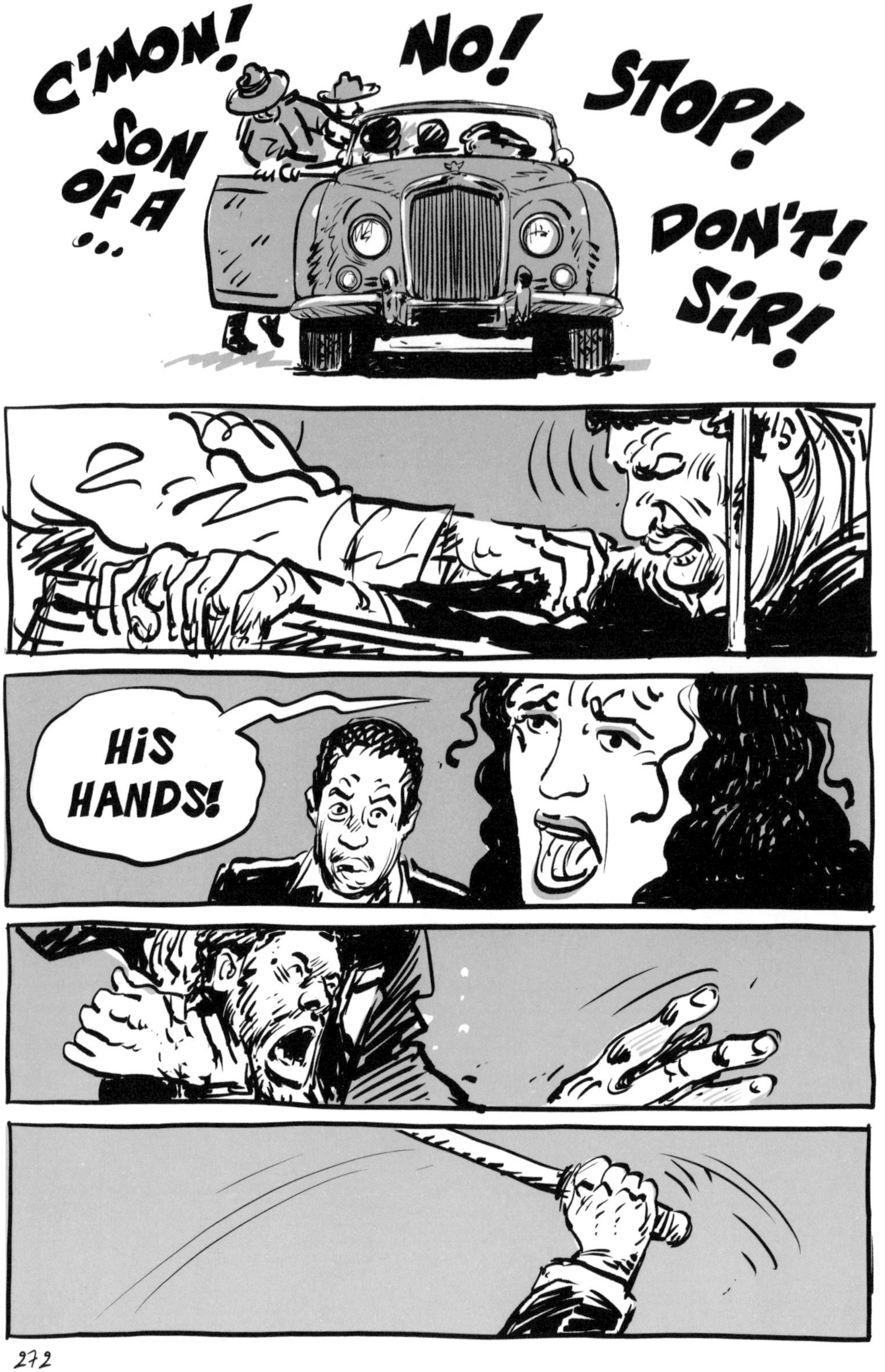
C'MON!
SON OF A ...
NO!
STOP!
DON'T!
SIR!
HIS HANDS!

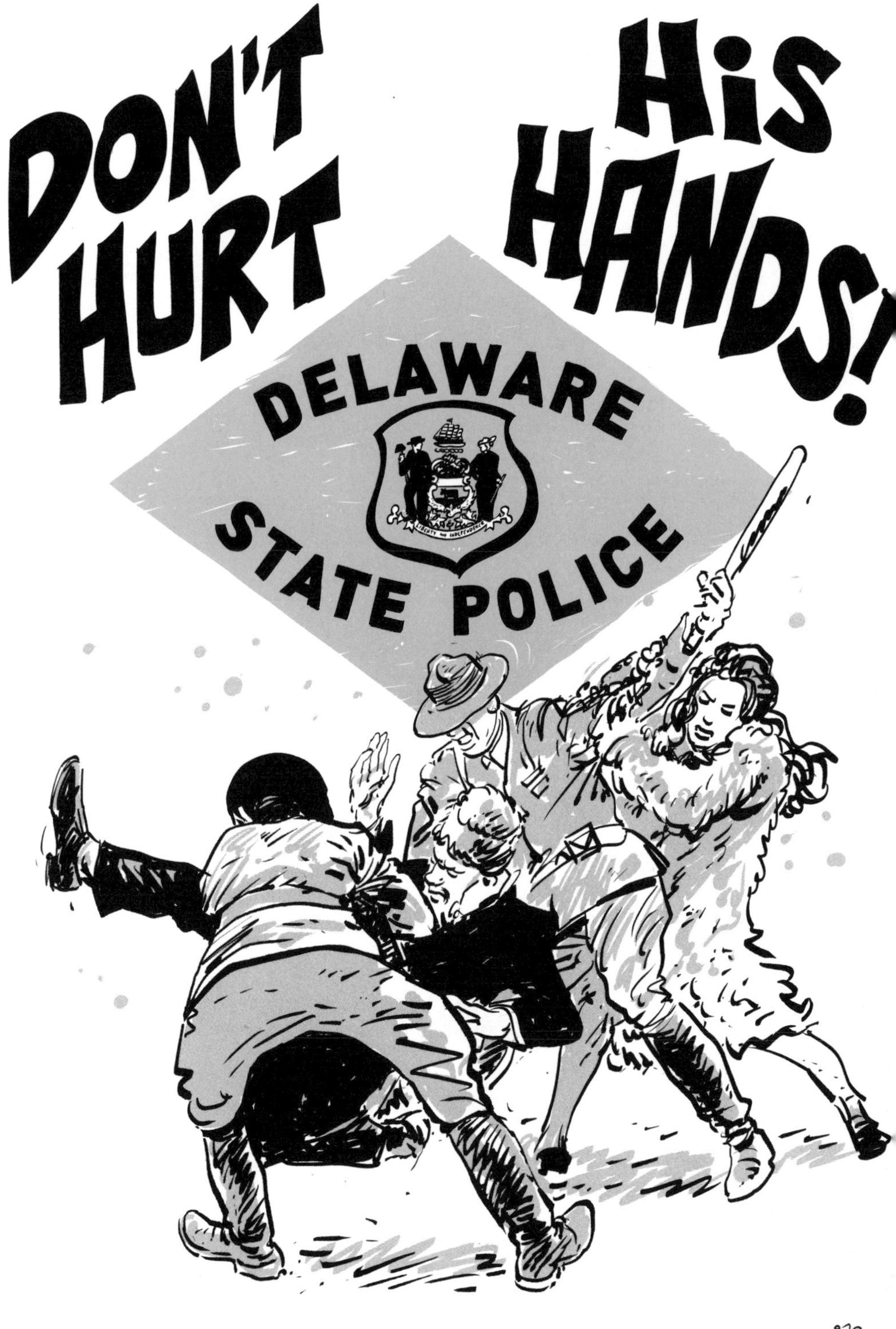
DON'T HURT HIS HANDS!
DELAWARE STATE POLICE

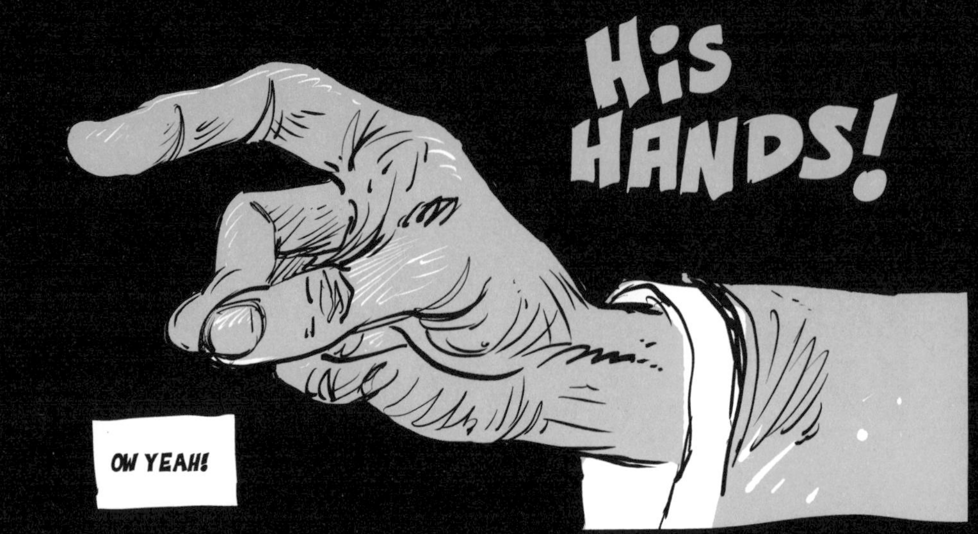
HiS
HANDS!
OW YEAH!

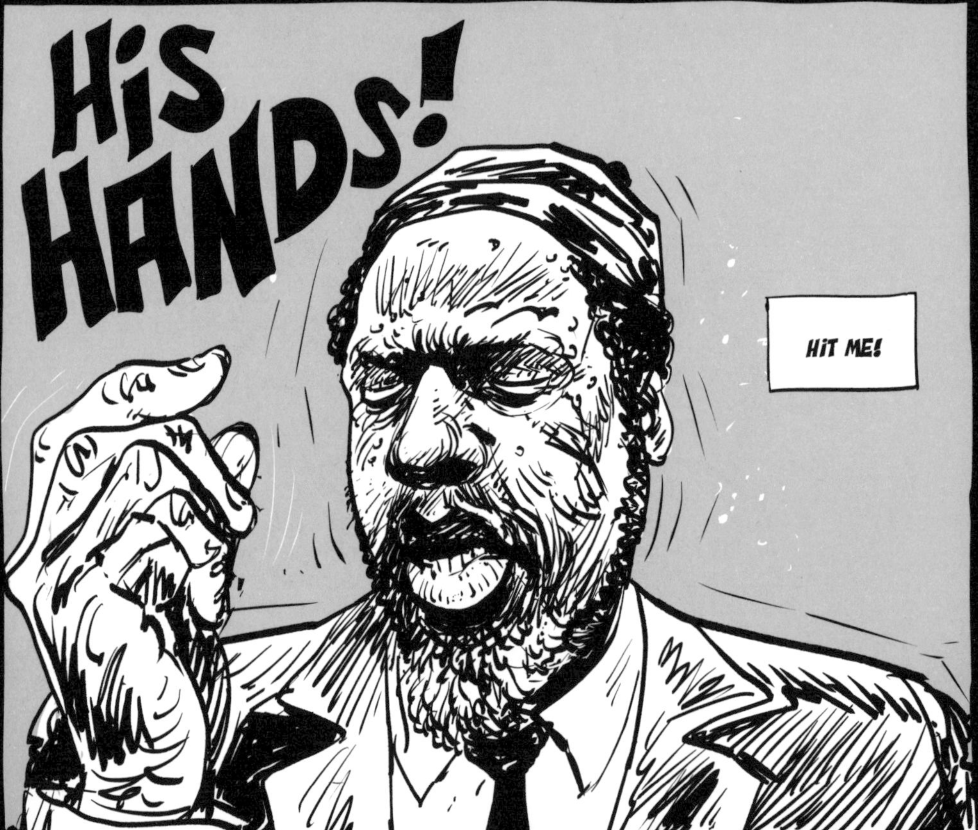
HiS
HANDS!
HiT ME!

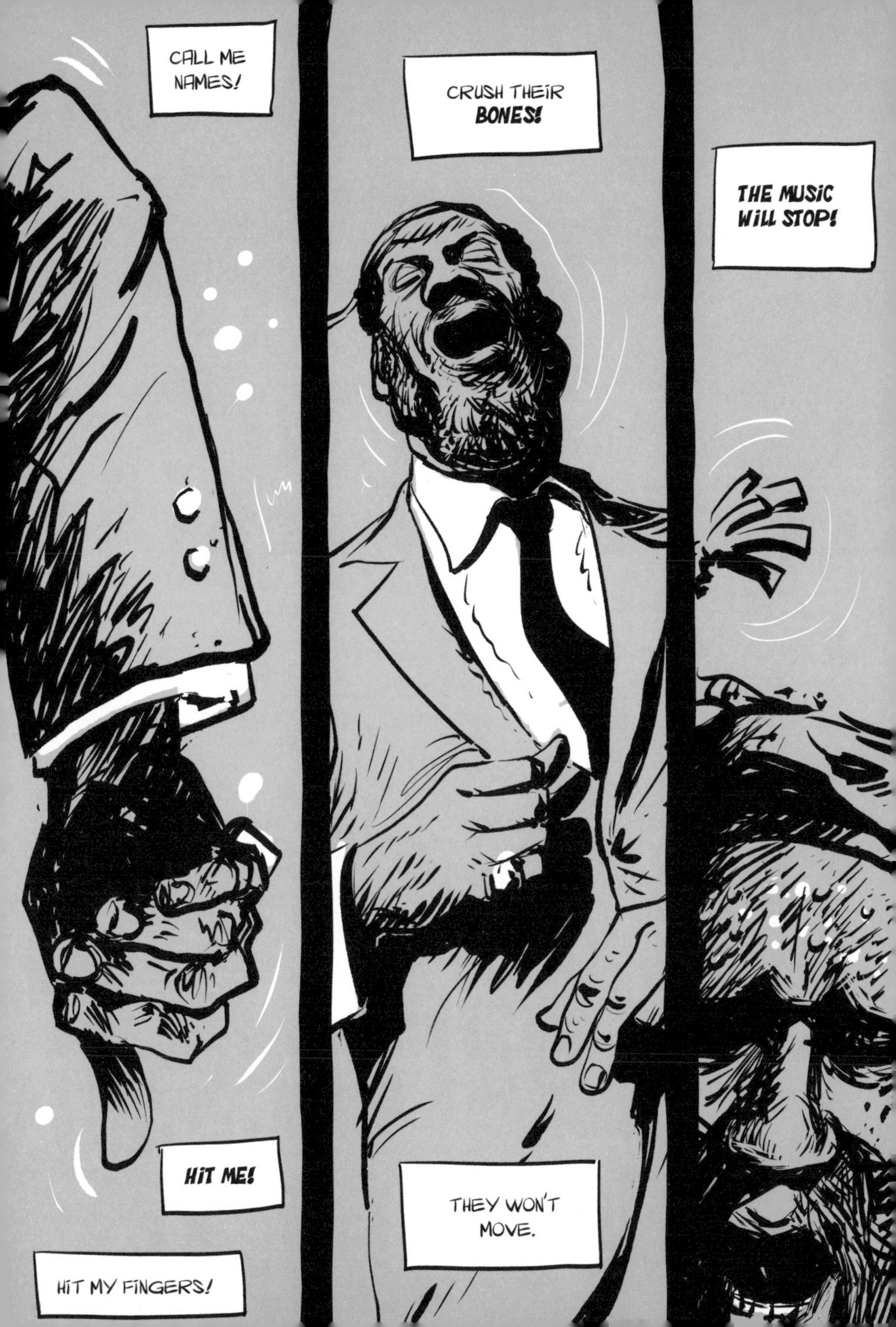
CALL ME NAMES!
HIT ME!
HIT MY FINGERS!
CRUSH THEIR BONES!
THEY WON'T MOVE.
THE MUSIC WILL STOP!

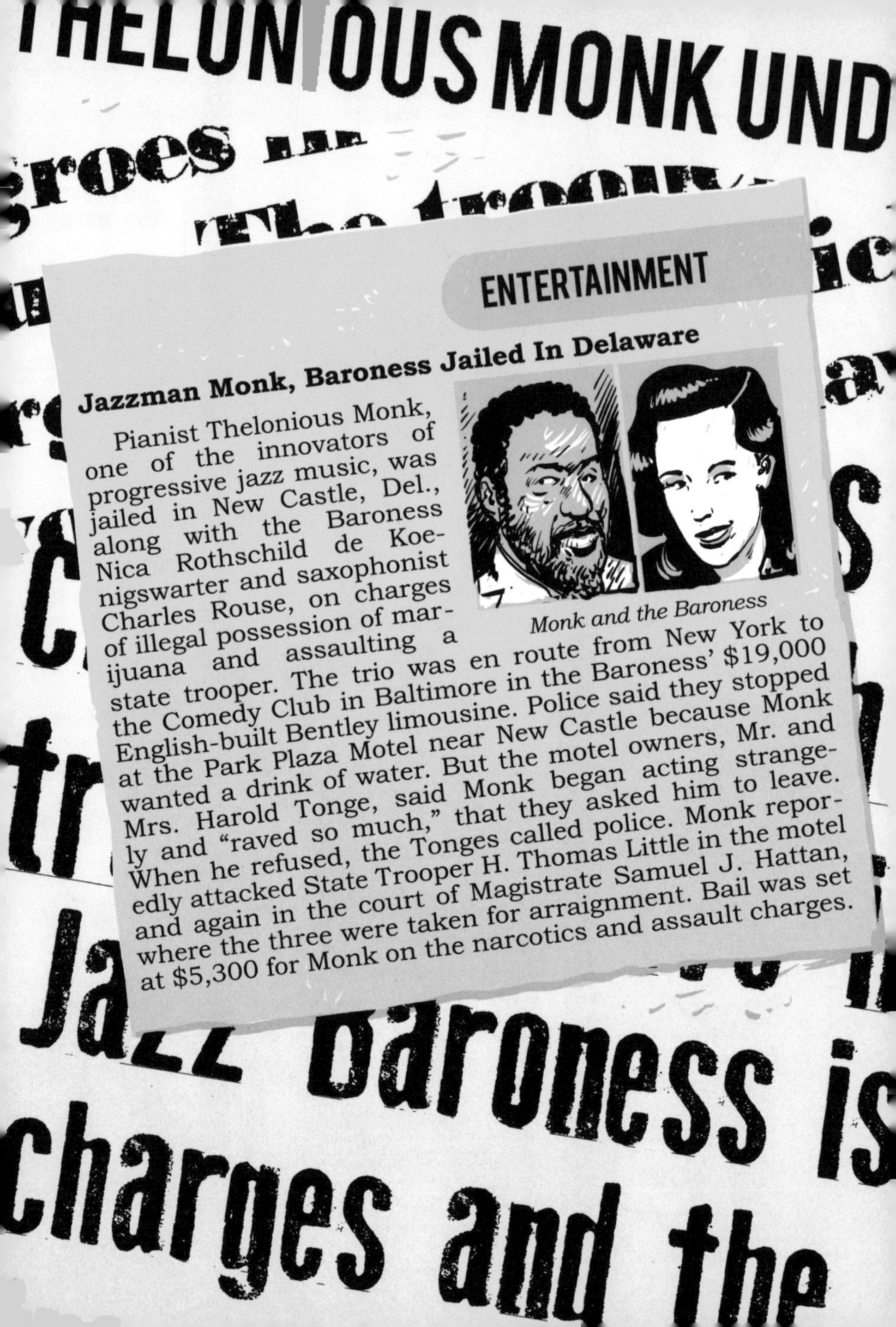
THELONIOUS MONK UND
ENTERTAINMENT
Jazz Baroness is
charges and the

Jazzman Monk, Baroness Jailed In Delaware

Pianist Thelonious Monk, one of the innovators of progressive jazz music, was jailed in New Castle, Del., along with the Baroness Nica Rothschild de Koenigswarter and saxophonist Charles Rouse, on charges of illegal possession of marijuana and assaulting a state trooper. The trio was en route from New York to the Comedy Club in Baltimore in the Baroness' $19,000 English-built Bentley limousine. Police said they stopped at the Park Plaza Motel near New Castle because Monk wanted a drink of water. But the motel owners, Mr. and Mrs. Harold Tonge, said Monk began acting strangely and "raved so much," that they asked him to leave. When he refused, the Tonges called police. Monk reportedly attacked State Trooper H. Thomas Little in the motel and again in the court of Magistrate Samuel J. Hattan, where the three were taken for arraignment. Bail was set at $5,300 for Monk on the narcotics and assault charges.

Monk and the Baroness

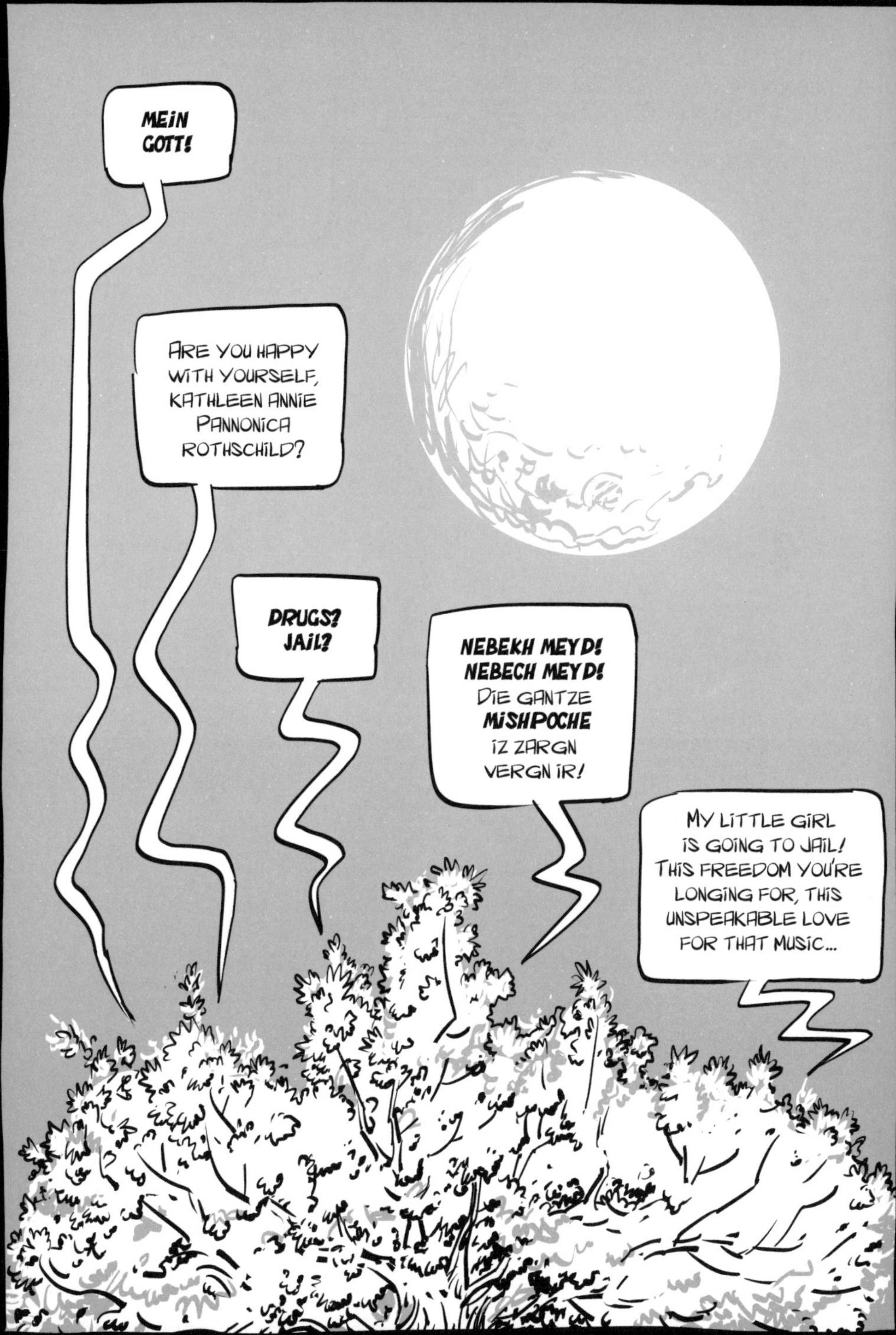
MEIN GOTT!
ARE YOU HAPPY WITH YOURSELF, KATHLEEN ANNIE PANNONICA ROTHSCHILD?
DRUGS? JAIL?
NEBEKH MEYD! NEBECH MEYD! DIE GANTZE MISHPOCHE IZ ZARGN VERGN IR!
MY LITTLE GIRL IS GOING TO JAIL! THIS FREEDOM YOU'RE LONGING FOR, THIS UNSPEAKABLE LOVE FOR THAT MUSIC...

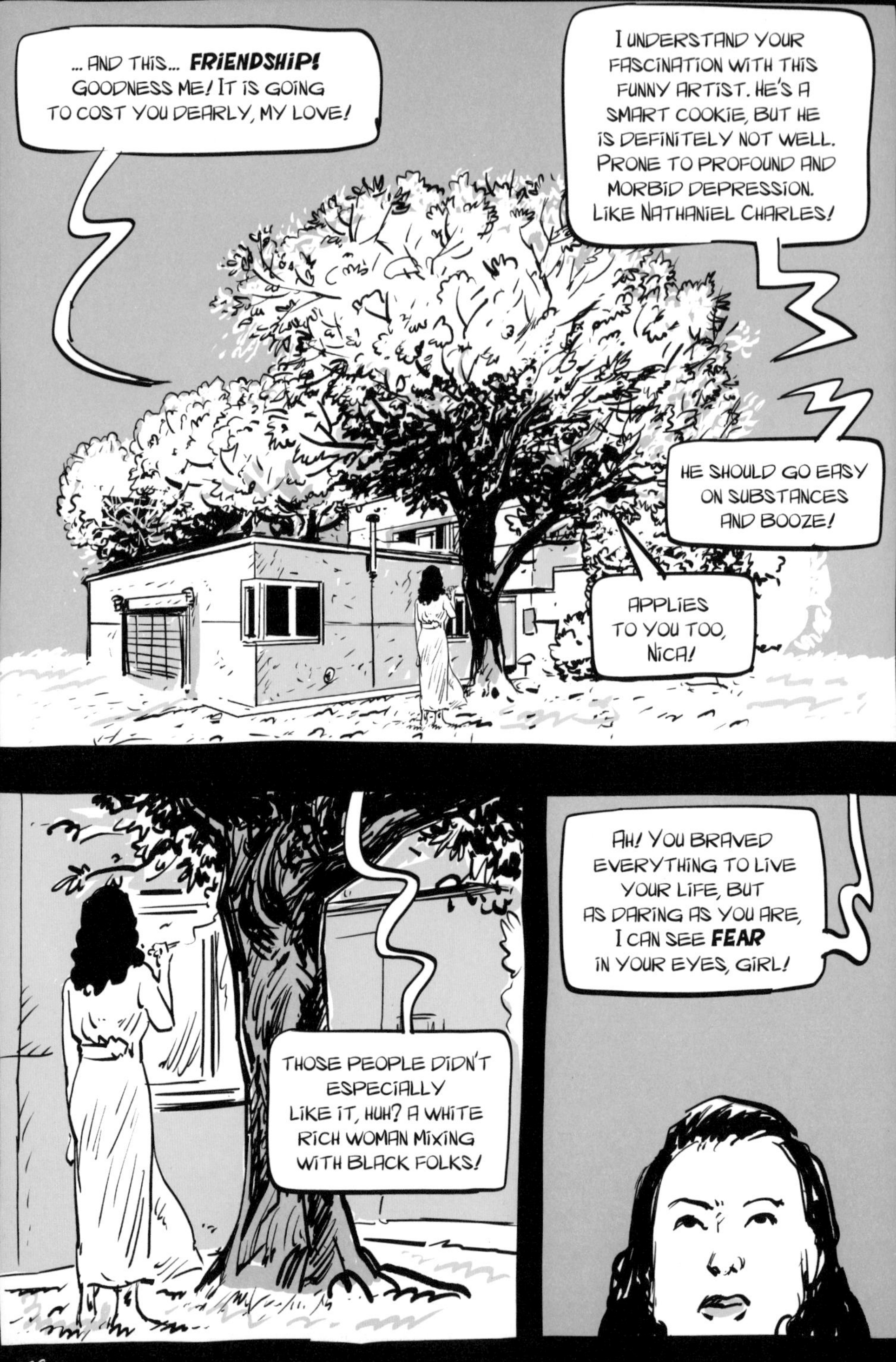

... AND THIS... **FRIENDSHIP!** GOODNESS ME! IT IS GOING TO COST YOU DEARLY, MY LOVE!
I UNDERSTAND YOUR FASCINATION WITH THIS FUNNY ARTIST. HE'S A SMART COOKIE, BUT HE IS DEFINITELY NOT WELL. PRONE TO PROFOUND AND MORBID DEPRESSION. LIKE NATHANIEL CHARLES!
HE SHOULD GO EASY ON SUBSTANCES AND BOOZE!
APPLIES TO YOU TOO, NICA!
THOSE PEOPLE DIDN'T ESPECIALLY LIKE IT, HUH? A WHITE RICH WOMAN MIXING WITH BLACK FOLKS!
AH! YOU BRAVED EVERYTHING TO LIVE YOUR LIFE, BUT AS DARING AS YOU ARE, I CAN SEE **FEAR** IN YOUR EYES, GIRL!

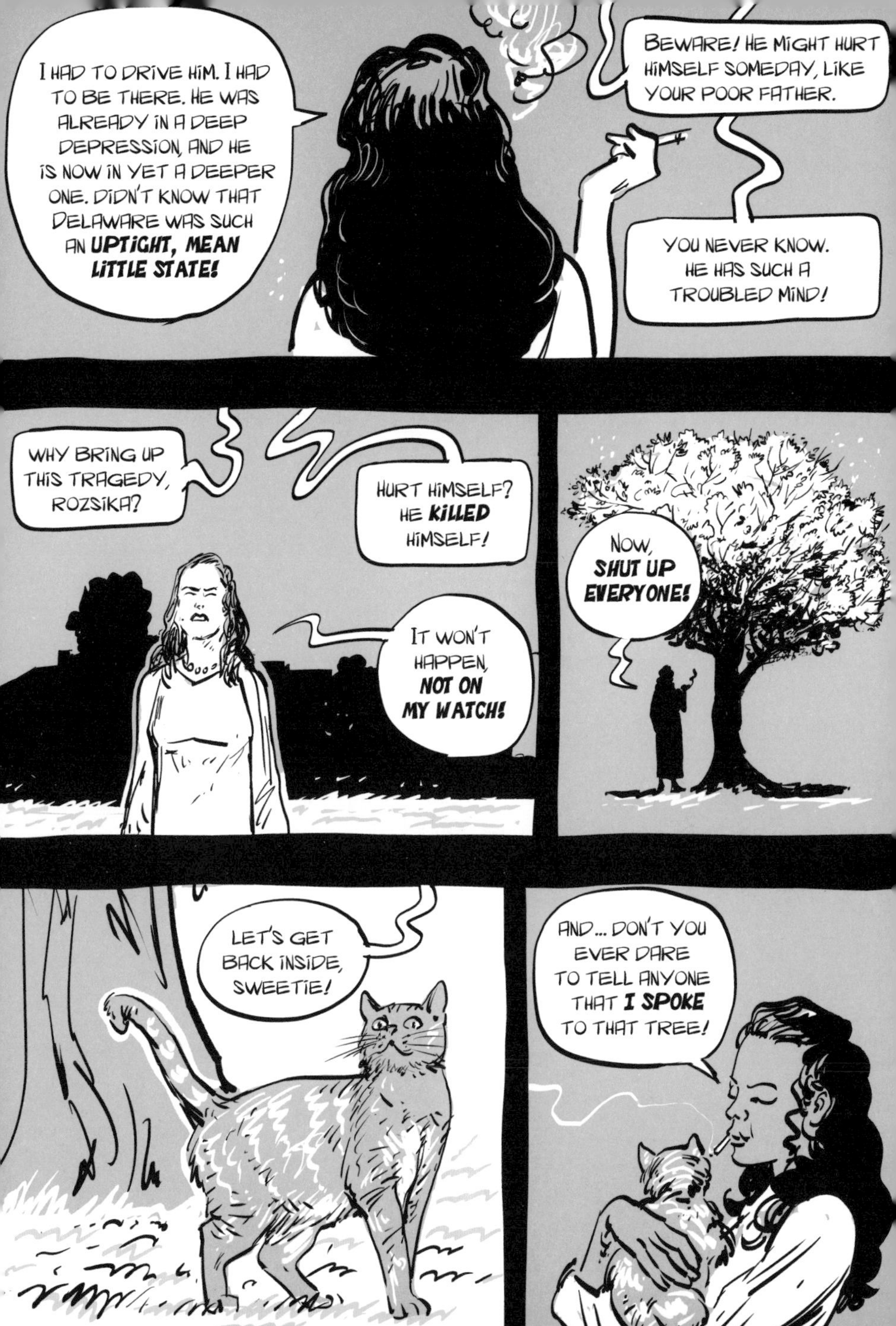

I HAD TO DRIVE HIM. I HAD TO BE THERE. HE WAS ALREADY IN A DEEP DEPRESSION, AND HE IS NOW IN YET A DEEPER ONE. DIDN'T KNOW THAT DELAWARE WAS SUCH AN UPTIGHT, MEAN LITTLE STATE!
BEWARE! HE MIGHT HURT HIMSELF SOMEDAY, LIKE YOUR POOR FATHER.
YOU NEVER KNOW. HE HAS SUCH A TROUBLED MIND!
WHY BRING UP THIS TRAGEDY, ROZSIKA?
HURT HIMSELF? HE KILLED HIMSELF!
IT WON'T HAPPEN, NOT ON MY WATCH!
NOW, SHUT UP EVERYONE!
LET'S GET BACK INSIDE, SWEETIE!
AND... DON'T YOU EVER DARE TO TELL ANYONE THAT I SPOKE TO THAT TREE!

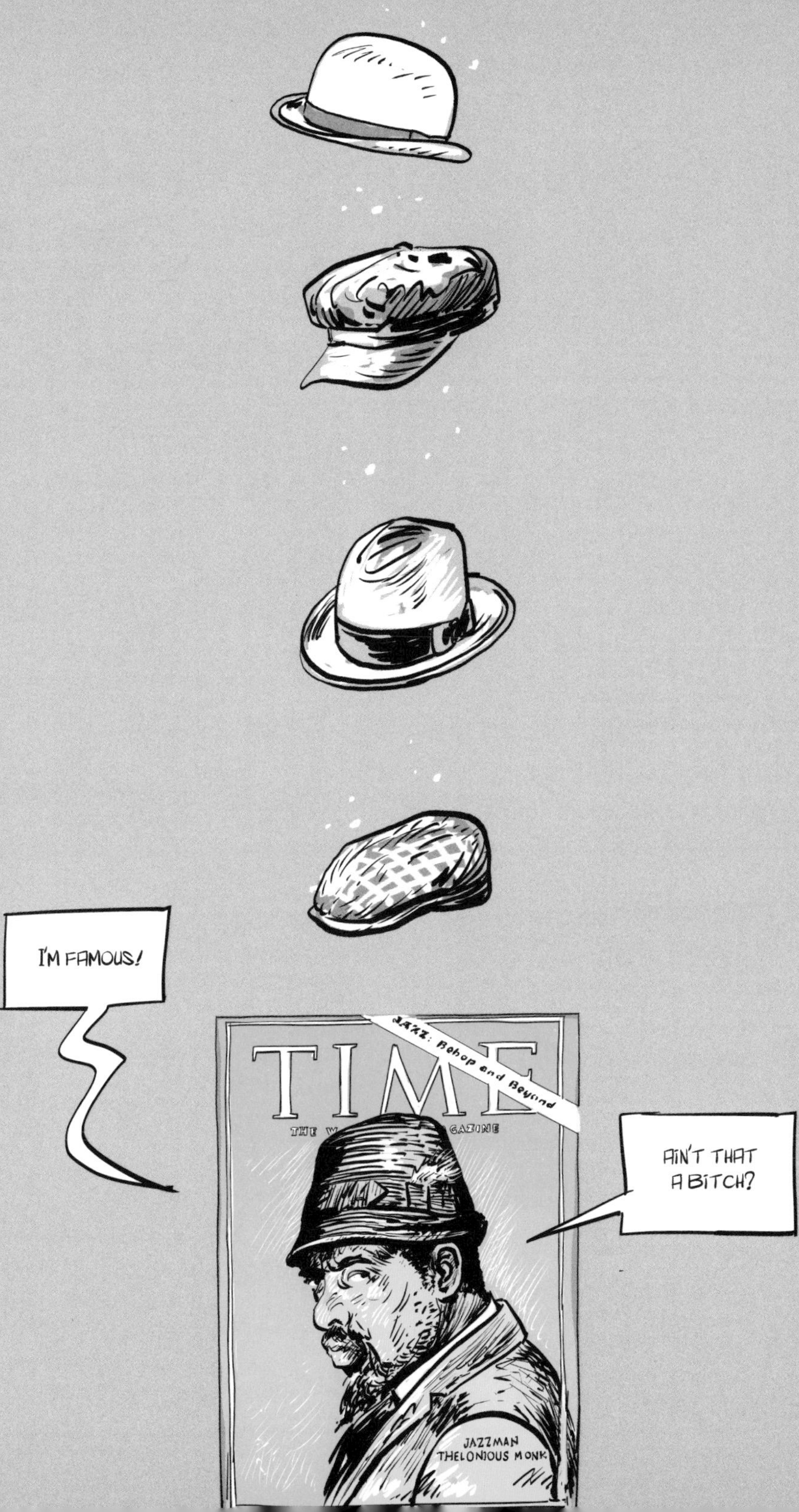
I'M FAMOUS!
TIME
JAZZ: Bebop and Beyond
AIN'T THAT A BITCH?
JAZZMAN THELONIOUS MONK

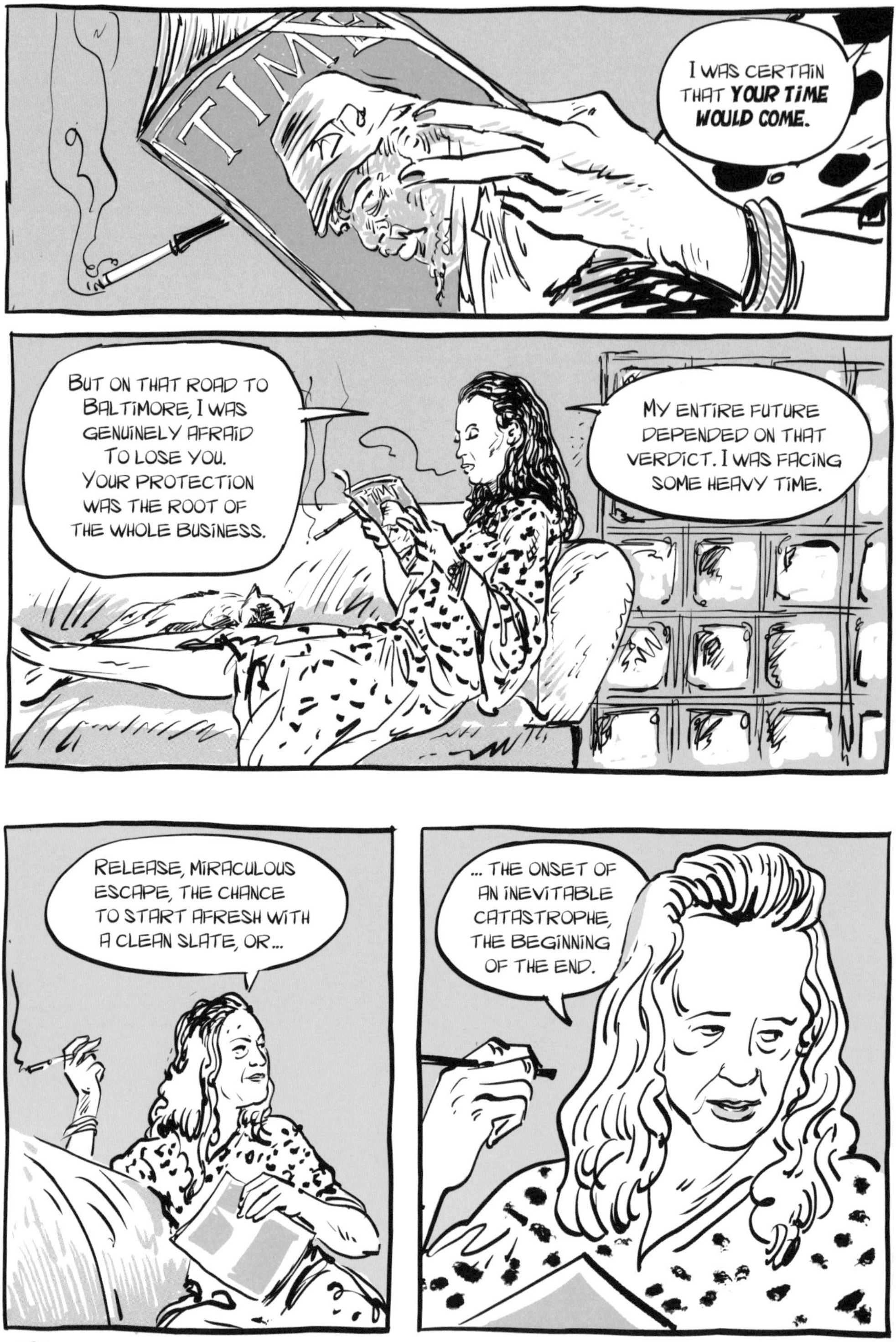
I WAS CERTAIN THAT **YOUR TIME WOULD COME.**
BUT ON THAT ROAD TO BALTIMORE, I WAS GENUINELY AFRAID TO LOSE YOU. YOUR PROTECTION WAS THE ROOT OF THE WHOLE BUSINESS.
MY ENTIRE FUTURE DEPENDED ON THAT VERDICT. I WAS FACING SOME HEAVY TIME.
RELEASE, MIRACULOUS ESCAPE, THE CHANCE TO START AFRESH WITH A CLEAN SLATE, OR...
... THE ONSET OF AN INEVITABLE CATASTROPHE, THE BEGINNING OF THE END.

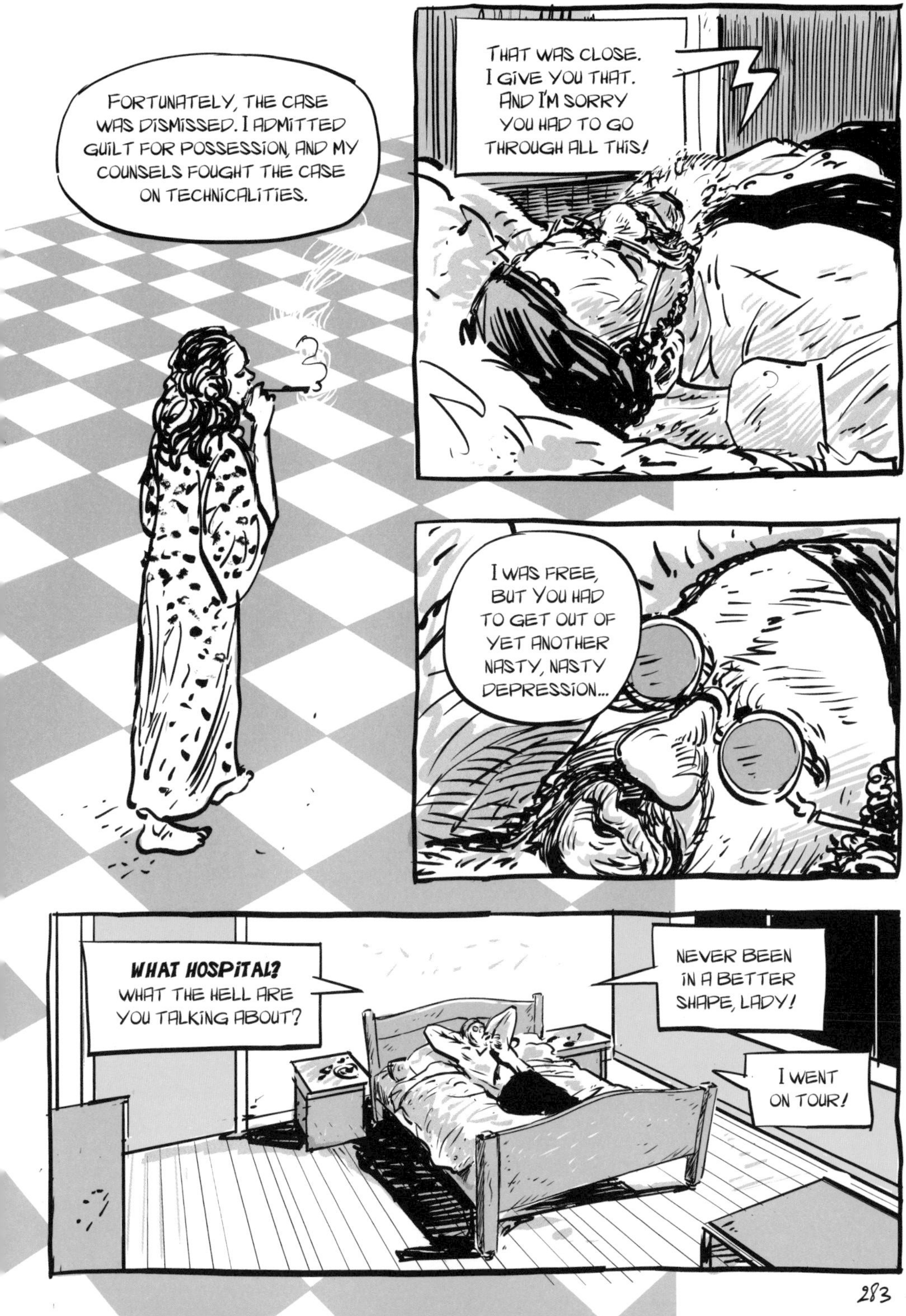
FORTUNATELY, THE CASE WAS DISMISSED. I ADMITTED GUILT FOR POSSESSION, AND MY COUNSELS FOUGHT THE CASE ON TECHNICALITIES.
THAT WAS CLOSE. I GIVE YOU THAT. AND I'M SORRY YOU HAD TO GO THROUGH ALL THIS!
I WAS FREE, BUT YOU HAD TO GET OUT OF YET ANOTHER NASTY, NASTY DEPRESSION...
WHAT HOSPITAL? WHAT THE HELL ARE YOU TALKING ABOUT?
NEVER BEEN IN A BETTER SHAPE, LADY!
I WENT ON TOUR!

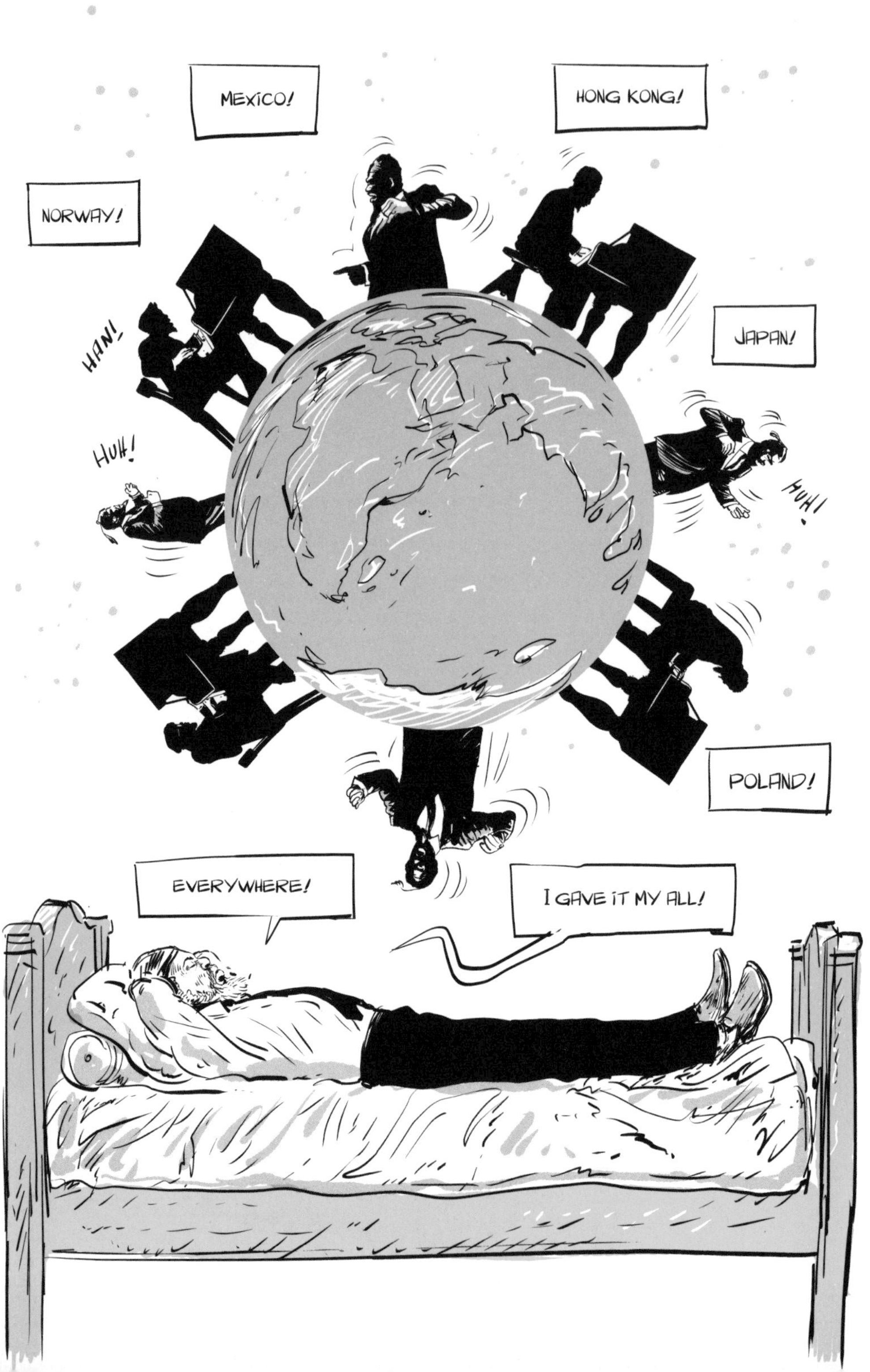
MEXICO!
HONG KONG!
NORWAY!
HAN!
JAPAN!
HUH!
HUH!
POLAND!
EVERYWHERE!
I GAVE IT MY ALL!

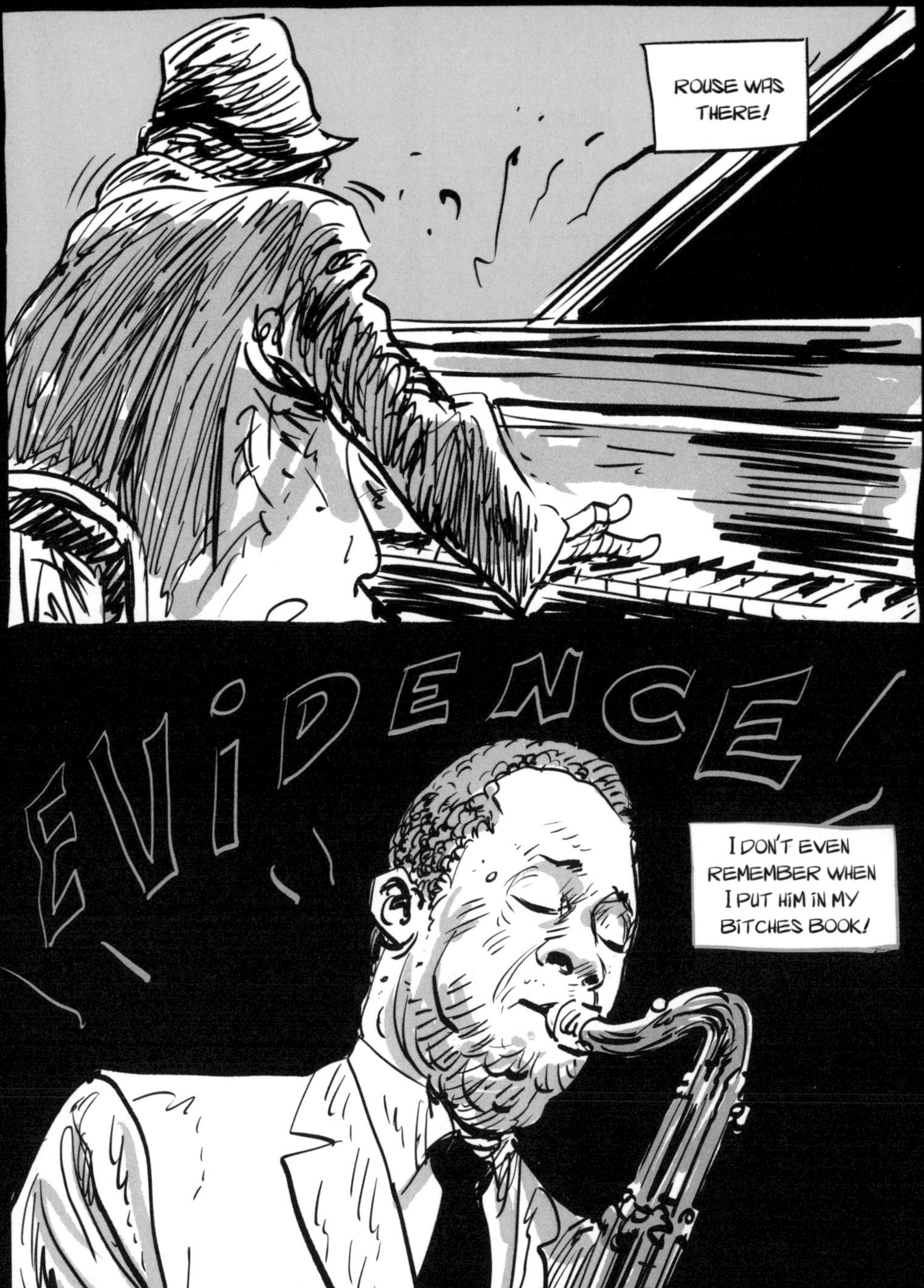
ROUSE WAS THERE!
EVIDENCE!
I DON'T EVEN REMEMBER WHEN I PUT HIM IN MY BITCHES BOOK!

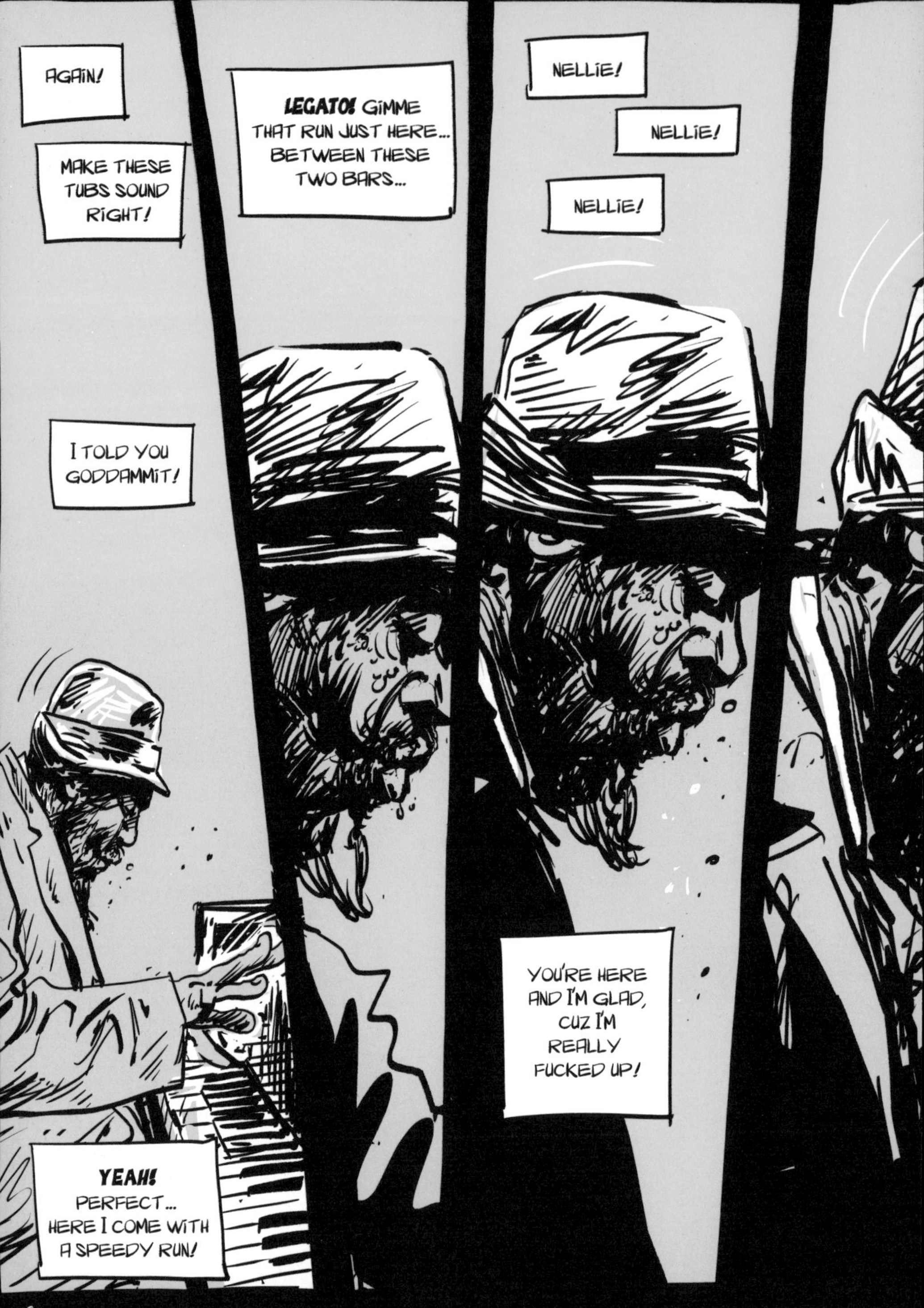
AGAIN!
MAKE THESE TUBS SOUND RIGHT!
I TOLD YOU GODDAMMIT!
YEAH! PERFECT... HERE I COME WITH A SPEEDY RUN!
LEGATO! GIMME THAT RUN JUST HERE... BETWEEN THESE TWO BARS...
NELLIE!
NELLIE!
NELLIE!
YOU'RE HERE AND I'M GLAD, CUZ I'M REALLY FUCKED UP!

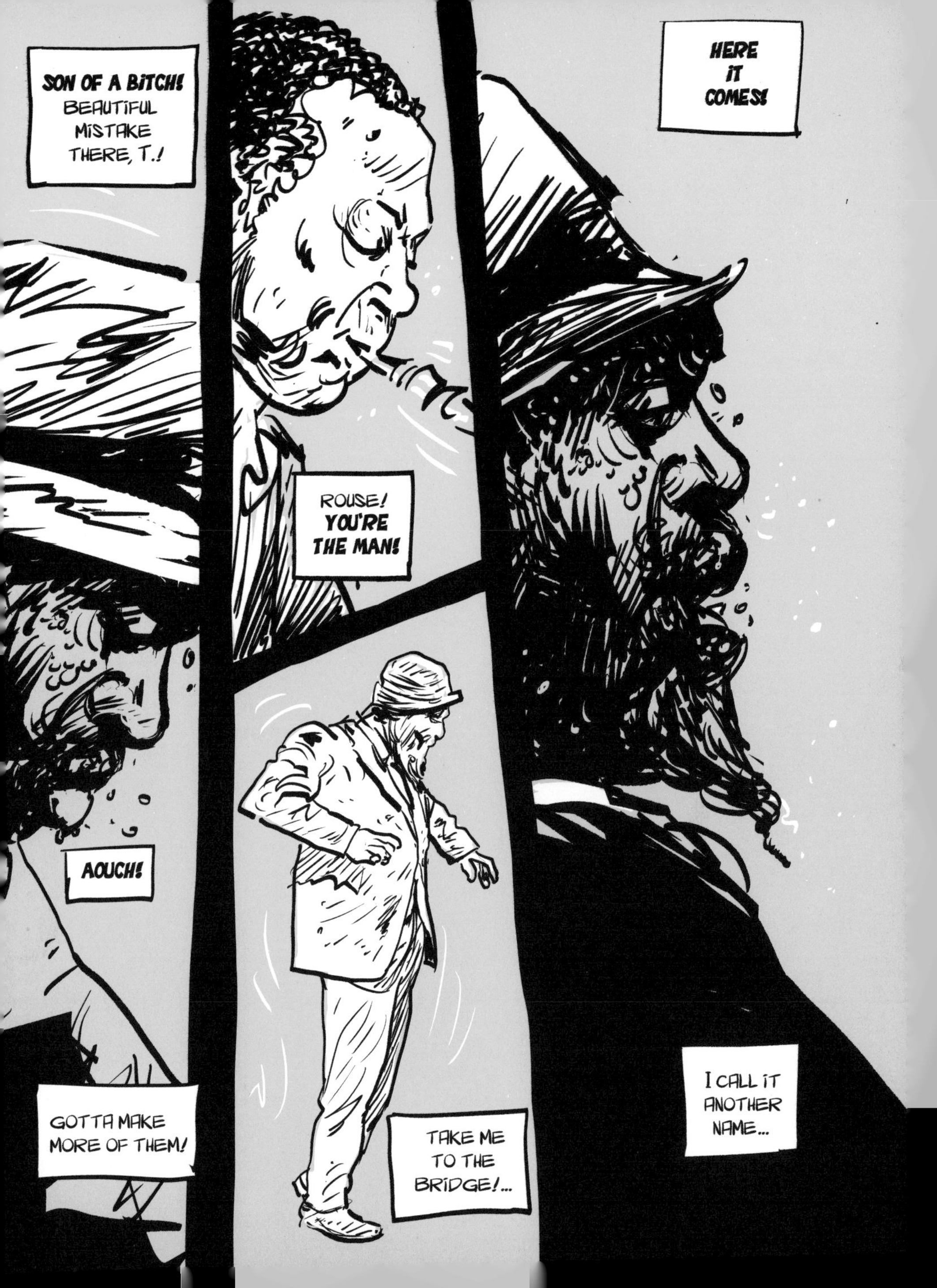
SON OF A BITCH! BEAUTIFUL MISTAKE THERE, T.!
AOUCH!
GOTTA MAKE MORE OF THEM!
ROUSE! YOU'RE THE MAN!
TAKE ME TO THE BRIDGE!...
HERE IT COMES!
I CALL IT ANOTHER NAME...

THE INSIDE

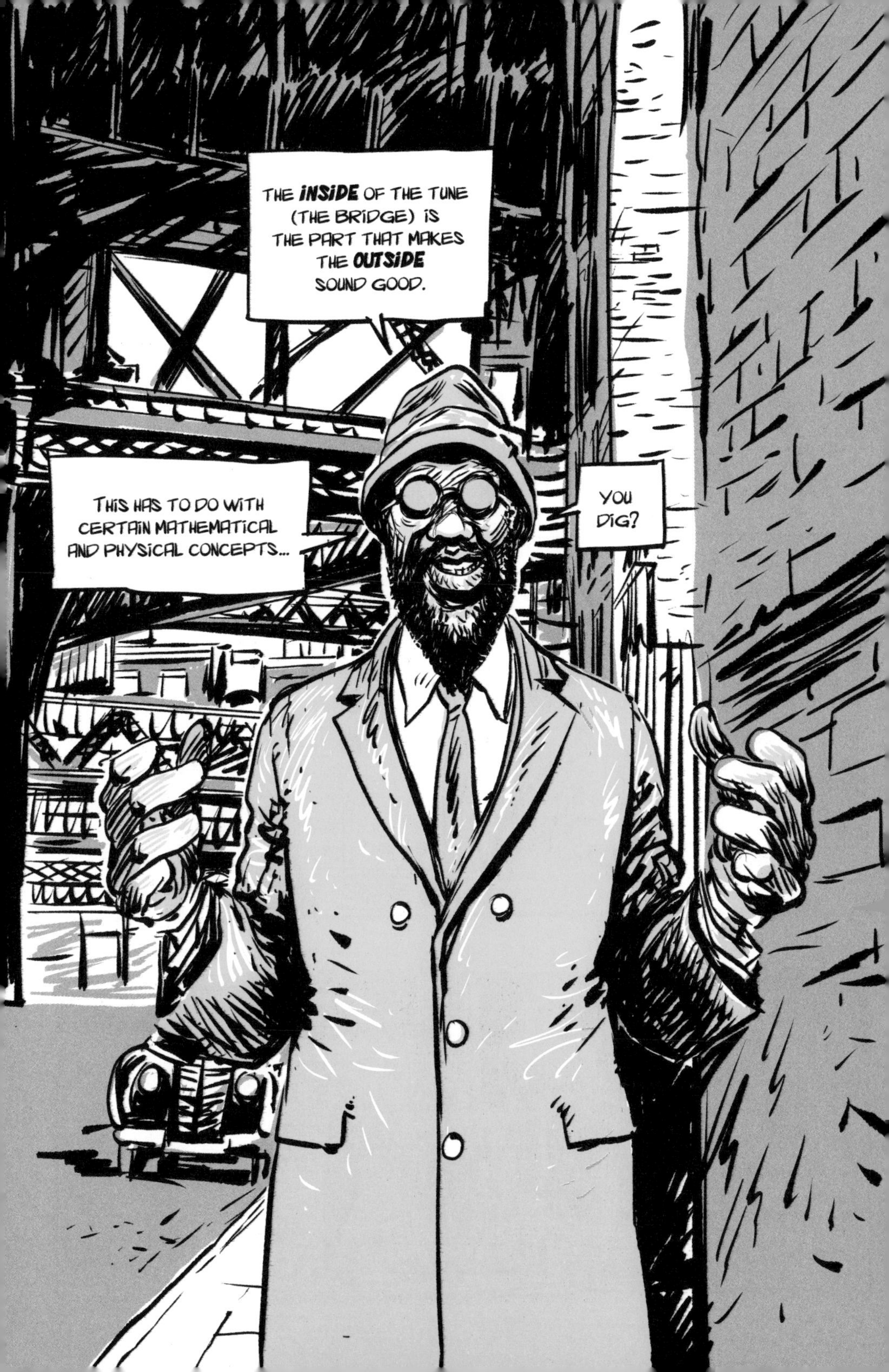
THE INSIDE OF THE TUNE (THE BRIDGE) IS THE PART THAT MAKES THE OUTSIDE SOUND GOOD.
THIS HAS TO DO WITH CERTAIN MATHEMATICAL AND PHYSICAL CONCEPTS...
YOU DIG?

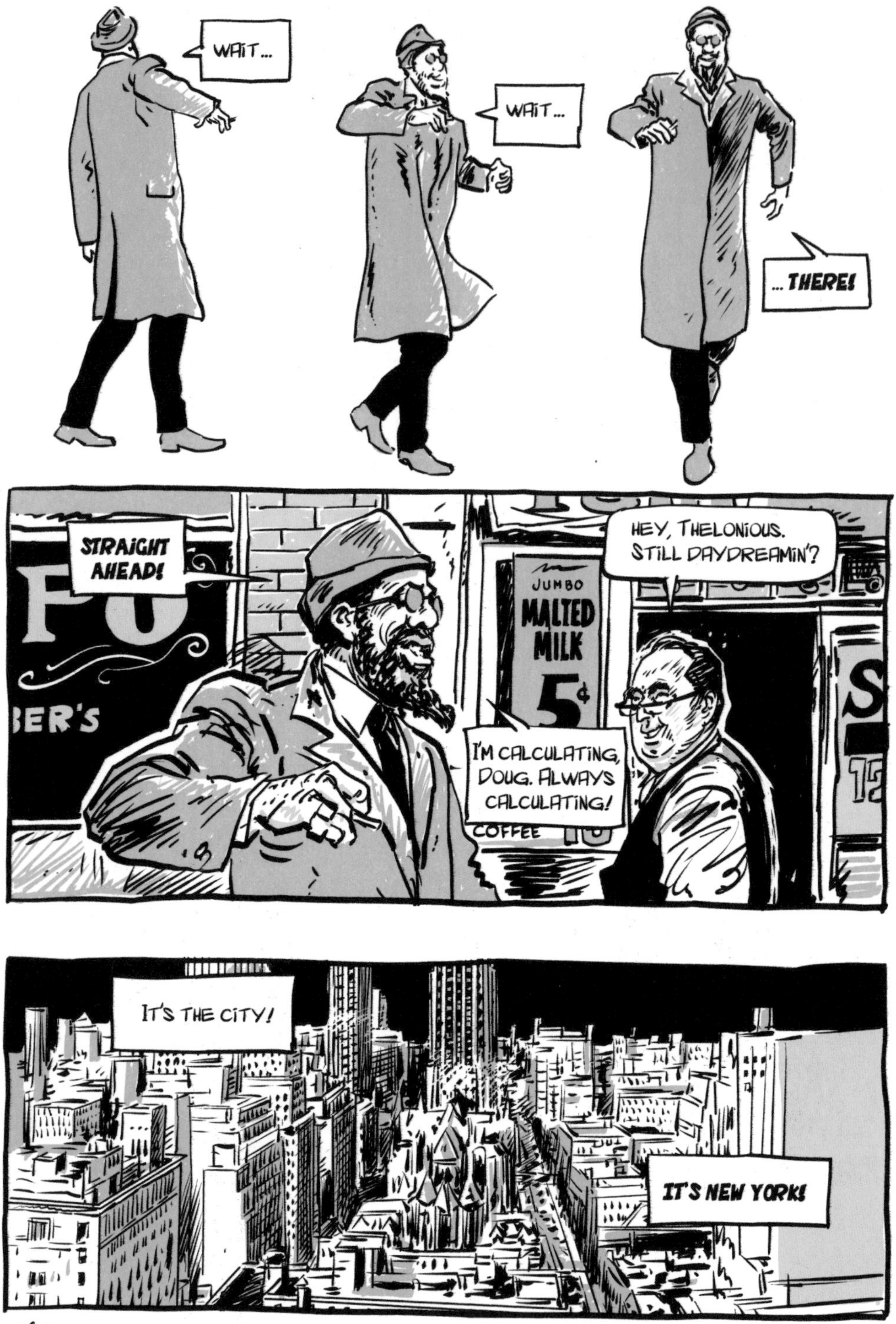
WAIT...
WAIT...
...THERE!
STRAIGHT AHEAD!
FO
BER'S
JUMBO
MALTED MILK
5¢
HEY, THELONIOUS. STILL DAYDREAMIN'?
I'M CALCULATING, DOUG. ALWAYS CALCULATING!
COFFEE
IT'S THE CITY!
IT'S NEW YORK!

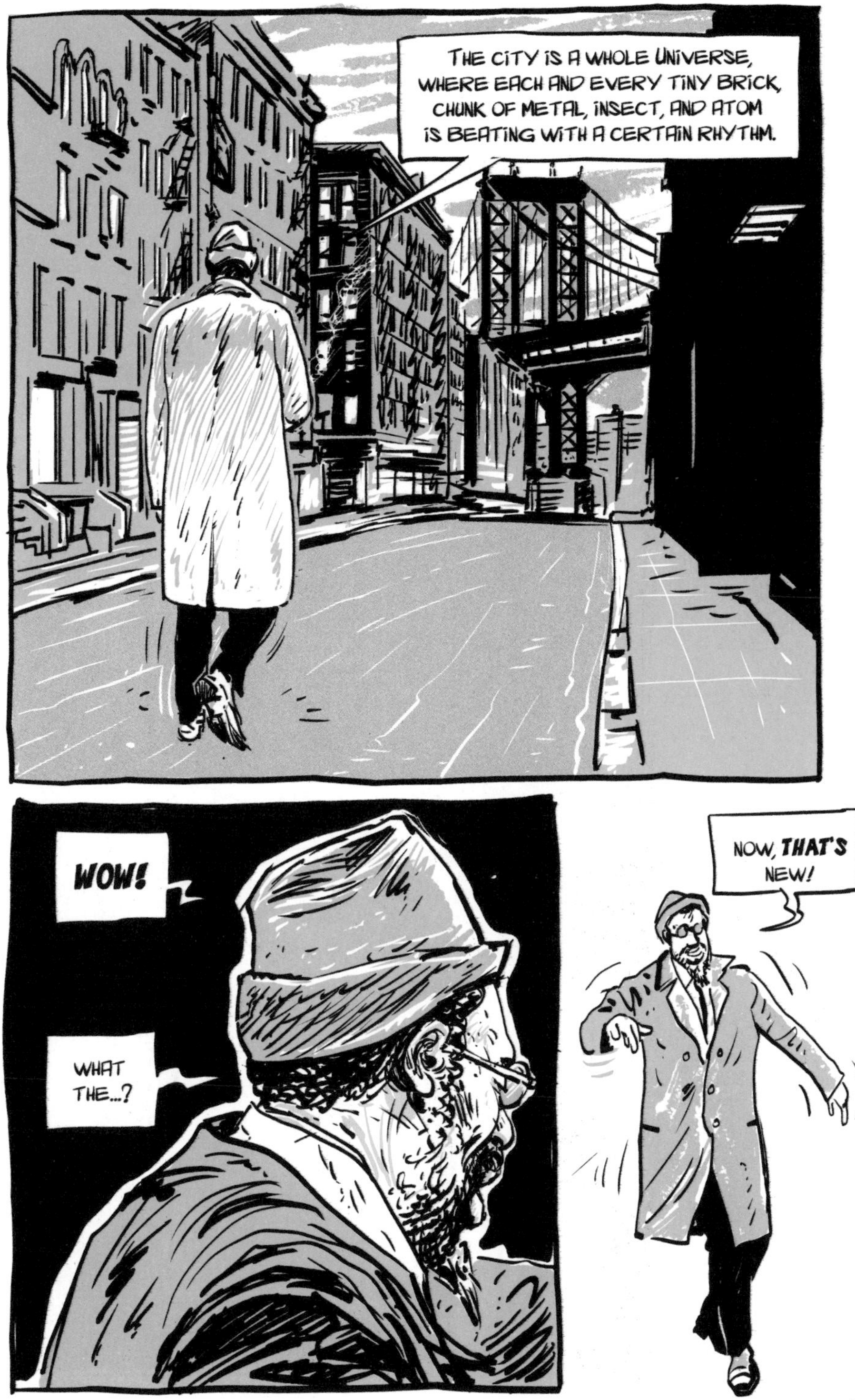
THE CITY IS A WHOLE UNIVERSE, WHERE EACH AND EVERY TINY BRICK, CHUNK OF METAL, INSECT, AND ATOM IS BEATING WITH A CERTAIN RHYTHM.
WOW!
WHAT THE...?
NOW, **THAT'S** NEW!

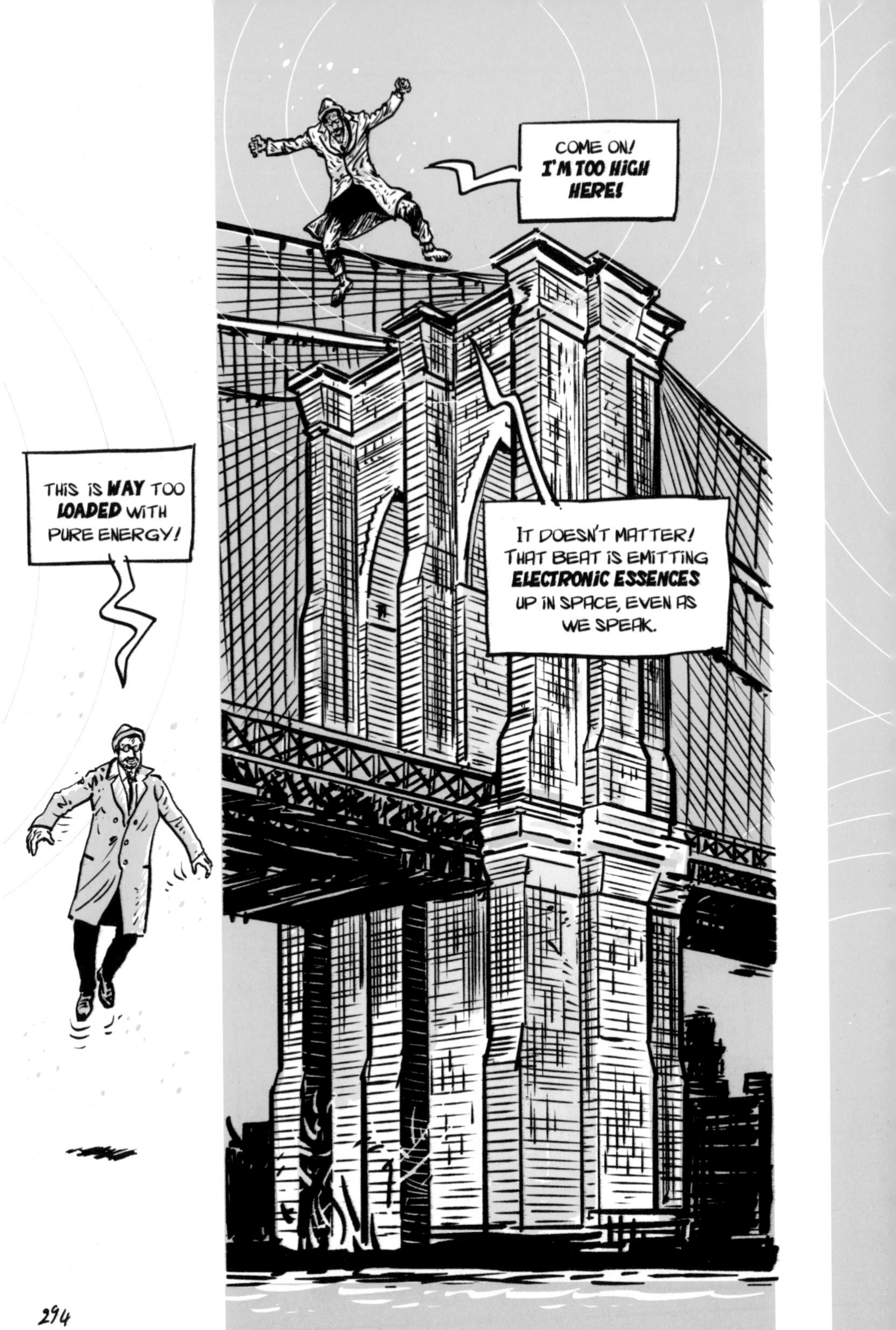
COME ON! I'M TOO HIGH HERE!
THIS IS WAY TOO LOADED WITH PURE ENERGY!
IT DOESN'T MATTER! THAT BEAT IS EMITTING ELECTRONIC ESSENCES UP IN SPACE, EVEN AS WE SPEAK.

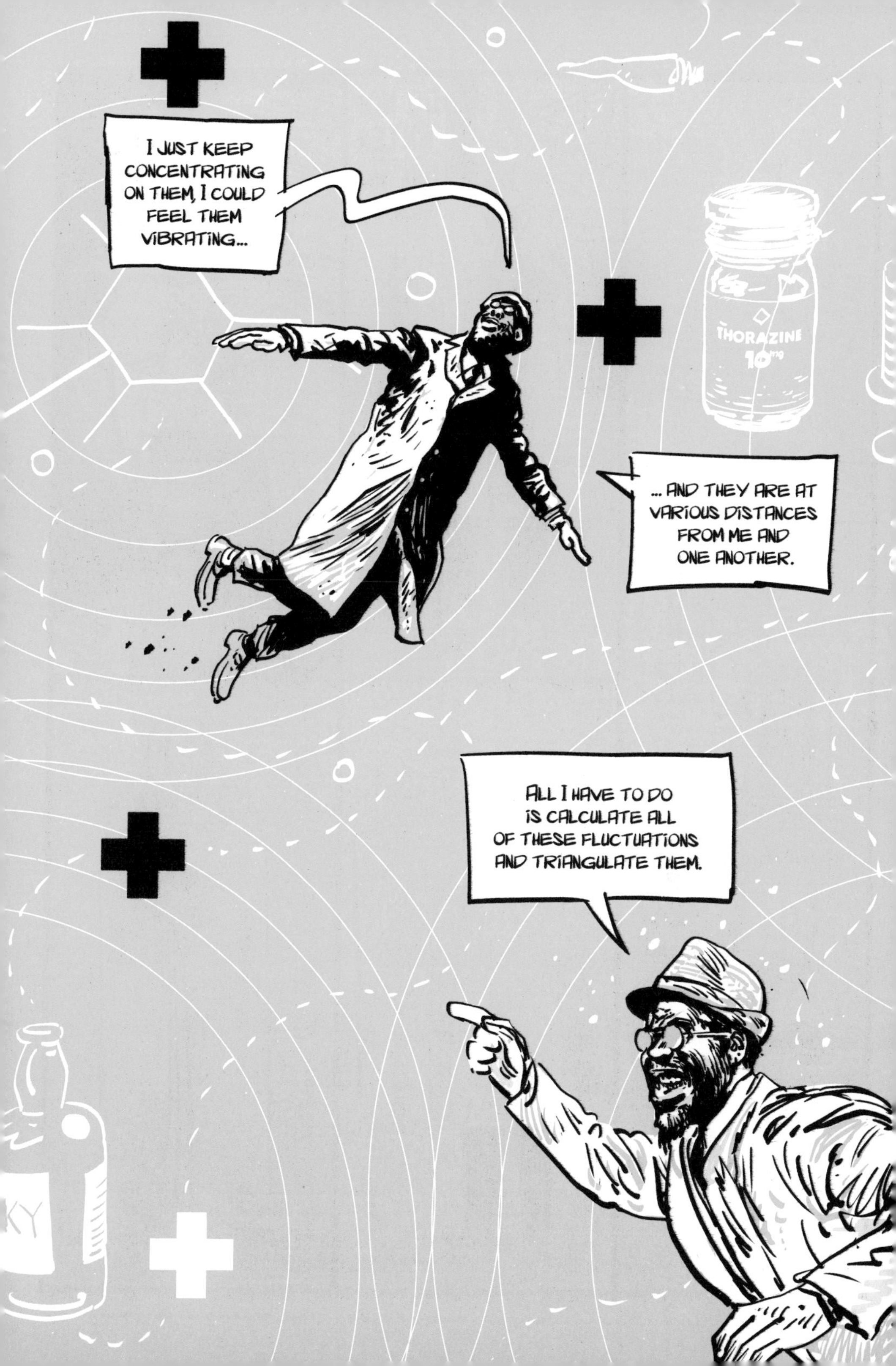

I JUST KEEP CONCENTRATING ON THEM, I COULD FEEL THEM VIBRATING...
THORAZINE 10mg
... AND THEY ARE AT VARIOUS DISTANCES FROM ME AND ONE ANOTHER.
ALL I HAVE TO DO IS CALCULATE ALL OF THESE FLUCTUATIONS AND TRIANGULATE THEM.

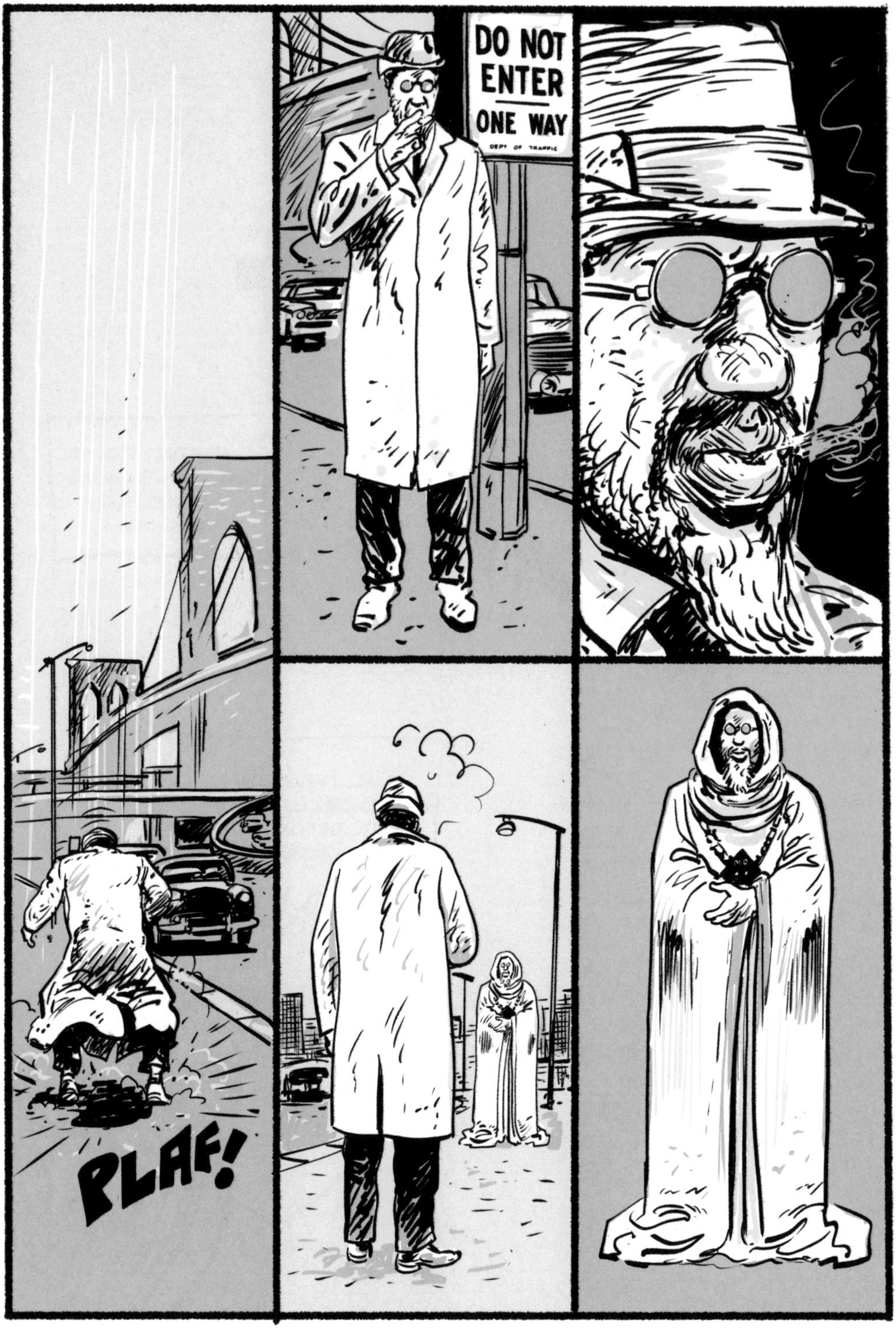
PLAF!
DO NOT ENTER
ONE WAY
DEPT OF TRAFFIC

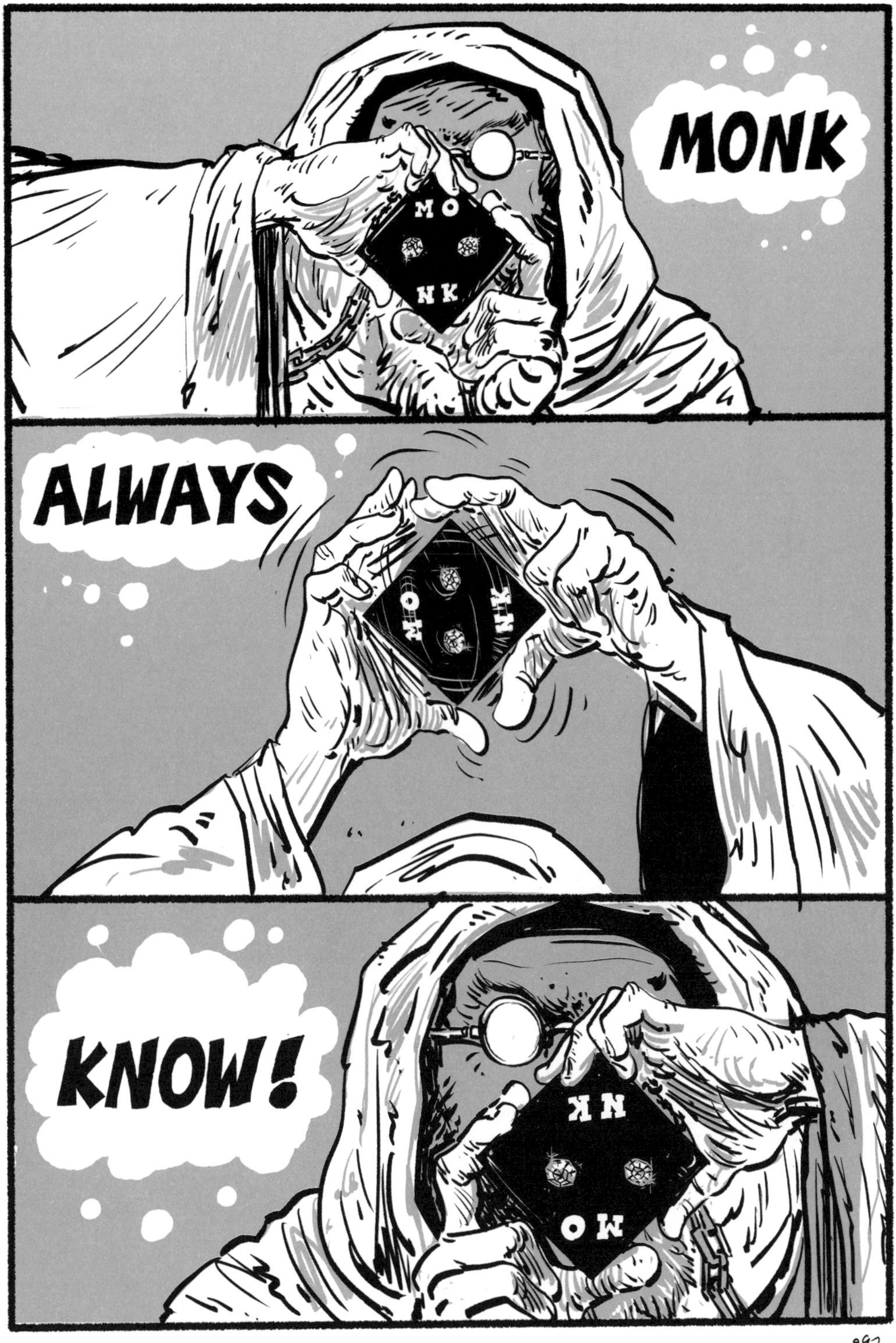
MONK
MO
NK
ALWAYS
KNOW!

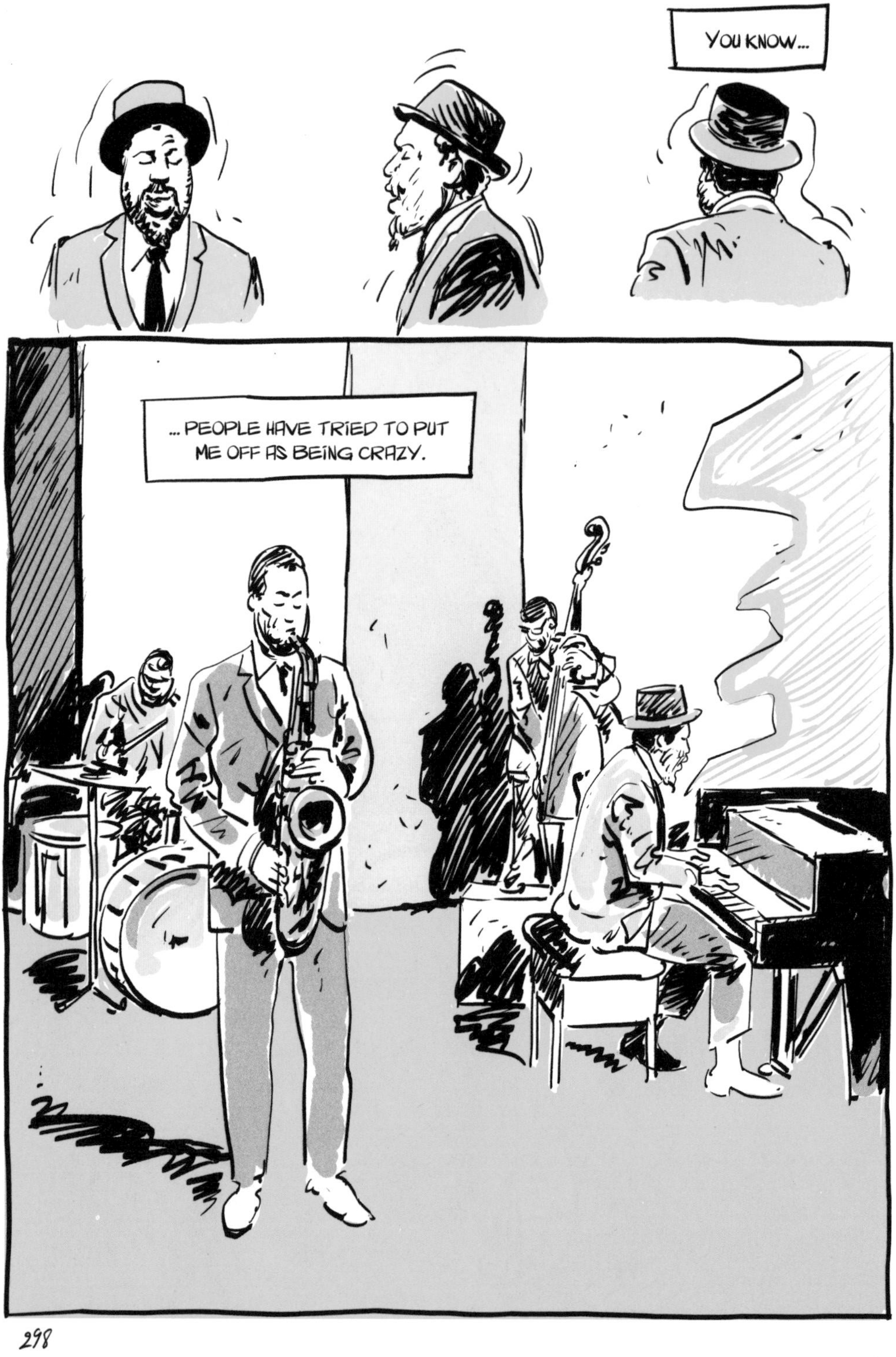
YOU KNOW...
...PEOPLE HAVE TRIED TO PUT ME OFF AS BEING CRAZY.

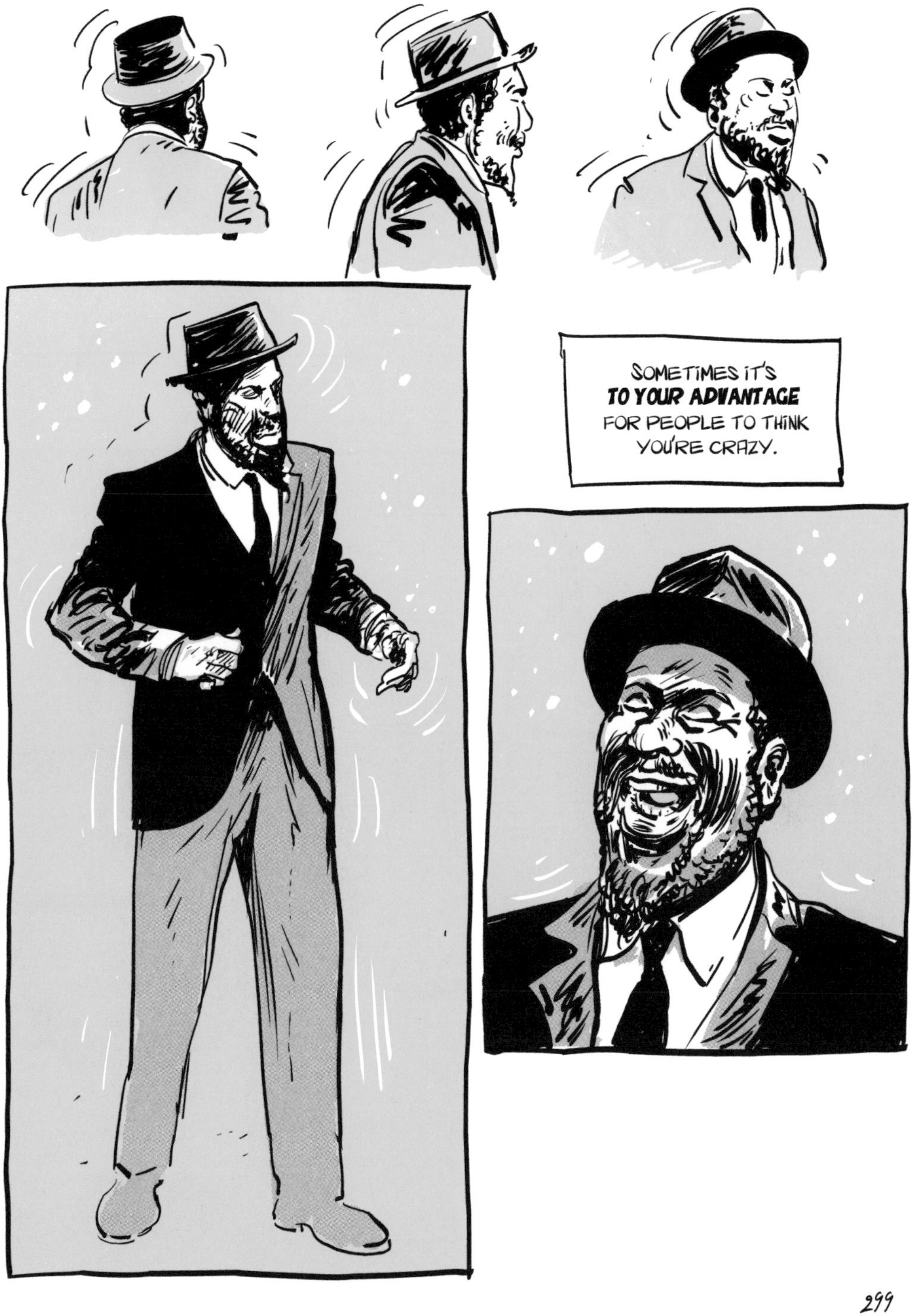
SOMETIMES IT'S
TO YOUR ADVANTAGE
FOR PEOPLE TO THINK
YOU'RE CRAZY.

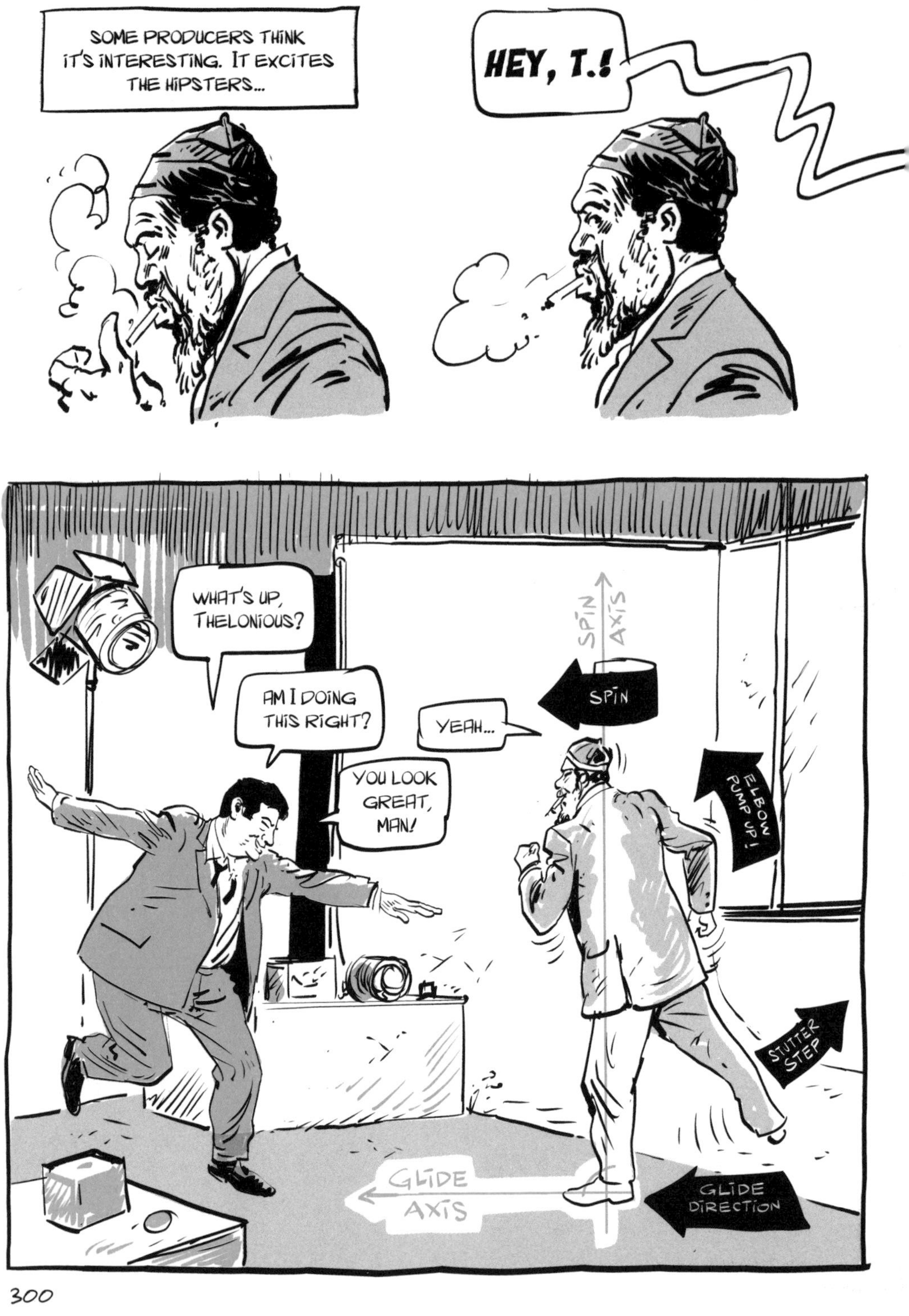
SOME PRODUCERS THINK IT'S INTERESTING. IT EXCITES THE HIPSTERS...
HEY, T.!
WHAT'S UP, THELONIOUS?
AM I DOING THIS RIGHT?
YEAH...
YOU LOOK GREAT, MAN!
SPIN AXIS
SPIN
ELBOW PUMP UP!
STUTTER STEP
GLIDE AXIS
GLIDE DIRECTION

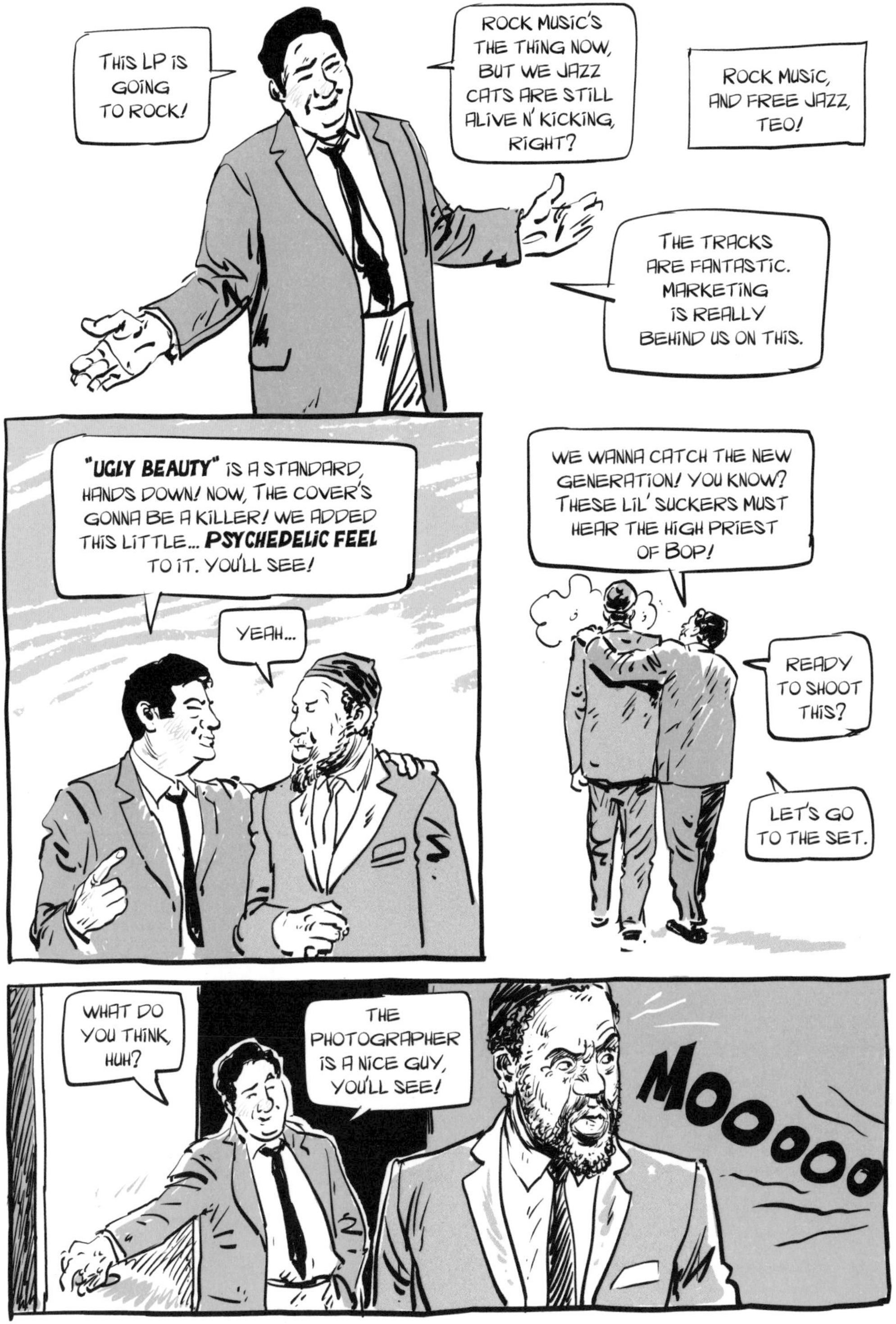
THIS LP IS GOING TO ROCK!
ROCK MUSIC'S THE THING NOW, BUT WE JAZZ CATS ARE STILL ALIVE N' KICKING, RIGHT?
ROCK MUSIC, AND FREE JAZZ, TEO!
THE TRACKS ARE FANTASTIC. MARKETING IS REALLY BEHIND US ON THIS.
"UGLY BEAUTY" IS A STANDARD, HANDS DOWN! NOW, THE COVER'S GONNA BE A KILLER! WE ADDED THIS LITTLE... PSYCHEDELIC FEEL TO IT. YOU'LL SEE!
YEAH...
WE WANNA CATCH THE NEW GENERATION! YOU KNOW? THESE LIL' SUCKERS MUST HEAR THE HIGH PRIEST OF BOP!
READY TO SHOOT THIS?
LET'S GO TO THE SET.
WHAT DO YOU THINK, HUH?
THE PHOTOGRAPHER IS A NICE GUY, YOU'LL SEE!
MOOOOOO

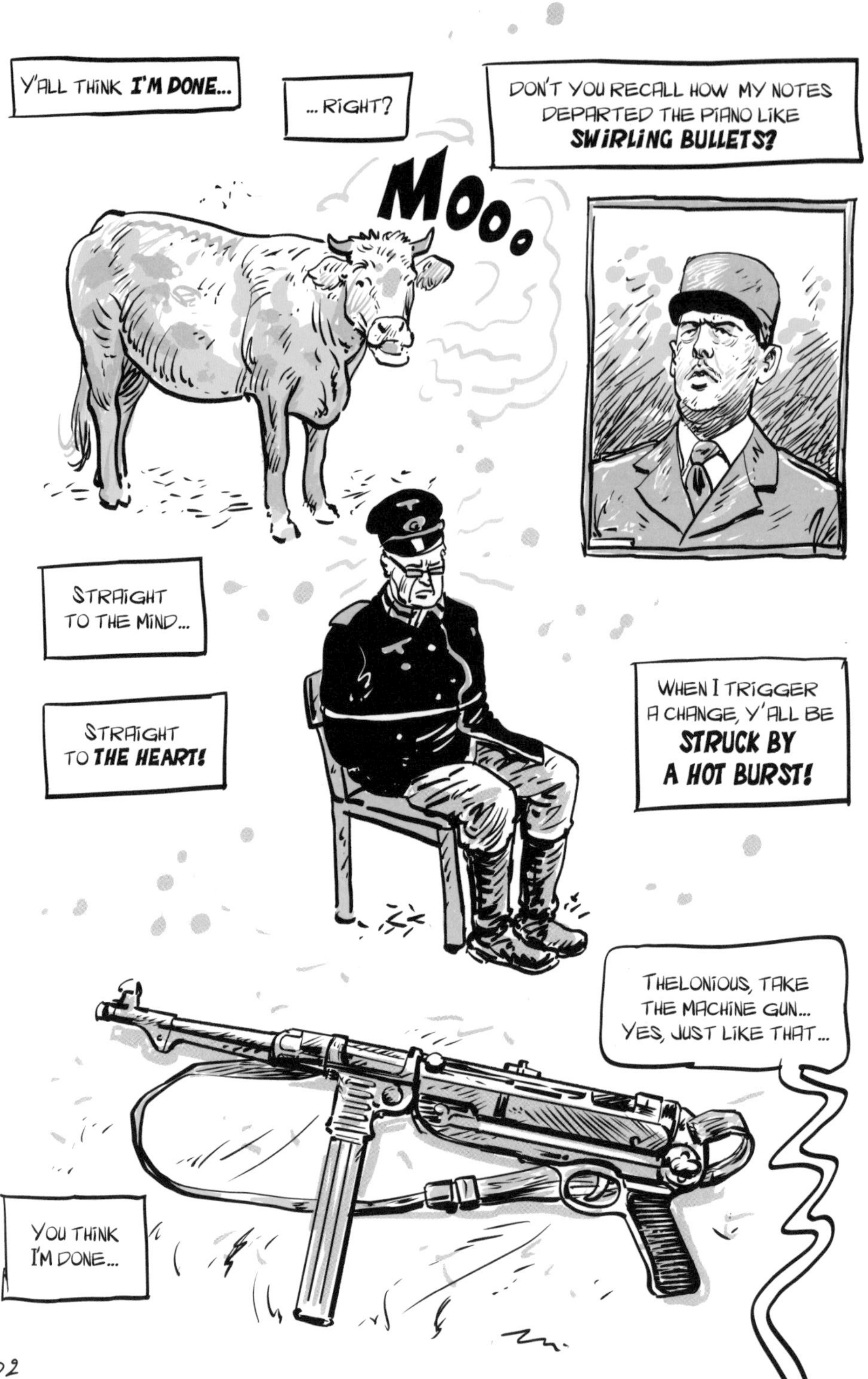
Y'ALL THINK I'M DONE...
... RIGHT?
DON'T YOU RECALL HOW MY NOTES DEPARTED THE PIANO LIKE SWIRLING BULLETS?
MOOO
STRAIGHT TO THE MIND...
STRAIGHT TO THE HEART!
WHEN I TRIGGER A CHANGE, Y'ALL BE STRUCK BY A HOT BURST!
THELONIOUS, TAKE THE MACHINE GUN... YES, JUST LIKE THAT...
YOU THINK I'M DONE...

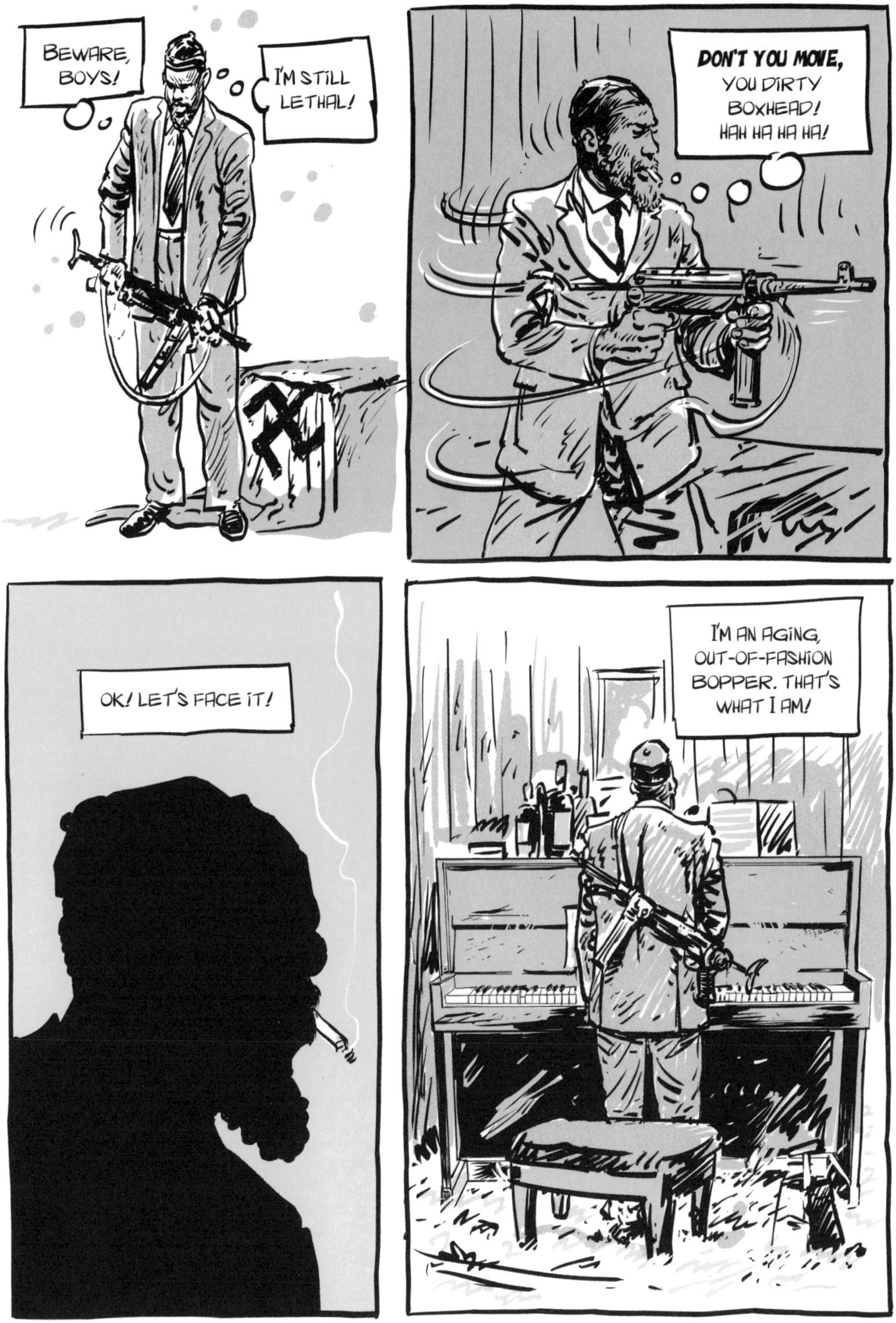
BEWARE, BOYS!
I'M STILL LETHAL!
DON'T YOU MOVE, YOU DIRTY BOXHEAD! HAH HA HA HA!
OK! LET'S FACE IT!
I'M AN AGING, OUT-OF-FASHION BOPPER. THAT'S WHAT I AM!

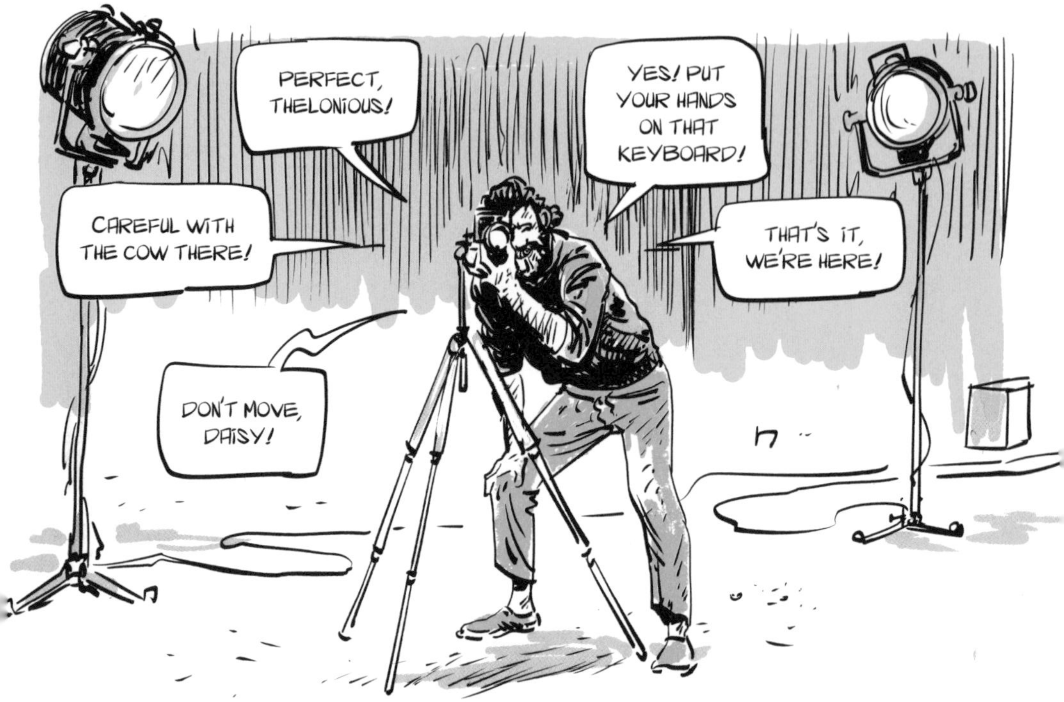
PERFECT, THELONIOUS!
YES! PUT YOUR HANDS ON THAT KEYBOARD!
CAREFUL WITH THE COW THERE!
THAT'S IT, WE'RE HERE!
DON'T MOVE, DAISY!

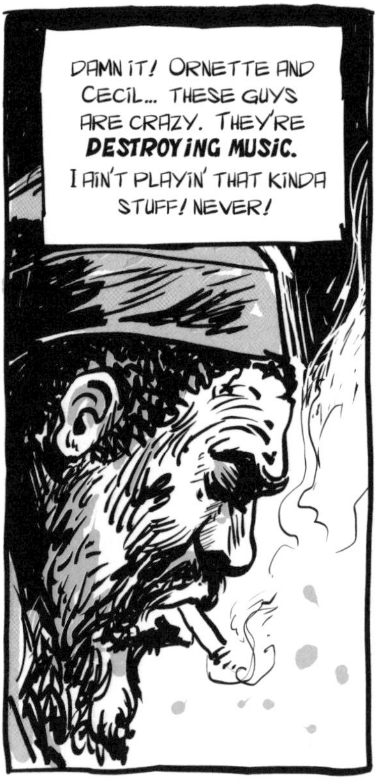
DAMN IT! ORNETTE AND CECIL... THESE GUYS ARE CRAZY. THEY'RE **DESTROYING MUSIC.** I AIN'T PLAYIN' THAT KINDA STUFF! NEVER!

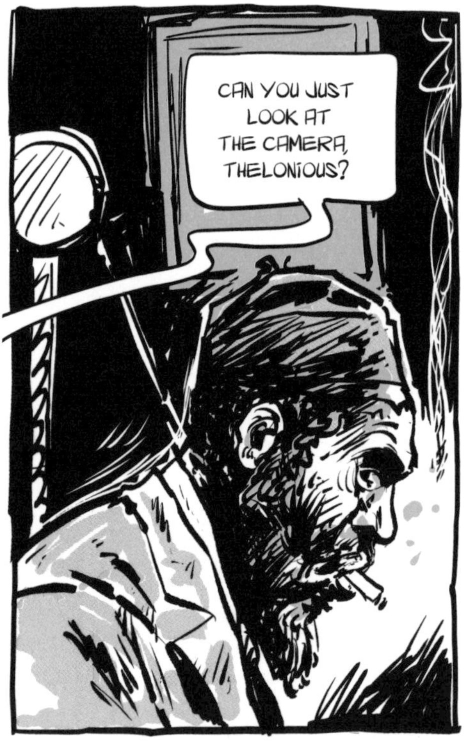
CAN YOU JUST LOOK AT THE CAMERA, THELONIOUS?

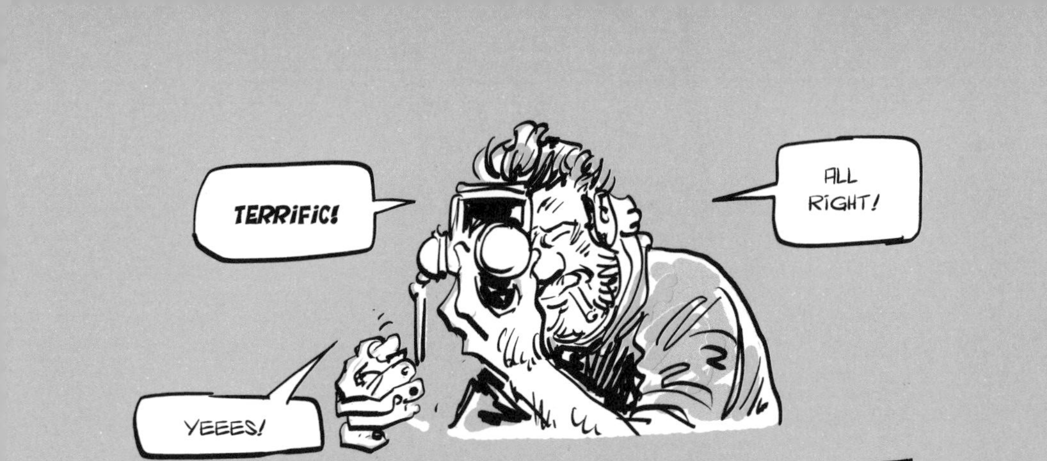
TERRIFIC!
ALL RIGHT!
YEEES!

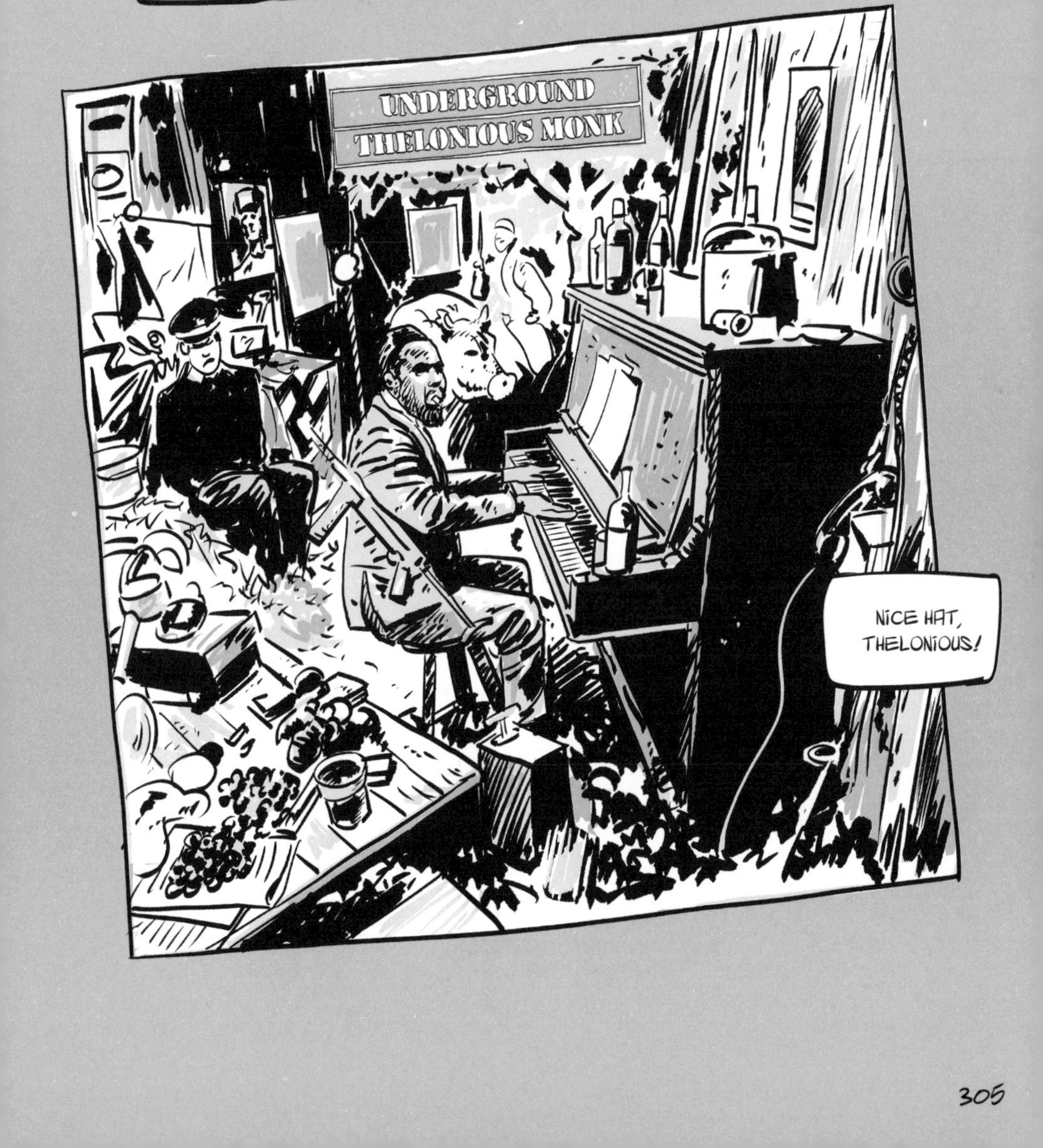
UNDERGROUND
THELONIOUS MONK
NICE HAT, THELONIOUS!

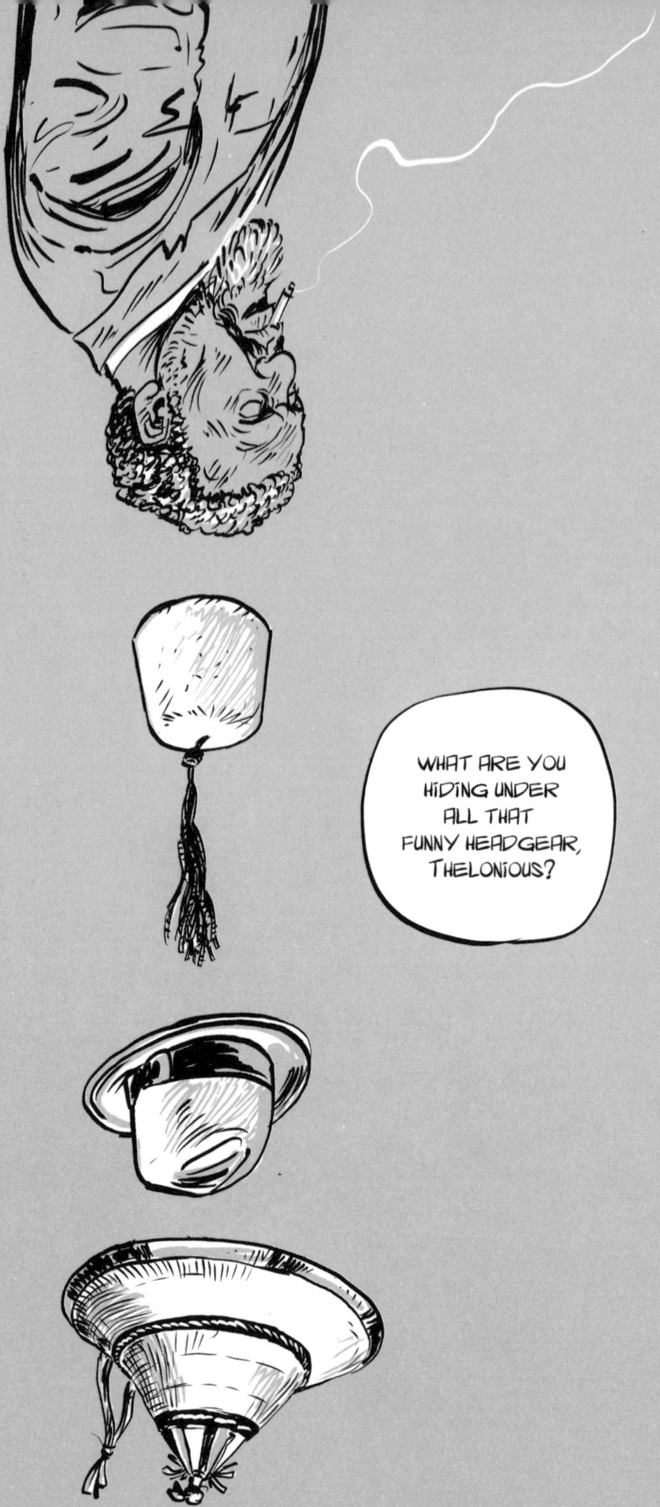
WHAT ARE YOU HIDING UNDER ALL THAT FUNNY HEADGEAR, THELONIOUS?

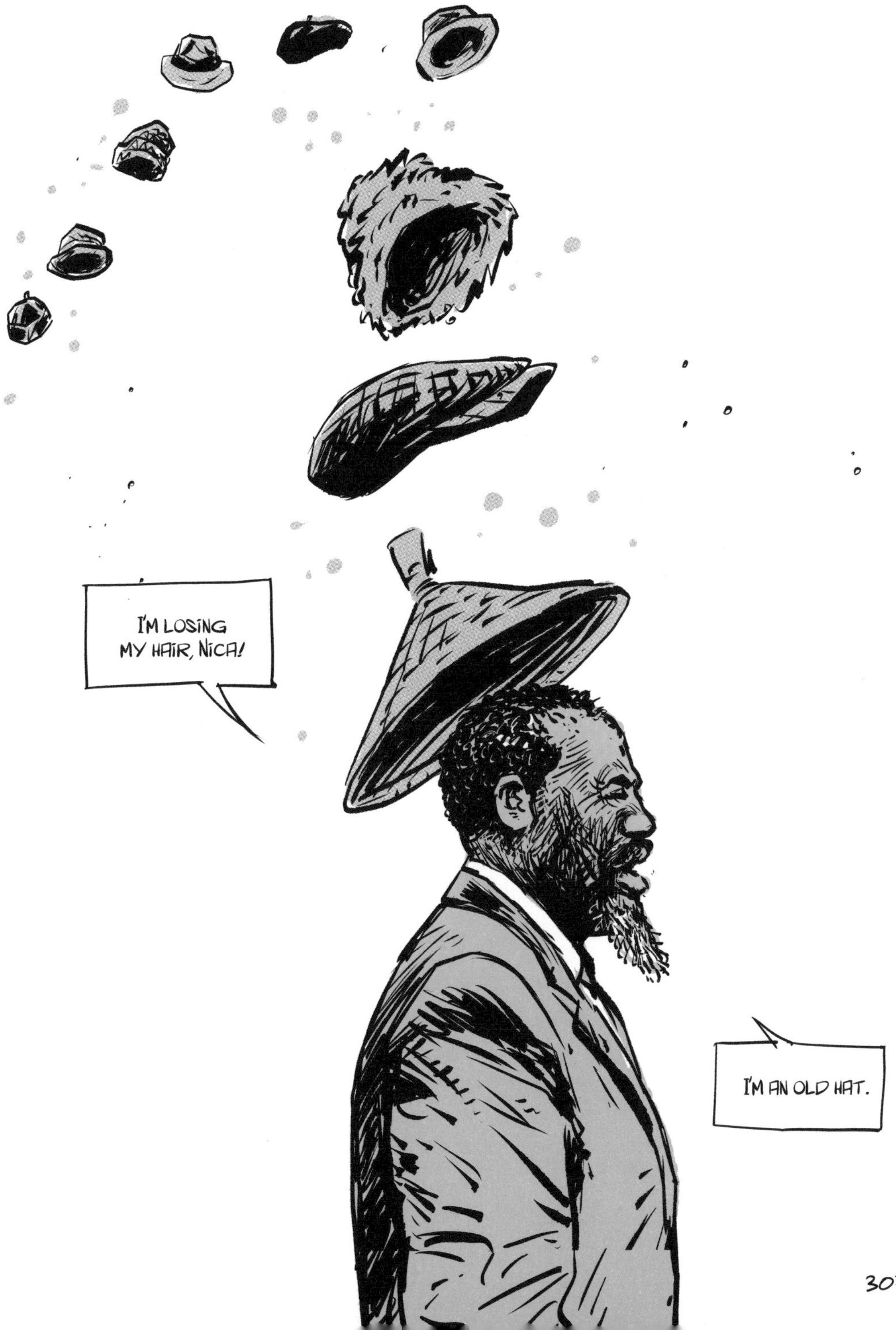
I'M LOSING MY HAIR, NICA!
I'M AN OLD HAT.

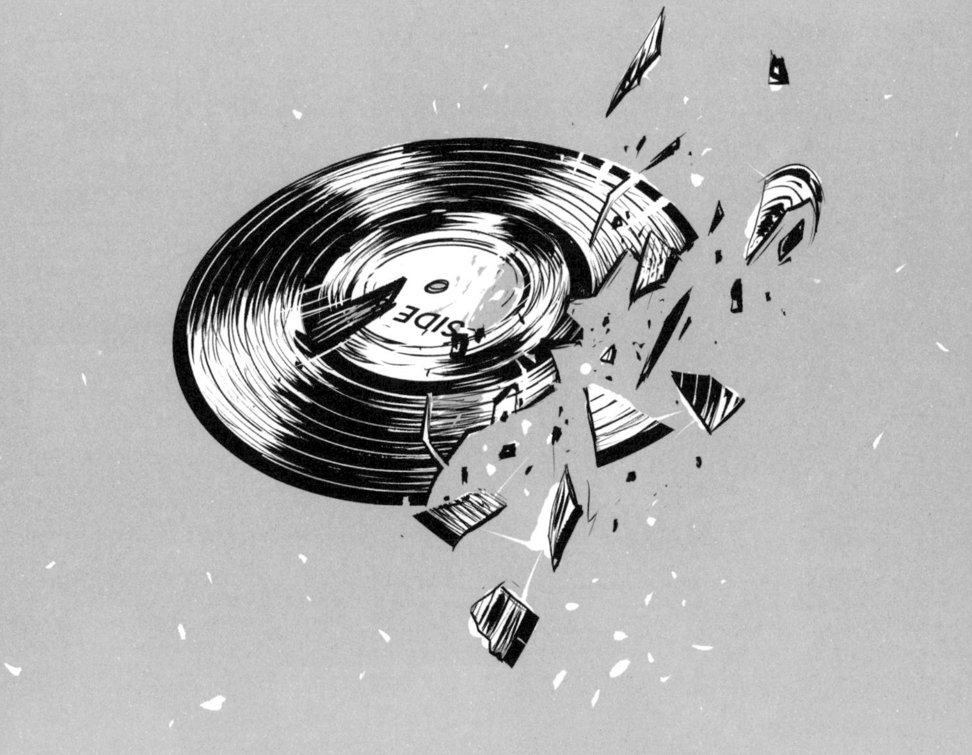
SIDE

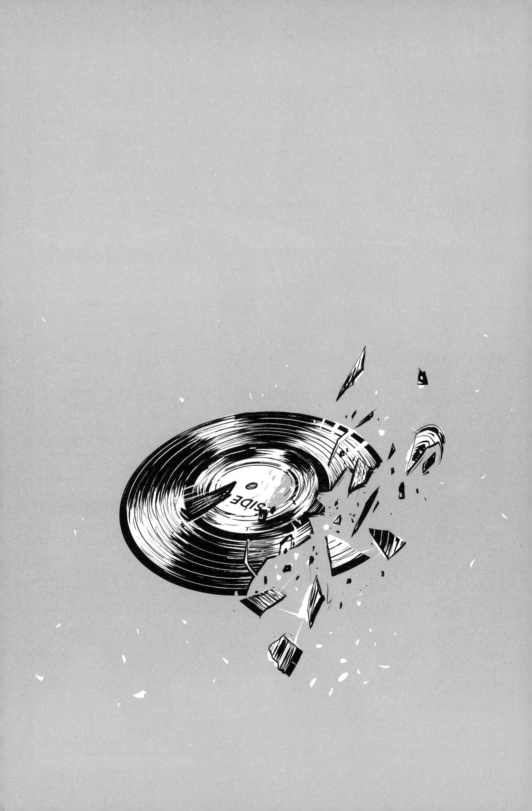

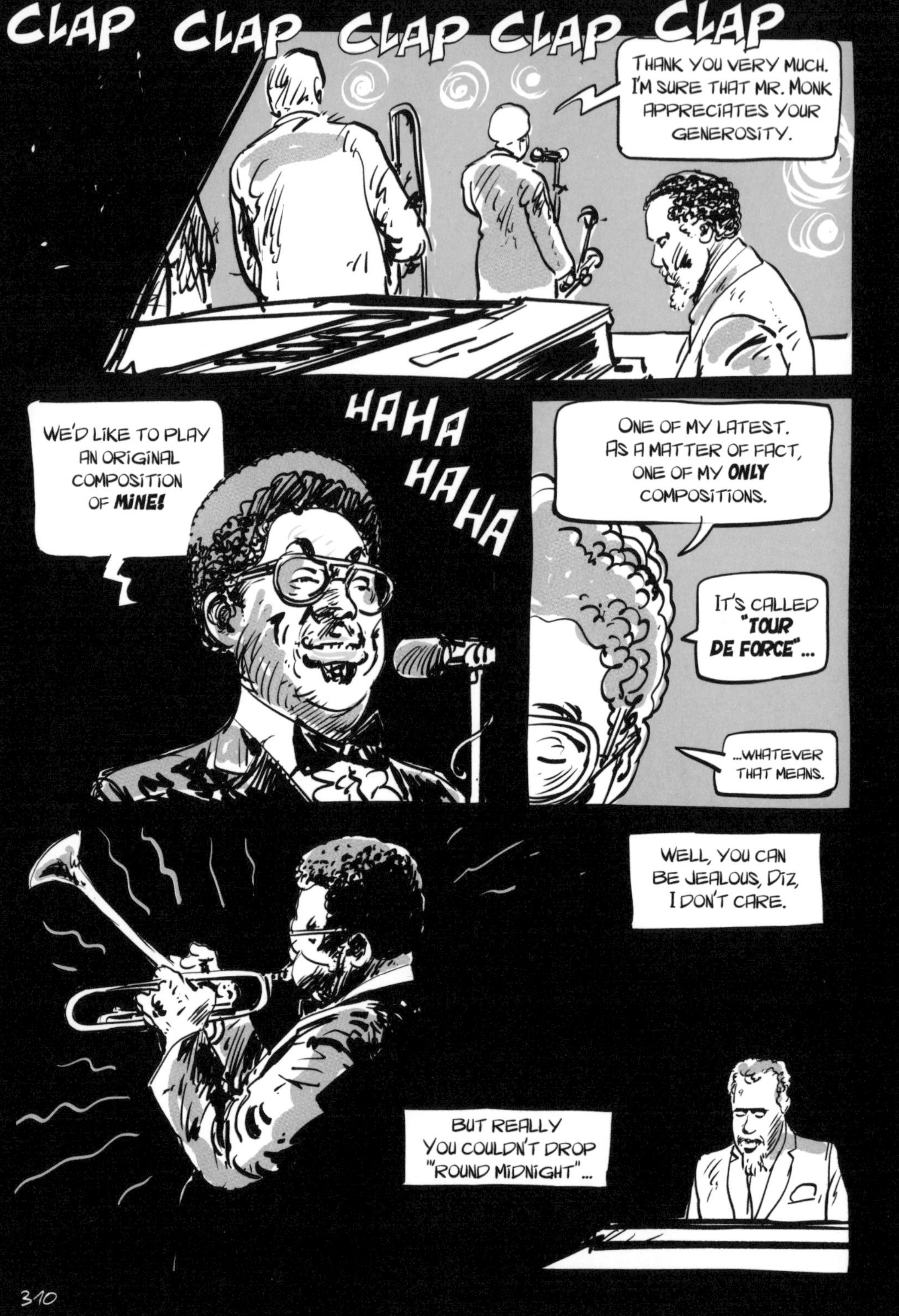
CLAP CLAP CLAP CLAP CLAP
THANK YOU VERY MUCH. I'M SURE THAT MR. MONK APPRECIATES YOUR GENEROSITY.
WE'D LIKE TO PLAY AN ORIGINAL COMPOSITION OF MINE!
HAHA HAHA HA
ONE OF MY LATEST. AS A MATTER OF FACT, ONE OF MY ONLY COMPOSITIONS.
IT'S CALLED "TOUR DE FORCE"...
...WHATEVER THAT MEANS.
WELL, YOU CAN BE JEALOUS, DIZ, I DON'T CARE.
BUT REALLY YOU COULDN'T DROP "ROUND MIDNIGHT"...

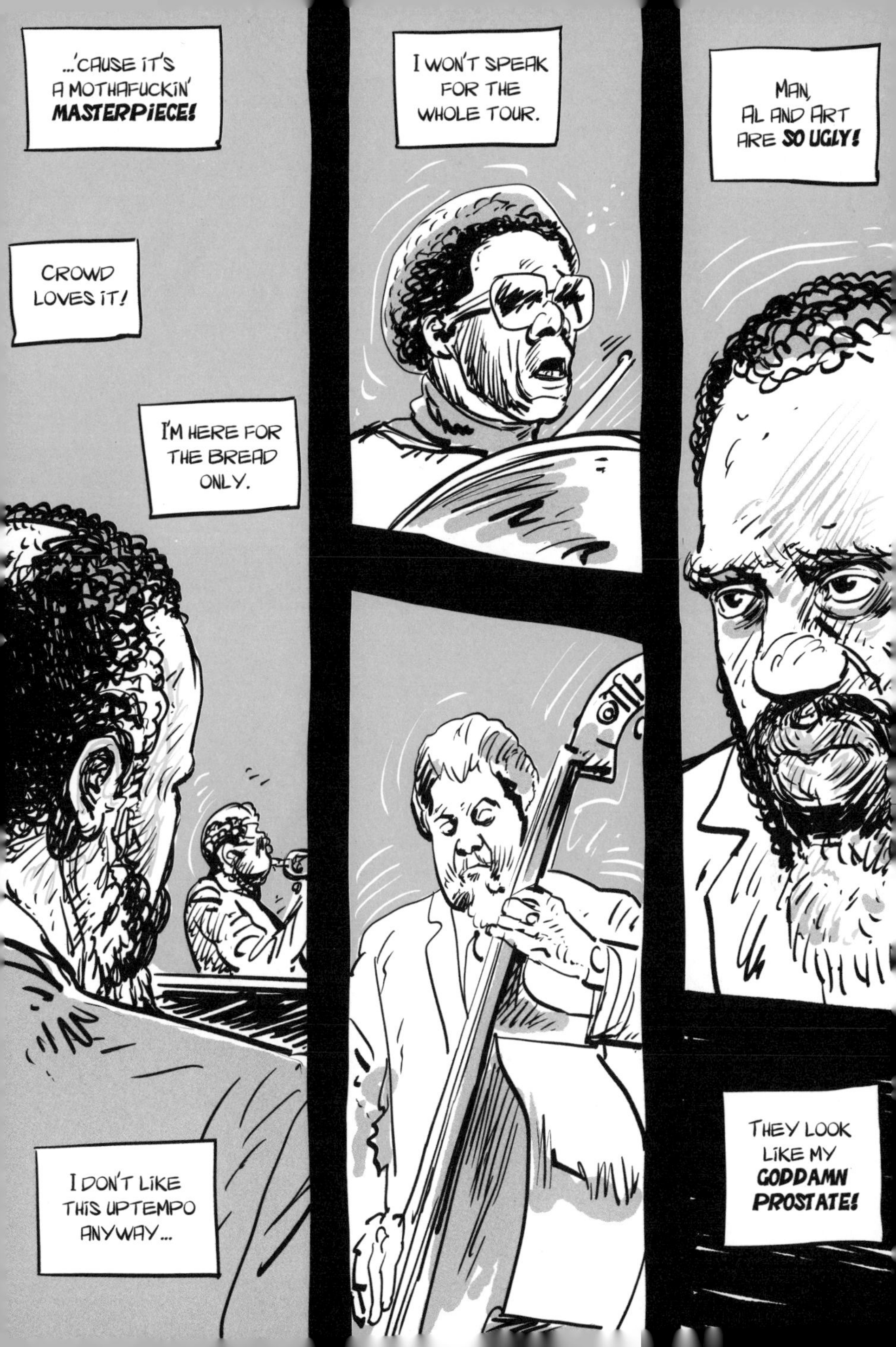
...'CAUSE IT'S A MOTHAFUCKIN' **MASTERPIECE!**
CROWD LOVES IT!
I'M HERE FOR THE BREAD ONLY.
I DON'T LIKE THIS UPTEMPO ANYWAY...
I WON'T SPEAK FOR THE WHOLE TOUR.
MAN, AL AND ART ARE **SO UGLY!**
THEY LOOK LIKE MY **GODDAMN PROSTATE!**

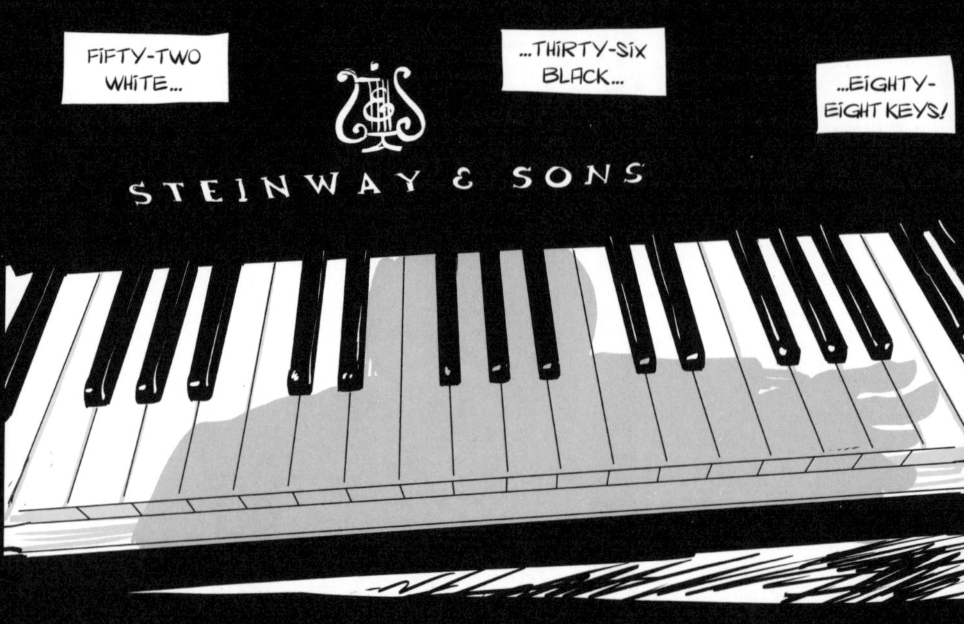
FIFTY-TWO WHITE...
...THIRTY-SIX BLACK...
...EIGHTY-EIGHT KEYS!
STEINWAY & SONS

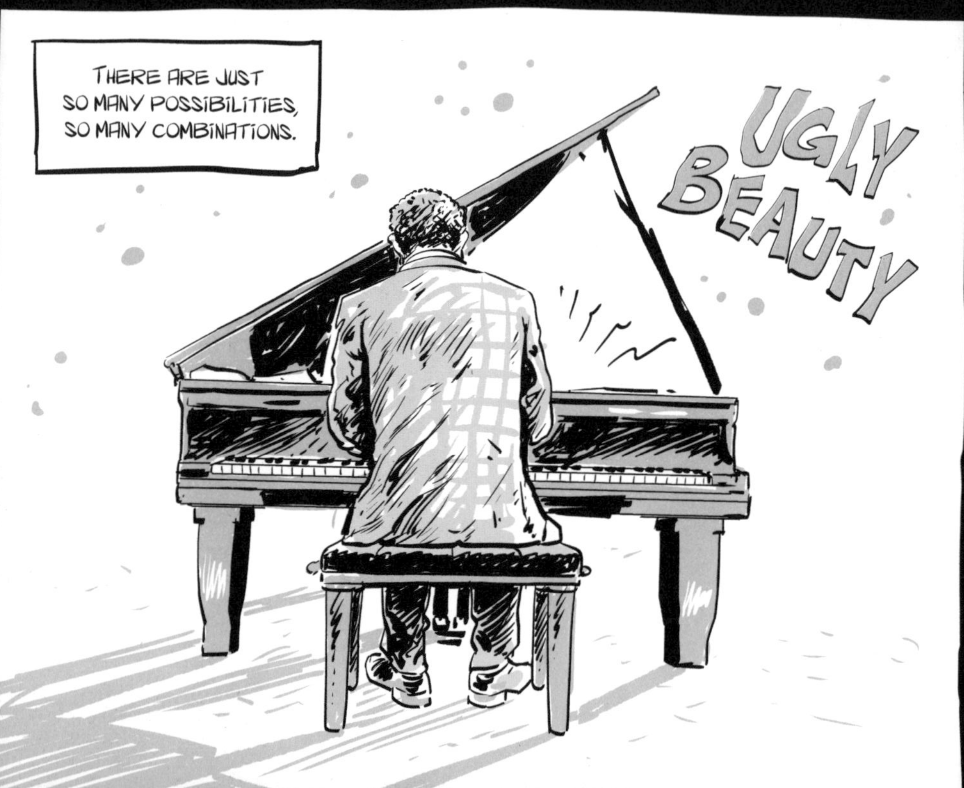
THERE ARE JUST SO MANY POSSIBILITIES, SO MANY COMBINATIONS.
UGLY BEAUTY

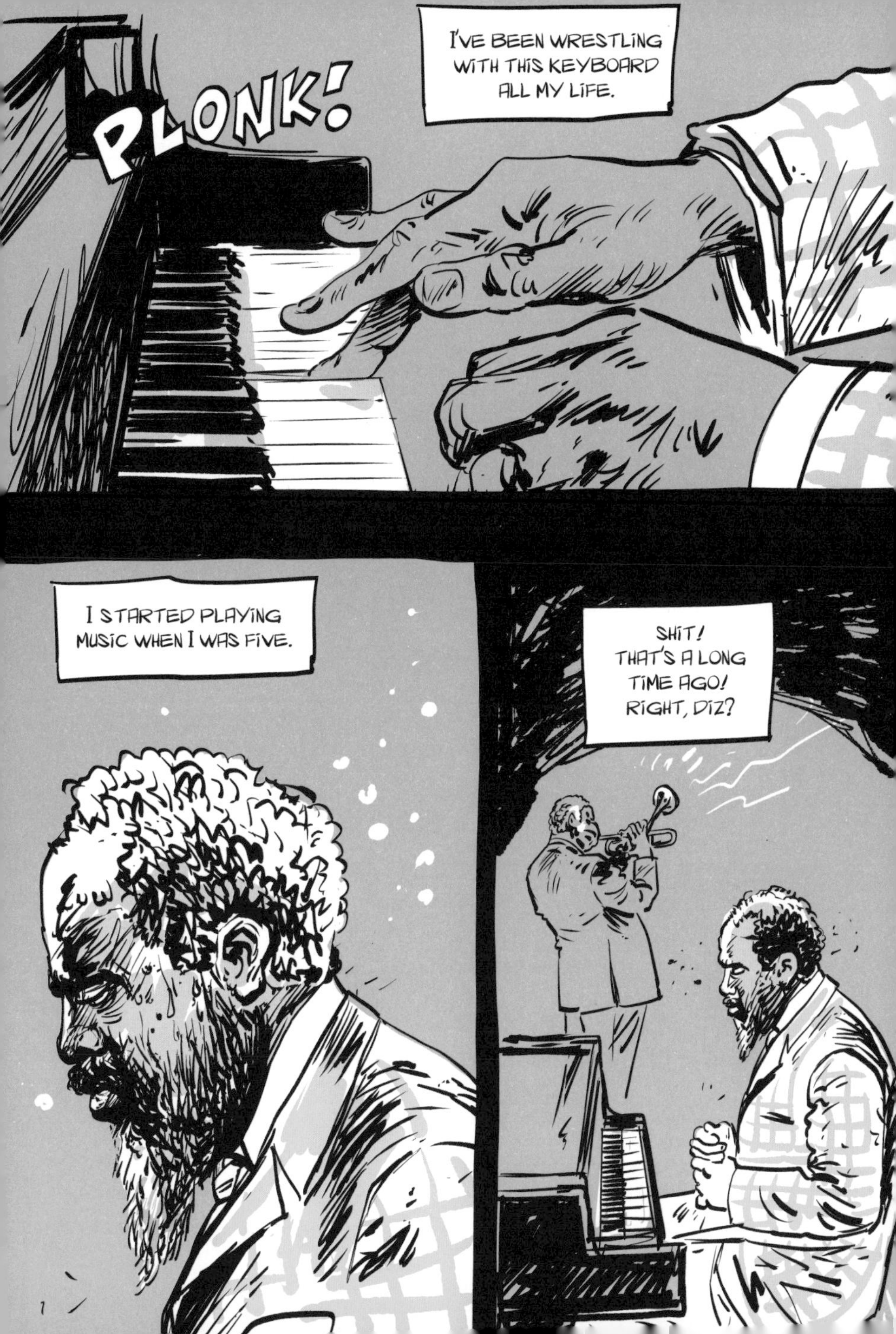
PLONK!
I'VE BEEN WRESTLING WITH THIS KEYBOARD ALL MY LIFE.
I STARTED PLAYING MUSIC WHEN I WAS FIVE.
SHIT! THAT'S A LONG TIME AGO! RIGHT, DIZ?

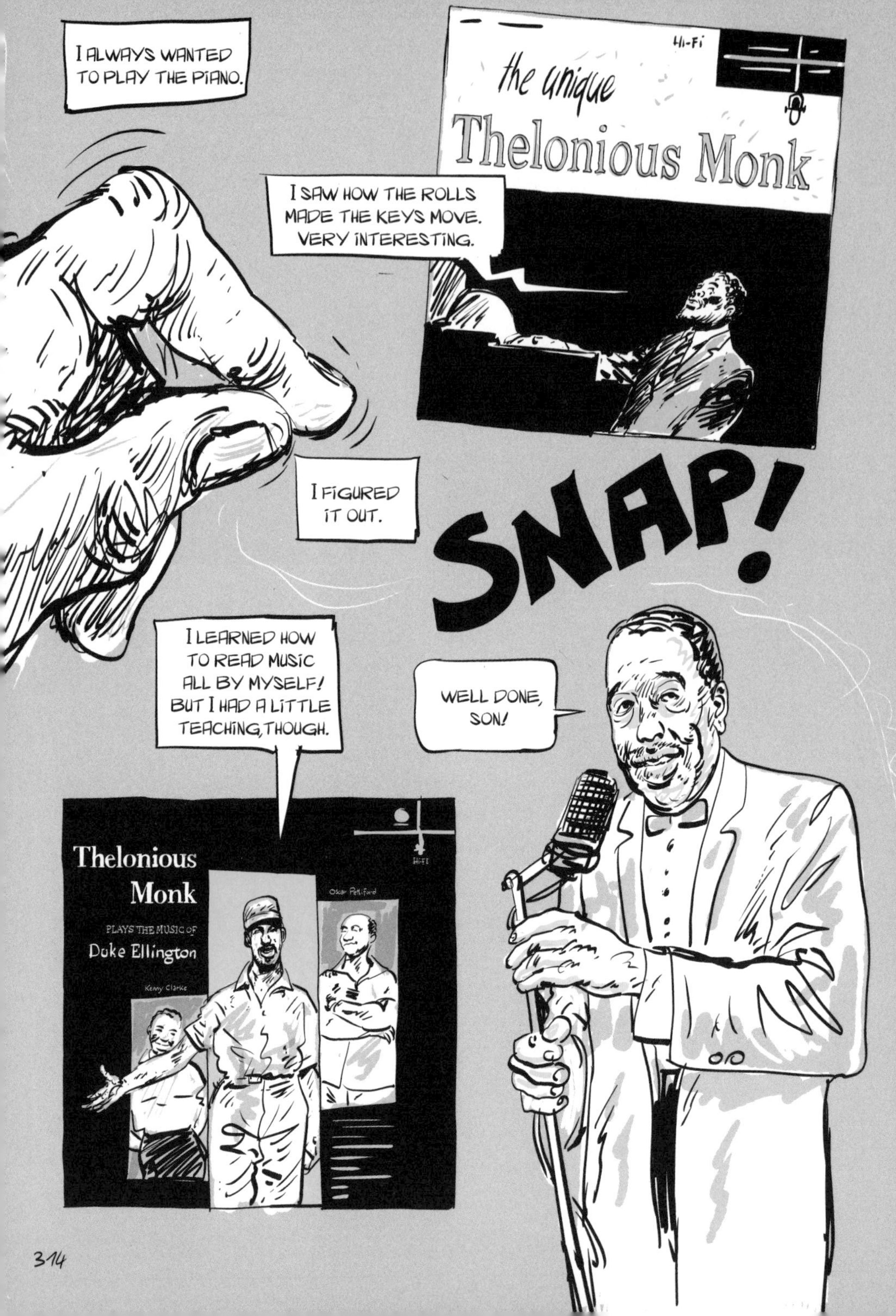
I ALWAYS WANTED TO PLAY THE PIANO.
Hi-Fi
the unique
Thelonious Monk
I SAW HOW THE ROLLS MADE THE KEYS MOVE. VERY INTERESTING.
I FIGURED IT OUT.
SNAP!
I LEARNED HOW TO READ MUSIC ALL BY MYSELF! BUT I HAD A LITTLE TEACHING, THOUGH.
WELL DONE, SON!
Thelonious Monk
PLAYS THE MUSIC OF
Duke Ellington
Hi-Fi
Oscar Pettiford
Kenny Clarke

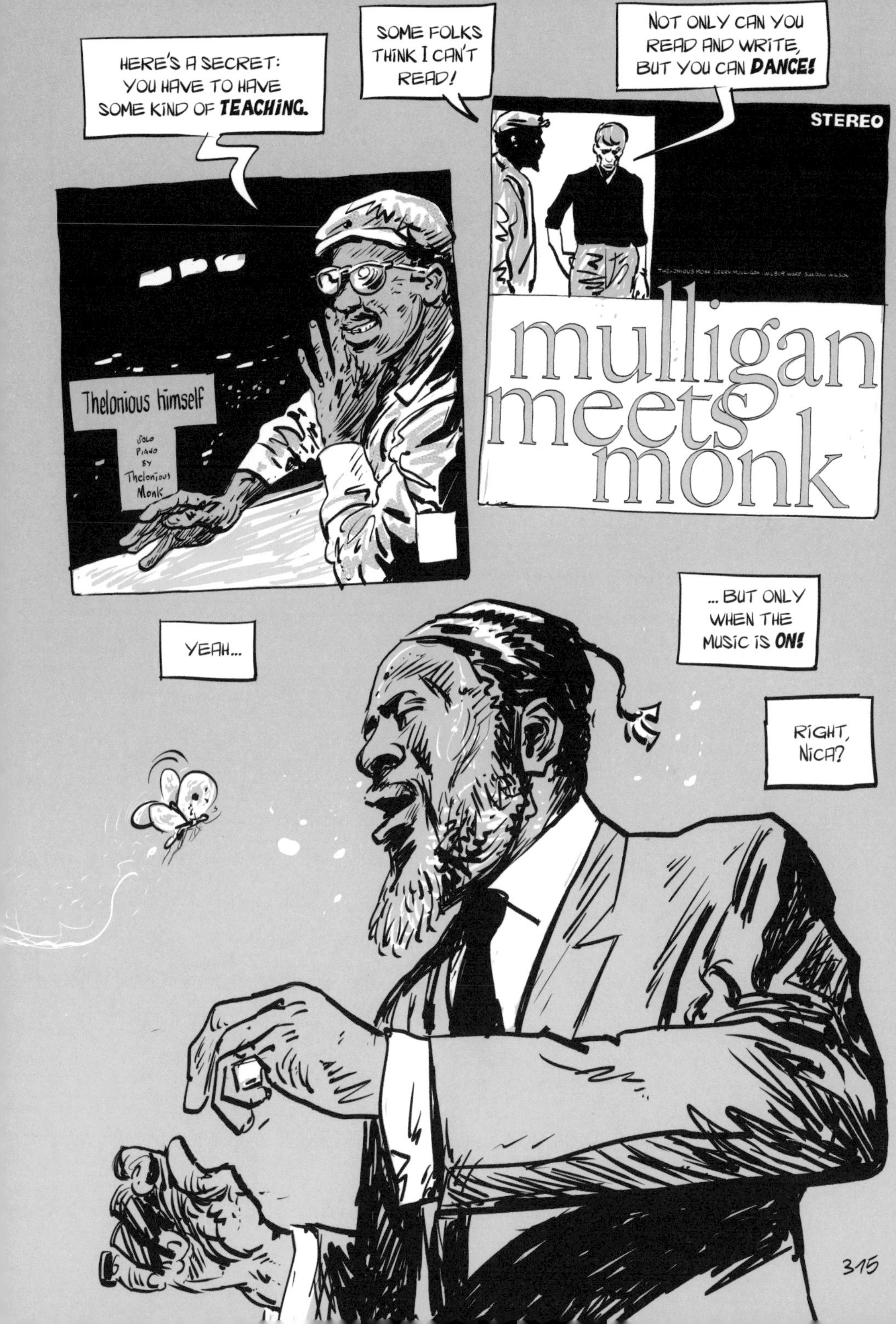
HERE'S A SECRET: YOU HAVE TO HAVE SOME KIND OF TEACHING.
SOME FOLKS THINK I CAN'T READ!
NOT ONLY CAN YOU READ AND WRITE, BUT YOU CAN DANCE!
Thelonious himself
SOLO PIANO BY Thelonious Monk
STEREO
mulligan meets monk
YEAH...
... BUT ONLY WHEN THE MUSIC IS ON!
RIGHT, NICA?

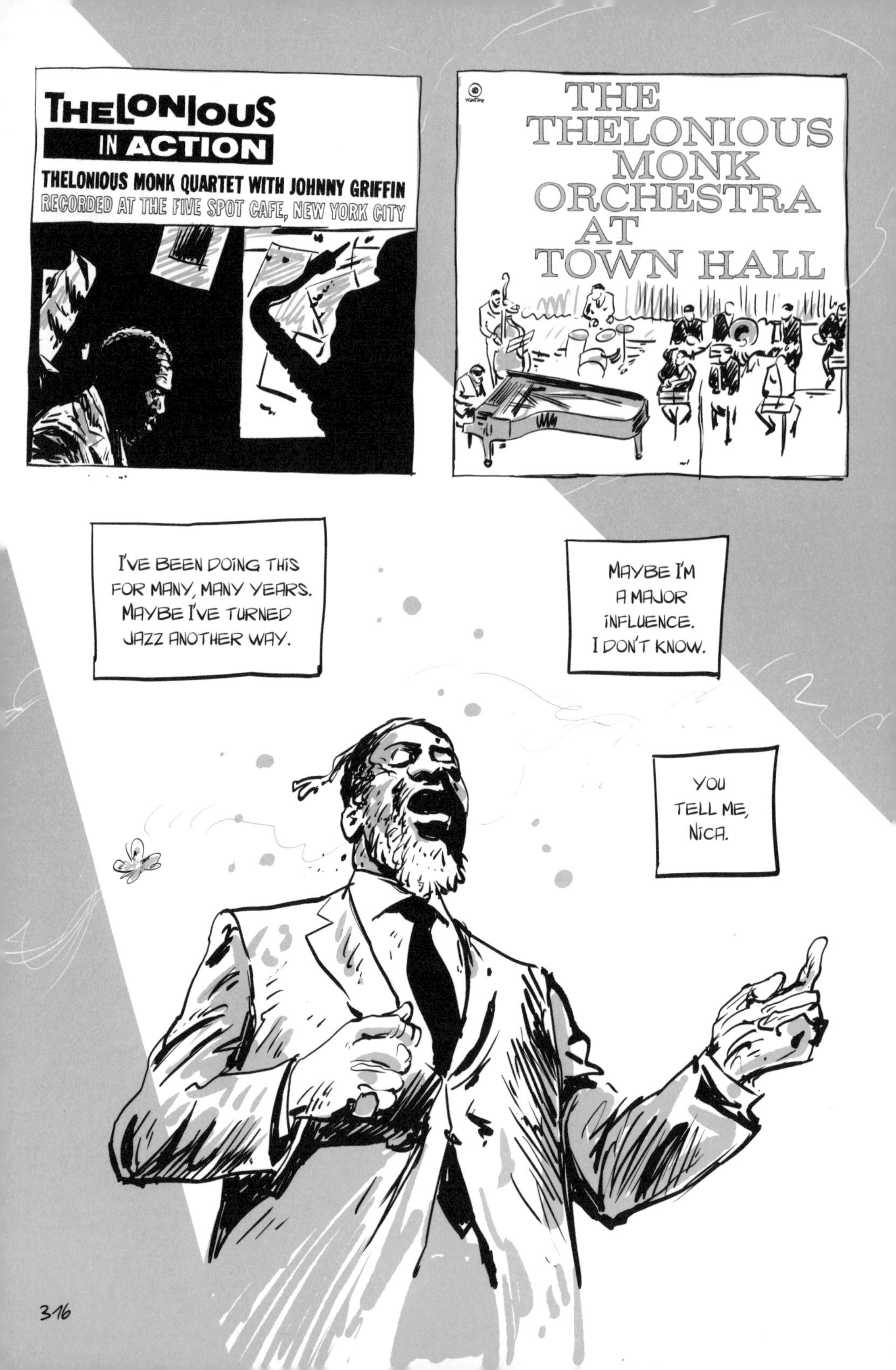
THELONIOUS IN ACTION
THELONIOUS MONK QUARTET WITH JOHNNY GRIFFIN
RECORDED AT THE FIVE SPOT CAFE, NEW YORK CITY
THE THELONIOUS MONK ORCHESTRA AT TOWN HALL
I'VE BEEN DOING THIS FOR MANY, MANY YEARS. MAYBE I'VE TURNED JAZZ ANOTHER WAY.
MAYBE I'M A MAJOR INFLUENCE. I DON'T KNOW.
YOU TELL ME, NICA.

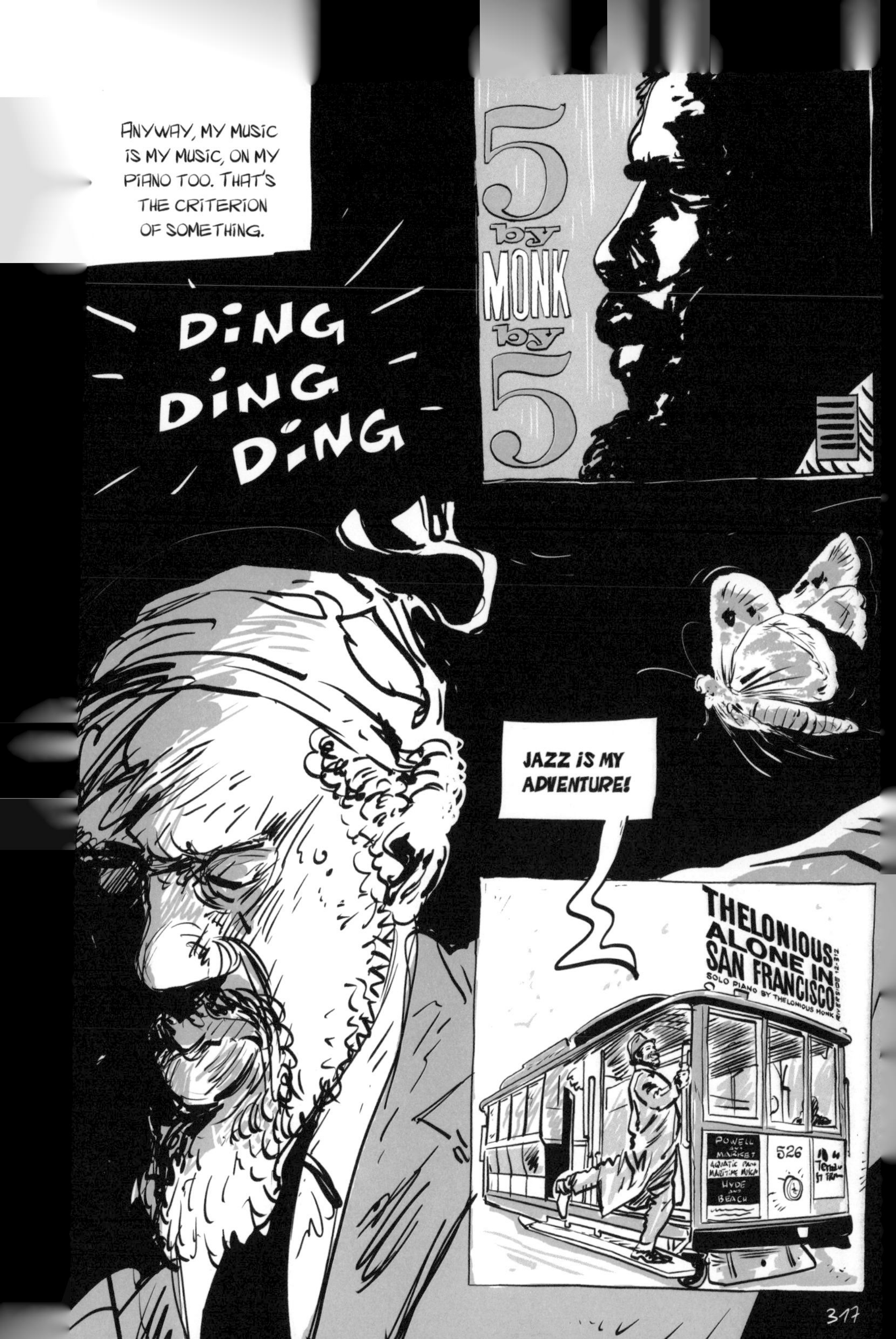
ANYWAY, MY MUSIC IS MY MUSIC, ON MY PIANO TOO. THAT'S THE CRITERION OF SOMETHING.
DING DING DING
5 by MONK by 5
JAZZ IS MY ADVENTURE!
THELONIOUS ALONE IN SAN FRANCISCO
SOLO PIANO BY THELONIOUS MONK
RIVERSIDE 12-312
POWELL AND MARKET
HYDE AND BEACH
526

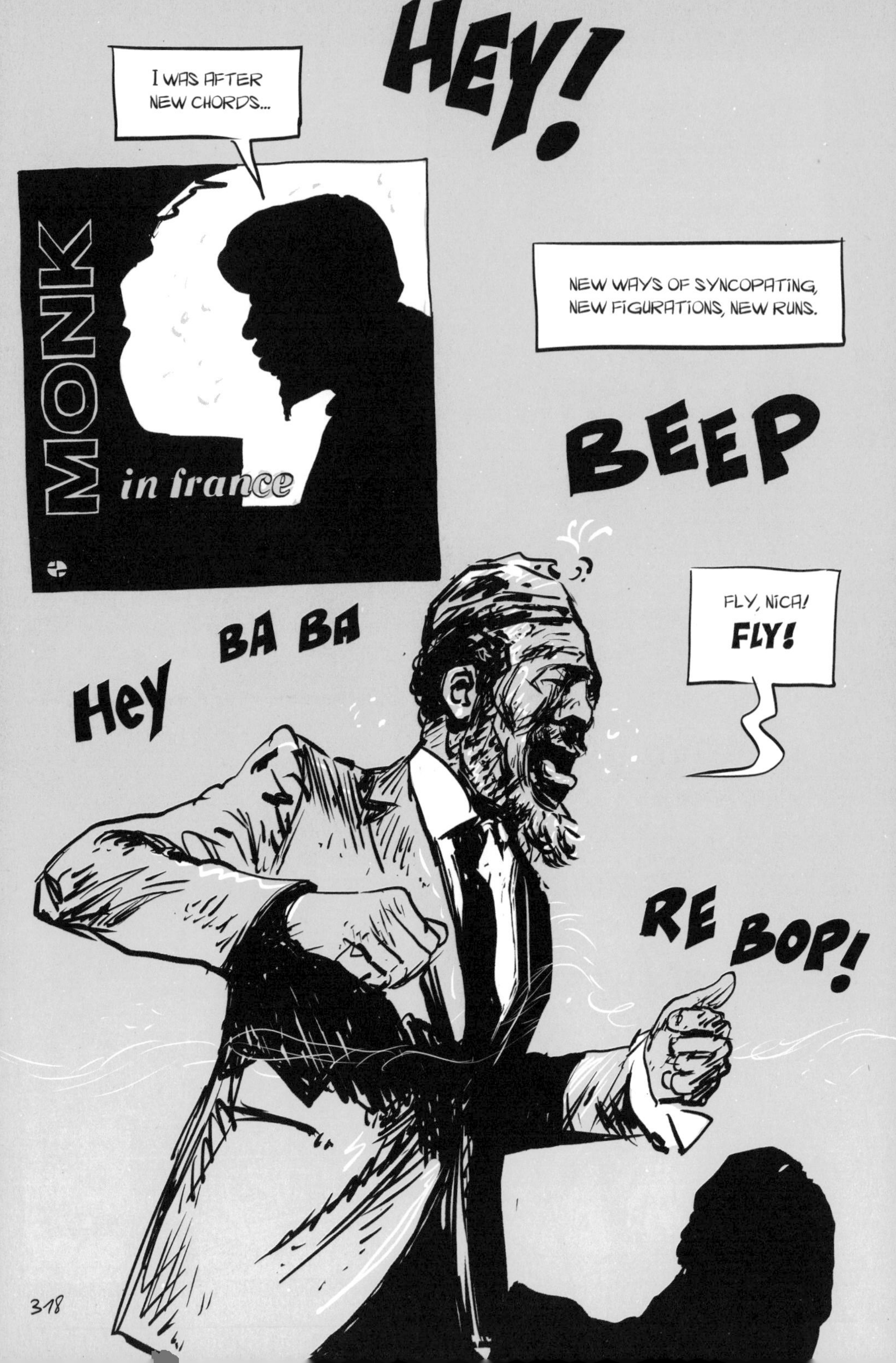
I WAS AFTER NEW CHORDS...
HEY!
MONK in france
NEW WAYS OF SYNCOPATING, NEW FIGURATIONS, NEW RUNS.
BEEP
Hey
BA BA
FLY, NICA! FLY!
RE
BOP!

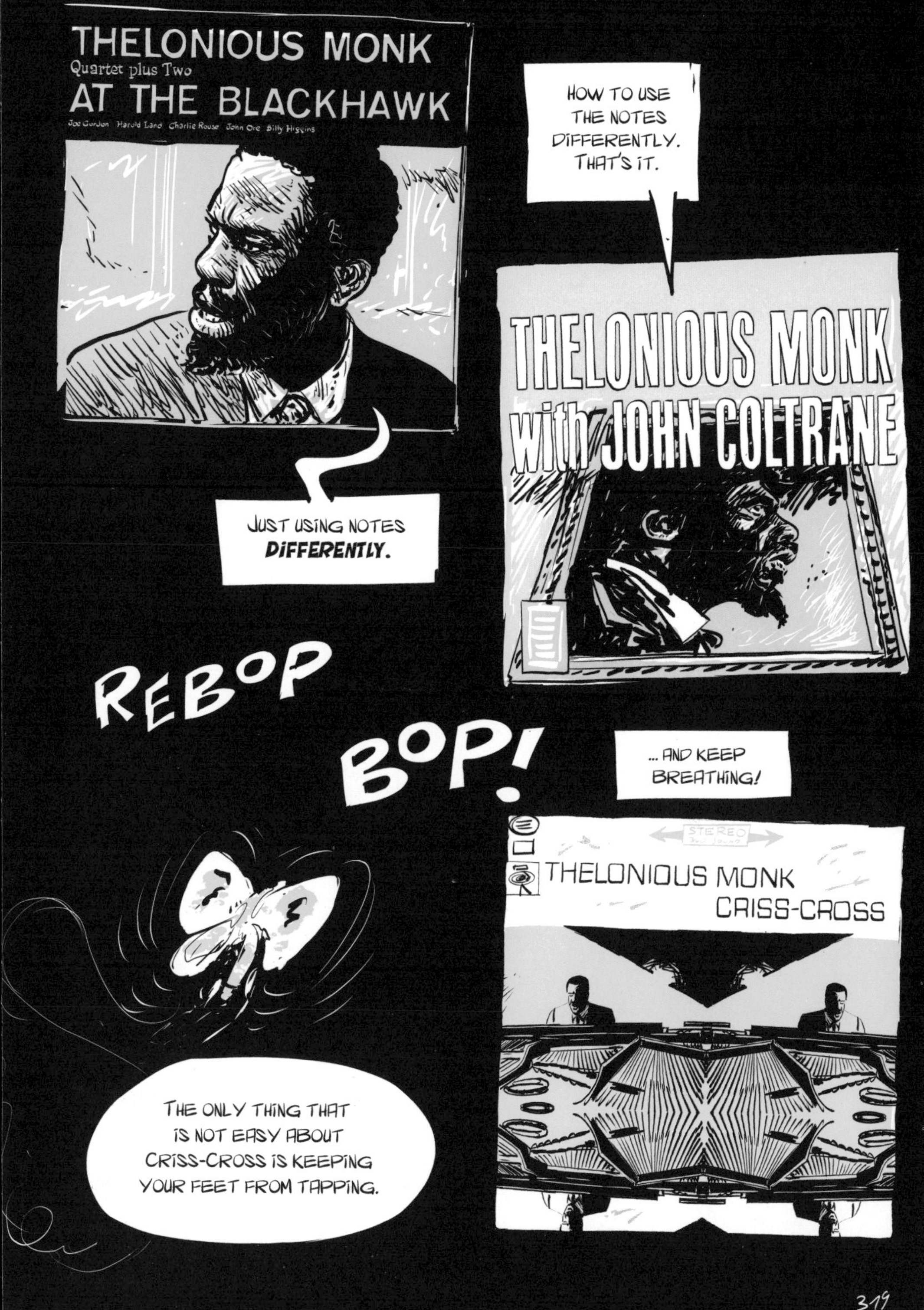
THELONIOUS MONK
Quartet plus Two
AT THE BLACKHAWK
Joe Gordon Harold Land Charlie Rouse John Ore Billy Higgins
HOW TO USE THE NOTES DIFFERENTLY. THAT'S IT.
THELONIOUS MONK with JOHN COLTRANE
JUST USING NOTES DIFFERENTLY.
REBOP
BOP!
... AND KEEP BREATHING!
STEREO
THELONIOUS MONK
CRISS-CROSS
THE ONLY THING THAT IS NOT EASY ABOUT CRISS-CROSS IS KEEPING YOUR FEET FROM TAPPING.

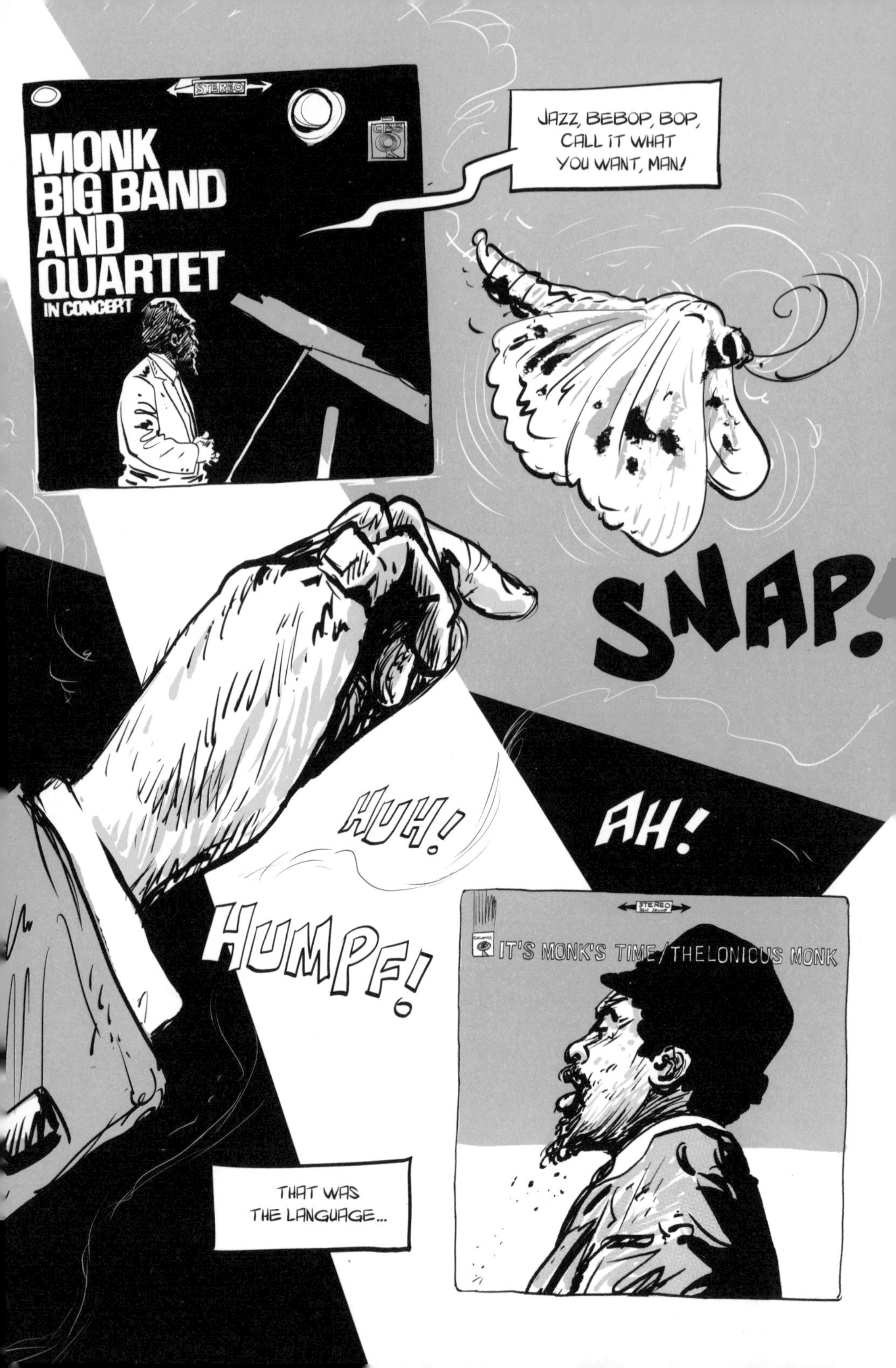
STEREO
MONK BIG BAND AND QUARTET IN CONCERT
JAZZ, BEBOP, BOP, CALL IT WHAT YOU WANT, MAN!
SNAP.
HUH!
AH!
HUMPF!
STEREO
IT'S MONK'S TIME / THELONIOUS MONK
THAT WAS THE LANGUAGE...

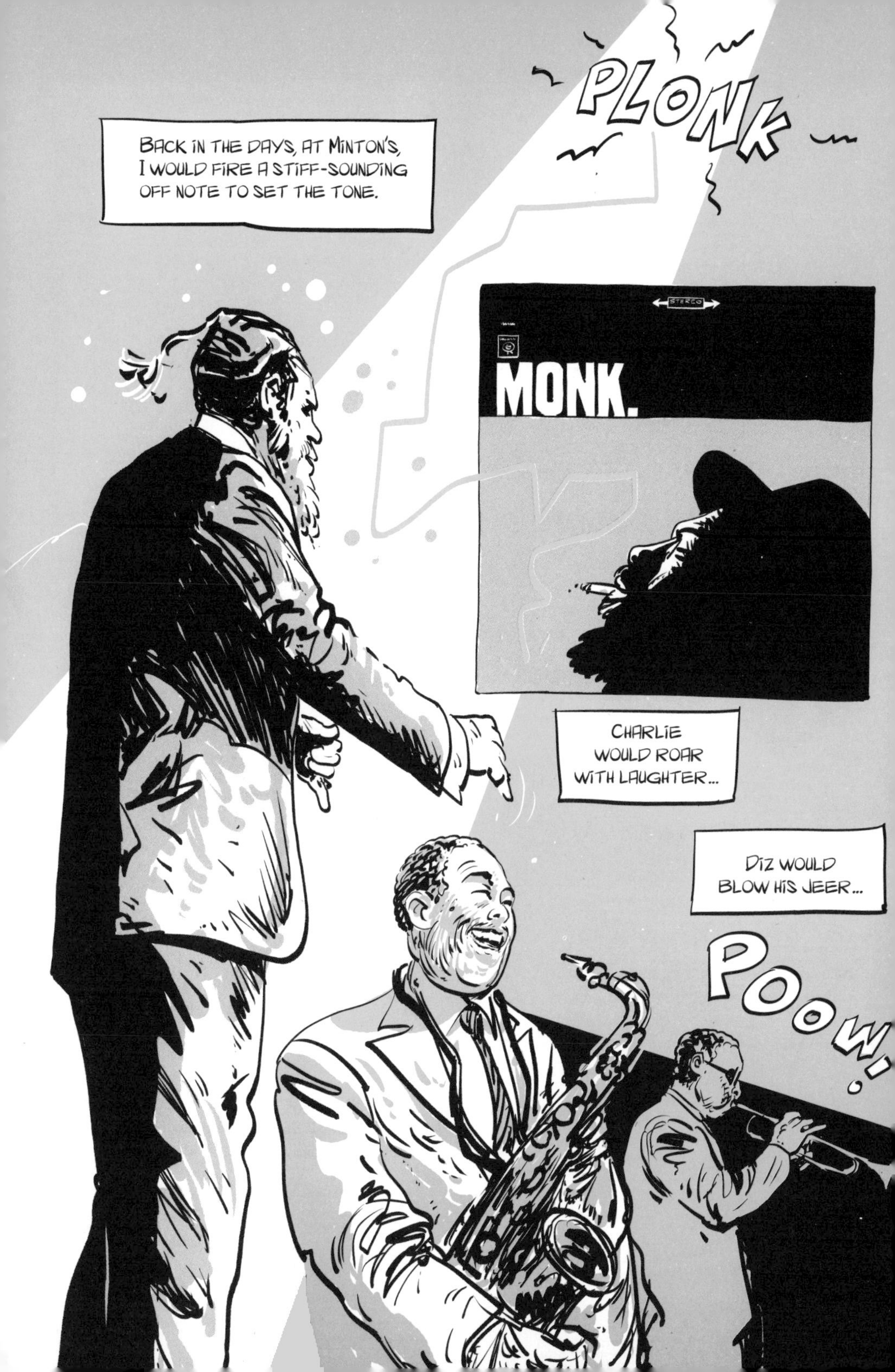
BACK IN THE DAYS, AT MINTON'S, I WOULD FIRE A STIFF-SOUNDING OFF NOTE TO SET THE TONE.
PLONK
STEREO
MONK.
CHARLIE WOULD ROAR WITH LAUGHTER...
DIZ WOULD BLOW HIS JEER...
POOW!

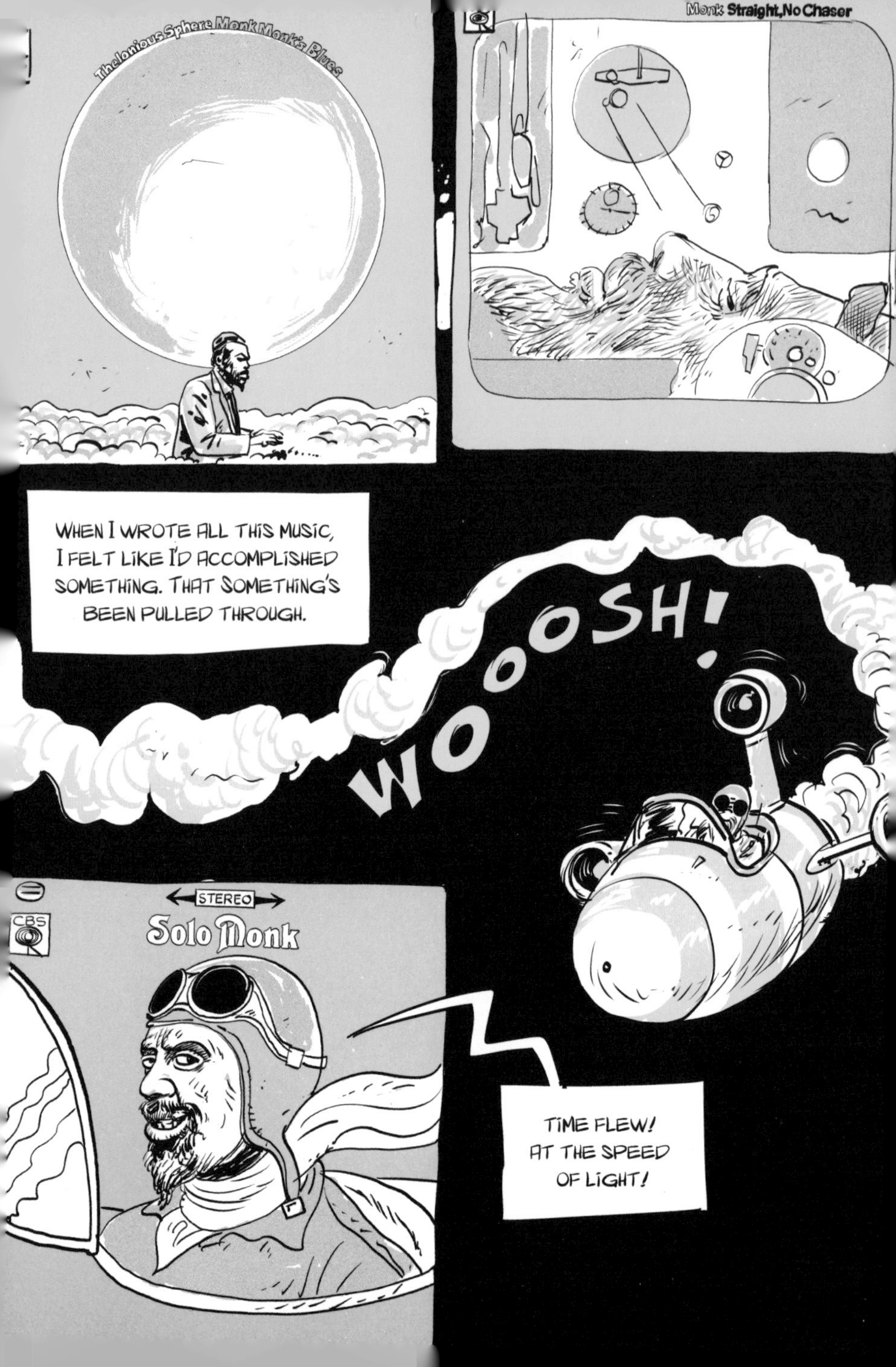
Thelonious Sphere Monk Monk's Blues
Monk Straight, No Chaser
WHEN I WROTE ALL THIS MUSIC, I FELT LIKE I'D ACCOMPLISHED SOMETHING. THAT SOMETHING'S BEEN PULLED THROUGH.
WOOOOSH!
STEREO
CBS
Solo Monk
TIME FLEW! AT THE SPEED OF LIGHT!

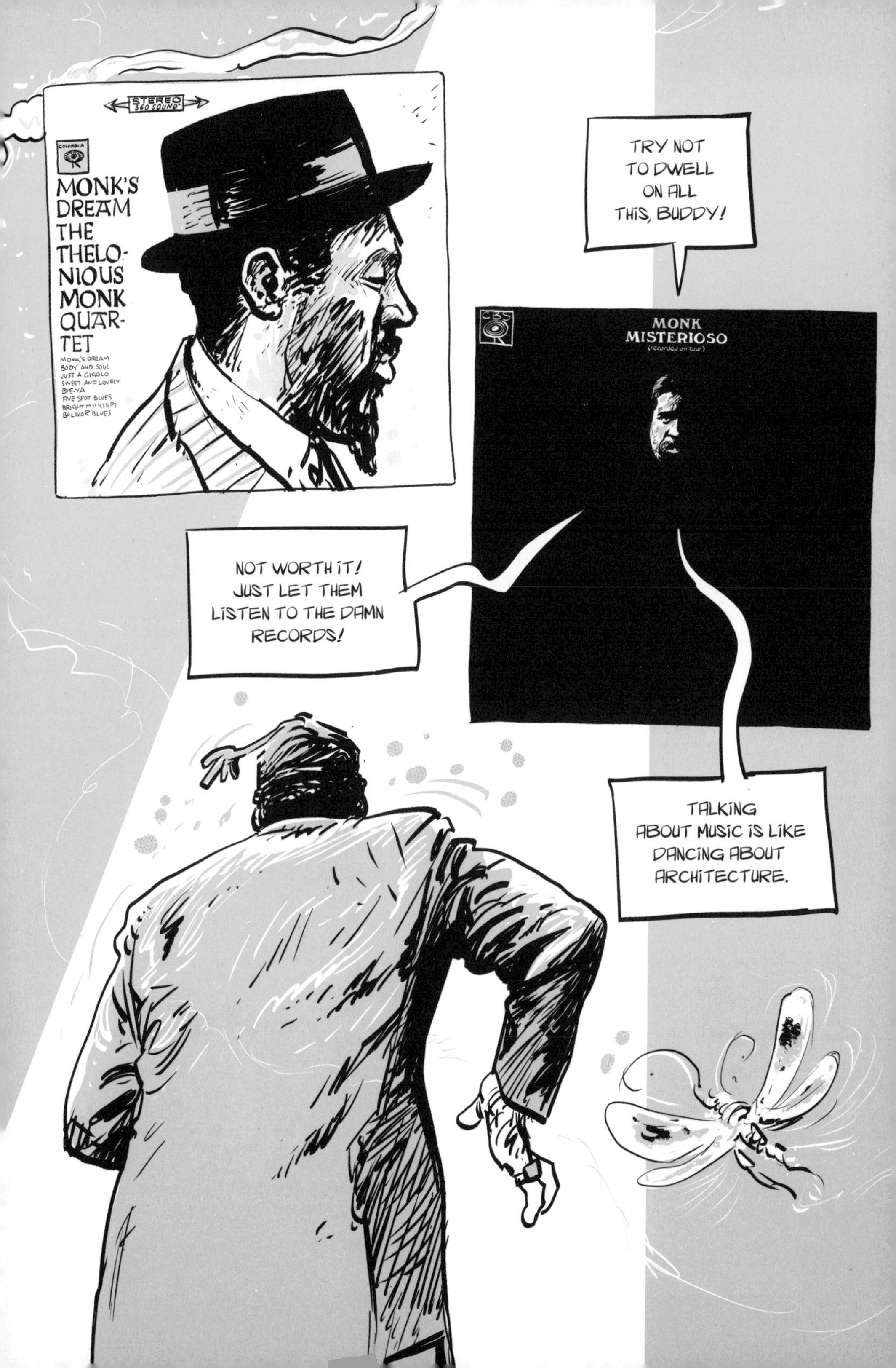
STEREO 360 SOUND
COLUMBIA
MONK'S DREAM THE THELONIOUS MONK QUARTET
MONK'S DREAM
BODY AND SOUL
JUST A GIGOLO
SWEET AND LOVELY
BYE-YA
FIVE SPOT BLUES
BRIGHT MISSISSIPPI
BOLIVAR BLUES
TRY NOT TO DWELL ON ALL THIS, BUDDY!
CBS
MONK MISTERIOSO
(recorded on tour)
NOT WORTH IT! JUST LET THEM LISTEN TO THE DAMN RECORDS!
TALKING ABOUT MUSIC IS LIKE DANCING ABOUT ARCHITECTURE.

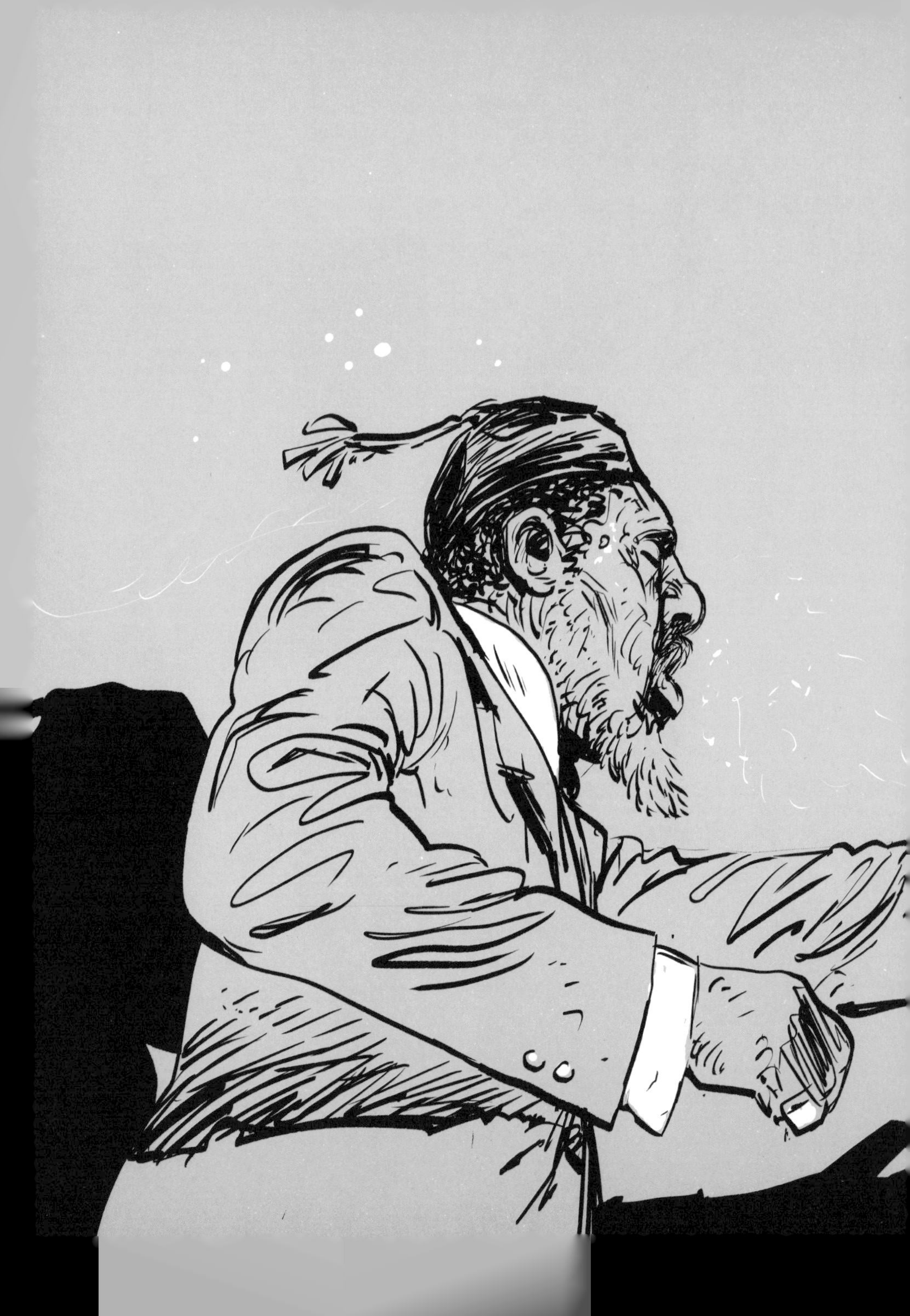

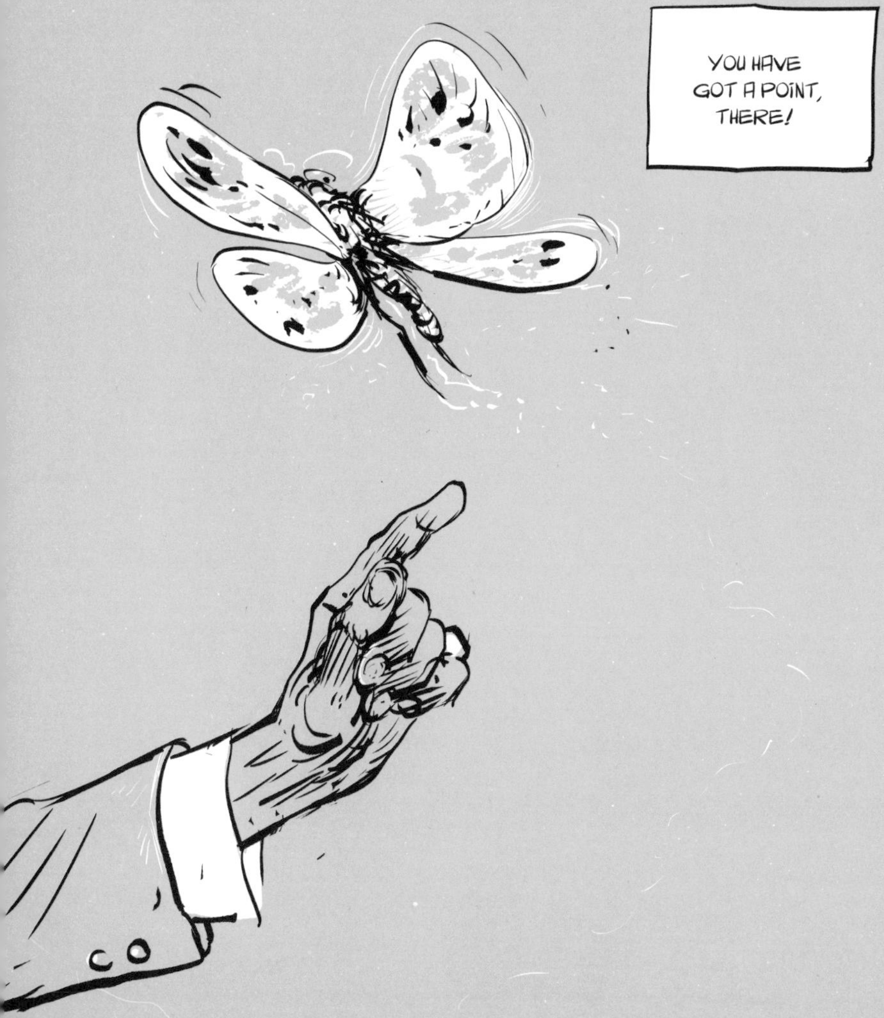
YOU HAVE GOT A POINT, THERE!

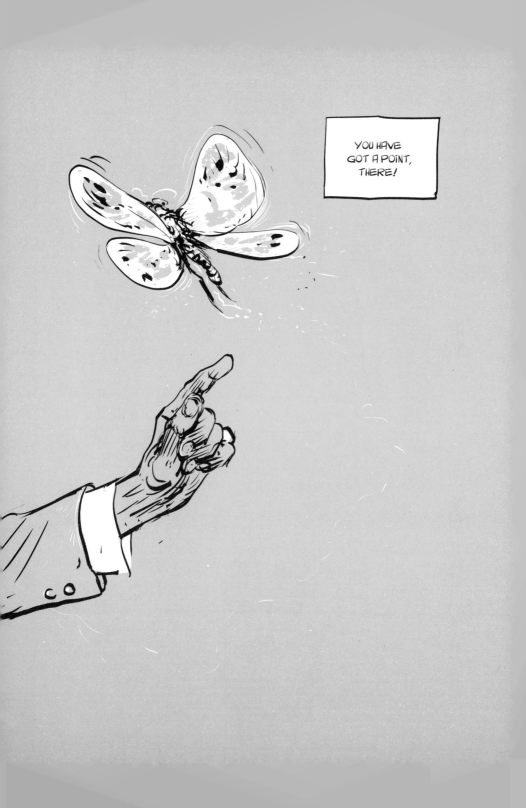

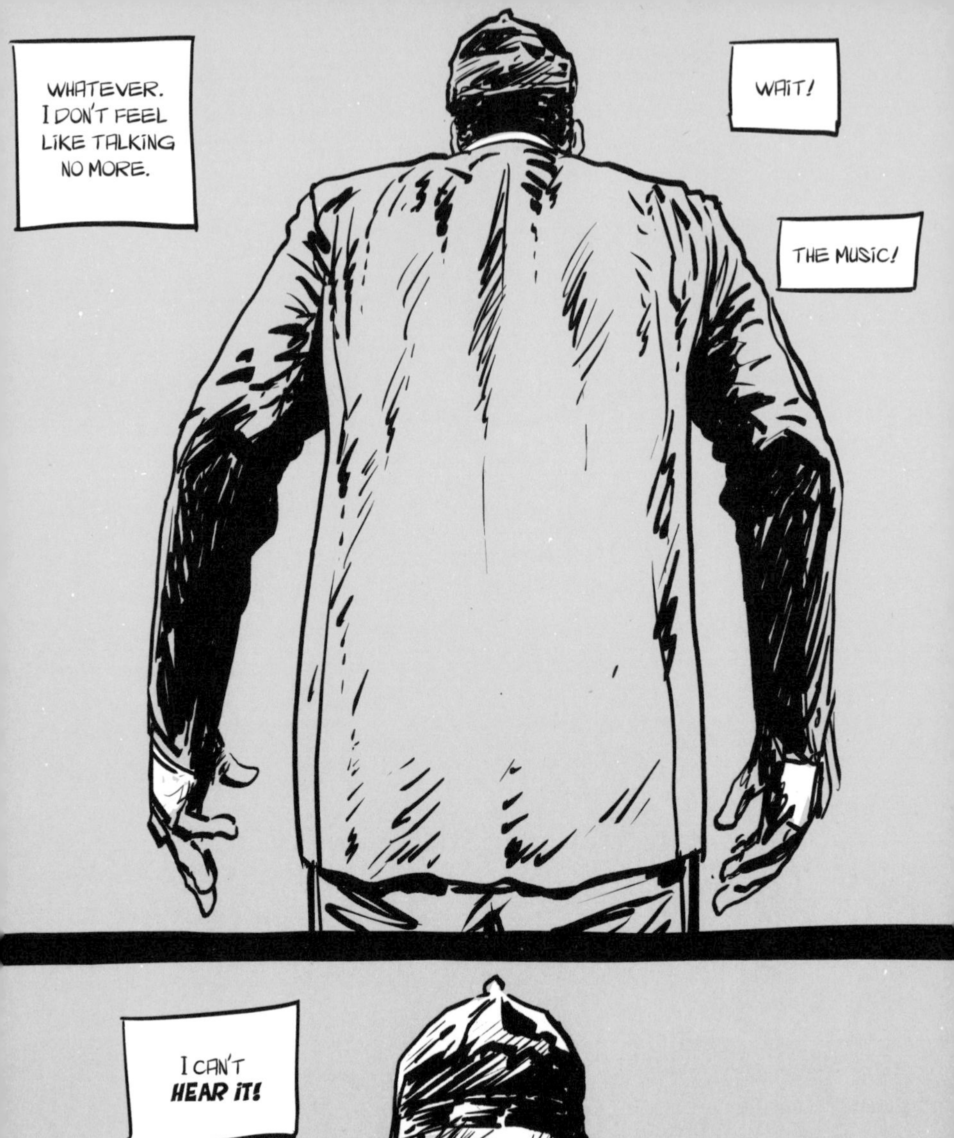
WHATEVER. I DON'T FEEL LIKE TALKING NO MORE.
WAIT!
THE MUSIC!

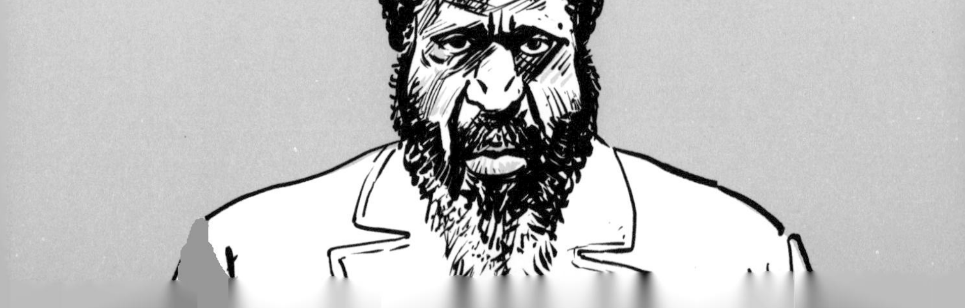
I CAN'T **HEAR IT!**

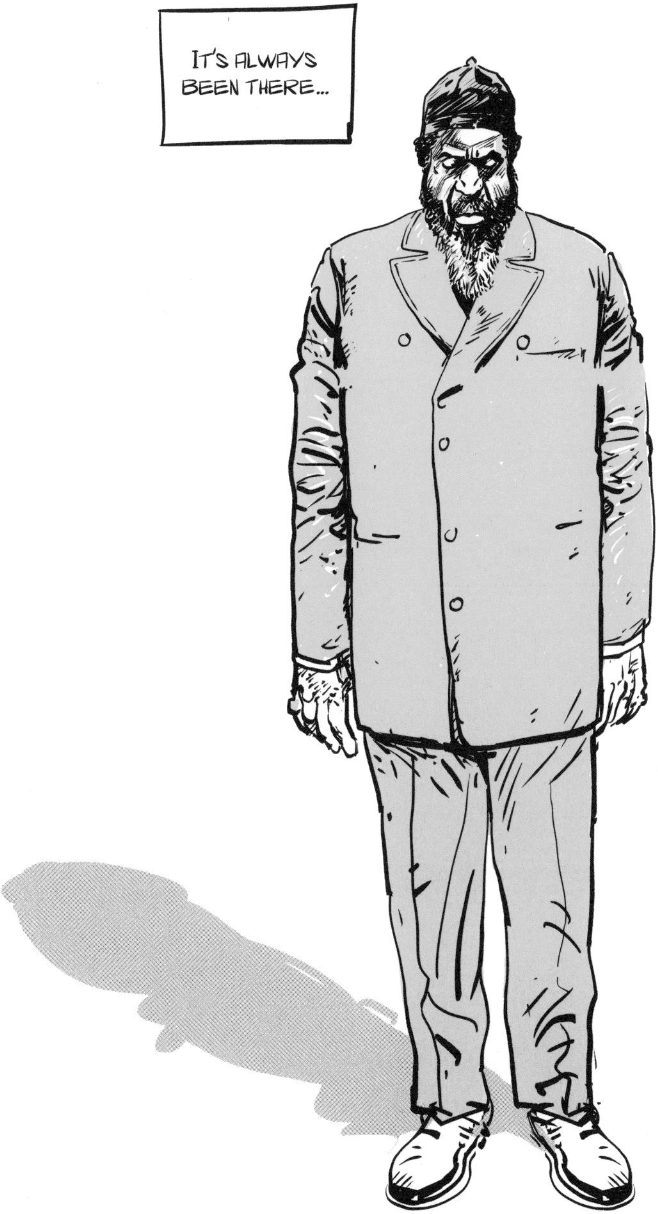
IT'S ALWAYS BEEN THERE...

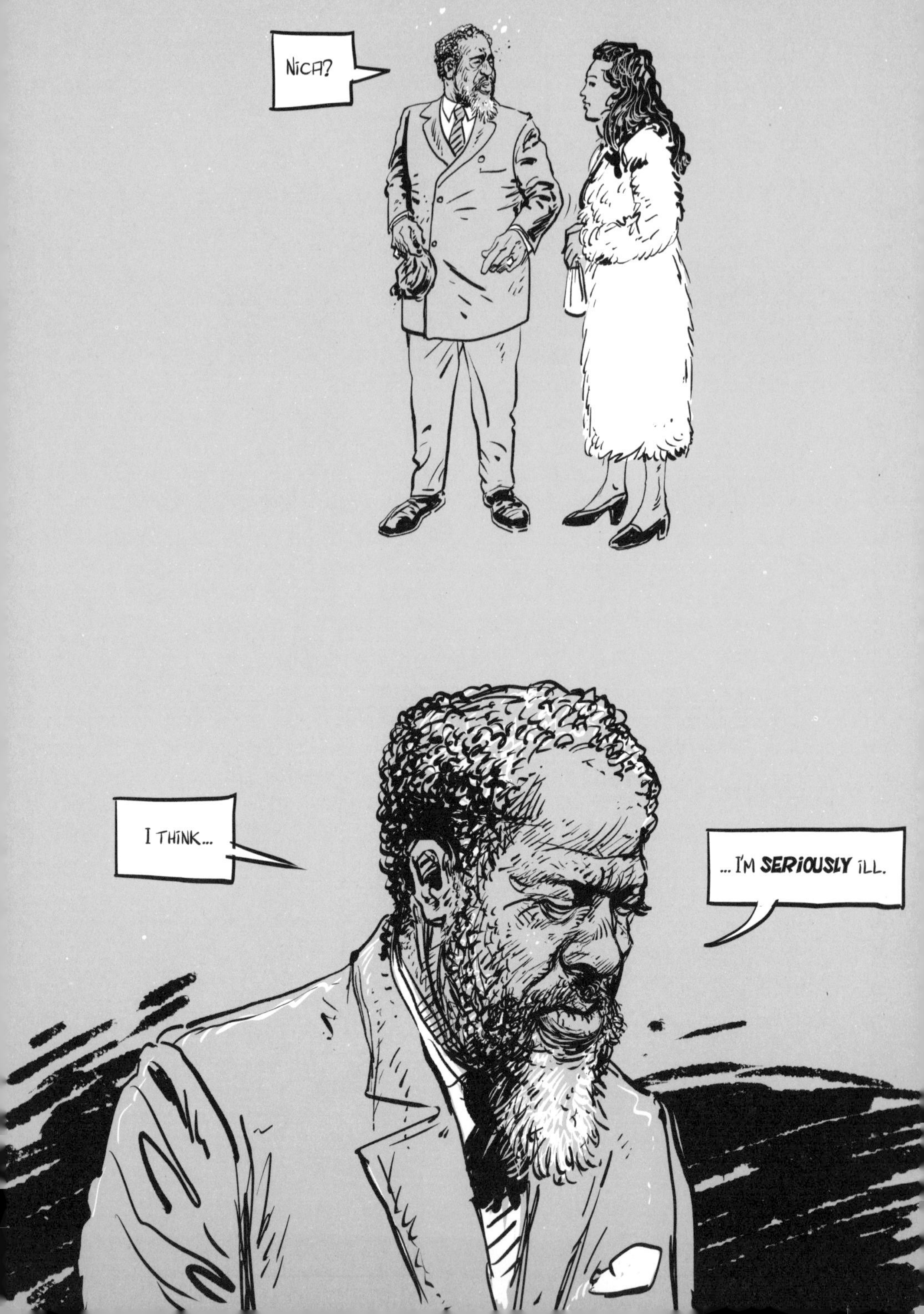
NICA?
I THINK...
... I'M SERIOUSLY ILL.

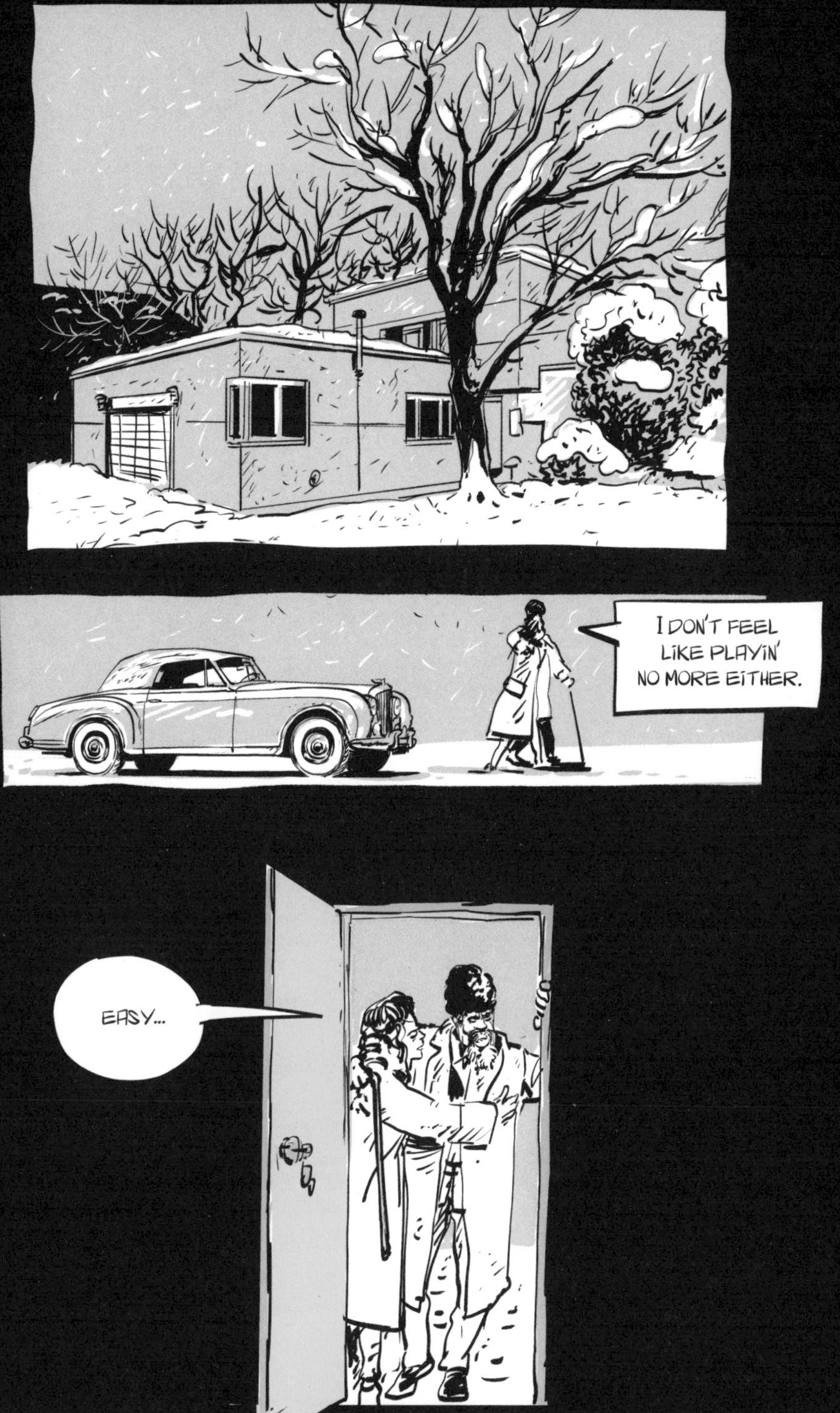
I DON'T FEEL LIKE PLAYIN' NO MORE EITHER.
EASY...

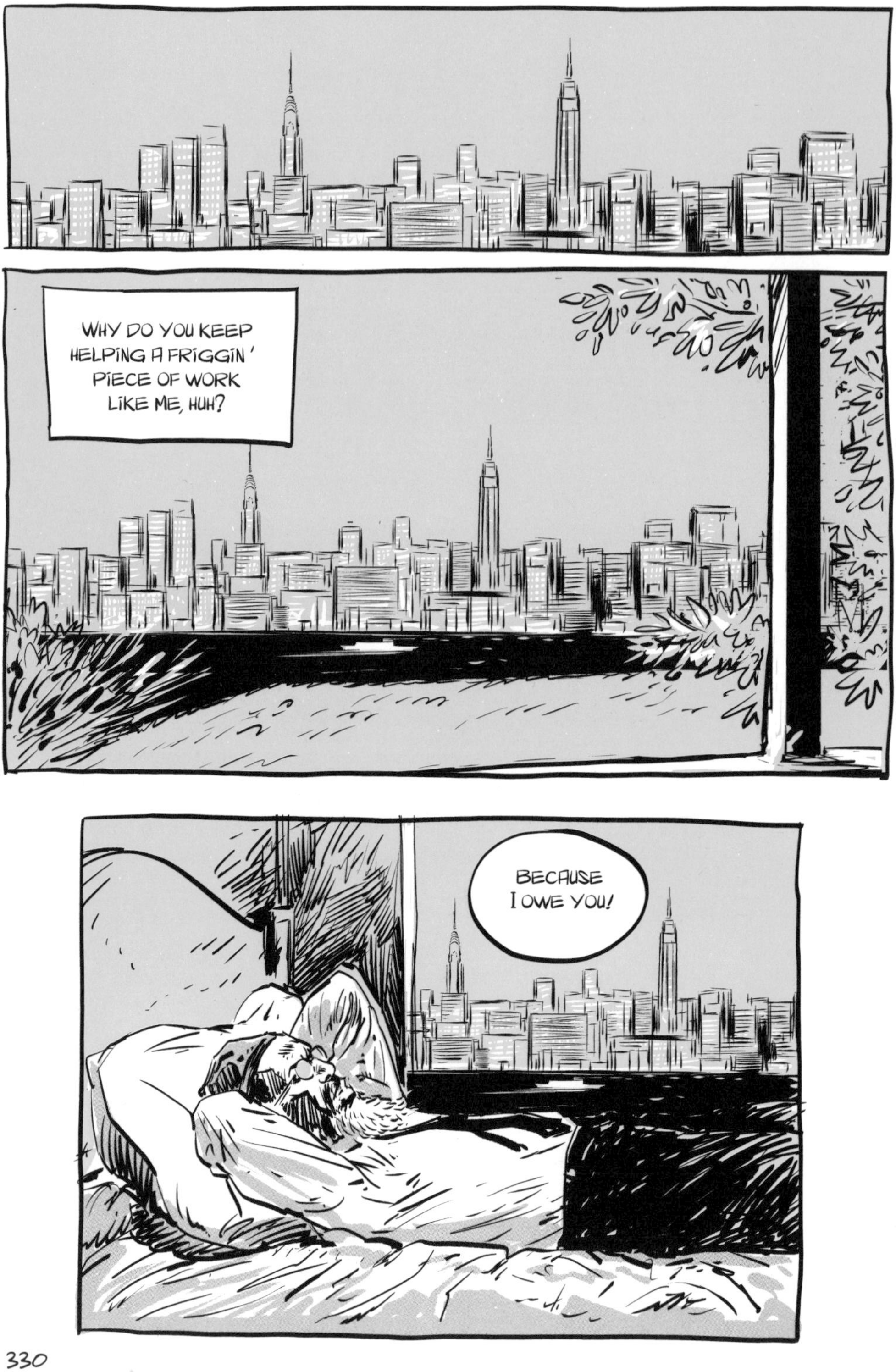
WHY DO YOU KEEP HELPING A FRIGGIN' PIECE OF WORK LIKE ME, HUH?
BECAUSE I OWE YOU!

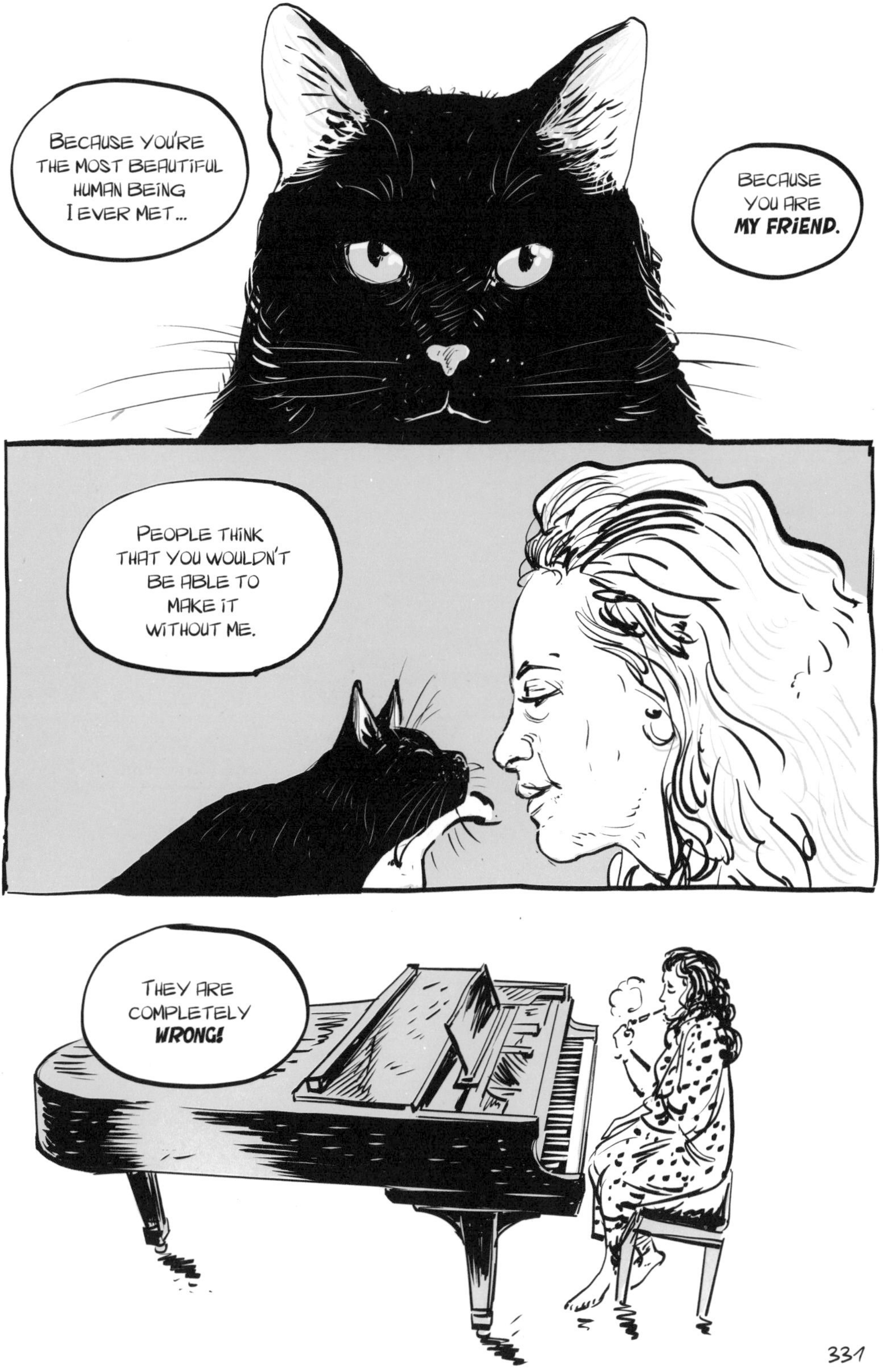

BECAUSE YOU'RE THE MOST BEAUTIFUL HUMAN BEING I EVER MET...
BECAUSE YOU ARE **MY FRIEND.**
PEOPLE THINK THAT YOU WOULDN'T BE ABLE TO MAKE IT WITHOUT ME.
THEY ARE COMPLETELY **WRONG!**

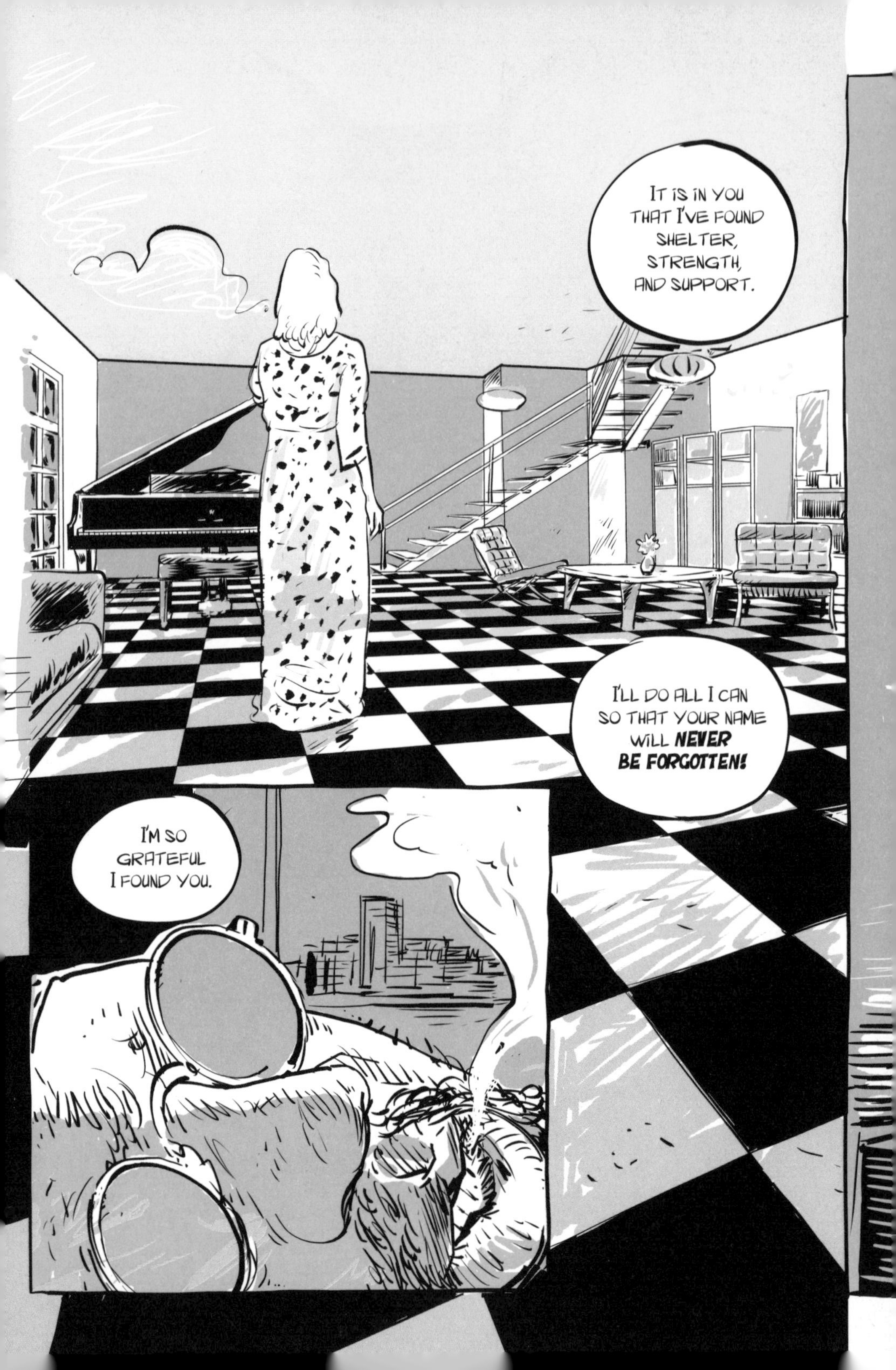
IT IS IN YOU THAT I'VE FOUND SHELTER, STRENGTH, AND SUPPORT.
I'LL DO ALL I CAN SO THAT YOUR NAME WILL **NEVER BE FORGOTTEN!**
I'M SO GRATEFUL I FOUND YOU.

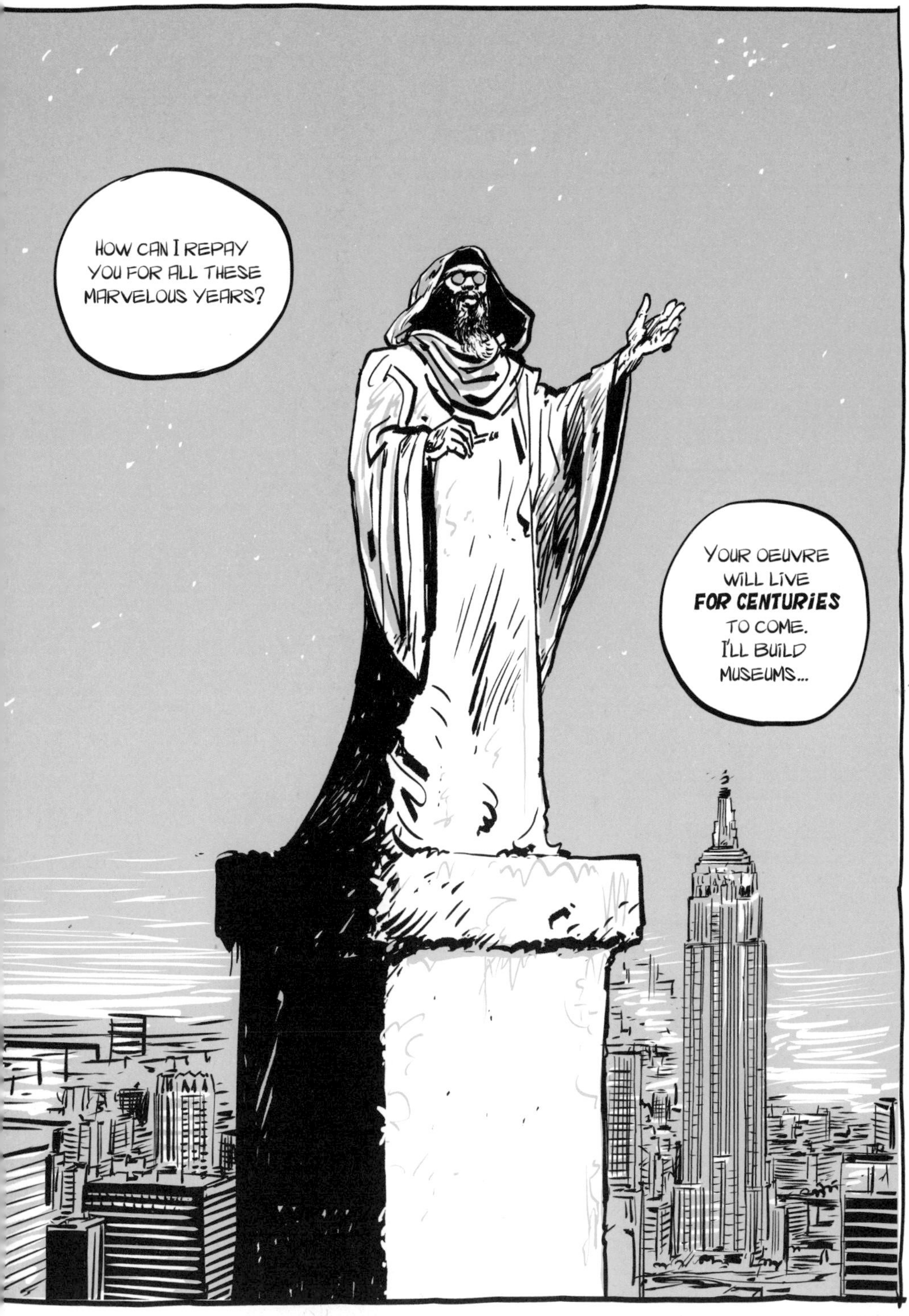
HOW CAN I REPAY YOU FOR ALL THESE MARVELOUS YEARS?
YOUR OEUVRE WILL LIVE **FOR CENTURIES** TO COME. I'LL BUILD MUSEUMS...

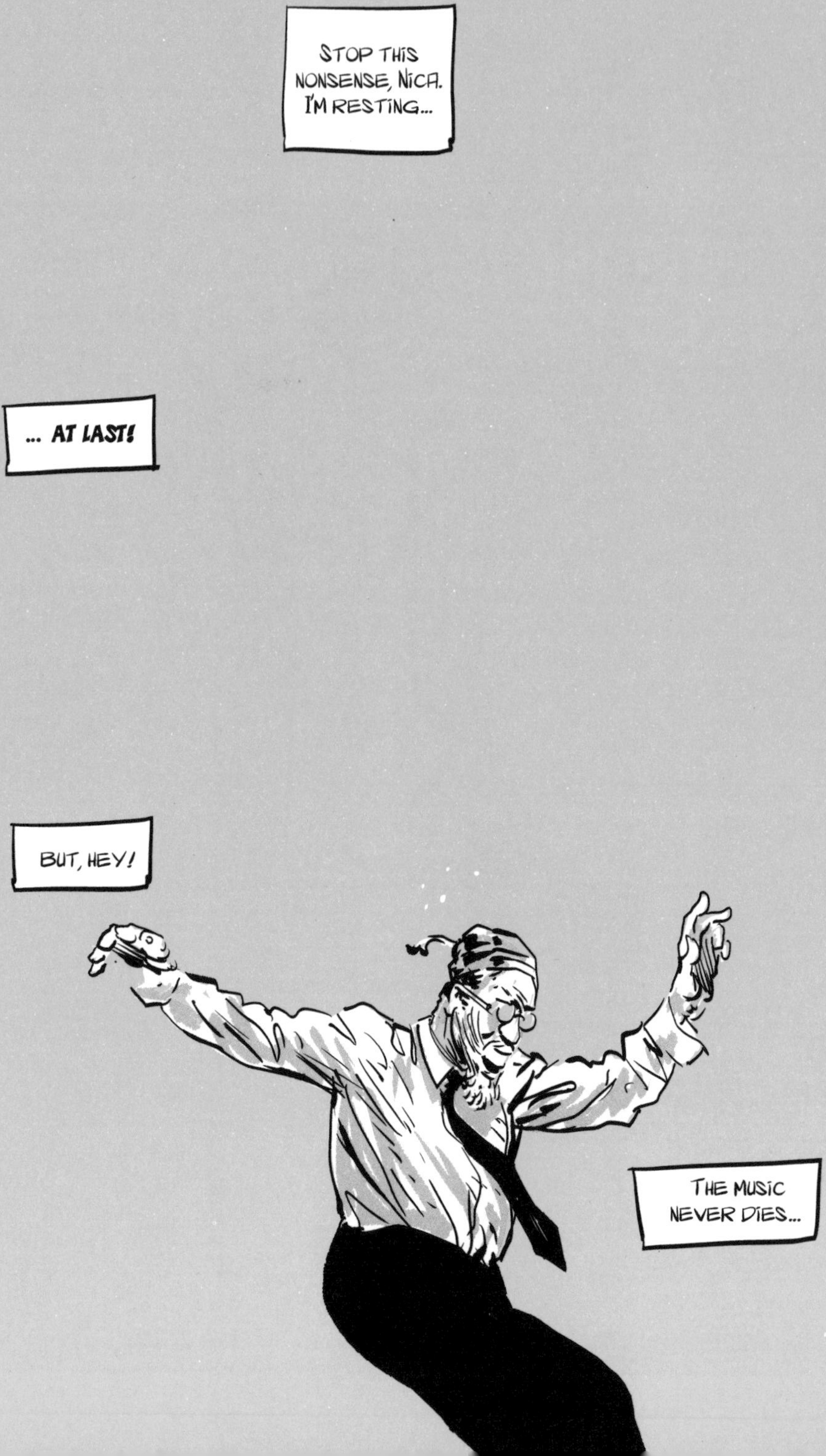
STOP THIS NONSENSE, NICA. I'M RESTING...
... AT LAST!
BUT, HEY!
THE MUSIC NEVER DIES...

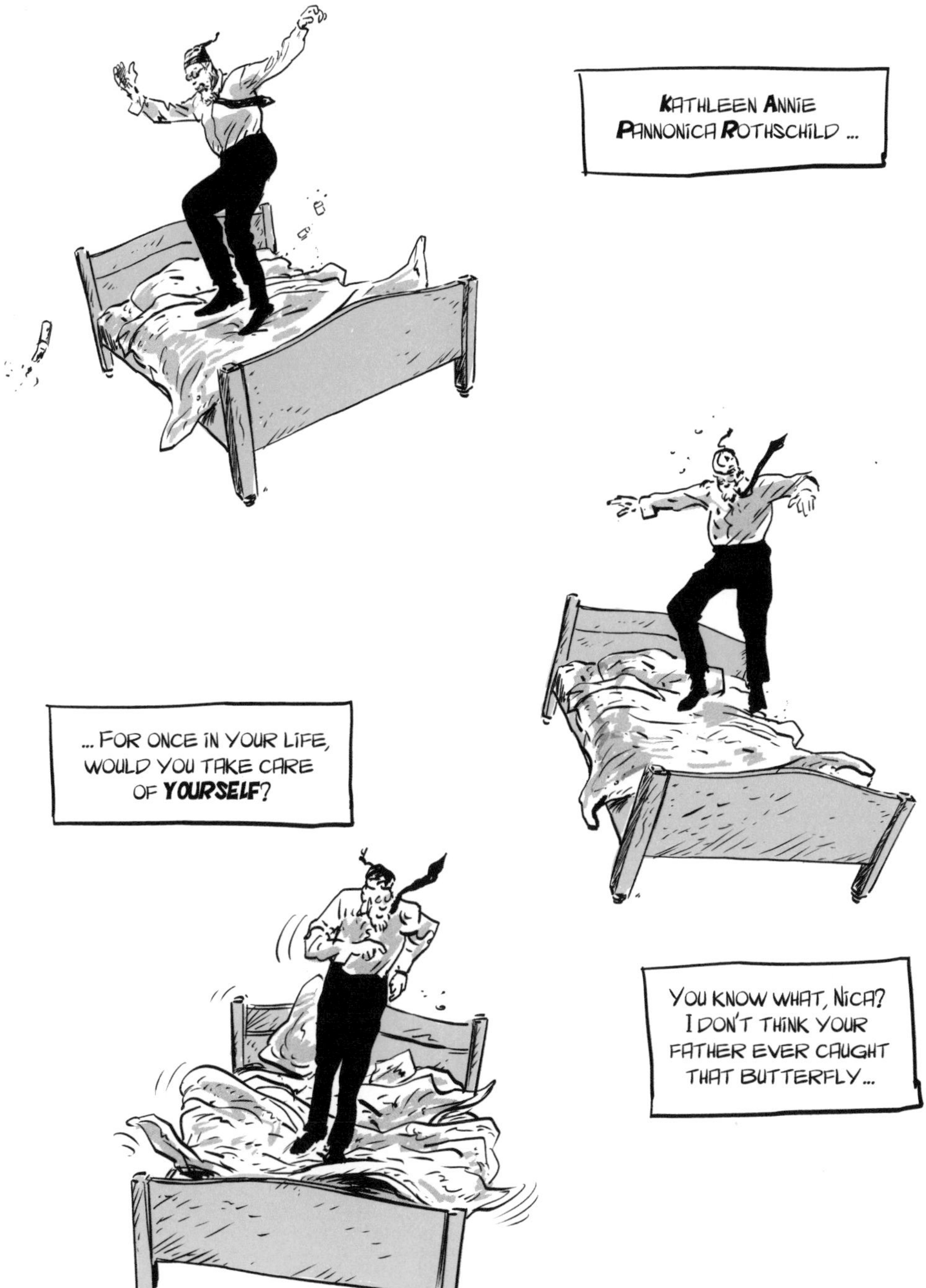
KATHLEEN ANNIE PANNONICA ROTHSCHILD ...
... FOR ONCE IN YOUR LIFE, WOULD YOU TAKE CARE OF **YOURSELF**?
YOU KNOW WHAT, NICA? I DON'T THINK YOUR FATHER EVER CAUGHT THAT BUTTERFLY...

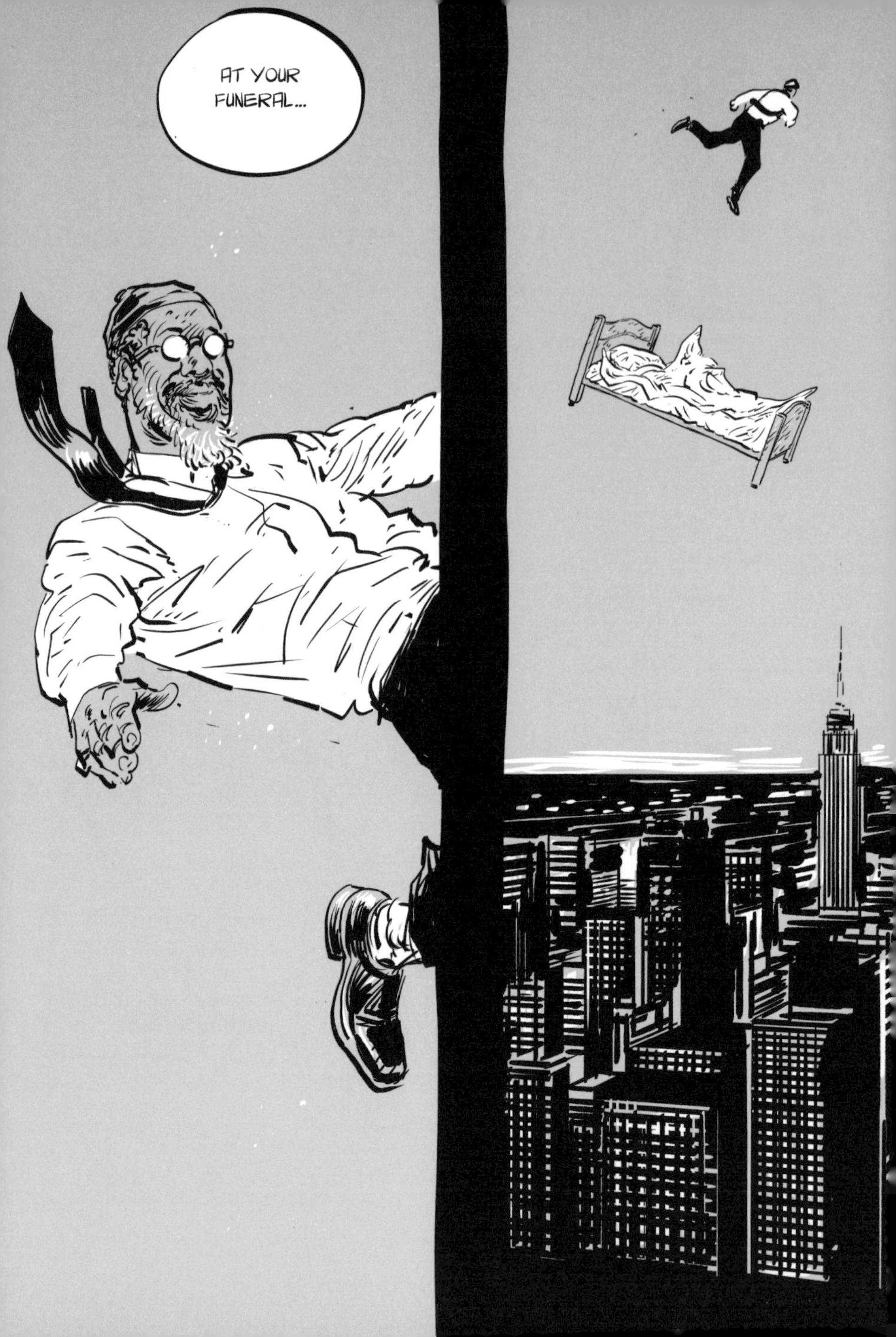
AT YOUR FUNERAL...

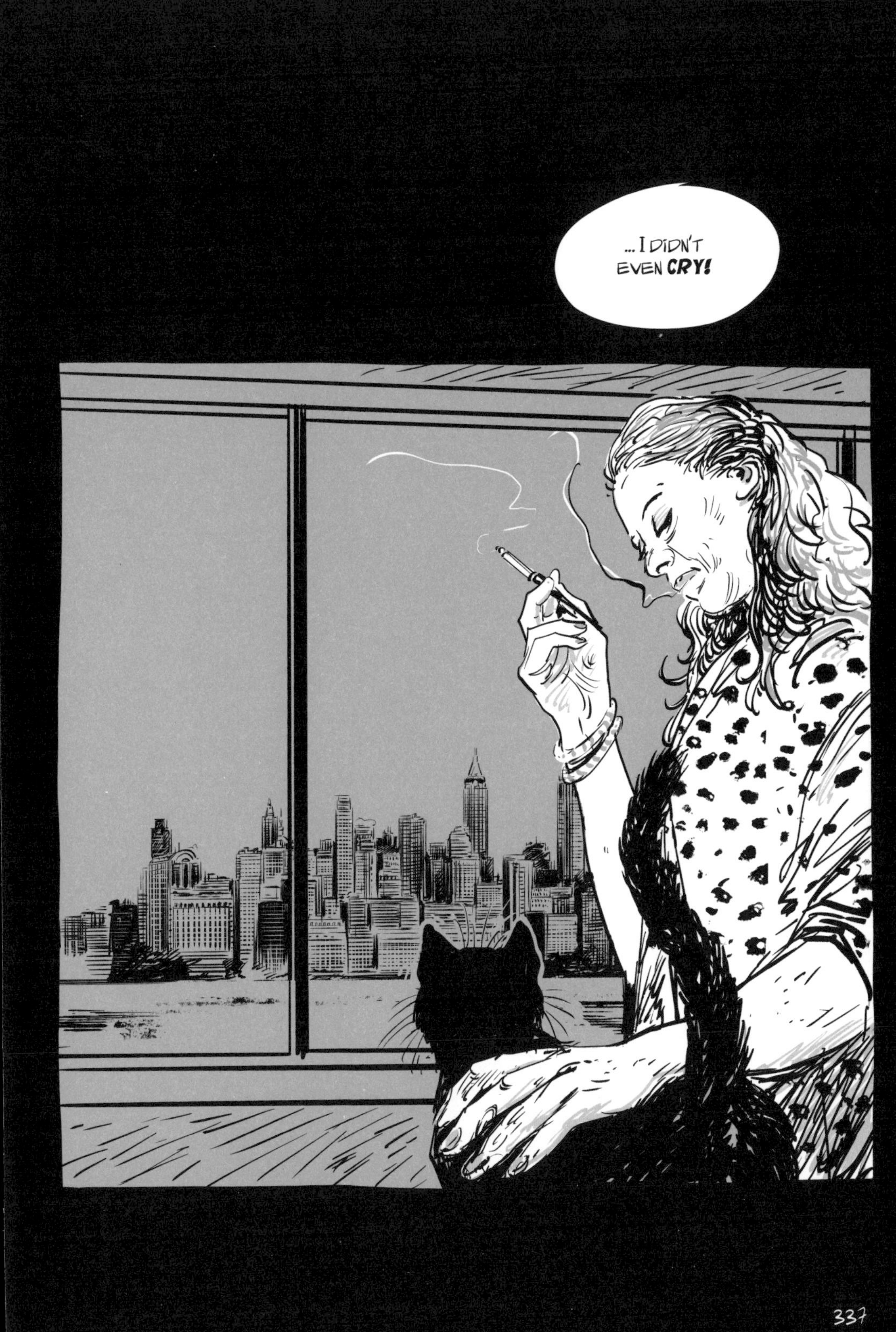
...I DIDN'T EVEN CRY!

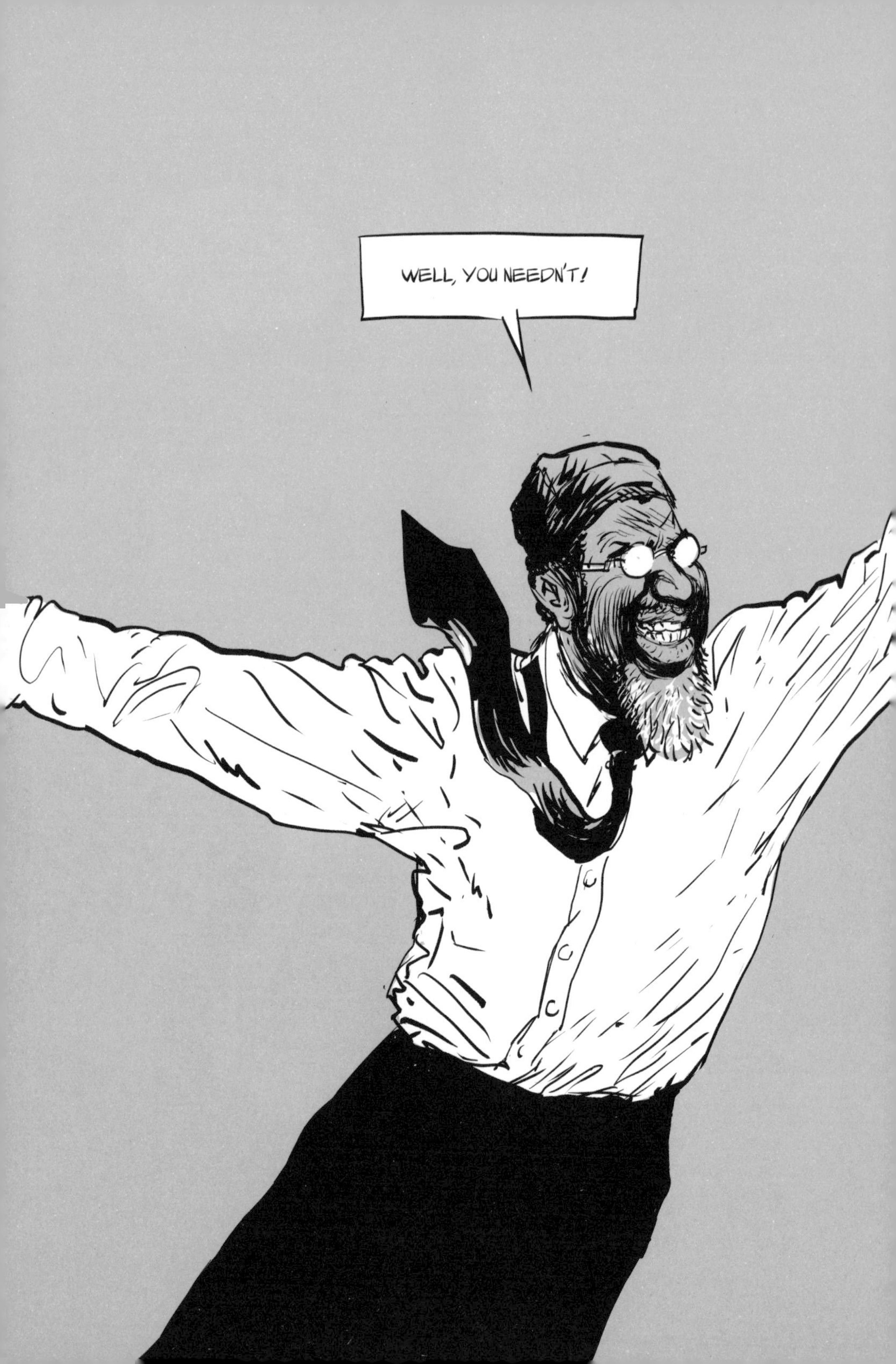
WELL, YOU NEEDN'T!

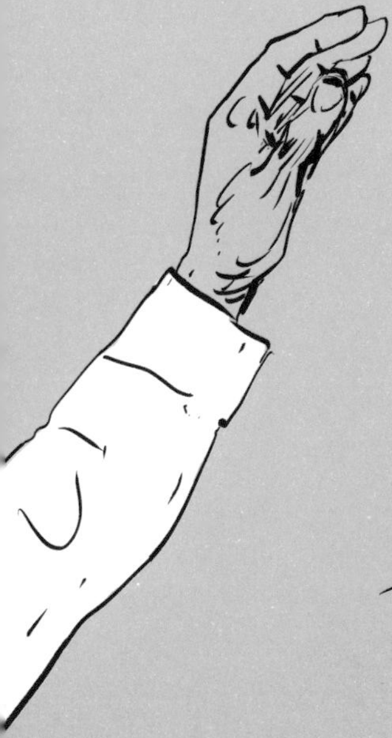

Thelonious Sphere Monk
1917-1982

Kathleen Annie Pannonica Rothschild
1913-1988

DAOUDI

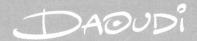

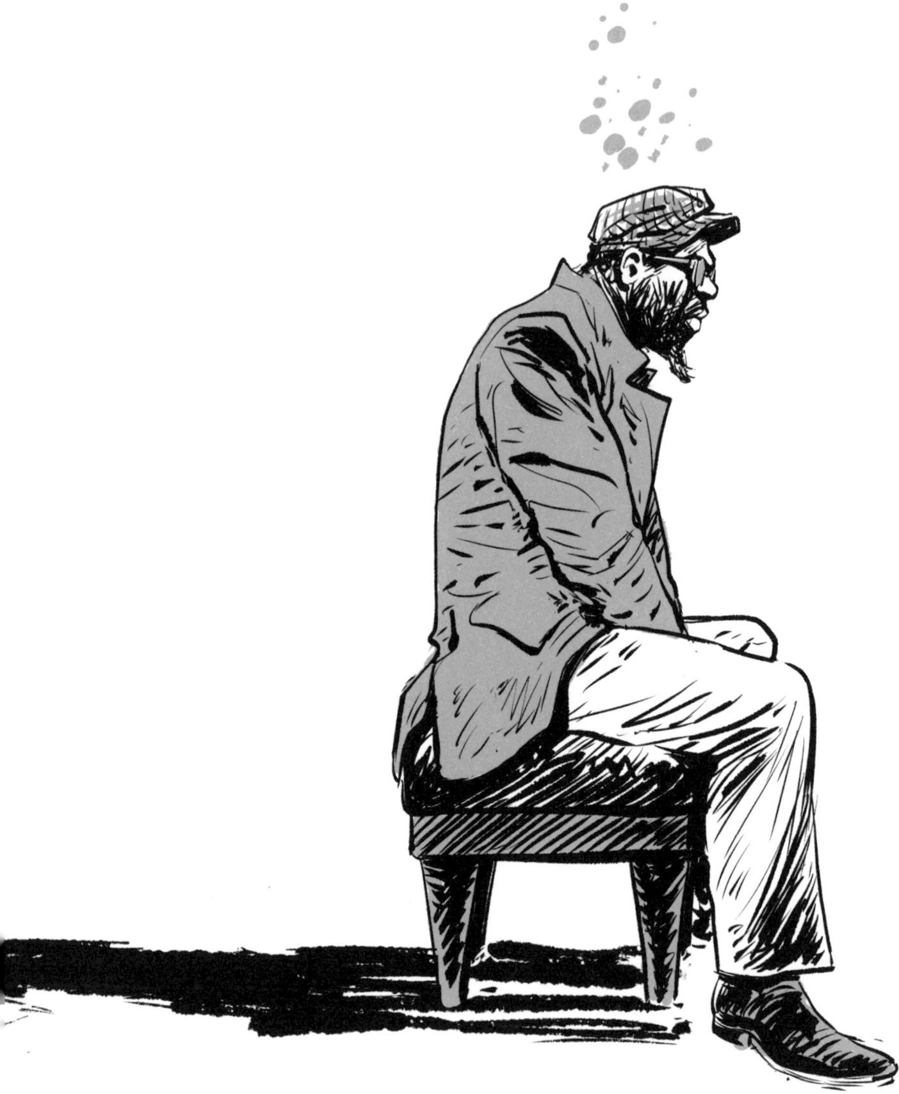

ORIGINS

Reflecting back on my early days as a cartoonist, I realize how Monk's music, spirit, and creativity inspired me during those long hours of reflection, writing, sketching, penciling, and inking. At that time, the idea of a graphic novel about Monk didn't occur to me, even though his music was teaching me so much.

Years later, when my wife and I visited New York, we went to see jazz pianist McCoy Tyner in concert. I was amazed that this legend, who needed assistance to walk to the piano, played like a young man! I realized that there was something about the air in this city. Jazz is New York, and New York is jazz.

My starting point for this story was the very special friendship between Nica de Koenigswarter and Thelonious Monk. Since the book was to focus on jazz, I wanted the style to reflect that, with a little melody and a lot of improvisation.

Jazz has saved my life, or at least, my sanity. The very fact that some cats could produce such dazzling music gave me hope for humanity. And one of the most beautiful examples of that is the work and life of Thelonious Sphere Monk.

— Youssef Daoudi

BIBLIOGRAPHY

BOOKS

Kastin, David. *Nica's Dream*. New York: W. W. Norton & Company, Inc., 2011.

Kelley, Robin G. *Thelonious Monk: The Life and Times of an American Original*. New York: Free Press, 2009.

Rothschild, Hannah. *The Baroness: The Search for Nica, the Rebellious Rothschild*. New York: Vintage Books, 2014.

De Wilde, Laurent. *Monk*. Translated by Jonathan Dickinson. New York: Marlowe & Company, 1997.

ARTICLES & JOURNALS

Brown, Frank London. "A Profile of Thelonious Monk: Exploring the Life of the Influential Jazzman." *Down Beat* (September 1958).

Clouzet, Jean, and Michel Delorme. "L' Amertume du Prophète." *Jazz Magazine* 93, no. 9 (1963): 39.

Givan, Benjamin. "Thelonious Monk's Pianism." *Journal of Musicology* 26, no. 3 (2009): 404–442.

Gonzales, Pearl. "Monk Talk." *Down Beat* (October 1971).

Monson, Ingrid. "Monk meets SNCC." *Black Music Research Journal* 19, no. 2 (1999): 187–200.

PLAYLIST

Thelonious Monk: Genius Modern Music vol. 1, Blue Note Records (1951)
Thelonious Monk: Genius Modern Music vol. 2, Blue Note Records (1952)
  Monk's Blue Note sessions recorded in 1947, 1951, and 1952

Brilliant Corners, Riverside Records (1957)
  Recorded in late 1956

Thelonious Monk with John Coltrane, Jazzland Records (1961)
  Recorded in three sessions in 1957

Monk in Tokyo, CBS/Sony Records (1973)
  A live album recorded on May 21, 1963

Readings by Jack Kerouac on The Beat Generation, Verve Records (1960)

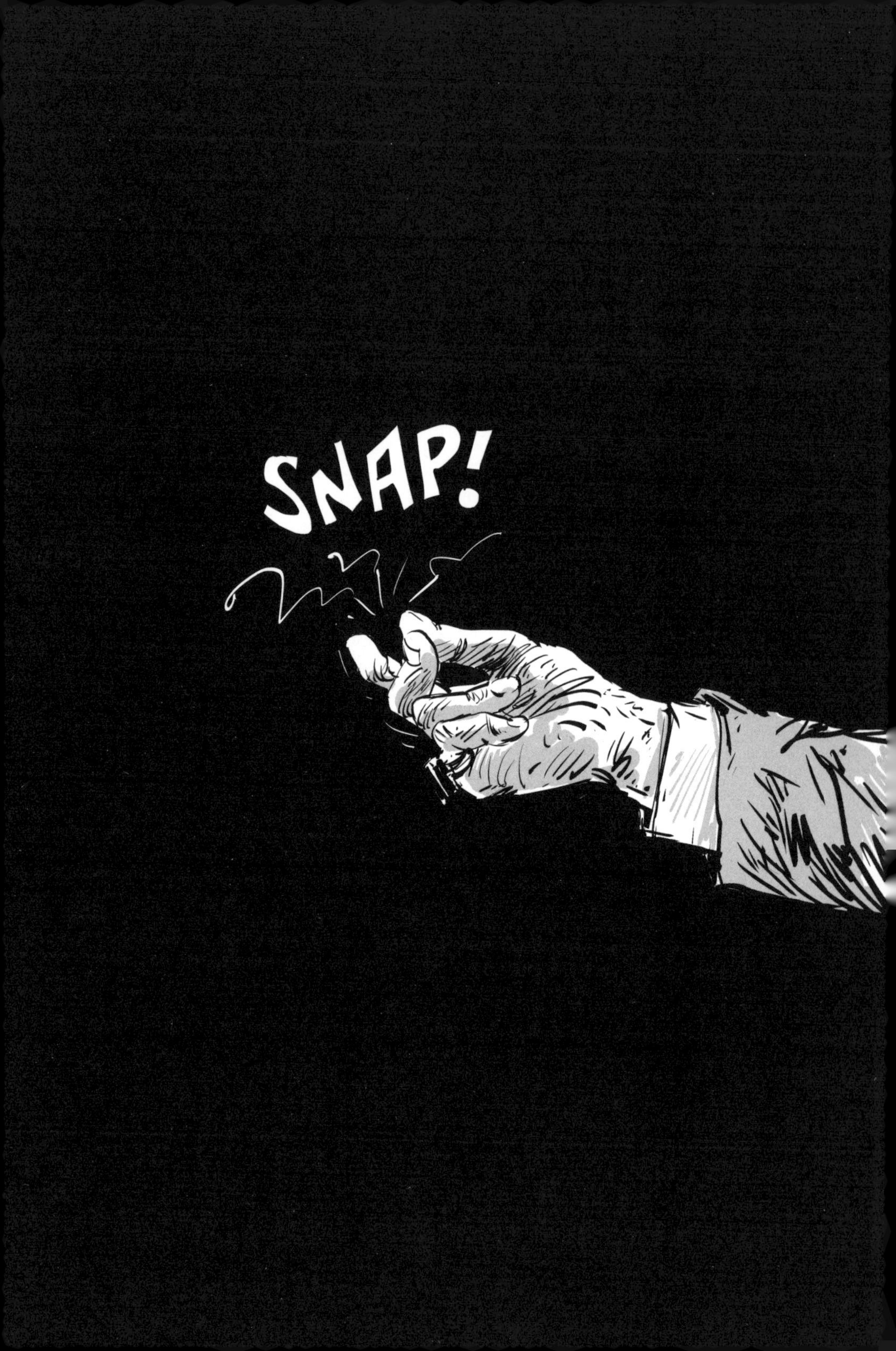
SNAP!

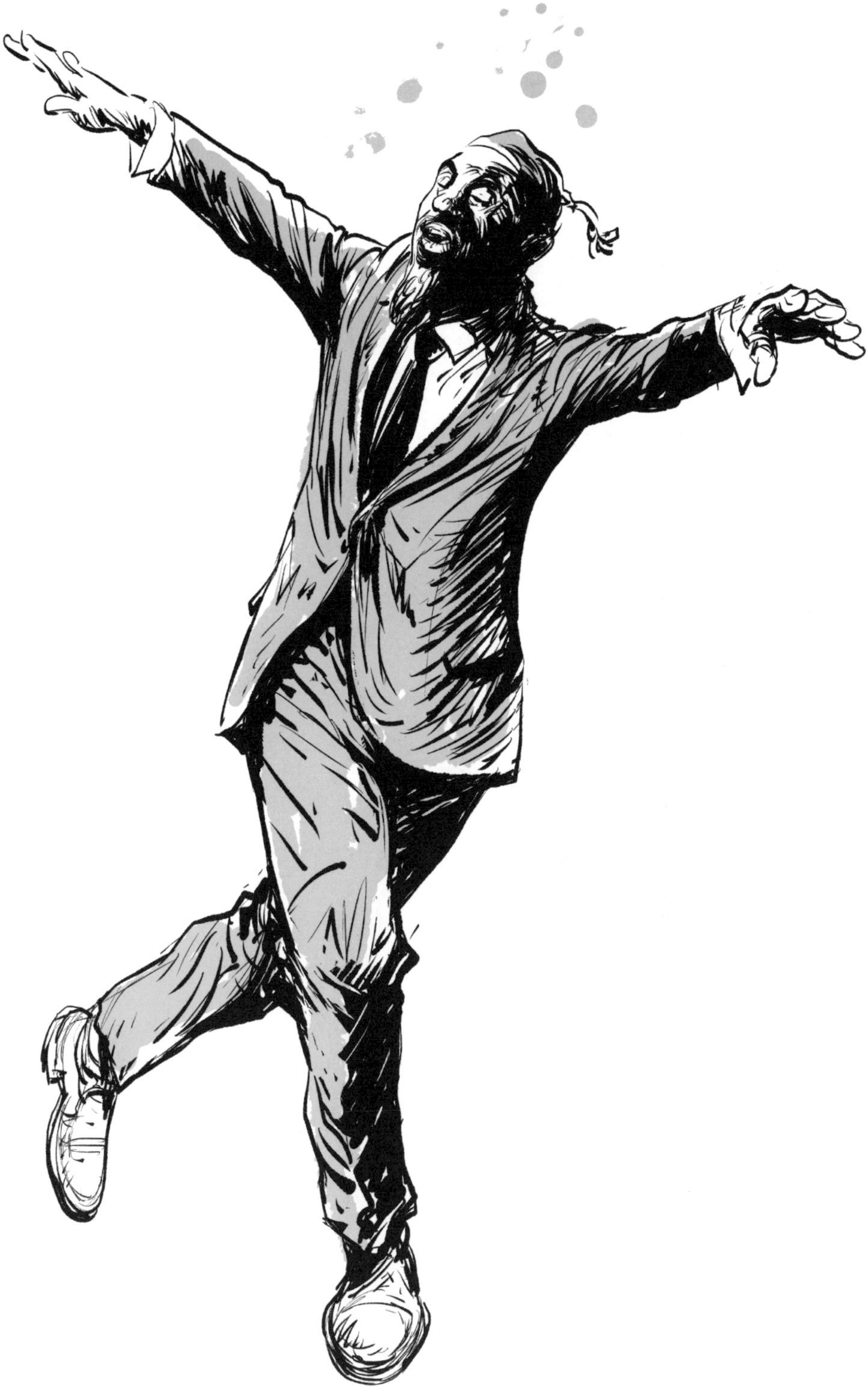

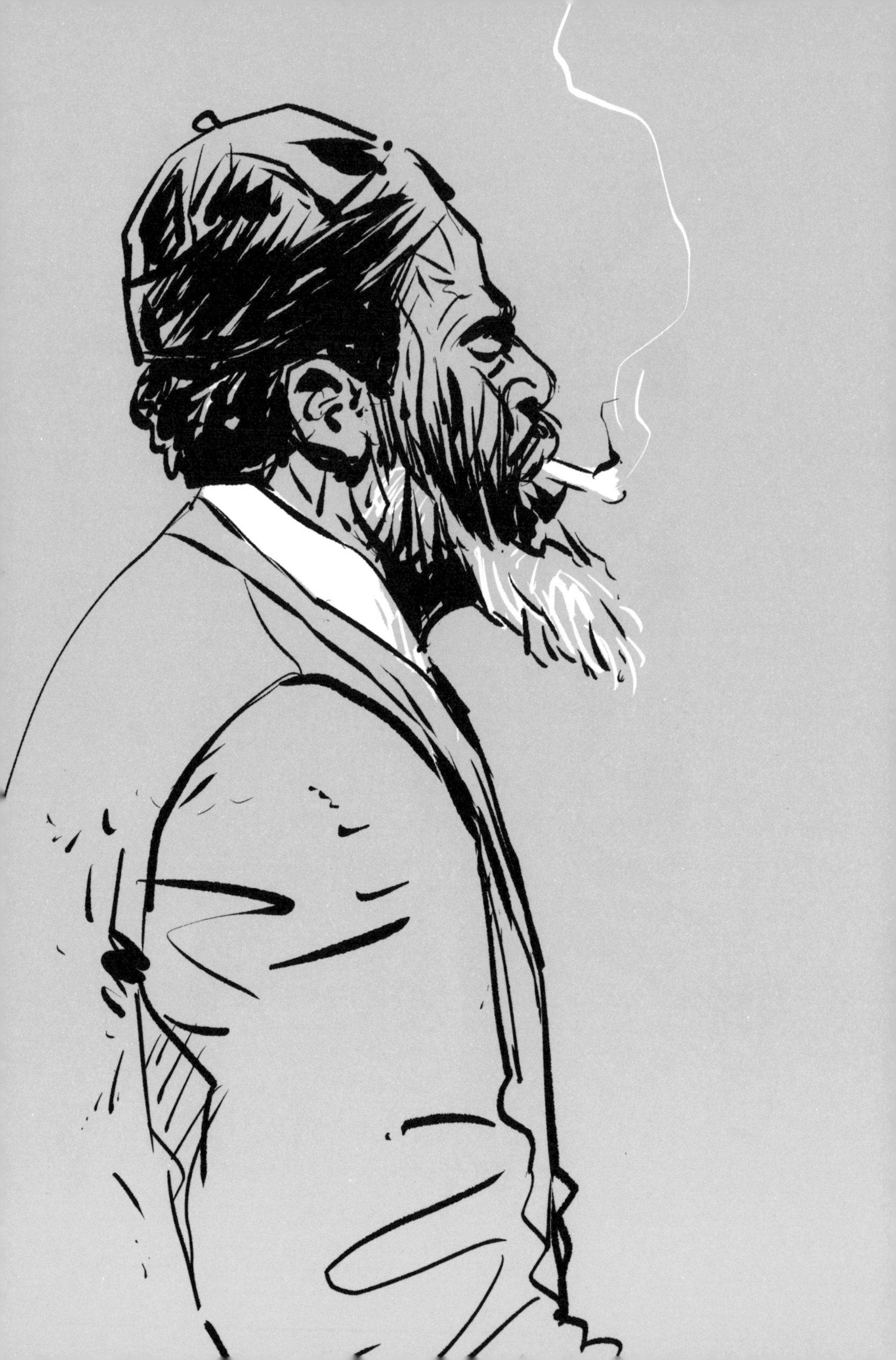

Thanks to Mark Siegel, Fabien Laze, Igor Olafs,
and Antoine Maurel for their help and support.

Youssef Daoudi is a comic artist and illustrator
living in France. He worked as an art director for
multinational advertising firms for fifteen years
before committing himself to writing and drawing
graphic novels. He is an avid traveler, and New York
is one of the most inspiring cities he's ever visited.

:01

First Second

Copyright © 2018 by Youssef Daoudi
Published by First Second
First Second is an imprint of Roaring Brook Press,
a division of Holtzbrinck Publishing Holdings Limited Partnership
175 Fifth Avenue, New York, NY 10010

All rights reserved
Library of Congress Control Number: 2017957413

ISBN: 978-1-62672-434-1

Our books may be purchased in bulk for promotional, educational,
or business use. Please contact your local bookseller or the
Macmillan Corporate and Premium Sales Department at
(800) 221-7945 ext. 5442 or by e-mail at
MacmillanSpecialMarkets@macmillan.com

FIRST EDITION

First edition, 2018

Edited by Mark Siegel and Whit Taylor
Book design by Andrew Arnold

Printed in China by RR Donnelley Asia Printing Solutions Ltd,
Dongguan City, Guangdong Province

1 3 5 7 9 10 8 6 4 2

BY ART
WE LIVE